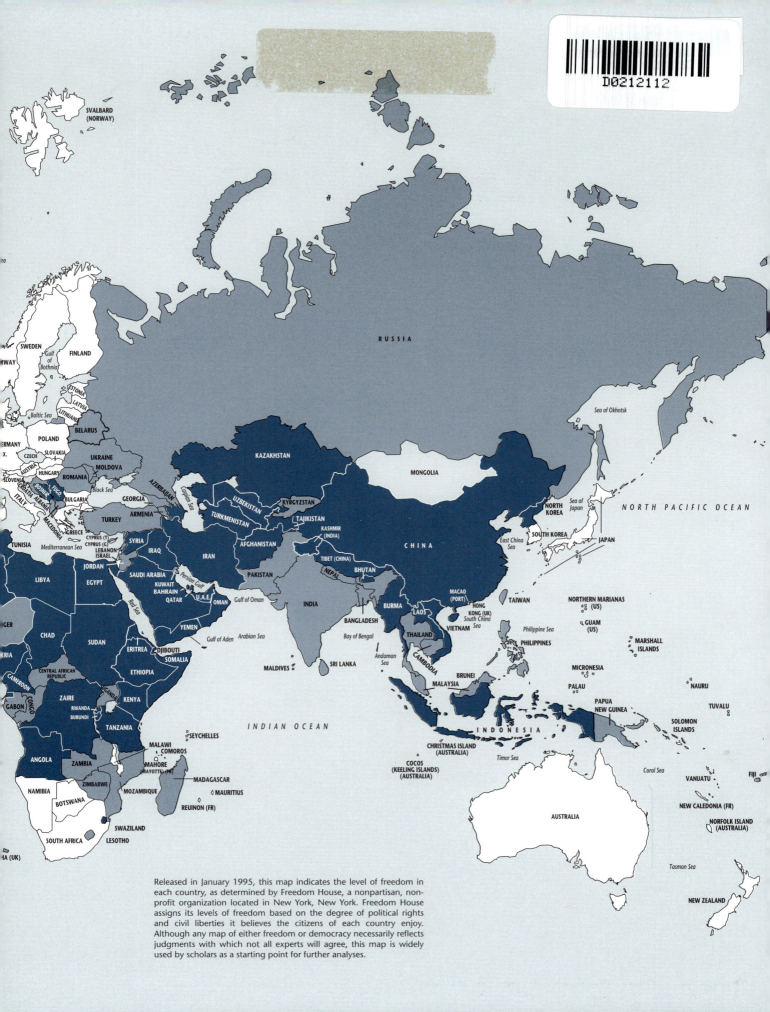

SVALBARD
(NORWAY)

SWEDEN
FINLAND
Gulf
of
Bothnia
ORWAY
Baltic Sea
ESTONIA
LATVIA
LITHUANIA
BELARUS

RUSSIA

Sea of Okhotsk

GERMANY
X.
POLAND
SLOVAKIA
CZECH
AUSTRIA
SLOVENIA
HUNGARY
ROMANIA
CROATIA
ITALY
YUGO.
ALBANIA
BULGARIA
Black Sea
MACEDONIA
GREECE
BOSNIA
UKRAINE
MOLDOVA

KAZAKHSTAN

MONGOLIA

Sea of Japan

NORTH PACIFIC OCEAN

AZERBAIJAN
Caspian Sea
GEORGIA
ARMENIA
TURKEY
CYPRUS (T)
CYPRUS (G)
LEBANON
ISRAEL
SYRIA
IRAQ
JORDAN
IRAN

UZBEKISTAN
KYRGYZSTAN
TURKMENISTAN
TAJIKISTAN
AFGHANISTAN

KASHMIR
(INDIA)
TIBET (CHINA)

CHINA

NORTH
KOREA
SOUTH KOREA
JAPAN

East China
Sea

TUNISIA
Mediterranean Sea

LIBYA
EGYPT

SAUDI ARABIA
KUWAIT
BAHRAIN
QATAR
U.A.E.
OMAN
Persian Gulf
Gulf of Oman

PAKISTAN

NEPAL
BHUTAN

BURMA

MACAO
(PORT)
HONG
KONG
(UK)
South China
Sea

TAIWAN

NORTHERN MARIANAS
(US)

GUAM
(US)

Red Sea
YEMEN
Gulf of Aden
Arabian Sea

INDIA
BANGLADESH

Bay of Bengal
Andaman
Sea

LAOS
THAILAND
VIETNAM

Philippine Sea

MARSHALL
ISLANDS

NIGER
CHAD
SUDAN
ERITREA
DJIBOUTI
SOMALIA

CENTRAL AFRICAN
REPUBLIC
ETHIOPIA
UGANDA

MALDIVES
SRI LANKA

CAMBODIA
BRUNEI
MALAYSIA

PHILIPPINES

MICRONESIA
PALAU

NAURU

ERIA
CAMEROON
GABON
CONGO
ZAIRE
RWANDA
BURUNDI
KENYA
TANZANIA

SEYCHELLES

INDIAN OCEAN

INDONESIA

TUVALU

SOLOMON
ISLANDS

ANGOLA
ZAMBIA
MALAWI
COMOROS
MAHORE
(MAYOTTE) (FR)
MADAGASCAR
MAURITIUS
REUINON (FR)
ZIMBABWE
MOZAMBIQUE

CHRISTMAS ISLAND
(AUSTRALIA)
COCOS
(KEELING ISLANDS)
(AUSTRALIA)

Timor Sea

Coral Sea

VANUATU

FIJI

NEW CALEDONIA (FR)

NAMIBIA
BOTSWANA
SWAZILAND
SOUTH AFRICA
LESOTHO

HA (UK)

AUSTRALIA

NORFOLK ISLAND
(AUSTRALIA)

Tasman Sea

NEW ZEALAND

Released in January 1995, this map indicates the level of freedom in
each country, as determined by Freedom House, a nonpartisan, nonprofit organization located in New York, New York. Freedom House
assigns its levels of freedom based on the degree of political rights
and civil liberties it believes the citizens of each country enjoy.
Although any map of either freedom or democracy necessarily reflects
judgments with which not all experts will agree, this map is widely
used by scholars as a starting point for further analyses.

THE ENCYCLOPEDIA OF DEMOCRACY

THE ENCYCLOPEDIA
OF DEMOCRACY

SEYMOUR MARTIN LIPSET

Editor in Chief

VOLUME I

 CONGRESSIONAL QUARTERLY INC.
Washington, D.C.

Book design and production by Kachergis Book Design,
Pittsboro, North Carolina

Printed and bound in the United States of America

The paper used in this publication meets the minimum requirements
of the American National Standard for Information Sciences—Permanence of Paper for Printed Library Materials, ANSI Z39.48-1984.

Photo credits and permissions for copyrighted material begin on page
1553, which is to be considered an extension of the copyright page.

Endpapers Map of Freedom courtesy of Freedom House, New York,
New York

Pericles' funeral oration reprinted by permission from *Thucydides History of the Peloponnesian War*, translated by Rex Warner (Penguin Classics,
1954). Translation copyright © Rex Warner, 1954.

African Charter on Human and Peoples' Rights copyright © Amnesty
International Publications. Reprinted by permission.

LIBRARY OF CONGRESS CATALOGING-IN-PUBLICATION DATA
The encyclopedia of democracy / Seymour Martin Lipset, editor in chief.
   p. cm.
  Includes bibliographical references (p.) and index.
  ISBN 0-87187-675-2 (set : alk. paper)
  ISBN 0-87187-886-0 (v.1 : alk. paper)
  ISBN 0-87187-887-9 (v.2 : alk. paper)
  ISBN 0-87187-888-7 (v.3 : alk. paper)
  ISBN 0-87187-889-5 (v.4 : alk. paper)

  1. Democracy—Encyclopedias.   I. Lipset, Seymour Martin.
JC423.E53   1995
321.8'03—dc20   95-34217
                                 CIP

ABOUT THE EDITORS

GAIL W. LAPIDUS is senior fellow at the Institute for International Studies, Stanford University, and professor emeritus of political science at the University of California, Berkeley. She received her Ph.D. from Harvard University. She is the author of *State and Society in the USSR* and *Women in Soviet Society: Equality, Development and Social Change.*

AREND LIJPHART is professor of political science at the University of California, San Diego, and president of the American Political Science Association. He received his Ph.D. from Yale University. Among his many publications is *Electoral Laws and Party Systems in Western Democracies, 1945–1990.*

JUAN J. LINZ is Sterling Professor of Political and Social Science at Yale University. He received his Ph.D. from Columbia University. He is the author or coeditor of several books, including *The Breakdown of Democratic Regimes: Crisis, Breakdown, and Reequilibrium.*

THOMAS L. PANGLE is professor of political science at the University of Toronto and a fellow at St. Michael's College. He received his Ph.D. from the University of Chicago. He is the author of several books, including *The Ennobling of Democracy as the Challenge of the Postmodern Age* and *The Spirit of Modern Republicanism: The Moral Vision of the American Founders and the Philosophy of Locke.*

LUCIAN W. PYE is Ford Professor of Political Science at the Massachusetts Institute of Technology. He received his Ph.D. from Yale University. He is a past president of the American Political Science Association. His many publications include *The Mandarin and the Cadre: The Political Culture of Confucian Leninism* and *Asian Power and Politics.*

GEORGE H. QUESTER is professor and chairman of the Department of Government and Politics at the University of Maryland. He received his Ph.D. from Harvard University. He is the author of *Deterrence before Hiroshima* as well as many other books, articles, and monographs.

PHILIPPE C. SCHMITTER is professor in the Department of Political Science at Stanford University. He received his Ph.D. from the University of California, Berkeley. He is coeditor of *Transitions from Authoritarian Rule: Prospects for Democracy* and *Private Interest Government and Public Policy.*

CONTENTS

PREFACE

AS A NEW CENTURY DAWNS, democracy seems to be gaining a foothold throughout the world, yet it remains fragile in all but a handful of nation-states. Understanding democracy is an essential part of nurturing its often tenuous hold on people and countries. In a world made small by swift transportation and instant communication, such an understanding is increasingly important as competing ideologies inevitably come into conflict.

What exactly is democracy? Where does it occur, and under what conditions? Is it limited to the largely Indo-European nations of the developed world? Wherever it exists, does it have common characteristics that make it instantly recognizable?

The *Encyclopedia of Democracy* seeks to provide readers with answers to these and many other questions about the complex subject of democracy. The editors of this work have undertaken to create a comprehensive reference on democracy that would be understandable to general readers and students, while at the same time providing useful information for scholars and other experts in various fields. No such concise, readable, and authoritative reference work has been published before.

The editors realize that there are no single, or simple, answers to many of the important questions about democracy. Therefore they encouraged the contributors to be flexible in presenting the circumstances of different nations or explaining the theoretical and philosophical principles that underlie democratic practice. Scholars will argue over the inclusion of this person or that in the encyclopedia, or the importance attached to one event or another. The editors' objective throughout was not to be definitive but provocative and, above all, to be useful.

Arrangement of the Encyclopedia

The four volumes are organized in the normal alphabetical format of an encyclopedia, allowing readers to move easily from place to place and idea to idea as their interests demand. There are 417 original articles on countries, geographical regions, historical eras, important individuals, philosophical concepts, and many other issues important to an understanding of democracy. The articles range in length from 300 to 8,500 words, totaling more than one million words in all; the longer entries include brief bibliographies to help students, scholars, and others who wish to pursue further reading. Many of the articles refer readers to related subjects in the encyclopedia and to important documents in the appendix .

In addition to the articles, the encyclopedia includes an introduction by editor in chief Seymour Martin Lipset. There is also an appendix that contains the texts of twenty primary source documents. These documents, which span the globe and 2,400 years, lend insight into how democracy was understood and articulated in different eras and in different societies. They range from Pericles' funeral oration of 431 B.C. to the Declaration of Principles issued at the 1994 Summit of the Americas. Brief overviews introduce the reader to the appendix and to the individual documents.

Acknowledgments

Preparation of the encyclopedia began in 1990, almost five years before its publication. It has been the work of hundreds of individuals under the direction of an editor in chief and the guidance of an editorial board composed of nine distinguished scholars. The signed articles have been prepared by 253 scholars from around the world.

In an undertaking of this magnitude it would be all but impossible to identify each person who made an important contribution. However, a few have been so closely associated with the effort from the very beginning that they must have special note. First is the editor in chief, Seymour Martin Lipset, professor of public policy at George Mason University and of political science and sociology at Stanford University. Members of the editorial board, all of whom participated actively throughout the preparation of the work, are Larry Diamond, the Hoover Institution; Ada W. Finifter, Michigan State University; Gail W. Lapidus, Stanford University; Arend Lijphart, the University of California, San Diego; Juan J. Linz, Yale University; Thomas L. Pangle, the University of Toronto; Lucian W. Pye, Massachusetts Institute of Technology; George H. Quester, the University of Maryland; and Philippe C. Schmitter, Stanford University. The editor in chief and the board were assisted by consulting editors Samuel P. Huntington, Harvard University, and Michael Saward, the University of London. Members of the editorial board read all of the material to ensure its quality and consistency.

On the staff of Congressional Quarterly, two persons were so crucial to the work that it can fairly be said publication was absolutely dependent upon them. One was Jeanne Ferris, who as the sponsoring editor of the encyclopedia was the single person most responsible for organizing and orchestrating the work for the entire five years of its preparation. The other was Ann Davies, a senior editor on the publisher's staff, who oversaw the editing of the manuscript pieces by a team of editors and who herself edited much of the material. Mark Barragry of Routledge shepherded the encyclopedia through to publication in its British edition.

Nancy Lammers, director of editorial design and production, showed her usual aplomb and creativity in managing the staff of editors, designers, and others involved in the production of the encyclopedia. Jerry Orvedahl wrote the introductory material to the appendix and provided invaluable help in many other ways. Martha Hawley-Bertsch and Megan Davis gave endless hours of general support throughout the preparation of the volumes. Jamie Holland identified and collected images for the encyclopedia with skill and care for the content of the work. The maps were meticulously prepared by Joyce Kachergis. Myra Weinberg of the Congressional Quarterly library staff was diligent and persevering in locating documents used in the appendix. Freelance editor Nola Healy Lynch deserves special thanks for her commitment throughout the project; she edited many articles with great care and precision. Other editors whose work was invaluable at various stages of the project were Joanne S. Ainsworth, Donna Brodsky at American Writing Corporation, Barbara de Boinville, Kristine A. Imherr, Steven B. Kennedy, Sabra Bissette Ledent, Madelyn C. Ross, Lys Ann Shore, Michelle Sobel, and Margery Boichel Thompson. Jodean M. Marks proofread the edited manuscripts with exemplary skill. Shirley Tuthill and Diane Koch provided bibliographic research. Joe Fortier and Leslie Rigby proofread the typeset volumes. Pat Ruggiero prepared the index with intelligence and insight under the pressure of deadlines. Kerry Kern and Christopher M. Karlsten were of immeasurable help during the final production.

The publisher wishes also to thank all of the numerous persons outside the company who made many useful suggestions at various times during the encyclopedia's preparation. Of special importance was the advice of Charles E. Smith, Claude Conyers of Oxford University Press, Ron Chambers of the Naval Institute Press, and Paul Bernabeo of Simon & Schuster. The publisher also appreciates the assistance of Elvira Clain-Stefanelli of the Smithsonian Institution, for locating the Greek coin that became the symbol for the *Encyclopedia of Democracy,* and thanks Numismatic Fine Arts for graciously giving us a photograph of the coin to use.

The encyclopedia was designed, composed, and paged by Joyce Kachergis with the skilled support of the staff at Kachergis Book Design.

DAVID R. TARR
Editor in Chief
Congressional Quarterly Book Division

PATRICK BERNUTH
Vice President and General Manager
Congressional Quarterly Book Division

ALPHABETICAL LIST OF ARTICLES

CONTRIBUTORS

A

ABRAMSON, PAUL R.
Michigan State University
Participation, Political

ADAMS, WALTER
Trinity University (Texas)
Laissez-faire economic theory
Regulation

ALEXANDER, JEFFREY C.
University of California, Los Angeles
Watergate

AMSDEN, ALICE H.
Massachusetts Institute of Technology
Markets, Regulation of

ANDEWEG, RUDY B.
University of Leiden
Low Countries

ANTONIO, ROBERT J.
University of Kansas
Weber, Max

ARONOFF, MYRON J.
Rutgers University
Zionism

ARUTIUNOV, SERGEI A.
Russian Academy of Sciences
Caucasus, The

B

AVINERI, SHLOMO
Hebrew University
Judaism

BAILEY, JOHN
Georgetown University
Mexico

BALDWIN, PETER
University of California, Los Angeles
Welfare, Promotion of

BARBER, BENJAMIN R.
Rutgers University
Justifications for democracy
Participatory democracy
Switzerland

BARKER, RODNEY
University of London
Civil disobedience

BARNES, SAMUEL H.
Georgetown University
Protest movements

BARONE, MICHAEL
U.S. News & World Report
Kennedy, John F.
Roosevelt, Theodore

BARTOL, FREDERICK
Yale University
Progressivism

BAUMAN, ZYGMUNT
University of Leeds
Marxism

BEINER, RONALD
University of Toronto
Religion, Civil
Social democracy

BENHABIB, SEYLA
Harvard University
Critical theory

BERRY, JEFFREY M.
Tufts University
Interest groups

BOLLEN, KENNETH A.
University of North Carolina at Chapel Hill
Measures of democracy

BORITT, GABOR S.
Gettysburg College
Lincoln, Abraham

BOSANQUET, NICK
University of London
Market theory

BOXILL, BERNARD R.
University of North Carolina at Chapel Hill
Theory, African American

BRATTON, MICHAEL
Michigan State University
Zambia

BROCK, JAMES W.
Miami University (Ohio)
Laissez-faire economic theory
Regulation

BRONNER, STEPHEN ERIC
Rutgers University
Luxemburg, Rosa

BROWN, ARCHIE
Oxford University
Gorbachev, Mikhail Sergeyevich
Sakharov, Andrei Dmitrievich
Yeltsin, Boris Nikolayevich

BRUBAKER, STANLEY C.
Colgate University
Freedom of speech

BRUNEAU, THOMAS C.
U.S. Department of the Navy,
   Naval Postgraduate School
Portugal

BRUNNER, RONALD D.
University of Colorado at Boulder
Lasswell, Harold D.

BRYM, ROBERT J.
University of Toronto
Intellectuals

BUFACCHI, VITTORIO
University of Manchester
Justice, Theories of

BUTLER, DAVID E.
Oxford University
Bryce, James
Commonwealth, British
Election campaigns
Referendum and initiative

BUTTERWORTH, CHARLES E.
University of Maryland
Islam

C

CAMPBELL, COLIN
Georgetown University
Cabinets

CANOVAN, MARGARET
University of Keele
Republicanism
Virtue, Civic

CHAI, MAY-LEE
University of Colorado at Boulder
Confucianism

CHAI, WINBERG
University of Wyoming
Confucianism

CHANDLER, JAMES A.
Sheffield (England) Business School
Local government

CHEHABI, H. E.
University of California, Los Angeles
Small island states

CITRIN, JACK
University of California, Berkeley
Tax revolts

CLARK, TERRY NICHOLS
University of Chicago
Class
Local government

COAKLEY, JOHN
University College, Dublin
Ireland

CONNELL, WILLIAM J.
Rutgers University
City-states, communes, and republics

COPPEDGE, MICHAEL J.
University of Notre Dame
Andean countries
Polyarchy

COSER, LEWIS A.
State University of New York at Stony Brook
Bernstein, Eduard
Communism
Engels, Friedrich
Marx, Karl

CROSSETTE, BARBARA
New York Times
Koirala, Bishweshar Prasad

CROUCH, COLIN
Oxford University
Industrial relations

CRUISE O'BRIEN, D. B.
University of London
Senegal
Senghor, Léopold Sédar

CUNNINGHAM, FRANK
University of Toronto
Macpherson, C. B.
Socialism

D

DALLIN, ALEXANDER
Stanford University
Russia, Post-Soviet

DANFORD, JOHN W.
Loyola University Chicago
Enlightenment, Scottish
Republics, Commercial

DANIELS, WILLIAM J.
Rochester Institute of Technology
Civil rights
King, Martin Luther, Jr.

DANNHAUSER, WERNER J.
Michigan State University
Existentialism
Nietzsche, Friedrich
Relativism

DAVIES, ANN
Congressional Quarterly, Washington, D.C.
Machiavelli, Niccolò

DAWISHA, ADEED
George Mason University
Egypt
Iraq
Jordan
Kuwait

DEEGAN, HEATHER
Middlesex University
Middle East

DELLA PORTA, DONATELLA
University of Florence
Corruption
Patronage

DEVINE, PAT
University of Manchester
Economic planning

DIAMANDOUROS, P. NIKIFOROS
University of Athens
Greece (modern)
Karamanlis, Constantine

DIAMOND, LARRY
Hoover Institution
Africa, Subsaharan
Colonialism
Legitimacy
Nigeria

DI TELLA, TORCUATO S.
University of Buenos Aires
Bolívar, Simón
Civil-military relations
Military rule and transition to democracy
Populism

DORFMAN, GERALD A.
Hoover Institution
Disraeli, Benjamin
Gladstone, William E.
United Kingdom

DOWNS, DONALD A.
University of Wisconsin—Madison
Censorship
Freedom of assembly

DRESCHER, SEYMOUR
University of Pittsburgh
Abolitionism

DREWRY, GAVIN
University of London
Bagehot, Walter
Unitary state

DUCH, RAYMOND M.
University of Houston
Rational choice theory

DUDWICK, NORA
George Washington University
Armenia

DUNLOP, JOHN B.
Hoover Institution
Orthodoxy, Greek and Russian

E
_____

EISENSTADT, S. N.
Hebrew University
Civil society

EKEH, PETER P.
State University of New York at Buffalo
Theory, African

EKIERT, GRZEGORZ
Harvard University
Poland
Solidarity
Veto, Liberum
Walesa, Lech

ELAZAR, DANIEL J.
Bar-Ilan and Temple Universities,
*   Jerusalem Center for Public Affairs*
Federalism

EMBERLEY, PETER C.
Carleton University
Montesquieu, Charles-Louis de Secondat,
    Baron de
Revolution, French
Sieyès, Emmanuel-Joseph

EMMERSON, DONALD K.
University of Wisconsin—Madison
Asia, Southeast
Indonesia
Sukarno

ENGERMAN, STANLEY L.
University of Rochester
Williams, Eric

EPP, CHARLES R.
Indiana University
Judicial systems

F
_____

FAGELSON, DAVID
University of Maryland
Property rights, Protection of

FEIGENBAUM, HARVEY B.
George Washington University
Gambetta, Léon-Michel
Thiers, Louis-Adolphe

FEWSMITH, JOSEPH
Boston University
China
May Fourth Movement
Three People's Principles

FINIFTER, ADA W.
Michigan State University
Political alienation
Polling, Public opinion
Public opinion
Socialization, Political

FINN, RICHARD B.
American University
Yoshida, Shigeru

FORREST, JOSHUA BERNARD
University of Vermont
Namibia

FORTIN, ERNEST L.
Boston College
Natural law

FOSTER, DAVID J.
Kenyon College
Education, Civic

FOX-GENOVESE, ELIZABETH
Emory University
Feminism

FRANKLIN, MARK N.
University of Houston and University of
    Strathclyde
Voting behavior

FRIEDMAN, STEVEN
Centre for Policy Studies, Johannesburg
de Klerk, Frederik Willem
South Africa

G

GARRETÓN M., MANUEL ANTONIO
Facultad Latinoamericana de Ciencias Sociales, Santiago, and University of Chile
Aylwin, Patricio
Chile
Frei, Eduardo

GERMINO, DANTE
University of Virginia
Critiques of democracy

GERSHMAN, CARL
National Endowment for Democracy, Washington, D.C.
Dissidents
Hook, Sidney

GERSTMANN, EVAN
University of Wisconsin—Madison
Impeachment

GLEASON, ABBOTT
Brown University
Kerensky, Alexander Fedorovich
Russia, Pre-Soviet

GOLD, STEVEN J.
Michigan State University
Americans, Ethnic

GOLDBERG, ROBERT
Kenyon College
Theory, Ancient

GOLDMAN, RALPH M.
Catholic University of America
Parties, Transnational

GRIMES, ALAN P.
Michigan State University
Hamilton, Alexander
Madison, James
United States Constitution

GRINDLE, MERILEE S.
Harvard University
Class relations, Agrarian

GROFMAN, BERNARD
University of California, Irvine
Districting
Downs, Anthony

GROSSMAN, JOEL B.
University of Wisconsin—Madison
Impeachment
Judicial systems
Majority rule, minority rights

GUNTHER, RICHARD
Ohio State University
Suárez González, Adolfo

H

HAGTVET, BERNT
University of Oslo
Rokkan, Stein

HAMBURGER, JOSEPH
Yale University
Burke, Edmund
Mill, John Stuart
Utilitarianism

HANCOCK, M. DONALD
Vanderbilt University
Adenauer, Konrad
Germany
Scandinavia

HARTLYN, JONATHAN
University of North Carolina at Chapel Hill
Colombia
Dominican Republic

HERBST, JEFFREY
Princeton University
Zimbabwe

HICKOK, EUGENE W.
Dickinson College
Accountability of public officials
Bureaucracy

HICKS, ALEXANDER M.
Emory University
State growth and intervention

HIGLEY, JOHN
University of Texas at Austin
Elite consolidation
Elite theory
Elites, Political
Mosca, Gaetano
Pareto, Vilfredo

HIRST, PAUL
University of London
Associations

HOCHSCHILD, JENNIFER L.
Princeton University
Racism

HOLM, JOHN D.
Cleveland State University
Botswana
Khama, Seretse

HOLMES, STEPHEN
University of Chicago
Constitutionalism
Kelsen, Hans

HORSTMANN, STACEY
Emory University
Feminism

HUBER, EVELYNE
University of North Carolina at Chapel Hill
Bustamante, Alexander
Caribbean, English

HUDSON, MICHAEL C.
Georgetown University
Lebanon

HUNTER, SHIREEN T.
Center for Strategic and International Studies, Washington, D.C.
Iran

I

ISHII, YONEO
Sophia University
Buddhism

J

JANOS, ANDREW C.
University of California, Berkeley
Europe, East Central
Hungary

JUNG, COURTNEY
Yale University
Africa, Lusophone

K

KAASE, MAX
Wissenschaftszentrum Berlin für Sozialforschung
Hermens, Ferdinand A.

KARATNYCKY, ADRIAN
Freedom House, New York, N.Y.
Ukraine

KARL, TERRY LYNN
Stanford University
Arias Sánchez, Oscar
Betancourt, Rómulo
Central America
Figueres Ferrer, José
Venezuela

KASSIMIR, RONALD
Columbia University
Uganda

KAUTZ, STEVEN
Emory University
Communitarianism

KELLER, EDMOND J.
University of California, Los Angeles
Africa, Horn of

KESSELMAN, MARK
Columbia University
France

KIM, ILPYONG J.
University of Connecticut
Roh Tae Woo
South Korea

KORITANSKY, JOHN C.
Hiram College
Tocqueville, Alexis de

KRAUSS, ELLIS S.
University of Pittsburgh
Japan

KRAYNAK, ROBERT P.
Colgate University
Hobbes, Thomas

L

LAKOFF, SANFORD
University of California, San Diego
Althusius, Johannes

LAMOUNIER, BOLÍVAR
*Institute of Economic and Political Studies
   (IDESP), São Paulo*
Brazil

LAND, HILARY
University of London
Thatcher, Margaret
Wollstonecraft, Mary

LAPIDUS, GAIL W.
Stanford University
Union of Soviet Socialist Republics

LAWLER, PETER A.
Berry College
Mass society

LEMARCHAND, RENÉ
University of Florida
African transitions to democracy

LEVIN, DANIEL M.
Ripon College
Majority rule, minority rights

LIJPHART, AREND
University of California, San Diego
Electoral systems
Multiethnic democracy
Proportional representation

LINZ, JUAN J.
Yale University
Authoritarianism
Fascism
Michels, Robert
Parliamentarism and presidentialism
Spain

LIPSET, SEYMOUR MARTIN
*George Mason University and Stanford
   University*
Colonialism
Development, Economic
Legitimacy

LOEWENBERG, GERHARD
University of Iowa
Legislatures and parliaments

LONGLEY, LAWRENCE D.
Lawrence University
Electoral college

LUTHARDT, WOLFGANG J.
Freie Universität, Berlin
Kirchheimer, Otto

LYONS, TERRENCE
Brookings Institution, Washington, D.C.
Sudan

M

MCALLISTER, IAN
University of New South Wales
Australia and New Zealand

MCCREA, ADRIANA
Dalhousie University
Levellers

MCWILLIAMS, WILSON CAREY
Rutgers University
Adams, John
Antifederalists
Federalists

MAHONEY, DANIEL J.
Assumption College
Aron, Raymond
de Gaulle, Charles

MARKS, GARY
University of North Carolina at Chapel Hill
Class relations, Industrial
Lipset, Seymour Martin

MARTY, MARTIN E.
University of Chicago
Protestantism

MARX, GARY T.
University of Colorado at Boulder
Police power

MATTAUSCH, JOHN
University of London
Popper, Karl

MELZER, ARTHUR M.
Michigan State University
Rousseau, Jean-Jacques

MENSKI, WERNER
University of London
Hinduism

MÉNY, YVES
European University Institute
Decentralization
Government, Levels of

MERKL, PETER H.
University of California, Santa Barbara
Popular sovereignty

MEYER, ALFRED G.
University of Michigan, Ann Arbor
Leninism

MEZEY, SUSAN GLUCK
Loyola University Chicago
Anthony, Susan B.
Pankhurst, Emmeline
Stanton, Elizabeth Cady
Women and democracy
Women's suffrage in the United States

MILLER, DAVID
Oxford University
Anarchism

MITCHELL, CHRISTOPHER
New York University
Caribbean, Spanish

MOUFFE, CHANTAL
Collège International de Philosophie (Paris)
Citizenship

MUNDT, ROBERT J.
University of North Carolina at Charlotte
Almond, Gabriel

MYERS, RAMON H.
Hoover Institution
Sun Yat-sen
Taiwan

N

NAGEL, JACK H.
University of Pennsylvania
Dahl, Robert A.

NEAL, PATRICK
University of Vermont
Theory, Postwar Anglo-American

NEHER, CLARK D.
Northern Illinois University
Abdul Rahman, Tunku
Magsaysay, Ramón
Malaysia
Philippines
Singapore
Thailand

NELSON, SAMUAL
University of Wisconsin—Madison
Censorship

NEWELL, WALLER R.
Carleton University
Dictatorship

NEWMAN, MICHAEL
University of North London
Laski, Harold

NICHOLS, JAMES H., JR.
Claremont McKenna College
Dewey, John
James, William
Pragmatism
Rhetoric

NOHLEN, DIETER
Universität Heidelberg
Voting rights

O

OFFE, CLAUS
Humboldt University, Berlin
Future of democracy

OLCOTT, MARTHA BRILL
Colgate University
Asia, Central
Kyrgyzstan

OLLMAN, BERTELL
New York University
Industrial democracy

OSBORNE, DENIS G.
Consultant, Dulwich, London
Aid policy

P

PALLEY, MARIAN LIEF
University of Delaware
States' rights in the United States

PANGLE, THOMAS L.
University of Toronto
Spinoza, Benedict de

PARRY, GERAINT
University of Manchester
Types of democracy

PASQUINO, GIANFRANCO
*University of Bologna and Bologna Center
    of the Johns Hopkins University*
Italy

PASTOR, ROBERT A.
Emory University
Elections, Monitoring

PEELER, JOHN A.
Bucknell University
Costa Rica

PELLICANI, LUCIANO
Libera Università Internazionale degli Studi Sociali, Rome
Ortega y Gasset, José

PETERS, B. GUY
University of Pittsburgh
Income, Equality of
Policy, Implementation of
Taxation policy

PLATTNER, MARC F.
Journal of Democracy, Washington, D.C.
Human rights

POGGI, GIANFRANCO
University of Virginia
De Gasperi, Alcide

POWELL, G. BINGHAM, Jr.
University of Rochester
Europe, Western

PRICE, H. DOUGLAS
Harvard University
Key, V. O., Jr.

PURKITT, HELEN E.
U.S. Naval Academy
Algeria
Morocco
Tunisia

PYE, LUCIAN W.
Massachusetts Institute of Technology
Dominant party democracies in Asia
Political culture

Q

QUAGLIARIELLO, GAETANO
Libera Università Internazionale degli Studi Sociali, Rome
Ostrogorski, Moisei Yakovlevich

QUESTER, GEORGE H.
University of Maryland
Foreign policy
Kant, Immanuel
League of Nations
National security
United Nations
Wilson, Woodrow

R

RANNEY, AUSTIN
University of California, Berkeley
Candidate selection and recruitment
Checks and balances
Media, Mass
Presidential government

REMPEL, MICHAEL
University of Chicago
Class

RIAL, JUAN
Peitho Sociedad de Análisis Político, Montevideo
Batlle y Ordóñez, José
Sanguinetti, Julio María
Uruguay

ROAZEN, PAUL
York University
Lippmann, Walter
Psychoanalysis

ROSANO, MICHAEL
University of Michigan, Dearborn
Obligation

ROSE, RICHARD
University of Strathclyde
Churchill, Winston
Monarchy, Constitutional

ROSE-ACKERMAN, SUSAN
Yale University
Progressivism

ROSENBLUM, NANCY L.
Brown University
Liberalism

ROTHCHILD, DONALD
University of California, Davis
Ghana
Nkrumah, Kwame
Secession

RUDERMAN, RICHARD S.
University of North Texas
Leadership

RUESCHEMEYER, DIETRICH
Brown University
Capitalism

RUSTOW, DANKWART A.
City University of New York
Atatürk, Kemal
Turkey

S

SAFRAN, WILLIAM
University of Colorado at Boulder
Furnivall, John Sydenham

SALISBURY, ROBERT H.
Washington University
Private governance of associations

SAVAGE, JILLIAN
University of Wisconsin—Madison
Freedom of assembly

SAWARD, MICHAEL
University of London
Complexity
Environmentalism
Globalization
Gramsci, Antonio

SAXONHOUSE, ARLENE W.
University of Michigan, Ann Arbor
Aristotle
Cicero
Classical Greece and Rome
Plato

SCARROW, HOWARD A.
State University of New York at Stony Brook
Ballots

SCHATZBERG, MICHAEL G.
University of Wisconsin—Madison
Zaire

SCHECHTER, MICHAEL G.
Michigan State University
International organizations

SCHEUERMAN, WILLIAM E.
University of Pittsburgh
Critical theory

SCHLESINGER, JOSEPH A.
Michigan State University
Politics, Machine
Spoils system

SCHMITTER, PHILIPPE C.
Stanford University
Consolidation
Corporatism
Democratization, Waves of
European Union
Future of democracy
Monnet, Jean

SCHWARTZ, MILDRED A.
University of Illinois at Chicago
Canada

SCHWARTZ, NANCY L.
Wesleyan University
Egalitarianism

SCIGLIANO, ROBERT
Boston College
Representation

SHELDON, GARRETT WARD
*Clinch Valley College, University of
    Virginia*
Declaration of Independence
Jefferson, Thomas
Paine, Thomas

SHELL, SUSAN M.
Boston College
Hegel, Georg Wilhelm Friedrich
Historicism
Idealism, German

SHUBANE, KHEHLA
Centre for Policy Studies, Johannesburg
Biko, Bantu Stephen
Mandela, Nelson
Sobukwe, Robert

SHUGART, MATTHEW SOBERG
University of California, San Diego
Duverger, Maurice
Election, Indirect
Terms of office

SIGMUND, PAUL E.
Princeton University
Catholicism, Roman
Christian democracy

SILBEY, JOEL H.
Cornell University
United States of America

SIMMONS, A. JOHN
University of Virginia
Consent

SKLAR, RICHARD L.
University of California, Los Angeles
African independence movements
Azikiwe, Nnamdi
Nyerere, Julius

SKOCPOL, THEDA
Harvard University
Revolutions

SMITH, DAVID HORTON
Boston College
Personality, Democratic

SMITH, STEVEN B.
Yale University
Theory, Twentieth-Century European

SMITH, WILLIAM C.
University of Miami
Argentina

SOTIROPOULOS, DIMITRIOS A.
*American College of Greece and University
    of Athens*
Civil service

SPAETH, HAROLD J.
Michigan State University
Marshall, John

SPENCER, METTA
University of Toronto in Mississauga
Education

SPRINZAK, EHUD
Hebrew University
Israel

STEINBERG, DAVID I.
Georgetown University
Aung San Suu Kyi
Burma

STEINER, DAVID M.
Vanderbilt University
Postmodernism

STEINER, JÜRG
*University of North Carolina at Chapel Hill
and University of Bern*
Decision making

STOESSINGER, JOHN G.
Trinity University
World War I
World War II

STONER, JAMES R., JR.
Louisiana State University
Revolution, American
Washington, George

STRØM, KAARE
University of California, San Diego
Coalition building
Government formation
Parties, Political
Party systems

SWEDBERG, RICHARD
Stockholms Universitet
Schumpeter, Joseph

T

TAAGEPERA, REIN
*University of California, Irvine, and Tartu
University*
Cube law

TAMIR, YAEL
Tel-Aviv University
Nationalism

TARCOV, NATHAN
University of Chicago
Locke, John

TARROW, SIDNEY
Cornell University
Social movements

TEMPERLEY, HOWARD
University of East Anglia
Slavery

THERBORN, GÖRAN
Göteborg Universitet
War and civil conflict

TIBI, BASSAM
Georg-August-Universität zu Göttingen
Fundamentalism

TITMA, MIKK
Stanford University
Baltic states

V

VARSHNEY, ASHUTOSH
Harvard University
Gandhi, Mohandas Karamchand
India
Nehru, Jawaharlal

VASSORT-ROUSSET, BRIGITTE
University of Nice
Mannheim, Karl
Maritain, Jacques

VERNON, RICHARD
University of Western Ontario
Contractarianism

W

WATSON, HARRY L.
University of North Carolina at Chapel Hill
Jackson, Andrew

WEINBAUM, MARVIN G.
University of Illinois at Urbana-Champaign
Jinnah, Mohammad Ali
Pakistan

WEINBERGER, JERRY
Michigan State University
Conservatism
Science
Technology

WEINER, MYRON
Massachusetts Institute of Technology
Affirmative action

WHELAN, FREDERICK G.
University of Pittsburgh
Immigration

WIDNER, JENNIFER A.
University of Michigan
Kenya
Kenyatta, Jomo

WITTE, JOHN, JR.
Emory University
Reformation

WOLCHIK, SHARON L.
George Washington University
Czechoslovakia
Havel, Václav
Masaryk, Tomáš Garrigue

WOLFE, CHRISTOPHER
Marquette University
Separation of powers

WOLFF, JONATHAN
University College, London
Autonomy
Berlin, Isaiah

WRIGGINS, W. HOWARD
Columbia University
Sri Lanka

Z

ZAPRUDNIK, JAN
Columbia University
Belarus

ZVESPER, JOHN
University of East Anglia
Roosevelt, Franklin D.

LIST OF ARTICLES BY SUBJECT

BIOGRAPHIES

TWENTIETH CENTURY

Abdul Rahman, Tunku

Adenauer, Konrad

Almond, Gabriel

Arias Sánchez, Oscar

Aron, Raymond

Atatürk, Kemal

Aung San Suu Kyi

Aylwin, Patricio

Azikiwe, Nnamdi

Batlle y Ordóñez, José

Berlin, Isaiah

Bernstein, Eduard

Betancourt, Rómulo

Biko, Bantu Stephen

Bryce, James

Bustamante, Alexander

Churchill, Winston

Dahl, Robert A.

De Gasperi, Alcide

de Gaulle, Charles

de Klerk, Frederik Willem

Dewey, John

Downs, Anthony

Duverger, Maurice

Figueres Ferrer, José

Frei, Eduardo

Furnivall, John Sydenham

Gandhi, Mohandas Karamchand

Gorbachev, Mikhail Sergeyevich

Gramsci, Antonio

Havel, Václav

Hermens, Ferdinand A.

Hook, Sidney

Jinnah, Mohammed Ali

Karamanlis, Constantine

Kelsen, Hans

Kennedy, John F.

Kenyatta, Jomo

Kerensky, Alexander Fedorovich

Key, V. O., Jr.

Khama, Seretse

King, Martin Luther, Jr.

Kirchheimer, Otto

Koirala, Bishweshar Prasad

Laski, Harold

Lasswell, Harold

Lippmann, Walter

Lipset, Seymour Martin

Luxemburg, Rosa

Macpherson, C. B.

Magsaysay, Ramón

Mandela, Nelson

CHRONOLOGICAL LIST OF DOCUMENTS

INTRODUCTION

DEMOCRACY HAS DEVELOPED from a largely northern European to a worldwide phenomenon in the twentieth century. Many individuals, in almost every society, of every social and economic class, educational level, occupation, and religious faith, consider democracy to be the ideal form of government. Yet for many people, especially for those who have little or no experience with representative government or those who take its benefits for granted, democracy's allure is more emotional than intellectual; although the term inspires powerful feelings, few could offer more than a rudimentary definition. And now that democracy exists in different cultural settings around the world, those definitions will vary considerably.

The definition of a concept as complex as democracy will inevitably be culturally based; one would expect differences in outlook between a Central European trade union supporter and a subsistence farmer in Subsaharan Africa. The definition will also be historically conditioned; for example, citizens of countries that emerged from colonialism after 1945 will have different perceptions of democracy than will citizens of long-established countries. And a person's definition of democracy will be influenced by any number of other factors as well.

Even though differences of definition exist at the margins, it is still possible—and for the purposes of analysis and discussion absolutely essential—to identify the core features that set democratic systems apart from nondemocratic systems. The editors of the *Encyclopedia of Democracy* identified three such features. First, competition exists for government positions, and fair elections for public office occur at regular intervals without the use of force and without excluding any social group. Second, citizens participate in selecting their leaders and forming policies. And, third, civil and political liberties exist to ensure the integrity of political competition and participation.

With that definition as a unifying element, the editors of the *Encyclopedia* invited more than two hundred distinguished scholars from around the world to contribute a total of 417 articles on different aspects of democracy. The authors do not necessarily agree with one another—or, for that matter, with the members of the editorial board—on any particular issue. The goal, however, was not to reach a consensus but rather to present a wide variety of viewpoints on a complex concept.

The Contents of the Encyclopedia

Four types of articles are included in the *Encyclopedia*: biographical sketches, country studies, regional overviews, and topical analyses. The editorial board's desire to give a full picture was limited by the recognition that no set of articles, no matter how extensive, could address everyone's idea of democracy. Some choices had to be made.

The biographical sketches are of individuals who in the estimation of the editorial board contributed to the theory, practice, or understanding of democracy. Included are political theorists, scholars, philosophers, activists, dissidents, revolutionaries, and leaders. The biographies span more than 2,000 years—from Plato to Aung San Suu Kyi. And they span the globe as well, including Nelson Mandela of South Africa, Margaret Thatcher of the United Kingdom, and Sun Yat-sen of China. Political leaders, to reiterate, are included only if they contributed to theory or furthered democracy. Salvador Allende, for example, is not included because, although a Chilean political leader, he did not contribute to the theory or spread of democracy. By contrast, an article on Kwame Nkrumah is included because of his role as a leader of the movement for independence in Africa—even though later in his career he became a dictator.

Some people are so linked to a particular topic or philosophy (for example, John Stuart Mill and utilitarianism) that they are covered in both a topical article and a short biographical sketch. Longer biographical articles appear on thinkers who were not part of a philosophical group (for example, Alexis de Tocqueville, whose *Democracy in America* has influenced generations of thinkers).

The selection and treatment of countries and regions in the *Encyclopedia* are based on several considerations. Countries that have had unique experiences with democratic development and consolidation are treated individually. But some countries—Estonia, Latvia, and Lithuania, for example—are so politically homogeneous and their democratic development so integrally linked that they are treated as a region. And some countries are in effect discussed twice, once separately and once as part of a regional overview, if that treatment sheds light on both local and broader issues. For example, the Dominican Republic has undergone an interesting democratic development that merits individual attention, but that country is also part of the Spanish Caribbean, about which broader generalizations can be made.

Some readers might be surprised at the space devoted to certain of the countries and regions profiled in the *Encyclopedia*. Some countries, such as Costa Rica, that are of great interest as democracies but of limited strategic importance in world politics, are treated at greater length than some readers might expect. Space was allocated to each *Encyclopedia* entry—country studies, biographies, and topical pieces included—based on the editorial board's judgment of the topic's interest, relevance, and importance to democracy as a theoretical concept and as a practical system of governance.

The selection of topical articles in the *Encyclopedia* reflects the modern notion that politics and political thought must be considered in a broader context. Any society's political thought influences and is influenced by its economy, social structure, culture, and religion. The exact nature of the interrelationship among these factors is open to debate. Also open to argument is the influence of these anonymous forces relative to the influence of individual leaders and thinkers. Such considerations are important whether analyzing historical episodes, developments across time, or contemporary issues.

These broad theoretical considerations, when applied to questions of democratic development and consolidation, give rise to many of the issues addressed in the *Encyclopedia*. Why do some democracies thrive and others falter? What economic, social, and political conditions foster the emergence of democratic societies? What have thinkers, politicians, and statesmen contributed to the birth of democratic governments? How has democracy developed in different regions of the world?

Some topical articles focus on institutions and processes to illustrate how democracies work in practice: legislatures and parliaments, checks and balances, voting behavior, protest movements, and the promotion of welfare. Other articles examine the fundamental assumptions of democracy: the rights and duties of citizenship; freedom of speech, press, and assembly; mechanisms for making government responsive to the citizens; and legal protection of individual and group rights against arbitrary state action. In addition, readers will find articles that investigate democracy's links to ideas of self-determination and nationalism; to religion, civic education, and the media; to civil rights, human rights, and class relations.

And still others of the topical articles in the *Encyclopedia* address the complex interplay between democracy, political ideologies, and broad philosophical movements. How have various philosophies and beliefs affected democracy, and vice versa? The inclusion of certain political ideologies, communism for example, may at first glance appear odd. Ideologies are addressed if their adherents comment, positively or critically, on democracy. Communist theoreticians claim that democracy is simply a front for the power of the bourgeoisie.

The contributors to the *Encyclopedia of Democracy* have undertaken the task of analyzing the relationship of 417 individuals, countries, regions, and topics to the idea and practice of democracy through time and around the world. To facilitate the quick and efficient use of the Encyclopedia by researchers, each entry stands alone. Each is a discrete, self-contained examination of one element of the democratic phenomenon. For further research, cross-references to related entries are provided.

As any researcher well knows, however, the relationship of the parts to the whole is often complicated. The introductory comments that follow are intended to provide the reader with an analytical framework for conceptualizing how those discrete parts coalesce to form a comprehensive portrait of the democratic experience.

The first section, "Influences on Democratic Development," looks in turn at the economic, political and social, and religious factors that have influenced democratization through the ages. Historically, certain factors have abetted democratization and others have inhibited it. This section, drawing on examples from the distant as well as more recent past, examines those factors. Then, under the heading "Prospects," the newly emerging democracies of the late twentieth century are examined in light of the conclusions drawn about the factors abetting and inhibiting democratization.

Democratization or the lack thereof, however, is not an inevitable outcome of impersonal, immutable forces. To say that Latin America lacks the Protestant heritage and strong middle class of northern Europe is not to say that Latin America cannot follow a democratic path. The prospects for democracy may be affected by the personal will and conscious policy decisions of leaders. In the next section, "The Challenge of Democratic Consolidation," we review the factors that are essential for establishing a stable, popular, participatory democracy. Even where the economic, social, and religious traditions that historically fostered democratization are absent or weak, a government intent on solidifying a nascent democratic order can take steps in that direction.

Influences on Democratic Development

Democratization over the past two centuries has ebbed and flowed in waves. The most recent wave began in the mid-1970s, when Portugal, Spain, and Greece replaced autocratic regimes with democratic governments. In the early and mid-1980s democratization arose in Latin America and in Asian countries, including South Korea, Thailand, and the Philippines. The successor states to the Soviet Union and the countries of Eastern Europe, as well as parts of Subsaharan Africa, began the difficult transition from authoritarian rule to democracy in the late 1980s and early 1990s. The progress has been staggering. Whereas in 1970 the overwhelming majority of countries around the world had authoritarian systems, by 1995, by one count, 114 of 191 countries had a system of government that met the three core conditions of political democracy defined earlier.

The transition to democracy is not a simple one, however. We turn in order to the three most important influences on the development of democracy: economic factors, political and social culture, and religion.

Economic Development and Democracy

The correlation between economic development and the presence of democratic institutions has been noted by many people. Alexis de Tocqueville, a French aristocrat whose mid-nineteenth century observations on American society are still quoted today, observed that respect for individuals regardless of their economic condition contributes to democracy. Later, many political theorists, including the scholars Max

Weber and Joseph Schumpeter, noted the relationship between a free market economy and democracy. Schumpeter maintained that modern democracy is a product of capitalism. The reason? A free market is facilitated by democracy and vice versa.

Many of the old democracies of northern Europe and North America followed similar patterns of development. Political rights expanded in these societies during the early stages of capitalist development under pressure from the deprived classes of society. As economic development progressed and the societies became more affluent, an independent middle class arose. The middle class, buoyed by its economic power, created a civil society of powerful institutions—associations, parties, and interest groups of various types—that weakened state power. An independent trade union movement helped to create and strengthen free institutions. Lessened state power then led to increased respect for human rights and the rule of law—both essentials of democratic governance. In short, the rising economic power of the citizenry put a brake on the political power of the government, leading to democratic rule.

In a modern developing nation, however, economic power and political power are generally concentrated in the same class of people. If the working and middle classes are weak or forcefully repressed by an authoritarian government, the natural path to democratic governance is short-circuited. The income structure of the population of a developing nation is usually badly skewed, with wealth concentrated in the hands of a small number of people who also retain political power. The state is usually the most important source of capital, income, power, and status. For an individual or governing body in such a nation to give up control because of an election outcome would be astonishing behavior. The cards are stacked against the emergence of democracy in these states.

State allocation of resources and opportunity make corruption a major problem of governance and one that is inherent in polities built on mass poverty. In such systems, which describe many of the countries that have been making the transition to democracy during the past twenty years, it is almost impossible to eliminate personal networking (which can lead to corruption) in distributing resources controlled or influenced by the state. Formulating laws that require the application of impersonal standards based on merit (which reduce the effect of personal networks) is desirable. But it is difficult to institutionalize a merit-based system where none had existed.

A democratic political culture requires that the resources that are controlled by the state be distributed in a fair and impartial manner. Beyond formal, legal limits on the role of the state, ethical standards of propriety for officials have to be reformulated in new and poor regimes, and objective standards must be applied in allocating resources. Establishing these requirements, of course, would be facilitated by an efficient civil service selected by standards based on merit. It took many decades for civil service reforms to take hold in Britain, the United States, and various European countries. Changing the norms and rules in contemporary impoverished countries and institutionalizing new mechanisms of resource distribution are not easy to do, especially in a short time frame.

Political and Social Culture

Cultural factors appear to play an even more important role than economic ones in fostering democracy. To flourish, democracy requires the acceptance by the citizenry and political elites of freedom of speech, assembly, religion, and the press. More fundamentally, democracy requires universal respect for the institutions and processes of political life such that the outcomes they create—laws, regulations, policies, and election returns—are respected and obeyed even if they are disliked. In a democratic political culture, the processes and institutions confer legitimacy on the outcomes, however unpopular they may be.

But a democratic culture does not evolve overnight. In the United States and the countries of northern Europe, freedom, suffrage, and the rule of law grew piecemeal, not in a planned fashion. Governmental parties only gradually and reluctantly recognized the right of oppositions to exist and to compete freely. (Almost all the heads of young democracies, from John Adams and Thomas Jefferson in America to Indira Gandhi in India in the mid-twentieth century, attempted to repress their opponents.) In solidifying their democratic political cultures, those early democracies had an advantage not shared by the emerging democracies of today: the state in the eighteenth and early nineteenth centuries was less a source of prestige and advantage than it is now, and therefore those in power could yield office more easily. Furthermore, the agrarian societies of the earlier period, with their simpler class relations, placed fewer demands for rights, benefits, and services on the young governments of the United States and northern Europe than those that are faced by contemporary democracies. Consequently, democratic systems in the earlier era could develop gradually, at first with a limited suffrage linked to ownership of property, literacy, or both. Elites yielded slowly in admitting the masses to the franchise and in tolerating and institutionalizing opposition rights. In the states of northern Europe, democratization left the monarchies and aristocracies with their elite status, even though their power was curtailed—a process that contributed to legitimacy.

Such a gradual evolution toward a democratic political culture is not possible in contemporary societies. But is it possible to transplant a democratic political culture? Of all the nations formerly ruled by colonial powers, those once governed by Great Britain are most likely to be democracies today. Part of the reason for that lies in the fact that many areas under British control—such as North America before the American Revolution, or India, Ireland, and Nigeria in more recent times—had elections, political factions or parties, and the rule of law while ruled by Britain. The pre-independence experiences of the former British colonies helped to ease the transition to representative government after independence. In contrast, Belgium, France, the Netherlands, Portugal, Spain, and the Soviet Union did not allow for the gradual incorporation of indigenous populations into the polities of their countries.

Revolution and upheaval have proved to be ineffective means of establishing a democratic political culture. Most rebellions—from the French Revolution in 1789, to Russia's February revolution in 1917, to the Latin American turnovers in the nineteenth century, to those in Africa and Asia after World War II—failed to establish democratic regimes. In fact, only four of the seventeen countries that adopted democratic institutions between 1915 and 1921, in the wake of World War I, were able to maintain them for even two decades. Breakdowns were frequent in the post–World War II years as well.

Democracy has developed by plan in only two cases: in Germany and Japan after World War II, when it was imposed by democratic conquerors on nations that had been utterly destroyed socially, economically, and politically.

All in all, democratic political cultures that evolve gradually are likely to be the most enduring. The imposition and transplantation of democratic values and institutions have produced mixed results.

Religious Tradition

Observers since Tocqueville's time have noted that, among European countries and their overseas offspring, Protestant countries have been democratic more often than have Roman Catholic ones. The Roman Catholic Church, which is hierarchical and authoritarian in spiritual matters, has fostered a disinclination on the part of many of its followers to believe that counting heads is the best way to run a country. Protestantism, by contrast, is less authoritarian and more participatory and individualistic.

Catholic countries, nonetheless, have contributed significantly to the wave of democratization that began during the 1970s. This development reflects the drastic modifications in church doctrine and the political pronouncements of the church since the 1960s. The changes occurred in part because of the decline in influence of what has been called ultrarightist or clerical fascism in Catholic thought and politics. This is a result of the defeat of fascism in Europe, and the considerable postwar economic growth in many major Catholic areas, such as Italy, Spain, Quebec, Brazil, and Chile.

Conversely, Islamic (particularly Arab) states have not been part of the latest wave of democratization. Almost all remain authoritarian. In most Islamic countries the future growth of democracy and political freedom is uncertain. Because Islam views all law as God's law—permanent and unquestionable—Islamic states have had a history of autocracy that is unlikely to change in the near future.

Like Islam, Orthodox Christianity closely links the religious and political spheres, particularly in Russia but in other parts of Eastern Europe as well. The Orthodox

Church has not actively supported either human rights or religious tolerance. Historically, democracy has been weak in Orthodox Christian lands.

Similarly, in Confucian China religious and cultural organizations were part of the state. Most Asian experts agree that traditional Confucianism was either undemocratic or antidemocratic. The People's Republic of China remains an autocratic one-party state, although the growth of a market economy in recent years has led to a decline in authoritarian control. Among the Confucian countries, only Japan had institutionalized a democratic government before 1990, and that development stemmed largely from the American occupation after World War II. The other countries with a Confucian tradition—Korea, Singapore, Taiwan, and Vietnam—were autocratic. As in China, however, rapid economic growth and a free market system in recent years have tempered the autocracies in these countries.

In stark contrast, India, a predominantly Hindu country, became democratic before industrialization came about, in large part because of the legacy of British colonial administration but also because of the doctrinaire character of Hinduism. The religious and political orders were fairly distinct in India, a situation that allowed the process of democratization to proceed unhampered by the country's traditional cultural orientation.

Prospects

What do the foregoing generalizations about economics, culture, and religion imply about the prospects for the further spread of democracy around the world? They suggest a very difficult road ahead for some of the nations that began to emerge from authoritarianism in the latest wave of democratization. The nascent democracies—in East and Southeast Asia, Latin America, Eastern Europe, the Balkans, and the former Soviet Union—enjoy few of the advantages that were crucial to the institutionalization of democratic processes and the internalization of democratic political cultures in the United States and northern Europe. Although the economies of many of the new polities are doing well, raising hope that a strong middle class will evolve and assert its independence of and power over the state, cultural and religious factors as well as the legacy of corrupt authoritarianism overshadow the prospects for the long-term entrenchment of democratic rule and governance in many of these countries. Furthermore, as noted earlier, the rising expectations of the citizenry—for improvements in services and benefits and, above all else, for progress toward stable government—have placed enormous pressure on the new democracies for immediate results.

None of the emerging democracies of the past two decades share the Protestant background that contributed so greatly to the cultures of northern Europe and the United States. In Poland, although the Catholic Church played a substantial role in the country's move away from Soviet-style communism, the nation is now troubled by conflicts flowing from the church's efforts to affect politics in Eastern Europe (such as raising the abortion issue) even as it relaxes those efforts in Western Europe and most of the Americas.

The picture is similar elsewhere. The Orthodox Christian Church, which has a long history of subservience to the state (in contrast to the Protestant religions' autonomy), is dominant in Russia and Belarus, and Ukraine is divided between both the Catholic and Orthodox Churches. In the Central Asian regions of the former Soviet Union—areas that are among the least democratic of the Soviet successor states—Islam is a significant influence. Yugoslavia is being torn apart along ethnic and religious lines. Led by the Orthodox Serbians, but assisted by the actions of the Catholic Croats and Muslim Bosnians as well, the country has been devastated by war and "ethnic cleansing." No peaceful, much less democratic, end is in sight.

But there is still cause for hope for democratization. Belief systems change. Capitalism, a large middle class, an organized working class, and increased wealth and education are all associated with secularization and the institutions of civil society. They can help create autonomy for civil society from the state and accelerate other preconditions for democracy. In recent years, this possibility of change has been most apparent in the economically successful Confucian states of East and Southeast Asia—states once viewed as nearly hopeless candidates for either development or democracy. Today they are booming economically. And two previously authoritarian states—South Korea and Taiwan—are institutionalizing competitive electoral systems, following the model of Japan. Democracy is clearly possible in the Confucian societies.

Likewise, democratic values are progressing in many previously totalitarian countries, including many of those that were communist controlled. Granted, the cultures must change further. But except for the most fundamentalist and least industrialized of the Muslim states and some nations in Africa and the former Soviet Union, these countries seem to be moving in the right direction.

The Challenge of Democratic Consolidation

Governments, democratic and otherwise, are made by people. Their forms are influenced greatly by impersonal economic, social, cultural, and religious factors, but those cannot "determine" the form of government. For democracy to succeed, governments and their leaders must create institutions, adopt procedures, and institute policies that will command the support of the citizens.

Casting off an authoritarian ruler is only the first step toward democratic rule. To gain the support of the people, an emerging democracy must quickly establish institutions and processes that are viewed as fair, effective, and stable by all elements of society. New democracies face many challenges: they must create a growing, preferably more egalitarian economy; reduce the tensions with the old civil and military elites, perhaps replacing them with new elites; and formulate workable democratic electoral and administrative systems that are based on stable political parties and a dispassionate bureaucracy. These important topics and others that relate to consolidating democracy are discussed in various articles in this encyclopedia. I would like to introduce a few of them now: legitimacy and the rule of law, parliamentary versus presidential government, electoral systems, civil society and political parties, structural tensions, and economic and social order.

Legitimacy and the Rule of Law

Political stability in democratic systems cannot rely on force. The alternative to force is an accepted "title to rule," or what scholars call legitimacy. Max Weber, the fountainhead of legitimacy theory, identified three types that governments use to justify their rule.

Most of the nations of northern Europe and the British Commonwealth relied on what Weber termed "traditional legitimacy." These nations developed democratic institutions while retaining the legitimacy derived from a continuing monarchy. The institutions and traditions of the monarchies were employed to sanction and buttress early democratic reforms. Without that bedrock of royal authority, democracy might not have developed as it did in those areas, if at all.

According to Weber, legitimacy can also come from popular acceptance of the system of rules under which a government has won and held office ("rational-legal legitimacy"). In the United States, for example, the Constitution is today the basis of all authority; election outcomes, laws, and court decisions are respected because they are "constitutional," because they derive from processes and institutions that themselves are considered legitimate. But this type of legitimacy is based on performance over an extended period of time. The governments of the United States, the United Kingdom, and other "old" democracies base their legitimacy in part on the age and durability of their institutions. Rational-legal legitimacy, therefore, is weak in most new government systems that have not had time to demonstrate effectiveness. In such systems, much of the population will likely identify the law with the interests of a foreign exploiter or with a deposed domestic dictator.

A third type of legitimacy ("charismatic legitimacy") exists when authority rests on faith in a leader believed to be endowed with great personal worth—either from God, as in the case of a religious prophet, or simply from the display of extraordinary talents. The "cult of personality" is an extreme form of charismatic legitimacy. Because authoritarian regimes lack the means to establish legal-rational legitimacy (the rule of law), they often seek to gain legitimacy through cults of personality. Napoleon Bonaparte, Benito Mussolini, and Adolf Hitler readily come to mind. Even communist governments—whose Marxist ideology explicitly denies the importance of "great men" in history and stresses the role of materialist forces and "the people"—resorted to the use of charismatic legitimacy. Communist states produced the cults of V. I. Lenin, Joseph Stalin, Mao Zedong, Josip Broz Tito, and Fidel Castro, among others. The legitimating power of charismatic leadership is demonstrated in the breach: the four communist regimes that experienced large-scale re-volts—East Germany (1953), Hungary (1956), Poland (1955–1980), and Czechoslo-vakia (1968)—were also those with very weak personality cults, much like the Soviet Union when it came apart in 1989–1991. Charismatic legitimacy, however, is inherent-ly unstable in the long run because it does not separate the source of authority from the agent of authority. If rulers and their policies are seen as oppressive or exploita-tive, the regime and its rules will eventually be rejected. Force alone cannot convey a "title to rule."

It is not at all unusual for a government to manipulate national symbols, to coin slogans, to embellish, rewrite, or even create the national history, and to take other measures in an effort to fabricate legitimacy where there is little or none to begin with. Recent history is rife with examples, some successful and others not, of efforts to establish the legitimacy of a new order. Many such efforts failed after World War I, as mentioned earlier. Of the new countries carved from the remains of the German, Austro-Hungarian, and Ottoman empires, only four still had democratic institutions two decades later, largely because the new governments lacked legitimacy in the eyes of a majority of their citizens. Germany is a case in point: Winston Churchill, among others, strongly opposed the Allies' insistence that the German kaiser be deposed, correctly anticipating that the new democratic system would be opposed by adher-ents of the old empire and would not command their allegiance.

The victors of World War II had learned a lesson about legitimacy from the bitter legacy of the earlier war. After World War II, Japan was permitted to retain the em-peror, who remained in the eyes of many Japanese the only legitimate ruler of the na-tion. The emperor was able to lend power, authority, and legitimacy to the new order, just as the monarchs of northern Europe had smoothed the transition to democratic rule in their countries. Over the course of five decades of stable government and eco-nomic growth, the Japanese constitutional order, which had been imposed by the victorious Allies, seemingly acquired a legal-rational legitimacy in its own right.

Over time, governments can best gain legitimacy by performing effectively, by sat-isfying the basic needs of societies as most of the population and important power groups (such as the military and economic leaders) see them. New democracies must go one step further and separate the agent from the source of authority. Citizens must respect and obey the laws and rules even if they dislike those who enforce them. Respect for the laws and, more generally, for the rule of law, is enhanced by enhanc-ing the prestige of the courts, which should be as independent of the rest of the polity as possible. New democracies must draw up a constitution as soon as possible, to provide a basis for legitimacy, to define limits on state power, and to ensure political and economic rights.

As we have noted, most of the democracies established in Europe after World War I as a result of the overthrow of the German, Austro-Hungarian, and czarist Russian empires did not last. The post–World War II Latin American and African records were equally poor, and most have witnessed considerable ups and downs in political rights. Beyond failures of economic effectiveness, these countries lacked the resources needed to win over the loyalties of both ordinary citizens and elites. Efforts to create democracy thus have broken down in several of them.

The postwar democratic regimes of Italy and Germany, former fascist states, were established—like the Weimar Republic—under the auspices of the conquerors. Clearly, these democracies had no legitimacy at their onset. But they had the advantage of the postwar "economic miracles," which produced jobs and steadily rising standards of living, and this legitimized the regimes. These new systems have been economically effective for five decades. Their stability is also linked to the discrediting of antidemocratic, right-wing tendencies—forces that were identified with fascism and military defeat.

Democracy, then, can be seen as a means of facilitating stability. Stability in turn can encourage economic growth. Democracy enables citizens to see the polity as inclusive of all elements in a society, not simply those in power. The electorate becomes part of the legitimating structure. It, rather than the government, holds the ultimate authority. Voters are encouraged to work for a change of government while remaining loyal to the system.

The argument has occasionally been put forth that, because democratic systems rely on popular support and must constantly compete for such backing, they are "weaker" and less resolute than dictatorships. Observers as diverse as Max Weber and Mikhail Gorbachev, however, have noted the reverse: the cacophony of interests and competing demands are positive elements that strengthen authority. Oppositions serve as a communication mechanism, focusing attention on problems in government and society. Freedom of opposition encourages a free flow of information about the economy as well as about the polity.

Weber noted that an autocrat is often less powerful than a democratic ruler. Because of the restrictions on the free flow of information, a dictator may not know when his orders are ignored by the bureaucrats or interest groups that oppose them. Weber cited as an example the failure of the land reforms attempted by Frederick the Great in eighteenth-century Prussia. The Prussian bureaucracy and local authorities, which were linked to the landed aristocracy, simply ignored the new laws. And no one told the king.

In a democracy, by contrast, the opposition or the press can expose such sabotage. Gorbachev, in speeches during his first few years as Soviet leader, remarked on the dysfunctional consequences of one-party regimes in terms similar to those of Weber. Pointing out that the bureaucracy ignored the orders and reforms it opposed, Gorbachev noted that this situation could not happen in a multiparty system. He, of course, did not advocate more parties. Rather, he called on the Soviet press and the intelligentsia to carry out the communication and exposure functions that the opposition handles in democratic countries.

An important concern of democracies as they seek to establish their legitimacy is protecting the rights of minorities from the majority. If minorities—particularly ethnic, linguistic, and religious minorities—feel that they cannot share power, they may try to gain local autonomy or secede from the state. This occurred in parts of the former Yugoslavia and Soviet Union in the 1990s. One solution to this problem is a constitutional structure that gives minorities veto power in the policy development process when their interests are affected. Efforts to construct such an arrangement failed in Cyprus and Lebanon but have apparently been successful in Switzerland. Canada and South Africa are currently looking for comparable arrangements to give their minority populations access to political power and thereby instill their governments with broad legitimacy.

Federalism, in which powers are divided between a national government and lower-level governments such as states or provinces, is another means of enhancing the legitimacy of a government in the eyes of minority groups. In fact, federalism is one of the oldest and in many ways the most satisfactory means to manage conflicts between ethnic or other groups. But federalist arrangements clearly are no panacea. There have been failures (Yugoslavia) as well as successes (Switzerland and to some extent Canada).

Parliamentary Versus Presidential Government

Governments that are seen as representative of and responsive to the needs and aspirations of the citizens are more likely to be viewed as legitimate by the people than are governments that appear aloof and unresponsive. The structure of a government—its institutions, the power relationships among them, and the mechanisms for changing governments—greatly affects the people's perceptions. Over the past two centuries, two major types of democratic government have evolved: presidential and parliamentary. Their relative merits have been debated at length by scholars and other observers. In practice, each has produced model democratic regimes. Each has produced disappointments as well.

In a presidential system, the executive is head of state and head of the government: symbolic authority and effective power are combined in one person. In a parliamentary system, symbolic authority and real power are divided between a usually titular head of state (sometimes a president or monarch) and a powerful head of government (a premier or prime minister).

It has often been said that in a presidential system, with a single person at the top of the power structure, it is hard for the public to separate its feelings toward the regime from those it holds toward the president. In a well-established presidential democracy such as the United States, however, no such difficulty arises. Because of the hallowed nature of the American constitutional order, the office of the presidency, rather than the person who occupies the presidency, is revered. Similarly, the constitutional traditions of some other states are so entrenched that the institutions of government transcend the personalities of a given presidential term.

A related criticism often leveled against presidential governments is that they generally have been considered to be more unstable than parliamentary systems. In the latter, a relatively powerless constitutional monarch, or elected head of state who acts out the role of constitutional monarch, stands above the partisan, political fray. That figurehead lends an aura of stability and dignity to the seeming "chaos" of a vibrant democratic system. Presidential systems lack even that minimal decorum, with the chief executive often at the center of public squabbles. The difficulties many Latin American presidential regimes have had in institutionalizing democracy during the past century and a half may reflect this problem.

But parliamentary systems can be unstable too, especially if the legislative body is splintered among many political parties. If no one party has a clear majority in the parliament, a government cannot be formed without a coalition of two or more parties. Coalitions are inherently unstable, and if a multitude of weak parties cannot come to an agreement, deadlock is a possibility. The pre–World War II parliamentary systems in Germany, Italy, Spain, and many Eastern Europe countries collapsed because of partisan stalemate. Similarly, in 1958 Charles de Gaulle attributed the instability of the Third and Fourth French Republics to their multiparty parliamentary systems. These republics produced short-lived and ineffective cabinets. As a remedy, de Gaulle introduced a complex system with a powerful president who shares power with a prime minister and a legislature. These reforms brought more effective and longer-lived governments. In the new Russian Federation, the constitution proposed by Boris Yeltsin and adopted in December 1993 attempted a similar institutional arrangement.

The inability of parliamentary systems to produce stable governments because they lack operating legislative majorities persists in many places today. Some of the countries of Eastern Europe now moving away from communism have this problem. In Poland, twenty-nine parties won seats in the parliament in 1991. The implications for deadlock were so dire in that country that the constitution was manipulated to try to produce more manageable partisan outcomes before the next elections. As a result only seven parties were represented in 1993. Before Yeltsin introduced electoral reforms in the early 1990s, Russia was bogged down with fourteen organized factions. Of these, each had 48 or more deputies in the Congress of People's Deputies; in addition, almost 200 deputies did not belong to any faction. Even after electoral reform, the parliament contained twelve factions plus 120 independent deputies.

Another criticism that is often made of presidential systems is the amount of power concentrated in the hands of a single person. The debate is not simply academic: generally, the more diffuse the power, the more stable the democracy and the more likely the government will be viewed as legitimate. In fact, presidents are frequently less powerful than the head of government in a parliamentary system. In presidential regimes, the power to enact legislation, pass budgets, appropriate funds, and make high-level appointments is divided between the president and the legislature (itself usually divided into two houses). Parliamentary regimes, by contrast, usually are unitary, permitting the prime minister and cabinet to have their way legislatively.

A prime minister with a parliamentary majority—the usual governing arrangement in most nations of the British Commonwealth and a number of countries in continental Europe—is much more powerful and less constrained than a constitutional president. A president under a constitution can only "propose while Congress disposes." Here again, however, the practical experience is mixed. The weak, divided authority system has worked in the United States. As noted, however, the presidential system repeatedly has broken down in Latin America. One could argue that the explanation for failure in Latin America is not the constitutional arrangement but cultural legacies and the social discontent caused by a grossly unequal distribution of wealth.

Electoral Systems

The procedures for choosing and changing administrations also affect legitimacy. Electoral rules that offer voters a regular and effective way to change the government provide stability. Just as there are two predominant governing systems, presidential and parliamentary, so there are two predominant electoral systems: those based on single-member districts and those that use proportional representation.

Single-member districts, such as those in the United States and much of the British Commonwealth, for the most part press the electorate to choose between two major parties. Voters know that if they turn against the party in power, they can replace it with the opposition. Because the opposition usually promises to reverse the course, incumbents can be punished for unpopular policies or for happening to preside over unfortunate events (such as an economic downturn). Although many voters frequently feel they are opting for the "lesser evil," they still have an opportunity to "throw the rascals out."

In systems based on pure proportional representation, the parties are assigned a number of seats in the legislature based on their proportion of the vote. This type of system has certain advantages in that small minority parties gain some say in the legislature. But a drawback is that the electorate may be unable to determine the composition of the government. Proportional representation was used in pre-Hitler Germany, prefascist Italy, and much of Eastern Europe during the 1920s and early 1930s.

It currently exists in Germany, Israel, Italy, Scandinavia, much of Eastern Europe, and the Russian Federation.

As mentioned above, if no party wins a majority under a proportional system, alliances must be formed from diverse forces. A party in a government coalition may gain votes but then may be excluded from the new cabinet formed after the election. Small, opportunistic, or special-interest parties may hold the balance of power and determine the shape and policies of coalitions. Some countries have reduced the tendency toward this kind of instability by setting up their electoral systems so that a minimum number of votes is required before a party can gain representation. For example, Germany and Russia instituted a 5 percent cutoff. In any case, whether based on single-member districts or proportional representation, both types can still be considered democratic.

Civil Society and Political Parties

More important even than electoral rules in encouraging a stable democratic system is a strong civil society. Civil society comprises the myriad institutions that operate independently between individuals and the state, such as associations and the media. Citizen groups enable people to affect the policies of the state and help to ensure that the central power apparatus does not dominate society. Citizen groups thus support the institutionalized parties that are a necessary condition for a modern democracy.

We owe our awareness of the importance of civil society in a democracy to Tocqueville. He saw in the flourishing of civil associations in the United States the secret to America's political and economic success as compared with the experiences of the European nations of his day. Tocqueville called political associations "large free schools." Through them the members of the community learned how to work together in harmony and toward a shared goal.

A fully operative civil society is likely to be a participatory one as well. Organizations stimulate interest and participation in the larger polity. Political institutions can consult civil organizations about projects that will affect them and their members, and the organizations can transfer information back to the people. Civil organizations reduce resistance to change. They prevent the isolation of political institutions from the people and can smooth over, or at least recognize, differences of interests early on. Finally, by competing with one another and with the state for the power to carry out their own aspirations, various groups—class, religious, economic, and professional—legitimate themselves by encouraging the rights of other groups to oppose them. Thus they provide a basis for democracy. Through conflicts and their differing ideologies, these groups form an alternative to the state and to its control of society.

Effective civil societies do not exist in totalitarian systems, and they are weak under authoritarian regimes. Totalitarian regimes seek either to eliminate groups mediating between the people and the state or to control these groups to eliminate any competition or independent communication among members. Although the regimes may successfully undermine the possibility for organized opposition, in the process they also lessen group effectiveness generally and reduce the capability of individuals to innovate.

In the countries of Eastern Europe and the successor states to the Soviet Union, the absence of a modern civil society makes it difficult to institutionalize democratic polities. These countries have had little opportunity to form the civil groups that are the basis for stable political parties. Among the few groups that flourished were the churches in some countries, such as Poland, and small, autonomous illegal networks. Consequently, the fledgling democracies of the former communist world have had to create political parties from scratch. The former communists, who have been well organized for many years and have constructed their own coalitions, have been opposed mainly by ideologically splintered groups. Fragmentation rather than consolidation has been the result.

If democracy is to succeed, political parties must be viewed as the most important mediating institutions between the citizens and the state. A crucial condition for a stable democracy is the existence of at least two major parties that have an almost permanent base of support. If this condition is not met, parties may be totally wiped out, thus eliminating effective opposition. The Republican Party in the United States, for example, although tagged by many with responsibility for the Great Depression, remained a major opposition party. Despite the fact that the country suffered unprecedented levels of unemployment, bankruptcies, and stock market instability, the Republican Party survived. If parties do not command such allegiance, they can easily be eliminated, and democracy itself jeopardized.

Given that strong political parties are a precondition for democracy, the prospects for democracy in Eastern Europe seem cloudy. Opinion polls reveal that Eastern Europeans hold conflicting views about political parties and about other ingredients of democracy as well. Although the people in the region favor popular government, they are unhappy with the political parties, parliament, and press that are the vital cornerstones of popular government. They like social welfare legislation and equality but dislike trade unions, which historically have been the force propelling social welfare legislation and equality.

Structural Tensions Within the Polity

Twenty-five years ago Stein Rokkan and I examined the party alignments and voting patterns underlying the European party systems. In *Party Systems and Voter Alignments* (1967), we explained modern political voter alignments as being the result of two kinds of revolution: national revolutions and the Industrial Revolution.

These revolutions created class, ethnic, and other tensions that became linked to party lines and voting behavior.

National revolutions were political in nature and created political tensions. They resulted in cleavages between the central state and majority culture on the one hand, and minority cultures—such as ethnic, linguistic, or religious groups often located in the outlying regions—on the other. The national revolutions also often led to tensions between church and state: the state sought to dominate, and the church tried to maintain its historic corporate rights. The Industrial Revolution, which was economic in nature, gave rise to cleavages between the landed elite and the growing bourgeois class. Cleavages between capitalists and workers followed; these were the struggles on which Karl Marx focused.

The voting alignments that resulted from these four cleavages—the two political cleavages between center and periphery and state and church, and the two economic cleavages between agriculture and industry and capitalist and worker—largely persist today. They are the framework for the party systems of the stable democratic polities, particularly in Europe. Class became the chief source of conflict and determining factor of voting behavior, particularly after the extension of suffrage to all adult males. Both Tocqueville in the early nineteenth century and James Bryce at the end of it noted that at the bottom of the American party conflict lay the struggle between aristocratic and democratic interests and sentiments.

The partisan expressions of these four sources of division have varied greatly internationally. The divisions have been fully expressed in multiparty systems and condensed into broad coalitions in two-party systems like those of Australia and the United States. Despite the transformations in Western society over the first half of the twentieth century, the formal party divisions remain little changed. Essentially, the voting alignments became institutionalized: the party systems in the Western world of the 1990s resemble those that existed before World War II.

Nevertheless, a few important changes have occurred. The most important ones were the disappearance of fascist movements and the melding of the various working-class parties following the collapse of communism. Leftist parties had gained strength after World War II, but in recent decades the social democrats and many of the communists and reformed communists dropped their ideological opposition to market-driven economies.

By the mid-1960s the Western world appeared to have entered a new political phase. This development has been characterized by the rise of "postmaterialist" issues: concern for the environment, use of nuclear power, equal status for women and minorities, quality education, strong international relations, democratization, and a permissive morality (particularly as it affects family and sexual issues). Some analysts perceive these issues as the basis for a third revolution—the "postindustrial revolution." This revolution, like the national and industrial revolutions before, is introducing new social and political cleavages. For example, several scholars have pointed to a new political realignment over the issues of industry versus ecology. In this conflict, those people who emphasize industrial production (who also tend to hold conservative or trade unionist positions on social issues) confront those who emphasize quality-of-life issues and liberal social views toward ecology, feminism, and nuclear energy. Quality-of-life concerns are difficult to formulate as party issues, but educated, middle-class groups such as the green parties and the new left have sought to foster them.

The instability, or potential instability, created by this emerging third revolution need not lead to the weakening of democratic institutions. Just as the democracies of earlier eras coped with the cleavages wrought by the national and industrial revolutions, so the contemporary democracies will have to adjust to the new social tensions.

The third revolution is not the only, or even the greatest, challenge facing today's emerging democracies. The nascent democracies of Eastern Europe, East and Southeast Asia, and elsewhere are emerging from authoritarian pasts in which there often were no truly independent and viable political parties. The social tensions that elsewhere had given rise to political parties and to political competition had not found expression in stable party alignments or voting blocs. Hence, the emerging democracies have had to create political parties from scratch, as democracy, by our definition, requires party politics.

History provides some solace, however. In the past, a number of totalitarian and authoritarian states that made the transition to democracy were able to institutionalize political parties patterned on the four traditional lines of social cleavage. Stable parties and voter alignments recurred in the postfascist systems of Germany and Italy, as well as in more recent postauthoritarian democracies like Spain and Chile. But, as mentioned earlier, stability has not yet appeared in most of the postcommunist electoral "democracies." The former members of the communist parties have reassembled in "socialist" parties, while the noncommunists have formed a hodgepodge of unstable liberal (free market) populist-nationalist, regional, and religiously linked parties. The one traditional basis of party differentiation that is clearly emerging in Russia is the center-periphery conflict, the cleavage that also developed first in Western societies. The church-state (or church-secular) cleavage is just beginning to take shape to varying degrees, and the land-industry (or rural-urban) tension is also apparent. Ironically, the capitalist-worker struggle is the weakest, perhaps because a capitalist class and an independently organized working class do not yet exist.

In short, democracy by definition requires stable parties with permanent bases of support among voters and an appreciation among the citizenry of the merits and legitimacy of party politics. Without parties and party competition, there is no democracy.

Economic and Social Order

Order and predictability are vital for the well-being of the economy, the political system, and the society. They are essential if a democratic regime is to achieve legitimacy. The Canadian Fathers of Confederation, who drew up the newly unified country's constitution in 1867, described the constitution's objective as "peace, order, and good government." Basically, they were talking of the need for the rule of law—that is, for rules of due process and an independent judiciary. Where power is arbitrary, personal, and unpredictable, citizens will not know how to behave and will fear that any action may produce an unforeseen consequence. Essentially, the rule of law means that people and institutions will be treated equally by the institutions administering the law—the courts, the police, and the civil service—and that they can predict with reasonable certainty the consequences of their actions, at least as far as the state is concerned.

As I said at the beginning of this introduction, economic development and democratic government seem to go hand in hand. Some of the countries that have moved toward democracy in recent years demonstrate this relationship. Chile, Spain, South Korea, and Taiwan are among them. Before democratization, they made rapid advancements on economic measures as well as in providing the necessities of human welfare. But the links between economy, welfare, and democracy are far from consistent. The economic characteristics of India, the most populous democracy in the world, contradict the overall correlation between affluence and democracy, as do those of Botswana, Papua New Guinea, and Sri Lanka. The diffusion of democracy to other poor developing countries in recent years also challenges the generalization.

Socioeconomic factors alone do not explain the nature of a political system. Other variables also come into play. Cultural factors, the course of domestic politics within the country, events in neighboring countries (and even outside the region), and the behavior of leaders and movements all play a role. The outcome of the Spanish civil war of the 1930s, which placed Spain in an authoritarian mold, was influenced by the behavior of other European states. Similarly, the Western acquiescence to Soviet domination of Eastern Europe after World War II determined the political future of that area. It also led Western nations to seek to prevent electoral victories of forces aligned with the Communist Party. Today international agencies and foreign governments openly work to influence the form of domestic politics in developing countries and postcommunist nations; they generally try to foster pluralistic regimes. This development is in large part due to the end of a bipolar world: dictators in developing countries can no longer take advantage of the cold war tension between the Soviet Union and the West to solidify their rule and hold back pro-democratic forces.

It is inevitable that any given factor or policy will result in contradictory out-comes because of the different contexts. As noted, even the most obvious generalizations concerning the beneficent effects of economic development, for example, need not work in any one country. We know that development efforts, which disrupt the lifestyles and social relationships of people and change their expectations, may leave countries open to extremist movements, religious or secular. As Tocqueville emphasized in his study of the French Revolution, and as Gorbachev discovered with dismay as his reforms spun out of his control, a political system may break down precisely when conditions are improving. This is a common result of people's rising expectations and the undermining of traditional beliefs and loyalties.

Conclusion

Democracy today is an international cause. A host of democratic governments and parties, as well as nongovernmental organizations dedicated to human rights and international development, are working to create and sustain democratic forces in newly liberalized polities and to press autocratic ones to change. Various international agencies like the European Union, the North Atlantic Treaty Organization, the World Bank, and the International Monetary Fund require a democratic system as a condition for membership or aid. The costs of avoiding free elections—in terms of lost foreign aid, lost foreign trade, and lost productivity from a repressed populace—are becoming prohibitive, particularly in Southeast Asia, Eastern Europe, Latin America, and to some extent in Africa. Yet the solution in many countries—superficial or even sham elections—do not address the problems. Elections that lack integrity are meaningless. And although the outside world can encourage democratic institutions, political parties, and meaningful competition among the parties, party systems and values must develop from within.

The long-term prospects for stable democracy in a number of the new systems are questionable. Most new democracies inherently are low in legitimacy in the eyes of their citizens because they lack the traditional loyalties or a record of effectiveness. Moreover, in many of the states political democratization is emerging against a backdrop of severe economic crisis. And a dysfunctional economy, the source of massive poverty and social animosities, is democracy's worst enemy. Such conditions have already endangered democratization in Algeria, Haiti, and Nigeria as well as in Egypt, Kenya, the Philippines, and the Central Asian successor states to the Soviet Union.

What new democracies need, above all, to attain legitimacy is to be effective, particularly in the economic arena but also in governance. If they can manage economic development effectively, they can keep their political houses in order. But the immediate strains that arise from economic growth may undermine long-term democratic stability.

We have made a number of assertions, with a good measure of confidence, about the structural, cultural, and institutional factors that lead to democracy. But specific outcomes depend on particular contexts: on whether the electoral system and other political institutions are appropriate to managing the ethnic and other strains in the country, on the state of the economy, and, of course, on the abilities and tactics of the major actors involved. George Washington and Abraham Lincoln, V. I. Lenin and Mikhail Gorbachev, Jawaharlal Nehru and Charles de Gaulle, to name just a few, all profoundly affected the prospects for democracy in their times and countries.

The various forces for and against democratization reviewed here and in many articles in the *Encyclopedia* influence the possibilities for democratization, but they cannot determine outcomes. Whether democracy succeeds or fails continues to depend significantly on the choices and behaviors of political leaders and groups.

SEYMOUR MARTIN LIPSET

THE ENCYCLOPEDIA OF DEMOCRACY

A

Abdul Rahman, Tunku

Leader of the independence movement in Malaya and the first prime minister of that nation. The relative stability of democracy in Malaya, which has been called Malaysia since 1963, can be attributed largely to Tunku Abdul Rahman (1902–1990). As the architect of Malayan independence, Abdul Rahman played a vital role in creating a political culture that supported democracy and in establishing democratic institutions of government.

In 1951 Abdul Rahman was elected president of the United Malays National Organization, the major political party in Malaya. He sought cooperation with the Malay Chinese Association and the Malay Indian Congress to form the coalition Alliance Party, which ultimately became the vehicle for the independence movement.

The overriding characteristic of Malayan politics was its communal (multiethnic) nature. Ethnic Malays constituted about half the population, and Chinese made up about one-third; Indians, aborigines, and Europeans were smaller minority groups. Abdul Rahman's alliance party system was established to cope with the severe tensions arising from the conflicting cultures and ambitions of the major ethnic groups.

Abdul Rahman led the movement for independence under the principles of constitutionalism. He did not advocate armed struggle. He favored the British system of democracy as the model for Malaya. He recognized the importance of retaining the monarchy and traditional rulers, while simultaneously establishing a secular system of democratic rule. Under his leadership, the Alliance Party brought about peaceful independence from Britain in 1957.

The establishment of the multiethnic alliance was Ab-

Tunku Abdul Rahman

dul Rahman's most important contribution to democratic stability and the easing of ethnic tensions in Malaya. Abdul Rahman also undermined the Malay Communist Party by opening the political and economic system to the Chinese, many of whom otherwise would have affiliated with the Communists in the 1950s, when their numbers were growing.

In 1963 Abdul Rahman oversaw an agreement to incorporate Sabah, Sarawak, and Singapore into a Federation of Malaysia. The merger of these states with Malaya was seen as a way to stabilize the region. The Federation of Malaysia lasted only two years in its original form. In August 1965

Prime Minister Abdul Rahman requested that Singapore leave the federation. The prime minister of Singapore, Lee Kuan Yew, called for a "Malaysian Malaysia"—that is, a Malaysia with equal participation from all areas and groups. In contrast, Abdul Rahman advocated a "Malayan Malaysia," with special privileges reserved for the dominant ethnic group.

The removal of Singapore in 1965 did not resolve the problems engendered by the communal character of Malaysian politics. Indeed, Abdul Rahman's commitment to democracy was tested in May 1969, when racial tensions led the government temporarily to dismantle democratic institutions. Authority was granted to a National Operations Council under the leadership of Tun Abdul Razak, the deputy prime minister. Abdul Rahman resigned in 1970, and Abdul Razak became prime minister. Parliamentary government returned to Malaysia in a modified form in 1971.

The significance of Abdul Rahman's role in the democratization of Malaysia cannot be overstated. His commitment to parliamentary government, his emphasis on communal inclusion, and his effective policies for economic development formed the foundation for democracy. After leaving office, Abdul Rahman became the nation's senior statesman, the national "conscience," and a respected journalist who unfailingly opposed his successors' moves to undercut the rule of law.

See also *Malaysia; Singapore.*

Clark D. Neher

BIBLIOGRAPHY

Abdul Rahman, Tunku. *As a Matter of Interest.* Kuala Lumpur: Heinemann Asia, 1981.
Ahmad, Zakaria Haji. "Quasi Democracy in a Divided Society." In *Democracy in Developing Countries: Asia,* edited by Larry Diamond, Juan J. Linz, and Seymour Martin Lipset. Boulder, Colo.: Lynne Rienner; London: Adamantine Press, 1989.
Ishak, Enche Abdul Aziz. *The Architect of Merdeka.* Singapore: Tan Kah Jee, 1958.
———. *Contemporary Issues in Malaysian Politics.* Petaling Jaya: Pelanduk, 1984.

Abolitionism

A social movement and ideology aimed at the legal prohibition of the international slave trade, slavery, and other forms of coerced labor. Historically, the institution of slavery implied a system of authority that denied specific individuals or groups enforceable claims to rights of kinship, property, and family, while giving slaveholders socially enforceable access to the bodies and labor of the enslaved as chattel (personal) property. The collective movement to eliminate slavery began only in the last quarter of the eighteenth century. Before the institution was abolished, only selective manumission (or emancipation of individuals), flight, or resistance offered a way out of slavery.

From the Premodern Period to Colonization

Although democratization and the elimination of slavery are sometimes assumed to be mutually reinforcing processes, democracy, in its earliest form, was considered to be compatible with, and even dependent on, slavery. In the ancient Greek *polis,* or city-state, the idea of democracy implied the participation of all citizens in lawmaking and office holding. In the classical world, however, a system of slave labor supported the material and psychological independence of the citizenry. The existence of slavery sharpened boundaries between citizens and noncitizens.

As the Greeks emerged from the pre-*polis* stage, membership in the community was inextricably bound up with possession of land and military participation. When the local peasantry won the status of freedom from involuntary labor they also won "citizenship" in the *polis.* Given the impossibility of compelling peasant or artisan citizens to become hired labor in preindustrial conditions, slavery was established for "outsiders" brought into the *polis,* without claims to rights in the community. Although Aristotle's theory of "natural" slavery as the basis of political participation in the *polis* was not shared universally, the expansion of Athenian citizenship increased pressures for the expansion of slavery.

In antiquity, domestic slavery was far more common than was political democracy. Personal dependency and fundamental inequality were characteristic features of most premodern societies throughout the world, regardless of the political system. Most expansions and contractions of chattel slave systems occurred without widespread popular hostility to slavery or any expressed intention to replace the institution by free contractual labor. In the world of imperial Rome, slavery was gradually and incompletely displaced by other servile forms of labor. These included laborers bound to the land rather than to persons—serfs and debt bondsmen, for example.

The decrease of slave labor in late antiquity must therefore be seen in the context of increased coercion of non-slave labor. When societies placed constraints on enslavement by virtue of shared ethnic or religious affiliations, opportunities for recruiting outsiders as slaves still continued. For example, Muslims and Christians did not customarily enslave followers of their own religions. Royal prohibitions of domestic slavery in fourteenth-century France and eighteenth-century Russia were made in the context of continued servile status for rural agricultural laborers. Both chattel slavery and the slave trade could be tolerated or reintroduced as distant territories were added to the royal domain.

Nevertheless, the political and social roots of modern abolitionism reach back into medieval Europe. In northwestern Europe the virtual disappearance of slavery in the twelfth and thirteenth centuries was followed by the gradual diminution of serfdom in the next two centuries. Medieval urban communes often proclaimed the principle of "free soil" within their jurisdictions—that is, within the walls of a town the air was legally "too free" for slaves to breathe. Such municipal legislation was intended to undermine the power of neighboring feudal lords to control the flow of labor, but it could also be applied to individual foreigners traveling with slaves or, occasionally, to whole cargoes of slaves. In the sixteenth century a prototype of the American Underground Railroad ran across the Pyrenees Mountains from the Iberian peninsula to "free soil" Toulouse in France.

Despite the secular trend toward the disappearance of servile labor in western Europe, the first three centuries of European overseas expansion stimulated new boundary-drawing opportunities for Europeans. In Asia, Africa, and the Americas, where the institution was already endemic, slavery was also sanctioned in every European settlement. Governments provided for the increased use of transplanted European indentured labor. Indentured servants agreed to work for a master for a certain period of time, usually in exchange for passage to a new country. Governments allowed still more leeway for coercing native labor, although the enslavement of native people in the Americas and in East Asia was gradually prohibited. In the case of African slaves, a full range of property rights in regard to persons were sanctioned.

For two and a half centuries after the successful transoceanic expeditions of the Portuguese and the Spanish, slavery and empire both expanded without serious political impediment. Free-soil principles for New World slaves were sometimes eroded even in Europe. As late as the last quarter of the eighteenth century, legal provisions were made in France and the Netherlands to ensure that free-soil status could be suspended for those slaves temporarily brought to France and the Netherlands by overseas slaveholders.

An institutional dualism deepened between the zones of civil liberty in northwestern Europe and their colonies "beyond the line." The Dutch and English revolutions against royal, feudal, and ecclesiastical authority stimulated no corresponding movement against expansion of their overseas slave empires. On the contrary, the Dutch Republic and the English Commonwealth both vigorously encouraged overseas expansion of plantation colonies using coerced labor. Yet even during three centuries of tolerated overseas slave expansion (1450–1750), the social development of northwestern Europeans continued in the direction of freedom for labor in the home countries. In England, France, and the Netherlands the dependence of employers upon wage labor or contractual labor did not diminish during the expansion of those countries' slave colonies; rather, the notion was ceaselessly articulated that any slave who set foot on free soil was free.

By 1700 the language of hostility to slavery ran through the rhetoric, the rituals, and the riots of Great Britain. Overseas slavery and slaves brought to Europe impinged only minimally on Britain's legal institutions. Economically, slave capital was important only to a few British merchants and members of the gentry. Eighteenth-century philosophers generally condemned the institution of slavery. Unlike the situation in the premodern Mediterranean world, the boundary between freedom and slavery was geographic.

On the eve of the American Revolution, Arthur Young, an English gentleman farmer and writer, estimated the world's servile population as nineteen in twenty. All the inhabitants of eastern Europe, Asia, Africa, and Central and South America were casually consigned to slavery, while all the inhabitants of northwestern Europe and the whites of British North America were numbered among the free.

The Anglo-American World

Democracy and abolitionism first converged in the Anglo-American world, where the line between colonizing and colonial societies became blurred. Britain's North American colonies, with their uniquely predominant European and free labor populations, first made it possible for Anglo-Americans to imagine their New World settlements as extensions, and even democratizations, of the free civil society that had emerged in northwestern Europe. Polemical attacks against "enslavement" of the Americans by the mother country were often linked to attacks on chattel slavery in America.

More than rhetorical escalation accompanied this anti-imperial mobilization. In 1774 the Continental Congress achieved a unified colonial boycott of the African slave trade. The potentially egalitarian implications of the Declaration of Independence (1776) were embedded in some free-soil constitutions of the northern colonies, beginning with Vermont in 1777 and Massachusetts in 1780. Emancipation legislation was introduced into the other northern colonies of the new United States, beginning with Pennsylvania in 1780.

The arguments for expanding political suffrage for free white males, the nationalization of the boycott against the slave trade, and the antislavery overtones of antiestablishment religious mobilization were, however, ultimately set aside in the interest of fostering national unity with the slave states of the South. The Constitutional Convention of 1787 postponed the abolition of the slave trade for at least another twenty years. The Constitution implicitly recognized slavery as the preserve of the individual states. By 1807, when the transatlantic slave trade to the United States was prohibited, democratization of voting rights for white males in the South was proceeding in tandem with a general strengthening of the institution of southern slavery.

A second democratic wave in the northern states after 1830 was accompanied by a revival and radicalization of mass abolitionism. In the North the same postindependence consolidation that had lowered electoral qualifications for white males had also systematized the exclusion of women and free blacks. Northern abolitionism stimulated the U.S. women's rights movement and was frequently linked to radical communal experiments. By 1860 slavery had become the central issue in the geographical extension of political democracy. As antislavery principles became increasingly characteristic of northern democratization and decreasingly characteristic of southern democratization, the growing northern majority clearly threatened the continuation of the institution of slavery. In 1860, on the eve of the American Civil War, the Democratic Party, which was dedicated to keeping slavery from becoming the nation's primary political issue, ruptured over just that issue. The victory of the Republican Party triggered southern secession.

Abolitionism played a more central role in the democratization of Great Britain than in the democratization of the antebellum United States. In Britain the rise of abolitionism preceded the first expansion of the suffrage (1832) by decades. This interval has inclined many historians to misinterpret the first generation of abolitionism as an elite or capitalist-led movement, directed against democratizing forces. Between the late 1780s and the early 1830s abolitionism became the most exemplary of Britain's national social movements in democratizing public organization and public rhetoric.

Popular abolitionism emerged during the "British miracle" of the 1780s, reflecting the restoration of economic, political, and international confidence after the war with the colonies. Abolitionism became Britain's popular reaffirmation of its prewar self-proclaimed status as the world's standard-bearer of liberty. Abolitionists expanded the claims of justice to incorporate descendants of Africans. They recruited women as political canvassers. The cause offered an opportunity for the politicization of ordinarily cautious religious dissenters. Through their pioneering use of the petition, abolitionists legitimized the concept of public opinion as a responsible "actor" in the legislative process during a period when popular politics was under suspicion in reaction to the French Revolution, which began in 1789, and the 1791 slave revolt in Saint-Domingue (the modern Haiti).

For almost fifty years before the Reform Act of 1832, abolitionism provided an organizational shelter for class, gender, and religious protest in Britain. Abolitionists encouraged colonial slave resistance through agitation at home and through Britain's expanding missionary network in the Caribbean. From the 1780s to the end of British colonial slavery in 1833–1838, waves of abolitionist agitation coincided with mobilizations of movements for other rights and with the expansion of vehicles for nonviolent agitation. For example, abolitionist petitions to Parliament increased from 100 in 1788 to more than 5,000 in 1833. The average of all petitions to Parliament rose from about 200 per year to 10,000 per year during the same period. Movements working on behalf of disenfranchised men, for women's suffrage and child labor laws, and for religious minorities, workers, and consumers drew on the organizational model provided by abolitionist agitators.

In Britain, as in the United States, the link between abolitionism and democratization was sectional, though the regions were far less polarized. Abolitionism and political democratization were most closely connected in the industrializing areas of northern England and southern Scotland. In the three generations following American independence, there was also much transatlantic interaction between abolitionists. Britain and the United States legislated the end of their respective Atlantic slave trades almost simultaneously. During the late 1820s in Britain, and the early 1830s in the northern United States, the "gradualist," nonconfrontational abolitionism after the abolition of the slave trades changed into a more radical "immediatism."

The last popular abolitionist revival in Britain was stimulated by conflict over slavery during the American Civil War. It became linked to British workers' demands for further electoral reform in 1866–1867. The emancipation of the slaves in the United States also stimulated liberal reformers in the French Second Empire, making the late 1860s a high water mark of democratization in the Atlantic world.

Europe and Latin America

Beyond the Anglo-American North Atlantic, the link between abolitionism and democratization is less clear. The processes of emancipation of slaves in the civil sphere and of expansion of participation in the political process often operated at cross-purposes. Continental European abolitionism offers few parallels with Anglo-American abolitionism.

Mainland European governments did not have to deal with mass abolitionist agitation at home on the same scale as did Great Britain and the United States. On the Continent, abolitionist movements were geographically confined and transitory. Continental governments tended to move against slavery in response to external international pressures, such as British diplomacy or demands created by insurrections in their overseas colonies. Abolitionist initiatives came in the forms of bureaucratic plans and revolutionary decrees. Neither form was particularly responsive or conducive to broader patterns of democratization. The Swedish, Danish, Dutch, Spanish, and Portuguese colonial emancipations conform largely to this model. All had meager abolitionist organizations before emancipation and no connection to internal democratic agitation.

French abolitionism was an anomaly in some ways. France was unique in having had two slave empires divided by a revolutionary interregnum. On the eve of the French Revolution in 1788, French abolitionists founded the *Amis des Noirs* (Friends of Black People). This elite organization was never able to generate a mass movement because it was stalemated by a counter-abolitionist mobilization of French overseas interests and then dispersed by waves of revolutionary purges. Purges were directed against members of the *Amis des Noirs* less because of their positions on slavery than because of their affiliations with political groups considered to be tainted during the Jacobin period.

Meanwhile, revolutionary propaganda and political turmoil in France stimulated political division and mass slave uprisings in France's Caribbean islands. By 1794 France had to deal with the combined threats of British colonial conquest and the most successful slave revolution in history in its largest slave colony—Saint-Domingue. The first French emancipation of slaves, in February 1794, was accomplished by emergency decree. Like all continental antislavery, it was in response to an external crisis. Reaction against the revolutionary violence of the Caribbean blacks encouraged racism among some French philosophers and scientists. In 1802 Napoleon Bonaparte restored slavery in every colony of the French tropical empire except Saint-Domingue, where his forces were defeated by a renewed uprising of freedmen in 1803.

The second French slave emancipation deceptively resembled the first. It was decreed by the provisional government of the French Second Republic, which was established after the revolution of 1848. Yet this emancipation, unlike the previous one, was preceded by a popular abolitionist movement. Although unimpressive when compared with its Anglo-American counterparts, the brief French abolitionist campaign of 1846–1847 was a popular movement by continental standards. In the 1860s the Civil War in the United States and the Reconstruction era that followed stimulated a brief renewal of abolitionism in France. The northern cause became a rallying point for liberals and other supporters of democracy in the Second French Empire.

Spain and the Spanish colonies conformed to the continental European model in their reaction to abolitionist pressures. In the early nineteenth century the demands fueled by the wars of independence initiated a process of emancipation without abolitionism in mainland Central and South America. The new South American nations generally freed their slaves very gradually and without political democratization. In the Spanish Caribbean, international pressure, mainly British, finally ended the slave trade to Cuba in the 1860s. Thereafter, revolutionary insurgency within Cuba combined with a liberal revolution in Spain to accelerate gradual emancipation in the 1870s and 1880s.

Brazil was the largest and last of the Latin American countries to abolish slavery. For most of the nineteenth century, Brazilians followed the continental model without initiating either abolitionism or democratization. The ending of the Brazilian slave trade was precipitated by British naval action in 1850. Until the 1880s steps toward gradual abolition were managed by an oligarchical regime of imperial notables chosen by a restricted franchise. In its final days of slavery (1880–1888), Brazil became the only Latin American country to develop an Anglo-American style of antislavery movement, with mass rallies and new forms of collective action. Although the national legislature remained relatively passive, popular abolitionism took an extralegal but nonviolent path. Emancipation spread from province to province, with mass flights of slaves matching or exceeding the flight of southern slaves during the U.S. Civil War. Brazil's emancipatory "Golden Law" of 1888 ratified the death of an institution undermined by abolitionist protests and slaves already voting with their feet.

Asia and the Middle East

Abolition and democracy diverged again in the late nineteenth century, in both the Old World and the New. After Brazilian emancipation in 1888, European attention shifted to those areas of the Eastern Hemisphere that were under European domination. Cardinal Charles Martial Allemand Lavigerie, an outstanding figure in the Catholic missionary movement in Africa, made a grand tour of Europe in the late 1880s. He sparked a mass continental crusade against the slave trade and slavery in Africa. The ending of slavery in Africa and Asia, however, was characterized by a profound divergence between democracy and abolitionism. Emancipation became a legitimization of overseas European imperial domination, not of democracy.

The process of abolition in the Eastern Hemisphere conformed to what some historians have called a bureaucratic British–East Indian model of emancipation rather than the Anglo-American models of complete emancipation driven by mass agitation. Gradual, often drawn-out, emancipations served as a means of accommodation with native elites. In the vast areas of Africa and Asia under European political control, the ending of slavery and the emergence of self-government were historically unconnected phenomena. The process of civil emancipation

usually ended long before that of political democratization began. Imperialist governors frequently argued that emancipation of slaves required European domination.

In the nominally independent countries of Asia the abolition of slavery had only a minor role in discussions of democracy. In China, for example, a full-scale attack on the market in human beings did not begin until the twentieth century. That market was finally abolished under the aegis of a communist "people's democracy" after 1949. In Communist China liberal notions of democracy were proscribed along with the market in humans. In India and in the Islamic world, the slave trade and slavery were ended either under direct European imperial rule or by native rulers under Western diplomatic pressure. In either case, popular abolitionism played little role in the process. Slavery did not occupy a prominent place in twentieth-century discussions of democracy in developing nations.

After Emancipation

The creation of democratic polities was not a prominent feature of most former slave societies. In Saint-Domingue, the first postslave society, former slaves gained both nominal civil liberty and nominal national independence as Haitians. However, Haiti's revolutionary national liberation generated two centuries of militarism and oligarchic state exploitation. Nearly a century later, in 1889, Brazil inaugurated a republic. The republic was at least as oligarchical and authoritarian as its imperial predecessor. Before 1881, when popular abolitionism emerged in Brazil, the franchise was open to a million potential voters, enabling 10 percent of the adult population to vote. Under the literacy-based franchise of the early republic, the percentage of voters declined to between 1 and 3 percent.

The British Caribbean retreated from democracy in the wake of emancipation. A generation after the ending of slavery, parliamentary colonial regimes were abolished in favor of Crown colonial rule. In the French tropical colonies and in the U.S. southern states, where emancipation initially included the introduction of universal male suffrage, curtailments or dilutions of popular rights were prevalent. Racial discrimination continued nearly everywhere long after legal emancipation. Because New World abolitions occurred in a historical context in which adult male suffrage was the outermost boundary of political participation, the political goals of abolitionism were confined to the acquisition of rights for men. In the northern United States, Reconstruction was followed by a distancing of many former abolitionists from the women's suffrage movement. Women's suffragists, in turn, did not actively oppose the segregationist tide at the end of the nineteenth century.

In the Eastern Hemisphere the transition of civil status from slavery (or serfdom) to freedom was a complex process of negotiation and struggle. The extension of political rights was limited, grudging, and fragile. In a global perspective, even nineteenth-century abolitionism and democratization were linked processes only in a few instances. Events since the emancipation of black slaves in the New World have further demonstrated that there is no general convergence of abolition and democracy. Just when forced labor seemed to have receded into insignificance and antislavery measures were being codified in the declarations of the League of Nations after World War I, major new zones of coerced labor emerged in parts of Europe and Asia.

The same newspapers that reported the triumphant centenary celebrations of British slave emancipation in 1933 carried vivid accounts of Jews being driven into the streets of German cities and forced to perform degrading tasks. Ten years later the servile labor force in Nazi-dominated Europe was far greater in numbers than the total slave population of the Americas had been a century before. In the democratic people's republics of the communist-dominated world, millions were uprooted in vast systems of penal servitude. Formal representation, universal suffrage, and civil equality were combined with massive new systems of coerced labor well into the second half of the twentieth century.

The processes of democratization and the abolition of legally coerced labor seem to have converged once more in the closing decades of the twentieth century. Although semiclandestine forms of coercion such as debt bondage and child labor continue to be widespread, the most massive forms of coerced labor ended in another wave of democratization.

See also *Brazil; China; City-states, communes, and republics; Classical Greece and Rome; Colonialism; Communism; Revolution, American; Revolution, French; Slavery; Theory, Ancient; Union of Soviet Socialist Republics; United Kingdom; United States of America; Women and democracy.* In Documents section, see *American Declaration of Independence (1776).*

Seymour Drescher

BIBLIOGRAPHY

Blackburn, Robin. *The Overthrow of Colonial Slavery, 1776–1848.* London: Verso, 1988.

Davis, David Brion. *Slavery and Human Progress.* New York: Oxford University Press, 1984.

Drescher, Seymour. *Capitalism and Antislavery: British Mobilization in Comparative Perspective.* New York: Oxford University Press; London: Macmillan, 1986.

———. "The Long Goodbye: Dutch Capitalism and Antislavery in Comparative Perspective." *American Historical Review* 99 (February 1994): 44–69.

Finley, M. I. *Ancient Slavery and Modern Ideology.* New York: Viking, 1983.

Foner, Eric. *Reconstruction: America's Unfinished Revolution, 1863–1877.* New York: Harper and Row, 1988.

Genovese, Eugene D. *From Rebellion to Revolution: Afro-American Slave Revolts in the Making of the Modern World.* Baton Rouge: Louisiana State University Press, 1979.

Miers, Suzanne, and Richard Roberts, eds. *The End of Slavery in Africa.* Madison: University of Wisconsin Press, 1988.

Perry, Lewis, and Michael Fellman, eds. *Antislavery Reconsidered: New Perspectives on the Abolitionists.* Baton Rouge: Louisiana State University Press, 1979.

Scott, Rebecca J., et al. *The Abolition of Slavery and the Aftermath of Emancipation in Brazil.* Durham, N.C.: Duke University Press, 1988.

Accountability of public officials

The ability to determine who in the government is responsible for a decision or action and the ability to ensure that officials in government are answerable for their actions. Accountability is a critical concern in democratic government. For a democratic political system to function, it is imperative that citizens have ways to hold public officials accountable for their actions and decisions.

The most basic premise of democratic government is that the government is responsible to the people. The idea of government being responsible has two dimensions, however. In one sense, it means that the government must be accountable to the people. In another sense, it means that the government is expected to act with a sense of responsibility.

A system of campaigns and elections resulting in officials holding office at the pleasure of the voters is the most elementary device designed to ensure the accountability of public officials. But elections pertain only to this one aspect of responsibility and apply only to elected officials. Other strategies have been introduced to provide mechanisms to ensure that all public officials—those appointed as well as those elected to office—act in a responsible fashion and that they are held accountable for their actions.

Exercise of the Ballot

In democracies the ballot is the most basic way to ensure the accountability of elected public officials. A system of competitive elections and terms of office provides a systematic vehicle for voters to evaluate their elected officials and their performance in office. This is a system of popular accountability that can work. But problems are inherent in the process. Voters need not be informed in order to participate. People vote for a variety of reasons, many having little or nothing to do with the candidates running or the issues involved. Because of this ostensible deficiency, elections may not be the most effective way to keep public officials accountable.

For those voters seeking to exercise the franchise because of a concern with accountability, there are problems as well. Getting accurate information in a timely and usable fashion can be difficult, given the character of contemporary political campaigning. Moreover, officials need not respond to every voter's concerns—nor even to the concerns of a majority—in order to win reelection. Talented candidates can fashion winning coalitions that may not reflect majority sentiment. Prudent use of campaign materials and resources can forge winning results even when the record of a candidate, or a candidate's controversial actions, would seem a serious political liability.

Electoral competition is critical to the functioning of democracy. When there is a lack of competition, voters do not have adequate opportunity to hold officeholders accountable. And even where high levels of political competition exist, the character of the system of campaigns and elections may not facilitate holding public officials accountable. Where citizens elect individuals according to their political party affiliation by voting for a party rather than a candidate, the direct link between the citizens and the public official is missing. In such a system, it is the party that is being held accountable. That party's elected officials are being held accountable only indirectly. In addition, the policy-making process within modern governments is often quite complex; the procedures and rules are hard to follow, making it difficult for voters to determine who is responsible for actions and decisions. In fact, the nature of the policy-making process in modern government represents a serious challenge to political accountability.

Alternatives to the Ballot

In most democracies, numerous alternatives to the ballot have been devised to hold public officials accountable. Many have the effect of promoting popular accountability of appointed officials as well as of elected officials.

Public opinion polls emerged during the latter half of the twentieth century as an effective device for promoting accountability and responsibility in government. Officials look to polls as a gauge of their performance in office and of the popular sentiment surrounding issues and policies they confront. Officials in democracies tend to read public opinion polls as a measure of their popularity, influence, and legitimacy among the citizens. In addition, polls can help to shape the direction government follows in the deliberation of issues, and they can determine what issues will reach the political agenda. An issue generating significant popular attention as reflected in polling data quickly becomes the focus of government scrutiny. Similarly, a government official whose conduct generates popular controversy usually becomes a focus of official scrutiny. The history of modern democracies is replete with examples of the influence of public opinion and polling on the conduct of government and those who serve in government.

In most modern democracies the system of popular accountability created through elections and polling is supported by ethics laws and procedures aimed at ensuring that government officials behave responsibly. A concern with the ethical conduct of government officials has always been associated with democracies. But comprehensive ethics laws and procedures are a relatively recent phenomenon. Their primary purpose is to provide those who serve in government with guidance so that incidental or unintended misconduct may be avoided. In other words, ethics laws and procedures are established to set standards for conduct. They also provide mechanisms for punishing ethical offenses.

Most modern democracies have ethics laws and procedures in place to protect against such things as conflict of interest; they also have policies regulating the investigation of alleged misconduct and punishment for proven misconduct. Many governments maintain offices of government ethics so that officials can resolve any concerns relating to ethics before engaging in conduct that might be questionable. Individuals are usually required to provide information regarding personal wealth and assets prior to joining government and to update that information regularly. Such public disclosure requirements provide a means to guard against official misconduct while underscoring the point that government service in a democracy is not supposed to lead to personal profit or wealth.

In addition to these kinds of ethics laws, many governments have passed freedom of information acts that enable individuals and groups outside government to obtain both personal and job-related information about government officials. Although a relatively recent development, these freedom of information acts have emerged as one of the primary means by which the public attempts to hold officials accountable for their actions.

From time to time, individuals within government, motivated by a concern for the public interest or by personal outrage, will speak out publicly when unethical, illegal, or improper conduct is taking place within government. This sort of whistle-blowing usually takes place only after formal complaint resolution strategies within government have exhausted. But whistle-blowing will quickly bring the conduct of public officials to the attention of the citizens and often leads to official action.

Ethics policies aside, however, the political process remains the primary vehicle for ensuring accountability in democratic governments. Whereas it was once standard practice among democracies for much of the business of government to take place behind closed doors, today the political process is far more accessible. In most democracies the passage of laws and the creation of regulations can no longer be shielded from popular scrutiny. Sunshine laws, for example, require official meetings to be accessible to the public. In some places the bureaucracy must adhere to relatively stringent requirements for public input and comment while promulgating rules and regulations. Many governments have created positions especially designed to resolve concerns and complaints citizens might have about the government. These ombudsmen act as a direct link between the individual and the government and provide a personal service for citizens seeking redress of some grievance. The office of ombudsman originated in Sweden early in the nineteenth century; the term is Swedish for "agent."

Many governments have established relatively sophisticated policy-analysis and auditing agencies. The purpose of such agencies is to determine how well government programs work and what can be done to improve them. The findings of these agencies are usually available to the public and can be a valuable source of information to those interested in holding officials accountable.

Most democratic governments provide additional means by which public officials may be held accountable for their conduct. Some systems have established mechanisms through which citizens may recall elected officials.

Both popular referendums and citizen initiatives have been employed to force governments to deal with issues when public officials have refused to act. Popular grassroots movements have emerged periodically in response to perceptions of government waste, abuse, or ineffectiveness. In most democracies there are established procedures for impeaching and removing from office public officials judged to have violated their oath of office, those found guilty of malfeasance or misfeasance in office, or those convicted of violations of law.

Complexity and Accountability

The modern liberal democratic state that has emerged during the last half of the twentieth century—a state that is charged with dealing with a vast array of complex issues—contrasts sharply with the rather simple vision of popular accountability and governmental responsibility that rests at the heart of democratic theory. A complex government is more difficult to understand and to keep under control than a simple one. A large and active government is, by definition, more difficult to hold accountable. And it is more difficult to ensure that it acts responsibly. But the ability of a people to hold officials accountable for what they do remains the truest measure of a democracy.

See also *Complexity; Corruption; Media, Mass; Polling, Public opinion; Referendum and initiative.*

Eugene W. Hickok

BIBLIOGRAPHY

The Federalist Papers. Edited by Clinton Rossiter. New York: New American Library, 1961.

Goldman, Alan H. *The Moral Foundations of Professional Ethics.* Totowa, N.J.: Rowman and Littlefield, 1980.

Mosher, Frederick C. *Democracy and the Public Service.* 2d ed. New York: Oxford University Press, 1982.

Redford, Emmette S. *Democracy and the Administrative State.* New York: Oxford University Press, 1969.

Wilson, James Q. *Bureaucracy: What Government Agencies Do and Why They Do It.* New York: Basic Books, 1989.

Adams, John

First vice president and second president of the United States. Adams (1735–1826), who was the descendant of

John Adams

ings are driven by the "passion for distinction," a yearning that can be ennobling but that is also the source of jealousy and conflict. In most human beings, Adams argued, passion overrides virtue and reason unless restrained by force. Over time, consequently, the government decisively affects what a people thinks of as honorable and dishonorable; influencing such definitions and goals is the art of governance.

Adams came to believe that Americans had no special civic virtue, particularly given the role of the "spirit of commerce" in promoting the private pursuit of wealth. A sounder basis for government lay in using competing forces to balance each other. Adams supported ratification of the Constitution, although he would have preferred a more classical structure in which the upper house was reserved for "the rich, the well-born and the able." Adams—who was often charged with favoring aristocracy—feared that the rich would dominate both houses unless the aristocracy was made identifiable. Similarly, although he favored limiting the vote to those who possessed at least some property, he wanted a broad electorate and supported policies to promote widespread ownership of land.

Adams died on the same day as Thomas Jefferson, July 4, 1826, fifty years to the day after the signing of the Declaration of Independence.

See also *United States Constitution*. In Documents section, see *American Declaration of Independence (1776)*; *Constitution of the United States (1787)*.

Wilson Carey McWilliams

Massachusetts Puritans and a graduate of Harvard, was influenced both by religion and by newer secular ideas. His wife, Abigail, was an early champion of women's rights; his son, John Quincy Adams, became the sixth president of the United States.

During the Continental Congress, Adams had been a member of the committee that drafted the Declaration of Independence (1776). He was a moderate Federalist, but he remained at odds with the orthodoxy of both the Federalist and the Antifederalist Parties. In his books on the principles of politics, including *A Defense of the Constitutions of Government of the United States of America* (1787) and *Discourses on Davila* (1790), he contended that human be-

Adenauer, Konrad

First chancellor of the Federal Republic of Germany and a principal architect of the post–World War II political and economic recovery of Germany and of European integration. Adenauer (1876–1967) was praised by Winston Churchill and others as Germany's greatest statesman since Otto von Bismarck. He played a decisive role in the creation and legitimation of the Federal Republic of Germany as an effective constitutional democracy.

Adenauer became leader of the newly founded Christian Democratic Union (CDU) shortly after the end of World War II and served as federal chancellor from 1949 to 1963. During these critical years, West Germany emerged from wartime devastation and Allied occupation to become one of the most prosperous and politically stable nations in Europe and a respected member of the Atlantic alliance. Under Adenauer's leadership, West Germany also helped initiate the postwar movement for European integration.

Adenauer's political career spanned four German regimes. Born into a Catholic family only five years after German unification, Adenauer studied law and became active in local government in his native city of Cologne as a member of the Catholic-based Center Party. In recognition of his administrative skills, the city council elected him lord mayor of Cologne in 1917. Adenauer was initially in contact with a separatist movement to establish an autonomous West German republic at the end of World War I. He saw this as a territorial buffer against a possible socialist revolution elsewhere in Germany. Once national leaders in Berlin had restored order with the assistance of the German army, Adenauer declared his political loyalty to the fledgling Weimar Republic.

Adenauer continued to serve as mayor of Cologne during the republic's tumultuous existence, but he was abruptly dismissed when the National Socialists (Nazis) seized power in 1933. In the following years he was periodically arrested by the Gestapo and marked several times for execution. For most of the Third Reich, he lived with his family in seclusion in a village south of Bonn.

As U.S. military forces moved into the Rhineland during the final months of World War II, U.S. officials—who knew of Adenauer's anti-Nazi record—invited him to resume his duties as lord mayor of Cologne. Adenauer, however, promptly angered British occupation officials because of his independent views on Germany's future. In October 1945 he was summarily dismissed as mayor for a second time. In the following months, he devoted his attention to establishing the Christian Democratic Union as a "supra-confessional" organization (that is, one uniting Catholics and Protestants) that would be a successor to the Center Party. Under his leadership the CDU emerged as one of the principal political parties in the western zones of occupied Germany.

Adenauer was elected chair of the Parliamentary Council, which convened in September 1948 in Bonn with instructions from the U.S., British, and French governments to draw up a constitution for a West German state. He used his authority to help engineer a broad consensus among the delegates on the legal and institutional basis for the new Federal Republic. At the same time he gained do-

Konrad Adenauer

mestic and international visibility for himself as an astute politician. Following national elections in August 1949, a narrow majority of the members of the parliament (the Bundestag) elected him federal chancellor at the head of a coalition cabinet dominated by the Christian Democrats. At seventy-three years of age, Adenauer assumed executive responsibility for the rebirth of Germany's democracy.

Adenauer's Catholicism, Rhineland origins, and antipathy to communism determined the course of his domestic and foreign policies during the formative years of the Federal Republic. He established a political rapport with fellow Catholic leaders in France, Belgium, and Italy. His distrust of Protestant eastern Germany was due to its traditions of Prussian militarism and radical socialism as well as to the difference in religion. This lack of trust underlay his determination to lead West Germany into a firm economic, political, and military alliance with the West, even at the cost of deepening Germany's postwar division.

In rapid succession, Adenauer negotiated the lifting of

Allied restrictions on economic recovery, German membership in postwar regional economic and political organizations (including the Organization for European Economic Cooperation and the Council of Europe), and the restoration of West German sovereignty. He was receptive to Allied initiatives to rearm West Germany as a bulwark against potential communist expansion after the outbreak of the Korean War in 1950. In 1955 he led the Federal Republic into the North Atlantic Treaty Organization (NATO). He joined with France, Italy, Belgium, the Netherlands, and Luxembourg in launching the West European integration movement through treaty agreements to establish the European Coal and Steel Community in 1951 and the European Economic Community in 1957.

Adenauer's diplomatic prowess was accompanied by the rapid reconstruction of West Germany's cities and infrastructure, economic growth, and the integration of millions of political refugees and exiles from East Germany during the 1950s and early 1960s. German voters responded by continuing to reelect the Christian Democrats and their Free Democratic coalition partners. Adenauer was reelected federal chancellor in 1953, 1957, and 1961.

Ultimately, Adenauer's advancing age and increased resistance to domestic and international change undermined his parliamentary support. He reacted hesitantly to the erection of the Berlin Wall in August 1961. In October 1962 the involvement of senior government officials in an unconstitutional raid on the office of one of Germany's leading news periodicals triggered a cabinet crisis. The Free Democrats insisted on Adenauer's resignation. In October 1963 he reluctantly yielded the chancellorship to Ludwig Erhard, the former minister of economics. Adenauer continued to serve as CDU chair until shortly before his death in 1967.

Adenauer was frequently criticized, at home and abroad, for his authoritarian style of leadership and political inflexibility, especially during his last years in office. Nonetheless, he contributed significantly to West Germany's successful transition to democracy and to its postwar status as an equal partner with other Western nations.

See also *Germany; World War I; World War II.* In Documents section, see *Constitution of the Federal Republic of Germany (1949).*

M. Donald Hancock

BIBLIOGRAPHY

Adenauer, Konrad. *Memoirs, 1945–1953.* Translated by Beate Ruhm von Oppen. Chicago: Regnery, 1965.

Heidenheimer, Arnold J. *Adenauer and the CDU.* The Hague: M. Nijhoff, 1960.

Hiscocks, Richard. *The Adenauer Era.* Philadelphia and New York: Lippincott, 1966.

Neumann, Erich Peter, and Elisabeth Noelle. *Statistics on Adenauer: Portrait of a Statesman.* Allensbach am Bodensee: Verlag für Demoskopie, 1962.

Wighton, Charles. *Adenauer: A Critical Bibliography.* New York: Coward-McCann, 1963.

Affirmative action

Policies and programs of government and nongovernmental institutions intended to redress inequalities among racial, linguistic, gender, and caste groups by providing individuals with special opportunities or benefits on the basis of their membership in these groups. The mechanisms of affirmative action include laws, regulations, administrative rules, court orders, and various public interventions and private actions to provide certain public and private goods—such as admissions into schools and colleges, jobs, promotions, business loans, and land rights—on the basis of membership in a particular ethnic, racial, or other group for the purpose of achieving greater equality among these groups. Thus the central feature of affirmative action is that efforts are made on behalf of individuals because they belong to particular groups. Affirmative action is not intended to bridge the gap between rich and poor but to bridge the gap between groups.

The term *affirmative action* originated in the United States in the 1960s. Although other countries (for example, Canada, the Netherlands, and Switzerland) have adopted elements of affirmative action, the most extensive and comprehensive affirmative action policies in addition to the United States are those in India, Sri Lanka, and Malaysia. These programs—under such nomenclature as *reservations, compensatory discrimination, positive discrimination,* and *preferential policies*—rest on the belief by policymakers that disparities among groups are the result of one group's discrimination against or oppression of another; that they are a consequence of the state's systematic denial of equal resources; or that they are the byproduct of historic circumstances that have given one group advantages over another. These disparities often persist and perpetuate themselves from one generation to another, in some instances as a result of the legacy of the past but in other instances as the result of persisting barriers to equal opportunity. When differences are reproduced from one generation to another, externally imposed barriers are presumed to exist.

Opposition to affirmative action policies has come from those who want to build a nonracial, color-blind, caste-blind, ethnically blind society and who therefore are uncomfortable with the idea that benefits should be allocated on the basis of race, caste, gender, or ethnic identity. Opposition also comes from those who are concerned that individual merit and achievement will be downgraded if admissions to universities and professional schools as well as jobs are granted on the basis of group membership. Such policies, it is argued, erode individual accomplishment, create a new class of excluded (and therefore demoralized) individuals, and make industry and universities less competitive and government less efficient.

The United States

The first legislation to use the term *affirmative action* was the U.S. Civil Rights Act of 1964, Title VII. The act stated that employers who had engaged in discriminatory practices had to take "affirmative action" to compensate for their wrong practices. A year later, President Lyndon B. Johnson issued an executive order requiring affirmative action in all employment and promotion for all federal contractors, even if they had never been known to discriminate. In the early 1970s the Equal Employment Opportunity Commission, during Richard Nixon's administration, went a step further by establishing quotas, or statistical goals, for the employment of certain minority groups.

Affirmative action acquired a double meaning in the United States. To some, it meant an active or affirmative effort to recruit and promote minorities and to end discriminatory practices. It included efforts by universities, firms, and governments to recruit minorities and women and to create special programs to improve the skills that minorities needed in order to compete effectively in the labor market. To others, it meant mandatory results that were to be obtained through quotas.

This debate moved through the U.S. courts to the Supreme Court *(University of California Regents v. Bakke,* 1978). The medical school at the University of California at Davis had reserved sixteen seats for African American applicants. A rejected white candidate, Allan Bakke, whose test scores were higher than those of the sixteen admitted

African American students, filed suit, charging that his civil rights had been violated. The Supreme Court ruled in a five-to-four decision that race could be taken into account in the university's admission practices, but in another five-to-four decision the Court ruled that the system of quotas established by the medical school was unacceptable because it made race the exclusive factor for a fixed number of admissions. The case thus captured the American ambivalence toward affirmative action: there should be equal opportunity for all based on merit but at the same time there was a national need to take positive steps to remedy historical injustices and dismantle continued barriers to equal opportunities for African Americans.

India, Malaysia, and Sri Lanka

Even before the United States introduced affirmative action programs, India in its constitution of 1950 provided for the establishment of reservations, or quotas, for former untouchables (known in India as the "scheduled" castes) and tribes ("scheduled" tribes). The scheduled castes, who comprise 15 percent of the population, and the scheduled tribes, who comprise 7 percent, were given seats in Parliament and in other elected bodies in proportion to their total population. Quotas were set for their admission into schools, colleges, and medical and engineering schools and for their employment in government services. The constitution also provided for special benefits for other "backward" classes designated by the government. This category refers to member of other lower castes, some of whom are actually well off. The Indian government subsequently extended reservations for this category in university admissions and government employment, providing these communities with a quota of 27 percent. In all, nearly half the admissions into colleges and medical and engineering schools, and nearly half the appointments in government service, were set aside for castes and tribes constituting an estimated three-quarters of the population.

In Malaysia and Sri Lanka, affirmative action programs were put in place to benefit the majority communities, who regarded themselves as disadvantaged in relation to minorities. In Malaysia, the Malay-dominated government argued for "special rights" for the Malays, who constitute a bare majority. The Chinese minority had migrated to Malaysia in the nineteenth century, when they were able to take advantage of the market economy created by the British. The Malay community was divided between a small aristocratic class and a large, poor, rural, uneducated population. After riots in 1969 in which Malays and Chinese clashed, the government introduced what was called the New Economic Policy in order to accelerate economic growth and provide the Malays with special benefits. Appointments in the civil service were made at a ratio of four Malays to one non-Malay; preferences were given to Malays in admission into universities; arrangements were made to expand Malay equity in firms; and land settlement schemes, agricultural credit, and price supports were designed to benefit rural Malays.

In Sri Lanka a Sinhalese-dominated government set out in 1956 to eliminate English as the official language and to replace it with Sinhalese. (Sinhalese constitute 75 percent of the population; the Tamil-speaking minority constitute 18 percent.) Within a decade, the Tamil composition of the civil service dropped from 50 percent to 15 percent because few Tamils spoke Sinhalese. Entrance examinations to the universities, medical schools, and engineering schools continued to be offered in both Tamil and Sinhalese, but the government decided to standardize marks so that Sinhalese and Tamil pass rates would be in proportion to their population. As merit-based opportunities for Tamils declined, resentment by young Tamils against the government's policies grew. They regarded the government's affirmative action policy as an instrument of the majority Sinhalese to use their political power to restrict opportunities for the Tamils. Young Tamils soon turned to arms and called for the creation of an independent Tamil state on the island.

Policy Goals

Although all affirmative action programs share the principle that efforts are made on behalf of individuals because they belong to a designated group, two types of affirmative action policies exist—one directed at opportunities, the other at outcomes.

The first type might be called affirmative action for expanding opportunities. In this category are all policies to eliminate discrimination, including unintended discrimination in job requirements that are not job related and that have a disproportionate effect on minorities. These affirmative action policies include race- or ethnically conscious policies intended to expand the pool of qualified individuals, such as training programs to upgrade the skills of workers, special bridge programs in higher education that enable students who lack adequate preparation to catch up, financial assistance to students who are qualified for higher education but cannot afford it, loans to business owners in disadvantaged communities, and subcontracts to minority businesses. These policies are intended to improve access to education and employment. They entail positive efforts by universities, government, and the private sector to include groups that previously had been excluded. The beneficiaries are explicitly intended to be members of designated communities.

A second type of affirmative action policy emphasizes fixed outcomes based on designated quotas. These are result-oriented policies; they set out to ensure that the distribution of education, employment, income, and wealth among ethnic groups or races will correspond to the proportion in the population of each ethnic group or race. According to this view of affirmative action, every group ideally would be proportionately represented in the universities and professional schools, in legislative bodies, in the higher levels of the bureaucracy, medicine, law, education, and business. Under this model, targets are set and the goal of affirmative action is not achieved until there is proportional representation. If necessary, requirements for admissions and standards of performance are lowered. In each of the countries that have adopted affirmative action programs, the quota route has created the greatest controversy by eroding the notion of equality of opportunity for all and by threatening to erode the performance of institutions.

Affirmative action policies have costs. They generate conflicts between beneficiaries and nonbeneficiaries; strengthen identities on the basis of race, religion, language, and caste; induce politicians to mobilize groups along these lines; encourage individuals to assert group claims and identities; and generate demands by various groups for inclusion under the system of preferences. Affirmative action can be a policy to improve the position of disadvantaged minorities, but it can also be an instrument to enable a numerically dominant social class to exercise its political power against high-achieving minorities.

Affirmative action policies often have a double and sometimes contradictory goal: to diminish inequalities and to diminish ethnic conflict. The latter can best be avoided if affirmative action grows out of a process that leads to a consensus about what constitutes appropriate and acceptable measures to benefit one group without inflicting too great a loss upon another. Such measures would provide special benefits to some while creating equal opportunities for all.

See also *Americans, Ethnic; Citizenship; Egalitarianism; Furnivall, John Sydenham; India; Malaysia; Multiethnic democracy; Racism; Sri Lanka; United States of America.*

Myron Weiner

BIBLIOGRAPHY

"Affirmative Action in India, Malaysia, Sri Lanka, and the USA." *Development and Democracy* 6 (September 1993): 1–86.

Cohen, Marshall, Thomas Nagel, and Thomas Scanlon, eds. *Equality and Preferential Treatment.* Princeton: Princeton University Press, 1977.

Galanter, Marc. *Competing Equalities: Law and the Backward Classes in India.* Berkeley: University of California Press, 1984.

Glazer, Nathan. *Affirmative Discrimination: Ethnic Inequality and Public Policy.* New York: Basic Books, 1975.

Goldmann, Robert B., and A. Jearatnam Wilson. *From Independence to Statehood: Managing Ethnic Conflict in Five African and Asian States.* London: Pinter, 1984.

Lipset, Seymour Martin. "Two Americas, Two Value Systems: Blacks and Whites." In *American Exceptionalism: A Double-Edged Sword.* New York: Norton, 1996.

Weiner, Myron, and Mary Fainsod Katzenstein. *India's Preferential Policies: Migrants, the Middle Classes and Ethnic Equality.* Chicago: University of Chicago Press, 1981.

Africa, Horn of

The northeast African countries of Djibouti, Eritrea, Ethiopia, Somalia, and sometimes Sudan (which is treated separately in this encyclopedia). Although there have been historic political openings that might have led to democratic consolidation, the countries of the Horn of Africa have actually had little experience with democracy.

Somalia, which was nominally democratic at independence in 1960, succumbed to authoritarian military regimes in the first decade. In Djibouti the party in power at independence in 1977 became increasingly authoritarian in the first decade. In Eritrea multiparty democracy flourished in the years leading to federation with Ethiopia in 1952, but it was almost immediately eliminated on federation. And in Ethiopia pluralist democracy was untried until a halting experiment in the 1990s.

Underlying the political authoritarianism and turmoil of this region of Africa have been common problems: profound underdevelopment; limited or no preparation for democratic politics during the colonial period; deep ethnic and clan rivalries that often have exploded into vio-

lence; protracted civil wars generating humanitarian as well as political crises; and a bitter legacy of superpower proxy involvement in the Horn region during the cold war.

Ethiopia

Ethiopia is one of the few African countries that was never colonized by Europeans. The modern imperial state was consolidated between 1855 and 1908. Emperor Haile Selassie I introduced its first written constitution in 1931. Patterned after the Japanese constitution of 1889, it established Ethiopia as a constitutional monarchy, guided by an emperor who traced his ancestry back to King Solomon of Jerusalem and the Queen of Sheba.

The constitution also provided for the secularization and centralization of the bureaucracy. Rules were drawn to professionalize the bureaucracy, judiciary, and budgetary institutions. Perhaps the most remarkable innovation was the inauguration of legislative institutions, the Chamber of Deputies and the Senate. Although these bodies were meant to recommend democratic reforms to the Crown, they were not empowered to make laws autonomously. Neither house was popularly elected. The Chamber of Deputies, it was envisioned, would eventually be elected by the people when they were prepared to accept this weighty responsibility.

The 1931 constitution left little doubt that the authority of the Crown was absolute. Almost half of the fifty-five articles related to the power and prerogatives of the emperor. What few rights were accorded the citizenry could be suspended at will by the emperor or any of his agents.

A new and different constitution, reflecting the influence of American advisers, came into effect in 1955. Like the American Constitution, it provided for a separation of power among the three branches of government. Furthermore, it gave new power to the legislative branch, and fully twenty-eight of its articles addressed the rights and duties of citizens. This constitution, like the previous one, however, imposed no formal restraints on the powers of the emperor, who continued to rule in an authoritarian fashion. Although deputies but not senators were now popularly elected, political parties were still forbidden, and candidates had to meet property qualifications to stand for office.

Between 1955 and 1974 popular pressures for democracy grew rapidly, in part inspired by the winds of change sweeping across the colonized world. Emperor Haile Se-

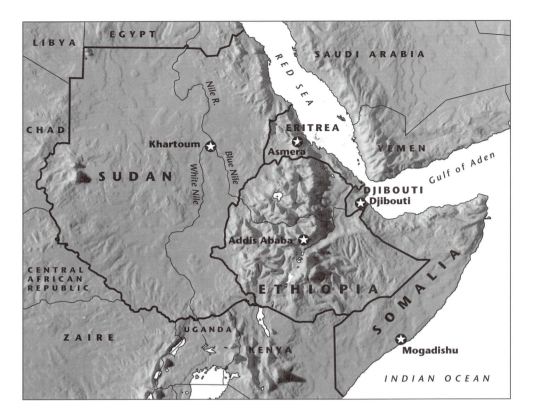

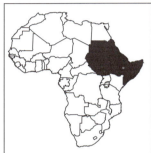

lassie responded to the times by convening yet another constitutional reform commission, but a new constitution never went into effect. A military coup toppled his regime in September 1974. In the immediate aftermath of the coup, the political climate opened as never before. Exiled intellectuals returned home to contribute to the debate over the character of the "new Ethiopia." This openness was short lived, however. Over the next two years the new regime either neutralized, co-opted, or liquidated voices that questioned its own vanguard role in the revolution. In response to urban terror campaigns by various leftist opposition groups, the government responded with its own "Red Terror Campaign." Its aim was to wipe out all voices of opposition and to lay the groundwork for an authoritarian, statist development strategy. Between 1977 and 1978 roughly 5,000 people were killed in the Red Terror Campaign. This massacre was followed by a fifteen-year attempt to organize society according to the principles of Marxism-Leninism.

Under the regime of Mengistu Haile-Mariam, all rural and urban property was decreed to be state owned. The state attempted to gain complete control of the means of production, distribution, and exchange and to engage in central planning. In an effort to promote collectivization

in the agricultural sector, it set up state farms and forced the rural population into village communities and resettlement schemes. These coercive policies were pursued at great cost to human life. Government repression, arbitrary military conscription and arrest, and strict surveillance of the general population became the order of the day. The government used the Workers' Party of Ethiopia to carry out its brutal mission.

Introduced in 1984, the vanguard Workers' Party proclaimed a commitment to the principles of democratic centralism. In practice, however, the party favored centralized, bureaucratic control of all aspects of civil life. By 1990 it was clear that the socialist experiment had failed. Ethiopia's leaders disbanded the Workers' Party and declared themselves amenable to multiparty democracy. This gesture proved to be too little, too late. Ethiopia's second revolutionary government assumed power in April 1991 after a bloody civil war of almost a decade.

The new regime, headed by the Ethiopian People's Revolutionary Democratic Front, convened a reconciliation conference in July 1991 involving thirty-one political organizations. The Revolutionary Democratic Front sought to form a broad-based pact that included most of the substantial political groups, except for those that seriously opposed its leadership, such as former members of the Workers' Party and the deposed Mengistu regime. Consequently, radical leftist groups, along with several conservative Ethiopian nationalist groups, were excluded from the conference. By mid-1992 the number of registered political parties had grown to almost 200, but only a few had significant popular support.

Conference participants signed a charter calling for a transitional period of no more than two years and the creation of a Representative Council to facilitate the drafting of a new constitution and to prepare for democratic national elections. The council promulgated two controversial resolutions: one agreeing to Eritrean self-determination and the other administratively reorganizing Ethiopia into regions based on ethnicity. Both of these resolutions heightened tensions and forced the Ethiopian People's Revolutionary Democratic Front to act in undemocratic ways although it did implement some new liberal policies. By mid-1993 the ruling coalition, led by Meles Zenawe, had become very narrow. The transitional government forged ahead, however, and drafted a new constitution. National elections were finally held in May 1995, but they were boycotted by several of the major ethnically based parties. Democracy is still in doubt.

Eritrea

Italy colonized Eritrea in the 1880s and remained there until the British captured it in 1941. The British tried to enlist the support of the Eritreans in World War II, promising them self-determination. After the war, however, it became apparent that Eritrean self-determination was not guaranteed.

At the Paris Peace Conference between 1946 and 1947, a formula was negotiated for the disposal of former Italian colonies in Africa. The matter of Eritrea was turned over to the General Assembly of the United Nations (UN), which established a special study commission. In response to the commission's recommendations, which were submitted in June 1949, the United Nations finally agreed to federate Eritrea with Ethiopia, an arrangement not favored by all Eritreans. Nevertheless, the federal constitution was implemented.

Eritrean political organizations emerged as early as 1944. By 1952 the various factions had coalesced into three political parties: the Unionist Bloc, which favored union with Ethiopia, and the Democratic Party and the Muslim League of the Western Province, both of which favored independence. In the March 1952 elections for the legislative assembly, the Unionists won thirty-two of the sixty-eight seats, the Democratic Party won eighteen seats, and the Muslim League won fifteen seats.

On the assumption that Eritrean autonomy was protected, the new assembly ratified the federal constitution. Throughout the deliberations, Haile Selassie had lobbied to ensure that the Unionists could influence who would secure the most important positions in the new government. Those efforts continued throughout the period of federation and facilitated the undermining of Eritrean autonomy.

The year 1952 was a watershed. It marked the beginning of federation, and it was the year the Eritrean constitution was suspended. A year later all trade unions were banned. In 1956 political parties were banned, and the national assembly was "temporarily" suspended. Eritrea was completely annexed by Ethiopia in 1962.

Political groups went underground, formed movements of national liberation, and waged a thirty-year war against Ethiopia. The most successful group was the Eritrean People's Liberation Front, which in 1991 defeated the Ethiopian army, setting the stage for a UN-sanctioned referendum on Eritrean self-determination. In the April 1993 referendum more than 98 percent voted for independence. A month later the Republic of Eritrea was declared. Although the new government of Eritrea claims to be committed to multiparty democracy, the first priority has been given to drafting a new constitution by 1996.

Somalia

Immediately upon securing their separate independence from the British and Italians, respectively, in July 1960, the national assemblies of northern and southern Somaliland voted to merge the two polities into the Republic of Somalia. Because all citizens were ethnic Somalis, many felt that this would be a lasting union. However, the different colonial experiences of the two regions and endemic clan rivalries among the Somalis caused immediate tensions. The political system left to Somalia was a liberal democracy based on the principles of multiparty competition. Rather than contributing to a smoothly functioning political system, this legacy proved disastrous.

Democratic politics compounded the problems of nation building and state building. By March 1969 there were sixty-four political parties, most of them organized along clan lines. The election for the national assembly held that month resulted in unimaginable chaos. Corruption, intimidation, and political assassination abounded. In the confusion Gen. Mohamed Siad Barre launched a military coup, promising to eliminate corruption and unify the country.

Siad Barre ruled repressively for more than twenty years until he was overthrown in a civil war in January 1991. Toward the end of his rule, he abandoned his scientific socialist program and claimed to be open to multiparty democracy. His regime was overthrown before reforms could be implemented, however. In Somalia, unlike in Ethiopia, opposition groups had not formed a united front before they overthrew the dictator. A viable pact for a transitional government was not formed. Civil war, based upon clan and subclan rivalries, escalated until Somalia virtually ceased to be a viable state.

Djibouti

During the European "scramble for Africa" in the late 1800s, France laid claim to a small enclave on the coast of the Red Sea, calling it the Territory of the Afars and the Issas. The colony was valued mainly for its strategic location. France granted the territory, or Djibouti, independence in June 1977. The new government was headed by an Issa, Hassan Gouled Aptidon, and his party, the African People's League for Independence. The Issa and their Somali relatives make up about 80 percent of the population; the remainder are mostly from the Afar ethnic group. The Afar collaborated with the French during the waning days of colonial rule; this collaboration enhanced Hassan's reputation among the Issas as a liberator.

In 1979 Hassan formed a new party, the Popular Rally for Progress, and created a de jure one-party state. In response, the Afar formed an opposition party in exile, the Democratic Front for the Liberation of Djibouti. By the mid-1980s overt opposition to the hegemony of the Popular Rally for Progress had surfaced. In 1986 a former minister in the Hassan government was expelled from it; he formed his own party, the Djiboutian National Movement for the Installation of Democracy, with the stated purpose of restoring multiparty democracy. In January 1990 the Democratic Front merged with this party, forming the Union of Democratic Movements.

Alleging systematic ethnic discrimination, a significant segment of the Afar population flocked to the guerrilla-based Front for the Restoration of Unity and Democracy, a new party created in 1991. From this point Afar opposition to the government became more intense, culminating in what some Afar termed a "massacre" in the Afar quarter

of the capital, Djibouti, in December 1991. Some well-respected members of the Popular Rally government consequently defected, calling for a return to multiparty democracy. Finally, Hassan acceded, agreeing to a constitutional reform that would allow for up to four political parties.

The first test of this new dispensation was the parliamentary election of December 1992. Only two parties participated: the Popular Rally for Progress and the Party of Democratic Renewal. Many observers, and the party itself, felt that this arrangement favored the Party of Democratic Renewal. However, the Popular Rally for Progress won by a margin of more than three to one. Two reasons for the victory were Hassan's personal popularity and a party-list, winner-take-all system heavily weighted in favor of the urban-based Popular Rally. Most Afar boycotted the vote. There were considerable electoral irregularities, but the results stood.

In May 1993 presidential elections were held. Again most Afar boycotted the vote. Hassan faced four opponents, and he secured about 60 percent of the vote, avoiding a runoff. There was evidence of massive vote rigging, but again the results were upheld.

Outlook for the Future

Although the political upheavals of the early 1990s created new possibilities for democracy in the Horn of Africa, severe obstacles to the successful functioning of democracy remain. Prominent among these obstacles are the difficulty of finding viable formulas for managing ethnic and regional conflict, the lack of tolerance and trust among competing political forces, and the extreme weakness and fragmentation of political parties and democratic institutions more generally. The prospects for democratic evolution have dimmed in Ethiopia, they remain clouded in Eritrea, and they appear elusive in Djibouti. In Somalia the road to democracy—or to political order of any kind—looks long and arduous.

See also *African independence movements; African transitions to democracy; Sudan.*

Edmond J. Keller

BIBLIOGRAPHY

Africa Watch. *Somalia: A Government at War with Its People.* New York: Africa Watch, 1990.

Clapham, Christopher. *Transformation and Continuity in Revolutionary Ethiopia.* Cambridge and New York: Cambridge University Press, 1988.

Harbeson, John W. *The Ethiopian Transformation.* Boulder, Colo.: Westview Press, 1988.

Keller, Edmond J. "Drought, War, and the Politics of Famine in Ethiopia and Eritrea." *Journal of Modern African Studies* 30 (December 1992): 609–624.

———. *Revolutionary Ethiopia: From Empire to People's Republic.* Bloomington: Indiana University Press, 1988.

Laitin, David, and Said S. Samatar. *Somalia: Nation in Search of a State.* Boulder, Colo.: Westview Press; Aldershot: Gower, 1987.

Okbazghi, Yohannes. *Eritrea: A Pawn in World Politics.* Gainesville: University of Florida Press, 1991.

Pateman, Roy. *Eritrea: Even the Stones Are Burning.* Trenton, N.J.: Red Sea Press, 1991.

Saint Varan, Robert. *Djibouti: Pawn of the Horn of Africa.* Metuchen, N.J.: Scarecrow Press, 1981.

Africa, Lusophone

The five former Portuguese colonies of Angola, Cape Verde, Guinea-Bissau, Mozambique, and São Tomé and Principe (the last two are one nation). Portugal's five African colonies gained independence in 1974 and 1975, in large part because of popular opposition in Portugal to costly wars in the distant colonies. All the colonies had nationalist movements, some of which had been fighting Lisbon for more than a decade.

Colonial Rule and Beyond

The Portuguese arrived in Africa in the late fifteenth and early sixteenth centuries to establish trading outposts at ports along the coast. It was not until the early twentieth century, however, that Portugal established colonial rule over African territory. Even within the context of European colonialism, the Portuguese ruled their colonies in a highly exploitative fashion and gave them no preparation for self-rule. Thousands of Portuguese, fearful of retribution and African rule, fled after independence was granted, often destroying the property they did not take with them. Most of the former colonies could count only two or three lawyers and five or six doctors in their entire population. There also was very little administrative, technical, or professional expertise to sustain the new regimes because few Africans had served as local administrators in the Portuguese colonial governments.

All the former Portuguese colonies instituted single-party systems, incorporating varying degrees of socialist rhetoric and policies. Both Angola and Mozambique declared themselves Marxist-Leninist. They modeled their nascent political and economic structures on Eastern European blueprints and courted Soviet and Eastern bloc aid. The government of São Tomé espoused Marxist ideas but never formally embraced Marxism-Leninism as its official ideology. Cape Verde and Guinea-Bissau were strictly nonaligned; they courted Western aid but had single-party systems and centrally planned economies.

Beginning in the late 1980s, Lusophone Africa, along with many other developing and former Eastern bloc countries, began to liberalize under pressure for reform from foreign donors as well as internal democratic movements. Often reform was used, albeit unsuccessfully, as a conservative measure to mollify popular opposition to one-party rule while retaining control of the government. In Angola and Mozambique liberalization was part of a strategy for negotiating an end to civil war.

Angola

Three rival nationalist movements—the Popular Movement for the Liberation of Angola (MPLA), the National Front for the Liberation of Angola (FNLA), and the National Union for the Total Independence of Angola (UNITA)—formed a transitional government and took power from Lisbon in January 1975. The MPLA quickly seized control of the government, and within months the three groups were engaged in a bloody civil war that soon attracted outside support for all sides. Zaire assisted the FNLA, South Africa and the United States aided UNITA and the FNLA, and Cuba and the Soviet Union provided aid and troops to the MPLA.

Although the FNLA was soon marginalized, UNITA and the MPLA kept fighting, spurred on by ethnic and power rivalries and competition for superpower support. UNITA, which professed a commitment to democracy and a free market system, controlled a large section of southeastern Angola, from which it launched sabotage attacks that rendered much of the country impassable. Angola's infrastructure was destroyed and its economy paralyzed (except for the country's significant oil reserves in Cabinda). Between 1975 and 1991 Angolan society was decimated: an estimated 500,000 Angolans were killed, and the war left many more displaced and starving.

The withdrawal of South African and Cuban troops after 1988 and the gradual lessening of assistance to the warring parties from the Soviet Union and the United States forced UNITA and the MPLA to negotiate a settlement, which was reached in May 1991. The internationally monitored transition to democracy in Namibia then became a blueprint for peace in Angola.

Angola's attempt at democratic transition coincided with reconciliation between the warring parties. Prompted by increased international pressure for peace, Angolan president José Eduardo dos Santos led the MPLA Third Congress to establish a multiparty democracy in December 1990. Despite opposition from intransigent members of his politburo, dos Santos favored a multiparty system because he believed it would provide a mechanism for peaceful opposition and the integration of UNITA into national politics. The MPLA laid the foundation for political pluralism by approving a new constitution to provide for fundamental freedoms, granting the right to strike, ensuring an independent judiciary, and protecting private property. The MPLA officially abandoned Marxism-Leninism in 1991 and adopted a democratic socialist platform.

After the peace agreement was signed, the two parties—in addition to eleven other parties that emerged to vie for power—began to prepare for elections that were held in September 1992. Elections were partially funded and monitored by the United Nations. However, the money and personnel provided by the UN were insufficient to oversee the elections adequately, given the country's tremendous size, logistical obstacles, and UNITA's recalcitrance. The MPLA won the 1992 elections under terms that the United Nations called generally free and fair. UNITA leader Jonas Savimbi rejected the election outcome, however. Revealing his shallow commitment to democracy, Savimbi declared that the election was rigged and returned to war. In November 1994 the MPLA and UNITA signed another peace agreement that continues to hold, for the most part, and they have begun to discuss terms for a new democratic arrangement.

Mozambique

Mozambique achieved independence in June 1975 under the leadership of Samora Machel, head of the Mozambique Liberation Front (Frelimo), which had waged a campaign for independence since 1962. The new regime faced the challenge of governing an extremely poor and unevenly developed country. (The lion's share of infrastructural resources were deployed in the south.) Although Frelimo was a strictly nationalist organization at its inception, it moved into the socialist sphere after its first leader, Eduardo Mondlane, died in 1969.

At independence, Frelimo declared itself Marxist-Leninist and was formally allied with the Soviet Union and the Eastern bloc. The government tried to achieve rapid development through central direction of the economy, big heavy-industry projects, and state-run farms. By forcibly moving thousands of people to state farms, undermining the authority of traditional ethnic leaders, and confiscating church properties, Frelimo alienated a significant portion of the population, particularly in the rural areas of central Mozambique.

Adding to Frelimo's woes was a violent terrorist challenge by Renamo, the Mozambique National Resistance. Renamo was created by the Rhodesian Central Intelligence Organization to counter Mozambican support for the liberation of Rhodesia (now Zimbabwe). Renamo drew volunteers from disaffected Frelimo members, former criminals, traditional leaders, and ethnic groups, such as the Ndau, that were underrepresented in the Frelimo government. When Zimbabwe gained independence in 1980, South Africa assumed sponsorship of the rebel group, which grew in size and scope under Pretoria's tutelage. By 1985 Renamo had some 15,000 members and conducted sabotage operations throughout Mozambique.

Although Renamo had only a vague political agenda, it professed commitment to multiparty democracy and a free market system (no doubt at the insistence of South Africa and of right-wing backers in Europe and the United States). Recognizing that a military solution to the civil war was probably unattainable because of a massive reduction in Soviet support, Mozambican president Joaquim Chissano began to move toward a multiparty system in 1989 in order to preempt the rebels' political agenda and to deny them substantive leverage in negotiations. In November 1990 the government ratified a new constitution providing for universal suffrage, direct legislative and executive elections, multiple parties, private ownership, basic social and religious freedoms, and the right to strike.

Mozambique's first multiparty elections, held in October 1994, were narrowly won by Frelimo. Chissano (Frelimo's leader) won 53 percent of the vote in a separate presidential poll; Renamo's leader, Afonso Dhlakama, won 34 percent. Despite problems ironing out Renamo's precise role in government, both sides rejected a coalition arrangement, and Dhlakama appeared committed to working within the system rather than returning to war.

As in Angola, the pressures for democracy in Mozam-

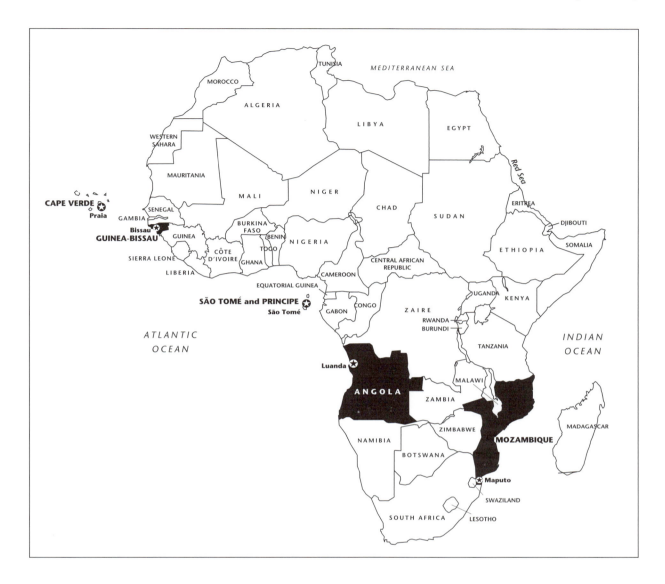

bique were primarily external: the collapse of Eastern Europe and the Soviet Union as ideological models, the end of the cold war and the withdrawal of Soviet military and advisory support, the consequent need to court the West as a source of aid, South African support for a settlement, and negotiations for peace in Angola. As in Angola, democratic transition was closely intertwined with the peace process: reform was designed to undercut the insurgents and bring them into the political system. The West had firmly set democracy as a precondition to much-needed aid, and Chissano, a pragmatic politician, recognized the value of espousing democracy.

São Tomé and Principe

São Tomé's first president, Manuel Pinto da Costa, ruled under a one-party constitution from independence in 1975 until multiparty elections in 1991. In an effort to rescue the country from economic ruin and to stem the rising tide of political discontent, his government began a process of economic and political liberalization in 1985. Although political reform was somewhat slower than economic reform, the ruling Movement for the Liberation of São Tomé and Principe started to implement long-promised liberalization in 1987. It recognized factions within the ruling party and invited exiled opposition groups to return home. The movement finally agreed to multiparty democracy in 1989, when increasingly vocal internal opposition was reinforced by events in Eastern Europe. In an August 1989 referendum 72 percent of the electorate ratified the decision.

A number of exiled parties returned to São Tomé to contest elections in 1991. The ruling party tried to position itself for elections by adopting a social democratic platform, but it was no challenge to the Party of Democratic Convergence–Reflection Group. This breakaway faction of the ruling party backed the former prime minister to win 82 percent of the vote in the presidential elections and thirty-three of fifty-five parliamentary seats.

Cape Verde

The African Party for the Independence of Guinea and Cape Verde (PAIGC) was founded in 1956. Its goal was freedom from Portugal and unification of the two countries. After independence in July 1975, it led the postcolonial governments of both countries under a one-party system. Following the 1980 coup in Guinea-Bissau, however, Cape Verde's PAIGC was dissolved and replaced by the African Party for the Independence of Cape Verde (PAICV).

The Third Party Congress in 1988 marked a turning point in Cape Verde's postcolonial history by moving decisively to liberalize the country politically and economically. The government enacted sweeping constitutional reforms and opened the economy to the private sector, allowing private health care and education. In 1990 the ruling party amended the constitution to allow multiparty elections and enacted legislation guaranteeing opposition parties freedom to organize and use the media. The transition was motivated by the eloquent pro-democracy demands of a small but strategic group of some 600 technocrats in Praia, who later formed the main opposition party, the Movement for Democracy.

Cape Verde held its first multiparty presidential elections in February 1991. The leader of the Movement for Democracy, António Monteiro, was elected by direct universal suffrage for a five-year term. The PAICV moved into the role of loyal opposition, although considerable ill feeling between the two leading parties slowed promised liberalization and political decentralization.

Guinea-Bissau

Guinea-Bissau's first postindependence government was formed by the African Party for the Independence of Guinea and Cape Verde in 1974, and Luis Cabral became president under a one-party system. In 1980 Cabral was deposed by his prime minister, João Vieira, in a coup that enjoyed considerable popular support because of the shortage of food in the country. Legislative elections in 1989 suggest that the ruling party did not face significant internal demands for change. Vieira was reelected presi-

dent, and PAIGC candidates garnered 95 percent of the vote. Nevertheless, the government faced some internal opposition to one-party rule among local elites, as well as vocal dissent and demands for democracy from opponents exiled in Portugal and Senegal.

In response to this pressure and to external pressure from donor countries, Vieira announced in 1990 that he favored a multiparty system. Over the next three years the government adopted a new constitution, legalized opposition, and provided for freedom of expression. In 1992 emerging political parties demanded the creation of a multiparty transition commission. This commission, which included the ruling party and eight legalized parties, drafted legislation to prepare for the country's first free elections, which were held in 1994 and won by Vieira.

Prospects for Democratic Consolidation

The wave of democratic transitions in Lusophone Africa in the 1990s was driven in large part by economic failure (which undermined the ruling parties' domestic support) and external pressure. The ideological hegemony of democracy in the world today is likely to produce formally democratic and procedurally accountable governments in most, and maybe all, of these countries. It is unlikely, however, that these governments will extend full rights and liberties to most of their poorly organized and ill-informed citizens. The institutions of power will almost certainly remain concentrated in the hands of a small elite. Although the governments may be responsive to the demands of a visible urban segment, remote, uneducated, and poor rural populations are not likely to be much affected by a multiparty system. Absent a strong civil society that will hold the leadership accountable beyond the transition period, few elites will retain a commitment to a democratic system that could undermine their power base.

Lusophone Africa's attempt to democratize will also be troubled by poverty and other socioeconomic and development problems. Most years Mozambique (with a per capita income of less than $90) vies with Bangladesh for the status of the poorest country in the world. Angola's per capita income is deceptively high because of its substantial oil reserves; roads, schools, and medical facilities have been destroyed, and thousands of Angolans have been displaced by the civil war. The other three countries are slightly better off but well below even the middling levels of economic development conducive to democracy.

Nevertheless, these five countries, which were extremely disadvantaged by colonial rule, have made significant strides toward better governance since independence. In particular, Mozambique and Angola—with the end of civil war and the anticipated end of civil war, respectively—have better conditions and prospects for economic development, human rights and liberties, and democracy than at any point since 1960.

See also *African independence movements; African transitions to democracy.*

Courtney Jung

BIBLIOGRAPHY

Alden, Chris, and Mark Simpson. "Mozambique: A Delicate Peace." *Journal of Modern African Studies* 31 (March 1993): 109–130.

Hamilton, Kimberley A. *Lusophone Africa, Portugal, and the United States: Possibilities for More Effective Cooperation.* Washington, D.C.: Center for Strategic and International Studies, 1992.

Hanlon, Joseph. *Apartheid's Second Front: South Africa's War Against Its Neighbours.* Harmondsworth and New York: Penguin Books, 1986.

Hodges, Tony. *Angola to the 1990s: The Potential for Recovery.* London: Economist Publications, 1987.

Isaacman, Allen F., and Barbara Isaacman. *Mozambique: From Colonialism to Revolution, 1900–1982.* Boulder, Colo.: Westview Press, 1983; Aldershot: Gower, 1984.

Isaacman, Allen F., and David Wiley, eds. *Southern Africa: Society, Economy, and Liberation.* East Lansing, Mich.: African Studies Center at Michigan State University and the Department of African American and African Studies at the University of Minnesota, 1981.

McCulloch, Jack. *In the Twilight of Revolution: The Political Theory of Amilcar Cabral.* Boston: Routledge and Kegan Paul, 1983.

Pereira, Anthony W. "The Neglected Tragedy: The Return to War in Angola, 1992–93." *Journal of Modern African Studies* 32 (March 1994): 1–28.

Silva, Josue da. *Era uma vez: Tres guerras em Africa.* Cacem, Portugal: Edicoes Ro, 1981.

Soremukun, Fola. *Angola: The Road to Independence.* Ile-Ife, Nigeria: University of Ife Press, 1983.

Africa, Subsaharan

The forty-eight independent countries of the African continent (and islands in the region as far away as Mauritius) that lie in and to the south of the Saharan desert. Subsaharan Africa encompasses all the African countries except the five North African countries that border the Mediterranean Sea: Egypt, Libya, Tunisia, Algeria, and Morocco. The region has had a turbulent and largely unsuccessful experience with democracy since Sudan and Ghana led the way to independence in 1956 and 1957, respectively.

In a relatively short period of time, virtually all the formally democratic systems left behind by the departing colonial rulers gave way to authoritarian regimes of one kind or another. In most cases the demise of constitutional democracy began with the movement to one-party, and typically one-man, rule. In some countries, such as Senegal and the Côte d'Ivoire, this development followed from the electoral supremacy of the ruling party and the cohesiveness of the country's elites before independence, although authoritarian rule was not consolidated without repression. In other countries, primarily former British colonies such as Kenya, Zambia, Ghana, and Uganda, one-party regimes (officially or effectively) were established only a few years after independence, but with extensive coercion and concentration of power in one person.

In Nigeria's First Republic (1960–1966), turbulent multiparty competition was diminished by the consolidation of single-party rule in each of the three regions; there followed increasingly severe constraints on liberty and electoral competition. In Nigeria and elsewhere (as in Sierra Leone and Zaire), growing instability surrounding electoral competition paved the way for military intervention, which also swept away the more fragile one-party regimes.

By the early 1970s virtually all the independent regimes in Subsaharan Africa were either military or one-party. When Portugal's African colonies finally broke free in 1974–1975, after years of armed challenge to some of the most exploitative and authoritarian of all African colonial regimes, those new countries (principally Angola and Mozambique) also became one-party states, with Marxist-Leninist orientations.

Success and Near Success

Multiparty democracy endured for several decades in three African countries: Botswana, Gambia, and Mauritius (all of them small in population and former British colonies). In Botswana, where the bureaucracy dominates, democracy, although paternalistic, has nevertheless become more vigorous and pluralistic over time. The island nation of Mauritius has consistently maintained the most liberal and competitive political system in Africa since it won independence in 1968; the nation is multiethnic (predominantly Indian) and prosperous. By contrast, after thirty years of continuous rule by the same party and pres-

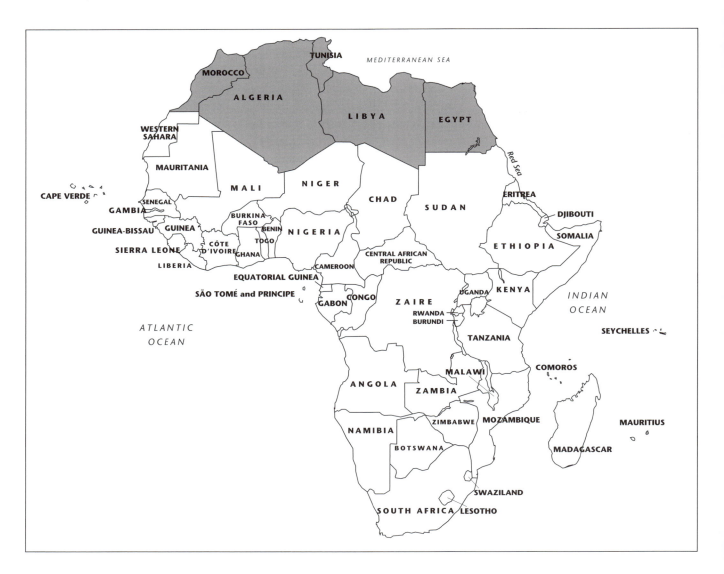

ident (Dawda Jawara), and rising discontent over corruption, Gambia's democracy fell to a military coup in 1994.

Yet by the end of the twentieth century, numerous other African countries had legalized party competition and established democratic constitutional forms. Most of these had no previous experience with multiparty democracy or had seen it expire quickly after independence. These included several former French colonies (Benin, Mali, Niger, Madagascar, the Republic of Congo, and the Central African Republic); two former British colonies (Zambia and Malawi); two former Portuguese colonies (the tiny island states of Cape Verde and São Tomé and Principe); and two former apartheid states (Namibia and, most significantly for the drama of its transition and the implications for the entire continent, South Africa).

A number of African countries that experienced politi-

cal transitions during the early 1990s fell short of the mark of fully democratic rule. These included Niger, the Central African Republic, Comoros, the Republic of Congo, Ghana, Seychelles, and Mozambique (which held a successful transition election in 1994). In these countries, multiparty constitutional regimes were installed. But significant abridgments of democracy remained, such as lingering military influence over government, limitations on rights of opposition and dissent, compromise of judicial independence, and electoral biases and irregularities. Despite the great promise of its pathbreaking electoral transition in 1991, Zambia witnessed a significant narrowing of competition and liberty because of states of emergency, crackdowns on the opposition, corruption, and political intolerance.

Some African countries (such as Uganda, Tanzania, and

Ethiopia) had yet to clearly establish their constitutional form and political identity. Several promised transitions fizzled out or were quashed by authoritarian rulers, as in Togo and Zaire. In Nigeria a continually delayed and almost completed democratic transition was aborted by the military in June 1993, when it annulled the results of the freest and fairest presidential elections in that country's history; for the first time Nigeria appeared to have elected a southerner from the Yoruba ethnic group to the country's highest office.

Such regime ambiguity, or dissonance between form and substance, has been a familiar story in postindependence Africa. Since the restoration of multiparty competition in 1976, Senegal has lived uncomfortably with some genuine pluralism and liberty, matched with the state manipulation, electoral fraud and pervasive clientelism, patronage, and corruption necessary to maintain the dominance of the ruling Socialist Party. Zimbabwe has perpetuated a similar type of semidemocracy since it came into being as an independent country in 1980, though with rather less liberty and greater use of violence and intimidation by the ruling party.

Ghana, Kenya, Cameroon, and Gabon adopted ambiguous regime forms in the early 1990s. In each case, the authoritarian rulers—Jerry Rawlings, Daniel arap Moi, Paul Biya, and Omar Bongo, respectively—were forced by domestic and international pressures to concede to multiparty elections. In each case the incumbent dictators won dubious and disputed election or reelection as president in 1992 or 1993 through force, fraud, intimidation, and heavy manipulation of state power and electoral rules (though Ghana's election was somewhat cleaner than the others). In each case, subsequent abridgments of opposition and individual rights put the regimes on the margin between semidemocracy and authoritarianism. There was an improvement in tolerance for political opposition and the operation of civil society, but Kenya and Cameroon soon reverted to harsh repression of opposition.

Postcolonial Failures

Two types of developments, distinct but not mutually exclusive, signaled the failure of democratic systems in Subsaharan Africa following independence. In a great many countries, especially the former French colonies, the new rulers and ruling parties eliminated political competition, more or less quickly, and established one-party regimes. Where political support was too divided or political leadership insufficiently willful and authoritarian to permit the construction of single-party dominance, political competition typically tore the polity apart in spasms of political deadlock and crisis, ethnic polarization, partisan violence, state repression, and electoral fraud, paving the way for military intervention.

In Ghana, Senegal, Kenya, Uganda, and elsewhere the first postindependence elected leaders eliminated democracy through various measures that amounted to executive coups. After three years of political insecurity, authoritarian overreaction, and abuse of power, Ghana's coup was carried out by Prime Minister Kwame Nkrumah through a national referendum in 1960, which established a centralized presidential system under Nkrumah's leadership. A highly personalized, one-party dictatorship followed; it decimated the country's economy and brought on a military coup in 1966. Significantly, the transition from political pluralism to authoritarianism was also marked and consolidated in Senegal, Uganda, and Kenya by constitutional change from a parliamentary to a presidential system, with extreme concentration of power in the presidency and marked diminution of legislative authority. These were among a number of African countries that descended into authoritarianism not by military coup (at least not initially) but through various political measures constraining and ultimately proscribing opposition parties.

Colonial Background

Several factors account for the failure of democracy in the new states of postcolonial Africa. Many of these had their origin in European colonial rule. To be sure, colonial rule left behind some of the infrastructure and institutions of a modern economy and society—transportation and communication grids, monetary systems, public education, and a state bureaucracy. Under French and especially under British colonial rule, there also emerged for the first time modern elements of political pluralism and civil society: political parties, trade unions, churches, organized interest groups, newspapers, universities, and intellectuals. Even during long periods of subsequent authoritarian rule, this societal pluralism would endure and evolve in many English-speaking and French-speaking countries, exerting crucial pressure for democratization.

The British saw preparation of the colonies for self-rule as part of their mission. In contrast to India and the Caribbean, however, that preparation came quite late in the British colonies of Africa, even later in the French ones (save for Senegal, especially Dakar), and not at all in the Belgian and Portuguese colonies. Thus, while the former

British colonies had some limited success with competitive party politics, at least for a time, and some intellectual and social pluralism survived in countries like Nigeria, Ghana, and Kenya (and among the former French colonies, most notably Senegal), what democratic processes there were quickly collapsed in most of the rest of Africa.

A number of underlying features of colonial rule throughout Africa left a highly unfavorable legacy for democracy. It was in the nature of colonial rule everywhere to be authoritarian and paternalistic. Even the more liberal systems, like the British colonies in West Africa, allowed only limited participation in government, confined mainly to a small elite and to the local levels of governance until a few years before independence. For most of the sixty or so years of formal colonial rule, colonial officials enjoyed extraordinary powers with exalted status and few checks. In contrast to India, which had gradually built up a strong, indigenous "steel frame" of public administration under its much longer British colonial rule, African countries had few of their own in the upper reaches of the state bureaucracy when independence came. Most newly independent states thus quickly embarked on sweeping programs of "Africanization" as a means of asserting political control and, symbolically, of national identity as well. These programs opened wide opportunities but diminished governmental capacity and integrity. (Perhaps not coincidentally, Botswana, the one country to have maintained democracy continuously since independence, also took a much more gradual and cautious approach to Africanization of the state bureaucracy.)

The paternalism of colonial rule was particularly damaging in its transmission of institutional frameworks borrowed almost wholly from the colonizer, with little concern for incorporation of indigenous practices and symbols. As a result, African peoples and politicians alike felt little sense of ownership of, or identification with, the new, postcolonial constitutional structures. Aspiring autocrats, civilian and military, thus encountered little resistance in sabotaging or overthrowing them.

The colonial state was not simply authoritarian and paternalistic, it was often brutal as well. Resistance and protest were readily, and if need be, bloodily repressed. Dissidents and nationalist "agitators" were jailed. It was this model, and not the model of British or French democracy, that was to be emulated by the postcolonial elite and that helped to breed from the start a political culture of intolerance.

The Statist Legacy

The colonial legacy was not only authoritarian but also statist. The colonial bureaucracy (like the military) was surprisingly small, and in the case of the British, often ruled indirectly through traditional systems of authority. Nevertheless, the state imposed extensive controls over internal and external trade; established monopoly control over the marketing of agricultural cash crops, the largest source of cash income; and awarded itself exclusive control over the mining of minerals and the development of infrastructure. This incipient statism, along with favoritism toward capital and imported goods from the colonizing power, preempted the emergence of an independent, indigenous capitalist class in the colonies. Even more significantly, the bureaucracy provided a welcome means for the new African political elite to accumulate personal wealth and consolidate its grip on power after independence. At the same time, African economies were left dependent on international trade and capital and vulnerable to abrupt swings in commodity prices.

Colonial rule, and the carving of Africa into colonial territories (formally initiated with the Berlin Conference of 1884–1885), produced the seeds of modern ethnic conflict as well. The colonial demarcation of African boundaries followed European rather than African political logic, splitting up some cultural and historical groups while throwing together others with little in common—except perhaps a history of warfare and enmity. This initial cultural complexity was aggravated by the uneven spread of education, economic development, military recruitment, and other Western influences; thus some regions and peoples were distinctly advantaged over others. Colonial policies and institutions emphasized ethnic differences as part of a strategy of "divide and rule." British imperial policy deliberately encouraged ethnic and regional consciousness, as opposed to an incipient national consciousness, and strengthened institutions of traditional rule. In Nigeria, Sudan, and Uganda, British colonial rule crystallized and tenaciously preserved regional structures and cleavages that ultimately led to civil war.

In at least a few countries where decolonization occurred without mass mobilization and violence, such as Nigeria, Ghana, Senegal, Gambia, and Botswana, some currents of pluralism and democratic culture were felt. Where decolonization occurred through armed struggle, a militant, ideological, or at least rhetorically revolutionary authoritarian regime was typically the result, as in the Portuguese colonies of Angola, Mozambique, and Guinea-Bissau and, to a lesser extent, Zimbabwe. There the black majority government of Robert Mugabe rigorously respected the protections for white minority rights codified in the 1979 constitution but gradually assumed much of the repressive character of the African one-party state. Given this legacy, it is all the more remarkable that South Africa has found its way to democracy after apartheid, despite the considerable violence, mass mobilization, and state repression that attended the decades-long struggle for a society that would not be based on race.

Postcolonial Politics and Society

The problems and contradictions of colonial rule were greatly exacerbated by the African political leaders who came to power with independence. Some historians maintain that failures of democracy, and more broadly of governance, in this period were virtually predestined by the structural patterns, conflicts, and weaknesses inherited from colonial rule. Others maintain that the problems were produced by self-serving elites who did little to forge a different style of politics and governance. Where similar historical outcomes occur in several dozen countries, one cannot dispute the powerful role of common structural and historical factors. In the context of extreme poverty and economic dependence, deep ethnic divisions, little democratic experience, weak and artificial governmental structures, shallow constitutional legitimacy, meager civil societies, and sweeping state controls over the formal economy, the maintenance of a relatively liberal and democratic regime would probably have required political leadership exceptional in its self-discipline, democratic commitment, and skill at coalition building.

In virtually every country—save for a few with small populations, like Mauritius and Botswana, where the challenges were less daunting—such leadership was missing. Yet leadership was not irrelevant. During the 1960s and 1970s Senegal and Kenya managed to preserve some elements of pluralism and constitutionalism and to avoid the more grotesque degrees of repression and state failure, partly because of the leadership of Léopold Senghor and Jomo Kenyatta, respectively. For five years the accommodating style and personal restraint of Nigeria's prime minister, Abubakar Tafawa Balewa, helped to hold disaster at bay and a multiparty regime in place. Botswana's democratic development was heavily shaped from the beginning by the strong convictions and political vision and skill of Seretse Khama, who governed with more self-restraint and success (despite a paternalistic style) than perhaps any other African ruler of his time. And South Africa's largely peaceful transition to democracy, and its subsequent embrace of racial and political reconciliation and power sharing, owed much to the leadership, vision, direction, and charisma of Nelson Mandela.

For the most part, however, newly independent African states succumbed more or less quickly to centralizing and authoritarian political temptations. In some cases (particularly in French-speaking countries) this process was facilitated by the relative paucity of organized opposition and the more centralized political character of French colonial regimes and of France's own political system. Elsewhere, ethnic fragmentation and rising opposition led political leaders like Kwame Nkrumah in Ghana and Milton Obote in Uganda to abandon democracy in order to maintain control. In Zambia, President Kenneth Kaunda tolerated multiparty competition for almost a decade after independence in 1964. But when his ruling party was threatened with defeat in parliamentary elections, he clamped down the lid of repression in 1973, having amended the constitution to ban opposition parties.

A common feature behind all these movements to authoritarian rule was the weakness of democratic norms and values. In some cases—as with Sékou Touré in Guinea and Julius Nyerere in Tanzania (and Nkrumah in Ghana as he moved to the socialist left)—one-party rule was declared out of ideological commitment to a communitarian socialist ideology and to African cultural traditions emphasizing consensus.

Through the 1960s and 1970s ideas of developmentalism and dependency gained favor. Leaders stressed the necessity for centralized authoritarian rule to preempt class divisions, manage relations with exploitative economic forces in the world economy, and organize the society for rapid development. Marxist revolutionary doctrines—which took hold in Angola, Mozambique, Ethiopia, Guinea-Bissau, and a few other African countries—went further, justifying terrible repression in the battle against imperialism, class privilege, and ethnic consciousness. Increasingly, democrats in Africa were on the defensive intellectually as well as politically. By the 1970s most African states that were not under military rule had a one-party system, a form of government they proclaimed to be distinctively appropriate for Africa.

A number of postindependence African political leaders had intellectual (and, in effect, political) training in Britain and France; Senghor had even served in the French National Assembly. The Nigerian nationalist leaders Nnamdi Azikiwe and Obafemi Awolowo manifested in their speeches and extensive writings a broad, passionate, and sophisticated appreciation of the value and character of liberal democracy. However, even where these expressions of principle were sincere, as with Awolowo and Azikiwe, they were often undermined by abrasive or autocratic political styles, or by the pressures of political conflict in structural circumstances that were not conducive to the mutual security, trust, and tolerance among competing political forces that make democracy possible.

Seeds of Corruption

These structural factors were probably more important than ideas or ideology alone in explaining the almost universal absence or failure of democracy in Africa during the first three decades of independence. Mostly rooted in colonial rule, the failures took on more crippling dimensions after independence. At the hub of all these structural factors was the swollen African state—too large and interventionist to allow market forces to generate growth, yet too weak to undertake the quest for the kind of state-led development that took place at the same time in East Asia. The typical African state owned or controlled by far the greatest share of wealth outside the subsistence economy—in mining, agriculture, and even industry and services. It became the leading purchaser of goods and services; the provider of schools, roads, clinics, and markets for communities; the principal source of wage employment, contracts, careers, commissions, and scholarships.

Because of the pervasive poverty and the extreme underdevelopment of indigenous entrepreneurship, the African state became the primary arena of class formation after independence, the chief means (through political corruption and patronage) for the accumulation of personal wealth and the opening of economic opportunities to family, friends, clients, and ethnic kin. State power became extremely valuable. Those who held it became rich and had resources available to them; those who did not were virtually without opportunity.

Politics became a zero-sum game, in which winning was everything and no one could afford to lose. What democratic ideals and inclinations there were could not survive these structural pressures and insecurities. The idea of "anything goes" prevailed in the struggle for power: violence, vituperation, demagoguery, intimidation, as-

sassination, rigging of elections, census manipulation, arrests, repression.

Where civilian politicians did not put an end to multiparty competition, it became so chaotic and corrupt that the military was easily able to seize control, initially with enthusiastic popular support. Invariably, however, military rulers fell victim to the same temptations as had civilian politicians. But the military rulers displayed even less respect for law and opposition, even weaker capacity to build multiethnic coalitions, and even greater disposition to use violence and repression as substitutes for legitimacy. Political decay and popular alienation and disengagement thus intensified.

Statism and corruption had other devastating consequences for democracy. Pervasive state controls stifled incentives for investment to raise agricultural productivity and launch new business ventures. Unchecked by any restraints from independent institutions, such as the judiciary or the mass media, nepotism and corruption turned into gross mismanagement and brazen plunder of public resources. Economies were driven into effective bankruptcy, with massive foreign debt, staggering inequality, and explosive public anger. Subsequent attempts at democracy in Ghana, Nigeria, and Sudan failed even more dramatically than the initial attempts; public patience evaporated more quickly, and the military, fattened from the previous spoils of office, proved hungrier to intervene again. No country fell further than Nigeria, which squandered billions of dollars in oil revenue during the four-year Second Republic while generating massive shortages of basic consumer goods and $20 billion of foreign debt.

Institutional arrangements did little to soften the competition for power throughout Africa. In most countries, power was highly centralized and was monopolized by a single ethnic group or narrow coalition. Groups that did not find their way into the ruling coalition could expect short shrift in the distribution of resources. The most far-reaching and imaginative experiment in federalism on the continent, in Nigeria, did generate a significantly more complex and fluid political pattern. The splitting up of the three major regions of the First Republic into first twelve and then nineteen states, many of them dominated by ethnic minorities, activated divisions within ethnic groups and facilitated cross-cutting alignments. However, the premium on control of the central government remained intense, since that was the locus of most state resources. Although polarized ethnic and regional conflict did not figure prominently in the breakdown of the Second Republic in 1983, corruption and mismanagement did. Constitution makers had failed to create effective mechanisms to monitor the conduct of public officials and check the abuse of power.

The need for federalism, decentralization, and power sharing constitutes one of the principal lessons of Africa's postindependence political experience. Only by giving different ethnic groups some sense of political security and autonomy—and some control over their own resources—can ethnic and regional conflict be effectively managed. Only by inducing or requiring political parties to forge broad ethnic coalitions can stability be achieved.

Such mechanisms would probably have prevented the destructive civil wars that occurred in Nigeria, Uganda, and Sudan. For a time during the 1970s the granting of substantial political autonomy to the southern region did bring a halt to the civil war in Sudan, until President Jaafar Muhammed al-Numeiri effectively abrogated the agreement in 1983 in an effort to consolidate his waning support in the north.

Fortunately, South Africa seems to have learned something from previous African experience. Despite the strong historical disposition of the African National Congress toward a unitary system, it agreed to a new political system of nine regions, with independently elected assemblies and premiers and some significant autonomous powers. Power sharing has also been facilitated in South Africa and Namibia by the use of proportional representation in legislative elections and the formation of coalition governments.

A final factor that must be weighed in assessing the causes of democratic failure in Africa is international politics. Throughout the period of decolonization and postindependence politics—from the 1950s through the late 1980s—the principal powers in the cold war viewed Africa primarily as an arena of competition for geopolitical and occasionally military advantage. The Soviet bloc provided crucial support to Marxist and quasi-Marxist regimes like those in Ethiopia, Angola, and Mozambique. Without Soviet support these regimes might have fallen (though probably not to any democratic alternative). Soviet bloc nations also supported liberation movements in Zimbabwe, South Africa, and Namibia.

The United States, Great Britain, and France backed their own allies and surrogates in the struggle, especially the authoritarian regime of Mobutu Sese Seko in Zaire. This regime became pivotal in the United States's strategy to stem and undermine the spread of Soviet influence in Africa. The United States also offered close support to al-Numeiri in Sudan; to Samuel Doe's dictatorship in Liberia; to Moi's increasingly repressive one-party state in Kenya; and to the dictatorship of Mohamed Siad Barre in Somalia after it bolted from its pro-Soviet alliance. France turned a blind eye to pervasive corruption and repression while maintaining intimate and even heavily controlling ties with the governments of its former African colonies. Despite rhetorical and diplomatic objections, Western countries, including the United States, also supported and did business with the apartheid regime in South Africa into the 1970s (and, more discreetly, the 1980s). If there was one thing that did not seem to matter much to the major world powers in their aid, trade, and military assistance relationships with Africa, it was democracy.

The Second Liberation

In February 1990 two historic political events took place that were to transform the character of politics in Africa. In Benin, the National Conference of Active Forces of the Nation, called by the one-party state to consider constitutional reforms that might revive its depleted legitimacy, instead seized sovereign power and effective authority from President Mathieu Kerekou, established a transitional government, and prepared the way for multiparty elections under a new constitution. And in South Africa, recently installed President Frederik W. de Klerk lifted the ban on the African National Congress (as well as the Pan-Africanist Congress and the South African Communist Party) and released Mandela from prison, effectively initiating a transition to democracy.

Over the next three years a wave of democratic transitions swept across Africa. Inspired by Benin's experience, several French-speaking African countries—Togo, Niger, Madagascar, Zaire, the Republic of Congo, and Mali (following a military coup to depose the stand-pat dictator)—organized national conferences. In four of the six (Mali, Niger, Madagascar, and the Republic of Congo), constitutional change and multiparty elections followed. Under rising domestic and international pressure and criticism, one African dictator after another legalized the opposition and agreed to hold multiparty elections: Kaunda in Zambia, Moi in Kenya, Rawlings in Ghana, Bongo in Gabon, Biya in Cameroon. Malawi joined the list when 63 percent of the voters in a June 1993 referendum endorsed the multiparty option in a stunning rejection of Hastings Kamuzu Banda's twenty-nine-year dictatorship.

In two years the political map of Subsaharan Africa was

transformed. At the end of 1989 thirty-three of the then forty-seven Subsaharan African states were rated "not free" by Freedom House (an organization headquartered in New York City); in 1991 only twenty were so rated, and the number of "free" states had risen from three to eight. Three years later the number of free states held at eight, and another dozen or so countries had multiparty systems that approached democracy to varying degrees. But some of the countries with democratic openings had slipped back into authoritarianism and state breakdown, and twenty-six of the Subsaharan countries were classified as not free.

The early 1990s was a time of democratic mobilization and experimentation in Africa. Between 1990 and 1994 more than two dozen African countries held multiparty elections. Only about two-thirds of these were judged free and fair by independent observers. Yet in eleven countries—including South Africa, Zambia, Madagascar, and Malawi—incumbent parties and rulers were voted out. And those dictatorships that survived through fraud at the polls, as in Kenya, Cameroon, and Gabon, had to contend with more vigorous civil societies and more energetic political oppositions.

International and domestic factors converged powerfully to generate this wave of African democratic movements, which has been called Africa's second liberation. It was no coincidence that the two igniting events in Benin and South Africa came on the heels of the collapse of the Berlin Wall in 1989. The downfall of communism in Europe transformed the international environment, discrediting the main ideological rival to political and economic liberalism on the African scene. And the end of the cold war freed the United States from its absorption with countering Soviet influence on the continent, enabling it to give democracy and human rights a much higher priority in diplomacy and foreign aid allocations.

International Pressures

Beginning in 1990 the United States moved increasingly to integrate the promotion of democracy and human rights into its foreign aid programs worldwide and to impose democratic conditions for assistance. Britain and France moved in the same direction.

A turning point came in June 1990, at the Franco-African summit at La Baule, when French President François Mitterrand announced a dramatic turn in France's traditionally dominating and commercially driven relations with its former African colonies. Henceforth, Mitter-

rand warned, France would link its aid to institutional progress toward democracy, as evidenced by free and fair elections between competing parties, press freedom, and judicial independence. In fact, France's determination to pull the plug on Kerekou's political life-support system, by suspending aid, had been a prime factor in the Beninois president's decision to call the National Conference four months previously. Now other former colonies were put on notice that badly needed French aid would be directly linked to democratic and human rights reforms. Political openings soon swept through French-speaking Africa, some leading to genuine transitions to democracy and others to more cosmetic reforms that nevertheless created more space for opposition and dissent.

In English-speaking Africa, external pressure had its most visible effects in Kenya and Malawi. For years, both the foreign policy aid agencies of individual states and international agencies had become increasingly offended by the growing scale and brazenness of corruption and repression under the Moi regime in Kenya. Finally, in November 1991, after months of warnings of an aid cutoff by the United States and Scandinavian countries, Kenya's aid donors suspended new aid for six months and established explicit political conditions for its resumption. One week later Kenya's ruling party repealed the ban on opposition parties, paving the way for multiparty elections—a change that Moi bitterly attributed to Western pressure. A similar decision by international donors in May 1992 to freeze $74 million in aid to Malawi (following the first mass protests in twenty-eight years) was similarly critical in prompting the Banda regime to release political prisoners, legalize opposition movements, and conduct the 1993 referendum on the existence of multiple parties, which proved its undoing.

Western pressure was pivotal in prying open the heavy lid of authoritarianism in Africa. Private foundations and groups in the West, as well as publicly funded democracy initiatives like the U.S. National Endowment for Democracy, also played an important role in giving assistance to African democratic movements and civil society organizations. External pressure and support could not have succeeded, however, were it not for the emergence of indigenous democratic movements of unprecedented scope and vigor, demanding a new political order.

The rise of civil society from the cynicism, repression, and chaos of authoritarianism in Africa provided the driving wedge for Africa's democratic resurgence in the 1990s. In the face of economic and political decline during the

1970s and 1980s there emerged a host of independent associations, movements, networks, and media to advance popular interests and challenge or displace the predatory power of the African state. In addition to more traditional professional associations—of lawyers, doctors, journalists, teachers, university staff, and students—human rights and pro-democracy groups formed specifically around issues of democratic reform. Groups included the Civil Liberties Organization, the Constitutional Rights Project, and the Campaign for Democracy in Nigeria; the Law Society of Kenya and the Federation of Women Lawyers in Kenya; and the Zimbabwe Human Rights Association and the Forum for Democratic Reform in Zimbabwe. These were on the forefront of campaigns for democracy in their countries.

Intellectuals—disillusioned with socialism and what they increasingly came to see as the inevitable corruption and abuse of one-party rule—eloquently argued that Africa could not advance without the pluralism and accountability of multiparty democracy. Successful movements require broad coalitions across civil society, however. In Zambia the powerful trade union movement, led by the Zambian Congress of Trade Unions and its chairman, Frederick Chiluba, spearheaded a coalition of labor, students, businesspeople, and dissident politicians; it eventually took shape in (and won power as) the Movement for Multiparty Democracy.

In many African countries, religious figures and organizations took the lead in denouncing authoritarian rule and providing both legitimacy and sanctuary to vulnerable opponents. Powerful moral impetus for the anti-apartheid movement in South Africa came from outspoken black clergy like Anglican Archbishop Desmond Tutu and iconoclastic white clergy like the Reverend Beyers Naude. Clerics like Bishop Henry Okullu, chairman of the National Council of Churches of Kenya, and the Reverend Timothy Njoya rallied popular sentiment for multiparty democracy in Kenya. In several countries, well-publicized sermons and pastoral letters gave moral support and political momentum to the democratic cause. Such a letter by seven Catholic bishops helped to inspire the popular movement for democracy in Malawi. In both Benin and the Republic of Congo, Roman Catholic prelates presided over the national conferences.

Popular movements for democracy arose out of longtime frustration with the mounting failures and injustices of every type of authoritarian rule. During the 1980s Subsaharan Africa's per capita gross national product shrank at a rate of 1.1 percent annually. By 1989 its total external debt stood at $147 billion, 99 percent of gross domestic product and four times the annual export earnings. On virtually every dimension of economic and human development, African countries ranked among the poorest and most miserable in the world, despite an annual aid inflow of $15 billion. Decades of decay in education, infrastructure, health, and other public services were capped by fiscal crises that left states like Benin unable even to pay civil servants' salaries (a critical factor in stimulating protest).

In the midst of such intense poverty and economic decline, the gross venality and arrogance of ruling elites, their arbitrary use of power and abuse of human rights, and their reliance on increasingly narrow and exclusive ethnic bases of support ruptured the remaining bonds of political legitimacy. Alternative, informal channels of production and exchange proliferated as people sought to escape the predation of the state, and political opposition grew in breadth, boldness, organization, and moral fervor. Where such movements could not congeal, the alternative in several states, such as Liberia, Somalia, Sudan, Angola, and Rwanda, was civil war and state disintegration.

Toward Democratic Development?

Africa gained a new chance at democratic development in the 1990s, but with no assurances of success. Although one-party, socialist, and military regimes have been utterly discredited, democracy has yet to garner positive and broad legitimacy as an alternative. The movements that brought down authoritarianism were largely critical and oppositional in nature. Africa has yet to develop a healthy symbiosis between state and civil society. Civil society organizations and mass media generally have yet to find the balance between democratic vigilance and oversight, on the one hand, and positive engagement with the state and respect for its authority, on the other. And, for the most part, rival political factions and ethnic groups have yet to work out enduring modes of accommodation and coexistence among themselves. As Africa's past political travails have poignantly shown, democracy encompasses more than competition and participation. It requires tolerance, trust, moderation, accommodation, and accountability.

To be successful, democracy in Africa thus will demand broad changes in political culture, beginning with the political elite. No challenge is more important for the future of democracy in Africa than structuring institutions wisely. Strong autonomous institutions are needed to build a rule of law, regulate electoral contestation, and monitor conduct in public office. Layers of insulation are needed so that the judiciary and electoral administration will not be politicized again but can gain the confidence of all factions and groups through high standards of professional recruitment and operation.

To control corruption, two types of institutions are essential: an audit agency to monitor all government accounts and transactions and a commission to scrutinize the assets and conduct of all public officials. These institutions as well need rigorous professional standards and powerful insulation from partisan politics; top officers must be appointed from outside the political process (perhaps by the judiciary) and enjoy tenure of office that can be removed only by special procedures for demonstrated cause. They also need the resources to exercise effective oversight and to deter and punish corruption: sizable staffs of trained investigators, lawyers, and accountants; substantial computer technology; sufficiently competitive salaries to attract qualified professionals and deter temptation; and tough, savvy, truly independent administrators.

These structures of oversight will not come cheaply, but they will more than pay for themselves by deterring waste and theft or recovering monies wasted or stolen. Unless the virulent malignancy of corruption is contained and diminished, and a new ethic of public service and developmental purpose is generated, competitive, multiparty politics in Africa cannot possibly develop the mutual restraint and popular legitimacy necessary to survive.

Institutional innovations are also needed for managing Africa's ethnic diversity democratically. One institutional imperative for ethnically divided societies is federalism—or some functional equivalent that devolves meaningful power, autonomy, and resources to regional and local governments. Only through such devolution can the stakes of controlling political power at the center be reduced and governmental responsiveness to grassroots concerns and initiatives increased. Devolution of power will improve accountability as well as the sense of responsibility on the part of citizens for their own development and for monitoring the political process.

In this way, citizenship—the most basic building block of democracy—will be actively nurtured in Africa for the first time, as Africans learn that democratic participation means more than electing an ethnic "son of the soil" and waiting for him to bring back from the capital their "share of the national cake," in the form of contracts, jobs, money, and other patronage. In addition, by raising through taxation even modest funds for community development,

local governance might teach the important lesson that the state is no longer some alien colonial entity but that it belongs to all citizens and requires vigilant scrutiny and responsible participation from all.

Innovative provisions for ethnic power sharing and accommodation must also be crafted. Presidentialism offers the advantage of a single, unifying symbol of national political authority. Nigeria has led the way in showing how a presidential party system can generate incentives for transethnic politics. Nigeria's system requires a broad ethnic and regional distribution of support for election to the presidency, mandates broad ethnic representation in government appointments, ensures ethnic and regional balance in the "zoning" of party offices and nominations to different ethnic regions, and bans avowedly ethnic or regional parties.

Yet presidential power is also easily aggrandized and abused. An alternative strategy for encouraging ethnically broad electoral alliances or coalition governments would involve a parliamentary system coupled with proportional representation in districts small enough to provide effective linkages between voters and representatives.

Whatever the electoral system, political parties must develop greater institutional depth, reach, and capacity if they are to be effective instruments for representing and aggregating interests. An effective system requires not only appropriate institutional incentives but also creative political entrepreneurship to develop party structures that are independent of particular personalities and ethnic groups—to make parties into cross-cutting, issue-based political associations. The same is necessary with respect to independent organizations and interest groups in civil society. Yet institutionalization also requires patience and time; it will occur in Africa only if competitive, constitutional politics can, for the first time there, gain a long run without interruption by a military or presidential coup or by civil war.

Economic and International Prerequisites

Market-oriented reforms are indispensable to the future of democracy in Africa for two reasons: first, to reduce the scope for politicians to manipulate state economic regulations and controls for their own corrupt profit; and second, to unleash the entrepreneurial energy and investment that have been evident in the African informal sector and that must be mobilized formally, and on a large scale, if Africa is to develop. Yet the transitional costs of reform are enormous: socially, in terms of lost jobs and consumer subsidies; financially, in terms of the needs for government restructuring and social safety nets to ease adjustment; and politically, in terms of the instability that can result if the other costs of adjustment are not somehow met. One of the most pressing dilemmas facing the new and emerging democracies of Africa is thus financial: how to obtain the resources to manage adjustment and rekindle economic development.

Except for a few mineral-rich countries like Botswana, Nigeria, and Angola (and the last two have bankrupted themselves), most African countries have little prospect of economic recovery without renewed international assistance. Properly conditioned on open, liberal, accountable governance and responsible macroeconomic policies, international assistance could do much to ease the costs of structural adjustment, reduce crippling burdens of external debt, attract new business investment, and raise productivity through well-managed public investments in infrastructure, education, health, and capital funds for small businesses.

Yet the end of the cold war has been a mixed blessing for Africa. Although it has largely ended the proclivity of the major world powers to manipulate Africa's internal conflicts and embrace its authoritarian regimes, it has also greatly diminished their interest in Africa altogether. With Africa accounting for a virtually invisible 1 percent of world trade, internationalist forces in the West find it difficult to summon other than humanitarian and idealistic justifications for continued engagement in Africa. Africans have thus found themselves in the paradoxical position of being urged to reform and democratize—and making progress in doing so—while receiving less interest and support from the established democracies, especially the United States, than they did before reform and democratization.

To be successful, democracy in Africa will also require more support from within the community of African nations. Although the Organization of African Unity has increasingly committed its member nations to human rights and democracy in recent years, it has barely ventured beyond rhetoric. Two efforts in 1994 were auspicious. In August the presidents of South Africa, Zimbabwe, and Botswana successfully pressured the monarch of Lesotho to reverse his decision to disband the parliament. And in October the leaders of the former Front-Line states in the anti-apartheid struggle, joined by those of South Africa, Lesotho, Swaziland, and Malawi, met with the leaders of the two major competing parties in Mozambique on the eve of its United Nations–supervised elections. These outsiders obtained the parties' pledges to respect the results—thus enhancing mutual trust and helping to pave the way for a peaceful electoral transition.

Even in the face of a hopeful "second beginning," the future of democracy in Africa faces troubling questions. How long can the new democracies (and quasi-democracies) of Africa survive without renewing economic development and improving their peoples' material lives? How long will elected governments in Africa stick with painful economic reforms if those reforms fail to rekindle economic growth? In the face of so much economic scarcity and uncertainty, what ruling elite will summon the courage and self-discipline to institute the hard measures necessary to ensure public accountability? Will South Africa find the political stability and economic dynamism to become the democratic model and developmental engine that many Africans have been looking for on the continent? Will the Western democracies realize that the cost of investing in democracy and economic reform in Africa is far cheaper than the likely alternative of responding to an endless stream of humanitarian emergencies, civil wars, and collapsed states?

Increasingly, Africans recognize that democracy is not a luxury or a mere ideal but a necessity for development, justice, and conflict management in their countries.

See also *Africa, Horn of; Africa, Lusophone; African independence movements; African transitions to democracy; Botswana; Dominant party democracies in Asia; Electoral systems; Federalism; Ghana; Kenya; Namibia; Nigeria; Senegal; South Africa; Sudan; Uganda; Zaire; Zambia; Zimbabwe.*

Larry Diamond

BIBLIOGRAPHY

Ake, Claude. "Rethinking African Democracy." *Journal of Democracy* 2 (January 1991): 32–44.

Diamond, Larry. "Promoting Democracy in Africa." In *Africa in World Politics,* edited by John W. Harbeson and Donald Rothchild. 2d ed. Boulder, Colo.: Westview Press, 1995.

Diamond, Larry, Juan J. Linz, and Seymour Martin Lipset, eds. *Democracy in Developing Countries: Africa.* Boulder, Colo.: Lynne Rienner; London: Adamantine Press, 1988.

Harbeson, John W., Donald Rothchild, and Naomi Chazan, eds. *Civil Society and the State in Africa.* Boulder, Colo.: Lynne Rienner, 1994.

Hyden, Goran, and Michael Bratton, eds. *Governance and Politics in Africa.* Boulder, Colo.: Lynne Rienner, 1992.

Joseph, Richard. "Africa: The Rebirth of Political Freedom." *Journal of Democracy* 2 (October 1991): 11–24.

Luckham, Robin. "The Military, Militarization and Democratization in Africa: A Survey of Literature and Issues." *African Studies Review* 37 (September 1994): 13–75.

Nyong'o, Peter Anyang'. "Africa: The Failure of One-Party Rule." *Journal of Democracy* 3 (January 1992): 90–96.

Oyugi, Walter O., E. D. Atieno Odhiambo, Michael Chege, and Afrika K. Gitonga, eds. *Democratic Theory and Practice in Africa.* Portsmouth, N.H.: Heinemann; London: James Currey, 1988.

Robinson, Pearl T. "The National Conference Phenomenon in Francophone Africa." *Comparative Studies in Society and History* 36 (July 1994): 575–610.

Rothchild, Donald, and Naomi Chazan, eds. *The Precarious Balance: State and Society in Africa.* Boulder, Colo.: Westview Press, 1988.

Sklar, Richard L. "Democracy in Africa." *African Studies Review* 26 (September–December 1983): 11–24.

———. "Developmental Democracy." *Comparative Studies in Society and History* 29 (October 1987): 686–714.

———. "The Nature of Class Domination in Africa." *Journal of Modern African Studies* 17 (1979): 531–552.

Tordoff, William. *Government and Politics in Africa.* 2d ed. London: Macmillan; Bloomington: Indiana University Press, 1993.

Widner, Jennifer A., ed. *Economic Change and Political Liberalization in Sub-Saharan Africa.* Baltimore: Johns Hopkins University Press, 1994.

Wiseman, John A., *Democracy in Black Africa: Survival and Revival.* New York: Paragon House, 1990.

African independence movements

African independence movements were the democratic responses to European rule and decolonization in Africa. Nationalism in colonial Africa signified redemption from servitude enforced by means of racial oppression and alien rule. Accordingly, racial emancipation and national self-determination were core values for the African nationalist intelligentsia.

The related value of political freedom emerged from more complex intellectual origins. During the colonial era, African thinkers freely subscribed to the progressive ideals of Western liberalism and socialism. Many of them opted for principled cooperation with the colonial powers. For example, Edward Wilmot Blyden (1832–1912), a renowned father of African nationalism, expressly welcomed the advent of colonial rule. A patriotic citizen of the independent Republic of Liberia, Blyden supported, in word and deed, African cooperation with European colonial administrations if they demonstrated respect for African cultural values and provided opportunities for the advancement of African interests. Similar attitudes motivated pioneer nationalists everywhere in Africa. Hence both cooperation with colonial governments and resistance to colonial rule left their imprint on African democratic thought.

Although African nationalist thought incorporates pre-colonial precepts, its principles were formulated mainly in response to the partition and occupation of Africa by Europeans. Taking into account all forms of European rule in colonial Africa, one can distinguish three basic patterns of power: autochthony, diffusion, and despotism. Autochthonous forms of colonial rule relied on the adaptation of indigenous African political institutions. Rule by diffusion transferred European institutions to the colony. Despotic rulers did not recognize subordinate African authorities and acknowledged little, if any, legal restraint on their exercise of power over Africans. In practice, these three forms were mixed, but one type of rule was always predominant. Furthermore, each type regularly produced its characteristic nationalist response.

Democratic Responses to Colonial Rule

In colonial Africa the principle of autochthony underpinned a widely practiced policy known as "indirect rule," the exercise of political power through the medium of indigenous authorities. Indirect rule was the method of choice in British colonies, particularly those where the white settler element was relatively small and insignificant. In such countries African democrats confronted two kinds of rulers who were not accountable to their subjects: colonial officials and African "chiefs," who were recognized as traditional rulers by the colonial governments. For example, in the theocratic Muslim emirates of northern Nigeria, radical democrats attacked the biracial alliance between ruling African dynasties and their British imperial overlords.

The method of diffusion, or re-creating European institutions in African societies, was pursued more systematically in the French colonies than elsewhere. African democrats challenged the architects of the French Fourth Republic (1946–1958) to honor their promise of emancipation to the people of France overseas. In 1946 the interterritorial, federated African Democratic Rally of French West Africa called for equal social and political rights within a freely accepted union of the peoples of Africa and the people of France. Not until 1957, by which time France had set arbitrary and inequitable limits to African representation in the metropolitan National Assembly, did the

African Democratic Rally proclaim the goal of independence as an inalienable right.

Far removed from the dialogue on African rights in most of British and French colonial Africa were the despotic systems of rule in the Belgian, Portuguese, and Spanish colonies, as well as in the white settler states of Kenya, Rhodesia, and South Africa. In these places a latent tendency toward messianic or revolutionary violence was never far beneath the surface of manifestly dependent behavior. In the Belgian Congo a rigidly paternalistic regime granted few political rights or opportunities for postprimary education to Africans. Consequently, national leaders were ill prepared to cope with independence when it was granted precipitously by a demoralized Belgian government in 1960. Congolese nationalists were also deeply divided among themselves. One faction favored a unitary state; its opponents preferred a federal union with a high degree of regional autonomy. These rivals united for a bold experiment in democracy that was aborted, tragically, by an army mutiny only four days after independence.

In the European settler states of British East and Central Africa, and in Portuguese Africa, nationalists of the post–World War II era spurned reformist substitutes for the goal of sovereign independence based on majority rule. For example, in 1953 the Federation of Rhodesia and Nyasaland was created by British settlers who proposed to maintain a relatively liberal form of white minority rule compared with apartheid in South Africa and the authoritarian Portuguese regimes in Angola and Mozambique. The federation was bitterly opposed by African nationalists in Northern Rhodesia and Nyasaland. They perceived it to be an attempt to perpetuate white rule by extending the range of white power in Southern Rhodesia to the northern protectorates, where the white settler communities were smaller and still subject to salutary supervision by the British imperial government. In Southern Rhodesia, Africans were more inclined to believe that an interterritorial federation based on multiracial principles might actually mitigate the severity of racial repression in their own country. The federation, however, eventually was destroyed by resolutely antifederal African nationalism in the northern protectorates.

In 1962 African nationalists in Southern Rhodesia faced a difficult choice. Relatively moderate whites sought their support for a new constitution that offered some African representation in the parliament in return for a promise by white leaders to reduce, and gradually eliminate, white supremacy. But no mainstream African nationalist movement of the post–World War II era had ever accepted a constitution designed to perpetuate African political subordination. Following a debate on the merits of incremental reform, the Rhodesian (now Zimbabwean) nationalists rejected the white moderates' proposed constitution. As a result, the white electorate lost confidence in the ability of moderate leaders to resolve racial questions and entrusted its fate to a party of extreme racialists who favored a Rhodesian variation of the South African system of apartheid. The Africans then resolved to win their freedom and independence by means of armed struggle, which culminated in the replacement of Rhodesia by Zimbabwe in 1980.

The Pan-African Movement

The question of armed struggle, as an alternative to nonviolent methods of agitation for racial equality and national self-determination, was debated by delegates to the All-African People's Conference of December 1958. Prime Minister Kwame Nkrumah of Ghana convened the conference in fulfillment of a commitment made by leaders of the pan-African movement in 1945 to hold their next general meeting in a liberated country on African soil. Representing nongovernmental organizations from all parts of Africa, including liberation movements, political parties, trade unions, and women's groups, the conferees shared their hopes, fears, and proposals to liberate and democratize African societies.

The merits of nonviolent political action were strongly defended by Tom Mboya, conference chairman and general secretary of the Kenya Federation of Labor, and by Jordan Ngubane, delegation leader of the South African Liberal Party. Algerian delegates, reflecting the circumstance of guerrilla warfare against French rule in their country, were foremost among proponents of armed struggle. At length, a compromise resolution pledged support to all fighters for freedom in Africa—those using peaceful means of nonviolence and civil disobedience as well as those compelled to retaliate against violence. This measured endorsement of liberating violence in response to repressive violence was widely understood to express a preference for nonviolent political strategies, reserving violence as a method of last resort.

Scarcely two months earlier, in September 1958, Julius Nyerere, leader of the Tanganyikan African nationalist movement, had invited delegates from seven countries to a conference at Mwanza, Tanganyika. This conference inaugurated the Pan-African Freedom Movement of East and

Central Africa (PAFMECA). Its constitution contained a declaration of intent to champion nonviolence in nationalist struggles. Eventually, in 1962, membership in this organization was offered to the freedom movements of southern Africa, entailing a name change to Pan-African Freedom Movement of Eastern, Central, and Southern Africa (PAFMECSA). In 1963 Nelson Mandela, leader of the underground military wing of the African National Congress of South Africa, addressed a PAFMECSA conference in Addis Ababa, Ethiopia. He explained that, regrettably, violence in his country could not be avoided. PAFMECSA then repealed its constitutional commitment to nonviolence.

At its inaugural (1958) conference, PAFMECA had adopted a freedom charter that pledged to oppose white racialism and black chauvinism and to uphold the Universal Declaration of Human Rights. Comparable resolutions relating to the protection of individual rights and minority racial rights, however, had divisive effects at the subsequent inaugural meeting of the All-African People's Conference. Three delegations—the Action Group of Nigeria (one of three leading parties in that country), the United Party (an opposition party) of Ghana, and the ruling party of Liberia—sponsored a resolution calling on African states to give legislative effect to the Universal Declaration of Human Rights. This proposal was rejected.

Soon thereafter the United Party succumbed to Nkrumah's intolerance of opposition. Paradoxically, the Action Group, under pressure to restrict its activities in Nigeria after independence, obtained paramilitary assistance in 1960 from Nkrumah. Given its notorious record of repression at home, Liberia's gesture of support for political rights was dubious. Concerning racial minority rights (particularly the rights of Europeans and Indians in African countries), there were memorable statements by delegates from Kenya and South Africa. Ezekiel Mphalele, chief delegate of the African National Congress of South Africa, declared that an African was a person of any color who was born in Africa and considered it home. Although the conference resolutions skirted the question of African identity, they did condemn racial discrimination as such and called for the formation of a committee to examine alleged abuses of human rights anywhere in Africa.

These early debates about universal standards of human rights, minority racial rights, and armed struggle for freedom culminated with the establishment of the Organization of African Unity at Addis Ababa in 1963. The charter and related resolutions, adopted by that summit conference of independent African states, followed the example of PAFMECSA by both endorsing the Universal Declaration of Human Rights and establishing a permanent committee to coordinate all forms of assistance to national liberation movements.

Democracy and the Party System

At midcentury there were only four independent countries in Africa—Ethiopia, Liberia, Egypt, and South Africa (in order of their attainment of sovereignty in modern times). During the 1950s six more African states became independent—Libya, Sudan, Morocco, Tunisia, Ghana, and Guinea. In the watershed year 1960 no fewer than seventeen African states attained independence. Fifteen more followed between 1961 and 1970. With few exceptions—notably Algeria and the former Belgian colonies—decolonization involved the creation of democratic political institutions for these newly independent states. In all but a few cases, the postcolonial democracies perished during the first decade of national independence. The causes of democratic decline in postcolonial Africa are complex and variable, but one cause is clearly attributable to the impact of revolutionary ideology on the anticolonial freedom movement.

During the late 1950s and the 1960s many intellectuals in Africa, as elsewhere, became convinced that some form of political dictatorship would be required to facilitate rapid economic development and social reconstruction. Although this viewpoint was expressed more frequently, clearly, and precisely after independence than before, antidemocratic tendencies were evident in the pre-independence thought and practice of various leaders, particularly those who fostered the creation of personality cults and the organization of political parties designed to dominate the state. Eventually some of those leaders embraced Leninist and Maoist concepts of party organization and rule, although no African party in power ever tried to restrict its membership as rigorously as was required by the tenets of orthodox Leninism. The Marxist-Leninist leaders of Angola, Mozambique, and Rhodesia during the 1970s, however, did emulate the doctrinaire political thought of Nkrumah in his later years.

The effect of communitarian socialist thought on democracy in Africa is more difficult to assess. Many African socialists were inclined to believe that traditional communalism had minimized divisive class conflicts.

Hence, they concluded, socialist societies could be consolidated in Africa without class struggles by returning, ideologically, "to the source," that is, to Africa's own cultural tradition. Such revolutionary thinkers as Nkrumah and Ahmed Sékou Touré (who defied Charles de Gaulle and persuaded the voters of Guinea to choose independence in 1958 rather than association with the French community) subscribed to that belief.

No one questions the democratic pedigree of communitarian socialism, but problems for democracy emerged when communitarians disputed the desirability of more than one political party once the "correct" political party had taken over. In Africa, communitarian socialists frequently resorted to the Marxist idea that political parties represent the conflicting interests of social classes. Absent class conflict, they argued, a genuine people's party would be morally legitimate, while other parties would be dysfunctional at best, agents of imperialism at worst. When populist myths of political unity and social harmony no longer sufficed, communitarian socialists shifted easily to other justifications of one-party rule: the inexorable growth of class conflict in Africa, solidarity against capitalist imperialism, the threat of ethnic political separatism.

Renowned for his intellectual integrity and consistency, Julius Nyerere is Africa's preeminent communitarian socialist. Unlike contemporaries who forgot their communitarian roots and lost touch with the people, Nyerere, as president of Tanzania, remained faithful to his nationalist ideals. He advocated a one-party state on the ground that it would actually enhance freedom of choice and democratic participation because one national party would be universally identified with general interests rather than sectional or class interests. He also continued to apply egalitarian standards of judgment in criticizing the oligarchic tendencies besetting his one-party government. Yet the basic contradiction between his egalitarian precepts and the enforcement of a one-party state by high officials would never be resolved in his theory or practice of government.

The multiparty persuasion in African nationalist thought was silenced unceremoniously by advocates of one-party rule in most of the newly independent African states. A few nationalist leaders, however, were able to create durable multiparty systems at the dawn of independence. They include Seretse Khama in Botswana, Dawda K. Jawara in Gambia, Seewoosagur Ramgoolam in Mauritius, and the Nigerian democratic nationalists, principally Obafemi Awolowo and Nnamdi Azikiwe.

Awolowo believed that cultural-linguistic groups were entitled to self-determination within multicultural federations. In addition to reasonable autonomy as compared with other groups, they should have the right to restore positive elements of traditional government that had been suppressed or distorted by colonial rulers. In societies that were constitutional as well as monarchical before colonial rule (for example, Awolowo's own Yoruba people), federal systems of government would protect regional reformers who wished to restore the constitutional balance between kings, chiefs, and people. Thus did Awolowo's party, the Action Group, turn the colonial principle of autochthony into a rampart of constitutional democracy. Largely because of its efforts, the federal principle was firmly established as the essential bedrock of Nigerian national unity. In practice, however, Awolowo and his followers compromised this ideal of cultural federalism by supporting the creation of large, multicultural constituent regions (subsequently states) of the Nigerian federation.

Meanwhile, during the final decade of colonial rule in Francophone Africa, the diffusionist vision of African emancipation within a unitary French empire was discarded by nationalists in favor of political autonomy. Léopold Sédar Senghor, poet, philosopher, and Senegalese statesman, cherished the idea of a Franco-African federation. At the very least, he hoped to preserve the multiterritorial federation of French West Africa as a sovereign, postcolonial entity. But federalism in Francophone West Africa succumbed to the balkanizing drive for territorial separatism, fostered principally by Senghor's rival, Félix Houphouët-Boigny, of the Côte d'Ivoire. Had Senghor's federal concept prevailed, the defense of democratic principles in Francophone Africa might have fared at least as well as it has in federal Nigeria, despite the travails there of persistent political instability.

Democratic Response to Decolonization

The concept of decolonization has provoked controversy because it implies the primacy of European rather than African initiatives in the movement for colonial freedom. In reality, complex patterns of shared agency were unmistakable: Britain and France employed various democratic measures, consistent with African nationalist values, to protect their interests and control the pace of political change.

Among British colonial thinkers, there was broad agreement on the desirability of three distinct phases of transition from the empire to a commonwealth of independent nations. These were identified as good government, responsible government, and self-government, in that order. Good government implied effective administration by local officials who had accepted full responsibility for development. Responsible government meant that high officials had become accountable for their actions to a territorial parliament, consisting of elected representatives of the people. Self-government signified the transfer of state power to indigenous officeholders. The architects of decolonization were deeply convinced that a premature transfer of power to politicians and administrators who did not believe in good government would be disastrous: responsible government could not then be maintained, and self-government would soon degenerate into bad government.

Nationalist thinkers, in British and French colonies alike, reversed the order of sequence. They were inclined to put self-government, based on democratic representation, first. They expected that responsible governments would then be chosen freely, resulting in good government for the independent countries. Hence they made every effort to mobilize the people to demand immediate democratic representation. By 1955 their demands had become virtually irresistible in British West Africa; by 1958 independence was on the agenda in most of Francophone Africa. Eventually, the democratic revolution prevailed against paternalistic caution and reluctance everywhere.

As a colonial creed, "good government" captured few hearts among passionate nationalists in Africa. Moreover, the leaders of independence movements readily identified public finance as a resource that could be used to fund their political machines as well as their ambitious programs for national development. Thirty years later a more cautious generation of African intellectuals, having experienced the failures of economic statism and the damage caused by rulers who were scarcely accountable to anyone for their performance in office, has revived the colonial idea of good government. Now it is widely espoused as the principle of "governance," which is understood to mean public accountability for officials, honesty in fiscal management, and respect for the rule of law.

To be sure, the African independence movements made their own crucial contributions to the ideal of good government. Nationalists, in general, assigned the highest priority to educational opportunity in their plans for a renascent Africa. In the eyes of most of the early beneficiaries of that commitment, the nationalist political leaders were authentic heroes; but the role models for upwardly mobile graduates were their professional predecessors who pioneered pathways to success in the public services, legal systems, and comparable institutions of modern society. A few of these pioneers are widely renowned; for example, Simeon Adebo, the quintessential Nigerian civil servant whose distinguished career was capped by an appointment as assistant secretary general at the UN Institute for Training and Research, and William Ndala Wamalwa, a Kenyan civil servant who is esteemed for his many contributions to public administration in Africa and who has been elected to successive terms as president of the African Association of Public Administration and Management. Thousands of their kind, bred for public service during the advance to independence, are unsung heroes of the movement for democracy and good government.

See also *African transitions to democracy; Azikiwe, Nnamdi; Khama, Seretse; Mandela, Nelson; Nkrumah, Kwame; Nyerere, Julius; Senghor, Léopold Sédar; Theory, African.* In Documents section, see *African National Congress Freedom Charter (1955); African Charter on Human and Peoples' Rights (1981).*

Richard L. Sklar

BIBLIOGRAPHY

Awolowo, Obafemi. *Path to Nigerian Freedom.* London: Faber, 1947.

Cox, Richard. *Pan-Africanism in Practice.* London: Oxford University Press, 1964.

Hodgkin, Thomas. *Nationalism in Colonial Africa.* London: Frederick Muller, 1956.

July, Robert W. *The Origins of Modern African Thought.* New York: Praeger, 1967.

Lee, J. M. *Colonial Development and Good Government.* Oxford: Clarendon Press, 1967.

Legum, Colin. *Pan-Africanism: A Short Political Guide.* Rev. ed. New York: Praeger, 1965.

Morgenthau, Ruth Schachter. *Political Parties in French-Speaking West Africa.* Oxford: Clarendon Press, 1964.

Munger, Edwin S. "All-African People's Conference." American Universities Field Staff Reports, Africa, 1959.

Nyerere, Julius K. *Freedom and Unity.* Dar es Salaam: Oxford University Press, 1966.

Sklar, Richard L. "The Colonial Imprint on African Political Thought." In *African Independence,* edited by Gwendolen M. Carter and Patrick O'Meara. Bloomington: Indiana University Press, 1985.

African transitions to democracy

Democratic transitions in Africa are problematic but there is hope. This article assesses, country by country, democracy's progress in Subsaharan Africa during the early 1990s. The focus is on Francophone Africa, which witnessed the greatest share of democratic ferment in this period. Francophone Africa includes Mauritania, Senegal, Mali, Niger, Burkina Faso, Côte d'Ivoire, Benin, Togo, and Cameroon in West Africa; Gabon, Congo, Chad, and the Central African Republic in equatorial Africa; Zaire, Rwanda, and Burundi in Central Africa; and Madagascar in East Africa.

In 1993 four states went through genuine democratic transitions: Niger, Madagascar, Lesotho, and the Central African Republic. Each resulted in the displacement of the incumbents and, more surprising, the acceptance of the results by the displaced. Between October 1990 and October 1993 twenty-two multiparty elections were held in Africa; twelve of them ousted the incumbent.

Elsewhere on the continent a depressing picture emerged of autocrats unwilling to loosen their grip on power and opposition forces reluctant to accept defeat. Even where the passage to democracy seemed reasonably promising, there were plenty of signs that the military was not fully committed to the new civilian order. The destruction of Burundi's fledgling democracy by the army on October 20, 1993, exemplifies the deadly threats posed to democratic consolidations by armed factions within the military. In Nigeria the annulment of the presidential poll by Gen. Ibrahim Babangida in June 1993 shows the intractable difficulties involved in disengaging the military from processes of democratization. In one case an exemplary transition was nipped in the bud; in the other the goal of democracy suddenly receded after drawing near.

Although these failings have received extensive media coverage, there has been relatively little discussion of the success stories. Measured by what could be observed at the end of 1989—when Mauritius, Senegal, and Botswana were the only islands of democracy in a sea of authoritarianism—few would deny that momentum is on the side of democracy. This is not to say that liberal democracy will carry the day everywhere on the continent or that a successful transition will necessarily lead to enduring democratic achievements. Tempting though it is to reduce processes of democratization to a form of sportscasting, with appropriate ratings, innings, and box scores, there are few undisputed champions. For every move toward liberalization there looms a difficult transition, and for every successful transition there follows a problematic consolidation.

The purpose of this article is to put the recent and ongoing wave of democratization in broad historical and comparative perspective. Major dimensions include the background of this continental awakening; the effect of historical and structural constraints on the dynamics and modes of transition; the obstacles to democracy, including those associated with strategies of authoritarian restoration; and the problems and opportunities confronting African states as they try to consolidate their democratic gains.

Roots of Africa's Democratic Awakening

The wave of democratization that has swept across the continent since 1989 is traceable not to any single event but to a combination of factors, some internal to Africa and others external. Of these none has had a more decisive effect than the end of the cold war and the collapse of communism. No longer could Western support for compliant African dictators be justified in terms of strategic imperatives. Long blocked from the West's vision by its myopic concentration on East-West competition, the damning features of African autocracies finally came into focus—their disastrous economic performance, their appalling human rights record, and their indifference to social justice.

Belatedly, international donors reappraised their objectives for Africa. Because their former goal, containment of communism, was now irrelevant, the promotion of multiparty democracy quickly emerged as a central goal. International pressures for democracy came from several sources and in different forms, but none proved more effective—and controversial—than "conditionality." Substantial evidence of progress toward democratic governance became a condition for economic and financial assistance. Democratic governance was usually defined in terms of transparency of political institutions, accountability, multiparty elections, and constitutionalism.

Conditionality lay at the heart of French president François Mitterrand's declaration at the 1990 Franco-African summit in La Baule: from then on France's aid would be in proportion to presumptive recipients' efforts toward greater freedom. Anglophone nations were served similar notice by Great Britain at the 1991 Commonwealth conference in Harare (Zimbabwe). Kenya's international donors at the November 1991 Paris meeting of the Consultative Group for Kenya said that they would not resume bilateral assistance unless political reform was implemented. In particular, they wanted to see more pluralism, greater respect for human rights, and freedom of expression and assembly. Two weeks later Kenyan president Daniel arap Moi lifted the ban on parties other than his own and formally agreed to multiparty elections.

Forces at work within African societies also played a critical role in stimulating demands for democracy. Organized labor, teacher associations, student groups, and civil servants were at the forefront of the popular protests directed against African dictators in Mali, Benin, Niger, Togo, Congo, and Zambia. Catastrophic economic conditions and shrinking salaries sparked countless outbursts of social violence—food riots (Zambia, 1990), student protests (Mali and Niger, 1990), strikes by civil servants (Benin, Niger, and Congo, 1989–1990), and rural uprisings (Burundi, 1988). An estimated 15,000 people died in Burundi, and more than 200 people died in Mali. Public outrage over the human toll, and African rulers' impotence in dealing with critical challenges to their authority, set in motion the wheels of democratization in much of West and Central Africa.

Once a trailblazer of Afro-Marxism, Benin by early 1990 stood as the bellwether of democracy for the rest of Francophone Africa. Its National Conference, which stripped President Mathieu Kerekou of his dictatorial powers, became an institutional model for other states that wanted to pave the way for a transitional government and lay down the ground rules for multiparty democracy. Although the Benin precedent turned out to be a mixed blessing elsewhere, it nevertheless legitimized and accelerated a process of change that had deep roots in the social tensions generated by autocratic rule.

Structural Constraints and Strategic Choices

Human idiosyncrasies, leadership skills, and ideological commitments are major ingredients in the welter of forces that affect the outcome of transitions. There is a palpable contrast, for example, between the political style of Kenneth Kaunda in Zambia, Pierre Buyoya in Burundi, and Ali Saibou in Niger—all of whom were displaced from presidential office through free and fair elections—and the sternly authoritarian, stubbornly uncompromising attitude of Presidents Mobutu Sese Seko of Zaire and Gnas-

singbé Eyadema of Togo. The political styles of opposition leaders also vary widely. Much of the credit for the success of democratic transitions in Zambia and Niger goes to the opposition candidates, Frederick Chiluba and Mahamane Ousmane, respectively. Their inspired leadership and commitment to democracy were not shared by their counterparts in Togo, Zaire, Gabon, or Burkina Faso. In these states more impressive leadership skills might not make much difference, however, because of the structural impediments to democracy.

History and environment set important boundaries on the strategic options of political leaders. Social configurations—class, religion, ethnic and regional ties, or a combination of these—have a direct bearing on the structure of political conflict.

Almost everywhere on the continent, attempts at democratic transition are confronted with the legacy of neopatrimonial regimes. The hallmark of such regimes is a form of authority based on vertical dependency relationships between the ruler (or patron) and his underlings (or clients). Personal patronage holds the system together. Material rewards to subordinates are repaid by loyalty to the ruler; rent seeking is the rule, and public office the main source of "rents" for aspiring clients. As Michael Bratton has pointed out, neopatrimonial rule weakens civil society. Broadly based associational ties are virtually nonexistent; legal and institutional norms are extremely weak. Collective action is rendered all the more difficult by the dearth of social capital. In neopatrimonial settings trust is highly selective and vertically structured; there is no room for horizontal networks of social engagement.

Zaire and Togo are classic examples: the ability of their rulers to manipulate, buy off, or coerce opposition figures has been enhanced by the extreme weakness of their civil societies. This is graphically illustrated by the extraordinary proliferation of parties (numbering more than 500 in Zaire in 1993) and by the dominance of personal connections, cunning, and clientelism in political life. Zaire and Togo are extreme but by no means unique examples. Cameroon, Côte d'Ivoire, Gabon, Kenya, and Malawi share many of the characteristics of neopatrimonial regimes, including high levels of corruption, weak civil societies, and a rich proliferation of patron-client ties. Alone among these, Malawi experienced an electoral transition to democracy in 1994 with the defeat of the ruling party.

To the disabilities involved in the legacy of neopatrimonial rule must be added the handicaps inherent in the highly fragmented, factionalized social structure of most African states. Of these, ethnicity is the most familiar, although possibly the least understood. In transitional settings, mobilized ethnicity is often the flip side of patron-clientelism. Electoral competition draws opposition candidates to their ethnic constituencies like a magnetic field. Few are able to resist the temptation of giving a moral dimension to their platform, even if it means compromising their chances of success at the polls. And where ethnicity dissolves into ephemeral clan alliances (for example, in northern Chad, Somalia, and southern Ethiopia), fragmentation is an even more formidable obstacle, resulting in anarchic factionalism and clan warfare.

Kenya is an example of how mobilized ethnicity can play into the hands of the incumbent. The clinching element behind Daniel arap Moi's victory in the December 1992 multiparty presidential elections was neither ballot rigging nor intimidation (though both helped) but the factional nature of the opposition—the inability of the three main opposition candidates (Kenneth Matiba, Mwai Kibaki, and Oginga Odinga) to transcend the limits of their respective ethno-regional constituencies and unite. Even where legal and constitutional restrictions have been placed on the organization of ethnic parties (as in Nigeria and Burundi), ethnicity may still play a major role in obstructing democratic transitions. In Nigeria critics of the military regime of General Babangida insisted that the presumptive winner in the June 1993 presidential elections, Moshood Abiola, was denied the fruits of his victory for no other reason than that he was a Yoruba and thus unacceptable in the eyes of a Hausa-dominated officer corps.

In Burundi ethnic motives were a decisive factor in the October 1993 coup: perceptions of Melchior Ndadaye's victory as a victory of the Hutu (who constitute about 85 percent of the population) prompted one segment of the Tutsi-dominated military to seize power. The coup was precipitated by Ndadaye's plans to allow the Hutu refugees from a 1972 bloodbath to repossess their lands and houses (now mostly in Tutsi hands) and by his decision to sack a number of Tutsi civil servants and replace them with Hutu candidates. The country's descent once again into a grim spiral of ethnic violence underscored the seemingly intractable nature of the Hutu-Tutsi conflict. In Burundi, as in South Africa, social conflict is vertically structured. An ethnic (or racial) majority—the Hutu in Burundi, black Africans in South Africa—are oppressed by a privileged minority. In both instances the central issue is how to rec-

oncile the rights of a politically dominant minority with the requirements of majority rule.

Power sharing or consociational formulas are often seen as a necessary ingredient of democracy in deeply divided societies. Their merits, however, are very much in doubt where the rights of minorities are at stake. Consociationalism was at the heart of the consolidation efforts in Burundi before the coup. Although it remains a critical aspect of the leveling of the constitutional playing field in South Africa, only the future will tell whether a democracy based on political pacts is enough to ensure the loyalty of the army.

Modes of Transition

Although transitions unfold in very different contexts, they all fall into one of two categories: transitions from above and transitions from below. In the former, rulers respond to crises by initiating democratic reforms whose timing and substance they hope to control. In the latter, mounting popular pressures eventually shift the initiative to national conferences. Acting as surrogate constituent assemblies, these conferences determine the pace and manner of the transition to democracy. The national conference is a distinctly francophone phenomenon, traceable to Benin's National Conference of Active Forces in February 1990. It soon became a model for other African states (Chad, Congo, Gabon, Mali, Niger, Togo, and Zaire). Transposed to other settings, the Beninois experiment proved somewhat less than promising, however.

In general, transitions from above are more likely than transitions from below to lead to democracy because they feature more specific plans about the time frame, methods, and overall strategy of transition. Transitions from below involve more uncertainty. Mass mobilization may be the quickest way to challenge autocratic rule, but mobilized groups can seriously complicate transition negotiations. This is why national conferences—with the notable exception of Benin—have a disappointing record. Only in Benin were the delegates to the National Conference able to outline a clear, step-by-step strategy of transition. Elsewhere, strategic and procedural issues never received the attention they deserved because of investigations of presidential misconduct (Congo), bickering among delegates over qualifications and authority (Niger and Chad), preemption of these issues by presidential initiatives (Togo and Gabon), or a combination of all three problems (Zaire).

On closer inspection the picture that emerges is more

ambivalent. Transitions from above have yielded mixed results, ranging from unmitigated disasters in the cases of Nigeria and Kenya to relative success in Zambia. National conferences have varied widely, not only in outcomes, but in size (from 380 participants in Gabon to 3,400 in Zaire), representativeness (high in Benin; low in Mali, Niger, and Chad), duration (from a few weeks to more than a year), mandate (constitutional or advisory), and expenses ($1.4 million in Benin, $7 million in Congo, and perhaps as much as $15 million in Zaire).

Where national conferences were allowed to operate as "sovereign" transitional assemblies—as in Benin, Congo, Niger, and Chad—the result has been (1) the promulgation of a transitional constitutional document; (2) the establishment, by co-optation, of a transitional legislative organ, known almost everywhere as the High Council of the Republic; and (3) the election, either by the conference or the High Council, of a transitional prime minister, pending presidential and legislative elections. Only in Benin did the conference do without the office of prime minister and vest all executive powers in a popularly elected president. Almost everywhere else the appointment of a prime minister led to conflict with the incumbent president: to wit, the tug-of-war in Chad between President Idriss Deby and Prime Minister Fidèle Moungar, in Zaire between President Mobutu Sese Seko and Prime Minister Etienne Tshisekedi, and in Togo between President Gnassingbé Eyadema and Prime Minister Joseph Koffigoh—until the latter finally decided to join the presidential camp.

A major reason for the relative success of the Benin experiment lies in the representativeness of its National Conference. In other national conferences, specific social, ethnic, or religious groups were underrepresented (for example, students in Mali, the Tuaregs in Niger, Muslim fundamentalists in Chad, and the Banyarwanda in Zaire). Clear underrepresentation, or the perception that certain groups were the victims of political exclusion, often made the atmosphere at these conferences acrimonious. Denial of "access" and "voice" emerged as one of the most contentious issues among conference participants. Underrepresentation lies at the heart of the outbreaks of ethnic violence in Zaire (between Banyarwanda and Bahunde in Northern Kivu) and explains why, in Niger, the Tuareg insurgency has yet to be fully quelled.

Perhaps the most promising formula is what Samuel Huntington of Harvard calls "transplacement," a situation in which the government and the opposition try to negotiate a mutually acceptable compromise. Yet whether transplacement fulfills its promise depends on the bargaining skills of the negotiators and the type of opposition the government is dealing with. This is where the dramatically divergent paths followed by South Africa and Rwanda hold significant lessons. In South Africa former president Frederik W. de Klerk and Nelson Mandela deserve full credit for resolving the impasse between the unitarists (represented by the African National Congress and the National Party) and the federalists of the Concerned South African Group (which included both Chief Mangosuthu Buthelezi's Inkatha Freedom Party and the right-wing custodians of the Afrikaner cause led by Gen. Constand Viljoen).

There was no equivalent in Rwanda for the sustained dialogue and compromises achieved through the complex personal chemistry between Mandela and de Klerk. The transition bargain in Rwanda (which has a numerical balance between majority Hutu and minority Tutsi roughly identical to Burundi's but with the former politically dominant until 1994) emerges retrospectively as a recipe for disaster. The negotiations (known as the Arusha accords) were conducted under tremendous external pressures (from France, the United States, Belgium, and the Organization of African Unity). In part for this reason, the concessions made to the Tutsi-dominated Rwandan Patriotic Front (RPF) were seen by Hutu hard-liners within the ruling National Movement for Revolution and Development (NMRD) as a sellout imposed by outsiders. Allowing for the RPF "rebels" to claim as many cabinet posts in the transitional government as the NMRD could not be viewed by Hutu extremists as anything other than a surrender to blackmail. Rather than providing a framework for a peaceful settlement, the Arusha accords thus became the focus of violent disagreements between Hutu moderates and extremists within the NMRD.

A characteristic feature of democratic transitions is that they tend to unleash rising social and political demands and sharpen ethno-regional political competition. As a result, an unbridgeable gap is created between constitutional design and political realities. In case after case the evidence shows that democracy is generally perceived as a zero-sum game with definite winners and losers among competing ethno-regional groups. This is why the movement from autocracy to liberalization makes democratic consolidation so problematic.

Threat of Authoritarian Restorations

Ethnic conflict is more than the product of a specific political conjuncture. All too often it is the consequence of strategies designed by African despots to ensure their own political survival. They deliberately manipulate ethnicity to foster social conflict.

The 1994 genocide in Rwanda is a tragic example: planned annihilation, not the sudden eruption of atavistic hatreds, is the key to the Rwanda tragedy. The aim, first and foremost, was to wipe out Tutsi civilians so as to deprive the Rwandan Patriotic Front of a domestic constituency and at the same time eliminate all basis for compromise between moderate Hutu politicians and the RPF. The reassertion of Hutu solidarities through the wanton killing of Tutsi civilians would transcend differences among Hutus (regional and political) and make it virtually unthinkable for Hutu and Tutsi to agree on anything.

The shooting down of President Juvénal Habyarimana's plane, on April 6, 1994, was consistent with this strategy. Despite the absence of solid evidence in support of a Hutu plot, it is easy to see the logic that might have prompted such a move. Not only did Habyarimana's death remove once and for all the specter of Arusha, but by holding the RPF responsible for it, extremists within the NMRD could point to this "dastardly crime" as moral justification for genocide.

Rwanda is an extreme but by no means unique case. In Kenya, for example, President Daniel arap Moi has encouraged armed attacks by members of his group, the minority Kalenjin, against largely defenseless more sizable ethnic groups like the Kikuyus. Again, in Zaire, President Mobutu is widely perceived as the instigator of the killings and mass exodus of so-called Kasaians from the Shaba province—a move intended to make Shaba safe for his political allies since Kasaians are overwhelmingly of Luba origins and hence sympathetic to Etienne Tshisekedi's Sacred Union coalition. In each case, ethnicity emerges as a major vehicle of state-instigated violence designed to intimidate opponents and thwart challenges to the status quo.

Ethnic manipulation is only one of several tactics used by African rulers to subvert democratic transitions or to retain ultimate control over their timing, agenda, and outcomes. Another tactic is the use of the armed forces as a counterweight to the forces of democratization. In most cases the ethnic underpinnings of the military only reinforce its disposition to intervene on behalf of the incumbent. In Togo the Kabye-dominated army, in a destructive show of force resulting in the death of hundreds of peaceful demonstrators in 1992 and 1993, all but undid the work of the National Conference and reduced the prime minister to a figurehead. Much the same scenario can be seen in Zaire, where the Special Presidential Division, dominated by Ngbandi elements (Mobutu's own group), repeatedly displayed its loyalty to Mobutu by shooting peaceful protesters and political opponents, and by holding hostage the members of the High Council for their failure to comply with Mobutu's agenda.

A more subtle maneuver is buying off political clients with a view to weakening the opposition or creating loyal political parties. Here again, pride of place goes to Mobutu, whose unparalleled skill in the arts of co-optation and repression explains his impressive performance during the National Conference. In the best tradition of neopatrimonial rule, Mobutu was able to sate the appetites of enough presumptive clients to drive a deep wedge into the ranks of the opposition. The emergence of parallel institutions designed to challenge the authority of the National Conference and the High Council—a phenomenon euphemistically referred to in Zaire as *dedoublement*—bears testimony to Mobutu's skill in co-opting opposition figures. In 1993 Zaire was the only country in the world to claim two prime ministers, two governments, two parliaments, two constitutions, and two transitional constitutional charters.

In Zaire, as elsewhere on the continent, authoritarian restorations have implications that go far beyond the short-term prospects for free and fair transition elections. Elections are not entities in themselves, divorced from the social context in which they unfold. Ethnic hatred, distrust, and other devastating effects of neopatrimonial rule will linger long after its fragile institutional base has collapsed.

Problems and Prospects

It is one thing for a transitional election to be successful and quite another for it to be meaningful. Competitive multiparty elections may be declared free and fair by international observers, and hence successful. Only if they contribute to long-term prospects for democratic consolidation and good governance, however, can they be viewed as meaningful.

Many problems hinder the consolidation of fledgling democracies. Opposition forces are extremely fragmented and lack coherent political platforms. Moreover, they tend

TABLE 1. Party Profiles in Selected African Parliaments

Country and date of election	Number of parties in election	Number of parties in parliament	Dominant party or coalition in parliament [a]	Rate of electoral abstention (percent)
Benin March 1995	50	16	Benin Renaissance Party (20/83)	30
Burkina Faso May 1992	27	17	Organization for People's Democracy —Labor Movement (78/107)	60
Cameroon March 1992	32	4	Cameroon People's Democratic Movement (165/175)	NA
Central African Republic Sept. 1993	15	13	Movement for the Liberation of the Central African People (34/85)	50
Côte d'Ivoire Oct. 1990	17	3	Democratic Party of the Côte d'Ivoire (165/175)	38
Gabon March 1991	9	7	Gabonese Democratic Party (66/117)	NA
Mali April 1992	22	10	Alliance for Democracy in Mali (73/116)	65
Mauritania Feb. 1992	3	2	Democratic and Social Republican Party (76/79)	64
Niger Jan. 1995	15	6	National Movement for the Development Society–Nassara (43/83)	50
Senegal Jan. 1993	9	5	Socialist Party (87/120)	49

a. The first number in each pair of numbers is the number of seats held by the dominant party or coalition; the second number is the total number of seats in the parliament.

to gravitate around ethno-regional constituencies. These conditions impede constructive parliamentary debate and threaten governmental stability. In Benin, Congo, and Niger ruling coalitions are notoriously vulnerable to factional discord. Few parliamentary parties have deep roots in the countryside. Most of them can best be seen as fragile political machines, lubricated by shrinking patronage benefits that seldom reach the needy. And where the conditions of economic austerity enforced through structural adjustment are accompanied by spectacular salary increases for cabinet ministers and deputies—as happened in Senegal in 1993, when the salaries of both were doubled—disaffection toward the political class is likely to grow. The absence of effective links between parliamentarians and their rural constituencies does little to legitimize notions of democracy among the masses.

This is one possible explanation for the universally low voter turnout in legislative elections. (See Table 1.) Another is the decision of opposition candidates to boycott legislative elections after losing the race for the presidency (as happened in Ghana in 1992 when Jerry Rawlings was elected). Opposition leaders argue that if it had not been for massive fraud on the part of the ruling party their victory would have been assured.

As Michael Bratton has shown, the refusal of the losers to accept the verdict of the polls is a widespread phenomenon. In ten of eighteen presidential elections examined by Bratton, the losers refused to accept the results, and in every case the winner happened to be the incumbent. Where the ruling "bosses" have effectively rigged their way back into office (as in Togo, Cameroon, and Gabon), the discredit incurred by the incumbents is bound to rub off on the institutions and seriously jeopardize their legitimacy. And where the outcome of the elections is challenged by armed factions, the result is likely to be a resumption of hostilities, as in Angola, or a violent resurgence of ethnic hatreds, as in Burundi and Rwanda.

As Angola's experience makes tragically clear, countries emerging from civil wars have little hope that transitional elections will serve their intended purpose unless the combatants have been disarmed, dissident units have been brought under control, and appropriate steps have been taken to initiate a demobilization program. The failure to meet these conditions in Liberia and Chad inspires considerable doubts about these countries' chances of successfully managing their democratic transitions. The case of Mozambique, on the other hand, shows that reasonably effective demobilization programs can be a major factor in the success of transitional elections.

The dangers posed by a politicized military may not become apparent until after the transition, when ethnic polarities between soldiers and civilians suddenly crystallize into factional struggles, leading to the overthrow of democratically elected governments. Burundi is a prime example, but there are potential Burundis elsewhere on the continent. The issues at stake go beyond the realm of ethnicity, however. How can the military be disengaged from the electoral process? How can its size be reduced, its recruitment patterns restructured, and ultimately its relationship to civil society redefined? These are critical questions in any attempt to assess the future of democracy on the continent.

Democracy requires a great deal more than professional armies, parties, parliaments, and elections. It assumes an informed citizenry, capable of comprehending how electoral choices can affect their lives. It presupposes a strong civil society, built on a variety of intermediary groups ranging from women's associations and trade unions to cooperatives and chambers of commerce. Such groups are likely to serve as the most effective vehicles for communicating social demands to decision makers. They also can play a significant pedagogical role by explaining to their respective publics the meaning of democracy.

In the nations of Africa, democracy is neither inevitable nor impossible. In none of them is civil society wholly mature, but in none is it wholly absent. Even where prospects for the emergence of civil society seem dimmest, there are significant grounds for hope in the active watchdog role played by human rights and religious organizations. Nurturing the seeds of democracy is not beyond the capacity of international actors. Rather than making the continent safe for democracy—a quixotic agenda at best—they should endeavor to make democracy safe for Africa. In short, Africans need inducements to think constructively and imaginatively about the forms of governance that are best suited to their sociocultural heritage.

See also *Africa, Subsaharan; Consolidation; Majority rule, minority rights; Military rule and transition to democracy; Multiethnic democracy; Patronage; War and civil conflict.*

René Lemarchand

BIBLIOGRAPHY

Barkan, Joel. "Kenya: Lessons from a Flawed Election." *Journal of Democracy* 4 (July 1993): 85–99.

Boulaga, Eboussi. *Les conferences nationales en Afrique noire.* Paris: Editions Karthala, 1993.

Bratton, Michael. "Political Liberalization in Africa in the 1990s: Advances and Setbacks." *Michigan State University Working Papers on Political Reform in Africa.* Working Paper No. 2, 1993.

———, and Nicolas van de Walle. "Neopatrimonial Regimes and Political Transitions in Africa." *World Politics* 46 (July 1994): 453–489.

Buijenhuijs, Rob, and Elly Rijnierse. *Democratization in Sub-Saharan Africa.* Research Report 1993/51. Leiden: African Studies Center, Political and Historical Studies Division, 1993.

DeCalo, Samuel. "The Process, Prospects, and Constraints of Democratization in Africa." *African Affairs* 91 (January 1992): 7–35.

Diamond, Larry, Juan Linz, and Seymour Martin Lipset, eds. *Democracy in Developing Countries: Africa.* Boulder, Colo.: Lynne Rienner; London: Adamantine Press, 1988.

Heilbrun, John R. "Social Origins of National Conferences in Benin and Togo." *Journal of Modern African Studies* 31 (June 1993): 277–299.

Lemarchand, René. "Managing Transition Anarchies: Rwanda, Burundi, and South Africa." *Journal of Modern African Studies* 32 (December 1994): 581–604.

Nwajiaku, Kathryn. "The National Conferences in Benin and Togo Revisited." *Journal of Modern African Studies* 32 (September 1994): 429–448.

Sandbrook, Richard. *The Politics of Africa's Economic Recovery.* Cambridge and New York: Cambridge University Press, 1993.

Aid policy

Aid policy is concerned with the various forms of assistance given by governments of industrialized countries to developing countries. Aid policies are determined primarily by donor countries; they include efforts to protect and promote democracy. Donors are responsible for the use of their resources, but recipient countries have a right to refuse aid, and aid policies are modified by dialogue between donors and recipients.

Bilateral aid is given directly from one government to another. Multilateral aid is given indirectly, through agencies such as the World Bank and the United Nations. Most aid programs include technical assistance to strengthen human resources through training and the provision of advisers or consultants as well as capital aid for buildings, equipment, and infrastructure (such as roads and electrification).

Conditions for Granting Aid

At first, donor countries linked aid to the defense and promotion of democracy mainly by selecting the countries that would receive aid. During the cold war, several Western governments preferred to give aid to countries they perceived to be at risk from communism—whether or not those countries had democratic governments. Over time, there was increasing recognition that aid helps to keep recipient governments in power regardless of their policies, since governments are less accountable politically if aid funds enable them to provide development and services that reduce public discontent. Several donors withheld aid from countries that showed disregard for human rights (for example, at different times, Chile and Uganda). Other donors with different views of democracy used aid to promote democratic socialism, claiming that label for Marxist systems in which the people had little choice. The People's Republic of China, for example, funded a major project to construct a railway through Tanzania to Zambia in the 1960s.

In practice, developing countries ask for the aid they want, and donors examine and help develop proposals before deciding whether they will give the support requested. For their major aid programs, donors rely mainly on economic criteria, justifying the investment of aid by calculating what a project could produce and earn. But environmental and social criteria have become increasingly important. Different donors have different mandates, causing some to use aid only to promote economic development, while others promote social as well as economic goals.

Some donors give aid (in relatively small amounts compared with their main aid programs) indirectly through foundations that have the specific objective of promoting democracy. The Federal Republic of Germany has supported three foundations, associated with its own political parties, that aim to strengthen political parties and trade unions abroad. These German agencies and smaller-scale U.S. efforts such as the National Endowment for Democracy and the Human Rights and Democratic Initiative Program of the U.S. Agency for International Development have been credited with key roles in transitions to democracy in Chile, the Philippines, Portugal, and Spain. Other donor agencies, including the Westminster Foundation in Great Britain, have supplemented their work.

Changes in Aid Policy

Many mainstream (and less overtly political) aid projects failed to meet their targets for economic development, and by the 1970s and 1980s developing countries had accumulated large debts. Many donors began to offer grants rather than loans and canceled the aid debts of poorer countries. Aid from the World Bank continued as loans but with concessional rates (interest far below ordinary commercial rates) so that each loan could be considered partly as a grant.

Development still flagged, however, and countries in Africa experienced low growth or even losses in per capita income. Donors attributed failures to faulty economic policies. The International Monetary Fund and the World Bank in concert with other major donors made economic stabilization and structural adjustment new conditions for their further support. The private sector rather than government was seen as the main engine for development. Governments were to free the economy by removing controls and subsidies, and they were to maintain a financial and economic infrastructure in which markets could flourish. In recipient countries there were adverse social effects and problems of acceptability.

Development remained slow despite structural adjustments and reforms in public service to increase efficiency and reduce costs. The World Bank, in a 1989 long-term study of Subsaharan Africa, argued that successful development depended on "good governance" by politicians and officials more accountable to the people and more

Trucks from the Red Cross bring relief and supplies to people in Yugoslavia in December 1991.

open in their dealings. Following publication of that study, the Marxist governments in East Central Europe disintegrated, and good governance became a development objective that donors applied everywhere. Good governance came to be seen both as a commendable goal in its own right and as a means to promote political stability and economic growth. Western leaders advocated economic and political pluralism as necessary for development, some arguing for the adoption of multiparty democracy in countries that had one-party systems.

Donor agencies constrained by their mandates to finance only economic development sought evidence of a positive correlation between democracy and economic growth. Studies were inconclusive, suggesting that democracy had neither favored nor disfavored economic development or the development of liberal economic policies. In 1993 Lee Kuan Yew, former prime minister of Singapore, reiterated the view that authoritarian regimes had advantages at the early stages of development. Donors with more open mandates could argue that participation and giving people a voice in matters that concerned them were worthy development objectives in their own right. Donors under the aegis of the World Bank's Consultative Groups claimed responsibility at least in part for multiparty elections in Kenya in 1993 and in Malawi in 1994, though the Bank itself avoided political involvement in its member states.

Although it can be argued that economic and political realities lead donors to support multiparty systems, that argument has not gone unchallenged. Academic critics of donor policies and political leaders in some countries receiving aid have claimed that multiparty systems are culturally inappropriate and could lead to ethnic rivalries, that proportional representation could lead to a confusing proliferation of parties, that electorates are unlikely to vote for the economic austerity programs required by the World Bank, and that changes entail a risk of civil war or anarchy, as in Liberia, Ethiopia, and Somalia. Several countries, especially in Francophone Africa, have mounted constitutional or national conferences to hold governments to account without necessarily adopting multiparty systems.

Constitutional change is not easy. In several countries there have been conflicts between loyalty to the president as a representative of the nation and vilification of the president in election campaigns. These conflicts highlight a concern expressed by Larry Diamond and Juan Linz (in *Democracy in Developing Countries: Latin America,* 1989) about presidentialism in Latin America; they suggest the merits of a nonexecutive presidency.

Besides requiring signs of progress toward more democratic systems as a condition for further aid, donors have looked for ways in which aid might give more positive support for democracy. Donors help monitor elections (as in South Africa); strengthen the work of courts, police, and parliaments; fund training to improve accountability and competence; support efforts to reduce corruption; and encourage the growth of a more diverse and lively civil society in which the skills of participation and representation can develop. Attempts to promote the development of civil society have raised difficult issues about changes in culture, especially in some postcolonial societies and transitional economies—those turning from the command economics of Marxism to market systems—where a culture of corruption has emerged, inhibiting development.

In summary, donors first sought to promote democracy by targeting aid to the countries they thought most in need of protection against nondemocratic forces or to those they deemed meritorious for their democratic efforts. As donors and recipients have learned about the problems of development, donors have imposed increasingly stringent conditions for aid. They have moved from economic criteria for individual projects to policy-based aid dependent on structural adjustment of the economy and on administrative reform. After 1989 this "conditionality" became more political; that is, donors began to tie aid to political conditions they thought necessary to ensure competent management of development. Increasing concern for human rights strengthened donors' resolve on this point. Within country programs, donors sought to direct a higher proportion of aid to the support of democracy and the strengthening of civil society.

See also *African transitions to democracy; Civil society; Corruption; Development, Economic; Elections, Monitoring; Foreign policy; Human rights; International organizations; Military rule and transition to democracy; Socialism.*

Denis G. Osborne

BIBLIOGRAPHY

Bourguignon, François, and Christian Morrisson. *Adjustment and Equity in Developing Countries—A New Approach.* Paris: Organization for Economic Cooperation and Development, 1992.
Diamond, Larry, and Juan J. Linz. "Introduction: Politics, Society, and Democracy in Latin America." In *Democracy in Developing Countries: Latin America,* edited by Larry Diamond, Juan J. Linz, and Seymour Martin Lipset. Boulder, Colo.: Lynne Rienner; London: Adamantine Press, 1989.
Healey, John, and Mark Robinson. *Democracy, Governance, and Economic Policy.* London: Overseas Development Institute, 1992.
Lee Kuan Yew. "A Map Up Here, in the Mind." *Economist,* June 29, 1991, 18–19.
Osborne, Denis G. "Action for Better Government: A Role for Donors." *IDS Bulletin* 24 (January 1993): 7–8 and 67–73.

Pinto-Duschinsky, Michael. "Foreign Political Aid: The German Political Foundations and Their U.S. Counterparts." *International Affairs* 67 (winter 1991): 33–73.
Riley, Stephen. "Africa's New Wind of Change." *World Today* 48 (July 1992): 116–119.
World Bank. *Sub-Saharan Africa, from Crisis to Sustainable Growth: A Long-Term Perspective Study.* Washington, D.C.: World Bank, 1989.

Albania

See *Europe, East Central*

Algeria

A predominantly Islamic republic situated in northwest Africa and bordered on the west by Morocco, on the south by Mauritania, Mali, and Niger, and on the east by Libya and Tunisia. Since a successful military coup on January 11, 1992, military leaders have appointed Algeria's political rulers. The military intervened to stop a runoff legislative election when early returns indicated that the Islamic Salvation Front (Front Islamique du Salut, or FIS), a diverse group of Islamic fundamentalists, would win the national election.

The coup brought to an end a political reform process that had begun in the late 1980s and reforms that had promised to transform Algeria from a socialist, one-party state into a multiparty democracy. Military leaders who participated in the 1992 palace coup pressured Chadli Benjedid, who was then president, to dissolve the National Assembly and step down as president. After the coup the struggle with Islamic militants intensified. By the end of 1993 nearly 2,000 Algerians had been killed; by 1994 the number had risen to more than 4,000 Algerians and nearly 60 foreigners. The death toll increased dramatically during 1994, as militants increasingly targeted civilians, including foreigners. Although official figures stated that 6,388 civilians died from political violence in 1994, many unofficial observers estimated that the total number killed by the end of 1994 was 30,000. By 1995 many feared that the country was sliding toward an all-out civil war. The key question was whether Algeria would be able to restore peace and develop a governmental system able to blend Islamic fundamentalism and democracy.

The political crisis engulfing Algeria as it approaches the twenty-first century reflects longstanding tensions between the influences of Islamic culture (which began to dominate in the seventh century) and Western culture (which arrived in the thirteenth century), the loss of legitimacy of the postindependence political system, and the growing economic problems heightened by a marked drop in oil and natural gas revenues, which account for most foreign revenue.

Early Cultural Tensions

Throughout history a succession of outsiders challenged the political status of the Berbers, the earliest inhabitants and the largest ethnic group in the region today. The northern portions of Algeria, known as Numidia, were ruled as Berber kingdoms until the second century B.C., when the area became a Roman province. Rome again ruled the region after a brief reign by the Vandals, a Germanic tribe who crossed from Spain in A.D. 429, but during this early period much of the interior remained independent and was organized into a loose confederation of tribes.

Arab raids during the seventh century culminated in the incorporation of the region into the great medieval Moorish empires that eventually extended across North Africa to Spain. Most Berbers converted to Islam while continuing to resist Arab political rule. Throughout the next three hundred years the area experienced conflicts among various Arab dynasties and Berber tribal lines. The Berber tribes of the Almoravids, from Morocco, restored order in the twelfth century. The Almohads, who succeeded the Almoravids, unified the entire North African area and ruled this region and Muslim Spain as a unified and highly prosperous entity. But the region had become politically unstable and was in a period of decline by the mid-thirteenth century.

The rise of the Christian kingdoms in Spain led to a series of Spanish crusades against Muslim power in North Africa at the end of the fifteenth century. Spain met little local resistance and gained control of a number of enclaves. In the early sixteenth century the capital city of Algiers and several other towns were formally placed under the protection of the Ottoman sultan. Portions of the country were ruled as a nominal province of the Ottoman Empire for three hundred years, but effective political

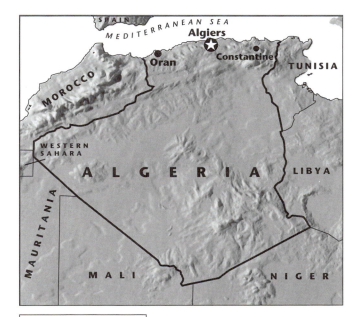

power remained in the hands of local rulers.

In coastal areas, local rulers (deys) retained power as long as they sent tribute to the Ottoman sultan, were able to satisfy the demands of local merchants and military forces, and permitted the pirate trade to flourish. European maritime countries, and the United States after independence, routinely paid local deys huge sums to protect national vessels from pirates. The United States ceased payments only in the early nineteenth century after a U.S. naval force and a combined English and Dutch naval force forced the dey of Algiers to end piracy off the coast of North Africa.

France, which had replaced Spain as the principal Western power in the region by the eighteenth century, sent military expeditions to Algeria in 1827 and in 1830 and formally annexed the territory in 1834. But France confronted fierce local opposition, the most formidable organized by Abd al-Kadir, who claimed to be a direct descendant of the prophet Muhammad. Abd al-Kadir unified the Berbers and Arabs against the French in a war that lasted from 1839 until 1847. But even after his defeat, sporadic rebellions against French rule continued. Much of this opposition was organized by the *moudjahidines*, early Islamic religious militants, who fought the French during a period when nationalism was defined largely by Muslim heritage and religious leaders.

France countered local opposition by encouraging large-scale European emigration to Algeria and by confiscating large tracts of land from rebellious Muslims. By the twentieth century European settlers dominated economic and political life. Modern nationalism surfaced among Algerian Muslims after World War I, but France refused to compromise until after World War II, when a new constitution promising French citizenship was formulated. But the 1947 constitution was never fully implemented. Instead, the nationalistic National Liberation Front (Front de Libération Nationale, FLN) led an open revolt against the French in 1954. As a result, one million Algerians died and more than two million were interned in camps before France granted independence in 1962.

Postindependence Problems

After independence, the Republic of Algeria operated as a secular state controlled by the army and secular factions of the FLN. A civilian government led by a hero of the war for independence, Ahmed Ben Bella, was established in 1963, and the FLN became the sole political party. Ben Bella consolidated power by suppressing political opponents and assuming the positions of secretary general of the party, head of state and government, and commander in chief of the armed forces. A split in leadership and a near collapse of the economy, however, presented serious problems for the new FLN-led state. An emergency austerity plan carried out in the name of Algerian socialism failed to lessen concerns about the economy or about Ben Bella's dictatorial tendencies.

In 1965 a bloodless military coup led by the minister of defense, Col. Houari Boumedienne (another hero of the war for independence), deposed Ben Bella, and the National Council of the Algerian Revolution became the supreme political authority, presiding over a major reorientation of the country's international and domestic policies. In 1967 Algeria joined other Arab states in declaring war against Israel. Diplomatic ties between Algeria and the United States suffered as Algeria established closer political and military ties with the Soviet Union and the Eastern bloc countries, while maintaining an active role as a leader of the nonaligned movement. Domestic policies also were reoriented to stimulate rapid economic growth, based on industrialization and funded by oil and natural gas exports. A new class of technocrats ran nationalized industries and government agencies.

In 1976 Boumedienne, who had called for major reforms in Algerian society, was elected president. A new constitution, drafted the same year and approved by referendum, reaffirmed Algeria's commitment to socialism under FLN guidance and recognized Islam as the state religion. The national legislature consisted of members selected by the FLN.

When Boumedienne died suddenly in 1978, the military supervised the political transition by decreeing that the National Council of the Algerian Revolution, which had no official status in the 1976 constitution, would maintain continuity. Col. Chadli Benjedid, a compromise candidate of the military, technical, and party cadres, was selected as leader of the council. In 1979 Benjedid was elected president in a national referendum.

Growing Political and Economic Problems

The army remained Benjedid's main supporters throughout his tenure. But he acknowledged the country's serious problems: dependence on hydrocarbons, reduced agricultural output, shortages of food and consumer goods, bureaucratic corruption, and extreme inequality in the distribution of wealth and growing unemployment, especially among the 70 percent of the population under thirty. A new national charter, adopted by the FLN in 1985, encouraged private enterprise and proposed a balance between socialism and Islam as the state ideology.

Despite these steps, the declining price of oil, government-imposed austerity programs in the face of widespread corruption, and growing foreign debts led to political unrest, increased support for Islamic fundamentalists, and a surge in migration to France. Widespread riots in 1988 in response to rising bread prices indicated the extent of discontent with the political status quo.

In the aftermath of the riots the FLN's thirty years of one-party rule came to an end. Beginning in July 1989 the government sponsored a series of constitutional amendments and laws that represented a break with the past. Among other things, Benjedid ended the identification of the state with the FLN, relinquished his post as secretary general of the party, and supported a move to make the prime minister responsible to the National People's Assembly. In a referendum more than 73 percent of the voters supported the proposals. Benjedid was reelected president for a third term, and the National People's Assembly passed a bill permitting opposition political parties to contest future elections.

In the 1990 elections the Islamic Salvation Front, an amalgam of several groups ranging from political moderates willing to work within the existing framework to militants calling for a holy war, gained control of about 80 percent of the country's municipal and departmental councils by winning almost 65 percent of the votes cast. The FIS victory, in the first competitive elections held since 1962, underscored just how out of touch the ruling elite had become.

In 1991 national elections were postponed after an FLN effort at gerrymandering triggered large-scale protests. The military intervened by arresting the top leaders of the FIS. In September 1991 the state of siege was lifted, and the Islamic Salvation Front again functioned as a political party. In December 1991 the FIS won the first round of voting for a new National People's Assembly. Candidates representing nearly fifty political parties, including the first green party in the Arab world, participated. The FIS won the majority of the ballots cast (but only 25 percent of all registered voters, due to low voter turnout), and its victory in the second round of elections was virtually assured. The military then pressured Benjedid to suspend the National People's Assembly and resign as president.

After the coup, Muhammad Boudiaf, a veteran politician and leader during the war for independence, was brought back from self-imposed exile to serve as the figurehead of a newly formed High State Council, which was to act as an interim government. The council curtailed a nascent free press, abolished the FIS as a political party, suspended all local assemblies, and removed local FIS elected officials. A state security system detained FIS leaders and sent thousands of sympathizers to Sahara detention camps.

Promises of jobs, housing, and food subsidies, together with a campaign against violence, a crackdown on corruption, and efforts by Boudiaf to encourage talks among all parties about an alternative to an Islamic republic or a militarized secular state, failed to stem Islamic fundamentalism. Boudiaf was assassinated in June 1992 by a member of his own security guard. The murder, as well as the government's claim that the assassin was an FIS sympathizer, increased polarization.

The military appointed a series of political figures to the figurehead position of head of state after Boudiaf's assassination. Ali Kafi, a lesser known independence war veteran who was named head of state in mid-1992, resigned by 1993. The former prime minister Redha Malek, who was appointed president at the end of 1993, after the High State Council dissolved itself, was replaced by Liamine Zeroual in 1994. Zeroual, former minister of defense and current president and leader of the National Transitional Council, has presided over two rounds of national talks with five of the eight recognized political parties about proposed reforms. But the government has failed to gain additional support for the political status quo. Most observers doubt that official promises to hold elections by 1996 will be honored. Meanwhile, the spiral of violence escalates.

Future Outlook

In the future, higher oil and gas revenues and a lowering of the national debt may improve the economy and reduce the fervor of many Algerians for a political change that would transform the country into an Islamic state. So far, however, increased repression and efforts to initiate a national dialogue between the government and selected political parties and individuals have only contributed to instability. Several radical militant Islamic groups now operate underground, independent of FIS. They are financed by Algerian shopkeepers and farmers as well as—according to government allegations—funds from Iran. Terrorist acts continue despite expanded security crackdowns.

See also *Colonialism; Fundamentalism; Islam.*

Helen E. Purkitt

BIBLIOGRAPHY

"Algeria." In *The Middle East and North Africa 1993.* 39th ed. London: Europa Publications, 1993.

Entelis, John P. *Algeria: The Revolution Institutionalized.* Boulder, Colo.: Westview Press, 1986.

———, and Phillip C. Naylor, eds. *State and Society in Algeria.* Boulder, Colo.: Westview Press, 1992.

Zartman, I. William, and William Mark Habeeb, eds. *Polity and Society in Contemporary North Africa.* Boulder, Colo.: Westview Press, 1993.

Almond, Gabriel

American scholar and pioneer in the behavioral study of politics and its application in cross-national comparisons. After completing a Ph.D. at the University of Chicago, Almond (1911–   ) taught at Brooklyn College and Princeton and Yale Universities before moving to Stanford in 1963. He headed Stanford's political science department and was president of the American Political Science Association (1965–1966).

During World War II, Almond served in the Office of

Gabriel Almond

War Information and in the War Department's Strategic Bombing Survey. He developed an abiding interest in authoritarianism at both the individual and collective levels. His first major works, *The American People and Foreign Policy* (1950) and *The Appeals of Communism* (1954), used behavioral and quantitative methodologies (rather than exclusively legal and historical approaches) to explain political attitudes and behavior. With *The Politics of the Developing Areas,* coedited with James S. Coleman in 1960, Almond extended behavioral analysis to politics in developing countries.

With Sidney Verba, Almond directed research that was published in *The Civic Culture* (1963), one of the landmark studies of contemporary comparative politics. Interviews were administered to large samples in five countries—Britain, Germany, Italy, Mexico, and the United States. From these surveys (and with acknowledgment of Aristotle's ideal of a "mixed government" combining oligarchic and democratic principles), Almond and Verba suggested that a stable democracy is composed largely of citizens who combine both subject and participant attributes in their political attitudes. These citizens carry a sense of obligation and loyalty to the system, but they also believe in their right to be consulted about policy, and they are willing to act on that belief.

The Civic Culture stimulated several decades of work on countries around the globe that drew on its methodology and built on the body of empirical democratic theory that it produced. The purpose of *The Civic Culture* was to explain why some contemporary governments are able to maintain a high level of democratic stability. The principal legacy of Almond's work, however, was to inspire interest in the process by which democracy is achieved. The introductory chapter lays the foundation for Almond's approach. He presents the slow, incremental development of Britain's democratic institutions as a successful model for other countries.

To encourage further exploration of the process through which political systems change, Almond led a group of young scholars through a research project that resulted in the publication in 1973 of *Crisis, Choice, and Change: Historical Studies of Political Development.* In this work, which examined historical cases of changes in regimes, he attempted to bring together the separate explanatory traditions of choice and determinacy in a single model. (Rational choice accumulates individual preferences and resources to explain social outcomes. Determinacy assumes that political change is caused by long-term economic and social trends.)

In 1966 Almond and G. Bingham Powell published *Comparative Politics* (revised as *Comparative Politics: System, Process, and Policy* in 1978), which gives an overview of the systems concept in comparative analysis. It also contains a synthesis of theoretical work on the concept of political development. Development is defined as having the cultural aspect of secularization (movement away from sacred or religious explanations) and the structural aspect of differentiation (more complex forms and structures of decision making). Movement is achieved along these two dimensions as systems confront various challenges. One of those challenges is that of participation, or pressure from outside groups to be included in policy making. Almond and Powell argued that achieving greater participation simultaneously with other goals, such as economic justice, may not be possible. They evaluated various strategies in terms of the likelihood that these strategies, in the long term, would achieve the democratic value of liberty along with other such universally sought values as welfare and security.

Almond defended the models and methods of comparative political analysis from attacks by dependency theorists, who claimed that underdevelopment in the modern world (in both the economic and the political sense) was caused exclusively by unequal exchanges between advanced industrial countries and developing countries, resulting in the dependence of the latter on the former. Accepting the criticism that systems analysis had in the beginning overemphasized the values of stability and order, Almond adjusted his model to allow more explicitly for change. He argued, however, that the dependency approach was crudely deterministic and that the effects of international economic forces could be accommodated in refined systems approaches. He also challenged the tendencies in the discipline to split off into isolated research schools based on specific methodologies.

Almond returned to the integration of methodologies developed in *Crisis, Choice, and Change* by working with area specialists on a comparative study of changes in regimes, focusing exclusively on democratization (generally defined according to Robert Dahl's two dimensions of the extent of participation and the degree of competition). In selected cases of complete and incomplete democratization, the project explores the influence of long-term socioeconomic trends, the effects of coalition and bargaining processes, and the role of leadership in achieving and consolidating a stable democracy. This work appears to support Almond's long-held premise that stable democratization is more likely to result from an incremental bargaining process than from a single revolutionary breakthrough that erases previous social and political institutions.

See also *Aristotle; Dahl, Robert A.; Theory, Postwar Anglo-American.*

Robert J. Mundt

BIBLIOGRAPHY

Almond, Gabriel A. *The American People and Foreign Policy.* New York: Harcourt, Brace, 1950.
———. *The Appeals of Communism.* Princeton: Princeton University Press, 1954.
Almond, Gabriel A., and James S. Coleman, eds. *The Politics of the Developing Areas.* Princeton: Princeton University Press, 1960.
Almond, Gabriel A., Scott C. Flanagan, and Robert J. Mundt. *Crisis, Choice, and Change: Historical Studies of Political Development.* Boston: Little, Brown, 1973.
———. "*Crisis, Choice, and Change* in Retrospect." *Government and Opposition* 27 (summer 1992): 347–367.
Almond, Gabriel A., and G. Bingham Powell. *Comparative Politics: System, Process, and Policy.* 2d ed. Boston: Little, Brown, 1978.
Almond, Gabriel A., and Sydney Verba, eds. *The Civic Culture.* Princeton: Princeton University Press, 1963.
———, eds. *The Civic Culture Revisited.* Boston: Little, Brown, 1980.

Althusius, Johannes

German Calvinist political theorist who was a noted antiroyalist, a champion of federalism, and the originator of the theory of consociationalism. Born in Westphalia and educated in Basel and Geneva in civil and ecclesiastical law, Althusius (1557–1638) taught in Herborn and became rector of an academy at Heidelberg. In 1604 he was invited by the city council of Emden, in East Friesland, to become its syndic, a post that combined the functions of city attorney, advocate, and diplomatic negotiator. Because of its intense Calvinism and influence over the Dutch Reformed Church, Emden was known as the Geneva of the North. The inhabitants of Emden, who nominally were within the jurisdiction of the German empire, yearned for the independence that had been won by other northern German cities and looked to their Dutch neighbors and coreligionists for help in attaining it.

Althusius was chosen to manage the city's difficult political maneuvering because of his *Politica methodice digesta* (Politics Methodically Set Forth) (1603), which summarized Calvinist and antiroyalist political thought. He later was made a member of the council of church elders. His influence on religious and political thinking in Emden has been compared with that of John Calvin in Geneva.

Althusius's theory of society resembles that of other Calvinist writers but is unique in important respects. Although steeped in scriptural references, it is much more naturalistic than other Calvinist accounts. And although it is couched in the language of emerging theories of social contract, and embodies the then-radical view that authority requires the consent of the governed, it is pluralistic rather than individualistic and aimed at conciliation rather than at justification of resistance.

Althusius's naturalism followed the Aristotelian tradition, according to which people are naturally gregarious and the aim of society is harmonious association, rather than the individualistic and mechanistic view that would emerge later in the century in Thomas Hobbes's *Leviathan* (1651). Hobbes, who conceived of the human being as a moving mechanical apparatus, would characterize the state of nature as one of isolation, fear, and antagonism. Althusius, however, defined politics as "the art of associating men for the purpose of establishing, cultivating, and conserving social life among them." Society is a symbiotic association of communities on successive levels. The family is the natural association; the collegium in its various forms (mainly the guild and corporation) is the artificial, or civil, association.

From this beginning, Althusius constructed what he called a consociational model of society, one with a federal political structure based on a succession of free unions, from village to town to province to kingdom (or state) to empire. In effect, Althusius replaced the hierarchical structure of feudalism (built on the principle of subordination) with a cooperative federation of associations. In this reformed model, authority and power are distributed among constituent groups that are roughly equal in status. The whole is knit together by shared morality (based on the Ten Commandments) and common interests. Aware of the distinction between confederation and federation, Althusius allowed for both, depending on the actual degree of integration, while insisting that in either case the political system should be understood as an association of associations or a community of communities.

Althusius's federalism contrasts sharply with the early and far more influential defense of absolutism by the French political theorist Jean Bodin in his *Six Books of the Commonwealth* (1576). Although Bodin accommodated the notion that sovereignty can be located in a legislature, his refusal to recognize the feasibility of a mixed constitution best suited the claims of absolute monarchs and ruled out any effort to divide sovereignty, including the idea of federalism. Althusius's thinking, while indebted to Bodin's scholarship, reflected a concern with preserving the benefits of medieval constitutionalism, with its limitation of the power of royalty and the nobility and its functional devolution of authority among the estates, the church, the guilds, and the corporations.

Mindful of medieval experience, especially that of the leagues of German cities, and of federal practice in Switzerland and the United Netherlands, Althusius proposed that the social contract should be understood as a mutual exchange of promises among lesser associations to create a larger association. The larger body would not dissolve these lesser associations but would include them as integral constituents. In a deliberate departure from Bodin's central thesis, Althusius assigned sovereignty not to a ruler or ruling group but to the symbiotic process by which the entire body politic engages in self-government on the various levels.

As absolutism became the norm in much of Europe, Althusius's theories came to seem anachronistic and unrealistic. Bodin's defense of sovereignty was restated, without the religious underpinnings and customary limitations, in the starkly survivalist logic of Hobbes. Those who criticized absolutism did so in the name of popular sovereignty or individual rights and saw group autonomy as inimical to both. Althusius had argued not for the rights of the isolated individual or the "general will" of an entire society but for the rights of all social groupings, emphasizing the natural bonding of the individual to the group.

In recent times, Althusius's stock has risen, as scholars have called attention to his contributions to the development of democratic theory. In shaping his concept of the constitutional state, they have pointed out, he sought to prevent the new secular authority from becoming so powerful as to deprive all lesser associations of any standing. As the theorist who introduced the consociational model of society and politics, Althusius can rightly be considered a forerunner of the many later advocates of federalism, pluralism, and other forms of power sharing, including especially the theorists of consociational or consensual democracy.

See also *Consent; Contractarianism; Federalism.*

Sanford Lakoff

BIBLIOGRAPHY

Althusius, Johannes. *"Politica methodice digeste" of Johannes Althu-sius.* Edited by Carl Joachim Friedrich. Cambridge: Harvard University Press, 1932.

———. *Politics* [abridged]. Translated and edited with an introduction by Frederick S. Carney. Foreword by Daniel J. Elazar. Indianapolis: Liberty Classics, 1994.

Figgis, J. N. *Political Thought from Gerson to Grotius: 1414–1625.* New York: Harper and Row, 1960.

von Gierke, Otto. *The Development of Political Theory.* Translated by Bernard Freyd. New York: Howard Fertig, 1966.

Americans, Ethnic

Ethnic Americans are persons associated with the social categories—religion, language, nationality, ancestry, appearance, or region of origin—into which they are born. The topic of democracy and ethnic Americans constitutes *the* American dilemma: the desire for fairness and individual equality on the one hand and the maintenance of locally based economic and social privilege on the other.

Since the colonial era the United States has become home to more numerous and diverse immigrants than any other nation. The country has an impressive tradition of openness and has made significant progress toward the inclusion of ethnic groups in its institutions, especially in the post–World War II era.

These gains have been seen most clearly in the political realm (which is most amenable to legislation) and for white ethnic groups—the Irish, Italians, Jews, Greeks, and Poles, for example. Progress is more spotty in American society more broadly construed, for instance, in economic mobility, access to housing, education, attainment of elite positions in private industry, and representation in the mass media. Nonwhite groups, notably African Americans, Hispanic Americans, and Native Americans, are not yet close to achieving a level of involvement or representation equal to that of native-born whites.

The twin themes of including and rejecting ethnic groups can be traced back to the colonial era. For example, although Pennsylvania guaranteed religious freedom and promoted democratic law making, the Puritans of Massachusetts denied the franchise to non-Congregationalists and implemented laws based on church doctrine. In other colonies, Africans were treated as property, and Native Americans were driven out or exterminated.

Despite Puritan efforts to unify church and state, the first four U.S. presidents acknowledged that America was different from Europe because there was no state religion and all its people were equal. In a letter to the Jews of Newport, Rhode Island, in 1790, George Washington emphasized that citizenship was to be shared by all members of the new nation and rejected the patronizing concept of toleration of one class of people by another.

Paradoxically, the very same year that Washington offered his magnanimous pronouncements to Rhode Island's Jews, Congress passed the Federal Naturalization Act of 1790, which prevented nonwhite immigrants from becoming citizens. This bar to citizenship and voting was not lifted until 1943 for the Chinese and 1952 for the Japanese and other nonwhites. Asians were also singled out by various exclusion acts passed in the late nineteenth and early twentieth centuries. The "threat of disloyalty" was used to justify the wholesale internment of Japanese Americans during World War II, but the same fate was not shared by those of Italian or German ancestry. Similarly, state and federal laws continued to limit marriage, voting, and landowning according to racial, ethnic, or national origin criteria until the 1950s and 1960s. The specter of race-based policies was seen even in the 1990s, when the State Department gave thousands of mostly white Cubans and Eastern Europeans refugee status while denying such status to black Haitians.

Ethnicity and Party Loyalty

From the 1820s, when universal white male suffrage was established in the United States, until the Great Depression of the 1930s, ethnic and religious differences were major factors in shaping political loyalties. The arrival of myriad immigrants and the transformation of the nation's social, political, and economic landscape only served to enhance the political salience of ethnic and religious affiliation during this long period.

American ethnic groups have always held diverse attitudes on the key social and cultural issues of the day—whether they be immigration, slavery, prohibition, women's suffrage, government finances, or public schooling—thus conditioning their political outlook. Prior to the 1930s, African Americans voted with the Republican Party because the party of Abraham Lincoln offered a moral mandate for opposition to slavery and the promotion of civil rights. Catholics, Lutherans, and immigrant groups who feared the power of established elites tended to support Democrats, who often welcomed them with open arms, even to the point of advocating voting rights for noncitizens. Before and after the Civil War (1861–1865), some white southerners favored the Democratic Party because they sought to resist the Republicans' drives to end slavery and segregation.

The economic policies of President Franklin D. Roosevelt's New Deal, which offered little in the way of civil rights, brought about a major change in ethnic voting patterns. African Americans abandoned the Republican Party—to which they had been fiercely loyal—to become the most fully Democratic of all American ethnic groups. Jews, especially those of eastern European origin, also responded to the economic agenda of the New Deal. In New York, many deserted their socialist affiliations in order to support the Roosevelt ticket.

After World War II, African Americans continued to support the Democratic Party. In response, the party adopted a strong civil rights agenda. This policy had the effect of dampening the loyalty of many white southerners. Nevertheless, all three Democratic presidents since John F. Kennedy in the early 1960s have been white southerners, suggesting the continued importance of this group to the vitality of the Democratic Party.

Political Machines and Unions

Urban political machines and unions played an important role in helping to involve generations of ethnic Americans in the political process. Although they are depicted as corrupt, machines provided real benefits to ethnic groups. More important, they socialized newcomers to the American political system.

The basic building blocks of the political machine were the precinct captains. In direct communication with superiors in city hall, they made community contacts and provided jobs, gifts, and emergency aid in exchange for votes. This practice played a vital role in connecting the members of working-class ethnic communities to the larger political structure. Furthermore, involvement in the political machine provided a career path for ethnic youth whose chances for other careers were hindered by limited education and discrimination.

Irish immigrants, who knew English and, because of their contact with the British, had a history of creating alternative political organizations, are associated with the great political machines. Already established in the United States, Irish Americans were able to organize and mediate

between the many competing nationalities from southern and eastern Europe who settled in the United States between 1880 and 1920.

As time passed, big-city machines reached out to non-European groups as well. For example, Richard J. Daley, mayor of Chicago from 1955 to 1976 and one of the last great bosses, derived much of his political support from African Americans. Puerto Ricans, Mexicans, and other Latino groups, as well as Asian Americans, have now become vital actors on the urban political landscape.

Trade unions too have played an important role in the lives of American ethnic groups. Since the Asian exclusion laws of the late nineteenth century, unions have been at the vanguard of immigrant exclusion. At the same time, the organized labor movement has provided a setting where immigrant and ethnic group members have become organized and politically active. It has also helped them to mobilize their communities and has linked them to larger social institutions. For example, various industrial unions, the International Ladies' Garment Workers' Union, the United Farm Workers, and several unions of local, state, and federal government workers have played a vital role in bringing their ethnic constituencies into positions of some influence in local politics. Still, with the general downturn in the entire labor movement since the late 1970s, the influence of unions in the lives of ethnic Americans has steadily diminished.

Ascendancy of White Ethnics

Before World War II, ethnic America was perceived as a working-class community. By the mid-1960s, however, pundits began to celebrate the entrance of a large fraction of the white ethnic population into the middle class. In the mid-1970s the sociologist Andrew Greeley described how the descendants of the immigrant hordes were now among the richest religious-ethnic groups in the country, with incomes and rates of college enrollment that far exceeded those of other white groups.

The political power of white ethnics was indicated by the election of John F. Kennedy, an Irish Catholic, as president in 1960 and the passage of the Immigration Act of 1965 (against the opposition of "old American" interests such as the Daughters of the American Revolution and the National Association of Evangelicals). This law changed U.S. policy to permit more migrants from southern and eastern Europe to enter. (An unforeseen consequence was the arrival of large numbers of persons from Asia, Latin America, and the Caribbean.)

Since that time, Jews, Catholics, and other non-Protestant groups have been able to move en masse into the mainstream of society, holding jobs and attending colleges that previously limited or altogether excluded their presence. Jews, for example, who make up about 2.5 percent of the American population, now hold almost 9 percent of the seats in the U.S. Congress, including 10 percent of those in the Senate.

Many observers argue that the principle of conformity accounts for the difference between the great achievements of white ethnics and the more modest progress of nonwhites. They maintain that those groups who most closely approximate the appearance, values, family patterns, and cultural practices of the Protestant, northern European majority are offered more opportunities than are those who remain physically, linguistically, and culturally distinct.

The Civil Rights Movement

From the 1950s through the 1970s the civil rights movement, largely organized and led by African Americans, was responsible for a significant expansion of opportunities for African Americans and other Americans in public and private institutions. Chief among the accomplishments of the movement were the banning of most forms of racial segregation, the abandonment of the "separate but equal" doctrine, the passage of the Voting Rights Act of 1965, and societal rejection of racial bigotry.

The movement and the Voting Rights Act also fostered the growth of African American political power. From 1970 to 1992 the number of elected officials who were African American grew fivefold nationwide, from fewer than 1,500 to more than 7,500. During that time, most of the nation's major cities, including several with relatively small African American electorates (Denver, Los Angeles, New York, Seattle) elected African American mayors.

A lasting legacy of the civil rights movement has been its example to other disadvantaged groups. Ethnic populations such as Native Americans, Chicanos, Asian Americans, and white ethnics, as well as women, gays and lesbians, and people with disabilities, have drawn heavily from the experience of African Americans in their own attempts to assert a communal voice.

Trends

In the current era, we are faced with a number of disparate trends in ethnic Americans' involvement with de-

mocracy. On a purely institutional level, we see growing numbers of ethnic Americans voting and being elected to political office. Just as the figures previously mentioned demonstrate a surge in the number of elected officials who are African American, there is also a growth in the number of Hispanic Americans elected to office. From 1985 to 1992 the number increased 159 percent, to just under 5,000. Despite this evidence of progress, aggregate statistics tell only part of the story. A full 40 percent of Hispanic elected officials in the United States come from a single state (Texas), and almost 95 percent come from just six states (Arizona, California, Colorado, Illinois, New Mexico, and Texas). Two East Coast states often noted for their large and powerful Latino communities—New York and Florida—have fewer than 100 Hispanic elected officials each. Part of the problem is the relatively low rate of naturalization among certain groups. For example, less than a fifth of Mexican immigrants in California have become U.S. citizens; the voting power of this sizable population is severely limited.

Relatively few Asian Americans, the nation's fastest growing ethnic population, have been elected to office. There have, however, been signs of progress in West Coast states and especially in Hawaii, where Asians make up a large proportion of the population.

Several American institutions, including governmental agencies, the courts, and the educational system, have attempted to address the needs and concerns of an increasingly ethnically diverse society through a variety of programs, such as multicultural education, affirmative action, and court-mandated redistricting. Such programs have yielded benefits, but they have also produced angry responses from groups who oppose extraordinary means of addressing past injustices. At least since the mid-1960s many politicians have found that sections of the electorate respond well to thinly veiled appeals to ethnic, racial, and nativist prejudices. Political issues with a strong subtext of ethnic antagonism—such as busing students, affirmative action, multiculturalism, welfare dependency, illegal immigration, homelessness, and law and order—have thus divided America's political landscape for decades.

Several discouraging tendencies have been observed with regard to the participation of ethnic Americans in democracy. The most central of these is economic decline. Since the mid-1970s the life chances of Americans who lack high levels of education and skill have been in decline. Because a large fraction of the African American, Native American, and Hispanic American populations are in this category, many remain mired in poverty and, consequently, have limited potential to merge fully with the mainstream institutions of American society.

At the same time, the inner city areas, where many ethnic Americans reside, have suffered the brunt of recent economic troubles, resulting in the exodus of considerable numbers of people to the suburbs. Thus, just when ethnic Americans have increased their representation within the political system, the urban areas where they live have become less important places, socially, politically, and economically, in the life of the nation.

Ethnic nationalism, and with it interethnic tension and conflict, have increased in recent years. Although some observers and activists believe that "identity politics" can mobilize disfranchised groups, at the same time, extreme demands for group loyalty limit individual freedom and reduce the viability of multiethnic coalitions. For example, the highly publicized conflict between African Americans and Jews, as precipitated by statements of black nationalist leaders, and the multiethnic conflagration in Los Angeles in 1992 do not bode well for the future of constructive urban political dialogue.

Finally, the mass media, which make up a key institution in shaping the nation's political and cultural discourse, are frequently singled out as being unresponsive to the interests and needs of ethnic Americans, who often complain that they are depicted in terms of negative stereotypes or not at all.

The opposing tendencies of inclusion and exclusion have affected ethnic Americans throughout the nation's history. At present, we see white ethnic groups enjoying a level of acceptance that would have been unimaginable even a few decades ago. Similarly, members of nonwhite ethnic communities have achieved positions of leadership and visibility in government, the media, and other areas of society. At the same time, however, hostility against immigrants and ethnic minorities persists in many areas of life, and large segments of the nonwhite population continue to be plagued by poverty-linked social pathologies.

Although we may hope that economically disadvantaged nonwhite ethnic communities might share in the success of white ethnic groups, there seems little cause for optimism in the near future.

See also *Affirmative action; Civil rights; Multiethnic democracy; Politics, Machine; United States of America.*

Steven J. Gold

BIBLIOGRAPHY

Dinnerstein, Leonard, Roger L. Nichols, and David M. Reimers. *Natives and Strangers: Blacks, Indians, and Immigrants in America.* 2d ed. New York: Oxford University Press, 1990.

Glazer, Nathan, and Daniel Patrick Moynihan. *Beyond the Melting Pot.* Cambridge: MIT Press, 1963.

Greeley, Andrew. *Ethnicity in the United States.* New York: Wiley, 1974.

Hacker, Andrew. *Two Nations.* New York: Scribner's, 1992.

Kantowicz, Edward I. "Politics." In *The Harvard Encyclopedia of American Ethnic Groups,* edited by Stephen Thernstrom. Cambridge: Harvard University Press, 1980.

Kornblum, William. *Blue Collar Community.* Chicago: University of Chicago Press, 1973.

Pohlmann, Marcus D. *Black Politics in Conservative America.* New York: Longman, 1990.

Portes, Alejandro, and Ruben Rumbaut. *Immigrant America: A Portrait.* Berkeley: University of California Press, 1990.

Takaki, Ronald. *A Different Mirror: A History of Multicultural America.* Boston: Little, Brown, 1993.

Wilson, William J. *The Truly Disadvantaged.* Chicago: University of Chicago Press, 1987.

Anarchism

A political ideology whose central tenet is that the state must be abolished and society organized by voluntary means without resort to force or coercive authority. Whereas conservatives, liberals, and socialists all assign the state an essential role in their contrasting visions of the good society, anarchists seek its outright destruction.

In support of this position they make two general claims. First, those who staff the various branches of the state—politicians, civil servants, judges, the police, and the military—together form a ruling class that pursues its own interests and exploits the rest of society, especially the working class. Second, insofar as the state does attempt to promote general social interests, the means that it has at its disposal—laws and other directives emanating from the center and coercively enforced—are ineffective for this purpose. Societies, anarchists believe, are highly complex entities, and they should be organized from the bottom up, with full attention paid to the varying needs of individuals and localities.

Anarchists therefore look to voluntary associations to maintain social order, to organize production and exchange, to protect the environment, and to perform other necessary social functions. But different anarchists hold different views of how a society organized by voluntary means might function. Individualists, such as the American anarchist Benjamin Tucker (1854–1939), envisaged a market-based system of free exchange and contract, with private protective associations acting to safeguard the rights of each individual who has bought their services. In contrast, collectivists such as Mikhail Bakunin (1814–1876) and communists such as Pyotr Kropotkin (1842–1921) sought to transcend the market and believed that social needs could be met through voluntary cooperation in workplaces and local communes. These bodies might federate for specific purposes (such as organizing a transport system), but the federal body would not have the right to compel its constituent parts if they dissented from its decisions. These socialist forms of anarchism have had the greatest political influence, helping to radicalize the workers' movements of late nineteenth and early twentieth century Europe, especially in France, Italy, and Spain. Anarchism had its greatest practical success at the outset of the Spanish civil war in the 1930s, when many areas came for a time under anarchist control, but subsequently its influence has waned. Anarchists today are effective chiefly through their participation in the peace and ecology movements.

Anarchists have been harsh critics of representative democracy on the Western model. Their critique can be boiled down to three essential points. First, a democratic state is still a state: its way of operating shows the same insensitivity to social needs as do other, more overtly authoritarian political institutions. Second, democrats often claim that what is represented in representative democracy is the will of the people, which informs and controls government policy. But, according to anarchists, the idea of a single, consistent popular will is a myth. People are divided in their opinions, their ideas are shifting, some are better informed than others. It is absurd to suppose that a majority view, expressed in a ballot at one moment in time, constitutes the will of the people. Third, anarchists attack the idea of popular representation in legislative assemblies. They argue that people, when called upon to choose their representatives, are very likely to vote for those who appear well educated and articulate—in other words, aspiring members of the middle class. But even if members of the working class were willing to select representatives from their own number, these would soon be corrupted by their new position as servants of the state.

In a famous passage, Bakunin argued that workers elected to form a government would be transformed almost at once from democrats into a new authoritarian aristocracy. Pierre-Joseph Proudhon (1809–1865), the most influential of the French anarchists, confirmed this principle for himself when he was elected to the Constituent Assembly in 1848. Absorption in the business of government, he found, quickly distanced him from the needs and desires of his constituents.

Except in very special circumstances, therefore, anarchists have favored a policy of political abstention and have sought to encourage a revolutionary transformation of society through a variety of extraparliamentary means, including propaganda, direct action, syndicalism, and finally insurrection. But does democracy play any part in their ideal society of the future? For anarchists of an individualist persuasion there is little room, if any, for collective decision making in such a society. Each person would make his or her own contractual arrangements with others according to tastes and preferences. Agreeing to decide certain matters by democratic vote would not be excluded, but neither would it be required.

For other anarchists the issue is a little more complicated. Inevitably questions will arise within workplaces and local communities that require collective decision. Ideally, these would be resolved unanimously, but if unanimous consent proved to be impossible the majority would have to decide. The minority would then face a choice: either to go along with the decision reached or else to withdraw and allow the majority to proceed. No anarchist would allow the minority to be forced to comply with the majority decision. To force compliance would be to reintroduce coercive authority, the hallmark of the state.

Direct democracy would, then, have some place in the ideal visions of most anarchists, but it would be subordinate to the principles of free agreement and noncompulsion. Even this arrangement would be going too far for some: the English philosopher William Godwin (1756–1836), the first systematic exponent of an anarchist political philosophy, argued against popular assemblies on the ground that the consensus they tended to produce resulted from irrational forms of persuasion, corrupting the independent judgment of each participant. Anarchist suspicion of democracy in any of its forms runs very deep.

See also *Communitarianism.*

David Miller

BIBLIOGRAPHY

Bakunin, Mikhail. *Bakunin on Anarchy: Selected Works by the Activist-Founder of World Anarchism.* Edited, translated, and with an introduction by Sam Dolgoff. New York: Vintage Books, 1972.

Crowder, George. *Classical Anarchism: The Political Thought of Godwin, Proudhon, Bakunin, and Kropotkin.* Oxford: Clarendon Press, 1991; New York: Oxford University Press, 1992.

Krimerman, Leonard I., and Lewis Perry, eds. *Patterns of Anarchy: A Collection of Writings on the Anarchist Tradition.* New York: Anchor Books, 1966.

Kropotkin, Pyotr. *Kropotkin's Revolutionary Pamphlets: A Collection of Writings by Peter Kropotkin.* Edited by Roger N. Baldwin. New York: Dover, 1970.

Miller, David. *Anarchism.* London: Dent, 1984.

Ritter, Alan. *Anarchism: A Theoretical Analysis.* Cambridge: Cambridge University Press, 1980.

Woodcock, George. *Anarchism.* Harmondsworth: Penguin Books, 1963.

Andean countries

Three republics of South America—Bolivia, Peru, and Ecuador—which have substantial indigenous populations living in remote areas of the Andes. The Andes mountain range extends from southwestern Venezuela through Colombia, Ecuador, Peru, Bolivia, and most of Chile. For most purposes, only Ecuador, Peru, and Bolivia are considered Andean countries because they are the only three countries in which a sizable portion of the population lives in the remote Andean highlands, speaks an indigenous language, and preserves other aspects of a distinct ethnic culture.

Although the criteria for defining ethnic identity are subjective, one may say that approximately 40 percent of Peruvians are indigenous (mostly Quechua), as are 20 percent of Ecuadorians (mostly Quichua) and 60 percent of Bolivians (Aymará or Quechua). Most of the nonindigenous population is of European (mainly Spanish) descent or *mestizo* (mixed European and indigenous), although coastal Ecuador has a significant population of African descent.

The Andean countries are the poorest countries in South America (with the exception of Guyana) and are generally less urban and industrial than their neighbors. Their resources include minerals in Bolivia; guano, minerals, fishing, and oil in Peru; and cacao, bananas, and oil in Ecuador. As sources of wealth, these resources have been short lived and unreliable, giving rise to dramatic economic swings.

The twin problems of ethnic division and economic instability have hindered the development of stable democracy in the Andean region. The arrival of democracy was delayed, and when it came it was exclusionary and subject to frequent military intervention. Indeed, Bolivia and Ecuador were the two least stable countries in South America during most of the twentieth century. The democratic regimes that began in 1979 in Ecuador, in 1980 in Peru, and in 1982 in Bolivia have been the longest and most inclusive in their respective histories. Nevertheless, they all faced difficult problems and must be regarded as fragile.

Historical Background

Ever since the Spanish conquered the Andean region in 1535, a wide gulf has separated the indigenous people and those of European descent. Initially, Spanish colonial rule was simply superimposed on pre-Columbian indigenous communities. Local chieftains were made responsible for collecting tribute for a Spanish landholder. The colonial authorities also adapted to their own uses the Inca system of forced labor. They used the system to muster a captive labor force for mining in Bolivia and Peru and for textile workshops in Ecuador. This exploitation continued even though the authorities in Spain repeatedly banned tribute in the form of labor. It continued even after interracial marriage had blurred the distinctions between Europeans and indigenous people. As late as the early twentieth century local government officials in Peru still pressed peasants into service to build roads. Even today, to many residents of Lima, Quito, and La Paz, highland society is as alien as a foreign country. Many indigenous peasants scarcely identify with the larger states that claim to govern them. The process of national integration in the Andean countries is far from complete.

Peru proclaimed its independence from Spain in 1821, and Bolivia in 1825. Ecuador, at first part of the newly formed state of Greater Colombia, became a separate state in 1830. As in all of Spanish America except Chile, independence from Spain left a power vacuum, and most of the nineteenth century was spent in power struggles among regional *caudillos* (warlords). By the latter half of the century, however, certain *caudillos* had established dominance. Peru and Bolivia were temporarily thrown into turmoil when they lost valuable territory for mining

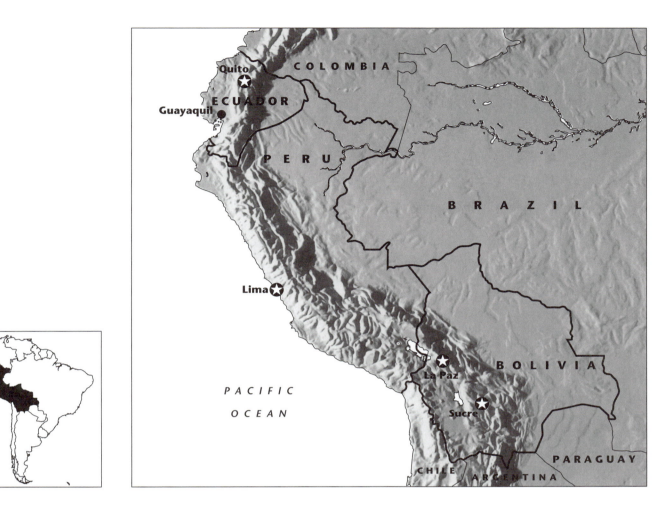

nitrates to Chile in the War of the Pacific (1879–1883). But before the turn of the century both countries had initiated a generation of stable rule by civilian oligarchs—their first approaches to democracy.

Bolivia experienced relative calm between 1884 and 1932 under rule by Conservatives, Liberals, and Republicans in succession. Peru was governed by the Civilistas during the "Aristocratic Republic" of 1895–1914. Elections were held during these regimes, but the suffrage was restricted to less than 5 percent of the population. In addition, the balloting was manipulated, and the outcomes were decided less by votes than by shifting economic and military resources, even if the contests remained peaceful. For example, the transfer of power from the Conservatives to the Liberals in Bolivia in 1890 was made necessary by the decline of the Conservative silver-mining elite and the rise of a new tin-mining elite. Intense rivalry between the cities of Quito and Guayaquil kept Ecuador from achieving stable civilian

rule at that time. A period of stability had been imposed earlier by the Conservative dictator Gabriel García Moreno (1860–1875), and a rather turbulent "Liberal Republic" claimed power from 1896 to 1925, roughly coinciding with a boom in the cacao industry. Such stability was short lived. Over the twenty-three years following the end of the cacao boom, Ecuador had twenty-seven governments and lost half of its Amazonian territory to Peru.

Limited Democracies

All three Andean countries encountered great difficulties in making the transition from civilian oligarchies to limited democracies with broader participation. In Peru and Ecuador little effort was made to extend participation to the indigenous population of the highlands. It was hard enough just to find a formula for governing that included the urban middle and working classes. In Peru the American Popular Revolutionary Alliance (APRA), a mass political party with strong middle-class and union support, gained strength in the 1930s. Its existence created a dilemma that remained insuperable for years: democracy was impossible without the party, yet unacceptable to the conservative social elite with it. Ecuador's lack of a strong mass party made it difficult for a series of populist presidents to govern. In both Peru and Ecuador limited democratic governments alternated with short periods of military rule.

In Bolivia a war with Paraguay created conditions for a social revolution that mobilized all groups in society, including the indigenous communities. This mobilization took the form of violence more than electoral participation, however, and the revolutionary coalition splintered into warring factions. Although elections were held regularly, democracy could not take root in such a violent and polarized atmosphere. Limited democracy gave way to longer periods of authoritarian rule by 1964 in Bolivia, by 1968 in Peru, and by 1970 in Ecuador.

Peru

In Peru the Aristocratic Republic ended with the dictatorship of Augusto Leguía (1919–1930). Although Leguía's rule was politically repressive, a period of sustained economic growth led by sugar exports fostered the emergence of new social groups. These included an urban middle class and an increasingly organized working class, especially in the sugar plantations of the northern coast. An elite intellectual, Víctor Raúl Haya de la Torre, began organizing these social groups to support his new party, APRA. APRA played a pivotal role in Peruvian politics for decades. Although Haya made rhetorical use of indigenous symbols, neither his party nor any other succeeded in winning much support in the highlands before the 1980s. Because of its large membership and tightly disciplined organization, APRA became a necessary partner in any relatively democratic government. Because of its radical ideology, however, the conservative economic elite was unwilling to accept it as either the governing party or a coalition partner.

APRA also quickly made an enemy of the military. The first presidential election with substantial middle-class participation took place in 1931. It appears to have been won fairly by Luis Sánchez Cerro, the popular army officer who had overthrown Leguía the year before. But Haya, who had also been a candidate, refused to recognize the election results, and Sánchez Cerro retaliated by exiling all APRA members of Congress. The Apristas, or members of

APRA, retaliated by killing sixty army officers, and the army in turn massacred one or two thousand Apristas. An Aprista then assassinated Sánchez Cerro. The continuing feud between APRA and the army made democratization difficult if not impossible.

For the next thirty-six years Peru alternated between military governments that banned APRA and more democratic civilian governments that lifted the ban at first but found this tolerant policy difficult to sustain. After the military government of Gen. Oscar Benavides (1932–1938), a conservative elected civilian, Manuel Prado (1938–1945), legalized APRA. His successor, José Luis Bustamante (1945–1948), formed electoral and cabinet coalitions with APRA, but in the face of conservative opposition he forced the Apristas out of the government and banned the party once again. The ban was maintained during the dictatorship of Manuel Odría (1948–1956). Prado returned to office in 1956 with APRA support, but the party exercised little influence during his government's tenure. When Haya came close to winning the presidential election of 1962, the military nullified the election and called a new election the following year. Fernando Belaúnde of the centrist Popular Action Party won that election.

Only 16 percent of the population voted in these elections because literacy requirements remained in force and few parties made an effort to reach out to the peasants in the Andes. In fact, most of the highlands had been utterly neglected by the state and had become recruiting grounds for leftist guerrilla movements. President Belaúnde wanted to advance national integration in Peru by building transportation, energy, and communications infrastructure to connect the coast to the Andes and the Amazon beyond, but many of his programs were thwarted by APRA. Having abandoned much of its progressive platform after years of currying favor with conservative governments, APRA formed an obstructionist coalition in Congress with Odría's party. The failure of the Belaúnde government encouraged a progressive faction of the military to seize power in 1968. By 1975 that junta, led by Gen. Juan Velasco Alvarado, had largely destroyed the landed elite of the highlands, without bringing prosperity to the peasants.

Ecuador

In Ecuador the banana industry enjoyed a boom in the late 1940s and early 1950s. This economic growth finally made it possible to have a relatively stable, limited democratic government, which lasted from 1948 to 1960. As in

Peru, literacy requirements and neglect of the highland areas limited voting participation, so that only 9–13 percent of the population voted in elections. Another limiting factor was the low level of urbanization in Ecuador. Unlike Peru, Ecuador had little success at party building. One exception was the Concentration of Popular Forces, a personalistic patronage machine based in Guayaquil.

Because parties were weak, presidents were elected on the strength of their personal appeal and regional origins. They therefore lacked a firm base of support once in office. Typically, presidential candidates would patch together an alliance of tiny, ephemeral, and mostly personalistic parties to legitimate their campaigns. This alliance would dissolve as soon as the spoils of victory had been divided up, leaving the president isolated and unable to govern constitutionally. The best example of this tendency is José María Velasco Ibarra, a charismatic orator who claimed to be "above" parties and was elected president five times but finished his term only once (1952–1956). Frustrated by opposition during his last presidency (1968–1972), Velasco Ibarra assumed dictatorial powers with military backing. Because civilians, including Velasco Ibarra, seemed incapable of governing, Gen. Guillermo Rodríguez Lara seized power in 1972. His junta imitated the policies of the radical-authoritarian Velasco government in Peru without being quite so radical, but the successor junta of Vice Adm. Alfredo Poveda Burbano followed an even more moderate course.

Bolivia

In Bolivia the Great Depression in the 1930s caused the price of tin to drop. Economic hardship severely eroded support for the civilian oligarchic regime. President Daniel Salamanca desperately sought to rally nationalistic support for his government by declaring war on Paraguay. The war lasted from 1932 until 1935. Bolivia lost the war and with it 65,000 lives and a large portion of its territory.

The war had two important political consequences. First, it marked the end of oligarchic rule in Bolivia. The country lacked a legitimate alternative governing formula, however, so it fell into a period of chaos that lasted for seventeen years. In that period (1935–1952) short-lived juntas of the left, center, and right seized power and tried unsuccessfully to govern. Second, conscription during the war brought whites, mestizos, and indigenous people into close contact and gave them a shared resentment of the oligarchy. During the chaos that followed the fighting,

middle-class and lower-class leaders of all races began organizing political parties, labor unions, and peasant unions of all political persuasions. In the 1940s some of these coalesced into the Nationalist Revolutionary Movement (MNR).

In 1952 the Nationalist Revolutionary Movement allied with a military faction and seized power, beginning the Bolivian revolution. It disbanded the army, raided its armories, and distributed weapons to miners and indigenous peasants, who then occupied the mines and seized land for themselves. Elections were held throughout the revolution, but the MNR leadership never intended to establish a political democracy. Rather, it meant to create a regime modeled on authoritarian-corporatist rule in Mexico, in which peasant, labor, military, and middle-class organizations were subordinated to a dominant party. This plan failed because the party leadership was ultimately unable to restrain the demands of the various organizations. The miners, led by Juan Lechín Oquendo, were not satisfied with control of the mines; they demanded a "cogovernment" between the party and the unions. Increasingly, the government turned against the miners.

During a stabilization program in 1956, President Hernán Siles Zuazo, lacking a strong military, mobilized the armed peasant militias to break strikes in the mines. The government also began accepting U.S. assistance to rebuild the military. Under the direction of Gen. René Barrientos, the military began to forge its own ties to the peasant unions. In the meantime, the middle-class leadership of the Nationalist Revolutionary Movement split into several personalistic factions, most of which deserted the president, Víctor Paz Estenssoro, during his 1960–1964 term. When a military-peasant alliance seized power in 1964, the MNR was powerless to resist. For the next eighteen years Bolivia was ruled by military dictators, most of whom had little success in holding onto power.

Weak and Embattled Democracies

Transitions to democracy (as indicated by the inauguration of an elected president) took place in 1979 in Ecuador, in 1980 in Peru, and in 1982 in Bolivia. In each case, military governments had been in power during a period of economic decline and were being blamed for it. In Bolivia the military's reputation was further tarnished by corruption and a shocking record of human rights violations. The military high commands were either internally split or fearful that they would become dangerously divided by the responsibilities of governing. These internal divisions probably explain why transitions took place earlier in the Andean countries than in other South American countries, such as Argentina, Uruguay, Brazil, and Chile, where the military was more unified.

The new regimes were more inclusive than any others in their countries' history. Both Peru and Ecuador finally abolished literacy requirements for suffrage. Voting participation rose to about 30 percent of the population in Peru, and to 20–25 percent in Bolivia and Ecuador. These figures were still below the levels of participation in Argentina, Chile, Costa Rica, Uruguay, and Venezuela, where the voting rate sometimes exceeded 50 percent, but they were nearly double the previous levels in the Andean countries.

The new Andean democracies encountered challenges to their stability and did not always handle them in the most democratic fashion. One challenge was the inability of most Latin American governments to service foreign debts that had been incurred in the 1970s. The debt crisis, which hit Latin America hardest in 1982–1983, overlapped with the first democratic governments. It crippled economic performance, undermined political support, and tempted presidents to ignore the constitutional prerogatives of the legislatures. Cocaine trafficking increased sharply in the late 1970s. It had a particularly strong effect on the Andean region, as well as Colombia, financing corruption and channeling resources to nontraditional, even antidemocratic, political actors. An indigenous awakening began in the 1980s, as new Indian organizations made demands on the state that democratic governments were often unwilling or unable to satisfy. Bolivia came closest to meeting these challenges, while Peruvian democracy temporarily succumbed to them.

Siles Zuazo was reelected president of Bolivia in 1979, but the military prevented him from taking office. When the military abandoned power in 1982, he and the Congress elected earlier simply assumed power. His government never quite recovered from the debt crisis. As a result, when Paz Estenssoro won the presidential election of 1985, he inherited hyperinflation and economic collapse. By the end of his term, Paz Estenssoro had managed to lower the rate of inflation and restore some minimal economic growth. He lacked broad popular support—he repressed frequent demonstrations by miners and students—but skillfully built coalitions at the elite level.

In the mid-1980s Bolivia had three important parties: Paz's party, the Nationalist Revolutionary Movement; the Revolutionary Left Movement, led by Paz's nephew Jaime

Paz Zamora; and the vehicle of former dictator Hugo Bánzer Suárez, the Nationalist Democratic Action. Bánzer placed first in the election, but because he did not win a majority, the constitution required Congress to choose a winner. Bánzer agreed to support second-place finisher Paz Estenssoro in exchange for a voice in economic policy. During this government the Nationalist Revolutionary Movement and the Nationalist Democratic Action gave Paz's economic team a free hand in managing the economy, with surprising success. Bánzer's advisers continued to have influence over policy during the next government (1989–1993) as the result of a bizarre coalition between the Nationalist Democratic Action and the Revolutionary Left Movement, which made the third-place candidate, Paz Zamora, president. Rewarding the success of these governments' economic policy efforts, Bolivians elected Paz Estenssoro's principal policymaker, Gonzalo Sánchez de Lozada, president in 1993.

As the drug trade prospered, Bolivia became the world's second largest producer of coca leaf. Consequently, corruption spread among police, the military, members of Congress, and government officials, tarnishing the legitimacy of the supposedly democratic regime. Coca production also provided a livelihood for many peasants. They organized coca producers' *sindicatos,* which became an important lobby. While the *sindicatos* sometimes resorted to road blockades and other acts of civil disobedience, indigenous groups also became involved in electoral politics through the Tupac Katarí Revolutionary Movement. One indication of the success of efforts to expand political participation to the indigenous population was the election of Víctor Hugo Cárdenas, an Aymará Indian leader, as vice president in 1993.

In the same decades Ecuador was less successful than Bolivia in both the economic and indigenous spheres. The government of Jaime Roldós Aguilera (who died in a plane crash) and Osvaldo Hurtado Larrea achieved respectable economic growth at first, but that changed when the debt crisis hit. Their successor, conservative business leader León Febres Cordero, attempted to impose a neoliberal orientation, but his efforts were frustrated by a Congress dominated by the opposition. Contests of will between the president and Congress brought Ecuador to the brink of military intervention. At one point a group of air force officers held the president hostage until he agreed to sign a law passed by Congress. Rodrigo Borja Cevallos of the Democratic Left was elected president in 1988. His administration had fewer confrontations with Congress because his program of gradual economic liberalization made fewer demands on Congress. But Sixto Durán Ballén, elected in 1993, had a neoliberal agenda as ambitious as that of Febres and ran into equally stiff congressional opposition.

In 1992 an uprising by a large and well-organized council of indigenous associations, called the Confederation of Ecuadorian Indigenous Nationalities, presented the Borja government with a different sort of challenge. The confederation preferred direct action, such as road blockades, to party building or electoral participation. It demanded regional autonomy, environmental protection, and a share of the proceeds from oil production in the Amazon. Borja negotiated with these indigenous groups and set aside a generous land preserve for them. Durán Ballén, however, reneged on his predecessor's concessions, an act that made the indigenous question an explosive issue once again.

Peru was the only Andean democracy to suffer a definite reversal after 1980. It faced formidable challenges: economic collapse, the most violent guerrilla movement in the hemisphere, and the world's highest level of coca production. All three problems worsened during the presidencies of Fernando Belaúnde (1980–1985) and Alan García (1985–1990). Belaúnde's government presided over an economic collapse that caused his party, the Popular Action Party, to fall from 45 percent of the vote in 1980 to 7 percent in 1985. The young and charismatic García led his party, APRA, to a decisive victory in 1985. However, he unexpectedly nationalized the banks in 1987, which shook confidence in his government. Over the next three years production dropped by 22 percent and inflation became uncontrollable. By the time of the 1990 presidential election, the party system of the past had imploded. Neither APRA nor the Popular Action Party got its candidate into the runoff, and a dark-horse technocrat, Alberto Fujimori, swept into office.

Meanwhile, the Maoist guerrilla movement, Shining Path, had won adherents among the indigenous peasants, who had been ignored for decades. Its cadres attracted genuine support at first by punishing the peasants' enemies: managers of state cooperative farms, tax collectors, and local merchants. The movement was also strengthened by resources siphoned off from coca producers, processors, and shippers in exchange for protection.

Under García and Fujimori more than half of Peru's territory was placed under the control of military governors, who allowed their troops to commit countless human rights abuses with impunity. In April 1992 Fujimori, complaining about corrupt and irresponsible parties, closed Congress, arrested most of its members, imposed censorship, and initiated a purge of the politicized court system. This coup, carried out by an incumbent president, met with international condemnation. Fujimori then released the legislators and promised elections for a constituent assembly. Those elections, held in November 1992, produced a working majority for the president, who was popular despite his authoritarian tendencies. The new Democratic Constituent Congress quickly amended the constitution to make Fujimori eligible for reelection in 1995.

The histories of Peru, Ecuador, and Bolivia illustrate the difficulty of creating a fully inclusive democratic regime where there is a large, ethnically distinct, subjugated population, and especially where periodic economic crises and military defeats interfere with the consolidation of any regime, democratic or not. Despite these obstacles, the Andean countries have made progress toward both inclusiveness and stability. Their record so far, however, suggests that progress will continue to be slow, qualified, and intermittent.

See also *Chile; Colombia; Colonialism.*

Michael J. Coppedge

BIBLIOGRAPHY

Conaghan, Catherine M. *Restructuring Domination: Industrialists and the State in Ecuador.* Pittsburgh: University of Pittsburgh Press, 1988.

———, James M. Malloy, and Luis A. Abugattas. "Business and the 'Boys': The Politics of Neoliberalism in the Central Andes." *Latin American Research Review* 25(2) (1990): 3–30.

Graham, Carol. *Peru's APRA: Parties, Politics, and the Elusive Quest for Democracy.* Boulder, Colo.: Lynne Rienner, 1992.

Hilliker, Grant. *The Politics of Reform in Peru: The Aprista and Other Mass Parties of Latin America.* Baltimore: Johns Hopkins University Press, 1971.

Klein, Herbert S. *Bolivia: The Evolution of a Multi-Ethnic Society.* New York: Oxford University Press, 1982.

Kuczynski, Pedro-Pablo. *Peruvian Democracy under Economic Stress: An Account of the Belaúnde Administration, 1963–1968.* Princeton: Princeton University Press, 1977.

Malloy, James M., and Eduardo Gamarra. *Revolution and Reaction: Bolivia, 1964–1985.* New Brunswick, N.J.: Transaction, 1988.

Mitchell, Christopher. *The Legacy of Populism in Bolivia: From MNR to Military Rule.* New York: Praeger, 1977.

Morner, Magnus. *The Andean Past: Land, Societies, and Conflicts.* New York: Columbia University Press, 1985.

Schodt, David W. *Ecuador: An Andean Enigma.* Boulder, Colo.: Westview Press, 1987.

Angola

See *Africa, Lusophone*

Anthony, Susan B.

Leader of the women's suffrage movement in the United States. Anthony (1820–1906) was born in Adams, Massachusetts. The daughter of Quakers, she was educated in private schools and became a teacher.

In 1851 Anthony began collaborating with Elizabeth Cady Stanton, a suffragist orator and writer. She was committed to three areas of social reform: temperance, abolition, and women's equality. She joined the Daughters of Temperance and organized the Woman's State Temperance Society in 1852. She campaigned for equality for married women. An outspoken abolitionist, she was the principal New York agent of William Lloyd Garrison's American Antislavery Society. After Abraham Lincoln issued the Emancipation Proclamation of 1863, Anthony and Stanton organized the Women's Loyal League, which mobilized women and men to petition Congress to end slavery. The league disbanded when the Thirteenth Amendment abolishing slavery was ratified in 1865.

With the end of slavery, Anthony and Stanton renewed efforts to enfranchise women. Feminists and abolitionists formed the American Equal Rights Association to urge democratic reform for women and blacks. Under the organization's male leadership, however, support for women's rights diminished. The group lobbied to ratify the Fourteenth and Fifteenth Amendments, which, among other things, guaranteed freed slaves citizenship and the vote but made no mention of women's rights.

Anthony and Stanton formed the National Woman Suffrage Association in 1869. A rival group, the American Woman Suffrage Association, was founded the same year by Lucy Stone and others. The organizations merged in 1890 to form the National American Woman Suffrage Association, which Anthony headed from 1892 to 1900.

To publicize women's disenfranchisement, Anthony and fourteen other women voted in the 1872 congressional election in Rochester, New York. She was arrested and fined but refused to pay the fine. Because no action was taken against her, she could not appeal her case to a higher court.

From 1868 to 1870 Anthony helped publish the weekly suffragist newspaper *Revolution*. She also contributed to the six-volume *History of Woman Suffrage*. She remained politically active until her death in Rochester at age eighty-six.

See also *Abolitionism; Pankhurst, Emmeline; Stanton, Elizabeth Cady; Women and democracy; Women's suffrage in the United States*. In Documents section, see *Declaration of Sentiments (1848)*.

Susan Gluck Mezey

Antifederalists

Those who opposed the ratification of the Constitution of the United States, as proposed by the Federal Convention of 1787. The Antifederalists were a diverse movement, most united by what they opposed but also by certain common persuasions. Their leaders included Richard Henry Lee, Samuel Adams, George Clinton, Patrick Henry, and Mercy Otis Warren.

The Antifederalists shared with their Federalist opponents a devotion to the principles of the Declaration of Independence, but Antifederalists were more inclined toward the ancient view that the shaping of souls is a necessary and proper role of government. Antifederalists saw civic virtue—subordinating oneself to the common good—as the first principle of republics, and especially of democracies. Self-government, they observed, requires more than a say in making law; it demands a willingness to obey law, a determination to govern oneself. Antifederalist theory grouped governments on a scale, the end points of which are force (the principle of despotism) and persuasion (the principle of republics). Recognizing that even the best regime sometimes will need coercion, they argued that republics must seek to minimize its use. In the Antifederalist view, to the extent that government depends on enforcement, it ceases to be republican, whatever the outward form of its laws. Correspondingly, the critical concern of republics is the development of citizens who combine freedom with self-restraint and take pride in both.

The Constitution, by contrast, is purposefully silent on the question of civic virtue, and Antifederalists charged that Federalists took the patriotism and civility of the American people too much for granted. Many Antifederalists regretted the absence of any support for religion—or even any acknowledgment of it—in the Constitution. And Antifederalists, who sometimes worried that the American Revolution might too greatly have weakened respect for law, were troubled that the terms for ratifying the Constitution violated the provisions for amendment in the Articles of Confederation, the original framework for the federal union. To Antifederalists, American political culture was rare and precious, requiring nurturance rather than the Constitution's apparent indifference.

Antifederalists noted, moreover, that commercial society—which they supported, on the whole—adds special dangers because the pursuit of gain slides easily into avarice and private spirit. Some, like George Mason, looked to government to set limits to luxury, and virtually all Antifederalists agreed that a republican people must be taught that liberty and self-government are beyond price.

Antifederalists adhered to the classical teaching that republican virtue is most easily learned in small political societies. In such polities, government is relatively easy to watch and comprehend. Citizens can experience the benefits of projects in the public interest, and because individuals are more likely to be known and to make a difference, public life may even enhance a citizen's sense of dignity. Above all, in small publics, more citizens can engage in the practice of citizenship—not merely voting but also sharing in deliberation and in holding office. Democracy, Antifederalists held, is naturally at home in small places.

They acknowledged that in the modern world larger states had become necessary. Seeing themselves as the true champions of federalism, almost all Antifederalists supported some sort of stronger central government and accepted representative government as an alternative to direct rule by citizens. Antifederalists urged, however, that the regime be kept as small and as simple as possible. Scenting in the Constitution a design to consolidate the states under the authority of the national government, they also disliked its complexity, as likely to mystify citizens. Antifederalists were not attracted by the diversity of the United States, on which Federalists relied. They observed that a single rule cannot justly govern widely differing communities: a large republic must either rely on force, to compel uniformity, or on bureaucracy, to vary law to circumstance.

Moreover, Antifederalists contended that individual representatives can speak for their constituencies only to the extent that they are part of its world of acquaintance, speech, and feeling. This rough political friendship, they held, would also be likely to afford representatives a respectful hearing when defending unpopular measures. Every step away from such deliberative communities would weaken the quality of public assent to law. Similarly, Antifederalists thought it important to represent all classes in a society. They recognized that, because elites form effective political associations more easily than the poor and the middle class, large-scale politics works to keep ordinary citizens out of government. Finally, Antifederalists argued that small districts should be supplemented by rotation in office and frequent elections to keep representatives close to citizens. Legislatures modeled on Antifederalist theory would be large, amateurish, and discursive but would be able to speak for the people with great authority. By Antifederalist standards, representation under the Constitution was inadequate and tilted toward oligarchy. Although they understood that their principles could not be realized fully at the national level, Antifederalists regarded these principles as standards to be approximated as far as circumstances permitted.

Antifederalists were most effective in their demands for a Bill of Rights, which they urged as a standing instruction in the first principles of politics, indispensable in the curriculum of civic education. Their advocacy was largely responsible for the first ten amendments to the Constitution, but they had aimed at a somewhat different Bill of Rights. First, they wanted a proclamation of natural rights, principles that precede and limit all governments. The first ten amendments, enacted by Congress and ratified by the states, are rules of positive law, theoretically subject to repeal. Second, Antifederalists were much less concerned with strictly individual liberties than with the right to a republican civic life. Antifederalists defended rights to privacy—limits on search and seizure, for example, or the quartering of troops—but their theme was the safeguarding of the foundations of democratic politics: freedom of the press, "adequate" representation, frequent elections. Even trial by jury they upheld less as a right of the accused than as the "democratic branch of the judiciary power," the peoples' role in interpreting law. Their insistence that citizenship is the soul of a democratic republic is the Antifederalists' truly enduring legacy.

See also *Communitarianism; Federalism; Federalists; Participatory democracy; Religion, Civil; Republicanism; United States Constitution; Virtue, Civic.* In Documents section, see *American Declaration of Independence (1776); Constitution of the United States (1787).*

Wilson Carey McWilliams

BIBLIOGRAPHY

Gillespie, Michael Allen, and Michael Lienesch, eds. *Ratifying the Constitution.* Lawrence: University Press of Kansas, 1989.

Kenyon, Cecilia, ed. *The Antifederalists.* Indianapolis: Bobbs-Merrill, 1968.

Main, Jackson Turner. *The Anti-Federalists: Critics of the Constitution, 1787–1788.* Chapel Hill: University of North Carolina Press, 1961.

Miller, Joshua. *The Rise and Fall of Democracy in Early America, 1630–1789.* University Park: Pennsylvania State University Press, 1991.

Rutland, Robert A. *The Ordeal of the Constitution: The Antifederalists and the Ratification Struggle of 1787–1788.* Norman: University of Oklahoma Press, 1966.

Storing, Herbert J. *What the Anti-Federalists Were For.* Vol. 1 of *The Complete Anti-Federalist.* Edited by Herbert J. Storing. Chicago: University of Chicago Press, 1981.

Argentina

A republic that dominates the southern portion of South America and is bounded by the Atlantic Ocean to the east and the Andes Mountains to the west and southwest. Argentina has had a troubled democratic history, even though its 34.5 million people enjoy levels of per capita income, literacy, urbanization, and social welfare that rank among the highest in Latin America.

The consolidation in the early twentieth century of a relatively strong and sophisticated civil society—with a dynamic and entrepreneurial capitalist class, a large middle class, and a comparatively well-organized working class—together with the absence of an ethnically distinct and oppressed rural peasantry distinguished Argentina from most other Latin American societies. But Argentina's prosperity and political development in the early decades of the twentieth century contrast sharply with its subsequent history of political and economic instability and vulnerability to authoritarianism. Nevertheless, the transition from military to civilian rule that began in the 1980s, along with far-reaching market-oriented economic reforms, points to the consolidation of democratic institutions.

Historical Background

Argentina's independence from Spain in 1816 inaugurated a succession of civil wars that pitted Buenos Aires, with its control of the nation's principal seaport and the surrounding fertile *pampas* (grasslands), against the regional elites of the interior provinces. The overthrow of Juan Manuel de Rosas and his authoritarian brand of federalism in 1852 presaged momentous social, economic, and political changes. The next seventy years witnessed the unfolding of a successful project of capitalist development, which combined the construction of a national state espousing liberal principles of constitutional law and representative government with oligarchical practices featuring political patronage, electoral fraud by conservative elites, and the skillful use of military might.

By World War I, rapid modernization under the hegemony of the agricultural and commercial elites, who controlled the country's highly productive grasslands, had consolidated Argentina's status as a prosperous semiperipheral society that exported beef and grains to the advanced industrial nations of Western Europe. From 1870 to 1914 a threefold rise in per capita income—slightly lower than income growth in Switzerland and higher than income growth in Sweden or France—permitted all social classes access to lifestyles and levels of consumption similar to those of the more advanced industrial countries of the time. Massive immigration by Italians, Spaniards, and Jews from eastern Europe during this period resulted in a fivefold increase in Argentina's population. In the process, Argentina became a predominantly urban society—unlike the rest of Latin America, which remained overwhelmingly rural.

Social, political, and cultural transformations gradually eroded the legitimacy of a liberal, albeit highly exclusionary, system of oligarchical domination. The founding in 1891 of Argentina's first modern, mass-based, reformist political party, the Radical Civic Union, along with the rise of militant labor organizations with anarchist and socialist orientations, accelerated the liberalization and democratization of oligarchical rule. The approval by conservative elites of universal male suffrage paved the way for the election to the presidency in 1916 of the leader of the Radical Civic Union, Hipólito Irigoyen, and the incorporation of the middle classes into the rapidly expanding arena of electoral politics.

From 1916 to 1930 Argentina seemed to be firmly on the road to liberal democracy. Electoral participation and the associated rights of citizenship were extended to the recently naturalized contingents of European immigrants, many of whom belonged to the rapidly growing urban working class. The conservative elites were partially displaced from political power, but they retained control over most economic resources—particularly the vital export sector—as well as hegemony over cultural life. The steps toward democratization and the modest redistribution of income and wealth carried out under successful Radical party governments ultimately proved to be acceptable to conservative elites only as long as the economy continued to prosper.

The economic crash of 1929 and the disruption of international trade caused by the Great Depression raised the stakes inherent in competitive elections and imbued ongoing struggles between the Radicals and their conser-

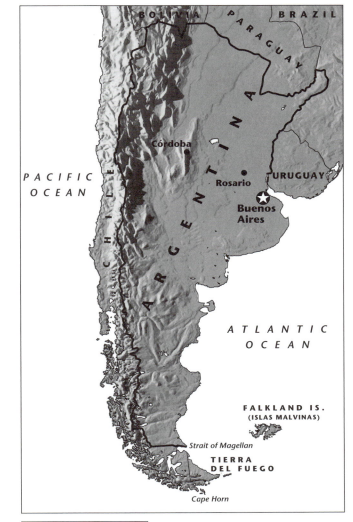

vative rivals with a new bitterness. A coup d'état in September 1930—carried out by the army with broad support from the landed classes, commercial elites, and parts of the middle classes—interrupted the process of gradual liberalization and democratization. The ensuing "infamous decade" (1930–1943) witnessed a partial restoration of conservative dominance by means of electoral fraud and repression against Radical party reformers, labor unions, and other democratic forces. A fifty-year period of mediocre economic performance and political stalemate was inaugurated, during which weak, semidemocratic civilian governments alternated with weak, illegitimate military dictatorships.

From Populist Compromise to Authoritarian Apotheosis

During the interwar period, economic and social policies played a large role in shaping the outcome of distributive struggles among contending groups in civil society. The expansion of state intervention and regulation of the economy—together with major transformations in the class structure, including large-scale migration from rural to urban areas—set the stage for a 1943 coup against conservative rule by a new generation of nationalist military officers. Among them was Juan Domingo Perón.

Perón's charismatic leadership and appeals to the "people" and the downtrodden *descamisados* ("shirtless ones") among the urban and rural poor won him the presidency in free elections held in 1946. His national-populist regime combined elements of representative government and electoral democracy with corporatist ties to organized labor (the "backbone" of Perón's Justicialista movement), to industrial entrepreneurs, and to the armed forces. Under Perón, populist and neo-Keynesian economic policies were relatively successful in the immediate postwar years in promoting economic growth and significant income redistribution in favor of urban workers, the middle classes, and industries that produced goods domestically rather than importing them.

By the early 1950s Perón's charisma, his populist discourse of social justice (the "humanization of capital"), and his aggressive nationalism began to wear thin, and Argentina's populist variant of a democratic class compromise began to unravel. The Peronist regime accentuated its authoritarian and repressive characteristics in response to severe balance-of-payments problems, worsening inflationary pressures, and a deepening state fiscal crisis. A military coup in 1955, supported by the dominant classes and middle sectors, toppled the regime and sent Perón into exile.

The decade following Perón's overthrow saw deepening polarization between Peronist and anti-Peronist forces in the electoral arena. Conservative groups in the armed forces and among the dominant classes insisted on the proscription of the majoritarian social actors represented by Peronism. Political fragmentation and electoral stalemates resulted. The weak electoral mandates of the semidemocratic governments of this period made them vulnerable to a politics of blackmail driven by military threats and sharp distributive conflicts among organized labor, urban consumers, domestic and transnational business interests, and agricultural producers. The military

overthrew the weak civilian governments of Arturo Frondizi in 1962 and Arturo Illia in 1966. In the latter instance, a military coup led by Gen. Juan Carlos Onganía proclaimed an "Argentine revolution," a coherent attempt to revamp the state and modernize the crisis-ridden economy. Ultimately, however, this attempt failed. Growing popular discontent culminated in the 1969 mass uprising known as the *Cordobazo,* and Onganía fell victim to a palace coup in 1970.

Confronted with mounting social and economic turmoil, Gen. Alejandro Lanusse orchestrated the armed forces' extrication from the direct exercise of state power and facilitated Juan Perón's return from Spanish exile in 1972. The subsequent electoral victory of Peronism over the Radical party in 1973 paved the way for a transition to civilian rule, with the aging leader himself assuming the presidency.

The early 1970s gave rise to a macabre dialectic between surging popular mobilization and a new revolutionary project spearheaded by Marxist and radical Peronist guerrilla movements, on the one hand, and rising state repression, on the other. The result was a bloody escalation of political violence and the militarization of politics. This perverse turn of events cast a pall over efforts to consolidate democratic institutions and practices, as soon became apparent in 1974, when Perón's death shattered hopes for stable economic growth under democratic auspices. In 1976 a military coup toppled the ineffectual constitutional government headed by Perón's widow, María Estela (Isabel) Martínez de Perón.

The post-1976 military regime headed by Gen. Jorge Rafael Videla proclaimed a crusade in defense of "Western and Christian civilization" and used systematic state terrorism to wage a "dirty war" against leftist militants, labor organizers, intellectuals, and ordinary citizens who dared harbor dissident opinions. Official sources have estimated the number of dead and "disappeared" at 10,000, although human rights groups place the number of victims at 25,000 to 30,000.

This so-called Process of National Reorganization was also aimed at carrying out a capitalist revolution through implementation of an extremely dogmatic version of monetarist-inspired "free-market" economics. The country's industrial base was decimated by persistent triple-digit inflation, financial speculation, and an overvalued exchange rate. The restructuring of the manufacturing sector meant the loss of tens of thousands of blue-collar and white-collar jobs. Under military rule, Argentina's foreign debt rose from less than $7 billion to more than $43 billion; the detonation of the Latin American debt crisis in 1982 made the debacle virtually irreversible.

The collapse of the authoritarian regime was most directly a consequence of the military's disastrous April 1982 invasion of the *Islas Malvinas* (Falkland Islands), whose ownership had been disputed by Argentina and Britain for almost 150 years. The resounding defeat inflicted by Great Britain on the poorly prepared Argentine expeditionary forces left the economy in tatters; the military regime was humiliated and isolated both domestically and internationally. Their own factionalism, combined with a reawakening of moderate civilian opposition, left the armed forces with no choice except to accede to elections.

Surprisingly, the October 1983 elections were won by the Radical party, whose presidential candidate, Raúl Alfonsín, a respected opponent of military rule and a champion of human rights, was perceived as better suited to lead Argentina toward democracy than the Peronists, who were tainted by their association with sectarian violence and populist mismanagement of the economy.

Return to Democracy and Economic Restructuring

During Alfonsín's administration, Argentines displayed a new appreciation for limited, representative government and a strong commitment to democratic political values. Alfonsín demonstrated considerable courage in bringing to trial the members of military juntas who were responsible for massive human rights violations and in facing down several rebellions from dissident sectors of the army. But the government proved less capable in managing the economy.

Whipsawed by a combination of its own policy failures, the loss of a stable congressional majority, the opposition of many business sectors, and constant pressures from the Peronist-controlled organized labor movement, Alfonsín's government was unable to reconcile popular expectations for income redistribution and social justice with the harsh realities of stabilization and structural adjustment policies and the exigencies of servicing Argentina's huge foreign debt. (The debt had surpassed $60 billion by the late 1980s.) The failure of "heterodox shock" policies (wage, price, and foreign exchange controls), in addition to conventional fiscal and monetary policies, to stabilize the economy prompted a catastrophic hyperinflationary crisis. From August 1988 through July 1989 consumer prices rose 3,610 percent, and wholesale prices skyrocketed 5,062

percent. This crisis assured the victory of Peronist Carlos Saúl Menem in the May 1989 presidential election.

Repudiating the populist and statist policies defended by Peronism since the 1940s, the Menem government launched an ambitious project of neoliberal free-market restructuring, which featured privatization of state enterprises, deregulation, liberalization of international trade, and promotion of foreign investment. In addition, labor market reforms were instituted that undercut the bargaining power of trade unions. In 1991 the Menem government implemented an austere plan (the so-called Convertibility Plan) for stabilizing and reforming the economy; it succeeded in bringing inflation strictly under control and achieving several years of spectacular economic growth. Menem also significantly reduced the defense budget and dismantled much of the arms industry. Consequently, the military's institutional and political prerogatives were sharply curtailed, and Argentina moved from only de jure to both de jure and de facto civilian constitutional control over the armed forces.

On the negative side of the balance sheet, Menem's neoliberal policies exacerbated tendencies toward deepening inequality and growing concentration of income and wealth. Moreover, the growth associated with market-oriented restructuring did not generate enough jobs to compensate for those lost to privatization and market pressures; unemployment reached unprecedented levels of more than 12 percent in 1995. Although the abolition of the "inflationary tax" on the poor was a positive outcome of Menem's market-oriented strategy, poverty worsened in the first half of the 1990s, with "paupers" and the "structurally poor" estimated to constitute at least one-fifth of the population.

The redressing of the lingering social trauma of earlier episodes of hyperinflation, as well as the government's newfound image of credibility, won Menem considerable support among all classes in Argentine society—mitigating voter concerns about executive branch corruption, poverty, and unemployment. As a result, Menem was able to garner consistent congressional support for key government initiatives and to win endorsement from the Radical Civic Union for constitutional reforms that included his right to stand for immediate reelection.

A preference for continuity carried Menem to an impressive victory in the May 1995 presidential election. He won nearly 50 percent of the vote, becoming the third Argentine president in the twentieth century to win election to a second term. The Radical Civic Union, which received less than 18 percent of the vote, suffered the worst defeat in its long history, while the nearly 30 percent won by the candidate of a newly created electoral coalition known as FREPASO pointed to the possible emergence of a viable center-left party opposition.

Regime Consolidation and the Challenges of Democratic Deepening

Contemporary Argentina is well advanced in the process of consolidation of a liberal and competitive—but not necessarily fully inclusionary or participatory—democratic form of governance. This is a surprising outcome in a country that from 1930 until 1983 saw twenty-six successful military coups and counted sixteen army generals among its twenty-four presidents. Despite moments of peril, the threat of authoritarian regression has receded dramatically. The authoritarian and semidemocratic actors of the past—the armed forces, elements of the dominant classes, leftist revolutionary movements, sectors of organized labor, and right-wing groups within the Peronist movement—have all subordinated their pursuit of power to the rules and the calendar of electoral competition.

In its efforts to move beyond minimal electoral and procedural criteria for a democratic regime and to ensure its continuity, contemporary Argentina confronts several major challenges. First, in order to achieve a more stable institutional equilibrium, the autonomy of the National Congress and the judicial system must be expanded and the broad discretionary powers of the presidency and executive branch must be limited, making them more transparent and accountable to a revitalized party system. Second, to complete the subordination of the armed forces to civilian authority, recent institutional changes must be made irreversible by additional reforms in military culture, doctrine, and mission. Third, and equally significant, the values and actors of civil society—particularly the labor movement, autonomous social movements and other secondary groups, and a critical and independent mass media—must be strengthened and democratic public space guaranteed for debate and political contestation regarding the country's future.

In addition, many would argue the urgency of imbuing citizenship and the rituals of voting and popular participation in representative institutions with greater meaning by implementing social policies capable of demonstrably improving the lives of those segments of the population most hurt by the state's retreat from its traditional responsibilities for the provision of employment, education, and social welfare. Similarly, for democracy to endure and to become less elitist and more inclusionary, Argentina will need to restore long-term economic growth and thereby reduce poverty and social inequalities. For these changes to work together in a sustainable fashion, new development strategies will be required that incorporate more competitive participation in world markets and more democratic modes of public regulation of the emergent market-driven economy.

See also *Constitution of Argentina (1853)* in Documents section.

William C. Smith

BIBLIOGRAPHY

Acuña, Carlos H., ed. *La nueva matriz política argentina.* Buenos Aires: Editorial Nueva Visión, 1995.

Brysk, Alison. *The Politics of Human Rights in Argentina: Protest, Change, and Democratization.* Stanford, Calif.: Stanford University Press, 1994.

Díaz Alejandro, Carlos. *Essays on the Economic History of the Argentine Republic.* New Haven: Yale University Press, 1970.

Manzetti, Luigi. *Institutions, Parties, and Coalitions in Argentine Politics.* Pittsburgh, Penn.: University of Pittsburgh Press, 1993.

O'Donnell, Guillermo A. *Bureaucratic Authoritarianism: Argentina in Comparative Perspective, 1966–1973.* Berkeley: University of California Press, 1988.

Rock, David. *Argentina, 1516–1987: From Spanish Colonization to Alfonsín.* Berkeley: University of California Press; London: I. B. Tauris, 1987.

Smith, William C. *Authoritarianism and the Crisis of the Argentine Political Economy.* Stanford, Calif.: Stanford University Press, 1989.

———. "State, Market, and Neoliberalism in Post-Transition Argentina: The Menem Experiment." *Journal of Interamerican Studies and World Affairs* 33 (winter 1991–1992): 45–82.

Waisman, Carlos H. *Reversal of Development in Argentina: Postwar Counterrevolutionary Policies and Their Structural Consequences.* Princeton: Princeton University Press, 1987.

Arias Sánchez, Oscar

President of Costa Rica from 1986 to 1990 and recipient of the 1987 Nobel Peace Prize for his role in promoting democracy and peace in Central America. While Arias (1940–   ) was president, Costa Rica became a symbol of

Oscar Arias Sánchez

political independence in Central America: it rejected outside interference from the two superpowers, the Soviet Union and the United States; openly opposed the U.S. military intervention in El Salvador and Nicaragua; and designed nontraditional channels of diplomacy to encourage dialogue and democratization.

Arias's studies prepared him well for this role. He majored in law and economics at the University of Costa Rica, winning the 1971 National Essay Prize for his thesis on interest groups in Costa Rica. In 1974 he received a doctorate in political science from the University of Essex, England. Returning to Costa Rica, he combined his academic and political interests by becoming professor of political science at the University of Costa Rica and secretary for international affairs of the National Liberation Party. He first gained national prominence by serving as Costa Rica's minister of planning and economic policy from 1970 to 1978. He later was elected to Congress and also won the position of secretary general of the National Libera-

tion Party, a position that he held until his presidency.

The foreign policy initiatives that won Arias world renown were apparent even in his presidential campaign. Unlike his opponent, who took a belligerent position toward Nicaragua's revolutionary Sandinista government, Arias called for peaceful coexistence with Nicaragua. He argued that wars in neighboring Nicaragua and El Salvador threatened Costa Rica's economic health and democratic stability and urged that Costa Rica take the lead in seeking their resolution. Asserting that there could be no successful development in Central America without peace and no peace without democracy, he adopted "peace for my people, peace for my land" as the slogan of his candidacy and the mission of his presidency.

Arias's emphasis on democracy, political compromise, and demilitarization as the sole means for achieving peace distinguished his diplomatic efforts. It also put him on a collision course with the United States. President Ronald Reagan's administration was intent on the total defeat of Nicaragua's Sandinista government and pressured Costa Rica to support its views. The peace plan Arias designed—known as Esquipulis II—was based on interlocking agreements throughout Central America (especially in Nicaragua) calling for cease-fires, free elections, the end of foreign aid to all irregular forces and their demobilization, smaller armed forces, and national reconciliation. The Arias plan was eventually accepted throughout Central America and resulted, most importantly, in the demobilization of the U.S.-backed opposition forces (contras) and the holding of elections in Nicaragua.

In May 1990, at the end of his presidential term, Arias assumed the presidency of the Arias Foundation for Peace and Human Progress. Established in 1988 with the monetary award that accompanied his Nobel Peace Prize, the foundation under his leadership promotes demilitarization and development initiatives throughout Central America, with strong emphasis on environmental concerns and women's rights.

See also *Central America; Costa Rica.*

Terry Lynn Karl

BIBLIOGRAPHY

De la Cruz de Lemos, Vladimir. *Historia general de Costa Rica.* San José: Ediciones Costa Rica, 1989.

Karl, Terry Lynn. "Hegemons and Political Entrepreneurs: Democratization and Cooperation in the Americas." In *The Political Economy of the Americas,* edited by Clark Reynolds. Forthcoming.

Aristotle

Greek philosopher who offered the first theoretical analysis of democracy. Aristotle (384–322 B.C.) was the son of the court physician of Philip of Macedon (father of Alexander the Great). He studied in Athens with Plato. After Plato's death, he traveled extensively in Asia Minor, returning briefly to Macedonia to tutor the young Alexander. Back in Athens, he founded the Lyceum. When the Athenians charged him with impiety, he fled the city, supposedly claiming with reference to the execution of Socrates in 399 B.C. that he did not want the Athenians to sin twice against philosophy.

Aristotle's study of the Greek city-state, the *polis,* presents a theory of politics that emphasizes the relationship between participation and democracy. His *Politics* analyzes the human who is "by nature a political animal." Whoever does not live in the *polis* is either a beast or a god. Humans alone possess speech, which enables them to debate the advantageous and the harmful, the just and the unjust. Only in the setting of the *polis*—and particularly in the assembly—can humans engage in such debates. To be hu-

man, one must live in a community in which one exercises the powers of one's speech, debating the collective choices that a community must make. Aristotle defines the citizen as one who shares in the decisions of the community and its offices and takes turns ruling and being ruled. Citizenship appears possible only in a regime in which "the many" participate.

Aristotle categorizes regimes according to the numbers in authority (one, a few, or "the many") and whether those in authority rule in the interest of the whole or in their own interest (good or bad regimes). He calls a regime in which the many rule for the interest of the whole a *polity,* the generic term for all regimes; he calls a regime in which the many rule for their own interest a *democracy.* Although this classification of regimes focuses on the numbers of individuals in positions of authority, Aristotle argues that the many will always be poor and only a few will be rich. Thus democracies will be the rule of the poor.

Aristotle finds most regimes to be either democratic or oligarchic (ruled by a few). Because each type has limitations, he proposes as the best practical regime one that combines the qualities of both—namely the participation of a large number of individuals but not so large a number as to create instability or allow the poor to participate. He also calls this mixed regime *polity.* No regime can be a pure form; all practical regimes mix aspects found in each of the pure forms, such as monarchy or democracy.

See also *Classical Greece and Rome; Theory, Ancient.*

Arlene W. Saxonhouse

Armenia

A republic in the Transcaucasian region, formerly part of the Soviet Union. Armenia is a small, densely populated country, about the size of Belgium, with 3.7 million people (a figure which does not take into account the large emigration from the country in recent years). Mountainous, poor in natural resources, and landlocked, Armenia is bordered by Georgia, Azerbaijan, Iran, and Turkey.

During the Soviet period, Armenia's trade-dependent economy was based on light industry, agriculture, food processing, machine building, and metalworking. A well-educated, Western-oriented Christian people in a largely

Muslim region, Armenians now look toward Europe and America for models by which to structure their fledgling democracy.

Historical Background

Armenians first appeared as a distinct ethnic entity about 600 B.C. in Anatolia. Adoption of Christianity as the state religion at the beginning of the fourth century A.D. and the creation of an Armenian alphabet a century later under church sponsorship played major roles in establishing and preserving a distinctive ethnic identity. Early Armenia consisted of feuding dynastic principalities under a succession of Roman, Byzantine, and Ottoman empires in the West and Iranian empires in the East. Beginning in the eleventh century, Turkic and Mongol invasions stimulated extensive Armenian migration throughout Europe, Russia, and the Middle East, creating a far-flung diaspora.

In the Ottoman Empire, Armenians were ruled as an ethnoreligious community through their religious leaders. In the eighteenth and nineteenth centuries a nationalist awakening began in the Armenian diaspora, traditionally a conduit for European Renaissance and Enlightenment learning. In Constantinople the new middle class of Armenian doctors, lawyers, writers, teachers, and small manufacturers challenged the elite control of church leaders, forcing them to adopt democratic reforms.

For Armenians, as for other ethnic communities living in multiethnic empires or states, issues of democratization (self-rule) have always been tied up with nationalism (freedom from domination by different and more powerful ethnic groups). The second half of the nineteenth century saw the founding of several parties that combined a program of enlightenment and democratization with nationalism. The parties articulated a program of autonomy, even independence, for Armenians in the Ottoman Empire, the majority of whom lived in eastern Anatolia as an impoverished, semiliterate peasantry subject to persecution and government-organized massacres.

The nationalist movement ended during World War I, however, when the Ottoman authorities organized the destruction of the Armenian community because of its perceived pro-Russian sympathies and desire for independence. Between 1915 and 1917, an estimated 1 million Armenians were executed outright or died during forced marches across the Anatolian interior. Survivors poured across the border into Russia, into neighboring Middle Eastern countries, and eventually to Europe and the Americas. Today Armenians living outside Armenia (ap-

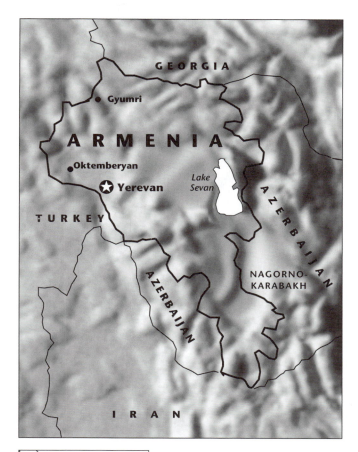

proximately 7 million) outnumber residents of the republic two to one.

As a prosperous commercial bourgeoisie, Armenians in the Russian empire had consistently fared better than those under Ottoman rule. After the genocide, hundreds of thousands of Armenian refugees entered Russian Armenia (annexed from Persia in the first decades of the nineteenth century). After the collapse of czarist power and the retreat of Russian forces in 1918, Armenians founded an independent republic and attempted to construct a functioning democratic government while coping with Turkish Armenian refugees, famine, and epidemics. In 1920, again threatened by Turkish forces, the defeated and discouraged Armenian government signed away its powers to the Bolsheviks.

As a result of the genocide, most Armenians accepted Soviet rule as the price of protection against Turkey. The small dissident movement in the 1960s, which called for independence from the Soviet Union, received little attention or support from the Armenian population. During the Soviet period, Armenians channeled political and economic grievances into protests about suppression of ethnic and cultural rights. It was only in 1991, with the dissolution of the Soviet Union imminent, that Armenians voted for independence in a national referendum.

Path to Independence

Since 1988 democratization of state and society in Armenia has been closely linked to a nationalist agenda. Indeed, the popular movement that launched the democratization process in 1988 developed in response to the ethnic activism of Armenians living in Nagorno-Karabakh, an autonomous region in Azerbaijan where Armenians made up about 75 percent of the population. Their demands to join Armenia mobilized the Armenian National Movement (ANM) in Armenia. The ANM's agenda rapidly broadened to address Armenia's serious ecological problems, widespread political corruption, and endemic violation of political rights.

Between 1988 and the formal achievement of national independence in 1991, the Karabakh conflict gradually escalated into violence and war between Armenians and Azerbaijanis (a conflict that was in part provoked by Communist Party authorities to divert attention from demands for democratization). An Azerbaijani blockade of fuel and other vital supplies was put in place. The December 7, 1988, earthquake in northeast Armenia—which leveled cities and towns, directly killed 25,000 to 30,000 people, made 530,000 homeless, and destroyed a significant portion of Armenia's manufacturing capacity—was a further blow to this beleaguered nation.

The war, blockade, and earthquake destruction all shaped political debate and policy. In 1990 the Armenian National Movement, running on a platform of democratic reform, attention to ecological issues, privatization, and support for the unification of Nagorno-Karabakh with Armenia, emerged as the strongest political force in multiparty elections to the Armenian parliament. Despite widespread anticommunist sentiment, independence was not part of the platform.

Building a democratic polity in Armenia has involved the daunting task of restructuring a unified party-state system in which legislative, executive, and judicial functions were combined in the Communist Party, and government functioned merely as the party's administrative

arm. In August 1991 the Armenian parliament established the post of president to address the leadership struggle between the executive and legislative bodies that emerged after the Communist Party's collapse. Levon Ter-Petrossian, a leading activist in the Armenian National Movement and chairman of the parliament since 1990, was elected president in a national election. Ter-Petrossian vowed to establish a democratic state and introduce a free market economy.

Although the government initiated consultations with Western experts in constitutional law, it resisted the early implementation of a constitution. Instead, Ter-Petrossian advocated a more gradual approach, constructing a workable governmental framework through incremental legislation. A strong presidential system developed, in which the president had the power to rule through decree, declare martial law, and appoint or dismiss ministers. The parliament retained the power to impeach ministers and override presidential vetoes.

Delineation of powers between governmental branches has remained weak. The judiciary has some protection of independence: judges are appointed (by the executive, or in some cases by the parliament) to five-year terms. Relations between central and local governments are still complicated by the fact that district governments have no way of raising their own revenues, so they remain dependent on the central government for financing. No decision has been made about whether municipal public property belongs to local governments or to the central government.

The constitution was expected to resolve many of the outstanding issues of governance. During the drafting stages the Armenian National Movement proposed a form of strong presidential rule, while the opposition called for a parliamentary form of government. A national referendum was expected to resolve the differences. Adoption of a constitution was expected to be followed by parliamentary elections in 1995 and a presidential election in 1996.

Constructing a Government

Formally, the Armenian government functions as a multiparty, pluralistic system. Despite the presence of more than a dozen parties and several groupings in parliament, and the relative freedom with which opposition parties operate, political parties remain weakly developed. Rather than representing articulated interests within society, they tend to appeal to the Armenian nation as a whole in the name of a single overriding vision of state and society. Politics remains focused on individuals rather than their parties.

Although the Armenian National Movement continues to be the strongest force in government, its popular standing has sharply fallen as a result of governmental failures and the flagrant corruption of some ANM representatives. The concentration of power in the Ministry of Internal Affairs, assassinations of several public figures, attacks on opposition newspaper offices, and the 1994 trial and sentencing of a security expert, allegedly due to his links with the opposition, raised fears about eroding civil liberties. The war with Azerbaijan also slowed development of an active opposition by encouraging opposition parties to restrain criticism of government in the interest of preserving a united front.

Processes and structures for negotiating and building coalitions to pass legislation barely exist. Given that the unicameral parliament (260 seats when filled) is dominated by large blocs, the requirement that an absolute majority of the members vote in favor of legislation has frequently caused legislative gridlock. The parties' difficulty in formulating and pursuing clearly articulated programs has also slowed the pace of legislative action. Many legislators show more interest in the privileges of their position (such as travel abroad) than in their job. Voters increasingly view the parliament as overly partisan and ineffective. As a result, cynicism and alienation are widespread among the electorate.

Armenia has taken steps to provide a legal basis for protecting the political and civil liberties of its citizens. The Armenian parliament has adopted the International Covenant on Civil and Political Rights as a bill of rights. All inhabitants of Armenian territory, regardless of ethnicity, have the right to become citizens of the republic (although a citizenship law had not been enacted by mid-1995). Armenian citizens now enjoy more freedom of speech, assembly, and press than they did before 1988. Although the government controls both television and radio, hundreds of journals and newspapers (some financed by parties based abroad) exist, some highly critical of the government.

Antigovernment demonstrations organized by opposition parties have taken place, usually without overt interference or arrests. Armenia's relatively positive human rights record was tarnished in December 1994, when the government suspended activities of the largest opposition party and closed down affiliated organizations and publications on the grounds that the party harbored a clandestine terrorist group engaged in racketeering, drug trafficking, and espionage. The ban was set to expire a week after the July 1995 parliamentary elections. Many Armenians ascribed the ban to the government's fear of losing control of parliament. The government has been slow to lift travel restrictions. Armenian citizens are unable to obtain passports or exit visas for travel outside the former Soviet Union without obtaining permission from the Ministry of Internal Affairs. By 1995, an estimated 700,000 Armenians, including businesspeople, scientists, and scholars, had left the republic in search of employment and stable living conditions.

Challenges to Armenian Democracy

Democratic governance cannot occur apart from a functioning economy. Serious shortages of energy and supplies have sharply curtailed industrial production and forced Armenians to endure successive winters virtually without gas or electricity. The government has tried to balance conflicting demands from international financial organizations and Armenian citizens regarding decentralization and privatization, but it is constrained by the need to coordinate limited resources. Shortly after independence, most collective and state farms were privatized, although absence of laws regulating conveyance of land, deeding, and titling have impeded development of a land market. Housing and commercial enterprises have since been privatized as well, and privatization of industry began in 1995.

Armenia still lacks an effective banking system and a legal infrastructure to protect local and foreign investments. This lack, in combination with the energy crisis and problems of transportation, has forced many local entrepreneurs to leave for other republics or the West. In addition, traditional links between the old Communist Party apparatus and the criminal underworld have penetrated new government structures and continue to dominate the economy, hindering development of an autonomous sphere of production and commerce.

Developed democratic polities are characterized by civic engagement on the part of an informed citizenry. In Armenia, however, several factors discourage civic engagement. During the Soviet period, civil society and a public sphere of free and informed debate and discussion were drastically reduced. The network of voluntary, religious, professional, and trade organizations; businesses; neighborhood groups; and clubs that links individuals to society and society to the state is still rudimentary. Armenians' primary ties traditionally have been to the extended family; society has remained an abstraction without practical implications. Moreover, the enormous hardships created by shortages and hyperinflation have meant that most citizens are too busy trying to survive to participate actively in public life.

Perhaps the most serious obstacle to developing a stable democracy is the weakness of the state. Old Soviet state structures have been seriously weakened, but new structures are not yet functioning effectively. The population lacks confidence in a government that cannot enforce the law, stop the disastrous fall in living standards, or control endemic corruption, rising crime, and war profiteering. This distrust also represents the pervasive antistate mood and fear of parties and ideologies that are a legacy of the Soviet era.

The Armenian government has yet to institute a civil service based on a merit system of recruitment, selection, and promotion. Loyalty and connections remain more important than ability, and old ways of getting things done tend to subvert change. Moreover, when a ministry does change leadership, a complete shake-up often results, and experienced personnel have to leave.

Prospects for Democratization

The state's weakness and the ongoing conflict with Azerbaijan remain grave obstacles to democratization. The war and blockade have led to continuing drops in industrial production and to dramatic emigration, providing the government with a ready excuse for failures and mistakes.

Despite its many disadvantages, Armenia nevertheless has a literate, well-educated population and a far-flung international diaspora that can provide technical assistance and contacts with other societies and states. In addition, since the 1988 deportation of 160,000 Azerbaijanis, Armenia is practically monoethnic. Its homogeneity will reduce opportunities for the kinds of manipulation of ethnic, religious, or linguistic differences for political ends that have disrupted other postcommunist states. When the war with Azerbaijan ends and Armenia normalizes relations with its neighbors, its citizens will be able to concentrate their energy and skills on building a civil society and functioning economy, both important prerequisites to a stable democracy.

See also *Caucasus, The; Russia, Pre-Soviet; Union of Soviet Socialist Republics.*

Nora Dudwick

BIBLIOGRAPHY

Dudwick, Nora. "Armenia: The Nation Awakens." In *Nations and Politics in the Soviet Successor States,* edited by Ian Bremmer and Ray Taras. Cambridge and New York: Cambridge University Press, 1993.

Libaridian, Gerard. *Armenia at the Crossroads: Democracy and Nationhood in the Post-Soviet Era: Essays, Interviews and Speeches by the Leaders of the National Democratic Movement in Armenia.* Watertown, Mass.: Blue Crane, 1991.

———, ed. *The Karabagh File.* Watertown, Mass.: Zoryan Institute, 1988.

Rutland, Peter. "Democracy and Nationalism in Armenia." *Europe-Asia Studies* (formerly *Soviet Studies*) 46 (1994): 839–861.

Smith, Hedrick. *The New Russians.* New York: Avon Books, 1990; New ed. London: Arrow Books, 1991.

Suny, Ronald Grigor. *Looking toward Ararat: Armenia in Modern History.* Bloomington: Indiana University Press, 1993.

Walker, Christopher J. *Armenia: The Survival of a Nation.* 2d ed. New York: St. Martin's, 1990.

Aron, Raymond

French philosopher, professor, and journalist who was known as a friend of liberal democracy. From 1930 to 1933 Aron (1905–1983) studied philosophy and sociology in Cologne and Berlin. His firsthand view of Germany's progression toward fascism profoundly transformed his intellectual orientation. He became interested in the importance of politics and looked in particular to Wilhelm Dilthey and Max Weber for guidance. His doctoral thesis (1938) provided the philosophic foundations for his lifelong opposition to Marxist-Leninism.

After spending the war years as a journalist in London associated with the Free French movement (1940–1944), Aron returned to France, where he gained recognition as a distinguished commentator, professor, and political thinker. A prolific writer, he investigated the characteristics of modern industrial societies and the nature of modern wars, criticized the indulgence of progressive intellectuals toward totalitarian regimes, theorized about interstate relations, and analyzed the most important political

Raymond Aron

and philosophical thinkers from Niccolò Machiavelli in the early sixteenth century to Karl Marx and Alexis de Tocqueville in the nineteenth century. In addition, Aron opposed the synthesis of Marxism and existentialism promoted by the twentieth-century French philosophers Jean-Paul Sartre and Maurice Merleau-Ponty and the pro-communist, antiliberal politics that flowed from that philosophical position.

Aron was critical of dogmatic democrats and recognized that democracy is not necessarily in accord with human liberty or human excellence. Still, like Tocqueville (for whom the primary meaning of democracy was the support of equality and egalitarianism), Aron believed that human liberty can flourish only if it supports the egalitarian values that are an essential element of the modern spirit.

In his *Essay on Freedom* and *Democracy and Totalitarianism,* Aron provided a thoughtful defense of the constitutional-pluralistic regime, as he called the modern representative state and society. Constitutional-pluralistic regimes are ruled by law and by a sense of compromise that moderates political fanaticism and allows for a substantial element of civic and social cohesion. These regimes attempt to moderate and regulate, but not eliminate or overcome, social conflict and division. Aron outlined four defining traits of constitutional-pluralistic regimes: they recognize and regulate political, economic, and social competition; they establish constitutional rules, mechanisms, and institutions; they accept a variety of social groups, interests, and associations; and they recognize that modern liberty is impossible without free and competing political parties.

In the modern world the significant democratic (in the Tocquevillian sense) alternative to the liberal or constitutional-pluralistic regime is the monopolistic party regime. The most extreme form of this kind of regime is ideological despotism, which is represented by the Nazi dictatorship in Adolf Hitler's Germany and the communist totalitarian states in eastern and central Europe under Vladimir Ilich Lenin and Joseph Stalin and their successors. Aron was fully aware of the imperfections of the liberal regime, with its propensity toward the corruptions of oligarchy or (more typically and dangerously) demagoguery. But he preferred the potential and partial corruption of the liberal regime to the fundamental imperfections of the monopolistic party regime, which are tied to its utopian efforts to create a society without serious conflict. In making this attempt, the monopolistic party regime eliminates the political liberty that is essential to genuine human universalism, and it hinders citizens' exercise of rational and civic virtues through participation in the deliberations of the state.

Although Aron accepted the need for a free market to fuel the engines of a productive economy, he recognized that modern democratic and representative societies contain unconstrainable egalitarian ambitions. Liberal societies must accept the fact that modern citizens desire freedom—understood as ample provision for all, guaranteed by social legislation—as much as they desire the liberties of the classical liberals, guaranteed by the limitation of the power of the state. Aron believed that the freedoms most threatened in his time were the freedoms upheld by liberals, such as freedom of speech, freedom of religion, and the right to property, as well as fundamental political liberties. But he could not agree with extreme free market liberalism, and he defended a social market welfare state—the synthesis of an essentially free enterprise economy with a welfare state—as the most exemplary compromise available. By this term he meant a state that does justice to the pluralistic aspirations and needs of a modern industrial society.

If Aron accepted without alarm the socialist aspects of peaceful modern societies, he also agreed with important conservative criticisms of democratic egalitarianism. For example, he recognized an irrepressible oligarchic element in all collective organizations. This element is a fundamental law of society ignored by many revolutionaries and dogmatic egalitarians. Aron encouraged a political moderation that respects the unavoidable tensions inherent in social life and recognizes obstacles to creating any purely egalitarian social order.

Toward the end of his life, particularly in *In Defense of Decadent Europe,* Aron's liberalism took on an increasingly neoconservative cast. Although reaffirming his essential philosophic position, Aron became increasingly concerned about the destructive consequences of doctrinaire egalitarianism—of utopian efforts to overcome or transform what he called biological and social nature. He believed that such egalitarianism leads to tyranny, not to equality or greater freedom. He also was concerned about the nihilistic implications of the thought of the 1960s, the hodgepodge of anarchism, socialism, and irrationalism represented by thinkers such as Michel Foucault and Jacques Derrida.

Finally, Aron became distressed by the movement toward social decadence, personal license, and civic indifference threatening the survival of the liberal democracies. He believed that liberal societies no longer appreciated the importance of institutions of authority and were incapable of resisting soft, humanitarian thinking. He worried about the decline of active citizenship in liberal societies. And he feared that liberal Europe was becoming less liberal and more democratic and decadent. Aron, however, refused to succumb to historical pessimism, the inverse of liberal or Marxist optimism. To the end he remained a friend of human liberty, properly understood. His thought is an intellectual antidote to any recurrence of the totalitarian temptation.

See also *Theory, Twentieth-century European.*

Daniel J. Mahoney

BIBLIOGRAPHY

Aron, Raymond. *Democracy and Totalitarianism.* Ann Arbor: University of Michigan Press, 1990.

———. *An Essay on Freedom.* New York: World, 1970.

———. *History, Truth, and Liberty.* Chicago: University of Chicago Press, 1985.

———. *In Defense of Decadent Europe.* Chicago: Regnery/Gateway, 1979.

———. *In Defense of Political Reason: Essays by Raymond Aron.* Edited by Daniel J. Mahoney. Lanham, Md.: Rowman and Littlefield, 1994.

———. *The Liberal Political Science of Raymond Aron: A Critical Introduction.* Lanham, Md.: Rowman and Littlefield, 1992.

Asia, Central

The collective name for the nations of Turkmenistan, Uzbekistan, Tajikistan, Kyrgyzstan, and Kazakhstan, which declared independence from the Soviet Union in 1991. The region is bounded on the north by Russia, on the west by the Caspian Sea, on the east by China, and on the south by Afghanistan and Iran.

Kazakhstan is by far the largest state, with 1,049,155 square miles. Its population is estimated to be 17 million, of whom about 41 percent are Kazakh and 38 percent are Russian. Uzbekistan, with about 20 million people (of whom 70 percent are Uzbek and 10 percent are Russian), is the most populous state. It has a territory of 186,400 square miles. Turkmenistan is about the same size, but with a population of only 3.8 million (of whom 70 percent are Turkmen, 10 percent are Uzbek, and 9 percent are Russian), it is the least populous state in the region. Kyrgyzstan is much smaller in area, with 76,640 square miles, and has a population of about 4.3 million, of whom about 54 percent are Kyrgyz, 20 percent are Russian, and 13 percent are Uzbek. Tajikistan—the smallest state, with 57,250 square miles—has a population of about 5.3 million, of whom 62 percent are Tajik, 23 percent are Uzbek, and 7 percent are Russian.

Historical Background

The peoples for whom the states are named have been established in the region for centuries. But the present states result from Soviet-era administrative divisions, which were designed both to create homelands and to make the states' independent existence impossible. As a

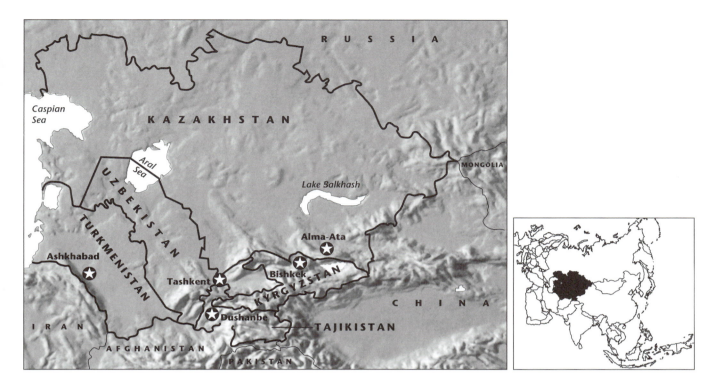

consequence, these new nations, and the region as a whole, face formidable impediments in the transition from dependency.

Central Asian peoples have been under Russian control for periods of approximately 100 years (Tajikistan, Turkmenistan, and parts of Uzbekistan) to 200 years (Kazakhstan), but they are very distinct from the Russians linguistically, culturally, and historically. All are of Sunni Muslim heritage, although they were converted to Islam at various times from the tenth to the eighteenth centuries. The Tajiks are Persian speakers, inheritors of cultures that have been in the region for millennia. The other four peoples are descendants of Turkic nomads who came to the area later; some, like the Kyrgyz, also have considerable infusions of Mongol culture.

In Soviet times (about 1920–1989) Central Asia was the most economically depressed and politically conservative area of the USSR. Most industry was administered from Moscow and staffed by Russians and other Europeans, whom the Soviet authorities imported in large numbers. These "stranded Russians" are now a significant problem in all the new Central Asian states.

Soviet policies encouraged the growth of large native administrations, which to a great extent were staffed by members of the old traditional elites. Thus large parts of traditional Central Asian society were virtually unaffected by Soviet power. As Soviet power has receded, these traditional elites have been content to part with communism but have shown no readiness to give up political power. One reason for Central Asia's political fealty to Moscow was that the region was tightly bound to Russia economically. Once the ties to Russia were severed or strained, the economies even of the areas richest in resources became depressed to the point of collapse.

The Struggle for Sovereignty

In the transition to nationhood (1989–1991), there was a groundswell of spontaneous or quasi-spontaneous mass political participation, usually stimulated by cultural issues. (The groundswell was much smaller in Central Asia than elsewhere in the Soviet Union, however.) Perhaps the two most common demands were to increase the role and status of the native languages and to rewrite the histories, so that conquest by Russian imperialists was no longer presented as a historically progressive act. Political activists, who early on began to call themselves democrats, were able to mobilize considerable support on these sorts of issues, some of which gelled into movements and political parties.

In Uzbekistan, language-rights demonstrations in 1989 spawned Birlik (Unity), which adopted a nationalist, pro-democratic platform that demanded sovereignty but stopped short of calling for secession. This group, and its women's auxiliary, participated widely in the republic's 1990 parliamentary elections. Ten of the candidates whom the Unity Party endorsed were elected, although all ten later disavowed the connection. In 1991, at the time of independence, the Unity Party claimed about 400,000 members. The other large Uzbek democratic party, Erk (Will), began when Unity cofounders Abdurakhim Pulatov and Muhammad Solikh disagreed and Solikh left to found his own pro-democratic party. Solikh ran for president in 1991. Although soundly defeated by Islam Karimov, whom Moscow had appointed as party and republic leader in 1989, Solikh and his campaign gave Uzbekistan one of only two contested presidential elections in the region.

The other contested election took place in Tajikistan, where two candidates, Davla Koudonazarov and Rakhman Nabiyev, contested the seat of Moscow appointee Khakhor Makhkamov, whom popular demonstrations had pushed from power in September 1991. The years 1989–1991 were also a period of mass political participation in Tajikistan, but the focus was regional and ethnic from the beginning. Because the republic was made up of disparate groups of peoples who had different histories, cultures, and even languages, and because it had a long history of rule by clans from one region, it was unstable well before the Soviet Union broke up. The three major parties that began to coalesce had different orientations, but they also had regional and clan underpinnings. The Democratic Party and Rastokhez (Renaissance) were secular parties, while the Islamic Renaissance Party was more religiously oriented. Nabiyev, a political boss from the era of Leonid Brezhnev whom Mikhail Gorbachev had dismissed, put together a coalition of democrats and the religious parties to come back to power, staving off a strong showing by Koudonazarov, who had the backing of democrats in Moscow.

In Kazakhstan the first political movement was ecological rather than national. Prominent Kazakh poet Olzhas Suleimenov organized the Nevada-Semipalatinsk movement to press for the end of the testing of Soviet nuclear weapons in the republic, a practice that had been devastating to the population and the environment. That movement was multiethnic, mobilizing large numbers of Russians and Kazakhs. So far it is the only group that has been able to appeal to both nationalities. Because its population is about equally Kazakh and Russian, Kazakhstan has attempted to inhibit the growth of nationalist parties. Nev-

ertheless, the period 1989–1991 saw the emergence of several Kazakh movements. These include Azat (Freedom), the Republican Party, the Civil Movement, and Zheltoksan (December). The most nationalist of the groups is Alash, named for the legendary founder of the Kazakh people, which also calls for a greater role for Islam. The Russians also spawned nationalist movements—Harmony, Unity, and Democratic Progress—as did the Cossacks, the descendants of imperial border guards, who see themselves as a separate nationality, although the Kazakhs regard them as Russians.

In Kyrgyzstan democratic parties appeared in society and within the Communist Party. The former were motivated by language issues and economic problems, while the latter were more concerned with issues of power. Ashar (Help) grew out of groups who were spontaneously seizing land. Ethnic riots in the republic's south in 1990 led to political crisis, during which a breakaway faction of the party formed Erkin (Freedom), which later became the parent party of the Kyrgyzstan Democratic Movement. In October 1990 the Democratic Movement succeeded in blocking the presidential aspirations of Moscow appointee Absamat Masaliyev and elected instead Askar Akayev, thus making Kyrgyzstan the first Soviet republic to select its own leader.

Independent but Not Democratic

Turkmenistan was the only exception to the general rising tide of pre-independence political participation. Appointed as republic leader by Gorbachev in 1985, Sapamurad Niyazov successfully controlled political participation in his republic. The first organizational meeting for the nationalist group Azy-birlik (Unity) was not held until March 1991, and it was attended by no more than twenty people. Since independence, even that degree of democracy has disappeared. Niyazov, who has begun calling himself Turkmenbashi, or "head of the Turkmen," has been elected president for life and has installed his own personality cult. There is little evidence, however, of any real opposition to Niyazov in this sparsely populated, oil-rich state. International human rights activists have learned of only four Turkmen "democrats," all of whom have disappeared.

Democracy has fared no better in Uzbekistan since independence. The Karimov government has suppressed the Unity and Will Parties with ruthless efficiency. Many of the leaders of the democratic groups were beaten or jailed, and all have been forced into exile. There is some effort to sustain a pro-democracy movement from abroad but without visible success.

The general hostility to broader political participation in Central Asia stems in part from the example of Tajikistan, which has essentially collapsed as a state. The Nabiyev coalition proved short lived. It was replaced in April 1992 by the government of Akbarsho Iskandarov, which included members of the Islamic Renaissance Party. Fears of "Islamification" led Russia and Uzbekistan in October 1992 to support the attempt by Speaker of the Parliament Imamali Rakhmanov to take power. This intervention precipitated a civil war that has spread to destabilize neighboring Afghanistan. The Rakhmanov government, with Uzbek and Russian support, has jailed or killed the political opposition within the territory it controls, but large portions of this mountainous, extremely poor nation remain beyond Rakhmanov's reach.

Relative Successes of Democracy

The only two Central Asian nations in which democracy may be said to be making some headway are Kazakhstan and Kyrgyzstan. All the Central Asian states have adopted post-Soviet constitutions, but only in these two countries is some serious effort being made to observe the rule of constitutional law.

After independence there was strong support for Akayev in Kyrgyzstan, but the rapidly deteriorating economy and growing evidence of favoritism and nepotism have soured relations between the democrats and the government. Akayev conducted a costly plebiscite on his presidency in January 1994, from which he secured a Soviet-style approval rating of 99 percent. Since then the democrats have complained of increasing harassment. Antidemocratic steps included the dissolution of the parliament and the closing of opposition newspapers in September 1994. Later in 1994, in violation of the constitution, a referendum was called on modifications to the constitution proposed by the president. The changes were ratified.

Demography and democracy work against each other in Kazakhstan. Consequently, the government maintains strict controls on the media and on the growth of political parties. Unlike the other Central Asian republics, though, Kazakhstan allows parties to function so long as they are not monoethnic and can demonstrate support across most of the state's huge territory. In practice, most postindependence parties have been government sponsored, due to President Nursultan Nazarbayev's search for a function-al (not ideological) replacement for the old Communist Party.

Because the country's constitution does not allow the president to hold office in other civic organizations, including parties, Nazarbayev has sponsored but not led these parties. The first was the Socialist Party, which initially inherited much of the Communist Party membership. The Congress Party was founded in 1992 by poets Suleimenov and Mukhtar Shakhanov, who at the time were pro-Nazarbayev. When that party remained small and unpopular, a Union of National Unity for Kazakhstan was formed but this too has been a disappointment. Nazarbayev's desire to make the Union of National Unity the dominant political force in the republic led to considerable manipulation of the March 1994 parliamentary elections. Stringent registration requirements, and the rigid, sometimes fraudulent, elimination of some independent candidates, combined to deny seats in the new parliament to strong nationalists from both ethnic groups.

What may spell trouble for the future is that Kazakhs are heavily overrepresented in the new parliament, while Russians are badly underrepresented. The Russians of Kazakhstan see the Kazakhs as an obvious threat, which will make the further democratization of Kazakhstan hazardous—and therefore unlikely. At the same time, though, the Russians see themselves as excluded from the political process, with nowhere except Russia to address their grievances.

Russia has tried to promote a policy of dual citizenship for Russians throughout Central Asia, but only Turkmenistan has agreed. Russian populations in Uzbekistan and Kyrgyzstan are small enough that emigration may solve the problem. In Kazakhstan, however, Russians constitute far too large a percentage of the republic's population to be ignored politically and are far too numerous to be absorbed into Russia proper. For that reason Russia will remain actively interested in Kazakhstan's politics, and intervention will be a constant possibility.

The biggest obstacle to the development of democracy in the region, though, is the general economic decline following independence. Although the elites of the Soviet era have managed to retain and even enlarge their privileges, life for the bulk of the population has worsened dramatically everywhere. The gap has sharpened antagonisms, so the compromises that are necessary for successful democratization have become much more difficult to design. The specter of Tajikistan's failure has led even the most democratically inclined of the present rulers, Nazarbayev in

Kazakhstan and Akayev in Kyrgyzstan, to see the preservation of stability as more important than democratization.

See also *Kyrgyzstan; Russia, Post-Soviet; Russia, Pre-Soviet; Union of Soviet Socialist Republics.*

Martha Brill Olcott

BIBLIOGRAPHY

Allworth, Edward A. *The Modern Uzbeks.* Stanford, Calif.: Hoover Institution Press, 1990.

Central Asia. Special issue of *Current History* (April 1994).

Fierman, William, ed. *Soviet Central Asia: The Failed Transformation.* Boulder, Colo.: Westview Press, 1991.

Mandelbaum, Michael, ed. *Central Asia and the World.* New York: Council on Foreign Relations Press, 1994.

Olcott, Martha Brill. "Central Asia's Catapult to Independence." *Foreign Affairs* (summer 1992): 108–130.

———. *The Kazakhs.* Stanford, Calif.: Hoover Institution Press, 1987.

Poliakov, Sergei P. *Everyday Islam: Religion and Tradition in Rural Central Asia.* Armonk, N.Y.: M. E. Sharpe, 1992.

Asia, Southeast

The region that encompasses the mainland or island nations of Brunei, Burma (Myanmar), Cambodia, Indonesia, Laos, Malaysia, the Philippines, Singapore, Thailand, and Vietnam. The number and variety of countries in Southeast Asia make it the most diverse region in Asia.

Culturally, the region is a kaleidoscope. In eight of Southeast Asia's ten states the most numerous ethnic community is different racially or linguistically from its counterpart in every other country in the region. (The exceptions are Brunei and Malaysia, both of which have Malay majorities.) In nine of the ten states the main religion—Islam, Theravada Buddhism, Mahayana Buddhism, Roman Catholicism, or Confucianism—is different from the main religion in at least one of its neighboring Southeast Asian states. (The exception is Burma, which shares Theravada Buddhism with its neighbors Laos and Thailand.)

Historically, different parts of the region have been influenced in different ways by a variety of outside cultures and powers. In religion, language, and the arts, legacies of Indian civilization can be found throughout Southeast Asia. Late in the second century B.C., the people of what is now Vietnam fell under Chinese suzerainty for about a thousand years. In the sixteenth century Spain Catholicized and colonized the Philippines. In the nineteenth century Britain acquired the territories that are now Brunei, Burma, Malaysia, and Singapore, while Vietnam, Cambodia, and Laos fell to the French. The Portuguese, the first Westerners to seize land in Southeast Asia, were the last to leave, abandoning East Timor, the sole remaining colony in the region, in 1975. Thailand, which was useful to the British and the French as a buffer between their Southeast Asian possessions, avoided colonization altogether.

Economically, as well, the Southeast Asian nations differ greatly. They include a tiny city-state specializing in services and manufacturing (Singapore); an even less populous enclave almost wholly dependent on oil and gas revenues (Brunei); small and still overwhelmingly agricultural countries (Cambodia, Laos); larger agricultural and manufacturing economies (the Philippines, Thailand); and the diverse and fourth most populous country in the world, Indonesia. Ranked by their per capita incomes in 1991, the nations of Southeast Asia ranged from very wealthy (Singapore, $13,900; Brunei, $8,800) to extremely poor (Laos, $220; Cambodia, $130). Economic performances also varied greatly; estimated rates of real growth in gross domestic product in 1992 ran from 8.0 percent (Malaysia) and 7.4 percent (Thailand) to 0.0 percent (the Philippines) and −1.0 percent (Burma). In the early 1990s these economies also differed in the extent to which their domestic markets were free from government intervention and protected from foreign competition, though all were more or less open to foreign investment.

Politically, nine different types of regimes were represented in Southeast Asia in the mid-1990s. These were an unconstitutional military junta (Burma); an absolute monarchy without parties or elections (Brunei); a nascent constitutional monarchy with two prime ministers (Cambodia); a military-influenced, multiparty, parliamentary-democratic constitutional monarchy (Thailand); a one-party-dominant parliamentary democracy under a rotating monarchy (Malaysia); a one-party-dominant parliamentary democracy with a directly elected president (Singapore); a military-dominant presidential autocracy with sponsored parties and elections (Indonesia); an American-style presidential-legislative democracy (Philippines); and two formally communist single-party states (Laos, Vietnam).

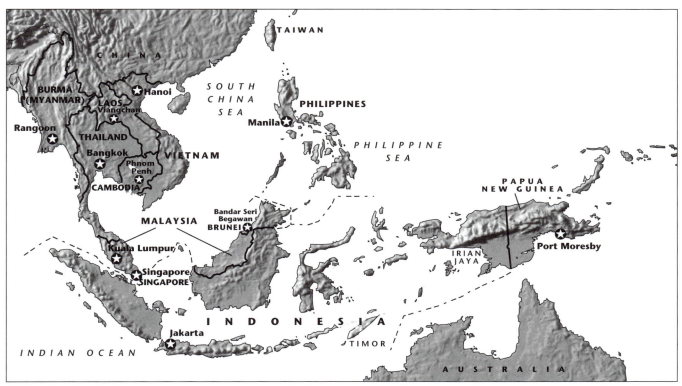

Levels of Growth and Freedom

According to the quantitative rankings released annually by Freedom House, a New York–based organization that monitors changing levels of freedom around the world, Southeast Asia was the least free region in Asia in the early 1990s. If Freedom House's country ratings for 1993 (drawn from *Freedom in the World,* 1994) are grouped and averaged for each of the four main parts of Asia, the results are these: with a perfect score of 1.0, Australasia (Australia, New Zealand) was Asia's only "free" region. "Partly free" were North Asia (China, Japan, Mongolia, North Korea, Russia, South Korea, Taiwan) with a score of 3.9 and South Asia (Bangladesh, Bhutan, India, Maldives, Nepal, Pakistan, Sri Lanka) with a score of 4.6. Southeast Asia, at 5.5, was "not free" by Freedom House's standards.

The location of Australia and New Zealand at the "freest" end of this ranking suggests an explanation: the higher the per capita income of a country, the "freer" that country is likely to be. Applied to three of the four Asian regions (Australasia, North Asia, and South Asia), this hypothesis works well. Ranked in order from freest to least free in 1993, Australasia, North Asia, and South Asia had levels of average real GDP per capita purchasing power parities of $14,766, $6,401, and $1,304, respectively, in 1991. Yet Southeast Asia, distinctly the "least free" region, registered a mean income level ($4,845) much higher than South Asia and not far below that of North Asia. The idea that freedom is a function of relative income levels also does not fare well in a comparison among Southeast Asian countries. Across the ten nations, the two variables are unrelated.

Faced with this negative result, one may question the dependent variable, freedom. But although freedom and democracy are not the same thing, the definition of "freedom" used by Freedom House has advantages in the present context. The definition incorporates twenty-two rights and liberties that are comprehensive and explicitly political, or have clear political implications, and that refer not to a country's constitution or formal regime but to actually prevailing conditions. The Philippines, for example, is a democracy in the legal-institutional meaning of the term. But the Freedom House rating of the Philippines as only "partly free" takes into account the actual operation of a full range of politically relevant rights and liberties. The Freedom House definition of "freedom," however, is imbued with the idea of a liberal democracy centered on the individual rather than on the group or community.

One could use economic growth rather than income level as the independent variable, arguing that even if wealthier polities are not consistently more democratic than poorer ones, rapidly growing ones ought to be more democratic than slowly growing ones. But there is no correlation across the ten Southeast Asian states between the rate of growth in GDP in 1992 and the level of freedom in 1993.

This independent variable may cover too short a time. Perhaps only the accumulated effects of economic growth over a period of years could be expected to differentiate the economy, enlarge the middle class, and open the political system to rising social pluralism. Applied to Southeast Asia, an independent variable showing economic growth over time does indicate that prolonged economic development encourages democracy, but mainly for places that have neither: Burma and Indochina (Cambodia, Laos, Vietnam). In these countries one may at least believe that future development will lead to democratization.

Poor and missing data make comparisons of Burma, Cambodia, Laos, and Vietnam difficult. But clearly they did regress, stagnate, or grow very little in the decades before 1993. In that year three of the four were "not free" by Freedom House's definition, and the one exception, "partly free" Cambodia, had only just been upgraded to reflect the multiparty elections held there in May. Indochina had been under Leninist dictatorships since 1975, while the military autocracy in Burma had lasted even longer, since 1962. In all of Southeast Asia, for 1993, Vietnam and Burma (both 7.0), and Laos, Indonesia, and Brunei (all 6.5) were rated "not free." Singapore (5.0), Malaysia and Cambodia (both 4.5), Thailand (4.0), and the Philippines (3.5) were labeled "partly free."

If the cases of Burma and Indochina support the idea that persisting economic stagnation inhibits democracy, however, Singapore, Indonesia, Thailand, Malaysia, and the Philippines do not show any correlation between sustained economic growth and democratization. Despite a stunning 6.5 percent average annual gain in gross national product per person from 1965 to 1990, Singapore had the second worst freedom score in the group for 1993. Indonesia, Thailand, and Malaysia also did well economically—

their respective rates of growth were 4.5, 4.4, and 4.0 percent—but in 1993 Indonesia was "not free," while Malaysia and Thailand were only "partly free." Almost a mirror image of Singapore was the Philippines, which had by far the worst economic performance in 1965–1990—a mere 1.3 percent growth per capita per year—yet achieved the highest freedom rating of any state in Southeast Asia in 1993.

Roughly speaking, for these five countries, the greater their economic growth, the less freedom their citizens enjoyed. If comparable data were available for Brunei, they might reinforce this finding. Brunei's oil-based economy surely grew rapidly during the petroleum industry boom of the 1970s, and the country still lacks political freedom. Brunei did suffer from falling oil prices in the 1980s, however, and it did not become independent from Great Britain until 1984.

Histories of Growth and Freedom

Considered historically, the proposition that a high or rising national income enlarges freedom and democracy does not even work very satisfactorily for that part of Southeast Asia where poverty has long coexisted with autocracy: Burma and Indochina. The authoritarian pasts of these four countries illustrate less the power of economics to determine politics than the autonomous influence of political variables, including violence, organization, and ideology.

Burma's civil wars have been more numerous and longer lasting than those of any other Southeast Asian state. The country gained its independence from Britain in January 1948. Three months later local communists revolted; two army battalions joined them. Despite constitutional safeguards for Burma's many ethnoregional minorities—in the early 1990s only 68 percent of all Burmese were ethnically Burman—the new government discriminated in favor of the Burman majority. In 1949 a revolt among the Christianized Karen ethnic group—Burmans are largely Buddhist—was strengthened by the defection of three battalions of Karen troops. Other ethnic groups also took up arms against the central government, which managed to avoid defeat in part because its many antagonists tended also to fight each other. From the late 1940s through the early 1990s, while the extent, severity, parties, and outcomes of these conflicts fluctuated, the general pattern—a debilitating welter of insurgencies—endured.

In Vietnam, in December 1946 the Viet Minh (Vietnamese Independence League) under Ho Chi Minh began fighting the effort by the French to regain control over their former colony. This First Indochina War ended in a French military defeat at Dien Bien Phu, a negotiated division of Vietnam at the seventeenth parallel in 1954, and the consolidation of a communist-ruled Democratic Republic of Vietnam north of that line. But within five years warfare resumed in the south, between the U.S.-backed state of Vietnam and its communist opponents. In 1975, following the withdrawal of U.S. forces and the deaths of well over one million Vietnamese, the communists won this Second Indochina War as well. A scant three years later Vietnam invaded and occupied Cambodia. Although Vietnam announced in 1989 that it had withdrawn its troops from Cambodia, the Cambodian core of this Third Indochina War was still in progress in the early 1990s. This summary does not cover the death toll in Cambodia and Laos from the First and Second Indochina Wars, the 1979 Sino-Vietnamese border war, or the deaths of up to one million Khmers under Pol Pot's reign of terror in Cambodia in 1975–1978.

Alongside endemic violence, centralized organization and socialist ideology further stymied whatever potential these countries may have had to become liberal democracies. Burma's military regime, for example, in power since Gen. Ne Win's coup in 1962, headed a one-party state (1964–1988) that badly mismanaged the economy in the name of a "Burmese way to socialism."

In Cambodia in the 1960s Prince Norodom Sihanouk advocated "royal Buddhist socialism." Political rivalries and a local communist revolt led Sihanouk to assume special powers in 1967, only to be ousted three years later in a military coup that plunged the country into civil war. In 1975 Pol Pot's Maoist-Leninist communists won that struggle. They erected a Leninist state with a fanatically anticapitalist agrarian ideology and set about destroying what urban educated class there was. The regime imposed on Cambodia by its Vietnamese invaders in 1979, though much less brutal and more pragmatic than Pol Pot's had been, brooked no opposition to the rule of its own Leninist party. Neither did its neighbor regimes in the Socialist Republic of Vietnam and the Lao People's Democratic Republic.

In Burma and Indochina, poverty alone cannot explain authoritarianism. Autocracy was at least as responsible for prolonging poverty as poverty was for prolonging autocracy. Only in the 1980s and early 1990s, when these began to open up and grow, was it possible to explore the positive side of the economic argument for democracy: not that deprivation and stagnation retard democracy but that development induces it.

Economic and Political Reforms

In Indochina market-oriented economic reforms were not set in motion by any renunciation of Marxism and conversion to capitalism. Rather, they arose from a pragmatic awareness that policies hostile to the private sector had failed to bring about desired growth. Along with that narrowly economic rationale came the idea that in politics the Leninist state, which had kept its rulers in power, was not broken and did not need fixing. Indeed, if economic liberalization could revive the economy, that would strengthen the authoritarian state and eliminate the need for significantly liberalizing political reforms and the instabilities they might trigger. In countries that had already demonstrated the relative autonomy of political elites and ideas, the justification of economic reform as a way of avoiding political reform did not augur well for democratization.

The Laotian case is of particular interest because its leaders preceded their counterparts in Burma, Cambodia, and Vietnam down the path of economic reform. In Laos the political consequences of economic loosening had more time to appear. In 1979 plummeting production and peasant unrest—brought on by earlier decisions to nationalize industry, control markets, and collectivize agriculture—obliged Laotian communist leaders to acknowledge a capitalist component within the national economy. Soon thereafter noncommunist technocrats were appointed to the government to help improve its efficiency. Orthodox socialist policies were modestly relaxed in the 1980s, and the economy revived just enough to embolden pragmatists within the ruling Lao People's Revolutionary Party (LPRP) to continue the reform process. By 1988 Laos had begun actively encouraging foreign investment and selectively reprivatizing nationalized firms.

At its Fifth Congress in 1991, a year in which real gross domestic product grew a respectable 5.0 percent, the LPRP reaffirmed its commitment to market principles. But the constitution finally adopted that same year, while acknowledging private ownership rights in the economy, reaffirmed the leading role of the LPRP. In 1992 three former officials accused of advocating a multiparty system were sentenced to fourteen-year prison terms. If the charges were true, they suggested that economic reform and growth were motivating some Laotians to press for political pluralism, which the regime was not ready to grant.

Short of democratization, three kinds of political reform can be observed in Laos and Vietnam: those concerning lawmaking, the electoral process, and the government. The writing and ratifying of constitutions and the specification of laws created a basis of authority other than that of the communist party. The process of lawmaking itself entailed the legitimate expression of disagreements. Vietnam's hotly debated 1992 constitution, for example, stated that the ruling Communist Party of Vietnam (CPV) was not above the law. Because Laos had had no constitution since 1975, the adoption of one in 1991 could be understood as limiting, at least in principle, the LPRP's freedom of action. But in both countries it proved difficult to implement written laws against the wishes of party conservatives.

In Laos (1988–1989) and Vietnam (1989–1992) elections were held in stages from local to national levels. For the first time in Vietnam candidates who were not CPV members were permitted to run. Market-minded leaders hoped in this way to bypass party hard-liners and create from the bottom up a constituency for economic reform. Often, however, the victors were local bosses more interested in payoffs than in reforms. For this reason, far from becoming the natural allies of decentralization, some reformist leaders favored tighter central control. The elections did not threaten party rule. Roughly one-tenth of the 601 candidates who contested the Vietnamese National Assembly's 395 seats in 1992 did not belong to the CPV, but only two of them were truly independent, and they both lost.

Liberal Democracy?

In the early 1990s the prospects for liberal democracy in Southeast Asia were not encouraging. In Cambodia the demand for the elections that were finally held in May 1993 arose not from the Khmer people but from international negotiations to end the Third Indochina War. Although the balloting succeeded in isolating Pol Pot's followers, the Khmer Rouge, who had boycotted it, it also resulted in a divided government whose two prime ministers were still unable to defeat the Khmer Rouge. In Burma the military leaders tolerated a free election in 1990 that rejected them overwhelmingly; they then annulled it and remained in power. In Thailand the promise of 1992, a banner year for democratization, faded into wrangling over constitutional amendments. In Indonesia labor unrest threatened to invite a crackdown by the armed forces, already anxious over the succession to President Suharto.

In Malaysia and Singapore years of rapid economic growth, far from bringing significant political liberalization, enabled the existing democracies to become even more institutionalized. By the early 1990s the long-awaited democratizing effect of Bruneian students returning from the West with Western ideas had not materialized.

As for the Philippines, that formally liberal democracy was in practice burdened with cronyism, venal elites, and stalemated institutions ill suited to achieving the rates of economic growth enjoyed by its more overtly authoritarian neighbors. Nevertheless, the economy improved in 1993. In 1994 a coalition of the governing party with its chief opposition in the Philippine Senate reduced the pluralism of party politics. Yet the move strengthened the hand of the government to make the difficult decisions necessary for further economic growth.

All this does not mean that democracy has no future in Southeast Asia. Rather, one may expect that diversity will probably continue to characterize the region's polities—including effective autocracies and illiberal democracies. In the long run, economic development could well liberalize these relatively closed polities. But in the near term, one should not overestimate the prospects for liberal democracy through economic growth in Southeast Asia.

See also *Burma; Dominant party democracies in Asia; Indonesia; Malaysia; Philippines; Singapore; Thailand.*

Donald K. Emmerson

BIBLIOGRAPHY

Chan Heng Chee. "Evolution and Implementation: An Asian Perspective." In *Democracy and Capitalism: Asian and American Perspectives*, edited by Robert Bartley, Chan Heng Chee, Samuel Huntington, and Shijuro Ogata. Singapore: Institute of Southeast Asian Studies, 1993.

Crouch, Harold A. *Economic Change, Social Structure, and the Political System in Southeast Asia.* Singapore: Institute of Southeast Asian Studies, 1985.

Diamond, Larry, Juan J. Linz, and Seymour Martin Lipset, eds. *Democracy in Developing Countries: Asia.* Boulder, Colo.: Lynne Rienner; London: Adamantine Press, 1989.

Emmerson, Donald K. "Walking on Two Legs: Polity and Economy in the ASEAN Countries." In *Asia in the 1990s: American and Soviet Perspectives*, edited by Robert A. Scalapino and Gennady I. Chufrin. Berkeley: University of California, Institute of East Asian Studies, 1991.

Hewison, Kevin, Richard Robison, and Garry Rodan, eds. *Southeast Asia in the 1990s: Authoritarianism, Democracy, and Capitalism.* St. Leonard's, Australia: Allen and Unwin, 1993.

Ljunggren, Börje, ed. *The Challenge of Reform in Indochina.* Cambridge, Mass.: Harvard Institute for International Development; London: Harvard University Press, 1993.

Neher, Clark D. "Democratization in Southeast Asia." *Asian Affairs: An American Review* 18 (fall 1991): 139–152.

Taylor, Robert, ed. *Elections in Southeast Asia.* Washington, D.C.: Woodrow Wilson International Center for Scholars, forthcoming.

Thayer, Carl, and David Marr, eds. *Vietnam and the Rule of Law.* Canberra: Australian National University, Research School of Pacific Studies, 1993.

Tønnesson, Stein. *Democracy in Vietnam?* Copenhagen: Nordic Institute of Asian Studies, 1993.

Assembly, Freedom of

See *Freedom of assembly*

Associations

Voluntary organizations created by private citizens to pursue a shared interest or activity. Associations are a significant feature of all liberal democratic societies with market economies. In such societies, voluntary associations independent of the state tend both to be numerous and to have a great diversity of organizational structures and purposes. Associations vary from highly organized bodies like major interest groups or large charities to smaller and relatively informal groupings like social and sports clubs. The term *associationalism* describes a body of thought in which voluntary organizations, rather than the state, are the organizing principle of democratic society.

The relationship between such associations and democracy has been seen differently in three distinct bodies of political theory. *Radical majoritarian democratic theory* has tended to see associations as a threat to political unity. In *liberal democratic theory,* associations are seen as providing additional support for representative democracy and political pluralism. *Associationalist theories of democracy* have seen such voluntary organizations as the main way in which the affairs of a free society should be conducted.

Negative and Positive Views of Associations

Radical majoritarian democrats, such as Jean-Jacques Rousseau, the eighteenth-century French political thinker, and those who have followed in his tradition, had a negative view of voluntary associations. They regarded them as dangers to democracy to the extent that they might frustrate or compromise the will of the people as expressed in its majority decisions. By consolidating particular interests, associations can divide the majority and distract the people from civic virtue and loyalty to the state. Proponents of such views fear that organizations that mediate between the state and the individual will create contrary loyalties and undermine the homogeneity of interests necessary for a true majoritarian democracy.

Modern liberal democratic theory was in large measure developed in direct opposition to such majoritarian views, in particular in response to the excesses of Rousseau's self-professed disciples during the French Revolution. Liberalism rejected simple majoritarianism, emphasizing the pluralism of modern societies as essential to a viable democracy. Liberal political theory has from its inception regarded voluntarily formed associations as an essential complement to the formal political institutions of representative democracy, such as political parties, legislatures, and popularly elected executives. The freedom of citizens to organize in civil society provides the basis for that plurality of interests and opinions that makes multiparty democracy possible and sustainable. A society composed of active, independent, and organized citizens is also a guarantee that government will not overstep its proper limits, intruding on the powers and liberties that individuals should enjoy without state interference.

The founders of liberal political theory in the eighteenth and nineteenth centuries—James Madison, Benjamin Constant de Rebecque, Alexis de Tocqueville, and John Stuart Mill—were all concerned that the participation of the masses in politics and the influence of ideas like Rousseau's would lead to the tyranny of the majority and the suppression of minority dissent. They saw in an open commercial society and in the freedom to form associations independent of the state the main means to prevent tyranny by the majority. Associations were a school for individual independence and a support for a variety of opinions.

Tocqueville, a nineteenth-century French aristocrat and conservative politician who wrote his most important work, *Democracy in America* (1835–1840), after a visit to the United States, remarked on the strength of Americans' willingness to organize their affairs by voluntary rather than by state action. He saw associations as a way of preserving liberty in a mass democracy and diversity in a highly egalitarian society.

Modern mainstream liberal political theory and pluralist political science has continued to see such voluntary bodies in this way, terming them *secondary associations,* the role of which is to sustain and reinforce freedom in the primary political association, the state. Centralized, dictatorial, and ideologically motivated regimes such as those of Adolf Hitler and Joseph Stalin, on the other hand, have sought to bring all social life under their control, in part by curbing the freedom of independent secondary associations. Bodies such as interest groups, labor unions, and sports clubs were controlled by the state in Hitler's Germany and Stalin's Russia; they became instruments for promoting the official ideology and mobilizing the population to meet the goals of the regime.

Foundations of Associationalism

For much of this century, politics has taken the form of a conflict between liberal democracy and the authoritarian ideologies of the extreme left and right, with their distinctive views on the role of associations in political life. But there have been other ways of conceiving the democratic contribution of associations, in particular the varied currents of thought that could be labeled "associationalist." Associationalist theories, which developed from the middle of the nineteenth century onward, gave rise to a variety of social and political movements that were fashionable in the early twentieth century before falling into a period of decline and neglect. They are now gradually becoming influential again. The remainder of this article will be devoted to the ideas and history of this political doctrine.

Associationalism gives voluntary organizations, rather than the state, the primary place in the organization of a democratic society. In their time, such ideas challenged the conventional liberal view of political life, in which voluntary associations were secondary, if vitally important, means of ensuring pluralism within the political system. Liberals accepted the notion of the state as "sovereign" and the nation-state as the primary organization in the community. Associationalists did not. Indeed, the one thing they had in common with liberals was the fear of excessive power wielded by the state over society. They charged liberals with inconsistency for believing that a strong central government was compatible with freedom. Unlike critics of liberal democracy of the extreme left and right, they were libertarians, not authoritarians. Unlike anarchists, they accepted the need for some kind of organized government, although they preferred a decentralized system with limited powers.

Associationalists tended to believe that voluntary associations should take over the running of most social affairs. Such organizations should be self-governing and controlled by their members. The state was to be, at best, a residual agency, responsible for those aspects of law and order that associations could not provide for themselves. Associationalists generally favored extensive decentralization of authority, preferring public government to be small in scale and to have strictly limited powers. Some associationalists were close to anarchism, others were anticollectivist socialists, others were conservatives opposed to state ownership, and still others were backward-looking utopians, seeking to reconstruct society by returning to such institutions of the Middle Ages as the craft and trade guilds.

The several distinct intellectual sources of associationalism never coalesced to form a single ideology or unified political movement. The easiest way to approach this diversity is to examine its many strands. It will then be possible to explain why associationalism never became a mainstream political doctrine like liberalism or socialism, and to consider why it may enjoy a new period of influence in the future.

Associationalist Theorists and Movements

The ideologues of the Cooperative Movement advocated and tried to practice cooperative production and distribution. The ideal was a self-regulating community based on common ownership and shared wealth. Two nineteenth-century Englishmen, Robert Owen and George Jacob Holyoake, were the movement's leading thinkers. Owen in particular was active in the first part of the century in creating cooperative communities in both Britain and the United States. Cooperatives have survived the failure of such radical utopian schemes, enjoying a limited measure of success as an alternative to the conventional commercial firm, rather than as a full-fledged social and political community. Cooperatives remain significant in the retail sector in Britain, in agricultural marketing in

France and Italy, and in industrial production, as in the Mondragon organization in Spain.

The French mutualist-socialist tradition was inspired by Pierre-Joseph Proudhon. Proudhon was not, as is often thought, an anarchist. His *Principle of Federation* (1863) shows his concern to develop an alternative theory of government. Proudhon advocated a decentralized economy based on nonprofit principles. Production was to be organized either by self-governing groups of artisans or by cooperatives. The financial system was to avoid rent and interest and was to be based on mutual institutions, such as credit unions. The political system was to be decentralized and based on the principle of federation; power would flow from the bottom up, controlled by democratic local authorities. Political institutions above the local level were to have strictly limited purposes and powers. Proudhon believed strongly in voluntarism as a principle of social action and rejected coercion as the basis for obedience to authority.

The German legal historian Otto von Gierke's most influential work was a massive history of the law and political theory of associations. He produced his four-volume *Das Deutsche Genossenschaftsrecht* (The German Law of Fellowship) over a period of four decades (1868–1913). He noted that, before the creation of the modern sovereign state in Europe in the sixteenth century, power had been dispersed among many different bodies. Authority was polycentric: overlapping powers could be found in the same territory. In particular, associations such as the craft and trade guilds had a major role in the government of their members' lives as well as their business affairs.

The English theorists of the plural state, including the eminent legal historian Frederick William Maitland and the theologian and historian of political thought John Neville Figgis were greatly influenced by Gierke. (Maitland translated Gierke's work.) Figgis (in *Churches in the Modern State,* 1913) argued strongly against the view that associations exist only because the state has permitted them to do so and with only such powers as it has given them in law. He held that this view threatened the freedom of such voluntary bodies to develop according to the wishes of their members. He noted the anticlerical attacks on the Catholic Church in Germany and France, and the 1903 case of the Free Church of Scotland, in which the wishes of the vast majority of the church's members were overruled by the courts. He was also concerned about the threat to English trade unions from the courts. Figgis argued that the claims of the state to sovereignty were unsustainable and a threat to liberty. He argued further that although a minimum of government is necessary to law and order, the centralization and concentration of power in the state ought to be reduced, and voluntary bodies should assume a greater role in running the affairs of society.

Perhaps the most sophisticated associationalist thinkers were the English anticollectivist socialists, George Douglas Howard Cole and Harold Laski. Both were greatly influenced by Figgis. Cole was the leading theorist of guild socialism, a doctrine that sought a third way between state ownership and the free market. In *Guild Socialism Re-Stated* (1920), he advocated a system of production based on cooperatively controlled enterprises. The activities of those enterprises were to be coordinated by national guilds for each major industry, and all the guilds were to participate in a system of economic governance by joint decision at the national level. Consumer and other public interests were to be protected by a decentralized state parallel to this system. Guild Socialist ideas were influential in Britain immediately after World War I.

At an early stage of his thinking, Laski too favored decentralization and the democratic self-government of industry. He advocated that state authority should be pluralized both territorially, into the smallest units compatible with good administration, and by social function. Thus institutions such as the national railways should become democratically self-governing bodies.

The French sociologist Emile Durkheim can be seen as having certain ideas in common with the associationalists. He argued (in *Professional Ethics and Civic Morals,* 1957) that political democracy and the market system were not in themselves sufficient to ensure the effective working of modern societies. The social conflicts resulting from these systems were exploited by the socialists. In order to forestall the danger to liberty represented by state socialism, institutions of mediation between the state and the individual were needed. The major occupational groups needed to be brought into association with one another and into partnership with the state in order to coordinate economic activity and prevent unorganized markets from undermining the social fabric. Durkheim contended that representative democracy had to be supplemented by the direct representation of social interests through their organizations. He was thus one of the main intellectual advocates of *corporatism.*

Like Durkheim, many other political thinkers in the late nineteenth and early twentieth centuries in France and Germany advocated versions of corporatism. Some advocated—for pragmatic reasons of economic efficiency—greater coordination of the capitalist system through collaboration among industry, labor, and the state. Others wanted to replace the capitalist system and the free market with a regulated economy modeled on the medieval guild system, in which indirect representation through guilds or corporations would be substituted for voting by individuals. Such conservative corporatists tended to differ from the associationalists in that they gave less attention to the voluntary nature of organizations and to democracy within them.

Loss of Influence

Associationalist ideas were most influential between the mid-nineteenth century and the middle of the 1920s, but they failed to displace the major competing ideologies of liberalism and socialism. To a great extent they failed because they were out of joint with the times. Associationalists favored weakening and decentralizing the state when many saw strong central government as necessary to protect countries against foreign enemies and internal social conflict. Associationalists also advocated cooperative and often small-scale production in a period when large firms were consolidating and appeared to represent the fastest route to industrial efficiency.

Many associationalists further supported functional democracy, that is, replacing democracy based on voter participation in elections with democracy based on the direct representation of producer and consumer organizations in the major decision-making bodies; individuals would participate through their membership in such organizations. Faced with threats from both the extreme left and the extreme right in the 1920s and 1930s, European democrats were unwilling to contemplate major experiments with the core political institutions. An example of such an explicit rejection of associationalist ideas is William Yandell Elliott's *The Pragmatic Revolt in Politics* (1928).

Associationalists were also ineffective in political action —even when they were quite influential, as were the British Guild Socialists—because they assigned a low priority to attaining political power. Because they saw voluntary action in civil society as primary and competing in elections as secondary, they behaved as if their political aims had already been achieved. In consequence, other political forces were able to compete for power and control the agenda of debate and policy making.

From the mid-1920s until the mid-1970s associationalist ideas were largely dormant. Liberal ideas had prevailed over fascism and communism. After 1945 Western economies proved capable of rapid recovery and growth. The success of the big corporation and of national economic management in securing full employment and growth made alternative forms of economic organization or any reduction in the powers of the centralized nation-state seem irrelevant.

Associations play an important but secondary role in liberal political theory, as we have seen. Throughout the twentieth century, however, voluntarism and democratic control in associations declined as the forces of increasing size and bureaucratic administration took hold. Corporations were not in fact answerable to large numbers of small shareholders. Unions often ceased to be "voluntary" organizations, since in many occupations and sectors it was difficult to work without a union card. Many large charities and clubs reduced the member's role to that of a mere subscriber.

This outcome was seen as the inevitable price of efficiency and economies of scale. It did mean that civil society was dominated by organizations that were only formally voluntary, that were not accountable to their members, and that were often bigger than were pre-industrial states. This development undermined the role of secondary associations in ensuring pluralism and citizen independence. Thus, in the 1980s, a mainstream American pluralist like Robert A. Dahl could advocate the need for the restoration of democratic control in civil society as a precondition for real citizen autonomy.

An Associationalist Renewal?

The pressures toward large size and bureaucracy began to lessen somewhat with the economic and social changes of the 1970s. The internationalization of trade and financial flows dramatically lessens the capacity of states to manage the economy. With the end of the cold war, Western countries are no longer likely to be faced with major international armed conflicts; thus another rationale for highly centralized power has been removed. Big business no longer finds sheer size an advantage. Management theorists favor more decentralized and less hierarchical organizations, and industrial economists stress the growth-generating role of small and medium-sized enterprises. Increasingly well-educated and self-directed individuals want more choice and control over their affairs. New communications and information technologies allow them to exercise it more easily.

Major social changes have begun to make centralization and the large-scale and hierarchical organization less necessary and less attractive. As national political leaders and institutions lose their ability to deliver jobs and growth, citizens become less involved. Citizen abstention from or dissatisfaction with national politics is now widespread in the West. Yet the public is not becoming less active. Single-issue campaigns and local affairs continue to attract strong citizen support and involvement.

Increasingly, citizens of Western countries are doing what Tocqueville observed in early-nineteenth-century America—namely, solving their common problems by acting together rather than waiting for government to act. Governments have become both remote and relatively ineffective. Greater decentralization and the active support of voluntary associations might do much to reduce the burdens on government and increase the accountability of government to the citizens.

See also *Civil society; Corporatism; Dahl, Robert A.; Decentralization; Interest groups; International organizations; Laski, Harold; Majority rule, minority rights; Private governance of associations; Tocqueville, Alexis de.*

Paul Hirst

BIBLIOGRAPHY

Black, Anthony. *Guilds and Civil Society in European Political Thought from the Twelfth Century to the Present.* London: Methuen; Ithaca, N.Y.: Cornell University Press, 1984.

Cole, G. D. H. *Guild Socialism Re-Stated.* London: Leonard Parsons, 1920. Reprinted with an introduction by R. V. Vernon. New Brunswick, N.J.: Transaction, 1980.

Durkheim, Emile. *Professional Ethics and Civic Morals.* London: Routledge and Kegan Paul, 1957.

Elliott, William Yandell. *The Pragmatic Revolt in Politics.* New York: Macmillan, 1928.

Figgis, John Neville. *Churches in the Modern State.* London: Longmans Green, 1913.

Gierke, Otto von. *Community in Historical Perspective.* Edited by Anthony Black. Cambridge and New York: Cambridge University Press, 1990.

Hirst, Paul. *Associative Democracy: New Forms of Economic and Social Governance.* Oxford: Polity Press; Amherst: University of Massachusetts Press, 1993.

———, ed. *The Pluralist Theory of the State: Selected Writings of G. D. H. Cole, J. N. Figgis, and H. J. Laski.* London: Routledge, 1989.

Nicholls, David. *The Pluralist State: The Political Ideas of J. N. Figgis and His Contemporaries.* 2d ed. London: Macmillan, 1995.

Proudhon, Pierre-Joseph. *The Principle of Federation.* Translated and introduced by R. Vernon. Toronto: University of Toronto Press, 1979.

Tocqueville, Alexis de. *Democracy in America.* 2 vols. New York: Doubleday, 1975.

Atatürk, Kemal

Founder and first president of the Republic of Turkey. Born in Salonika (then in Ottoman Turkey and since 1913 in Greece), Atatürk (1881–1938) was originally known simply as Mustafa and later, after his days in Ottoman military school, as Mustafa Kemal.

As a young officer, Kemal joined the Young Turk movement, which came to power in the 1908 revolution. Later he fought against the Italian invasion of Libya (1911–1912) and in the Balkan war (1912–1913). During World War I, he was the colonel in charge of repelling the British landing at Gallipoli (1915). After rising to the rank of general, he was assigned to the Russian and later to the southern (Syrian-Iraqi) front, returning to Istanbul at the end of the war.

When the victorious Allied powers occupied further parts of the defeated Ottoman-Turkish Empire within the 1918 armistice lines, including its capital of Istanbul, and Greece invaded its western regions, General Kemal assumed a command in eastern Anatolia—ostensibly to supervise the demobilization of Ottoman forces. His real goal, however, was to organize a military and popular resistance movement under the slogan "Defense of Rights." In public speeches he emphasized that the movement must be organized from the bottom up in every town and village. By 1920 he had convened a Grand National Assembly in Ankara attended by delegates from all regions of the country. Significantly, the name of the "nation" that the assembly represented was left unspecified so as not to open up divisive controversies about the country's Ottoman, Islamic, or Turkish identity.

After military victory over Greek forces and Ankara's full international recognition in the Treaty of Lausanne (July 1923)—and with much of the former Ottoman bureaucracy transferred from Istanbul—the Ankara assembly proclaimed the Republic of Turkey (November 1923), with Kemal as president. Afterward, assembly elections were held every four years, with candidates nominated by the regional branches of Kemal's Republican People's Party. Each new assembly duly reelected Kemal president.

An opposition party formed in 1924 by some of Kemal's associates was banned in 1925, when a conservative Islamic and nationalist Kurdish rebellion threatened the survival of the new republic. In 1930 Kemal encouraged Fethi Okyar, a former cabinet minister and ambassador, and his closest political associate, to form another opposition group, the Free Republican Party. Yet when that party began to attract major support, Kemal persuaded his friend to dissolve it. In 1935 the government allowed thirteen independent deputies not affiliated with the Republican People's Party to be elected, including several Christians and Jews. Thus Turkey under Kemal's leadership (1923–1938) remained, in effect, a benevolent single-party dictatorship.

In the fifteen years of his presidency, Kemal's government adopted fundamental political and cultural reforms, including abolition of the caliphate—the spiritual leadership of Islam—in 1924. It introduced European legal codes guaranteeing secular law, religious freedom, and equality between men and women (1926); shifted from the Arabic to the Roman alphabet (1928); replaced Islamic academies with universities based on the European model (1933); and adopted European-style family names (1934). With this last reform, the name Atatürk (or Father Turk) was conferred upon Kemal.

Atatürk made four essential contributions to Turkey's democratic future. First, he established a secure sense of Turkish national identity within the remnants of the defeated Ottoman Empire—based not on defeat but on victory in the war of independence (1919–1922). Second, he maintained friendly relations with all neighboring states, including the new Soviet Union, Greece (with which a friendship treaty was signed in 1930), and the British and French mandates of Iraq and Syria. Third, he adopted the principle of populism as the central tenet of his Republican People's Party; his successor, Ismet Inönü, invoked this principle in launching Turkey on its transition toward democracy in 1945. And, fourth, Atatürk initiated the reforms of 1924–1935, which secularized and Westernized Turkish society.

See also *Turkey*.

Dankwart A. Rustow

BIBLIOGRAPHY

Kazancigil, Ali, and Ergun Özbudun, eds. *Atatürk: Founder of a State*. London: Hurst, 1981.

Kinross, Lord [John Patrick Balfour]. *Atatürk: A Biography of Mustafa Kemal, Father of Modern Turkey*. New York: Morrow, 1965.

Rustow, Dankwart A. "Atatürk as Founder of a State." In *Philosophers and Kings: Studies in Leadership*, edited by Dankwart A. Rustow. New York: Braziller, 1970.

Aung San Suu Kyi

Nobel Peace Prize laureate, leader of the movement for democracy in Burma, and for several years political prisoner of the Burmese military. Aung San Suu Kyi (1945–) is the daughter of Aung San, the founder of independent Burma. Aung San was assassinated with most of his cabinet in July 1947, shortly before Burma gained its independence from Great Britain in January 1948. Aung San Suu Kyi's mother, *Daw* (Madam) Khin Kyi, later became ambassador to India.

After spending her early years in Burma, Aung San Suu Kyi accompanied her mother to India in 1960. She was educated at Oxford University and then worked for two years in the United Nations Secretariat. In 1972 she married Michael Vaillancourt Aris, a noted scholar on Bhutan, Tibet, and Central Asia.

In 1988, while Aung San Suu Kyi was in Burma tending her mother, who had had a stroke, disturbances convulsed

Aung San Suu Kyi

Suu Kyi has received many honors and awards for her advocacy of democracy and human rights. These include the Sakharov Prize for Freedom of Thought (European Parliament, 1991) and the International Simón Bolívar Prize (UNESCO, 1992). She assumed an unparalleled leadership role in the movement for democracy in Burma after 1988.

See also *Burma; Dissidents.*

David I. Steinberg

Australia and New Zealand

Pacific nations and members of the British Commonwealth that have a long tradition of maintaining democratic institutions. Although Australia and New Zealand share a common British heritage, their political development has diverged in several important respects. The two countries differ considerably in size. Australia is an entire continent, nearly as large as the United States in area. New Zealand comprises only slightly more than 100,000 square miles.

Historical Background

A long-established Aborigine population inhabited Australia when white settlers began colonizing the island continent in 1788. The separate colonies founded by the settlers—New South Wales, Victoria, South Australia, Tasmania, Queensland, and Western Australia—were effectively self-governing until 1901, when they entered a federal arrangement. Two territories, the Northern Territory (formerly part of South Australia) and the Australian Capital Territory (formerly part of New South Wales), joined the federation in 1911.

New Zealand, a small island nation, lies in the Pacific Ocean about 1,200 miles southeast of Australia. New Zealand's European settlers came somewhat later than Australia's, after the formal establishment of British sovereignty in 1840. In 1852 legislation passed by the British Parliament established an institutional framework of government. National elections were first held in 1854.

The populations of the countries are quite different in origin and outlook. Australia's early white population consisted mainly of convicts transported from Britain, togeth-

Burma and thrust her into politics. In August 1988 she gained national recognition as a leader of the National League for Democracy. The National League opposed the military regime of the Burma Socialist Program Party and later the State Law and Order Restoration Council, a military regime that came to power by coup and violent repression in September 1988.

As general secretary of the National League for Democracy, Aung San Suu Kyi electrified the country with her passionate speeches in favor of democracy. On July 20, 1989, she was placed under house arrest and was recognized as a prisoner of conscience by Amnesty International. She was forbidden by the military to run in the election of May 1990, in which her party received 80 percent of the seats in the National Assembly. The State Law and Order Restoration Council ignored the election results. She was released from house arrest in July 1995.

In addition to the Nobel Peace Prize (1991), Aung San

er with their guards. Since 1947 there has been a large influx of non-British immigrants. The nineteenth-century British working-class immigrants to Australia influenced the new country's class consciousness, attitudes toward women, and accent. Australia's Irish immigrants contributed anti-British sentiment and Catholicism. By contrast, convicts were never transported to New Zealand, and until very recently that nation has relied mainly on Great Britain for immigrants. New Zealand received more middle-class English immigrants than did Australia and had a larger proportion of farm owners, making its mainstream political values more like those of the English middle class.

Although both countries have indigenous populations, the Aborigines in Australia constitute only 1 percent of the population, whereas the Maori in New Zealand make up 12 percent of the population, and Pacific islanders comprise a further 4 percent. Questions of racial equity in democratic institutions have therefore been given greater priority in New Zealand.

Australian Federalism

Of several themes that have shaped Australia's twentieth-century experience of democracy, perhaps the most important is federalism, itself a consequence of size. The Constitution makes a clear distinction between the functions of the state and federal governments: the states accept responsibility for community services such as health and transportation, and the federal government handles foreign affairs, trade, and defense. Judicial interpretation of the constitution, the antipathy of the Australian Labor Party toward the states, and the increasing complexity of modern government, however, have led to a shift in political power in favor of the federal government. The most

States. The clearest political embodiment of these utilitarian values is the system of compulsory voting, adopted for federal elections in 1924 as a solution to the problem of declining turnout. Australia is one of the few democracies in the world to enforce compulsory voting.

A strong two-party system is another characteristic of Australian democracy. The Australian Labor Party is the nation's oldest party. Founded in 1891, it originated in the trades and labor councils of the 1870s and 1880s. Australia formed the world's first Labor government, which took office in Queensland for seven days in 1899. Between 1901 and 1993 the Australian Labor Party held federal office for thirty years. The Liberal Party was formed in 1944 on the instigation of Robert Menzies, who wanted to combine his United Australia Party with other non-Labor groups to form a single conservative party. A third party, the National Party of Australia, began as the Country Party during World War I and was renamed in 1982. The party has been in permanent coalition with the Liberals, with short breaks. With the exception of the 1990 election, since federation in 1901 no other party has won more than 10 percent of the vote in elections for the lower house, the House of Representatives.

This strong two-party system has conveyed great stability to Australian democracy during the course of the century. The stable two-party system reinforces the Westminster system of government, which was embodied in the constitution. The Westminster system (named for Westminster in London, where the British Parliament is located) is based on responsible party government: voters choose between competing parties that offer alternative social and economic policies. The executive, who is closely identified with one of the parties, is answerable to the legislature.

Parliament enacts legislation under a system of strong party discipline. Although Australian party discipline is a legacy of British practice, it exceeds anything found in the Westminster Parliament: voting against one's party in Australia is almost unheard of and is regarded as a cardinal political sin. Westminster conventions of collective cabinet responsibility and ministerial responsibility have also been adopted from British practice, although they are less frequently observed.

Australian society is based almost entirely on massive immigration. It has a higher percentage of foreign-born residents than any other advanced industrial society, with the exception of Israel. Despite the ethnic, cultural, and

significant event in this shift occurred in 1942, when the High Court, the nation's supreme legal body, upheld the federal government's right to deny the states income tax powers. Since then the states have been dependent on the federal government for revenue.

Australian democracy has placed the state in a central, regulatory role. The Australian state has traditionally taken on a wide range of social and economic responsibilities, including intervention in the economy, the regulation of trade, and the control of industrial relations. The role of the state originated in the political values of the early settlers, whose outlook reflected the Benthamite utilitarianism (a philosophy based on the work of Jeremy Bentham, 1748–1832) that was prevalent in early nineteenth-century Britain. The Australian state is regarded as an instrument for arbitrating disputes rather than as an agent for preserving individual liberty and freedom, as in the United

linguistic diversity of these immigrants, they have had comparatively little effect on the character or style of Australian democracy, including its institutions, political parties, or major actors.

Early in the twentieth century the policy of assimilation ensured that immigrants would conform to existing social norms. Since 1972 the policy of multiculturalism has relaxed this demand, though loyalty to Australian institutions remains a requirement. It is also clear, however, that many immigrants have been socialized into other political systems and have come to Australia for economic, not political, reasons; their interest in politics is therefore limited.

Australian Elections

Australia's electoral arrangements are complex. Since 1918 preferential voting based on single-member districts (known as electorates) has been used for the House of Representatives. Since 1949 the single transferable vote method of proportional representation has been used for the upper house, the Senate. (The states determine their own electoral arrangements for state elections, and they use a variety of systems.) The 148 members of the House of Representatives are elected for a maximum three-year term of office, although elections may be called early if the Senate twice rejects a bill from the lower house. The 76 members of the Senate are usually elected for a six-year term, with half the seats up for election every three years (in a "half Senate" election). When a "full Senate" election is held, half the members are elected for three-year terms and half for six-year terms.

In practice, the responsibility for calling an election rests with the government. The prime minister can request that the governor general (the head of state) dissolve the House of Representatives and half of the Senate or the House of Representatives and all of the Senate if the technical conditions are met. (The latter is called a double dissolution election.) In recent years, double dissolution elections have become more frequent, since governments often do not control the Senate, and they see such an election as an opportunity to extend their control to the upper house, thereby facilitating passage of their legislation.

The Senate was designed to represent the interests of the states and territories. The six states have an equal number of senators, despite their vastly different population sizes. The Senate was also seen as a house of review, like the British House of Lords; this concept was implicit

in senators' longer period of tenure. Party discipline, however, has come to dominate the Senate, like the House of Representatives, undermining its traditional function as a house of review. At the same time, the adoption of proportional representation in 1949 for Senate elections has frequently left the balance of power in the Senate in the hands of minor parties and independents. This has meant that governments have had to negotiate the passage of contentious legislation.

The federal constitution, drafted in 1900, did not guarantee universal suffrage. Those who were entitled to vote in elections to colonial parliaments were automatically given the same right in federal elections. Because women had the vote only in South Australia and Western Australia, only in those states could women vote in federal elections. This anomaly was rectified in 1908, when the last state to deny women the vote, Victoria, granted universal suffrage. In 1973 the voting age for all Australians was lowered from twenty-one years to eighteen years.

Racial discrimination in the franchise has persisted until comparatively recently. Aborigines were effectively denied the vote until 1949, when they were permitted to vote in federal elections if they were registered to vote in state elections or if they served in the military. In 1962 all Aborigines were given the right to vote, although registration remained voluntary. In 1984 enrollment for Aborigines became compulsory and they, like other Australians, were obliged to vote in federal elections.

Democratic Trends in Australia

In today's Australian federal democracy, two related themes are of increasing importance. There is greater discussion than ever before about the relevance of Australia's British heritage to an ethnically and racially heterogeneous society located on the edge of Southeast Asia. This debate has its origins in World War II, when Britain, engaged in the European war, was unable to help Australia in the fight against Japan, and Australia looked to the United States for military and economic assistance. More recently, Britain's entry into the European Community in 1972 altered Australia's traditional trading relations and forced Australia to look to Asia. The large number of non-British immigrants who do not identify with Britain or with British political traditions is an additional factor. Politically, the discussion has focused on proposals to make Australia a republic, to replace the queen as head of state, and to remove the British Union Jack from the Australian flag.

As Australia's traditional British ties weaken, there is increasing economic involvement in the Asian-Pacific region. This involvement is a logical consequence of Britain's withdrawal from Asia, completed with the reversion of Hong Kong to China in 1997. But it also reflects the changing power relations within the Pacific Rim, including the economic dominance of Japan, the rapid economic growth of countries such as Thailand and Malaysia, the collapse of the Soviet Union, and the withdrawal of U.S. military forces from the Philippines. All these factors have forced Australia to play a greater political, economic, and military role in the Asian-Pacific region and to reconsider its European, and specifically British, identity.

New Zealand's Democratic Setting

New Zealand, small in area and population, has always suffered from a greater sense of isolation than has Australia. This isolation, coupled with the nation's greater reliance on British settlers, has made New Zealand more conscious of its British identity. New Zealand's highly centralized government provides a perfect example of British parliamentary, or Westminster, democracy.

Egalitarianism is a major theme in New Zealand democracy—as it is in Australia. New Zealand established a strong welfare state early on. The commitment of successive governments to providing individual economic security was reflected in a very low level of unemployment until the 1980s, when unemployment rapidly increased. While the state played a major role, the economy was essentially a capitalist, free enterprise system. Within New Zealand political culture, the two themes are not contradictory but complementary.

The organized settlement of New Zealand dates from 1840, when the Treaty of Waitangi was signed between the British and some Maori chiefs. Later, Maori fought the settlers in a series of wars between 1860 and 1876. After the Maori were defeated, they were granted token separate representation in Parliament.

The 1852 New Zealand Constitution Act provided for six separate provincial assemblies (which were abolished in 1876) as well as for a national parliament. The legislature was made up of a lower house popularly elected every five years (reduced to three years in 1879) and a Legislative Council, whose members were appointed for life by the queen. The role of the Legislative Council was never clearly defined, and the council was abolished in 1950. Since then the legislature has been unicameral. Since 1911, after

brief experiments with a second ballot system and multi-member districts, elections have been exclusively conducted using the plurality system based on single-member districts (known as electorates).

In 1852 suffrage was restricted to men aged twenty-one years and over who could claim some property rights. The property qualification excluded almost all the Maori; the only ones who qualified were the few who owned or leased land under the European system of land titles. To permit Maori parliamentary representation, the 1867 Maori Representation Act provided for two separate electoral systems, one general and one Maori. Maori could choose to register in the Maori electoral roll and to vote in one of four Maori electorates. Although this separate system guarantees only minimal representation for the Maori, since 1975 they have been allowed to (and often do) choose instead to register in non-Maori electorates.

The property qualification was removed, and universal male suffrage was introduced in 1879. In 1893 full voting rights were extended to women, although women could not stand for election to the House of Representatives until the passage of the Women's Parliamentary Rights Act in 1919. In 1973 the voting age was lowered to eighteen years. Registration is compulsory, although voting is voluntary. Traditionally, turnout in New Zealand has been among the highest in the established democracies; in recent years, however, turnout has declined.

Parties in New Zealand

New Zealand has a fairly complex party history. The first political party to emerge was the Liberal Party, which was organized in 1890 and was elected to form the government early the following year. The Liberals held power until 1912. From that time until 1935 the farmer-based Reform Party dominated a situation of complex three-party politics. The Labour Party was formed in 1916, first came to power in 1935, and held office until 1949. It was succeeded by the National Party, formed in 1936 from the remnants of the various anti-Labour party organizations. By 1938 the modern two-party system had been formed. A variety of other minor parties have contested elections—New Zealand could boast, for example, the world's first national environmental party, the Values Party, formed in 1972—but in a plurality electoral system their success has been limited and they have not so far undermined the essentially two-party system.

Since the 1950s support for minor parties has fluctuated, but the long-term trend has been in their favor. As a consequence, increasing criticism of the unfairness of the plurality electoral system has been voiced. After two consecutive elections, 1978 and 1981, in which the major party with the most votes, Labour, secured fewer seats than its National opponent, such criticisms gained greater weight. In 1986 a Royal Commission on the Electoral System recommended that New Zealand adopt a modified version of the mixed-member proportional system used in Germany.

Both Labour and National governments had pursued radical economic liberalization, much to the dismay of many voters. In a 1992 referendum, voters were asked first to choose between the present plurality system and another system and then to choose among four alternative systems. Of the 55 percent of the electorate who voted in the referendum, 85 percent voted for change, with a clear preference for the mixed-member proportional system on the second question. A second referendum was held in 1993, in conjunction with the general election; voters were asked to choose between retaining the plurality system and adopting the mixed-member proportional system. Of the 83 percent of the electorate who voted, 54 percent favored the mixed-member proportional system and 46 percent favored the plurality system. Thus the proportional system would apply beginning in the 1996 general election.

Like Australia, New Zealand looked to the United States for military assistance during World War II. Defense arrangements were formalized in a mutual defense treaty among the three countries, signed in 1951. The Labour government elected in 1984, however, banned visits by ships carrying nuclear arms or powered by nuclear energy. As a result the United States cut all defense ties with New Zealand. Antinuclear popular sentiments have remained strong in New Zealand, and in 1987 the Labour government enacted its antinuclear policy into law. The 1984–1990 Labour government also undertook a thorough revision of the government's economic interventionist role, cutting state subsidies, reducing social welfare payments, and privatizing government-owned utilities—a policy called Rogernomics after the main instigator and Labour finance minister, Roger Douglas.

Although the character and style of New Zealand's democratic culture and institutions have changed little during the course of the century, recent events have suggested several directions in which New Zealand democracy may evolve in the twenty-first century. The change in the electoral system, given the long-term trend of increasing support for minor parties, may remove a substantial institutional foundation of the two-party system and perhaps lead to a period of political uncertainty. Changes to the traditionally interventionist role of the state under Labour have resulted in significant shifts in the distribution of wealth, although how much this alters popular democratic values is unclear. Meanwhile, the Maori are demanding compensation for past injustices and greater recognition of their language and culture in society and government.

Divergent Trends

While Australia is becoming a multicultural society, with increasing Asian influence, in New Zealand the future appears increasingly bicultural, with a new balance between European and Pacific influences. Finally, although a free trade area encompasses Australia and New Zealand, the absence of New Zealand defense ties with the United States places a question mark over a key aspect of New Zealand's long-term role in the region.

See also *Commonwealth, British; Electoral systems; Federalism; Multiethnic democracy; Proportional representation; Racism; Utilitarianism.*

Ian McAllister

BIBLIOGRAPHY

Aitkin, Don A. *Stability and Change in Australian Politics.* 2d ed. Canberra: Australian National University Press, 1982.

Catt, Helena, Paul Harris, and Nigel S. Roberts. *Voters' Choice: Electoral Change in New Zealand?* Palmerston North, New Zealand: Dunmore Press, 1992.

Collins, Hugh. "Political Ideology in Australia: The Distinctiveness of a Benthamite Society." *Daedalus* 114 (1985): 147–169.

Emy, Hugh V., and Owen E. Hughes. *Australian Politics: Realities in Conflict.* 2d ed. Melbourne: Macmillan, 1992.

Gold, Hyam. *New Zealand Politics in Perspective.* 2d ed. Auckland: Longman Paul, 1989.

McAllister, Ian. *Political Behaviour: Citizens, Parties and Elites in Australia.* Melbourne: Longman Cheshire, 1992.

———, Malcolm Mackerras, Alvaro Ascui, and Susan Moss. *Australian Political Facts.* Melbourne: Longman Cheshire, 1990.

Vowles, Jack, and Peter Aimer. *The Voters' Vengeance: The 1990 Election in New Zealand and the Fate of the Fourth Labour Government.* Auckland: Auckland University Press; New York: Oxford University Press, 1993.

Austria

See *Europe, Western*

Authoritarianism

A political system in which a leader or a small group exercises power without formal limits. Authoritarian rule does not permit two of the defining elements of democracy: free competition for political office and free participation of citizens in politics.

In authoritarian regimes, those in power are not accountable at regular intervals to an electorate or to representative bodies, although they might be responsive to certain interest groups. Some authoritarian rulers claim power for life; some are selected by the armed forces or the monarch. In authoritarian regimes, there is no freedom (or very limited freedom) to create political parties, and existing parties are usually dissolved or suspended. The regimes vary in the degree of institutionalization. Some are only temporary governments closer to the traditional concept of dictatorship as government for a crisis.

Characteristics of Authoritarian Regimes

Authoritarian regimes do not institutionalize a legal opposition, but—unlike totalitarian regimes—they do permit different forms of opposition. Some face opposition within the regime from those who have different goals—for example, the reestablishment of a monarchy. Others have an illegal, but tolerated and visible, opposition. In communist Poland the opposition of the Catholic Church and groups related to it, the illegal but visible Solidarity trade union, and the Committee for the Defense of Workers were part of political life. The existence of those various forms of opposition has made transitions to democracy less difficult and less traumatic than they might otherwise have been.

Authoritarian regimes limit the freedoms of their citizens and engage in political repression of their opponents. Often, "political" crimes are subject to military justice, which does not provide the same protection of the rights of the accused as civil courts and which can impose heavier penalties. Even when applied by civil courts, authoritarian codes of law define as criminal actions that are legal in liberal democracies: political propaganda, membership in parties, and participation in strikes. The police in authoritarian regimes have few limits on their power, and mistreatment and torture are not uncommon. Some regimes have engaged in repression that even their own legislation considers illegal—for example, "disappearances," secret detention centers, torture, and assassination.

In spite of the horrors of repression by some authoritarian regimes, however, they have not been comparable to the state terror of totalitarian regimes like the Soviet Union, particularly under Joseph Stalin, or the mass murder by the Nazis. But all authoritarian regimes violate basic human rights to varying degrees and do not recognize their citizens' political rights. Repression by authoritarian regimes has contributed to the international condemnation of their actions and to their loss of legitimacy. Democracies that succeed such regimes face a difficult legacy of official investigation of their crimes and restitution to their victims, particularly when the culprits are military officers claiming to have acted under orders or counting on the solidarity of their fellow officers.

Military Regimes

Many twentieth-century authoritarian regimes have been headed by military officers: Mustafa Kemal Atatürk in Turkey (1923–1938), Francisco Franco in Spain (1936–1975), Philippe Pétain in France (1940–1944), Juan Domingo Perón in Argentina (1946–1955, a period that includes his elected presidency), Gamal Abdel Nasser in Egypt (1956–1970), Lázaro Cárdenas in Mexico (1934–1940), Augusto Pinochet in Chile (1973–1990). But to distinguish between military and nonmilitary regimes is not adequate because the institutions and politics of military regimes themselves can be very different. Some civilian-led regimes might have more in common with some military regimes—for example, Portugal under António de Oliveira Salazar (1932–1968), Austria under Engelbert Dollfuss (1933–1934) and Kurt von Schuschnigg (1934–1938), and Brazil under Getúlio Vargas (1937–1945).

A more useful distinction is between a strictly military regime and a nonhierarchical military regime. In the first type, important decisions are made collectively by the top institutional leadership of the armed forces—the hierarchical military—with only limited participation by civilians and without the creation of a single party as a way to recruit elites. Examples are Argentina (1966–1973), Peru

(1968–1980), and Uruguay from the mid-1970s to 1985. In the second type, a group of officers has also taken power, but they do not necessarily consider themselves a permanent government (even though some last a long time), nor are they likely to develop institutionally. An example here is the Greek colonels (1967–1974). Such regimes tend to end when the armed forces consider it preferable to extricate themselves from power and return to the barracks, imposing only some conditions of immunity and guarantees for their corporate interests. In the case of nonhierarchical military regimes, other officers may question the rulers' continuity in office.

Modern Authoritarian Regimes

Authoritarian rule has dominated the politics of most of the world for a large part of the twentieth century, in spite of the waves of democratization in the first two decades and in the aftermath of World War II. A number of countries (such as the United Kingdom and the Scandinavian and Benelux monarchies) underwent a slow but continuous process of democratization starting from the constitutional liberal states of the nineteenth century. But in southern and eastern Europe, the Balkans, Latin America, and Japan, that process was interrupted in the 1920s and 1930s by dictatorships and a variety of authoritarian regimes. In some countries, like Yugoslavia, the conflicts between nationalities contributed much to the turn to authoritarian regimes.

In other cases, like Iran and Turkey, nontraditional authoritarian rule was linked with efforts at social and cultural modernization. Turkey successfully made the transition to democracy in 1947. But more often the revolutionary threat of communism, ethnic and cultural fragmentation, economic difficulties, and the threat of fascism led to authoritarian rule in newly independent states and democracies, such as Poland, Latvia, Lithuania, and Estonia.

Other Nondemocratic Regimes

Distinguishing sultanistic, totalitarian, and post-totalitarian regimes from authoritarian regimes aids in understanding the complex range of nondemocratic politics. One type of rule that is sometimes considered authoritarian can also be called neopatrimonial, despotic, or sultanistic, to use a term derived from Max Weber's discussion of a type of patrimonial regime.

Sultanistic rule is motivated largely by personal goals, rather than by pursuit of a particular concept of society or defense of the interests of a class or ethnic group. The pursuit of power and wealth for themselves or their family and friends, rather than collective goals, distinguishes despots like Rafael Trujillo in the Dominican Republic (1930–1961), the Somoza dynasty in Nicaragua (1937–1979, with interruption), Jean-Claude "Baby Doc" Duvalier in Haiti (1971–1986), even Ferdinand Marcos in the Philippines (1965–1986), and—to a large extent—Mohammad Reza Pahlavi, shah of Iran (1941–1979) from dictators like Miklós Horthy in Hungary (1920–1944), Salazar in Portugal, Dollfuss and Schuschnigg in Austria, Franco in Spain, and the Brazilian military (1964–1985).

Totalitarian political systems differ from authoritarian regimes in several ways. In authoritarian regimes there is a monistic (single) but not monolithic center of power, and whatever pluralism of institutions or groups exists derives its legitimacy from that center. In totalitarian regimes there is an exclusive, autonomous, and more or less intellectually elaborate ideology identified with the ruling group or leader and the party serving the leaders. The ruling group uses this ideology as a basis for policies or manipulates it to legitimize them. The ideology goes beyond the boundaries of legitimate political action to provide some ultimate meaning, sense of historical purpose, and interpretation of social reality. Citizens' participation in and active mobilization for political and collective social tasks are encouraged, demanded, rewarded, and channeled through a single party and its secondary groups. The passive obedience and apathy characteristic of many authoritarian regimes are considered undesirable by totalitarian rulers.

Some have included in the broad category of authoritarian rule the communist regimes in Eastern Europe after Stalin, which lost or modified their totalitarian characteristics after a more or less extended period of totalitarian rule. These post-totalitarian regimes cannot be understood without reference to their totalitarian past. Such regimes are characterized by both positive changes (liberalization) and by ossification—a degeneration of the totalitarian structures and ideology after losing their "utopian" and "idealist" components. Founders of regimes did not initially intend to create post-totalitarian regimes in the way that some founders chose to set up authoritarian regimes. Instead, post-totalitarian regimes are the result of changes in totalitarian systems along a continuum, from early post-totalitarianism to mature post-totalitarianism.

In post-totalitarian regimes, there is considerably more pluralism than in totalitarian regimes. This is due to the greater autonomy of institutions, bureaucracies, and public enterprises from the party, which retains in principle its totalitarian leading function. There is also an emerging "parallel" culture in civil society. However, that pluralism is different in degree and kind from authoritarian regimes because it appears after the "flattening" of the social landscape in the preceding totalitarian period. The leadership in such regimes is still largely recruited from the party, but some leaders come from the bureaucracy and the technocratic apparatus, and political or ideological loyalty becomes less important. Leaders are often aging, and there may be a collective leadership that tends to limit the former power of a totalitarian ruler. "Socialist legality" replaces the arbitrary use of power and state terrors. There is a growing skepticism and disregard for the official ideology, whose utopian and motivating value has been lost. With that loss, the regime is less able to mobilize its cadres and organizations, and there is a growing privatization of the people.

Corporatist Regimes

Authoritarian regimes, as distinct from totalitarian regimes, generally have not had a distinctive and intellectually elaborate ideological model of how to institutionalize politics. One exception is "organic statism"—also called "state corporatism" or "organic democracy"—as contrasted with the "inorganic democracy" of political parties and representation of the citizens. Corporatism is a system of representing interest groups in which each group is authorized by the state and given the sole right to represent citizens in its category. In exchange for such right, groups must accept certain state control over the selection of leaders and the expression of political views.

Corporatists reject the individualistic assumptions of liberal democracy and seek to provide an institutional channel for the representation of the heterogeneous interests in modern or modernizing societies, while rejecting class conflict. There have been a variety of theoretical-ideological formulations of corporatism and attempts to implement them through political institutions. The romantic-conservative idealization of the Middle Ages; the antiliberal, anticapitalist, antistatist, and antisocialist encyclicals of the Roman Catholic Church; the syndicalist current in the non-Marxist labor movement, which rejected parties and assigned to trade unions the revolutionary struggle and organization of society; even some liberal thought emphasizing the role of professional associations—all contributed to corporatist thought.

Those ideas were used in the 1920s and 1930s by the fascists, particularly in Italy under Benito Mussolini, and the authoritarians in Austria, Portugal, and Spain to create political institutions. Examples of corporatist regimes are Spain under Franco, Portugal under Salazar, Brazil under Vargas, Mexico under Cárdenas, and Argentina under Perón.

Corporative representation can disenfranchise the masses by allocating representation disproportionately to certain professions, the universities, employers, or—in the case of the Soviets—industrial workers. Elections for corporative representatives are usually organized as a multitier process from the workplace to the national level.

The assumption that such primary units share interests, rather than being internally divided, has not corresponded to reality. Nor has the related idea of "self-management" (democratic decision making, particularly in the workplace)—introduced by the dissident Communist Josip Broz Tito in Yugoslavia in the post–World War II years and adapted in Algeria, Peru, and other authoritarian regimes—ever turned into a promising new form of or road to democracy. In addition, such corporative representation cannot address major issues in society, such as religious policy, cultural conflicts, and foreign policy, as political parties can. Parties (particularly major parties) are organized to represent voters on a wide range of such issues, not on specific interests. Voters generally support them for their positions on more than one issue.

The allocation of seats in corporative legislative chambers can be made only by those in power. Authoritarian regimes therefore found corporatism a convenient form of pseudodemocracy. But since no authoritarian government has accepted the principle that it could be dismissed by a vote of no confidence in a corporative chamber, such chambers at most have had an advisory function.

Tutelary Democracies

The end of Western colonial rule in various parts of the world after World War II led to the creation of new states with democratic constitutions. After a first election, many of these became one-party states, which in turn often were overthrown by military coups that established authoritarian regimes. The regimes were initially characterized as tutelary democracies or modernizing oligarchies to highlight the continuing hope for democratization. Often inspired by the model of communist one-party rule, and strongly nationalistic, some regimes adopted an ideology labeled "African socialism" to indicate the goal of noncapitalist development. In reality, however, the single party was often a coalition of diverse groups, tribal leaders, notables, and leaders co-opted from other parties—what French-speaking Africans called *parti unifié* (unified party) rather than *parti unique* (single party). In other cases, the party had little presence beyond urban centers, without the mass membership and mobilizational characteristics of communist or fascist single parties.

A number of states in black Africa have adopted forms of highly personalized rule after a phase of single-party regimes. They range from various types of neopatrimonial or sultanistic regimes to tyrannies. Idi Amin in Uganda (1971–1979), Francisco Macías Nguema in Equatorial Guinea (1968–1979), Jean-Bédel Bokassa in the Central African Republic (1966–1979), and Sese Seko Mobutu in Zaire (1965–   ).

From Authoritarianism to Democracy

In all types of nondemocratic politics, it is important not to confuse democratization with liberalization, which entails greater legality; some freedom for voluntary associations, churches, and even trade unions; the freeing of political prisoners; greater freedom of the press; and the return of exiles. Although liberalization can facilitate democratization, democratization is often an unanticipated and unwelcome consequence rather than the intention of the rulers.

A transition to democracy requires authoritarian rulers to allow people to vote in free competitive elections and to be ready to give up power should the voters not support them. This does not necessarily mean that people identified with the former regime will be barred from competing in elections. Sometimes they win free elections, as has happened in Bulgaria, Poland, Hungary, and Lithuania in recent years.

See also *African transitions to democracy; Corporatism; Critiques of democracy; Democratization, Waves of; Dictatorship; Dominant party democracies in Asia; Fascism; Mass society; Military rule and transition to democracy; Types of democracy.*

Juan J. Linz

BIBLIOGRAPHY

Almond, Gabriel, and James S. Coleman, eds. *The Politics of Developing Areas.* Princeton: Princeton University Press, 1960.

Collier, David, ed. *The New Authoritarianism in Latin America.* Princeton: Princeton University Press, 1979.

Collier, Ruth Bevins, and David Collier. *Shaping the Political Arena.* Princeton: Princeton University Press, 1991.

Finer, S. E. *The Man on Horseback: The Role of the Military in Politics.* 2d ed. Boulder, Colo.: Westview Press; London: S. Pinter, 1988.

Hermet, G. "L'autoritarisme." In *Les régimes politiques contemporains.* Vol. 2 of *Traité de science politique,* edited by Madeleine Grawitz and Jean Leca. Paris: Presses Universitaires de France, 1985.

Huntington, Samuel P., and C. H. Moore, eds. *Authoritarian Politics in Modern Society.* New York: Basic Books, 1970.

Jackson, Robert H., and Carl G. Rosberg, Jr. *Personal Rule in Black Africa: Prince, Autocrat, Prophet, Tyrant.* Berkeley: University of California Press, 1982.

Janos, Andrew C. "The One-Party State and Social Mobilization: East Europe between the Wars." In *Authoritarian Politics in Modern Society,* edited by Samuel P. Huntington and C. H. Moore. New York: Basic Books, 1970.

Linz, Juan J. "An Authoritarian Regime: The Case of Spain." In *Mass Politics: Studies in Political Sociology,* edited by Erik Allardt and Stein Rokkan. New York: Free Press, 1970.

———. "Totalitarian and Authoritarian Regimes." In *Micropolitical Theory.* Vol. 3 of *Handbook of Political Science.* Edited by Fred I. Greenstein and Nelson W. Polsby. Reading, Mass.: Addison-Wesley, 1975.

O'Donnell, Guillermo. *Modernization and Bureaucratic Authoritarianism: Studies in South American Politics.* Berkeley: Institute of International Studies, University of California, Berkeley, 1973.

Perlmutter, Amos. *Modern Authoritarianism: A Comparative Institutional Analysis.* New Haven and London: Yale University Press, 1981.

Schmitter, Philippe C. "Still the Century of Corporatism?" In *Review of Politics* 36 (1974): 85–131.

Seton-Watson, Hugh. *Eastern Europe between the Wars, 1918–1941.* New York: Harper and Row, 1967.

Autonomy

Literally, self-rule or self-government. Autonomy has often been thought to bear a particularly close relation to democracy. Only in a democracy, it is sometimes said, can an individual or a people be truly autonomous. Spelling out why this should be so, however, takes some care.

In its ancient meaning, autonomy was taken to be a property of states, rather than of individuals. An autonomous people was one that was self-sufficient and self-governing, rather than being ruled by an outside force. In the modern world, we have not lost this understanding of the term: the "puppet" regimes of the former Eastern bloc, for example, were commonly contrasted with the apparently more autonomous regimes elsewhere around the globe. To have autonomy in this sense, no doubt, is part of what is required for a nation to be a democracy, but we should remember that in the ancient world even tyrannical states were often regarded as fully autonomous.

The modern understanding of the term attributes autonomy, or the lack of it, to individuals. In the philosophical literature, personal autonomy has been identified with a great variety of other notions, including self-government, freedom, responsibility, morality, dignity, independence, and self-knowledge. Yet the core concept seems to be simply that an autonomous person is one who makes, and acts upon, his or her own decisions.

The relationship between autonomy and democracy was perhaps most fruitfully worked out by the eighteenth-century French philosopher Jean-Jacques Rousseau, whose views were to inspire the moral and political works of the great German philosopher Immanuel Kant (with whom the term *autonomy* is most often associated). Rousseau's ideas were also to influence G. W. F. Hegel and Karl Marx in different ways.

Rousseau makes a powerful attempt to bring together the ancient and modern understandings of *autonomy*. The idea of individual autonomy is given perhaps its classic formulation by Rousseau in *The Social Contract* (1762). According to Rousseau, freedom is obedience to a law that we prescribe to ourselves. The problem of social order, then, becomes the problem of reconciling the individual's right to autonomy with the existence of the state, and in particular with the state's right to create and enforce laws. In Book 1, chapter 6, of *The Social Contract,* Rousseau sets out this problem as the need to find a kind of association "in which each, while uniting himself with all, may still obey himself alone, and remain as free as before."

Rousseau's solution is simple and elegant: all must equally play a part in the creation of laws to which all will equally be subject. In other words, individual autonomy is reconciled with the authority of the state by a form of direct, participatory democracy. At the same time, group autonomy is preserved: Rousseau's ideal state is self-governing.

That this solution works has often been doubted. Some critics have questioned whether we can identify "self-rule" with "rule by a corporate body which includes oneself." If an individual is outvoted, he or she may be made subject to disagreeable restrictions that normally would be thought to be a limit on autonomy. Thus some have even argued that the only form of government consistent with due respect for autonomy is a direct democracy in which laws are passed only if they are accepted unanimously. Because, in practice, such a state would be impossible to achieve, the contemporary American political philosopher Robert Paul Wolff, in *In Defense of Anarchism* (1973), has argued that giving autonomy its full due requires anarchism. According to this view, no autonomous person can obey the law simply because it is the law: for the autonomous person, there is no such thing as a command.

One response to this argument suggests that the claims made on behalf of autonomy are greatly exaggerated. On the contrary, an autonomous person can accept the advantages of government as a way of pursuing his or her own ends. This response, however, ignores the problem of those who are regularly outvoted. A more promising strategy is to concede that a concern for individual autonomy may well create a pressure toward anarchism but to insist that other values can be called on to provide a more powerful counterargument for the state. The state offers individual and collective security, together with a level of prosperity that could not be achieved without it. As the nineteenth-century English philosopher John Stuart Mill argued, in *On Liberty* (1859), all that makes anyone's life worth living depends on the existence of enforceable restraints on the behavior of others. In this view, life without the law would be worthless.

In sum, by combining respect for autonomy with recognition of the importance of security and prosperity, it is possible to provide a more robust and convincing defense of majoritarian democracy. Once we have accepted the necessity of government, concern for individual autonomy provides strong reason for favoring democracy over other forms of government. Even if it is wrong to say that the individual retains complete autonomy in majoritarian democracies, nevertheless democracy is the closest we can feasibly approach to the idea of individual self-government in a political context.

But are modern liberal democracies autonomous in the ancient sense of autonomy? The growing influence of the global market, of multinational companies and international banking and political organizations, has led to a decline in the ability of nations to control their own destinies, particularly with respect to economic policy. States in the contemporary world are becoming less autonomous than they were formerly. To the extent, then, that we see group autonomy as a condition of national democracy, we must conclude that increasing globalization has undermined the possibility of genuine local democracy.

See also *Anarchism; Berlin, Isaiah; Consent; Globalization; Hegel, Georg Wilhelm Friedrich; Justifications for democracy; Kant, Immanuel; Majority rule, minority rights; Marx, Karl; Mill, John Stuart; Participatory democracy; Rousseau, Jean-Jacques.*

Jonathan Wolff

BIBLIOGRAPHY

Berlin, Isaiah. *Four Essays on Liberty.* Oxford: Oxford University Press, 1969.

Dworkin, Gerald. *The Theory and Practice of Autonomy.* Cambridge: Cambridge University Press, 1988.

Held, David. "Democracy, the Nation-State and the Global System." In *Political Theory Today,* edited by David Held. Cambridge: Polity Press, 1991.

Mill, John Stuart. "On Liberty." In *Utilitarianism.* Edited by Mary Warnock. Glasgow: Collins, 1962.

Rousseau, Jean-Jacques. "The Social Contract." In *The Social Contract and Discourses.* Edited by G. D. H. Cole, J. H. Brumfitt, and John C. Hall. London: Dent, 1973.

Wolff, Robert Paul. *In Defense of Anarchism.* New York: Harper, 1973.

Aylwin, Patricio

First democratic president of Chile (1990–1994) after the military dictatorship of Gen. Augusto Pinochet. Patricio Aylwin Azócar (1918–) was a lawyer who was presi-

dent of the National Falange Party, a founder of the Christian Democratic Party (in 1957), and a senator from 1965 until the dissolution of Congress by the military in 1973.

As president of the Senate in 1971–1972 and president of the Christian Democrats from 1973 to 1976, Aylwin opposed the government of Salvador Allende (1970–1973) and rejected any compromise with its democratic socialist policies. When the Christian Democratic Party subsequently opposed the dictatorship of General Pinochet, Aylwin became a leader of the Group of Constitutional Studies, which put forward an alternative democratic constitution. He, among others, urged the opposition groups to focus their efforts on gaining the political space necessary to modify the 1980 constitution that Pinochet had imposed, rather than discussing its legitimacy. This view paralleled the growing conviction among opposition forces that political mobilization should use institutional means to remove the dictatorship. As president of his party, Aylwin became the spokesperson of the entire democratic opposition in the successful campaign to defeat Pinochet in the plebiscite of 1988.

Aylwin ran for president in 1989 as the candidate of a center-left coalition, the Coalition of Parties for Democracy. He carried 55 percent of the vote and took office in March 1990. During Aylwin's presidency the major institutions that had been put in place under the 1980 constitution were not modified, and Pinochet remained military chief of staff. Nevertheless, Aylwin's government eliminated the risk of a return to authoritarian rule and consolidated the fragile institutions of democracy. The center-left coalition that had elected Aylwin remained unified. In the 1993 presidential election it supported the successful candidacy of Eduardo Frei Ruiz-Tagle.

See also *Chile; Military rule and transition to democracy.*

Manuel Antonio Garretón M.

Azerbaijan

See *Caucasus, The*

Azikiwe, Nnamdi

Nigerian nationalist leader, governor general of the Federation of Nigeria (1960–1963), and president of the Federal Republic of Nigeria (1963–1966). Azikiwe (1904–   ) was the most influential African nationalist of an era that spanned the Great Depression, World War II, and the immediate postwar years. Unlike Winston Churchill and Charles de Gaulle, Azikiwe and his fellow nationalists believed that freedom from colonial rule was the logical and morally imperative corollary of principled antifascism.

Inspired by accounts of educational opportunity in America, the young Azikiwe in 1925 made his way to the United States, where he enrolled at Storer College in Harper's Ferry, West Virginia. During his nine years in the United States, he experienced poverty, racial discrimination, and utter despair, as well as success in athletic and academic pursuits. He earned a bachelor of arts in political science at Lincoln University, a master of science in anthropology at the University of Pennsylvania, and a certificate in journalism at Columbia University.

In 1934 Azikiwe accepted an offer to edit a daily newspaper in Accra, Gold Coast (now Ghana). Three years later, having been prosecuted by the colonial government and acquitted, on appeal, for the publication of a "seditious" article, he returned to Nigeria and established a daily newspaper, the *West African Pilot*, in the capital city, Lagos. He also published a collection of his articles and other works, entitled *Renascent Africa*, which became something of a bible for the nationalist intelligentsia of British West Africa.

One of the basic themes of Azikiwe's prewar writing was the principle of mental emancipation. He decried Africa's "miseducation" and consequent "mental enslavement" as a root cause of underdevelopment and political subjugation. Later, he fulfilled his youthful dream of building a university in Nigeria.

In 1944 Azikiwe and Herbert Macaulay, his mentor, founded the National Council of Nigeria and the Cameroons. When Macaulay died in 1946, Azikiwe became its president. His activities soon encompassed the distinct yet complementary roles of journalist, politician, publisher, and banker. He acquired a bank to finance the publications that supported his political activities. Eventually, his political career was threatened by alleged conflicts of interest arising from these diverse roles.

Azikiwe's career exemplifies the virtually inextricable interlacement of nationalist politics, private business, and ethnic loyalties in the African independence movements. Despite his dedication to universal purposes that transcended parochial ethnic identities, Azikiwe never neglected the political interests of his own Igbo-speaking people. He supported their struggle for secession (as Biafra) in 1967 but later played a significant role in the post–civil war reintegration of Igbos into the fabric of Nigerian political life.

Following the restoration of civilian government in 1979, Azikiwe ran for president in two successive elections. These candidacies reflected his continuing desire to ensure due consideration for Igbo interests in a governing coalition.

It could be said that Azikiwe loved to play the great game of democratic politics just as he loved the sporting world. He often praised the "spirit of sportsmanship" as a political virtue.

See also *African independence movements; Nigeria.*

Richard L. Sklar

B

Bagehot, Walter

English economist, journalist, and essayist. Bagehot (1826–1877) covered a wide range of subjects in his writings, including parliamentary representation and democracy. Chief among his contributions was his recognition and analysis of the distinction between, and interdependence of, the "dignified" (or ceremonial) and the "efficient" (or practical) characteristics of government.

Bagehot graduated with first-class honors in mathematics from University College, London, in 1846. He also qualified as a lawyer but never practiced. After working in his family's banking firm in Somerset, he succeeded his father-in-law as editor of the *Economist* in 1860. Editing, combined with a continuing interest in the family bank, remained his main occupation until his death.

On several occasions Bagehot tried and failed to enter Parliament as a Liberal. He became a close confidant of ministers, particularly on matters of economic and financial policy. Reputedly, British statesman William E. Gladstone, who served as prime minister four times between 1868 and 1894, once referred to him as "a kind of spare Chancellor of the Exchequer."

Bagehot's extensive political and constitutional writings were influenced by the works of, among others, political philosophers Jeremy Bentham and John Stuart Mill, historian Alexis de Tocqueville, and anthropologist Henry Maine. Sharing the alarm of many middle-class Victorians about being swamped by the votes of the uneducated masses, Bagehot wrote in a skeptical vein about the movement for working-class enfranchisement. Following passage of the 1867 Reform Act extending the franchise, however, he argued that the new electorate should be fitted for their new responsibilities through improved living conditions and by education. In *Principles of Political Economy* (1848), he had written that "the only effective security against the rule of an ignorant, miserable, and vicious democracy, is to take care that the democracy shall be educated, and comfortable, and moral."

Bagehot's best-known work, *The English Constitution*, was first published in book form in 1867. The Reform Act, passed that same year, heralded the rise of a mass, disciplined party system, which was destined to render some important parts of his analysis out of date. The enduring importance of the book, however, lies in its imaginative departure from obsolete constitutional doctrine about the separation of powers and the role of the monarch, inherited from, among others, philosophers John Locke and Baron de Montesquieu and legal writer William Blackstone. As Alastair Buchan noted (in *The Spare Chancellor*, 1959), Bagehot had for some years been impressed by the contrast between the omnipotence that the rural inhabitants of Somerset attributed to the Crown and the nobility and the reality as he saw it each week in London. Buchan pointed out that Bagehot's purpose was to look at the realities of power as they existed in 1867.

Bagehot began *The English Constitution* by observing that the importance that traditionally had been attached to the separation of powers, on the one hand, and to checks and balances, on the other, had overlooked the crucial distinction between the "dignified" and the "efficient" elements of government. For many centuries past, but no longer, those elements had united in one person, the monarch. The dignified parts—the pomp and ceremony surrounding the monarch and lords—appealed to people's deference to the "theatrical show of society," Bagehot wrote. He observed that the real rulers "are secreted in second-class carriages; no one cares for them or asks about them, but they are obeyed implicitly and unconsciously by reason of the splendor of those who eclipsed and preceded them."

In Bagehot's view the efficient secret of the English Constitution lay in the cabinet, which he described as "a combining committee—a *hyphen* which joins, a *buckle* which fastens, the legislative part of the State to the executive part of the State." In contrast to the separate legislative, executive, and judicial branches derived from the U.S. Constitution—with which Bagehot drew mostly unfavorable comparisons throughout the book—the cabinet embodied a fusion rather than a separation of legislative and executive powers.

Bagehot's analysis was a brilliantly original snapshot of the English Constitution as it had come to operate in 1867. The simple but effective dichotomy between "dignified" and "efficient" aspects of government remains a valuable example. The rise of mass political parties, however, quickly overtook his depiction of the House of Commons as the place where "ministries are made and unmade." (He had in fact conceded that the House of Commons embodied a dignified as well as an efficient role, a view that is even more appropriate today.) In his introduction to a 1963 edition of *The English Constitution*, English politician and political theorist Richard Crossman observed that Bagehot had not even a premonition about the nature of the modern political party—in part because he had never visited the United States, where parties already were firmly established.

Among Bagehot's writings are literary criticism and biography as well as politics, economics, and anthropology. His collected works run to fifteen volumes. After *The English Constitution,* he embarked upon *Physics and Politics* (1872), which was an attempt to apply evolutionary theories to political development.

Bagehot is not in the first rank of democratic theorists. Nor is he one of the great pioneers of social science: his views about popular deference and political naïveté were based upon a mixture of bourgeois prejudice and amateur psychology rather than upon systematic empirical investigation. But he was an astute, eloquent, and versatile political commentator who exerted considerable influence on his contemporaries, and his constitutional analysis throws valuable light upon the operation of representative government in an important formative era of modern British government.

See also *Gladstone, William E.*

Gavin Drewry

BIBLIOGRAPHY

Bagehot, Walter. *The Collected Works of Walter Bagehot.* Edited by Norman St. John-Stevas. 15 vols. Cambridge: Harvard University Press, 1965–1986.

———. *The English Constitution.* Introduction by R. H. S. Crossman. London: Collins, 1963.

Buchan, Alastair. *The Spare Chancellor.* London: Chatto and Windus, 1959.

St. John-Stevas, Norman. *Walter Bagehot.* London: Eyre and Spottiswoode, 1959.

Stephen, Leslie, and Sidney Lee, eds. *The Dictionary of National Biography.* Supp 1. *From Earliest Times to 1900.* Oxford and New York: Oxford University Press, 1953.

Ballots

Devices—paper, mechanical, or electronic—on which voters designate their choices for candidates or policy questions. With the expansion of the franchise in the nineteenth century, debate began in Europe and the British Empire over whether voting by oral expression should be replaced by voting on a printed paper ballot. A paper ballot could be secret and thus would discourage the intimidation and bribery of voters.

The Australian Ballot

The Australian colonies set the modern example. In 1856 a law was enacted to provide for a particular type of printed paper ballot. This Australian ballot was printed by the government; it contained the names of all duly nominated candidates (that is, it was a blanket ballot); and it was distributed by officials at officially administered polling places. Great Britain enacted its ballot law in 1872. At about the same time, other European countries provided their versions of the printed ballot. Today all European democracies follow the basic secrecy provisions of the Australian ballot, although the actual formats vary widely. In France, for example, each candidate in the single-member district legislative election prepares his or her own distinctive ballot to be distributed under government auspices.

The history of the ballot in the United States followed a different course. In the American colonies oral voting was replaced first by the use of corn or beans as ballots; later a voter could write the names of preferred candidates on a paper ballot. By 1780 all but one of the states required the use of such paper ballots. By the 1820s printed ballots had come into use. They were made necessary not only by the expansion of the franchise but also by circumstances peculiar to the country: the United States had an unusually large number of offices to be filled by voters, and the president was formally elected through an electoral college. To elect the president, voters had to support one or another list of electors who were pledged to a party's candidate. As in some European countries, these early ballots were printed by the political parties, not the government, and a party's ballot ("ticket") would contain only the names of its own candidates. Ballots were not secret—the parties' ballots might be of different colors, and any voter who took the time to strike out ("scratch") certain names and substitute others, either by writing them in or attaching a gummed "paster," was easily identified. In the United States as elsewhere the demand for the adoption of the Australian ballot was thus primarily a demand for ballot secrecy. The first state to enact a statewide Australian ballot law was Massachusetts in 1888. (A few months earlier such a law had been enacted for the city of Louisville, Kentucky.) By the presidential election of 1892, thirty-eight states had enacted such laws. By 1910 all but two had done so.

In the United States the Australian ballot was seen as a way to reduce the influence of powerful and often corrupt political machines. A significant source of a machine's power was its ability to extract "assessments" (payment) from candidates who wanted to appear on the party's ticket. Moreover, machine agents could readily bribe voters on election day and could observe how people voted. The existing ballot system also presented formidable obstacles to independent candidates. The enactment of Australian ballot laws in the various states thus marked the beginning of a wider antimachine, municipal reform movement that carried over into the 1890s and the early twentieth century and included proponents of a number of political movements, including the Mugwump, Single Tax, Populist, Progressive, and Good Government movements.

Questions Raised by the Australian Ballot

Wherever it was introduced, the Australian ballot implied certain political consequences perhaps unforeseen by its early advocates. First, it required government to define the rules by which candidates could be nominated and thus eligible to have their names included on the ballot paper. Usually the requirement was a certain number of nomination signatures. Second, there was the question of whether candidates on the ballot should be identified by party label. Great Britain did not print such labels until 1969, and Canada until 1972. Candidates appearing on the Australian ballot still are not identified by party.

In the United States the questions of ballot access and party labels were given distinctive answers. In recognition of the inevitability of political parties, state laws granted automatic ballot access to any political parties that demonstrated a certain level of public support and provided for the printing on the ballot of party labels and emblems. The two major parties (Republican and Democrat) thus were given an advantage over smaller parties, which were required to circulate petitions. The ballot legislation also sometimes attempted to regulate the procedures by which the officially recognized parties chose delegates to their nominating conventions. The introduction of the Australian ballot thus provided the legal foundation for what later became distinctive U.S. laws controlling political parties. That control was most dramatically reflected in the early years of the twentieth century, when most states enacted laws requiring the officially recognized parties to nominate their candidates by direct primary elections. As part of the same Progressive-inspired municipal reforms, many states also enacted laws requiring municipalities to omit party labels from their local election ballots, a requirement designed to produce nonpartisan government at the local level. About three-quarters of the cities and towns of the United States came to be governed by these laws. Far less successful was the "short ballot" movement, which urged a reduction in the number of elected municipal offices so that voters could give more careful attention to each ballot choice. Finally, in some states, as a consequence of Progressive reforms, ballots could be used to allow voters to record a "yes" or "no" vote in policy referendums.

Another question raised by the Australian ballot was the order in which candidate names should be listed. Possible options included listing by alphabet, by lot, by rotation, by incumbency, or—in the case of groups of candidates—by party strength. Studies have shown that candidates who are listed first, or whose party list appears first, have the advantage. The order of candidates on a list has been shown to be especially important in nonpartisan elections, including primary elections. In contrast, when policy questions are put to voters in a referendum, the place where these questions appear on the ballot has been shown to have little influence on outcome or participation.

Where many offices are to be filled in an election, an important question raised by the Australian ballot is whether candidates should be grouped by party affiliation. In countries using proportional representation systems for legislative elections, party grouping is essential. In the United States, where proportional representation is not used and where many types of offices are filled in a single election, the question of party grouping has been widely debated. The Massachusetts ballot arranged the names of candidates according to the office being contested. This office block ballot came to be preferred by reformers who wanted voters to focus on the qualifications of individual candidates and who also wanted to insulate state and local politics from national politics. In contrast, the ballot law enacted in Indiana grouped all of each party's candidates in a single vertical column, with each column having a party emblem and circle at the top to allow a "straight ticket" vote. By 1910 more than twice as many states had adopted this Indiana, or party column, ballot as had chosen the office block format. By the 1980s that balance had been reversed; only a minority of states used any device that allowed a straight party vote—whether on a paper ballot, a voting machine, or a punch card. By this time, however, the distinction between the Massachusetts and Indiana ballot types had become obsolete. Some states retained the office block format yet allowed a single pencil mark or "punch" to register a straight party vote. And the design of early voting machines made the office block format resemble the party column format, since all of a party's candidates were listed in separate horizonal rows or vertical columns, thereby allowing a quick sweep of the hand to register a straight party vote.

Scholars who have studied the consequences of ballot format agree that the use of any device that allows or facilitates a straight ticket vote—even a party column (or row) format on a voting machine—results in more straight ticket voting than does the traditional office block ballot. The amount of "ballot fatigue" (failure to vote for the less conspicuous offices) is also reduced.

The consequences of other ballot-related decisions are less certain. Was the sharp increase in split ticket voting that occurred in the United States about the turn of the century caused by the introduction of the Australian ballot, which guaranteed secrecy and presented all parties' candidates on the same ballot? Or should that change in voting patterns be attributed to changes in voters' attitudes about and orientation toward the party system? Also, does the downward trend in turnout statistics at the turn of the century reflect a reduction in voter participation or simply the fact that the Australian ballot eliminated large-scale ballot box stuffing?

Control of access to the ballot confronted U.S. states with an additional question. Should a person be allowed to appear on the ballot as the candidate of more than one political party? Joint candidacies were common in the 1880s under the party ticket system; the practice nourished small political parties by allowing them to wage "fusion" campaigns with one of the major parties. The adoption of the party column ballot allowed that practice to continue much as before, and the names of fusion candidates appeared in two or more columns of the ballot. By 1910, however, many states had put an end to joint candidacies either by including in their primary election laws prohibitions against "cross-filing" (filing petitions for entry into more than one party's primary) or by not allowing a candidate's name to appear more than once on a party column ballot. By 1990 all but three states had enacted such prohibitions. In New York, one of the remaining states to allow joint candidacies, the practice, known as cross-endorsement, has nourished that state's distinctive multiparty system.

Other Ballot Formats

Ballots for proportional representation elections can assume a variety of forms. When the single transferable vote form of proportional representation is used (as in Ireland and Malta, and for the Australian Senate), the basic form of the ballot does not vary much from country to country: in each district it contains all of the candidates' names, and voters are asked to rank order the candidates in the order of the voters' preferences by giving the number 1 to their most preferred candidate, the number 2 to their next preference, and so on.

There is greater variation in ballot forms when the more prevalent list system of proportional representation is used. For instance, the Belgian ballot contains the complete lists of candidates' names of each party printed side by side on the ballot paper; the voter can vote either for an entire list or for one preferred candidate on the list. In Switzerland, each party's list of candidates is printed on a different ballot; the voter selects one of these ballots and is then allowed to indicate preferences for candidates on this ballot. In Israel, each party also has a different ballot, but no candidate names are printed on it (and the voter does not have the option of indicating a preference for one or more of the party's candidates). Another variation is Finland's ballot, which contains neither the parties' nor the candidates' names; instead, each candidate is publicly assigned a number, and voters are asked to fill in the number of their preferred candidate on the ballot (which also signifies a vote for that candidate's party, unless the candidate is running as an independent). The large ballot used in Venezuela likewise omits the names on the party's list; to support the list, voters place a mark in one of the many brightly colored boxes containing party emblems.

See also *Participation, Political; Parties, Political; Politics, Machine; Progressivism; Proportional representation; Voting rights.*

Howard A. Scarrow

BIBLIOGRAPHY

Campbell, Angus, and Warren E. Miller. "The Motivational Basis of Straight and Split Ticket Voting." *American Political Science Review* 51 (June 1957): 293–312.

Epstein, Leon D. *Political Parties in the American Mold.* Madison: University of Wisconsin Press, 1986.

Fredman, L. E. *The Australian Ballot.* East Lansing: Michigan State University Press, 1968.

Gosnell, Harold F. "Ballot." In *Encyclopedia of the Social Sciences.* New York: Macmillan, 1930–1935.

Rusk, Jerold G. "The Effect of the Australian Ballot Reform on Split Ticket Voting, 1876–1908." *American Political Science Review* 64 (December 1970): 1220–1238.

Scarrow, Howard A. "Ballot Format in Plurality Partisan Elections" and "Cross-Endorsement and Cross-Filing in Plurality Partisan Elections." In *Electoral Laws and Their Political Consequences,* edited by Bernard Grofman and Arend Lijphart. New York: Agathon Press, 1986.

Baltic states

The countries Estonia, Latvia, and Lithuania, which border the Baltic Sea and were part of the Soviet Union until they were recognized as independent republics in 1991. Estonia, at 18,000 square miles and a population of about 1.6 million, is the smallest (and northernmost) of these states. Latvia is much larger, at almost 25,000 square miles and about 2.7 million people; Lithuania, the southernmost, covers 25,000 square miles and has about 3.7 million people. The Baltic states are bordered by Russia, Belarus, and Poland.

The Baltic states were independent from the time of the Russian Revolution until World War II. With their origins in peasant societies, the states of the region were remarkably democratic in the context of the era; they had democratic electoral systems and low levels of violence. But national statehood proved too brief to ensure the formation of stable multiparty systems.

During the 1930s the political situations of the three nations destabilized, and all three ended up under the rule of dictators. In Lithuania, the Nationalist Union ruled, and Antanas Smetona was president from 1926 to 1940. Latvia was initially a democratic state with a stable multiparty system, but the nation ended up under the dictatorship of Karlis Ulmanis in 1934. Estonia was also democratic until 1934, when president Konstantin Päts established personal rule.

The Molotov-Ribbentrop Pact of August 23, 1939, signed by the German and Soviet foreign ministers, effectively decided the fate of the Baltic states. Lithuania was occupied by Soviet authorities on June 15, 1940, and Latvia and Estonia on June 17, 1940. Both the Nazi occupation during World War II and the reoccupation by the Red Army dealt severe blows to the democratic elites of all three countries, leaving little of prewar democratic practices in public life. During the Soviets' repressive campaigns of 1940–1952 against former elites—as well as

status in the party, Lithuanians managed to control much more of their domestic affairs than did Latvians or Estonians.

Latvia was regarded as the most socialist of the Baltic nations by heritage. Even so, Latvian criticism of Moscow was met with severe measures. Estonia was under direct rule by Moscow until 1953, but local officials had some control over internal affairs between 1953 and 1978. Then new antinationalist leaders were installed, but they were unable to reverse the relative democracy of everyday life in Estonia. The Communist Party never had the support of the intellectual elite in Estonia.

Reemergence of the Baltic States

In 1988 Soviet leader Mikhail Gorbachev's perestroika, or "restructuring," allowed the restoration of democratic principles of life in the Baltics. Gradually, the fear in which Lithuanians, Latvians, and Estonians lived began to dissipate. The Estonian Popular Front was the first mass movement in the Union of Soviet Socialist Republics to support perestroika. Very quickly, however, the seeds of democratization grew into demands for national independence that could not be denied. Under pressure from mass movements in all three republics, a nationally oriented new leadership was established: Vaino Väljas in June 1988 in Estonia, Anatolijs Gorbunovs in October 1988 in Latvia, and Algirdas Brazauskas in Lithuania, also in October 1988. From the beginning these leaders accepted political pluralism and worked to reestablish the independence of their countries.

Gorbachev had not intended perestroika to be a means of dismantling the Soviet Union, and he attempted unsuccessfully to stop the republics from leaving. On November 16, 1988, the Estonian Supreme Soviet declared sovereignty, insisting on the supremacy of Estonian law. Estonia's move emboldened most of the other republics to challenge Moscow's rule in the following year. The elections to the Soviet Union's Congress of People's Deputies in March 1989 were the first multicandidate elections in the Baltics since Soviet occupation. In the Baltics those elections were held for all seats as multiparty contests between the ruling communist parties and the popular fronts.

In Lithuania the popular movement won outright; in Estonia each group gained half the seats; and in Latvia the Communist Party prevailed. As domestic politics became their main preoccupation, the Baltic representatives began to play a less active role in the political institutions of the

against those among the peasantry accused of resistance—more than 30,000 people were deported from Estonia, more than 57,000 from Latvia, and more than 120,000 from Lithuania.

With incorporation into the Soviet Union, the Baltic states became communist states under Soviet domination. At first the Soviet regime was ruthless, and all directives came from Moscow. Inside the Baltics, however, democratic traditions of popular culture continued; public opinion condemned abuses of power and offered victims support. The Baltic nations never accepted Sovietization, and much of the Communist Party leadership was Russian. Only Lithuania had a home-born first secretary of the Communist Party, Antanas Snieckus. More Lithuanians began to join the Communist Party in the mid-1950s. (In 1986 they made up about 70 percent of the party's 197,000 members in Lithuania.) Because of their majority

Soviet Union and instead influenced the democratization process from outside the Soviet bodies.

The multiparty elections to the Supreme Soviets of the three Baltic republics, held early in 1990, saw the establishment of noncommunist governments in all three states. The Lithuanian Popular Front (Sajudis) and Latvian Popular Front won decisively; the Estonian Popular Front fell short of a majority (42 of 101 seats). In Lithuania, Vytautas Landsbergis was elected chairman of the Supreme Soviet. In Latvia, Anatolijs Gorbunovs was elected chairman of the Supreme Soviet and Ivars Godmanis was named head of the government. In Estonia, Arnold Rüütel stayed as head of the Supreme Soviet, and the leader of the Popular Front, Edgar Savisaar, was nominated head of the government.

With the new governments, any efforts to improve the communist system were abandoned, and the move toward democracy was under way. The elections of 1990 also verified the individualization of the political processes in the three countries. The only common feature was their pursuit of independence as the basis for democratization of their future political life.

Lithuania declared independence from the USSR on March 11, 1990. In January 1991 the Soviet leadership tried to reestablish control over Lithuania by force. After this attempt failed, practical steps to rebuild the Lithuanian state went ahead rapidly. Lithuania did not attempt to restore the pre–World War II state, since Vilnius and the surrounding region had again become part of the country only in 1939. The legality of a restored state would be questionable.

An Estonian citizens congress was elected February 24, 1990 (90 percent of the citizens voted), and a Latvian citizens congress was elected April 8, 1990. For a while during 1990 and 1991 there was almost a dual system of government. The two nations' congresses claimed to represent their authentic national interests, while their Supreme Soviets claimed to play a transitional role between Soviet rule and renewed independence. The situation did not last long, however: the Estonian state was reestablished August 20, 1991, and the Latvian state gained independence the next day.

The New Governments

Democracy is grounded in citizens' loyalty to the state and its institutions. Having been part of a totalitarian, one-party state, the Baltic countries must struggle with their past. The rule of law and the rights of citizens over the state can be difficult to establish. Although the necessary laws may be adopted, it may take the coming of age of a new generation of citizens to put these principles of civil society into practice.

All three countries established the separation of powers in their constitutions. Estonia adopted its new constitution on July 3, 1992, and Lithuania adopted its new constitution on November 6, 1992. Latvia turned back to its 1923 constitution and readopted it in 1993. All three constitutions reflect the concept of the nation-state. The supremacy of human rights and of citizens is declared. Private property and the market as the basis of economic activity are among the basic principles of society in the new states.

All three countries are parliamentary democracies, with presidents elected by citizens in Lithuania and Estonia and by the parliament in Latvia. Presidents do not have executive power, which is given instead to the governments formed in parliament. As it turned out, of the new leadership established in 1988, only Lithuania's Brazauskas was elected to the presidency (in 1993, with 60 percent of the vote). In Estonia the parliament elected Lennart Meri to the presidency. The Latvian parliament (the Saeima) elected Guntis Ulmanis, the nephew of the late president, Karlis Ulmanis, to the presidency.

Because the division of power is ill defined and unstable, there is substantial rivalry between the presidents and the executive and legislative institutions. This rivalry is weaker in Lithuania, where the successor party to the Communist Party, the Democratic Labor Party, has a clear majority in the parliament and the president is a member of that party. Estonia suffers somewhat from the rivalry, but the struggle is most intense in Latvia, the country with the most diversified power base.

Civil servants in the Baltic states are beholden to the political groups in power, which use the state for their own ends. This situation inevitably creates corruption and a misuse of state power. In a democracy, independent civil servants have an institutionalized interest in protecting the state and preventing the abuse of power by the elected governments. To democratize fully, the Baltic states will need to establish civil services, with selection for positions to be based on merit principles rather than on political connections.

Another tool of a democratic state is an independent legal and law enforcement system. The Baltics have yet to devise such systems. It is common knowledge that the Soviet party-state used law in a declaratory manner and that the law enforcement system was entirely controlled by the party-state apparatus. The Scandinavian countries are helping the Baltic states, directly and by example, to establish judicial and legal systems.

Electoral Systems

In order to become functioning multiparty democracies, the Baltic states had to move quickly to develop parties in the electorate. The new countries based their electoral systems on European models of proportional representation. With minor differences, the systems of all three states combine party votes and candidate votes. Lithuania's system is closely modeled on Germany's two-tier parliamentary elections; one-half of the candidates are elected in single-member districts and the others from party lists. In Estonia and Latvia, quota systems are used to assign party and individual seats in multimember districts. Obviously, the political effect of the electoral laws can be assessed only after several elections.

Because the number of parties can become unmanageable, as happened in Poland's first free elections, it was important to assign seats in the parliaments only to parties that had received a reasonable number of votes. The threshold is 4 percent of the popular vote in Lithuania and Latvia, and 5 percent in Estonia.

In Estonia no one party or electoral list gained a majority. A government was formed by a coalition made up of the right-centrist Pro Patria election alliance, the Moderates, and the radical Estonian National Independence Party.

In the October 1992 elections to the Lithuanian parliament (the Seimas), the Lithuanian Democratic Labor Party won the majority of seats. In this case the democratic electoral system functioned as intended: the Sajudis government was voted out.

Latvia held its first parliamentary elections in June of 1993. The seats in the Saeima were distributed more evenly than were those in Estonia's parliament: the right-centrist Latvian Way won 36 of 100 seats; the radical National Independence Movement won 15 seats; and the left-centrist coalition Harmony for Latvia won 13 seats. The political center is stronger in Latvia than in the other Baltic countries.

In general, the new electoral systems functioned well and produced stable governments. Strong opposition parties were included in each of the parliaments. But over the long run the parties must have the experience of losing. It takes losing or the threat of losing to make parties and leaders accountable to the electorate. Those in government must take the opposition seriously, granting it respect and legitimacy.

The leaders of the popular fronts learned hard lessons. They had played a decisive role in the changeover from Soviet rule to independent rule. They had practically the total support of the native populations of their countries. Yet they failed to make the necessary transformation from political movement to electoral alliance. They failed to form stable parties.

At present, local elections are not important in the Baltic countries. These small nations have granted little power to their localities. Furthermore, the time and the will needed to establish a democratic sharing of power between the central government and the localities is so far absent.

Parties After Independence

Functioning democracies operate through stable party systems. In the Baltic states, with a few exceptions, the historically rooted parties did not reemerge after independence. In the early 1990s a number of groups were in the process of organizing into political parties. These groups formed alliances for the parliamentary elections. The groups fell into three basic categories: Soviet-era elites, popular fronts, and right-wing nationalist groups.

The Estonian Communist Party leadership in 1988 accepted its role as a transitional force from the party-state to a normal democratic state. The Estonian Communist Party released its members in March 1990, and new party membership was established through reapplication to the Communist Party. (Only one in forty Estonian party members reapplied.) This procedure created the most favorable situation for a peaceful transfer of power, in that the Estonian political elite from the socialist period did not try to use its party machine to stay in power.

In Lithuania and Latvia the former elite behaved differently. The Lithuanian Communist Party, which commanded much loyalty from the people as a national force, fought to hold on to the power it had before. Although the former political elite regained power in Lithuania, these former communists do not necessarily support communist ideology today. The Latvian party elite survived individually, but the re-formed party lost all its political positions. In the Latvian Saeima after the 1993 elections, 41 of the 100 seats were held by former Communist Party members.

The leaders of the popular fronts were active during the socialist period but did not form the top elite. In Estonia most of the Popular Front's leaders were members of the Communist Party. In Lithuania and Latvia somewhat fewer were party members. Most of these people had been heavily engaged in political movements, but they proved less ready to be integrated into political parties and day-to-day politics. Professionals from the arts and humanities dominated the popular fronts and had a huge effect on the transition period. They lost momentum, however, when their mass movements dwindled and they faced the need to become political parties. As a result, this elite produced important individual politicians but not dominant political parties. The exception is Sajudis in Lithuania, which makes up a thirty-member faction in the Seimas.

Typically, the Western press overestimates how much of the new elite comes from the earlier dissident movements. In Estonia those movements did at first lead the Estonian congress. Later, former dissidents were ousted by the younger generation, who organized anticommunist, right-wing parties. The electoral alliance of Pro Patria in Estonia had the best results in parliamentary elections. The young right-wing politicians won a stable majority in the parliament and formed the government. In Latvia right-wing parties emerging from the citizen movement and Latvian congress never gained enough support to influence national politics. The National Independence Movement is the strongest right-wing party in Latvia, and the Christian Democrats are the strongest in Lithuania.

The organization of political parties dragged on in Lithuania, and the emerging business and industrialist elite was very influential in the process. The delays resulted because the elite tended to ignore politics and concentrate on business. Leaders have had to learn the hard way that economics is not altogether independent from politics. Sooner or later they must declare their political preferences and support the appropriate political parties if they want to achieve their economic goals.

Obstacles to Democracy

Poor and socially divided societies are not the most fertile ground for democracy. The transition from the Soviet Empire to the nation-state, and from a command economy to a market one, has created both poverty and division. A strength of the Baltic states is the population's high level of everyday culture and education. These attributes constitute a firm base for developing a civic society with a functioning legal system, respect for human rights, and voluntary organizations, which help protect citizens from

the misuse of state power. Significant class cleavages are unlikely to appear in these small countries.

The Estonian economy is less vulnerable than the economies of the other Baltic states to the huge Russian market, and Estonia is clearly becoming more oriented to the Western European market. The Latvian and Lithuanian economies are more vulnerable to changes in Russia, since they lack their own energy resources and depend more on the Russian market. These two countries are likely to have more economic troubles in the future. Nevertheless, it is very unlikely that economic difficulties can destabilize the political situation, or that social divisions in these societies will influence the democratization process.

The most pressing social question facing these nations is what to do about their large non-native populations. During the Soviet period the government of the Soviet Union intentionally set out to Russianize the Baltic states, moving large numbers of ethnic Russians into them. Lithuania was the least affected; after independence, 80 percent of the population was of Lithuanian origin. That state readily adopted the normal policy toward citizenship in a new country: every person who lives within its borders has the right to become a citizen.

The Estonian and Latvian national populations, in contrast, felt threatened by the huge non-native populations that arrived during the Soviet period. When they became independent they adopted a policy of granting citizenship only to those who had been citizens of the pre-Soviet states and to their descendants. Speakers of Russian constituted more than one-third of the population of Estonia; some of these people have earned Estonian citizenship, but 28 percent of those living in Estonia have alien status. Their situation is difficult and potentially explosive. In Latvia almost one-half of the population is not Latvian, and more than one-quarter of the population does not have Latvian citizenship.

The citizenship policies have brought Estonia and Latvia into conflict with Russia—and, for that matter, with the international human rights community. Many, including the Russian government, argue that anyone who was born in Estonia or Latvia should have an automatic claim to citizenship. The governments involved must solve this problem, for large portions of a population cannot live without legal status. Russia seems unlikely to take the ethnic Russians back. As long as the economic conditions of Russian speakers are acceptable, the political situation will remain manageable. Problems within this population would immediately destabilize the political situation, however. If problems should occur, Russia might well act on behalf of these people. Therefore, for the democratic development of Latvia and Estonia in particular, a workable approach to this legacy of the Soviet years must be developed.

See also *Civil service; Electoral systems; Political culture; Proportional representation; Union of Soviet Socialist Republics.*

Mikk Titma

BIBLIOGRAPHY

The Baltic States: A Reference Book. Tallinn: Estonian Encyclopedia Publishers; Riga: Latvian Encyclopedia Publishers; Vilnius: Lithuanian Encyclopedia Publishers, 1991.

Estonia, Latvia, Lithuania: Statistical Data Book. Vilnius: Department of Statistics of the Republic of Lithuania, 1991–1994.

Lieven, Anatol. *The Baltic Revolution: Estonia, Latvia, Lithuania and the Path to Independence.* New Haven and London: Yale University Press, 1993.

Meissner, Boris. *Die baltischen Nationen: Estland, Lettland, Littauen.* Cologne: Markus, 1990.

Rauch, Georg von. *The Baltic States: The Years of Independence, Estonia, Latvia, Lithuania, 1917–1940.* Berkeley and Los Angeles: University of California Press; London: C. Hurst, 1974.

Senn, Alfred Erich. *Lithuania Awakening.* Berkeley and Los Angeles: University of California Press, 1990.

Sprudzs, Adolf, ed. *The Baltic Path to Independence.* Buffalo, N.Y.: W. S. Hein, 1994.

Taagepera, Rein. *Estonia: Return to Independence.* Boulder, Colo.: Westview Press, 1993.

Valgemae, Mardi, ed. *Baltic History.* Columbus: Ohio State University Press, 1974.

Barbados

See *Caribbean, English*

Bargaining, Collective

See *Industrial relations*

Batlle y Ordóñez, José

Leader of a reform movement that transformed Uruguay from a hotbed of revolutions into a "model country." The movement had a tremendous influence on twentieth-century Uruguayan society and politics.

Batlle y Ordóñez (1856–1929) was the son of General Lorenzo Batlle, former president of the republic (1868–1872) and a leader of the Colorado Party, one of the nation's two traditional parties. Deeply influenced by French radicalism as well as by rationalist and idealist doctrines, he believed that the reform of society should be based on the innate dignity of humankind. As a young man he opposed militarism, and in 1886 he took part in a revolt in Quebracho against the government of General Máximo Santos.

Batlle y Ordóñez founded an opposition newspaper, *El Día*, which was published until 1993. He struggled to strengthen and modernize the Colorado Party and to gain control over it. In 1903 he became president of the republic. From this position he fought the dissident nationalist elements led by Aparicio Saravia and in 1904 succeeded in effectively unifying the country. He then built and consolidated the central power of the state by depriving the rural chieftains, or caudillos, of their power and subordinating seditious elements. He was reelected in 1910.

During his second administration (1911–1915), he and his followers, called Batllistas, set themselves the task of reshaping the Uruguayan state and society. The Batllistas advocated the use of legislation and education as instruments of social and political reform. Batlle y Ordóñez made use of Uruguay's prosperity (based on the export of meat and wool) to give the state a major role as an economic and social agent in the redistribution of wealth.

Batlle y Ordóñez favored a party government in times of peace. He organized the Batllista wing almost as a separate party within the Colorado Party and gave it a modern organization. He sought a constitutional reform that included a collegial executive branch dominated by the majority faction of the winning party. He hoped that this would prevent the recurrence of governments dominated by a single individual while still maintaining party control over the executive. In 1916 his proposed reform was defeated in Uruguay's first open election with full guarantees (that is, secret and universal male vote).

He managed to ensure a mixed presidential-collegial government in the new Uruguayan constitution, which went into effect in 1919. A humanist, he also completed the process of secularization that had been begun by some of his predecessors. Church and state were formally separated in the new constitution.

Batlle y Ordóñez gave Uruguay a platform of social and political reform that endured through many crises. As a result, Uruguay became renowned for its democratic traditions and advanced social legislation.

Juan Rial

BIBLIOGRAPHY

Lindahl, Goran G. *Uruguay's New Path: A Study in Politics during the First Colegiado, 1919–1933.* Translated by Albert Reed. Stockholm: University of Stockholm, 1962.

Real de Azua, Carlos. *El impulso y su freno: Tres décadas de Batllismo y las raíces de la crisis uruguaya.* Montevideo: Ediciones de la Banda Oriental, 1964.

Vanger, Milton. *José Batlle y Ordóñez of Uruguay: The Creator of His Times, 1902–1907.* Cambridge: Harvard University Press, 1963.

———. *The Model Country.* Hanover, N.H.: University Press of New England, 1980.

Belarus

A state in Eastern Europe bordered by Poland, Lithuania, Latvia, Russia, and Ukraine, earlier known as Belorussia or colloquially as "White Russia." Belarus was a constituent republic of the Soviet Union, from which it became independent in 1991. Today, Belarus, like the other former republics of the Soviet Union, is on a tortuous road from a totalitarian regime to a democratic political system and a market economy. With a multiethnic citizenry of various religious faiths and an oversized army inherited from the old regime, Belarus has become a laboratory of peaceful democratic transformations and an example of the complexity of the process.

The idea of a modern Belarusian state evolved during the nineteenth century under the strong influence of socialism. The popularity of socialist views among the lower strata of the population was enhanced by the fact that the nobility in Belarus had been largely Polonized or Russified during five centuries of conflict between Poland and Russia for control of the region. The development of the native Belarusian language also played an important role in the political movement toward national statehood. Historical memories about Belarusian being the official language in the medieval Grand Duchy of Lithuania, Rus', and Samogitia still reverberate in Belarusian society.

The Belarusian-language code of laws—the Statute of the Grand Duchy of Lithuania, promulgated in 1588—serves as an early example of the country's legal culture. The heritage of Belarus is filled not only with wars over Belarusian territory between Russia and Poland but also with examples of tolerance and peaceful coexistence of diverse ethnic and religious groups, which are today the building blocks of democracy.

Problems of Transition

The difficulties for Belarus on the road to democracy are manifold: historical, geopolitical, economic, and psychological. Located directly on the line from Berlin to Moscow, Belarus remains a geostrategic hostage to Russia's military defense strategies. Landlocked and needful of markets and energy resources, Belarus relies heavily on economic ties with Russia, a circumstance that generates pro-Russian political currents. These currents are enhanced by traditional cultural and religious ties with the eastern neighbor. On the other hand, five centuries of association with Lithuania and Poland (from the fourteenth to the eighteenth century), which for a large part of their histories were in conflict with the Grand Duchy of Muscovy, stimulate pro-Western tendencies in Belarus. The call to "return to Europe" has become a popular slogan among the democratic parties.

The seventy-year Soviet period left Belarus with a citizenry whose social structure and psychological traits are not conducive to the development of robust political parties and democratic mechanisms of government. A lack of familiarity with democratic ways, compounded by an absence of social and economic groups that would defend their interests at the ballot box, severely reduces the scope and character of competitive politics.

The decline of the economy, which has continued since the collapse of the Soviet Union in 1991, aggravates the situation even more. The economic infrastructure remains largely in the hands of the old bureaucracy, while the privatization process is small-scale and hesitant. Spreading poverty breeds a psychology of heavy reliance on the state for economic and social tasks and initiatives and generates movements imbued with nostalgia for the Soviet past. The surviving concept of an all-encompassing state dampens the enthusiasm for individual rights and citizens' initiatives. The civil society, which would mobilize and launch public energies, is at its initial stage of development, and the number of nongovernmental organizations is very modest.

Birth of Political Parties

The growth of political parties in Belarus was propelled by a number of developments relating to Soviet general secretary Mikhail Gorbachev's perestroika ("restructuring") program, including the revelations in 1988 of Stalinist crimes of genocide, the exposure in 1989 of the government's cover-up of the 1986 Chernobyl nuclear disaster, and discussion of the pernicious effect of Russification on Belarusian culture. The policy of glasnost ("openness") provided the Belarusian intelligentsia with an opportunity to focus not only on their current grievances but also on their heretofore neglected national history, with its democratic features and ties to Western Europe. These developments stimulated the establishment of several parties with cultural, economic, or environmental goals. All were democratic in nature and supported the political independence of the republic.

As a result of a deepening postindependence economic crisis, a number of left-wing movements sprang up harking back to the fallen communist regime. Some right-wing, pro-Russian groups were founded advocating a return to the old Russian empire. There remains also an unstructured but potent force in former communists who, having abandoned their party membership, remain in power as government functionaries.

The Communist Party of Belarus, briefly banned, reconstituted itself under the new name of the Party of Communists of Belarus. Although the Party of Communists claimed to have about 15,000 members (which would make it one of the largest parties in the republic), its candidate in the 1994 presidential election received only 4 percent of the vote, underscoring the widespread disenchantment with communism. Among the democratic parties, the most viable are the Belarusian Popular Front, the Belarusian Social Democratic Union, the United Democratic Party of Belarus, the Belarusian Peasant Party, and the Belarusian Christian Democratic Association. Most of the other parties are tiny and ineffective. All in all, there were more than thirty political parties in Belarus at the beginning of 1995.

To reduce the proliferation of political organizations, the Supreme Council prepared a new electoral law that established a 500-member minimum for a party to function legally. The democratic parties argued for a lower threshold, of about 150 members, but failed to convince the conservative majority of the legislature. The cutoff rule of 500 will sharply reduce the number of organizations on both sides of the ideological spectrum.

Structure of Government and the New Constitution

In March 1990, when Belarus was still part of the Soviet Union, the Supreme Council, the highest legislative body in the republic, was elected for a five-year period. Favored by the electoral law, the Communists secured an overwhelming majority in the 360-member unicameral parliament. The democratic, reform-oriented opposition, led by the Popular Front, gained approximately 10 percent of the seats. But, in the course of the legislative process, it garnered up to 100 votes on occasion. These opposition deputies spearheaded the drive for national self-determination and democratic reforms. Through the efforts of this group the Supreme Council adopted the Declaration of State Sovereignty on July 27, 1990. This declaration was accorded the status of constitutional law when the Supreme Council proclaimed the independence of Belarus on August 25, 1991, in the wake of the failed communist putsch in Moscow.

Democratic reforms and privatization, however, were stalled by the conservative majority both in the government and in the Supreme Council. The opposition, led by the Popular Front, pressed for the government's resignation and new parliamentary elections. In the spring of 1992, more than 447,000 signatures were collected (30,000 over the legal requirement) to hold an early election for a new legislature. The Supreme Council, however, ignored the appeal, while the government of Prime Minister Viachaslau Kebich campaigned for a close union with Russia.

After almost four years of debate, the Supreme Council decided on the presidential character of the republic and, in March 1994, adopted a new constitution. Belarus was proclaimed to be a unitary, democratic social state with a diversity of political institutions, ideologies, and opinions. The constitution established a separation of powers among the legislative, executive, and judicial branches and established a unicameral legislature (Supreme Council) of 260 members elected for a five-year period.

Although basic human rights are enshrined in the law of the land, there is not much democracy at the lower level of the political system. The idea of self-government and local assemblies has been given short shrift by the constitution. Thus, in case of a conflict between lower and higher local councils, a decision of a lower council can be overruled by the next higher authority without recourse to the courts.

The constitution gave extensive powers to the president, who is elected for a five-year term and may serve a maximum of two terms. As head of state and the executive branch, the president appoints and dismisses ministers (key posts are filled with approval of the Supreme Council); introduces to the Supreme Council the nominations for other important positions; appoints justices; conducts international negotiations; signs treaties and laws; has the right to cancel acts and suspend decisions of lower executive authorities and local councils; heads the National Security Council; is the commander in chief; and can introduce martial law. The parliament, however, can overrule a presidential veto on any adopted bill if two-thirds of the deputies reconfirm the bill.

The constitutional provisions on the presidency were crafted by the conservative majority of the parliament with an eye on the strongly pro-Moscow prime minister Kebich. Kebich was heavily favored to win the election of June–July 1994, in which six candidates were vying for the post. However, Kebich lost dismally; he was beaten by a populist, Alaksandr Lukashenka, whose main attraction among the voters was his emotional outrage at corruption and thievery in the high echelons of government.

In the runoff election between Kebich and Lukashenka, 80 percent of the registered voters went to the polls, proving that there is strong support for the ballot as a way of expressing one's political choice. But the balloting also revealed the gullibility of the electorate, who, frustrated by bureaucratic disarray and poverty, readily responded to the shrill rantings of a populist avenger and his general promises of improvement.

At the same time, Lukashenka's resounding victory over Kebich, who abused his privileged access to the mass media, showed the electorate's ability to recognize the arrogance of power and to reject it. The two democratic candidates, Zianon Pazniak and Stanislau Shushkevich, backed by the Popular Front and the Social Democrats, respectively, collected a combined 23 percent of the votes, indicating that democracy in Belarus had a long way to go to be accepted as the best mechanism for solving problems. In Belarus, as elsewhere in Europe, the state is looked upon as the most reliable caretaker of popular needs.

Democratic Prospects

The first months of the Lukashenka presidency were a period of confrontation between the executive and the legislative branches of government, with the involvement of the Constitutional Court. The battle started when the president obtained from the Supreme Council a law empowering him to subordinate the local councils to his authority. This law precipitated court action. Eighty-two deputies requested that the Constitutional Court decide whether the president's move was in accordance with the constitution. The court ruled that it was not and nullified the reconstitution of the local councils but left the president's regional and local representatives in place.

At the end of 1994 debates were raging around the Constitutional Court, which was criticized for overstepping its authority and for being interventionist and politicized. The constitutional crisis reflected, on the one hand, a dearth of regulatory legislation, and on the other, the threat of authoritarianism to a society overburdened by economic hardships and lacking democratic experience.

In the latter part of 1994 the Supreme Council debated a new electoral law with a view to the parliamentary elections to be held in the spring of 1995. At issue was the principle of representation—majoritarian, proportional, or a combination of the two. The conservative communist majority prevailed over the democratic opposition and the legislature adopted the majoritarian principle. Majoritarian rule confines representation to single-member electoral districts, in most of which communist-era functionaries are still in power. This prevents the fledgling political parties, spread all over the nation, from winning a full measure of representation in the parliament. The democrats, led by the Popular Front, called on all parties that stand for national independence and a market economy to form a bloc to compete in an election that will profoundly influence the course of democratic reforms through the 1990s.

The development of democracy in Belarus has been inhibited by a generation of functionaries, still in power at all levels of the bureaucracy, who historically have been connected with the cause of a "great" Russia. For many Belarusians, there are psychological and cultural barriers against supporting an independent Belarus. It will be a generation or more before the idea of a sovereign and democratic Belarus will gain predominance among the population of the country and will be able to become a force in its political life.

See also *Europe, East Central; Union of Soviet Socialist Republics.*

Jan Zaprudnik

BIBLIOGRAPHY

Commission on Security and Cooperation in Europe. *Report on the Belarusian Presidential Election.* Washington, D.C.: U.S. Commission on Security and Cooperation in Europe, 1994.

Constitution of the Republic of Belarus in the Belarusian, Russian, English, French, and German Languages. Minsk: Belarus Publishers, 1994.

Edgeworth, Linda, Richard Messick, and Jan Zaprudnik. *Pre-Election Technical Assessment: Belarus.* Washington, D.C.: International Foundation for Electoral Systems, 1994.

"Human Rights in Belarus." *Belarusan Review* 7 (spring 1995): 1–6.

Kipel, Vitaut, and Zora Kipel, eds. *Byelorussian Statehood: Reader and Bibliography.* New York: Byelorussian Institute of Arts and Sciences, 1988.

Zaprudnik, Jan. *Belarus: At a Crossroads in History.* Boulder, Colo.: Westview Press, 1993.

Belgium

See *Low Countries*

Benin

See *Africa, Subsaharan*

Berlin, Isaiah

Political philosopher and historian of ideas. Berlin (1909–) was born in Riga, Latvia, but educated in England. His academic career has been spent at Oxford University, and he was knighted in 1957. As a historian of ideas, he is noted for his early account of the life and work of Karl Marx, first published in 1939 and never since out of print. In addition, Berlin has produced pioneering studies of many previously neglected figures in the history of thought, including Giambattista Vico (1668–1744), the Italian antirationalist philosopher of history, and Johann Herder (1744–1803) and Johann Hamann (1730–1788), figures of the German Counter Enlightenment.

Berlin's political theories are most famously set out in his 1958 Oxford inaugural lecture, "Two Concepts of Liberty" (reprinted in his *Four Essays on Liberty,* 1969). Two themes are given prominence. First is the distinction between positive liberty and negative liberty; second is the idea that human values, while objective, nevertheless do

Isaiah Berlin

erned?" The second of these questions asks, "What am I free to do?" or, as Berlin would say, "How much negative liberty do I have?" The first does not so much inquire about an individual's area of control but asks who is the source of control—who is master? One has positive freedom to the extent that one is one's own master.

As Berlin suggests, these two ideas at first do not seem very different; yet they can be made to come apart. Berlin argues that systems of positive liberty have sometimes tended to produce the opposite: tyranny. Suppose we agree that freedom requires self-mastery. Yet this supposition also suggests the idea of freedom as an act of overcoming—perhaps the overcoming of a "lower" self of base desires by a "higher" self of reason. In this view, if one is a slave to one's passions one is not free, even if no one else is restricting one's activities. Positive freedom, then, is acting as directed by one's rational self.

But who is to judge what my "rational self" directs? It is here that the possibility of tyranny enters. For others may claim to understand the nature of my rational self—my true interests—better than I do. Hence I may find that positive freedom, in practice, amounts to acting entirely as others direct. Thus totalitarian states have represented themselves as the only regimes of freedom—claiming that the individual's true interests are identical with the interests of "the party" or "the nation." On this basis, some have concluded that democracy must exclude appeals to the true interests of the citizen.

Critics have made several objections to Berlin's argument. One response is that the danger Berlin identifies is not so much a consequence of the adherence to the value of positive liberty but to the next two premises in the argument: the division of an individual into two selves and the identification of the higher self with a wider entity—the party or the nation. Further, as Berlin himself points out, negative liberty too can be perverted—this time in the direction of economic ultra-individualism, or anarchism. But Berlin's reply is that his argument is a historical one. Defenders of positive liberty have been prepared, in the words of the eighteenth-century Swiss-French philosopher Jean-Jacques Rousseau, to "force people to be free," whereas ultra-individualism has rarely been a consequence of those regimes that promote negative liberty: the absence of interference by others. Indeed, negative liberty is the distinctive value of much contemporary liberalism.

It is important for Berlin, however, that there is no necessary connection between positive liberty and tyranny. Insofar as he sees a connection between liberty and de-

not fall into a simple or coherent system—that is, plural and conflicting values coexist even within the life of a single individual. Both of these ideas have implications for democracy. Berlin sees democratic rule as a way of exercising positive freedom, yet pluralistic values cast doubt on the proposition that democracy can be conclusively justified.

Berlin's distinction between positive and negative liberty, while provocative, can be difficult to formulate. Sometimes it is represented—even by Berlin—as a distinction between freedom from interference (negative liberty) and freedom to act (positive liberty). But critics have pointed out that this interpretation does not mark a clear distinction: freedom is always freedom *for* a person, *from* some constraint, *to* act in a certain way (the so-called tripartite analysis of freedom).

Perhaps a more helpful way of approaching the distinction is to examine a pair of questions that Berlin sets out: "By whom am I governed?" and "How much am I gov-

mocracy, it is the positive concept of liberty that is relevant. Democracy is a particular sort—a particularly attractive and intrinsically valuable sort—of collective self-mastery, or self-government. And to be self-governing is to enjoy positive liberty.

Berlin sees the relationship between negative liberty and democracy as rather more precarious. For one may have more negative liberty—more freedom of action—under the rule of an easygoing or inefficient despot than in a strenuous but intolerant egalitarian democracy. Perhaps Berlin has in mind the tightly bound social contract of Rousseau: all citizens play an active role in the creation of laws, but, by contemporary liberal standards, they do not enjoy an extensive range of freedoms.

In Rousseau, then, we can see a conflict between positive and negative liberty, or between majoritarian democracy and liberty. This conflict is an example of Berlin's general thesis that it is impossible to achieve all that we value. Our values necessarily conflict, and so the values we advance in the social and political world are those we have selected. It would be natural to believe that the role of democracy is, in part, to facilitate choice between values. But Berlin's own view is that democracy is not a neutral or higher forum in which value conflict is to be played out. Rather democracy itself is one of the things we value, and, as we have seen, it is capable of conflicting with other values.

Democracy, then, is not the solution to the problem of conflicting values, for there can be no solution. On this view there can be no final, conclusive justification of democracy. The Western world, of course, has largely chosen to pursue democratic forms of government. According to Berlin this pursuit is certainly not something we should regret, but we should recognize it for what it is: a choice.

See also *Autonomy; Fascism; Justifications for democracy; Leninism; Rousseau, Jean-Jacques.*

Jonathan Wolff

BIBLIOGRAPHY

Berlin, Isaiah. *Against the Current: Essays in the History of Ideas.* London: Hogarth Press, 1979.

———. *Four Essays on Liberty.* Oxford and New York: Oxford University Press, 1969.

———. *Karl Marx: His Life and Environment.* 4th ed. Oxford and New York: Oxford University Press, 1978.

———. *Vico and Herder: Two Studies in the History of Ideas.* London: Hogarth Press, 1976.

Ryan, Alan, ed. *The Idea of Freedom.* Oxford and New York: Oxford University Press, 1979.

Ullmann-Margalit, Edna, and Avishai Margalit, eds. *Isaiah Berlin: A Celebration.* London: Hogarth Press; Chicago: University of Chicago Press, 1991.

Bernstein, Eduard

German socialist writer and politician who advocated a revised version of Marxism. Bernstein (1850–1932) was born in Berlin, the son of a Jewish railroad engineer. He worked as a clerk in a bank from 1866 to 1878. Unlike most early socialist leaders, he had no university education. He joined the German Social Democratic Workers Party in 1871 and became a Marxist under the influence of Karl Marx and Friedrich Engels, both of whom he met in 1880.

Engels's liking and respect for Bernstein led to his appointment as editor of the party organ, *Der Sozialdemokrat.* Because of antisocialist laws the paper was edited and printed outside Germany, first in Zurich and then in London. Bernstein lived in London from 1880 until his return to Germany in 1901.

Engels considered Bernstein a central figure in the growing German social democratic movement, and he chose Bernstein to be his literary executor. During his years in London, Bernstein was closely associated with the British Fabian socialists. He came to admire the democratic British labor movement with its reformist aspect. After his return to Germany, Bernstein published a series of articles in the social democratic theoretical paper, *Die Neue Zeit,* advocating reform. The articles shocked party leaders. While claiming that he still clung to the core message of the movement, Bernstein stated that the party functioned dogmatically, held outdated and unscientific premises, and needed an intellectual revision (hence the term *revisionism*) to stay in touch with contemporary philosophical and political trends. He expanded the articles into a book, *Evolutionary Socialism* (1899), which became the main handbook of revisionism in Germany.

Bernstein broke with Marxist orthodoxy on several issues. He claimed that Marx was wrong to expect an increase in the misery of the working class and the gradual destruction of the middle class. Although orthodox Marxists again and again proclaimed the impending demise of capitalist society in a series of catastrophic breakdowns, Bernstein predicted the gradual increase of both the power of the working class and its social and political weight.

The working class, he argued, would gradually gain influence through an increase in the number of social democratic deputies in the Reichstag, or parliament, and in the parliaments of the states that together formed the German state. The various parliaments could gradually move in the direction of democracy.

Bernstein appealed to his comrades to give up notions such as the proletarian revolution and the dictatorship of the proletariat. He urged them instead to become fully what they already were in part: a democratic socialist party of reform.

Bernstein wished to eliminate the utopian goals and language of his orthodox party comrades so as to concentrate on the everyday struggle in the real world. Various party congresses condemned Bernstein's views, but neither he nor his growing number of disciples were persuaded to bow to party discipline.

The dominant party center under the theoretical guidance of Karl Kautsky found it difficult to stamp out revisionism. In fact, the party in many instances followed a reformist line while at the same time proclaiming its orthodox faith.

The revisionist message was especially well received in the trade union movement. Although controlled by the party, this movement poured most of its energies into the daily struggle with employers and concerned itself with revolutionary thoughts only at May Day celebrations. Geographically, the effect of revisionism in the party was strongest in the relatively liberal states of southern and southwestern Germany, while autocratically run Prussia remained in the Kautskyan camp. This situation did not change until Prussia underwent democratization following World War I. In short, when and where the state and the ruling class refused to make concessions to the workers' movement, orthodox Marxism dominated. Wherever the ruling powers were willing to make concessions to the socialist movement, Bernstein's revisionism grew deep roots.

Bernstein was not content simply to propose a change in political tactics and strategy to his party. He tried to recast the philosophical premises on which the party had built its philosophy. He had little taste for the influence of the philosopher G. W. F. Hegel in the early work of Marx and Engels, and he also dissented from the historical materialism of their mature work. Instead, he proposed that the philosophical basis of the party should reflect the ideas of Immanuel Kant. This meant above all that the party should not rely on revolutionary hopes and on the

Eduard Bernstein

benevolent operation of an ever expanding economic infrastructure. The party should base itself on ethical appeals to the consciences of individual men and women.

Because of his ethical convictions, Bernstein joined leaders on the left of the party to agitate for a speedy peace in World War I. He did this at a time when many revisionists became superpatriots.

See also *Engels, Friedrich; Marx, Karl; Marxism.*

Lewis A. Coser

BIBLIOGRAPHY

Angel, Pierre. *Eduard Bernstein et l'évolution du socialisme allemand.* Paris: M. Didier, 1961.

Bernstein, Eduard. *Evolutionary Socialism: A Criticism and Affirmation.* London: Independent Labor Party, 1909; New York: Schocken Books, 1963.

Cole, G. D. H. *A History of Socialist Thought.* Vol. 3. London: Macmillan, 1956.

Gay, Peter. *The Dilemma of Democratic Socialism: Eduard Bernstein's Challenge to Marx.* New York: Columbia University Press, 1952.

Gneuss, Christian. "The Precursor: Eduard Bernstein." In *Revisionism: Essays on the History of Marxist Ideas,* edited by Leopold Labedz. New York: Praeger, 1962.

Kolakowski, Leszek. *Main Currents of Marxism.* 3 vols. Oxford: Clarendon Press, 1978.

Betancourt, Rómulo

President of Venezuela (1959–1963), founder of its leading political party, Democratic Action, and chief architect of a democratic Venezuela. With Costa Rica's José Figueres, Betancourt (1908–1981) was also one of the first Latin American leaders to make the promotion of democracy throughout the hemisphere a central tenet of his foreign policy.

Born in Guatire, Betancourt eventually studied law in Caracas. Student opposition to the tyranny of dictator Juan Vicente Gómez, culminating in a week of protests in February 1928, thrust Betancourt into his first political activity and led to his imprisonment on charges of subversion. After his release, he spent the next eight years in exile in Costa Rica.

For Betancourt, as for other members of the "Generation of 1928," these early events were formative: they brought the first serious demands for democratization and the revelation that popular movements, if organized and dedicated, could help shape Venezuelan history.

Following the death of Gómez in 1936, Betancourt returned to Venezuela to organize the country's first political party based on universal suffrage, agrarian reform, national control of economic resources, state planning, and civil liberties. Although he had earlier joined the Communist Party of Costa Rica, Betancourt later became strongly anticommunist, rejected class struggle, and was convinced that a multiclass coalition was the key to democratization. For the next several years, in hiding and in exile in Chile, he built the Democratic Action Party, which he considered his greatest achievement. Living his motto, "Not a single district nor a single municipality without a party organization," Betancourt crisscrossed Venezuela to establish the party in key cities throughout the country. This effort eventually gave him enormous control within the party directorate.

Democratic Action was Betancourt's political base for the rest of his life. When young military officers favoring the establishment of a democracy invited the party to form a government in 1945, Betancourt was designated unofficial head of a provisional junta. He later served in the leadership of the party's short-lived first democratic government (the *trienio*) until its overthrow in 1948, when he began a third period of exile. Although he remained abroad until 1957, when the dictatorship of Marcos Pérez Jiménez was finally brought down, Betancourt retained his position as president of Democratic Action. From that position he directed much of Venezuela's struggle against authoritarian rule.

Elected president in 1958 by a huge majority in Venezuela's first competitive elections, Betancourt established the political patterns and state-led economic development model that characterized Venezuela's democracy for years. He governed by developing a style of compromise, an emphasis on institution building, and a reputation for personal honesty. During his presidency, he rejected the sectarianism that had characterized the *trienio* and negotiated pacts (most notably, the Pact of Punto Fijo) with organized interests and opposition parties. He was intransigent only with the Communist Party and militants within his own party who criticized the moderating of Democratic Action's program and eventually launched a guerrilla war against his government. Betancourt's subsequent suspension of all guarantees of personal and civil liberties evoked the greatest controversy of his political career.

Betancourt emphasized the defense of democracy throughout the Americas as a corollary to the establishment of Venezuelan democracy. This view led him to oppose both the Cuban revolution under Fidel Castro and U.S. support for right-wing military regimes in Argentina and Peru. It also earned him the enmity of Dominican dictator Rafael Trujillo, who tried to have him assassinated in 1960. Betancourt eventually became a critic of the corruption that came to mar Venezuelan democracy and spent much of his later life in self-imposed exile in Europe. He died in New York in 1981.

Terry Lynn Karl

BIBLIOGRAPHY

Alexander, Robert. *Rómulo Betancourt and the Transformation of Venezuela.* New Brunswick, N.J.: Transaction, 1982.

Betancourt, Rómulo. *Venezuela: Politica y petroleo.* Mexico City: Fondo de Cultura Economica, 1956.

Martz, John. *Acción Democrática: Evolution of a Modern Political Party.* Princeton: Princeton University Press, 1966.

Biko, Bantu Stephen

Founder and leader of the black consciousness movement in South Africa and of the South African Student Organization. Biko (1946–1977) died in police detention from torture.

Biko's first encounter with politics was in high school, when he and his brother were detained for questioning following bombings by the Pan-Africanist Congress. After being tortured by the security police, Biko was released but was expelled from school; his brother was detained for ten months. In 1965 he enrolled in a Catholic school in Natal, where his political awareness was further advanced. He questioned the right of his teachers (black and white) to exercise arbitrary authority without any participation from the students in shaping their education. He also took

a keen interest in the decolonization process then sweeping the continent and came to admire African nationalist leaders.

In 1966 Biko began studying medicine at the University of Natal, at that time the only medical school in South Africa where blacks could study without the special consent of a government minister. A white institution, the university had a separate section for the medical school; in 1970 it was redesignated the University of Natal black section under pressure from the South African Student Organization.

When Biko entered the university, representation of students in South Africa was fragmented into a number of organizations. The National Union of South African Students, founded in 1924, reflected mainly the concerns of its majority white membership. Not until the 1960s did it begin to address political issues. The sense that the concerns of black students were slighted by the national union led Biko and his colleagues to break from it at a conference at Rhodes University in 1968. They founded the South African Student Organization as a black group to represent black postsecondary students.

Biko played a formative role in increasing blacks' consciousness by exposing the psychological roots of their passivity in the face of apartheid. Racially oppressed for so long, blacks had begun to despise themselves and to accept domination by whites. The black consciousness movement urged blacks (whom it defined politically as all those oppressed by apartheid for reasons of race) to liberate themselves psychologically by developing individual and collective pride. This new way of thinking moved an entire generation of young blacks to resist apartheid. Young people inspired by black consciousness led the 1976 popular revolts in South Africa, which dealt a devastating political blow to the apartheid system.

Biko's emergence as a political leader came at a critical time. The two leading resistance movements—the African National Congress and the Pan-Africanist Congress—had been banned after being routed in the early 1960s. Many members of the two groups were jailed or exiled. Draconian laws and heightened security sought to prevent formation of any new resistance movement by blacks. Fear to act politically paralyzed the black community. At a time when many black leaders were dying in detention, Biko courageously mobilized young blacks in higher education to rekindle the spirit of resistance that had characterized earlier movements.

In August 1977 Biko was arrested in Grahamstown on

Stephen Biko became a martyr of the anti-apartheid movement. In September 1987 activists gathered in his hometown of Ginsberg to commemorate the tenth anniversary of his death.

his way from Cape Town, where he had visited political colleagues in defiance of the order restricting him to the black township of Ginsberg. He was held in detention without trial. On the morning of September 6 he was subjected to an interrogation that continued until early evening. He was left chained to a chair overnight. By the next morning Biko had sustained head injuries that led to his death September 12, at the age of thirty.

Stephen Biko's life and death had a deep and lasting impact, especially on young South Africans. Through his thinking, organization, and personal example, he contributed significantly to the struggle for a democratic South Africa.

Khehla Shubane

BIBLIOGRAPHY

Biko, B. S. *I Write What I Like: A Selection of His Writings,* edited by Aelred Stubbs. New York: Harper, 1978; Oxford: Heinemann, 1987.

———. *Steve Biko: Black Consciousness in South Africa.* Edited by Millard Arnold. New York: Random House, 1978.

Maphai, V. "The Role of Black Consciousness in the Liberation Struggle." In *The Long March: The Story of the Struggle for Liberation in South Africa,* edited by I. Liebenberg et al. Pretoria: Haum, 1994.

Pityana, N. Barney et al., eds. *Bounds of Possibility: The Legacy of Steve Biko and Black Consciousness.* Cape Town: David Philip, 1991; London and New York: Zed Books, 1992.

Woods, Donald. *Biko.* Harmondsworth, England: Penguin Books, 1987; 3d ed. New York: Holt, 1991.

Bill of Rights

See *United States Constitution*

Bolívar, Simón

Political thinker and liberator of Venezuela, Colombia, Ecuador, Peru, and Bolivia. Son of a wealthy Venezuelan family, Bolívar (1783–1830) had the advantage of a prolonged grand tour in Europe during times of revolution. There he absorbed the main tenets of the Enlightenment and admired the feats of Napoleon with some ambivalence. Back in his native Caracas, he emerged as a political

Simón Bolívar

ing alliances and thus generated military anarchy. Governmental authority, in Bolívar's words, was alternately a contemptible stream or an impetuous torrent, and in neither case did it adequately perform its function.

Searching for a solution, Bolívar condemned the intellectuals' tendency to copy foreign models, including extreme liberalism and federalism, which he thought were "too perfect" to be applicable to Latin American societies. Bolívar tried to incorporate in his system some elements from the British model. In addition, some of his analyses and proposals were inspired by the eighteenth-century French writer Montesquieu, with an echo of Aristotle's search for a mixed government combining elements of monarchy, oligarchy, and democracy.

In his later years Bolívar devised a system of limited democracy that incorporated some monarchical features. He set forth his system in a constitution he drafted for Bolivia, the country that bears his name. He established a lifelong presidency, with the president appointed by Congress. The president had charge of the armed forces and foreign relations; the vice president, who would succeed the chief executive upon his death, directed the day-to-day administration. Congress had the usual two chambers, the lower one being elected on a limited franchise, as in England. Senators, selected from civilian and military leaders who had distinguished themselves during the revolution, were appointed for life, and their positions were inheritable. A third house, of "censors," oversaw the morality of officials and the practices of the press. Liberal opinion was opposed to this scheme.

In Colombia, Bolívar met with resistance from the Congress, which he dissolved through a coup d'état in 1828. After slightly more than a year of unrestricted presidential power, during which he tried to prevent the fragmentation of the three-nation entity called Greater Colombia, Bolívar resigned in the face of mounting opposition. Already seriously ill, he marched into exile and died along the way, before leaving Colombia.

Torcuato S. Di Tella

and military leader of the revolt against Spanish rule in 1810. After fifteen years of continuous fighting, he ended colonial rule in the Andean countries, becoming president of Greater Colombia (Venezuela, Colombia, and Ecuador) and Peru.

Bolívar considered the causes of the civil strife that beset the new nations. He observed that newly mobilized masses—often the result of changes brought about by war—created the conditions for populist leaders to emerge and threaten the orderly conduct of government and the accumulation of capital. At the same time, economic catastrophes caused unemployment or bankruptcy among members of the middle and upper classes. These citizens were bent on recouping their fortunes through political action. This objective set them against the traditional elites who were resisting the reforms necessary to co-opt the middle class and the potential mass leaders.

These were the conditions that created civilian anarchy and led to military takeovers, which often involved shift-

BIBLIOGRAPHY

Bolívar, Simón. *Doctrina del Libertador*. Caracas: Biblioteca Ayacucho, 1976.

Johnson, John J., with Doris M. Ladd. *Simón Bolívar and Spanish American Independence: 1783–1830*. Princeton: Princeton University Press, 1968.

Masur, Gerhard. *Simón Bolívar*. 2d ed. Albuquerque: University of New Mexico Press, 1969.

Bolivia

See *Andean countries*

Bolshevism

See *Leninism*

Bosnia

See *Europe, East Central*

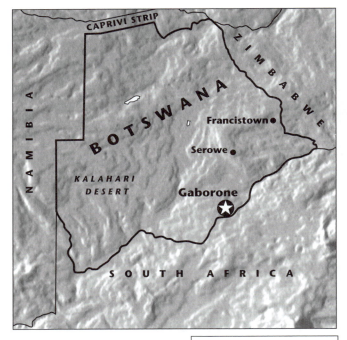

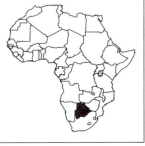

Botswana

A republic located north of South Africa and the only uninterrupted liberal democracy in postcolonial Africa. Most of Botswana's 1.3 million inhabitants reside along the eastern edge of the country, where rainfall is sufficient to sustain arid farming. The Kalahari Desert is in the southwest. The economy is based primarily on mining, cattle production, and labor migration to South Africa.

Since gaining independence in 1966, Botswana has conducted competitive elections every five years, established a record unequaled on the continent with respect to civil rights, and created a military that has remained firmly under civilian control. No other country on the African continent (and only Mauritius offshore) has maintained such a democratic record since independence.

Politics of Democratic Development

The structure of Botswana's government, established in the 1966 constitution, was the result of pre-independence negotiations between Botswana's political leaders and their British rulers. The constitution creates a parliament with two houses: the National Assembly and the House of Chiefs. The latter advises the former. The Assembly now includes thirty-four representatives (originally thirty-one) elected on the basis of single-member districts, four per-

sons selected by the Assembly, and an appointed attorney general. The elected members of the Assembly select the president of the country, who then appoints a cabinet from members of the Assembly. A no-confidence vote for the president by the Assembly mandates its dissolution.

Botswana's democracy is best characterized as developing. The process of liberalization for almost three decades provides insight into the realities confronting the current crop of states moving toward democracy. Slowly a transition is taking place in Botswana from party competition based on ethnicity to polarization of the parties on the basis of class, policy, and candidate personality. The Botswana Democratic Party has ruled continuously since independence. It forged its winning coalition based on the allegiance of the Bamangwato and the Bakwena, the two largest of the eight main Tswana tribes, which together constitute two-thirds of Botswana's population. In addition, the ruling party mobilizes varying degrees of support from several other Tswana and non-Tswana groups. The main opposition parties—the Botswana National Front and the Botswana People's Party—rely mostly on ethnic alienation from the ruling coalition to win supporters. The supporters of the National Front come mainly from Tswana groups, while the People's Party relies on the Kalanga, who are not Tswana.

The emergence of nonethnic competition has been slow. Beginning in the 1980s the Botswana National Front used populist Marxist appeals to secure a majority of the urban working class. This constituency is not sufficient to win control of the parliament. Thus the National Front has tried to establish an electoral coalition with the People's Party and other ethnically based parties. Despite repeated attempts, the conflict between class and ethnicity has prevented realization of this goal.

Botswana's democracy is also developing in the sense that the Democratic Party's domination of the parliament and the cabinet has not allowed it to set major policies related to land reform, urban housing, transportation, and agriculture. These and other initiatives come from the civil service and its dialogue with foreign aid agencies and the World Bank. Until the end of the 1980s the primary, if not the only, role of politicians was to sell new programs to their constituents. A new generation of Democratic Party parliamentarians has begun to exercise some policy leadership, especially with regard to privatization. Top civil servants have shown some resistance, but it is tempered in the case of privatization by the fact that civil servants can invest in the new enterprises.

A major challenge to the development of democracy in Botswana is its autocratic political culture. Particularly in the rural areas, an almost automatic deference exists toward authority figures, whether they are chiefs, elders, or top civil servants. At the time of independence, the Democratic Party took advantage of this tradition by selecting Seretse Khama to be the party's leader and then president of the country. Khama was heir apparent to the Bamangwato chieftaincy, which had long ruled over the largest ethnic group (one-third of the population) in the country. Many in the rural population perceived Khama's presidency from a traditional Tswana perspective. They saw it as a new form of chieftaincy and thus as a permanent, rather than elected, position. After voting for Khama in 1965, many did not vote again until 1984, when Quett Masire was the Democratic Party's candidate for president following the death of Khama.

Interest groups have been slow to secure influence in the policy process. Only in the 1980s did organized groups begin to think in terms of influencing government policy. In the 1990s their numbers are still small, and the most effective employer and environmental groups are led by

Europeans. African dominated groups lack funds and a will to exercise their influence. They are content with "advisory" councils, which make policy recommendations concerning incomes, land allocation, government purchasing, and rural development. In these councils civil servants solicit reactions to policy initiatives being developed. To retain the compliance of group leaders who participate, the government generously funds ongoing projects of their organizations. In addition, the government sometimes provides in-kind support such as free transportation to national conventions of the groups.

Most policy debate still takes place within the bureaucracy, where ministries compete with each other to shape and control programs. The Ministry of Finance plays a key role. No new initiatives are taken seriously until its permanent secretary announces that the ministry will provide major funding. Its officials preside over the ensuing debate and negotiation in interministerial committees. To enhance their power, weaker ministries solicit public opinion surveys and resolutions of support for policies from local councils and community groups.

Public opinion drives policy making only during the implementation stage, however. Ministries are obliged to gain community support before actual execution begins. This support is particularly important in the rural areas, where consultation takes place in the traditional community gathering, the *kgotla*. Prior to and during the colonial period the chiefs and headmen held *kgotlas* periodically as a means to consult and persuade their followers on a new policy. In the postindependence era civil servants have used local *kgotlas* to mobilize support, in part as a means of keeping politicians out of decision making. Although *kgotlas* are easily induced to go along with government plans, some refuse, often because of the leadership of a local chief or headman. Changes are then made; for example, a clinic is relocated, or certain roads are given priority over others for upgrading. On rare occasions the community resists proposals for a dam or a fencing scheme. The result of having this *kgotla* gauntlet to run is that ministries try to anticipate local reactions. Failure to do so is likely to embarrass the ministries and elicit inquiries by the cabinet, parliament, and press.

Another manifestation of the developmental character of Botswana's democracy relates to the role of women in politics. Traditionally, women were excluded from public affairs. They could not attend *kgotlas*, let alone speak. In the modern system they are free to speak but are hesitant to do so except on issues of manifest importance to them (for example, the upbringing of children). Although women make up 40–70 percent of most grassroots party organizations, they are rarely nominated to run in elections, and they hold almost no national offices within party structures. Women influence government policy largely through membership in organizations, which range from the conservative Red Cross and the moderate YWCA to the more radical Emang Basadi, which represents professional women. The government provides all these groups with significant funding to promote women's education related to health, family law, and employment.

The Economic Base

The steady expansion of Botswana's economy has provided a firm base for the stability of Botswana's developing democracy. The real rate of growth of the gross national product has been more than 10 percent annually for the past twenty-five years. The financial foundation of this expansion has been the government's joint development of diamond mining with Debeers, the international diamond marketing cartel. Botswana's diamond production is now larger in monetary terms than that of any other country in the world. The government, through the Ministry of Finance, has reinvested a major portion of its profits in accordance with very sophisticated five-year development programs. The ministry has also minimized corruption, especially compared with that of other African countries, and has constantly put pressure for reform on inefficient government programs and unprofitable public corporations.

This managed growth has had two critical consequences for Botswana's democracy. First, the government promotes development that expands employment at a rapid rate. The result is that social discontent arising from unemployment, particularly among the youth, has been greatly reduced. Second, to keep its rural electoral support, the Democratic Party government has provided extensive social services. These services include health clinics, clean water, free public education, numerous types of agricultural extension, and food relief in periods of drought. All are available even in the most remote villages. The net effect is to channel a significant portion of the country's economic growth to low-income groups, thus giving the regime widespread legitimacy.

The Future

The 1980s witnessed a number of developments that should put Botswana's democracy on a firmer foundation.

Most significant is the emergence of private newspapers as a significant force in politics. By 1990 five weeklies were distributed in the major urban centers and large villages. Each seeks to uncover government scandals as a way of increasing readership. As a result the ruling Democratic Party leadership and its civil service allies have been forced to reform a number of programs, particularly with respect to land allocation. One newspaper, *Mmegi*, has consistently presented sophisticated policy analysis as well. Although the government continues to publish its *Botswana Daily Mail*, the literate public increasingly looks to the private newspapers for serious reporting on national political conflicts.

There are some signs that government is beginning to lose control over its corporatist interest group structure. Trade unions are engaging in strikes, although no strike has yet been sufficiently crippling to force a major readjustment of the country's low wage scales. Some professional groups, especially the main teachers organization, are finding their constituencies eroded by new and competing groups that do not sit on advisory councils or take government subsidies.

Through the end of the 1980s Botswana's democracy functioned mostly for the benefit of the Tswana population. The Democratic Party and its allies in the civil service showed little inclination to recognize significant minority groups, including the Kalanga, the Bushmen, or the Bayei. The schools used only Tswana and English; the national radio station offered no programs in other languages; and government publications were likewise restricted. As nationalist groups have begun to emerge among non-Tswana populations, both the ruling party and the opposition are beginning to articulate some minority interests. In the not too distant future, government policy on language and culture is likely to recognize more cultural diversity.

In sum, recent developments in Botswana's democracy are expanding the scope of public debate, the role of interest groups, and minority group involvement in party politics.

See also *Africa, Subsaharan; Commonwealth, British; Khama, Seretse.*

John D. Holm

BIBLIOGRAPHY

Harvey, Charles, and Steven R. Lewis, Jr. *Policy Choice and Development Performance in Botswana.* London: Macmillan; New York: St. Martin's, 1990.

Hitchcock, Robert K., and John D. Holm. "Bureaucratic Domination of Hunter-Gatherer Societies: A Study of the San in Botswana." *Development and Change* 24 (1993): 305–338.

Holm, John. "Botswana: A Paternalistic Democracy." In *Democracy in Developing Countries: Africa*, edited by Larry Diamond, Juan Linz, and Seymour Martin Lipset. Boulder, Colo.: Lynne Rienner; London: Adamantine Press, 1988.

Holm, John, and Patrick Molutsi, eds. *Democracy in Botswana*. Athens: Ohio University Press, 1989.

Molutsi, Patrick P., and John Holm. "Developing Democracy When Civil Society Is Weak: The Case of Botswana." *African Affairs* 89 (1990): 323–340.

Sklar, Richard L. "Developmental Democracy." *Comparative Studies in Society and History* 29 (1987): 686–714.

Stedman, Stephen John, ed. *Botswana: The Political Economy of Democratic Development*. Boulder, Colo.: Lynne Rienner, 1993.

Brazil

The largest country of South America, once a Portuguese colony, and a republic since 1889. Brazil has a substantial tradition of democracy, though it is not fully consolidated.

Brazil was a Portuguese colony from 1500 to 1822 and a constitutional monarchy closely associated with Portugal from 1822 to 1889. Since then the country has been a presidential republic modeled on the U.S. system. Both transitions, from colonial to independent status and from monarchy to republic, were achieved without bloodshed. Although guaranteed for most of the republican period, democracy has been unstable. Thirty-three years of Brazil's past one hundred have witnessed nondemocratic rule.

Historical Background

Brazil's economy was essentially agrarian and dependent on slavery throughout the nineteenth century. Political competition within the landowning elite and parliamentary practices developed during this period but were limited by economic and social conditions.

In 1889 the first in a series of military interventions put an end to the monarchy and established a presidential and oligarchic federal system. Less than 5 percent of the population voted in the eleven direct presidential elections held under the so-called Old (First) Republic (1889–1930). Political life was dominated by one party in almost all states, and there were no truly national parties. In the 1920s opposition to the policies of the federal government emerged among the ruling groups of some of the weaker states, and unrest arose among the middle sectors, left-wing parties, labor organizations, intellectuals, and young military officers. Brazil's coffee-exporting economy suffered a major blow from the Great Depression of 1929, and the existing political arrangement was seriously weakened. In October 1930 a revolution headed by Getúlio Vargas, governor of Rio Grande do Sul, brought the Old Republic to a close.

Vargas headed a provisional government from 1930 to 1934. Elected president for a four-year term by the Constitutional Assembly in 1934, he imposed the authoritarian Estado Novo ("New State") from 1937 to 1945—a personal dictatorship that made few demands on its subjects. At the end of World War II the military, under strong liberal influence and backed by rising civilian opposition, deposed Vargas, paving the way for the "democratic experiment."

1945–1964: Democracy Reinstated

The two largest of the newly created political parties, the Social Democratic Party and the National Democratic Union, both nominated high-ranking military officers as their candidates in the 1945 presidential election—a clear indication that the military would continue to play a role in Brazilian politics. The winner, Gen. Eurico Dutra, never attempted to exceed the authority accorded him by the 1946 constitution. Within the multiparty system that emerged in the new constitutional framework, the Communist Party was outlawed in 1947. The former *integralista*, or protofascist, movement reappeared as a conservative electoral party but enjoyed little success. From the end of the Estado Novo until the early 1960s, the threat to democracy came primarily from disputes among the elite. A process of state-driven industrialization further polarized the country.

The legacy of Vargas's Estado Novo, far from damaging his political prospects, enabled him to reemerge as a formidable leader. Elected to the Senate in 1946, Vargas maintained a low profile but made a strong comeback in the 1950 presidential election, winning with 48 percent of the popular vote.

Vargas's Estado Novo had greatly extended labor rights. To retain the allegiance of organized labor, Vargas created the Labor Party. He could also rely on a substantial portion of the vote of the country's hinterland, channeled by the Social Democratic Party, which also was created through his influence. The Social Democratic Party became the vehicle through which a vast array of regional

and local politicians as well as a generation of state and local public employees entered national politics.

Facing intense civilian and military pressure, Vargas
committed suicide in 1954. Juscelino Kubitschek, the candidate of the Social Democrats, took office in 1955. Rapid
industrial growth and spectacular projects (notably, the
construction of a new capital city, Brasília) combined with
Kubitschek's political skill to create a climate of optimism.
But the Social Democrats' candidate was defeated in 1960
by Jânio Quadros, who won with 48 percent of the vote.
Quadros's inauguration as president seemed to indicate
that democracy had taken hold. But this optimism was
shattered by his sudden resignation in August 1961 because of "hidden pressures," to which he vaguely alluded
in his resignation letter.

Quadros's vice president, João Goulart, a member of
the Labor Party, was regarded as left of center in Brazil's
narrow ideological scale of the early 1960s. He was declared unacceptable by Quadros's military ministers. As a
result of a negotiated solution, Goulart took office as head
of state in a semiparliamentary system, and Tancredo

Neves, a conservative leader of the Social Democratic Party, became prime minister. This compromise worked pre-
cariously until January 1963, when a plebiscite returned
full presidential powers to Goulart.

1964–1985: Democratic Breakdown and Authoritarian Rule

Weak and fragmented, the Brazilian multiparty system
was not measuring up to the demands created by rapid
urbanization, economic stagnation, mounting inflation,
and ideological polarization. The explosive issue of land
reform loomed large on the country's political agenda. On
March 13, 1964, a military coup brought a period of prolonged authoritarian rule.

The military rulers did not break completely with traditional constitutional mechanisms. The generals who occupied the presidency did so for a fixed term of office.
And, although direct national elections were suspended,
military nominees had to be formally approved by the legislature (and later by an electoral college, which included
representatives of the state legislatures). The multiparty

system was replaced by a two-party system: the pro-government National Renovating Alliance and the opposition Brazilian Democratic Movement.

The military regime, which pledged to put an end to "communism and corruption" and to stabilize and modernize the economy, enjoyed substantial support during its first decade. Between 1967 and 1973 Brazil was transformed into a semi-industrialized and highly urbanized society through a process of accelerated structural change—the so-called Brazilian economic miracle. The military leaders and the civilian technocrats allied to them carried out this program using the same state-led, inflation-prone, and socially exclusionary strategy that Vargas and Kubitscheck had used. In 1968 military repression increased with further restrictions on political dissent, pervasive censorship of the press, and gross violations of human rights.

Chosen by his military peers for the presidency in 1973, Gen. Ernesto Geisel pledged to pursue a policy of gradual transition to democracy. It was a slow transition indeed. It gained momentum in 1982, when direct elections for state governorships were held and opposition candidates won ten of the twenty-two offices—including those of the key states of São Paulo, Minas Gerais, and Rio de Janeiro.

In 1984 huge demonstrations calling for direct elections failed to ensure that the successor of João Figueiredo, who was then president, would be chosen by direct popular vote. They did, however, change the political equation by creating uncertainty about the future of the electoral college. Tancredo Neves, governor of Minas Gerais, became virtually unbeatable as a candidate. He was the first civilian elected president since 1964.

1985: Beginning of Democratic Consolidation

Scheduled to take office on March 15, 1985, Neves fell ill on the eve of his inauguration and died thirty-six days later. An astonished Brazilian citizenry watched as Vice President José Sarney became the first civilian president since the military coup. Sarney, a longtime supporter of the military regime, had been chosen by Neves as a running mate only to balance the ticket.

Sarney's rise to power was an enormous blow to the consolidation of democratic legitimacy. Moreover, the country's long trajectory of high growth rates was over. Hard hit by the debt crisis of the early 1980s, Brazil entered a long cycle of stagnation and chronic high inflation. Long-repressed wage demands were strongly voiced. The broad coalition responsible for the process of redemocratization called a constitutional congress, which convened in early 1987. The constitution finally adopted on October 5, 1988, reflected the lack of leadership from both the presidential and party levels; it seemed destined to undergo numerous revisions.

Deep disappointment with the Sarney administration, continuing recession, and an inflation rate of 50 percent a month did not prevent Brazilians from placing great hopes on the first direct presidential election in twenty-nine years. In November 1989, for the first time in Brazilian history, the two-round ballot method was adopted in order to ensure an absolute majority for the winner. The electorate placed two young and sharply polarized candidates on the runoff ballot: left-of-center Luís Inácio Lula da Silva, a former labor leader who headed the Workers' Party, and Fernando Collor de Mello, governor of Alagoas, one of the smallest and poorest states.

Despite the certainty that neither candidate would have a majority in Congress and the fear of imminent hyperinflation, most Brazilians were convinced that democracy finally had come to stay. Collor's victory and his first hundred days in office left the impression that inflation would soon be ended and that tough, market-oriented reforms would reduce the size of the state. Less than one year later, however, these expectations were proved wrong. Collor was as weak a president as Sarney had been. Facing charges of corruption by a congressional investigating committee, Collor was impeached by overwhelming votes in the Chamber of Deputies and the Senate.

Popular support for Collor's impeachment and rigorous observation of constitutional procedures reinforced the public's confidence in democracy. Only six months later, however, the widespread perception that civilian politicians were unable to solve the country's economic problems, disappointment with Collor's successor, Itamar Franco, and continuing charges of corruption brought against public officials raised doubts about Brazil's democratic viability.

A plebiscite was held in April 1993, to decide whether the country should remain a republic or restore its monarchy and whether it should remain presidential or adopt a parliamentary system. Although 55 percent of the electorate voted against change on both counts, the campaign was marked by considerable apathy and hostility toward politicians. Opinion polls revealed the public's low esteem for Brazil's political parties and three branches of government. Discontent among the military was perceived as potentially dangerous, and rumors that a dictatorship or a civilian coup was imminent began to appear regularly in the press.

The public's confidence in the Franco administration was restored in mid-1993, when Franco appointed the respected foreign minister, Fernando Henrique Cardoso, to the Ministry of Finance. Cardoso's popularity increased when his economic stabilization program proved an initial success. He left the ministry in April 1994 to run for the presidency. Supported by his left-of-center Party of Brazilian Social Democracy and the more conservative Liberal Front Party, which agreed with his currency stabilization program and market-oriented reforms, Cardoso defeated the Workers' Party candidate, Luís Inácio Lula da Silva. His election reinforced hopes for stabilization and constitutional reforms, but these hopes dampened in early 1995 because of the instability of his congressional backing and the uncertainties created by the Mexican financial crisis and related difficulties in Argentina.

Prospects for a Democratic Future

Despite considerable progress, Brazil's democratic institutions still face major difficulties. Until 1945 democracy as a value was clearly subordinate to nation building. Viewed as the creation of a central bureaucratic machinery capable of controlling a large and diverse country, state-driven industrialization proved highly congruent with that preexisting "statist" ideological matrix. From 1945 to 1964 democracy grew stronger, but "development" was still a driving force. The acceptance of true representative democracy became dominant only in the course of resistance to the 1964 military regime.

Choosing presidents through direct elections was a major cause of political instability. Violent conflict over electoral rules and results were common before 1930. The Electoral Code of 1932, drawn up in the aftermath of the 1930 revolution, improved conditions significantly. An important institutional change was the establishment of the Electoral Court as an electoral umpire, which contributed strongly to the normalizing of electoral disputes. The expansion of the franchise was another extremely important change. Less than 5 percent of the population voted in the eleven direct presidential elections held under the First Republic (1889–1930). At the time of Jânio Quadros's election in 1960, only 22 percent of the population was entitled to vote. Over the next thirty-two years that proportion climbed to 60 percent, reflecting the highly inclusionary character of the franchise rules.

There are powerful forces of stratification in Brazilian society, but there are equally powerful forces—such as urban living and the spread of mass communications—that work in the opposite direction. The key condition for democracy, which clearly emerged from the reaction to the experience of military rule, is that the desire to preserve democracy as a value must emerge among the influential and high-income groups within the electorate. Recent research shows that democratic sentiment among low-income voters is less widespread in Brazil than in Argentina, Uruguay, or Chile, but it also suggests that a remarkable expansion has taken place since the early 1960s.

In a country with such a large population and enormous social and regional inequalities, democratic prospects cannot be dissociated from economic and social conditions. Many politicians and analysts, however, seem convinced that, in addition to intractable economic difficulties, mass poverty, and sharp income inequality, Brazilian democracy tends to be weakened by serious flaws in its underlying institutional architecture. The loss of authority of successive presidents dramatizes the weak presidential mandate derived from direct presidential elections—in spite of the popular majority ensured by the current system.

The belief that stability is better guaranteed by the rigid separation of powers that characterizes the presidential system than by a parliamentary system has also been called into question. Weak party organizations and extreme party fragmentation seem to be the Achilles' heel of Brazilian democracy. Proportional representation as practiced in Brazil is also a matter for continuing concern. Apportionment of the Chamber of Deputies in favor of the small and sparsely populated states of the north and center-western regions adds an element of regional tension.

Brazil's institutional difficulties seem to derive from the political system's inability to produce stable patterns of authority, a consequence of the precarious coexistence between an executive unable to convert its electoral capital into durable authority and congressional and party structures that are highly fragmented. From a structural point of view, the dilemma for democracy is clearly the tension between the degree of democratic development already achieved and the situation of mass poverty and income inequality. The recent enormous expansion of the democratic "arena" means that the country can no longer be governed by a small elite; however, stable and efficient governance on a pluralistic basis is difficult to achieve while intense redistributive conflict rages.

Bolívar Lamounier

BIBLIOGRAPHY

Keck, Margaret. *The Workers' Party and Democratization in Brazil.* New Haven: Yale University Press, 1992.

Kinzo, Maria D'Alvia G. *Legal Opposition Politics under Authoritarian Rule in Brazil.* Oxford: St. Anthony's/Macmillan Series, 1988.

Lamounier, Bolívar. "Brazil: Inequality against Democracy." In *Comparing Experiences with Democracy,* edited by Larry Diamond, Juan J. Linz, and Seymour Martin Lipset. Boulder, Colo.: Lynne Rienner; London: Adamantine Press, 1990.

Schmitter, Philippe C. *Interest Conflict and Political Change in Brazil.* Stanford: Stanford University Press, 1971.

Skidmore, Thomas E. *Politics in Brazil, 1930–1964: An Experiment in Democracy.* New York: Oxford University Press, 1967.

Stepan, Alfred, ed. *Authoritarian Brazil: Origins, Policies, and Future.* New Haven and London: Yale University Press, 1973.

———. *Democratizing Brazil: Problems of Transition and Consolidation.* New York: Oxford University Press, 1989.

British Empire

See *Commonwealth, British*

Brunei

See *Asia, Southeast*

Bryce, James

British political scientist, writer, politician, and diplomat. James, Viscount Bryce (1838–1922), was a true Victorian polymath. Lawyer, medievalist, journalist, teacher, and mountaineer, he could talk and write on equal terms with experts in classics, history, law, geography, and political science. His most important contributions to the study of democracy were two works: *The American Commonwealth* and *Modern Democracies.*

Although Bryce was born in Ulster, his schoolmaster father moved the family to Scotland when he was eight. Educated in Glasgow, Bryce was essentially a Scot. From Glasgow University he went to Trinity College, Oxford, where he distinguished himself. During his years at Oxford he produced the most elegant of his works, *The Holy Roman Empire,* an essay on the history of Europe from Constantine to Napoleon. After a brief practice as a barrister, he became Regius Professor of Law at Oxford (1870–1893). But his teaching duties did not prevent him from an extraordinary range of traveling and writing or indeed from representing Aberdeen, as a Liberal Party member of Parliament, from 1880 to 1907.

Bryce had an active political career. He took up the "Armenian question," which so exercised British politics in the 1870s and onward. Along with William E. Gladstone, leader of the Liberal Party and four times prime minister, Bryce denounced Turkish atrocities against the Armenians. He knew the area (he had been one of the first to climb Mount Ararat), and he felt passionately for the Armenians. He also became involved in Irish affairs and was a somewhat reluctant convert to home rule for Ireland. In 1885 Bryce served briefly as undersecretary at the Foreign Office, and, when the Liberals returned to power in the 1890s, he joined the cabinet as president of the Board of Trade. His main achievement in those years, however, was heading a path-breaking commission on secondary education.

After the Liberals left office in 1895, Bryce traveled to South Africa and wrote a book about his experiences. Later he became embroiled on the pro-Boer side in the troubles that culminated in the South African war between the British and the Boers (1899–1902). He was explicitly against imperial expansion by the British. When the Liberals returned to office in 1905, Bryce rejoined the cabinet as chief secretary for Ireland. In a relatively peaceful period, he administered that contentious island for a year before his career in the Commons was ended by his appointment as British ambassador to the United States (1907–1913).

Bryce's knowledge of the United States went back to 1870, when he had spent three months in the eastern United States, accompanied by A. V. Dicey, the constitutional lawyer. In 1881 and 1883 he made further visits, which provided material for his *American Commonwealth* (1888). He noted that no one since Alexis de Tocqueville (more than forty years earlier) had essayed a comprehensive picture of American democracy. But Bryce decided to be far more descriptive and less theoretical than de Tocqueville. He wanted to present a factual account of how contemporary American government operated at every level—federal,

James Bryce

state, and local. He saw the United States as the key example of the democratic ideal and he sought to report the reality—warts and all.

Bryce's writing was based on his insatiable questioning of everyone he encountered, from shopkeepers and chance fellow-travelers to important figures whom he met through his network of influential friends in Washington, Boston, and New York. He wrote analytically about the political machines in the large cities and the bosses who made their living by public office, and he explored the weaknesses at the heart of American government, entitling one chapter "Why Great Men Are Not Chosen President." He likened the two dominant parties, the Republican and Democratic Parties, to two identical bottles with different labels—both empty. But his enthusiasm for America and the American character shone through. In particular, he noted the hopefulness of the American people. Bryce revised and updated *The American Commonwealth* three times. For at least two generations it was the

major text on the United States, used by teachers on both sides of the Atlantic.

As ambassador, Bryce was imaginative and original. He was almost seventy, and not a professional diplomat, but he knew the United States as no other English person did, and the successive editions of *The American Commonwealth,* as well as his lecture tours, had made him a household name throughout the continent. He had almost as large a range of eminent friends and correspondents in America as, in his gregarious way, he had acquired in the United Kingdom. Among his warmest associates were Charles Evans Hughes, who later became chief justice of the United States, and Theodore Roosevelt, the American president. While ambassador, Bryce was notably close to three successive presidents—Roosevelt, William Howard Taft, and Woodrow Wilson. He used these links in a number of delicate negotiations, particularly in the field of U.S.–Canadian relations and in the Arbitration Treaty between the United States and the United Kingdom, which provided for disputes to be referred to the International Court at The Hague. He expanded enormously the public relations role of an ambassador, traveling constantly and giving lectures on a vast range of subjects.

While ambassador, Bryce took two long leaves to visit South America and Australasia in his quest to understand the nature of democratic government. His travels resulted in his last great book, *Modern Democracies* (1921). This work was the fulfillment of an earlier plan to produce the first comparative study of how democratic governments actually operate. Attempting a pragmatic, not a theoretical, definition of democracy, he claimed only to offer a set of personal observations based on the workings of government in Britain, America, Australia, and Switzerland. He concluded that "no government demands so much from its citizens and none gives so much back" as democracy. In this work he was retreading in a wider and more speculative way the path explored in *The American Commonwealth*—but without quite the same zest.

On his return to Britain, Bryce was made a viscount. During the First World War he chaired two important committees. The first one prepared an outline plan for what was to become the League of Nations, and the second provided a comprehensive scheme for changing the composition of the anachronistic House of Lords. He stayed fully active until his death at the age of eighty-three.

Although Bryce's long and virtuous public career left few policy landmarks, his vast output of books and articles—on classical scholarship, legal questions, history, political personalities, and travel—commanded a wide audience. If he left no great theoretical legacy, he provided a unique record of one long phase of American politics. A man of extraordinary energy, probity, and versatility, he, who had never seen America until he was thirty-two, became the ultimate Anglo-American. He wrote important books and held important offices. But it is as the author of *The American Commonwealth* that he will be most remembered.

David E. Butler

BIBLIOGRAPHY

Bryce, James. *The American Commonwealth*. 2 vols. London and New York: Macmillan, 1914.
———. *Modern Democracies*. 2 vols. London and New York: Macmillan, 1921.
Fisher, H. A. L. *James Bryce*. 2 vols. London: Macmillan, 1927.

Hacker, Louis. "Introduction to J. Bryce." In *The American Commonwealth*. Abridged ed. 2 vols. New York: 1959.
Ions, Edmund S. *James Bryce and American Democracy, 1870–1922*. London: Macmillan, 1968.

Buddhism

The religious system based upon the teaching of the historical Buddha, Siddhartha Gautama (c.563–c.483 B.C.). Buddhism originally developed in India but later spread over vast regions of Asia in various forms. It is an all-embracing term for a very diverse religious system. It includes the conservative Theravada Buddhism of Sri Lanka and Southeast Asia, the more liberal Mahayana Buddhism of East Asia, and the esoteric Tantric Buddhism of Tibet. Of these three the Theravada branch, which retains a portion of the original doctrine together with the early forms of its ecclesiastical institutions, is of special significance in the context of democracy.

Modern Political Influence

In its long history Theravada Buddhism has been deeply involved in the development and legitimation of political power in Sri Lanka, Burma (Myanmar), Thailand, Laos, and Cambodia. In the post–World War II history of the independent kingdoms of Laos and Cambodia, Buddhism was constitutionally made a state religion, while Sri Lanka and Burma experienced serious political crises over the legal issue of whether to grant Buddhism a privileged status as the state religion. During the early years of independence in Sri Lanka and Burma, this issue led to the assassination of political leaders and the collapse of governments.

In modern China the Chinese versions of Mahayana Buddhism— which are only one component of the Chinese religious trio of Confucianism, Buddhism, and Daoism—seem to have a limited role in the political arena, except perhaps in political protest movements, like those of Vietnam when Vietnamese Buddhist monks set themselves on fire to protest the Vietnam War in the 1960s. The Mahayana Buddhist sects of Asia are for the most part politically apathetic. One exception is the Sokagakkai, a lay Buddhist organization of Japan that has a strong political orientation. The Buddhism of Tibet, on the other hand,

In 1966, during the Vietnam War, Buddhist monks in South Vietnam protest against the South Vietnamese government and the United States. The war, which had begun as a civil war, became an area of international conflict that would not end until 1975.

has historically shown a strong political character; in Tantric Buddhism a religious leader was tantamount to a political leader, as in the case of the Dalai Lama.

In general, there has not been a close historical relationship between Buddhism and democratic government. Nonetheless, some tenets of Buddhism tend to support popular constraints on authority. One such is the concept of *dhammaraja,* which would constrain a king from oppression; another is the concept of the "great elect," which requires a monarch to keep worldly order for the benefit of his subjects. The concept of democracy has been called a secularized version of basic tenets of Christian theology. In other words, the will of God is replaced in the worldly arena by the omnipotence of the people and legislators of a democratic polity. How does Buddhism relate to this time-honored Western concept of democracy?

The Buddhist Brotherhood

The original tenets of Buddhism had a strongly elitist orientation. They were presented to disciplined monks in India to help them attain, by their own effort, the ultimate goal of emancipation from suffering. Buddhism presupposes neither a god nor a savior in this spiritual quest; instead, salvation comes through self-emancipation, as is clearly written in one of the verses of a sacred text called the *Dhammapada:* "Only a man himself can be the master of himself: who else from outside could be his master?" In the present context, one can say that this dictum clearly expresses respect for the dignity of the individual human being, a fundamental condition for democracy.

The social basis for the historical continuity of Buddhism was, in its original form, a brotherhood known as the *sangha,* a term originally referring to an aristocratic clan-republic of northern India. This brotherhood provided a center of spiritual practice among Buddhist monks. Buddhism was unique among the ancient Indian religions in that Buddhist monks, rather than leading a wandering life of solitary asceticism, usually joined the religious organization of the *sangha.* The *sangha* was structured around a code of conduct called *vinaya,* or "that which separates." The term aptly reflects the monastic character of a religion whose core members are "separated" in all respects from the ordinary way of life. Members of the *sangha* strictly followed the *vinaya,* the canonized precepts conducive to the final attainment of spiritual emancipation, or *nirvana.*

The *sangha* in its original form was an autonomous and democratic institution. Each member of this self-governing body had a voice in deciding on the group's adaptation of the *vinaya* and was entitled to express his views on the daily administration of the monastic community. Disputes within the *sangha* were settled according to the *vinaya.* A set of rules for Buddhist monks, which represents the core of the *vinaya,* lists Seven Cases of Settlement of Litigation about Faults, including "cancellation of litigation by the pronouncement of a majority." This practice resembles the principle of majority rule in Western democratic decision making.

Members of the *sangha* are called *bhikkhu,* or "one who begs for food." Traditionally, the monks were economically unproductive and depended for subsistence on the charity of householders. Such materially dependent communities found their most reliable supporters among Buddhist monarchs, who made vows to provide material as well as moral comfort to the monks. The relationship between the king and the *sangha,* however, was not one-sided but mutual: the king's support of the *sangha* helped to legitimize his rule. Any Buddhist king could enhance his political legitimacy by proclaiming himself a devoted "defender of the faith" and sustaining an otherwise declining community of monks.

Thailand and the Modern *Sangha*

Thailand affords the most significant example of how Buddhism has affected democratic development. The ancient *sangha* was loosely structured. Its organization had only such distinctions as senior and junior monk, fully ordained *bhikkhu* and novice, teacher and pupil. Modern communities generally are highly structured. A *sangha raja* or *sangha nayaka* ("king" or "lord" of the *sangha*) stands at the head, assisted by a council of elderly monks.

Within a decade after the constitutional revolution of 1932, the Thai *sangha* began to revise its administrative structure in imitation of the newly introduced secular democratic institutions. According to the *Sangha* Administration Act of 1941 of the kingdom of Thailand, the Thai *sangha* was reorganized upon the principle of separation of three powers, similar to the emerging constitutional

form of the Thai government, which had replaced the absolute monarchy of the previous decade. The reorganized Thai *sangha* still had a *sangha raja* as its supreme head, but under him were set up the three institutions of the *Sangha* Assembly (legislative branch), the *Sangha* Cabinet (executive branch), and the *Sangha* Courts (judiciary branch). Forty-five members of the Assembly were elected proportionately from among the two sects representing the Thai *sangha.* These sects were the large and traditional Mahanikai and the smaller but influential (thanks to its royal connection) Thammayut. Thus the whole administrative structure of the Thai *sangha* took on a tinge of democracy.

This democratic construct, however, was short-lived. Two decades later, during the highly centralized, despotic regime of Field Marshal Sarit Thanarat, the democratic *sangha* law was repealed. It was replaced with a law that reintroduced the traditional autocracy of the council of elders.

The Buddhist Polity

A democratic element of early Buddhism might be traced in its unique concept of an "elected king." This concept appears in some Buddhist scriptures, in which the image of an archaic king is depicted as the Mahasammata, or Great Elect, chosen by the people to maintain the worldly order. The Mahasammata was expected, according to scripture, to be angry when anger was right, to censure that which should rightly be censured, and to banish those who deserved to be banished. The Great Elect was said to receive a portion of the people's harvest for his meritorious service to the people who had elected him. A chronicle written in Pali states that some of the Sinhalese kings of Sri Lanka traced their descent from the Mahasammata.

One aspect of the traditional concept of Buddhist kingship is that a good Buddhist king must always behave as a protector of the *dhamma,* or the teachings of the historical Buddha that constitute social justice. When he is seen by his people to be properly performing his expected duty, he is praised as the *dhammaraja,* or "king of righteousness." In principle, the popular consent of his Buddhist subjects legitimizes the rule of a Buddhist king. As a corollary, it may be argued that popular consensus might even deprive a king of his claim to rule, if the king has been judged to be without *dhamma.* This can be seen in the case of King Taksin of Siam (1767–1782). Despite his admirable feat of freeing Siam from the occupation of the

Burmese army, King Taksin was eventually put to death by his former comrade in war because of his cruel behavior, which was judged to be unjustifiable for a Buddhist king. One of the royal chronicles poses the question: If the king becomes dishonest and unrighteous, what do you do? The ministers' reply is that any king who behaves dishonestly should be punished as a traitor. This chronicle gives an example of popular participation in the political process of the Buddhist polity.

According to the *Dhammasattham,* or the Buddhist-influenced Law of Manu, once adopted in many parts of Southeast Asia, the ideal monarch steadfastly follows the ten kingly virtues, upholds the five common precepts (for the laity), and on holy days keeps the set of eight precepts. He lives in kindness and shows goodwill to all beings. He also upholds the four principles of justice: to assess the rightness or wrongness of any deed that is done to him, to uphold what is righteous and truthful, to acquire riches only through just means, and to maintain the prosperity of his state only through just means. In short, a Buddhist king is destined to be always under the moral pressure of his subjects. If the king is unjust, his subjects might someday take part in a mass uprising to oust him from his throne.

The traditional Buddhist concept of a political leader being obliged to follow *dhamma,* or "righteousness," seems to be a persistent theme in the political culture of modern Buddhist Southeast Asia. This is true both for a kingdom with a constitutional monarchy, such as Thailand, and for a republic, such as Burma (Myanmar), Laos, or Cambodia. Sometimes one hears how a government of a Buddhist nation that is found to be corrupt comes under severe criticism from the populace (or the military) for its deviation from righteousness. Such logic was even followed by a Communist clandestine radio station in Thailand in the 1960s and 1970s, which accused the military regime in Bangkok of being unrighteous. The corrupt leaders, Thanom Kittikachorn and Prapas Charusathira, were eventually ousted in the wake of a student uprising in 1973.

Even democratically elected leaders are not immune to popular attack if they prove unable or unwilling to live up to the ideals of government according to righteousness. In 1991, when Chatchai Choonhavan's government in Thailand was found to be excessively corrupt, the Thai people gave tacit support to the so-called National Peacekeeping Council, which had staged a coup to overthrow the democratically elected cabinet on the pretext of its being a "parliamentary dictatorship." Similarly, the next year middle-class citizens of Bangkok revolted against the dictatorship of General Suchinda Kraprayoon, one of the leaders of the National Peacekeeping Council. The English political term *legitimacy* is usually rendered in Thai as "being in accordance with righteousness."

Buddhist Democracy

Liberty and equality are often called the twin essentials of modern democracy. These two values tend to come into conflict, however, whenever equality poses dangers to the survival of liberty. In Japan in the mid-1960s, with a view to overcoming this perennial contradiction, a novel concept of "dhammic democracy" was proposed by a leader of the Japanese Sokagakkai. Its advocates claim that only in the politico-religious ideal of *obutsu myogo,* or "the union of king and Buddha," can dhammic democracy eventually be achieved worldwide, creating a peaceful and harmonious coexistence of liberty and equality in the world.

Democracy, which was born in the West and has been nurtured in the Judeo-Hellenistic tradition of Europe, now demands universal applicability. No country in the world today can be accepted as a member of the family of nations without at least claiming to be democratic. It is therefore natural and understandable that a country with a totally different historical and cultural background should seek its own version of this Western political construct. A Buddhistic democracy would be just one among such varying versions of democracy.

Buddhism does not impose this political idea on its believers, but Buddhist doctrines and traditions do have a democratic vein. The fundamental tenet of this religion of ancient India is the dignity of each human being. The time-honored monastic tradition of Buddhism has a democratic tinge, as reflected in *sangha* autonomy. The archaic concept of the "great elect" suggests a modern application for participatory democracy. Buddhadasa Bhikkhu, a Buddhist monk and intellectual of Thailand, even goes so far as to claim the superiority of "dhammocracy" over democracy, calling the former the ultimate form of the latter. Whether a Buddhist version of democracy can help Asian countries survive and achieve further political development may depend upon the cultural tolerance of the rest of the world.

See also *Asia, Southeast; Burma; China; India; Japan; Thailand.*

Yoneo Ishii

BIBLIOGRAPHY

Aung-Thwin, Michael. *Pagan: The Origins of Modern Burma.* Honolulu: University of Hawaii Press, 1985.

Nival, Dhani. "The Old Siamese Conception of the Monarchy." In *The Siam Society Fiftieth Anniversary Commemorative Publication.* Vol. 2. Bangkok: Siam Society, 1954.

Smith, Bardwell L., ed. *Religion and Legitimation of Power in Thailand, Laos, and Burma.* Chambersburg, Pa.: Anima Books, 1978.

Tambiah, Stanley J. *World Conqueror and World Renouncer: A Study of Buddhism and Polity in Thailand against a Historical Background.* Cambridge and New York: Cambridge University Press, 1976.

Wijayaratna, Mohan. *Buddhist Monastic Life according to the Texts of the Theravada Tradition.* Translated by Claude Grangier and Steven Collins. Cambridge and New York: Cambridge University Press, 1990.

Bulgaria

See *Europe, East Central*

Bureaucracy

A form of organization for administration that is marked by a concern for rules and procedures, a chain of command defining superiors and subordinates, and precision in job descriptions and division of labor. The word *bureaucracy* comes from the French *bureau* and *cratie*. *Bureau* is derived from the cloth that covered the desks of the king's finance clerks; *cratie* comes from the Greek word for "rule." Bureaucracy literally means "rule by desks," or the rules and records stored in those desks. In modern liberal democracies bureaucracy is the primary organization for carrying out the administration of government at all levels in society. Management and reform of bureaucracy have become a principal focus of modern government.

Bureaucracy is not new. It existed in ancient Egypt and Sumer. But bureaucracy emerged as the principal form of organization for administration as society became technologically sophisticated. Advances in science and technology facilitated organizing for complex and difficult tasks, and bureaucracy became the primary organizing principle in both government and private industry. Virtually every form of government relies upon bureaucracy.

Weber and Bureaucratic Theory

Modern bureaucracy is the product of the philosophical movement known as German idealism. Perhaps the foremost theorist on the influence of bureaucracy in society was the German social scientist Max Weber (1864–1920). Weber published his theory of bureaucracy in the early twentieth century. According to Weber, in order to function effectively in a complex, democratic, and industrial society, organizations must be based on law and a rational arrangement of power and authority. The highly developed bureaucracy, he wrote in *The Theory of Social and Economic Organization,* should adhere to certain fundamental principles of organization. The bureaucracy rests on a body of law, which establishes the legitimate authority of the organization and defines the organization's purpose and responsibilities. The organization has established rules and procedures to govern how it will carry out its responsibilities. These rules and procedures are highly specialized and specific, governing the day-to-day operations of the personnel within the organization. They provide direction for the organization and limit the possibility of arbitrary action by individuals within the organization as well as arbitrary action by the organization itself.

Employees within a bureaucracy are appointed solely on the basis of their competence to perform specific tasks, and their competence is determined through testing and experience. All personnel decisions regarding hiring, promotion, and tenure are to be based on competence and achievement, as determined by superiors, and on seniority. Employees' salaries are determined by their rank within the organization. Within a bureaucracy, all positions are arranged hierarchically, with each position under a higher, or superior, one. Individuals supervise employees who occupy positions below them.

The highest ranking person within the bureaucracy is accountable to someone outside the organization. In democracies this is usually an elected official or office. All decisions and actions of the bureaucracy are written. This profusion of written records and files serves to guide future actions by the bureaucracy and helps to ensure that it remains accountable to outside authority.

The Rational Approach

The single most important organizing principle behind bureaucracy is procedural rationality. Procedural rationality is the belief that it should be possible to design an organization in such a way as to ensure that it accomplishes its goal in an efficient and effective manner. Advocates of procedural rationality argue that by establishing rules and procedures to direct the actions of the bureaucracy it is possible to construct an organization that will respond efficiently to instructions issued to it. The focus is on how to structure rules and procedures so as to minimize the amount of discretion left to individuals within the organization, thereby ensuring that the organization will act with precision in regard to whatever instructions it receives.

In the United States this approach to organization and administration was espoused by Woodrow Wilson (1856–1924), who was a professor of political science before he entered politics and was elected president. Wilson's essay "The Study of Administration" argued for a science of administration that could improve upon government by developing rational theories of administration. Wilson argued that it should be possible to determine the best way to organize the agencies of government in order to accomplish the purposes of government within a democratic society. He urged the study of the organization and administration of governments around the world in order to determine what works and why and to apply these lessons to the American system. According to Wilson, there is a dichotomy between politics and administration: politics is about making decisions and administration is about implementing those decisions. Bureaucracy is organization for administration.

The modern bureaucracy reflects the attention to procedural rationality and concern with a politics-administration dichotomy espoused by scholars such as Weber and Wilson. Modern bureaucracy is highly organized, and its personnel constitute a professional civil service who have been trained especially for careers within the bureaucracy. The political and legal authority of the bureaucracy is well established in most states. In highly developed democracies the bureaucracy constitutes a major portion of the government; it exists somewhat removed from the processes of partisan elections. Bureaucracy rests upon notions of political neutrality and merit, principles at odds with the overriding concern with public opinion that tends to drive elected officials in legislative and executive institutions. The makeup of the legislative and executive institutions may change frequently, but the responsibilities, authority, and character of the bureaucracy and the civil service are resistant to change. Bureaucracy therefore exerts something of a conservative force upon government and is oriented toward the status quo.

The influence of bureaucracy in modern government

and industry originates from the expertise it possesses. Bureaucracies bring together in a highly organized and concentrated way highly trained technical experts, and this expertise is then harnessed to accomplish the tasks set before the organization. In government, political leaders are responsible for defining those tasks. But the bureaucracy itself wields great influence in defining the tasks.

Challenges to Democracy

Bureaucracy and the bureaucratic state present special challenges to democratic government. The essence of democracy is self-government: citizens governing themselves through a system of elections and representation. It is a form of government that emphasizes the relationship between the individual and the government, the participation of citizens in politics, and popular accountability of government officials. Bureaucracy, however, emphasizes expertise, procedures, rules, and records. Those individuals employed by a bureaucracy are hired because of their fitness to fulfill specific tasks. The link between the bureaucracy and the people therefore is indirect. Citizens are served by the bureaucracy, but, as an organization, the bureaucracy is removed from popular accountability.

It is the responsibility of elected officials to provide the link between the citizens and the bureaucracy. In modern liberal democracies, much of the responsibility of elected officials is related to oversight of the bureaucracy in an attempt to keep it accountable. But the very nature of the well-established bureaucracy presents serious challenges to accountability.

In most democracies bureaucracy is accountable to elected officials within the government or to those who have been appointed by elected officials to oversee the operations of the bureaucracy. But the vast size and complexity of modern bureaucracy limit the degree to which the bureaucracy can be held accountable for much of what it does. In theory, a bureaucracy modeled after the image provided by Weber might respond efficiently to instructions issued to it by elected officials and might easily be held accountable for its actions. But because personnel within the bureaucracy respond to their superiors within the organization and to specific job responsibilities and procedures, bureaucracies tend to be resistant to changes introduced from outside by public officials responding to calls for change issued by the citizens. Moreover, any change in the responsibilities of the bureaucracy must be accompanied by the necessary changes in bureaucratic procedure, routine, and policy. Change, when it does occur within the bureaucracy, is usually slow.

The bureaucracy also represents a challenge to democratic government because of the expertise it possesses. Elected officials often come to rely on the bureaucracy for information and data on issues they confront. The bureaucracy often is the primary source of information for citizens as well. This reliance on the bureaucracy can undermine the independent political authority of elected officials in a democracy. Political leaders often find themselves reacting and responding to changes in the political environment that have been created by the bureaucracy. In addition, they become dependent on the bureaucracy to accomplish the purposes of legislation. And as citizens make more and more demands on government, bureaucracy increases. The size and expense of modern bureaucracy are such that it constitutes the major costs associated with government.

In light of all these considerations, the reform of bureaucracy is an ongoing concern in most developed democracies around the world. But bureaucracy has proved difficult to reform, resistant to change, and resilient to attack.

Endurance of the Bureaucratic State

The growth of the modern bureaucracy is considered by many to be an inevitable by-product of political development. The advent of the advanced bureaucratic state is a twentieth-century phenomenon associated with centralization of government and an industry-based economy. Highly decentralized states do not characteristically have large bureaucracies, nor do agricultural societies. As the state centralizes the institutions and processes of government, bureaucracy increases. This increase is true for virtually every form of government, not only for democracies. Moreover, as a society moves away from an agricultural economy toward an industrial economy, bureaucracy increases. Again, this is true regardless of the political system in place. When the Soviet Union was at the peak of its power, it possessed a vast bureaucracy that controlled virtually every aspect of the economy and the state.

A well-developed, functioning bureaucracy is the prime attribute of a modern, advanced state. It has evolved as the means by which government responds to the demands of the society as those demands are reflected in the political decisions reached by elected officials. Bureaucracy will, in all likelihood, be very influential in shaping the future of liberal democracy.

See also *Accountability of public officials; Civil service; Idealism, German; Participatory democracy; Weber, Max; Wilson, Woodrow.*

Eugene W. Hickok

BIBLIOGRAPHY

Downs, Anthony. *Inside Bureaucracy.* Boston: Little, Brown, 1967.
Mosher, Frederick C. *Democracy and the Public Service.* 2d ed. New York: Oxford University Press, 1982.
Redford, Emmette S. *Democracy in the Administrative State.* New York: Oxford University Press, 1969.
Simon, Herbert A. *Administrative Behavior.* 3d ed. New York: Free Press, 1976.
Weber, Max. *The Theory of Social and Economic Organization.* New York: Free Press, 1964.
Wilson, James Q. *Bureaucracy.* New York: Basic Books, 1989.
Wilson, Woodrow. "The Study of Administration." *Political Science Quarterly* (June 1887).

Burke, Edmund

British Whig politician and pamphleteer. Burke (1729–1797) was trained in the law but never practiced. After a brief career in literary journalism, he spent more than three decades in the House of Commons, where he was one of its leading orators.

Although Burke addressed contemporary issues in most of his writings and produced no formal treatise of political philosophy, he discussed all aspects of politics, including democracy, in his many pamphlets and speeches. Burke is well known for his defense of the American colonists in their dispute with the British government; for his belief that parliamentary representatives ought to form judgments in light of the broadest considerations of public policy and not by reflecting the local interests and wishes of their constituents; for his criticism of despotic British rule in India; for his condemnation of the oppressive penalties imposed on Catholics in Ireland; and above all for his critical analysis of the ideas and conduct of the French revolutionaries in *Reflections on the Revolution in France* (1790) and other works. His critique of the French Revolution defined debate about the revolution and provoked a considerable response from pamphleteers; among them was Thomas Paine's *Rights of Man* (1791).

Burke was deeply skeptical about democracy. He was not absolutely opposed to it, acknowledging that in some circumstances it might be necessary, even desirable. But he could not foresee what those circumstances might be, and he strongly believed they did not exist in his own time. Assessing the educational and economic conditions of eighteenth-century England, he concluded that democratic government would be not only inept but oppressive.

Burke's opposition to democracy, first of all, was based on his assumption that the qualifications for governing were not likely to be found within the general populace. Governing required knowledge and intelligence; moreover, those who made laws had to foresee their consequences. Foresight required prudence, which Burke called the first of political virtues. In addition to educated intelligence, prudence required experience and wisdom. All these qualities were more likely to be found among the privileged than among the common people. This antiegalitarian assumption did not prevent Burke from recognizing that many among the privileged did not possess these qualities. Although he was aware that occasionally a person in humble circumstances did possess them, he was convinced that among the common people such persons were rare.

Burke's opposition to democracy was also based on his belief that the common people had predatory and angry passions that would readily be aroused and vented if the people gained power. Normally such passions were moderated, for one of the functions of government was to restrain and discourage them. In a democratic government, however, the incentive to perform this moderating function would be removed. Moreover, the antiauthoritarian impulses unleashed in a democracy would lead to the undermining of tradition and religion, which, Burke argued, should supplement government by restraining popular passions and upholding authority. Once such controls were lifted, the result would be fraud, violence, rapine, and confiscation.

Burke offered a third argument against democracy: it had a tendency to tyrannize minorities. Democratic power—whether exercised by the people themselves or by demagogues acting in their name—could be as arbitrary and intolerant as any other power. Thus, Burke argued, the majority in a democracy was capable of inflicting on minorities greater oppressions with greater cruelty than would occur even under a tyrannical monarch. This tendency to oppress minorities was aggravated by a certain "fearless" character in democratic majorities, for they sensed that as holders of sovereign power and as makers

Edmund Burke

of positive law they were above punishment. Burke therefore emphasized that democratic majorities must not be allowed to believe that their will was the standard of right and wrong. The wishes and decisions of the populace, in other words, should be subject to an independent and higher moral law. The risk that a majority might seek arbitrary power was increased by its inclination to follow the lead of ambitious, selfish demagogues. Burke's fear of majorities was similar to James Madison's concern about majority factions and anticipated Alexis de Tocqueville's warning about the tyranny of the majority.

Although Burke had little opportunity to observe democracy directly, he based his views and assumptions about it largely on the writings of ancient philosophers, including Plato and Aristotle. He used these ideas in his analysis of the French Revolution, which was the occasion for his most notable work, *Reflections on the Revolution in France.* Burke regarded the Revolution as egalitarian and democratic: it used the rhetoric of the universal rights of man, made claims in behalf of those previously excluded from participating in government, and sought to overthrow many established institutions. Early in the Revolution, however, before its main features unfolded, Burke predicted that although it affected to be a pure democracy it would soon turn into a "mischievous and ignoble oligarchy." He complained that the revolutionaries were guided by abstract theories, including the egalitarian claim of the rights of man. He also noted the revolutionaries' wish to reduce everyone to the same level; their policy of destroying monarchy, aristocracy, and church in order to achieve this goal; and their efforts to undermine religious belief and traditional morality. This course, he argued, removed obstacles to despotic power and opened the door to rule by ambitious leaders who would claim to speak in the name of the people. Having made this analysis, he called the revolutionary government "a despotic democracy" and forecast an increasingly despotic outcome to the democratic revolution. This prediction was proved correct.

For all Burke's opposition to democracy in his time, he would probably approve of democracy today, at least as it has emerged in constitutional regimes that protect individual liberty, practice the rule of law, and provide constitutional protections against arbitrary rule and despotism. He would particularly approve of those democracies that allow the perpetuation of moral and religious traditions, which, he believed, also serve as obstacles to despotism. Because the prospect today for preventing despotism is greatest in constitutional democracies, we can be confident that Burke, were he alive now, would be among their most vigorous defenders.

Joseph Hamburger

BIBLIOGRAPHY

Burke, Edmund. *Burke's Politics: Selected Writings and Speeches of Edmund Burke on Reform, Revolution, and War.* Edited by Ross Hoffman and Paul Levack. New York: Knopf, 1949.
———. *Reflections on the Revolution in France and on the Proceedings in Certain Societies in London Relative to That Event.* Edited by Conor Cruise O'Brien. Harmondsworth, England: Penguin Books, 1982.
Canavan, Francis P. *The Political Reason of Edmund Burke.* Durham, N.C.: Duke University Press, 1960.
Cone, Carl B. *Burke and the Nature of Politics.* 2 vols. Lexington: University of Kentucky Press, 1957, 1964.
Freeman, Michael. *Edmund Burke and the Critique of Political Radicalism.* Oxford: Blackwell; Chicago: University of Chicago Press, 1980.
Mansfield, Harvey C., Jr. *Statesmanship and Party Government.* Chicago: University of Chicago Press, 1965.

Burma

The largest state in mainland Southeast Asia, with borders on China, Bangladesh, India, Laos, and Thailand. Burma has had limited experience with democracy since gaining independence from Great Britain in 1948. The military government that took power in 1988 changed the name of the state to Myanmar in 1989, though opposition groups did not accept the change. In this article, *Myanmar* is used only for the period since 1989, while the name *Burma* is retained for earlier periods. The adjective *Burmese* refers to the citizens of Burma/Myanmar, while *Burmans* refers to the major ethnic group.

In the precolonial era Burma traditionally was governed by an autocratic monarchy tempered only by the Buddhist clergy and its limited administrative capacity. Burma became a British colony after three Anglo-Burmese wars (1824–1826, 1852, and 1895–1896) that resulted in the partition of the Burmese state. Bent on revenue collection and law and order, the British governed Burma from India.

At the time of independence, in 1948, Burma adopted a civilian, multiparty democratic system dominated by a political coalition. This gave way to a military regime in 1958. Civilian, democratic rule was reinstituted through elections in 1960 and lasted until 1962. On March 2, 1962, the military launched a coup that kept it in power in the following decades and prevented the development of a democratic system of governance. Democratic and independence movements in Burma were linked to anticolonialism and nationalism, as well as to ethnic identity.

Traditional Decision Making

Burma traditionally has had many ethnic and linguistic groups. The Buddhist Burmans have been dominant in the heartland for most of the period since the eleventh century. In the south the Buddhist Mons established pre-Burman kingdoms, and in the Arakan Peninsula Hindu-Buddhist kingdoms existed from about the first century

A.D. to the end of the eighteenth century. In the northeast the Shans evolved a traditional Buddhist set of small hereditary kingdoms. The Chins and Nagas in the west, the Kachins in the north, and the Karens in the east all had tribal societies with animist religions. Christianity has made major inroads among the animist groups since the nineteenth century. Burman Buddhists traditionally have held women in high regard. Since early times women have had high literacy rates and equal rights, including the right to inherit.

Several types of consensual decision making were found in the traditional village-level societies within the boundaries of the present country. These were not democratic in terms of the election of leaders through some sort of formal or constitutional process, and they lacked the potential for a peaceful transfer of authority from one political group or individual to another. The Burman areas of Burma in the precolonial period, however, did have informal mechanisms whereby the village headmen—often hereditary positions—were viewed as representing the village to the central court. Some minority groups, such as the Kachins and Karens, showed a clearer pattern of consensual rule by elders or authority figures of the village or clan.

With a long history in Burma, Buddhism became established in the eleventh century. Theravada Buddhism is the religion of more than three-quarters of the Burmese, including most ethnic Burmans. Some scholars of religion argue that Theravada Buddhism fosters a sense of individualism and equality, both of which may contribute to the democratic process.

Beginning in 1922 the British rulers of Burma instituted a legislative council, with 80 of the 130 members elected by a limited electorate. The issue of separation from India dominated politics at that time, and a vote held in 1932 rejected separation. In 1935 a new constitution created a bicameral legislature: a Senate, of whose members half were elected and half were appointed by the British governor, and a more powerful elected House of Representatives.

The political process was characterized by the personalization of power. Burma had a strong tradition of personalism, dating back more than 900 years, in which loyalty was given to the individual monarch and not to the office of the throne.

Burma's experience with responsible parliamentary government proved fleeting; it lasted from 1937, when Burma gained separation from India, until 1941, when World War II began in Asia. Japanese forces occupied Bur-

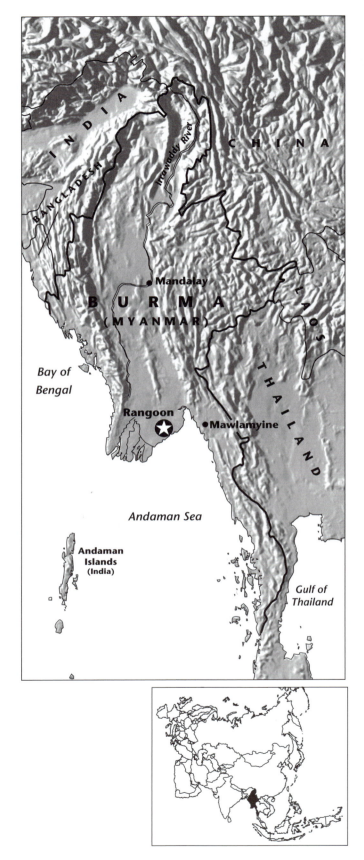

ma during World War II. That period saw the rise of a pseudo-independent state run by a dictatorship, or *adipati,* which soon became discredited. Eventually, resistance to the Japanese gave rise to a loose political confederation called the Anti-Fascist People's Freedom League (AFPFL). The AFPFL dominated Burmese political life for a decade after independence, until it formally split into factions in 1958. The split led to a constitutional coup in which the civilian regime, led by Prime Minister U Nu, authorized a temporary military takeover, led by the commander of the armed forces, General Ne Win. The AFPFL contained a broad spectrum of political opinion but excluded two separate communist parties, both of which were in revolt.

The decade of civilian control between 1948 and 1958 was characterized by a series of ethnic and political revolts that severely restricted the capacity of the state to develop. The rebels included two communist parties and elements of most minority groups. The government was elected under a constitution adopted in 1947, which established a republic with a bicameral legislature: an upper house of nationalities (that is, ethnic groups) and a dominant lower house. All seats were elected. A president was chosen from among those elected; the office rotated among various ethnic groups. A prime minister was appointed by the party in power, which in this period was continuously the AFPFL. Opposition parties were tolerated, although the Burma Communist Party was banned because it was in revolt. The judiciary was relatively independent, and its senior members were well trained in British law. A career elite bureaucracy was fostered. Suffrage was universal, especially because women had traditionally wielded considerable power in the society. The press was relatively free. This period was the most democratic of any in Burmese history.

The military caretaker government lasted from 1958 until 1960, during which time it ruled by decree. Military leaders unsuccessfully attempted to improve the economy and eliminate the rebellions. They did, however, abide by the results of the 1960 election, which was widely heralded as a fair contest. Two components of the now dissolved AFPFL were the main contenders; former prime minister U Nu won, and a civilian, democratic government was again installed.

The Coup of 1962

Ethnic unrest continued. On March 2, 1962, claiming that Burma was about to disintegrate as a result of the conflicts, the military launched an almost bloodless coup. This time the military leaders—most of whom had taken part in the earlier military caretaker government—clearly intended to stay in power. They established a military Revolutionary Council and ruled by decree for more than a decade, until 1974. They centralized control and eliminated any threats to their power, abolishing both the legislature and the judiciary. The executive branch was staffed and controlled by the military. A statement of intent, called the Burmese Way to Socialism, was established soon after the coup, and by the following year Burma was characterized by military mobilization, centralized control, an absence of political and media freedom, and a socialist economy.

By 1974 the military, led by General Ne Win, had taken a cadre party founded in 1962, called the Burma Socialist Program Party, and expanded it into a mass organization. It was enshrined in the Constitution of 1974 as Burma's sole party. The military leaders had somewhat liberalized the extreme socialism that characterized the 1960s. The 1974 Constitution also created the Pyithu Hluttaw, or national legislature, whose members were elected by voting for designated candidates on single-party slates. A system of "people's justice" was established, in which party officials replaced lawyers. The military controlled the press and censored all media. There was an elaborate system of military intelligence and reporting. With the military in complete command, human rights and democracy were suppressed.

The Events of 1988 and After

By 1988 the people of Burma were suffering from political malaise and economic deprivation. That March a massive uprising began, which lasted several months. It began among university students in Rangoon, the capital, and soon spread to the rest of the country. Attempts by the military to appease the populace with piecemeal reforms came too late. There had been mass killings of students and demonstrators that had discredited the regime. In the midst of this ferment, on September 18, the military launched its third coup to shore up military control and to replace the earlier military regime.

The new leaders, the State Law and Order Restoration Council, brutally suppressed popular dissent. This group, originally composed of eighteen senior military figures, continued to rule in the early 1990s. Until August 1992 the State Law and Order Restoration Council ruled by martial law. It abolished the legislature and disbanded the Burma

Socialist Program Party, establishing an even more autocratic military rule.

Promising an eventual move to a civilian, multiparty system, the State Law and Order Restoration Council allowed the formation and registration of political parties. The military promised to remain aloof from politics. Still, the National Unity Party was clearly the favored group. It had inherited many of the assets of the Burma Socialist Program Party. In all, 234 parties registered, and eventually 93 competed in the elections held May 27, 1990. An opposition party, the National League for Democracy, won 80 percent of the seats. It was led by *Daw* (Madam) Aung San Suu Kyi, whom the military had placed under house arrest. Taken aback by this sweeping rejection of the military's role in government, the State Law and Order Restoration Council refused to recognize the results of the election.

The council then promised to establish a multiparty civilian government under a new constitution and, in January 1993, began the long constitution-making process. The military called a national convention of more than 700 handpicked persons to establish guidelines for the constitution. No end date was set for the convention's deliberations. Following the convention, a new constitution would still have to be written (based, at least in theory, on the convention guidelines) and subjected to a national plebiscite, and then new elections would have to be held for the new government. The State Law and Order Restoration Council indicated that the military would continue in its traditional leadership role under any new government and would likely attempt to institutionalize its power.

Some members of the National League for Democracy held a rump, secret meeting in Mandalay of the majority of those elected to the Pyithu Hluttaw. They designated certain leaders to flee to a rebel-held area along the eastern (Thai) frontier. There they established, in December 1990, the National Coalition Government of the Union of Burma, a government claiming to represent the legitimate will of the people as expressed in the May 1990 elections. It was denounced by the Rangoon authorities.

Throughout its history Burma/Myanmar has been characterized by factional and personalized power. In the decades since independence the military has played the most conspicuous role and directly held power for more than three decades. The generation of leaders trained under the British in parliamentary democracy has grown too old to govern again.

International communications technology has kept the military from closing off the country from outside influences, as happened after the 1962 coup. Moreover, the military leaders have tried to encourage foreign tourists and investment. In 1988, when the old political, authoritarian structure was collapsing, there were continuous cries for democracy. There is considerable dispute concerning how far the Burmese people and some of their leaders understand the nature of the democratic system, in contrast to its forms. Many Burmese advocate democracy. Short of a popular uprising backed by some of the military, however, the military leaders seem unlikely to give up political control, whatever the nature of the new constitution.

See also *Asia, Southeast; Aung San Suu Kyi; Buddhism.*

David I. Steinberg

BIBLIOGRAPHY

Aung Cin Win Aung. *Burma: From Monarchy to Dictatorship.* Bloomington, Ind.: Eastern Press, 1994.

Gyi, Maurg. *Burmese Political Values: The Socio-political Roots of Authoritarianism.* New York: Praeger, 1983.

Shwe Lu Maung. *Burma, Nationalism and Ideology: An Analysis of Society, Culture, and Politics.* Dhaka: University Press, 1989.

Silverstein, Josef. *Burmese Politics: The Dilemma of National Unity.* New Brunswick, N.J.: Rutgers University Press, 1980.

Singh, Balwant. *Independence and Democracy in Burma, 1945–1952: The Turbulent Years.* Ann Arbor: Center for South and Southeast Asian Studies, University of Michigan, 1993.

Steinberg, David I. *The Future of Burma: Crisis and Choice in Myanmar.* Lanham, Md.: University Press of America, 1990.

Bustamante, Alexander

Founder of the Bustamante Industrial Trade Union and the Jamaica Labour Party, first prime minister of Jamaica (1962–1964), and one of Jamaica's national heroes. Bustamante (1884–1977) was born William Alexander Clarke and was related to Norman W. Manley, another Jamaican national hero and the leader of the People's National Party.

Bustamante grew up in rural Jamaica and spent many years in Cuba and Panama. He returned to Jamaica in 1934, setting up a money-lending business. He soon became known for his letters to the country's major newspaper on a wide range of public issues. He rose to prominence as a charismatic labor organizer and leader when

Alexander Bustamante

labor rebellions swept the island in 1937 and 1938. Victorious in conflicts with rival union leaders, he consolidated his control over the union movement, which became officially registered as the Bustamante Industrial Trade Union in January 1939.

Initially, Bustamante worked closely with the People's National Party, founded in 1938, but in 1942 he broke with that party. The next year he founded the Jamaica Labour Party, in anticipation of the electoral strength of the Bustamante Industrial Trade Union in Jamaica's first elections with universal suffrage. The Jamaica Labour Party won in 1944 and 1949, and afterward it alternated with the People's National Party in two-term cycles.

Bustamante's attitude to democracy was ambiguous. On the one hand, he made a major contribution to labor organization and to the formation of the alliance between unions and the middle-class People's National Party. This alliance was the basis of the nationalist movement, and the People's National Party component of the alliance became the driving force for democratization. On the other hand, Bustamante later divided the nationalist movement and for a long time opposed demands for self-government and independence. Moreover, he ran his own organizations, the Bustamante Industrial Trade Union and the Jamaica Labour Party, in a decidedly nondemocratic way. He made himself president general for life of the Industrial Trade Union and ruled the Labour Party as "the chief."

Evelyne Huber

C

Cabinets

Small groups of advisers selected by heads of state to assist in governing. Since the earliest civilizations, rulers have used cabinets not only to help with the workload but also to legitimize decisions—that is, to make decisions acceptable to the key forces that sustain the regime. Thus, in the past, the inner groups included representatives of various elements—usually military advisers, upon whom the ruler relied to maintain the security of the domain and, from time to time, expand its boundaries or pursue crusades against religious foes; nobles, who controlled large segments of the kingdom and the produce and taxes of those areas; scholars, who based their influence on their acumen; and religious leaders, who provided spiritual guidance and interpreted omens of good or bad fortune.

Modern cabinets owe their lineage to the practice in medieval Europe whereby kings would consult notables from the three "estates" of society upon whose cooperation they relied to stay in power and govern effectively. The estates were the military leadership, the landed aristocracy, and the clergy.

After the Middle Ages the military yielded much of its power to the landed aristocracy. As Europe secularized in the seventeenth and eighteenth centuries, the clergy played less of a role in monarchs' coteries. With the emergence of the modern state in the nineteenth century, bureaucrats who achieved their positions through merit-based selection began to dominate rulers' inner circles. As societies democratized, through the nineteenth and twentieth centuries, professional politicians increasingly assumed the key advisory roles in cabinets. Democratization gradually weakened the power of monarchs, and most of those who remain serve entirely as symbolic heads of state.

Head of State Versus Head of Government

The key function that has emerged with the decline of monarchy has been that of head of government. In many systems the ceremonial head of state and the effective head of government are two different people. The former is usually called a constitutional monarch or president and the latter a prime minister. The term *prime minister* connotes chairmanship of the ministry—that is, the group of political leaders that governs the country and manages its day-to-day affairs.

The American system is one very clear exception to this format. In the United States a president—chosen by an electoral college whose members are selected in federal elections—merges the functions of head of state and head of government. Several systems—most notably in Latin America—have copied this model. However, it has not been as successful in other systems as it has in the United States. The American political culture can sustain the policy ambiguities emerging from the separation of powers and the fragmentation of the cabinet system. In developing democracies, policy ambiguity often introduces pressures that result in military juntas and demagogues or dictators who run their cabinets autocratically.

The weakness of its cabinets distinguishes the American system even from most other systems with presidential constitutions. The Founders of the nation deliberately avoided mention of a cabinet in the Constitution. Subsequently, presidents have been careful not to impart the prerogatives of office in such a way that their cabinet secretaries could begin to see themselves as holding collective authority.

Many countries blend presidential and prime ministerial systems. The president might perform some roles belonging to a head of government as well as symbolic functions associated with the head of state. France deliberately pursues this approach in the Fifth Republic. Some countries achieve a de facto blend. This occurs largely in states dominated by one party, in which the president also operates behind the scenes as effective head of the party.

Cabinet Positions and Conduct of Business

Systems differ immensely in the ways in which individuals gain access to cabinet positions. In nations in which one party is dominant, normally only party operatives rise to such prominence. In highly "statist"—that is, rationalized—societies, such as France, Germany, and Japan, many cabinet members start their careers as government officials and then become professional politicians. Advanced democracies that follow the Westminster parliamentary system—the United Kingdom, Canada, Australia, and New Zealand—run their cabinets principally with elected politicians who have not served as bureaucrats. They also maintain a high degree of neutrality in their public services. Although they are not apolitical, officials do not publicly manifest their partisan sympathies, and they assume their careers as permanent vocations.

The United States runs a hybrid system. Cabinet secretaries do not hold elective office. Although some might have served as governors or as federal or state legislators, many simply worked their way up as professionals who parlayed a succession of appointive positions into prominence in a relevant policy field. In the typical U.S. executive department, the top four levels of officials and about half of the fifth level gained their posts through political appointment. Thus the reporting lines between a cabinet secretary and the merit-based career civil service have become attenuated. In other systems, career officials normally occupy all but the uppermost posts in ministries.

Cabinets also vary immensely in the way they conduct their business. Most cabinets meet regularly—in many cases, weekly. The sheer weight of government dictates that cabinets divide the labor. Many cabinets function with a steering committee that sets out the agenda for the term of the government or for a parliamentary session. Others have an inner group capable of devising macroeconomic policy or enforcing fiscal stringency.

Recourse to these various types of groups will depend on the nature of the times. For instance, the United Kingdom, Canada, and Australia found that a general-purpose priorities committee might enshrine policy objectives that violate the country's overall economic policy or break the budget. Thus in the 1980s all three nations resorted to inner groups that focused more on economics and stringency than on the programmatic policy agenda.

The United States has lagged in creating cabinet subcommittees. This absence of subcommittees has presented operational difficulties. In other systems the constitutional norms—either written in basic law or established by convention—strongly encourage collective decision making. In the United States no such norms prevail. Thus each president and the cabinet secretaries must become convinced of the usefulness of collective consultation and the division of labor into subcommittees. This point consistently has been difficult to sell to American presidents.

Other Cabinet Functions

Virtually every cabinet still performs at least some representational functions. Many regimes that depend on the support of the military continue to rely on some ministers from the armed forces, even if they are not formally a military junta. Often governments depend on the support of more than one party to sustain themselves. In some very mature democracies, such as Canada and Britain, the party with the greatest number of seats in the lower house might form a *minority* government if it does not have an absolute majority. Thus smaller parties would support the government without requiring representation in the cabinet. In other systems the smaller parties would insist on being represented in the cabinet. A *coalition* government would therefore emerge. Depending on the leverage smaller parties enjoy within such coalitions, they might demand control of specific ministries. For instance, a party of the far right that is suspicious of the national security policies of the largest coalition party might insist on controlling the ministry of defense.

Something of the old estates system, whereby the key elements necessary for sustaining the legitimacy of the regime must have a presence in the cabinet, survives into our current era. In the United States, presidents work mightily after the election to ensure that their cabinet appointees send the right signals to various groups. Treasury secretaries must have standing with Wall Street; secretaries of state, with the international affairs community; defense secretaries, with the military-industrial complex; and so on. The weaker the reference groups the less likely that a president will appoint for them a strong spokesman. For example, neither the Department of the Interior nor the

Department of Labor is always headed by someone with strong ties to their client groups.

Presidents and prime ministers putting together cabinets often must take into consideration the regional and ethnic roots of those whom they choose. Increasingly, they must also ensure that they appoint some women to significant roles in the administration. Some countries have encountered difficulty in fulfilling such requirements. The necessity for regional and ethnic representation has actually placed Canadian prime ministers under pressure to appoint large, unwieldy cabinets since confederation in 1867.

Cabinet discipline varies greatly among countries. British ministers typically leave the ministry rather than leak traceable information that hints of division within the cabinet. In the United States, in contrast, disputes occasionally erupt in which cabinet secretaries speak openly against one another. In some relatively authoritarian regimes, such as Thailand, newspapers report cabinet quarrels nearly blow by blow. Perhaps these systems can afford such undignified coverage because only the elites in society take any notice.

Providing executive leadership in any political system is a big job; it cannot be done by one person alone. This fact led rulers to create cabinets. Even in medieval times, however, cabinets played certain representational roles, though their focus was on maintaining the support of various elites whose cooperation was necessary to the viability of the regime. In our current era the representational role has expanded through democratization to include large segments of society. Here a trade-off emerges whereby cabinets that serve the representational function well might, in fact, make executive leadership more difficult and vice versa.

See also *Government formation; Parliamentarism and presidentialism.*

Colin Campbell

BIBLIOGRAPHY

Campbell, Colin. *Managing the Presidency: Carter, Reagan, and the Search for Executive Harmony.* Pittsburgh: University of Pittsburgh Press, 1986.

Hennessy, Peter. *Cabinet.* Oxford: Blackwell, 1986.

Mackie, Thomas Taylor, and Brian W. Hogwood, eds. *Unlocking the Cabinet: Structures in Comparative Perspective.* Beverly Hills, Calif., and London: Sage Publications, 1985.

Plowden, William, ed. *Advising Rulers.* Oxford: Blackwell, 1987.

Porter, Roger B. *Presidential Decision Making: The Economic Policy Board.* Cambridge and New York: Cambridge University Press, 1980.

Suleiman, Ezra N., ed. *Bureaucrats and Policy Making: A Comparative Review.* London and New York: Holmes and Meier, 1984.

Weaver, R. Kent, and Bert A. Rockman, eds. *Do Institutions Matter? Government Capabilities in the United States and Abroad.* Washington, D.C.: Brookings Institution, 1993.

Weller, Patrick. *First among Equals: Prime Ministers in Westminster Systems.* Sydney: Allen and Unwin; New York: Routledge Chapman and Hall, 1985.

Cambodia

See *Asia, Southeast*

Cameroon

See *Africa, Subsaharan*

Canada

A parliamentary democracy, member of the British Commonwealth, and second largest nation in the world in area. Canada is the northernmost country in North America, separated from the United States by a border of 4,545 miles along the south and 979 miles along the northwest. It was created a distinct state on July 1, 1867, from the remaining British North American colonies, including the former New France. The original provinces were Quebec, Ontario, Nova Scotia, and New Brunswick. Manitoba, British Columbia, and Prince Edward Island became provinces in the 1870s; Alberta and Saskatchewan, in 1905; and Newfoundland, in 1949. These ten provinces, together with the Yukon and the Northwest Territories, make up Canada today.

Encounters between native peoples and settlers from the two original colonial powers, between English and French speakers, between English and French speakers and immigrants from all parts of the world, as well as demands for a sovereign state and the attractions of its powerful southern neighbor, all continue to shape the contours of Canadian democracy.

Historical Background

To the British North American colonists in the middle of the nineteenth century, political union was the solution to political stalemate, economic depression, and threats from the neighboring United States, already mobilized as a result of civil war. The legislation resolving these problems was framed by the Fathers of Confederation, as the colonial politicians who devised the ensuing plan are known, and was passed by the British Parliament in 1867.

The British North America Act extended to Canada the kind of liberal democratic practices and protections then prevalent under British common law and at the same time gave Canada a written constitution. Although the act provided for elected legislative bodies, it gave executive authority to the queen and her representatives, a formal distribution of powers that remains to this day. This legal fiction accompanied the planned solution to the colonies' problems—the establishment of representative and responsible government within a federal system.

In the federal context, democracy meant an agreed-on division of powers between the center and the provinces. Legislative government was achieved through elected legislatures based on majority rule. Responsible government meant that executive authority would be exercised by ministers appointed from their legislatures. Principles of representation and responsibility, already characteristics of British government, were extended to federal and provincial parliaments. Over time, and especially since the 1960s, representation and responsibility have been transformed in the direction of greater participation.

Federalism

Because all political institutions in Canada are refracted through the lens of federalism, the search for an enlarged democratic life is itself conditioned by changes in federalism. To begin with, the incorporation of divided powers in the British North America Act opened the door to judicial interpretations, a limit on the parliamentary sovereignty understood to be the hallmark of British constitutional government. Because it was an act of the imperial Parliament, the highest authority for the British North America Act's interpretation was the Judicial Committee of the Privy Council. That authority was an additional limit on Canadian sovereignty.

After the Statute of Westminster (which, in 1931, created the British Commonwealth) removed barriers to sovereignty for self-governing dominions like Canada, there was theoretically no reason not to make the British North America Act a totally Canadian constitution. But because to do so would mean agreeing on amending procedures, something that had so far been carefully avoided, no changes were made until 1949. Until then, appeal on all constitutional issues continued to be made to the Privy Council; after that, the Supreme Court of Canada became the highest judicial authority, except on matters involving the provinces, parliamentary terms, and minority rights.

Even more important than Parliament or the courts, the institution of federal-provincial conferences became the mode for reconciling jurisdictional disputes. Regular meetings among first ministers (the prime minister and provincial premiers), other cabinet ministers, and top civil servants created a system of executive federalism in response to the growing complexity of government after World War II.

Only in 1982, following a request to the British Parliament from the Canadian House of Commons and Senate, was Canada's written constitution returned to its homeland. The British North America Act was renamed the Constitution Act, 1867, and new constitutional provisions, contained in the Constitution Act, 1982, included amending procedures for matters related to joint federal-provincial authority. Quebec did not agree to the new provisions, leaving a gap in the national consensus that continues to be a troubling weakness in the political fabric. It is possible to evaluate the practice of federalism, then, as both a limit on democratic practices of popular consultation and a source of conditions that foster intergroup conflict.

Especially relevant to limits on democratic rights and freedoms was the application of the Constitution's original provisions that the federal government had jurisdiction over "peace, order, and good government" and the provinces had jurisdiction over property and civil rights. The federal government was thus enabled to use orders-in-council to govern under emergency conditions. These provisions were most evident during and immediately after World War II, when they were used to intern West Coast residents of Japanese origin. Emergency powers were also invoked in 1970 in the aftermath of terrorist acts in Quebec. At that time they involved the suspension of civil rights for all Canadians. The provinces, in turn, had the authority to restrict individual freedoms. Persecution

of religious minorities, particularly Jehovah's Witnesses, by the Quebec government under Maurice Duplessis (who had been premier from 1936 to 1940 and again from 1944 to 1959), and measures taken against trade unionists in Quebec and Newfoundland were notable examples of such restrictive interpretations of provincial powers as late as the 1950s.

Federalism is also important for Canadian democracy in legitimizing concern with group rights. At the outset, federalism represented the interests of provinces and regions. It laid the foundation for arguing the special status of Quebec and, by extension, the status of French speakers (francophones) as a distinct people. From that came the concept of two charter groups, characterized as late as 1963 in the agenda set for the Royal Commission on Bilingualism and Biculturalism as two founding races or peoples—British and French—but then shifted to the more defensible linguistic division between francophones and anglophones. By analogy, federalism then became the basis for claims to recognition from other geographically based groups. Federalism as a system for dividing powers among jurisdictions can work to reconcile opposing interests. At the same time, it remains open to interpretation just when and where the divisions apply.

Political Structures

Impediments to the full exercise of the franchise associated with property and gender disappeared long before impediments based on race or beliefs. For example, conscientious objectors could not vote in federal elections until 1955. Asians and Doukhobors (descendants of a Russian religious group that had immigrated in the 1890s) were barred from voting in British Columbia until 1953. Inuit could not vote federally until 1950, and those who lived in areas of the Northwest Territories outside federal electoral districts were effectively disfranchised until 1962. Status Indians (those living on reservations) were not enfranchised federally until 1960, and Quebec maintained restrictions as late as 1970. Enfranchisement, however, led to the loss of the special rights of status Indians, a dilemma that was not resolved until 1985. With the Canada Elections Act of 1970, all voting restrictions in federal elections were removed for citizens eighteen and older except for convicts, the mentally disabled, federal judges, and certain election officials.

Elections are required at least every five years for both the national and the provincial legislatures. Typically, voters have a choice of two or more candidates from a changing repertoire of political parties. The two oldest parties are the Liberal and Progressive Conservative (what sounds like a contradiction in terms is the result of a 1942 name change in a move to incorporate the western-based Progressive Party). They resemble the two major parties in the United States more than they do their namesakes in Britain.

New parties have emerged most often in Quebec and in the four western provinces. Typically, even when new parties are successful in their home province, they have not been able to acquire broad-based national support. The only exception is the social democratic New Democratic Party. In general, the existence and relative strength of third parties remains a measure of the importance of regional forces in Canadian life. In the 1993 federal election, victory for the Liberals went along with a strong assertion of regional discontent through the election of members of the two largest opposition parties—the Quebec Bloc in Quebec and the Reform Party, which is concentrated in the western provinces. The Conservatives were reduced to two seats.

Today few restrictions are imposed on political parties, but in the past wartime and other emergencies have been the rationale for outlawing parties of both the left and the right. The Canadian Communist Party was an illegal organization in the 1930s but, after the Soviet Union became an ally during World War II, Communists were permitted to organize as the Labour Progressive Party. The cold war again put Communists under a cloud, but today they receive little attention.

The major complaint about elections in Canada in recent years is that the system of victory based on a plurality effectively disfranchises large segments of the electorate, even majorities, who do not select the winning candidate or party. In the past, electoral anomalies were associated with the ways electoral districts had been drawn, when boundaries were as much a partisan as a population consideration. Today every province has instituted nonpartisan electoral commissions that meet after the decennial census to draw up new districts. Complaints persist, however, because provinces' allotment of seats in the House of Commons is fixed and because rural districts are overrepresented. Party strength varies from province to province in what has become effectively a multiparty system; so the majority choice in one province may not be translated into commensurate power in the federal Parliament. Proposals for new voting systems that permit proportional representation are advocated as ways of nationalizing the party system and fostering greater democratic participation.

All provincial governments are now unicameral. The federal government alone has two chambers: the House of Commons and a centrally appointed Senate. Originally, there were expectations that the Senate would be responsible for protecting minority rights and representing the interests of the provinces. This arrangement never worked since the cabinet has always been the more significant source of power. Proposals to abolish the Senate have been made from time to time, but the argument has changed in favor of giving the Senate a more prominent role in representing the provinces by making it an elected body. The 1993 referendum on constitutional change had this proposal as a prominent component, but when the referendum did not receive majority support, Senate reform died. Proposals to change access to seats in the Senate are likely to reemerge as part of a move toward a more representative democracy.

Social and Legal Structures

The ability to live freely is enhanced where citizens can enjoy a minimal standard of living without threat of hunger or want and where they have access to resources that enable them to participate fully in the life of their community. The former is safeguarded through social welfare; the latter is stimulated through public education. Canada scores well in both regards. Although relatively slow in adopting national welfare policies, Canada made notable advances with the introduction of such universal entitlements as family allowances in 1944 (mothers' allowances were early measures in Ontario and Manitoba) and health insurance in 1968. Health insurance had been available earlier in some provinces, and its extension throughout the country was the result of federal-provincial diplomacy (Richard Simeon's apt description of the process of executive federalism).

Education is a provincial responsibility and consequently varies by province, less so now that all provinces have publicly supported, secular school systems. Denominational schools had been the rule in Newfoundland and Quebec; the advent of the Quebec Ministry of Education in 1964 was a major step in that province's "quiet revolution." The 1960s were also a period of great expansion in postsecondary education, as universities, community colleges, and technical institutes were established or expanded.

There is a uniform criminal code across Canada, since criminal law is a federal responsibility. Civil law remains under provincial authority, accommodating both the English common law and the Roman legal tradition of Quebec's civil code. Except at the lowest levels in the provinces, all provincial and federal judges are appointed, removed, and paid by the federal government.

Satisfaction with the common law protections of rights and freedoms lessened after World War II. The abuses of that period shocked Canadians into recognizing the need for more protections. The first effort to address these issues through legislation was a Bill of Rights, introduced by Prime Minister John Diefenbaker and passed in 1960. As an ordinary act of Parliament, the bill lacked constitutional authority. Yet cases brought before the Supreme Court that argued violations based on the Bill of Rights began to broaden conceptions of individual rights, in particular with regard to the free exercise of religion versus statutory restrictions on commerce and with regard to the rights of aboriginal peoples.

Bilingualism and Group Rights

After World War II it was widely recognized that the francophones were deprived of rights primarily on the basis of group characteristics. The appointment of the Royal Commission on Bilingualism and Biculturalism in 1963 was to bring about the first official admission that, even in Quebec, where they were the large majority, francophones were seriously disadvantaged in employment opportunities and income. Outside Quebec, francophones could not use their native language in such public forums as the courts or for advancement in the federal public service.

The Official Languages Act was passed in 1969 to redress these disabilities. This was a particularly significant piece of legislation for the new prime minister, Pierre Elliott Trudeau, who with it propounded his particular vision of Canada. According to the act, French and English would have coequal status as languages of the founding or charter peoples. Bilingualism would be a means for ensuring that francophone rights were not restricted to Quebec.

The unintended results of the language legislation were threefold. In the first instance, although there were serious efforts to increase bilingualism throughout the country, particularly in the federal public service, they did not result in large-scale upward mobility for francophones outside Quebec.

Second, politicians in Quebec were not very interested in what bilingualism might mean outside their province; they were more concerned about the inroads of English in Quebec and about constraints on mobility for francophones. Bilingualism simply did not address the general concerns of Quebec nationalists. Successive Quebec governments responded with a series of language bills, beginning in 1974, that made French the sole official language of the province. Each bill added restrictions on the teaching and public display of languages other than French and led to bitter court battles. Some retreat seems imminent, especially since the Human Rights Committee of the United Nations ruled in April 1993 that the ban on outdoor signs in languages other than French violated freedom of expression and basic human rights.

The third consequence was new demands for recognition from other ethnic groups. Canada might be bilingual, but it was more difficult to affirm that it was bicultural. Since many immigrants who were neither British nor French had settled in the western provinces, the issue of multiculturalism had a territorial locus that fit well with the general culture of federalism. Yet insofar as multiculturalism came to be part of official government policy, beginning in 1971, it led to greater estrangement for those of French origin, who took the policy as a message that their claims for recognition were no greater than those of other ethnic groups.

If official bilingualism was one pillar of Prime Minister Trudeau's vision of Canadian nationhood, the other was a Charter of Rights and Freedoms to be entrenched in the Constitution. Although others shared Trudeau's vision, the charter remained essentially a product of the federal government and the heart of the prime minister's own agenda. The Charter of Rights now begins the Constitution Act, 1982, with explicit guarantees of internationally recognized human rights.

The Charter of Rights includes protection of disadvantaged groups through affirmative action programs, along with guarantees of individual equality and freedom from discrimination. Men and women are guaranteed equality. The Charter also recognizes the rights of aboriginal peoples, defined as Indians, Inuit, and Métis (persons of mixed European and Indian heritage). This constitutional recognition came about largely through lobbying activities by those affected and marked an important step in continuing efforts at self-government by native peoples. Their representatives are involved in drafting alternatives to the federal Indian Act and in creating a self-governing territory for the Inuit. They have been active as well in establishing land claims with provincial governments.

The Charter of Rights also recognizes limits on rights and freedoms, so that the government does not relinquish emergency powers. Additionally, it provides a "notwithstanding" clause, allowing Parliament and the provincial legislatures to override provisions protecting individual rights and freedoms; any such legislation would still be subject to interpretation by the courts. The Quebec legislature has made greatest use of the notwithstanding clause, a symbolic show of its lack of support for the Constitution. Of course, the province is still bound by the Constitution.

The absence of Quebec from the original signatories to the Constitution Act has been a troublesome fact and has led to efforts to find a compromise. Prime Minister Brian Mulroney appeared to have achieved this by the Meech Lake Accord of 1987, when provincial premiers recognized Quebec's claim to be a "distinct society." However, the necessary ratification from all provincial legislatures was not forthcoming by the deadline of June 1990, and the sense of crisis continued. Opposition to Quebec's actions and to official bilingualism underlay that failure. Furthermore, many Canadians felt that they had had enough of executive federalism if it meant that important decisions were to be made by political leaders behind closed doors.

Continuing Struggle

The most recent round of constitution building in Canada began with citizen participation as a major component. Public discussion in local meetings, presentation of briefs, and public hearings were all widely advertised. One result was to continue the mobilization of disaffected groups, especially those with a territorial base—provinces, regions, and native peoples.

Some suggestions were incorporated into proposed constitutional changes developed by a joint House-Senate parliamentary committee. These proposals, in turn, served as the basis for negotiations between the federal government and provincial premiers. But the final Charlottetown Accord, signed on August 28, 1992, appeared to be the kind of compromise solution that satisfied mainly the politicians who hammered it out. In an advisory referendum held in October 1992, a majority withheld their approval on constitutional renewal based on the accord.

The results of the constitutional debates that have engaged Canadians since the 1960s have profoundly changed the character of their democracy. Instead of traditional common law protections of civil rights, explicit guarantees are now the rule. This new recognition of the importance of individual rights goes along with a new legitimacy for the rights of specific groups, among which women and native peoples are particularly prominent.

If Canadians were once inclined to trust their political leaders to carry out their responsibilities in the best interests of their constituents, that is no longer the case. A revolution in rights has brought with it a revolution in collective action. But, although more Canadians than ever believe that sovereignty belongs to the people, they still do not agree on the identity of that people, as Peter H. Russell has pointed out. Greater democracy has meant giving legitimacy to the expression of a wide range of collective grievances, but it has not yet provided the means for achieving solutions in the spirit of workable compromise.

See also *Commonwealth, British; Electoral systems; Federalism.* In Documents section, see *Canadian Charter of Rights and Freedoms (1992).*

Mildred A. Schwartz

BIBLIOGRAPHY

Asch, Michael. *Home and Native Land: Aboriginal Rights and the Canadian Constitution.* Toronto: Methuen, 1984.

Bothwell, Robert, Ian Drummond, and John English. *Canada since 1945: Power, Politics, and Provincialism.* Toronto: University of Toronto Press, 1981.

Cairns, Alan, and Cynthia Williams. *The Politics of Gender, Ethnicity, and Language in Canada.* Toronto: University of Toronto Press, 1986.

Careless, J. M. S., and R. Craig Brown. *The Canadians, 1867–1967.* Toronto: Macmillan, 1968.

Greene, Ian. *The Charter of Rights.* Toronto: Lorimer, 1989.

McRoberts, Kenneth. *Quebec: Social Change and Political Crisis.* 3d ed. Toronto: McClelland and Stewart, 1988.

Russell, Peter H. *Constitutional Odyssey: Can Canadians Be a Sovereign People?* 2d ed. Toronto: University of Toronto Press, 1993.

Simeon, Richard. *Federal-Provincial Diplomacy: The Making of Recent Policy in Canada.* Toronto: University of Toronto Press, 1972.

———, and Ian Robinson. *State, Society, and the Development of Canadian Federalism.* Toronto: University of Toronto Press, 1990.

Whitaker, Reg. "Democracy and the Canadian Constitution." In *And No One Cheered,* edited by Keith Banting and Richard Simeon. Toronto: Methuen, 1983.

Candidate selection and recruitment

Candidate selection and recruitment are essential components of the democratic process. Candidate selection is the mainly extralegal process by which political parties decide who will be designated on the ballot as their recommended candidates. Nomination is the legal process by which election authorities certify certain persons as qualified candidates for particular elective offices and print their names on official election ballots. Both selection and nomination play important parts in the more general process of recruitment, by which political organizations identify those who show promise for becoming organization members and encourage them to participate.

The problem these processes solve is one of numbers. Most democratic nations have millions of persons who would in principle be eligible for the offices open at each election. No voter, however devoted to civic duty, is capable of acquiring useful information about every one of the potential officeholders. Voters can make informed and meaningful election choices only when the number of alternatives before them is small enough that they can know something about each, weigh each against the others, and make the choices that seem best.

Nomination is a prerequisite for meaningful elections in any democratic polity larger than a small village. Although there are many variations in detail, most nominations are made by one or another of two basic procedures: petitions and party-list designations. In some jurisdictions, to be sure, voters are allowed to write in the names of persons not formally nominated for an office, but only in a handful of elections do more than a handful of voters write in their choices.

Nomination by Petition

Nomination by petition is the method employed in most polities that use electoral systems modeled on the single-member district system used for electing members of the British House of Commons. In Great Britain, eligible aspirants for election to the House acquire an official nomination paper from the election office in the district (constituency) they hope to represent. On that paper they write their name, address, and occupation. Each paper must be signed by one voter in the district acting as proposer, another acting as seconder, and eight others acting as assenters. The completed paper is filed with the election authorities and a substantial deposit is paid. The deposit is intended to discourage "frivolous candidatures" and is forfeited to the national treasury if the candidate wins less than 5 percent of the district's votes in the ensuing election.

When these undemanding conditions have been met, the candidate's name is placed on the ballot. Until 1969 British electoral law did not allow the candidate's political party affiliation to be printed on the ballot, and each party had to devote much of its campaign effort in each district to publicizing the connection between the candidate and the party. In 1969 the law was changed to allow each candidate to supply on the ballot an identifying phrase of up to six words. Since then the candidates of the established parties have chosen to have their party affiliations printed, and only the fringe-party or unaffiliated candidates have chosen slogans instead. Other countries that have similar electoral systems, such as Canada and New Zealand, use substantially the same nominating procedures, except that most routinely print the candidates' party affiliations on the ballots.

Party Lists

A majority of democratic nations use some form of party-list proportional representation, in which each election district elects several members of the national legislature and each ballot contains lists of the candidates nominated by each party for that district's seats. (The Israeli parliament, the Knesset, has one election district for the entire nation, and each party's list contains all of its candidates for the national legislature.)

In most of these nations an authorized agency (usually a national party executive committee but sometimes a regional party agency) draws up its list of candidates for each district, specifies the order in which it wishes the candidates to appear on the ballot, and submits the list to the election authorities. The authorities verify that the candidates are legally qualified to serve in the legislature and then print the parties' lists on the election ballot. In some countries, such as Israel, this is the only procedure by which candidates can get their names on the ballots, and write-in votes are not permitted. In others, such as Denmark and Finland, a hundred or so independent voters can also nominate a single candidate or a list of candidates by petition. In general, however, nomination procedures in the party-list countries are dominated—in some cases monopolized—by party organizations.

U.S. Primaries

Nomination procedures in the United States are unlike those of any other democratic system. The United States is the only country in which the direct primary is used. Through the direct primary, candidates for elective offices are selected by the voters in government-supervised elections rather than by party leaders. The system was first adopted by the state of Wisconsin in 1903, and it continues to operate largely under the laws of the different states rather than under national law.

There are some important variations among the states, but the essential features are the same. Any legally eligible person who seeks a particular party's nomination for a particular elective office files with election authorities a petition for that nomination. The petition must be signed by a legally designated number of voters in the jurisdiction. The authorities print election ballots containing the names of all the candidates for each party's nomination to each office. The voters mark their ballots in government-supervised primary elections, registering their preferences for one party nominee for each of the offices to be filled. The election authorities certify the person who receives the largest number of votes for each office in each party's primary as that party's nominee, and the nominees' names and party affiliations are printed on the ballot for the general election, which takes place some months later. At that time the voters choose one or another of the party nominees to fill the office.

The most significant variation in direct primary elections relates to which voters are eligible to vote in a particular party's primary. In closed primaries (now used in twenty-four states) only persons preregistered as members of a particular party can vote in its primary, and voters cannot switch parties on primary election day. In the crossover primaries of fourteen states, all voters, including registered independents, can vote in the primary of any

party they publicly choose. Nine states use open primaries, in which there is no party registration, all voters can vote in the primary of any party they wish, and voters make no public statement of their party choices. With blanket primaries, used in two states, there is no party registration; voters can vote in the primaries of both parties (although they are restricted to voting in one party's primary for each office). Louisiana holds nonpartisan primaries: all the candidates for each office are put on one ballot and each voter votes for one candidate for each office. Any candidate receiving a majority of the votes is elected. If no candidate receives a majority, a runoff election is held later between the two top finishers.

Some parties in a few nations (for example, Belgium, Canada, Germany, Norway, and Turkey) make nominations by party-conducted elections among enrolled dues-paying party members. The United States, however, is the only country that uses the direct primary in the strict sense: party nominations are made by government-conducted elections in which by law all registered voters may participate.

Candidate Selection Processes

In the United States, then, the distinction between legal nomination procedures and extralegal party processes is blurred and misleading. In all other democracies, however, parties select their candidates in ways that are largely or wholly unknown to the law, and extralegal candidate selection processes underlie the legal nomination procedures. Candidate selection procedures vary considerably, not only from one nation to another but also from one party to another within particular nations and even from one level of party organization to another within particular parties. Nevertheless, some generalizations can be made.

One widely studied variable is centralization—that is, the degree to which effective control over nominations is located in national, regional, or local party agencies. At one extreme, all candidates would be chosen by a national party agency with no participation or influence by regional and local party agencies. At the other extreme, all candidates would be chosen by regional or local party organizations with no participation or influence by national organizations. The studies of selection processes in particular nations suggest that control usually lies somewhere between the two extremes. The most common pattern is selection by district party agencies under some form of supervision by national or regional party agencies. The next most common is selection by national agencies after consultation with regional or local agencies.

Some parties in some countries give their national leaders the power to veto a candidate selected by a local party organization. National leaders thus can deny to a locally selected candidate the ability to contest the general election as the party's official candidate because he or she does not meet the party's requirements of ideological loyalty or personal ethics. Such vetoes are rare, but awareness of the possibility has inclined local "selectorates" to choose candidates they feel confident will be accepted by the national party authorities.

Some national party leaders also have the power to place candidates, by persuading or requiring local selectors (especially in districts the party is likely to win) to choose candidates the national leaders designate. Such central placements often arouse resentment among the local selectors, sometimes to the point where the local activists refuse to support the "parachuted" candidate and the party loses the election. Accordingly, most national leaders use their placement power rarely and gingerly.

Another variable is participation, the degree to which rank-and-file members of political parties participate in the selection of candidates. At one extreme is a situation in which a single party leader or a small group of party leaders would choose the candidates for all elective offices. Israeli parties come very close to this extreme. At each general election for the 120-member Knesset, each party submits one national list of up to 120 candidates for the 120 seats to be filled. Each party's national executive committee, sometimes after receiving suggestions from local activists, chooses the names for the list and also determines the order in which they will appear on the ballot. Getting positions high on the list is almost as important for candidates as being on the list at all, for each party elects a percentage of its nominees that matches its percentage of the popular votes cast for its list. The party's allotted seats are filled by the candidates on its list, taken one at a time in descending order until the party has filled all the seats to which it is entitled. Accordingly, if a party expects to win, say, about 20 percent of the votes, the top 24 or 25 candidates on its list are likely to be elected, and the candidates who are listed in places from, say, 26 to 120 are almost sure to lose. Thus, in Israel as in many other countries with party-list proportional electoral systems, the national party leaders' power to rank order the candidates on their lists is as important as their power to

choose small numbers of candidates from among large numbers of aspirants. In such systems the party's rank-and-file members have little or no role.

At the other extreme stand the selection procedures in U.S. parties. Under the direct primary system all registered voters are by law entitled to choose among the aspirants for their parties' nominations by casting votes in government-supervised, secret-ballot primary elections. As a general rule, to be sure, the turnout in primary elections is usually half or less of the turnout in the ensuing general elections. Even so, whereas fewer than a hundred leaders choose an Israeli party's candidates for the Knesset, many thousands, sometimes millions, of voters choose the Democratic and Republican parties' candidates for national and state offices. Moreover, the voters enjoy this power without assuming any obligation to the party. They do not have to pay party dues; they do not have to subscribe to the party's principles; they do not even have to support the party's candidates in the general election. They need only choose to vote in the primary election.

Most parties' selection processes lie somewhere between the Israeli and American extremes. In Great Britain and New Zealand, for example, parliamentary candidates are selected by small committees of dues-paying party members in the districts. In Belgium, Denmark, Germany, and Sweden candidates are selected by direct votes open to all local party members. In Italy and Switzerland they are selected by regional and district party committees. In general, national party agencies are stronger in countries with multimember district systems of proportional representation, and local and regional party agencies are stronger in countries with single-member district plurality systems.

Characteristics of Candidates

Studies have been made in several countries of the socioeconomic characteristics of the candidates who are eventually selected. Some studies have compared the candidates with rank-and-file party members or the general electorate. A few have compared persons selected with those who sought selection but were passed over.

In general, these studies have found that the candidates and persons who were passed over are very similar to each other and to persons who hold public office and lead party organizations. All four groups are quite different from ordinary party members and the general electorate. These politically active people have more formal education, higher incomes, and higher status occupations than do people who do not seek selection as candidates. In these groups there are also much higher proportions of men and of people aged thirty to fifty. In short, candidates, like all political elites, resemble one another much more closely than they resemble the general population.

See also *Ballots; Election campaigns; Electoral systems; Parties, Political; Proportional representation; Voting behavior.*

Austin Ranney

BIBLIOGRAPHY

Eulau, Heinz, and Moshe M. Czudnowski, eds. *Elite Recruitment in Democratic Polities.* New York: Wiley, 1976.

Gallagher, Michael, and Michael Marsh, eds. *Candidate Selection in Comparative Perspective.* London and Thousand Oaks, Calif.: Sage Publications, 1988.

Goodman, Jay S., Wayne R. Swanson, and Elmer E. Cornwell. "Political Recruitment in Four Selection Systems." *Western Political Quarterly* 23 (spring 1970): 92–103.

Harmel, Robert. "Environment and Party Decentralization: A Cross-National Study." *Comparative Political Studies* 14 (spring 1981): 75–99.

Keynes, Edward, Richard J. Tobin, and Robert Danziger. "Institutional Effects on Elite Recruitment: The Case of State Nominating Systems." *American Politics Quarterly* 7 (fall 1979): 283–302.

Putnam, Robert D. *The Comparative Study of Political Elites.* Englewood Cliffs, N.J.: Prentice Hall, 1976.

Ranney, Austin. "Candidate Selection." In *Democracy at the Polls: A Comparative Study of Competitive National Elections,* edited by David Butler, Howard R. Penniman, and Austin Ranney. Washington, D.C.: American Enterprise Institute, 1981.

Seligman, Lester G. *Recruiting Political Elites.* New York: General Learning Press, 1971.

Cape Verde

See *Africa, Lusophone*

Capitalism

A social system in which economic production is dominated by the owners of money, or capital, rather than by workers, landowners, political rulers, or religious leaders. Capitalism has been seen as bringing about a fundamental democratization of society and politics. Yet the specific political outcomes under capitalism have been varied and ambiguous. The precise relationship between capitalism and political democracy has long been debated.

Under capitalism, not only goods and services but also the major factors of production—capital, land, and labor—are exchanged on the market. Labor is contracted in exchange for wages in formally free agreements rather than being supplied through slavery, serfdom, or the obligations of citizenship. In capitalist systems, profit is the main criterion in economic decision making. Profit is realized in market exchanges by decentralized and more or less competitive private enterprises.

Capitalist production and exchange have proved to be a source of tremendous technical innovation and economic growth unequaled in history. At the same time, capitalism has disrupted cultural and traditional social orders and given rise to sustained conflicts between social classes. It was fostered by—and in turn fostered—the rise of the modern state. The transformations of society, culture, and politics due to capitalism have been the central theme of the classics of social science.

The State and Capitalism

The relationship between capitalism and the state is important for any analysis of capitalism. It is critical for an understanding of the interrelationships between capitalism and democracy.

A fairly high degree of separation—or, in technical terms, "structural differentiation"—between economic decision making and political rule is an essential characteristic of capitalism. It distinguishes capitalism both from earlier socioeconomic systems, such as feudalism, and from twentieth-century state socialism. Nonetheless, the rise of the modern state was closely related to the rise of capitalism.

Although state action and market functioning are often viewed as mutually exclusive opposites, a powerful state was a necessary condition for the rise of capitalism. Forceful state action was required to overcome obstacles to capitalist production and market exchange that were grounded in privilege and custom. State action also discouraged and if necessary repressed opposition from the victims of capitalist development. It gave legal shape and protection to new forms of property, contract, and enterprise organization—forms that were suitable to profit-oriented production and market exchange. This last point has been well understood since the eighteenth century, when it was formulated by the Scottish political economist Adam Smith. The new forms of economic relationships needed special protection because they often went against privileged interests, established social customs and mores, and popularly held ideas of fairness.

In turn, expanded market exchange and entrepreneurial profits made available the economic resources necessary for the rise of the modern state. Growing state revenues and large credits from merchant capitalists funded territorial conflict, expansion, and consolidation of control. They were also critical in converting the personalized, "patrimonial" state institutions of old into more impersonal and efficient "bureaucratic" structures. Only the more efficient states were capable of creating and protecting the legal infrastructure necessary for the spread of capitalist economic relations. Turning states away from military conflict and conquest and toward a peaceful role of service to the expanding capitalist economy was an important element of the self-understanding of early capitalism. This principle is illustrated in the theorem of a universal transition from military to "industrial" society, as advanced by the nineteenth-century English philosopher Herbert Spencer.

Different Forms of Capitalism

The model of competitive capitalism that has informed much of economic, social, and historical analysis does not exactly match the historical reality. Fully competitive capitalism never existed, and as the political economist Karl Polanyi persuasively argued in his book *The Great Transformation* (1944), the closest approximations to full competition lasted only a relatively short time. Karl Marx's attempt to identify inherent laws of development in capitalism turned out to be wrong in many respects. Marx was right, however, in his assumption that capitalism has a self-transforming dynamic, although this dynamic is less predictable and more dependent on different historical circumstances than he thought.

Advanced capitalist societies have typically undergone a number of changes. These include the concentration of productive property, the emergence of one or a few firms dominating an industry, collective organization of parts of the labor force, and increasing state action in the economy and society. In all capitalist countries there has been a long-term increase in politically imposed limitations on property rights, public regulation of production and market exchange, and state-provided supports for capitalist production and for the needs of the disadvantaged.

Although these trends represent broadly shared features of change in capitalism, they have varied from country to country in their speed, in their particular form, and in the ways they combined with each other. As a result capitalist societies differ substantially from each other. Relations of colonial domination and economic dependence between countries make for additional important differences. Yet even among advanced capitalist countries there are major contrasts, especially in state-sponsored social provisions. This is evident if one compares the limited welfare-state institutions in the United States with those in Europe and especially in Scandinavia. Japan presents yet another pattern.

Capitalism and Democracy: Diverse Accounts

Common wisdom, as well as much scholarly and political argument, assumes that democracy and capitalism are closely linked. In fact, they are often considered as the political and economic aspects of the same underlying socioeconomic system. Modern forms of democracy are indeed associated historically with the rise of capitalism. Furthermore, cross-national statistical research has established a significant, though by no means perfect, correlation between democracy and the level of capitalist development.

But historical association and statistical correlation alone do not yield an adequate understanding of the links between capitalism and democracy. There are many exceptions to the rule, and these cast doubt on any simple conception of democracy as the political expression of capitalism. For example, there are the successes of capitalist development engineered by authoritarian regimes in East Asia; the rise of fascism and National Socialism in Europe in the 1920s and 1930s; and the Latin American authoritarian regimes of the 1960s and 1970s. Postcolonial India had democratic government while its economy was poor and for a long time was a rather imperfect example of competitive capitalism.

Analysis of the relation between capitalism and democracy requires clarification of the concept of democracy. As used here, *democracy* entails (1) regular fair and free elections with a suffrage that is not limited by class, religion, ethnicity, or region; (2) the accountability of the state executives to the elected representatives; and (3) freedom of expression and association. This is a modest definition, which fits what political scientist Robert Dahl called "polyarchy," to distinguish it from the more demanding ideal of a society in which collective decisions are equally responsive to the preferences of all citizens.

While freedom of expression and association is widely recognized as a necessary condition for the democratic process, universal suffrage and the responsibility of the state to elected representatives are on occasion neglected. For example, some scholars view mid-nineteenth-century England as a democracy, even though only about 10 percent of all men were entitled to vote. Similarly, the limited responsibility of the government to the parliament in imperial Germany from 1871 to 1918 is sometimes considered secondary to the existence of universal male suffrage and a developed party system. In the second half of the twentieth century, it appears that restrictions of democracy are more often achieved by limiting the state's accountability to elected representatives than by denying the vote to large parts of the citizenry. For example, during the 1980s the elected president of El Salvador was unable to control the army and stop its involvement in terrorizing and killing civilians.

There are several explanations for the historical association of capitalism and democracy, as well as for the statistical correlation between level of capitalist development and democracy. One view holds that there is a structural correspondence between capitalism and democracy, with strong equilibrium tendencies favoring democracy. In this view, only democracy is sufficiently flexible and complex to deal with the political issues generated by an increasingly complex capitalist economy and society. This concept relies on problematic assumptions of a close systemic integration of economy, society, and politics. And it does not explain why democracy has failed in some relatively advanced capitalist countries.

A related position sees market choice and electoral choice as parallel and mutually reinforcing mechanisms. In this view, unfettered economic freedom provides the necessary underpinning of political freedom. But this assumption makes it hard to explain how capitalist economic rationality can justify the destruction of democracy, as it did in Argentina, Brazil, and Chile in the 1960s and 1970s. This view underestimates the potential level of conflict between the economically powerful interests of the few and the politically powerful interests of the many.

Other explanations of the association of capitalism and democracy focus on social classes—on their interests, their size and place in society, and their power resources.

Both classic liberal and Marxist-Leninist theories hold that the bourgeoisie—the class of major capital owners and thus the dominant class of capitalism—is the prime promoter and supporter of democracy. Comparative historical analysis reveals a much more complex pattern. It is true that the bourgeoisie does not rival large landowners in opposition to democracy. The bourgeoisie insisted on its own inclusion in the political decision-making process, and in doing so it typically supported public debate on policy and parliamentary government. But it did not uniformly support the inclusion of the working and middle classes, especially if strong working-class organizations threatened its interests. In Latin America the bourgeoisie participated in the termination of democratic rule because it perceived such a threat.

Perhaps the oldest argument about the relationship between the structure of society and constitutional form is one that goes back to Aristotle: that democracy rests on, and is advanced by, a large and vibrant middle class. This view holds that middle-class groups tend to support a culture of moderation and tolerance. Expanding with economic prosperity, they do not present a threat to the established order, nor do they have strong vested interests against broad participation in political decisions. This is certainly a strong argument, but it tends to overlook the influence exerted on the middle classes by more powerful classes and institutions. As a consequence, the middle classes' position on democracy is particularly ambiguous in a broadly comparative picture.

A similar consideration holds for peasants and farmers. Though frequently weak in their ability to organize, they are likely to support democratic participation. But they are often closely associated with, and thus strongly influenced by, large landowners. Large landowners are the most consistent opponents of democracy if they employ a large labor force and use political means for its control. Where influence from large landowners did not shape their political orientations, farmers played a major prodemocratic role, as in Switzerland, Norway, and the North of the United States.

Marx expected that an ever growing working class would organize itself politically and would ultimately win control of capitalist society. Universal suffrage was, in his view, one of the steps toward the classless society. Arguing about a democratic future not yet known, Marx anticipated with hope a dictatorship of the proletariat, while his contemporary the French political writer Alexis de Tocqueville feared a tyranny of the majority. Marx was right in claiming that the new urban working class had far better chances of collective self-organization than peasants had had in earlier times. And the working class has almost always been a pro-democratic force. The major flaw in Marx's prediction was that the working class was less unified and far weaker than he anticipated.

Capitalism and Democracy: The Relationship Reexamined

How, then, can we explain the historical association and the cross-national correlation between capitalism and democracy and, at the same time, account for the substantial inconsistencies and contradictions that characterize the relationship? It is no accident that so many of the theories just sketched focus on the position of social classes with regard to democratization. Promising to reduce inequality in politics, democracy is a matter of power and power sharing. A tension thus exists between democracy and a system of social and economic inequality. This insight points to two major conditions determining the chances of democracy: changes in the overall structure of social inequality and shifts in the balance of class power.

If all dimensions of inequality—income and wealth, honor and status, power and influence—are tightly linked, democracy is impossible. Democracy is possible only where political power and authority have become to some extent separate from the overall system of socioeconomic inequality. Feudalism had no place for democracy. An important prerequisite for democratic rule was established with the rise of capitalism, when political authority and economic property rights became institutionally separated. This separation, however, did not come about because of some inherent logic of capitalism but because of the power interests of new state elites and the rising bourgeoisie.

Neoliberal theories insisting on a one-to-one correspondence between economic and political freedom take this insight to the extreme. Such theories, however, are problematic even if the historical insight has contemporary relevance. The fact that the fusion of political authority and economic control in state socialism in Eastern Europe was incompatible with democracy does not mean that unfettered economic freedom and the resulting inequalities are favorable to democracy.

The tension between democracy and a system of social inequality points to another major condition for democracy: the interplay of class interests and thus the balance of class power. A shift in the balance of class power as a

consequence of capitalist development best explains the association of capitalism and democracy. Capitalism weakened the power of large landlords and increased the size and the power of subordinate classes, which previously had been excluded from political participation. These were the small and medium-sized farming class, the urban middle classes, and the new urban working class. The working class stands out among the subordinate classes of history because it shares with the urban middle classes a formidable capacity for collective organization due to urbanization, concentration in factories, and dramatic improvements in communication and transportation. At the same time, the working class has proved to be—with few exceptions—the most consistently pro-democratic social class.

The class interests actually pursued in particular historical situations cannot be simply read off from the material situation and the life chances of class members. They are formulated by leaders and associations that successfully organize and speak for large numbers of class members. The interests and political orientations of a class are thus historically constructed in the very process of organization that makes the pursuit of collective interests possible.

For this reason the positions of different classes with regard to the issues of democracy are historically variable, even though there are more or less strong typical tendencies. Particularly important factors in shaping such variations are the influence of dominant classes and institutions, the degree to which self-organization protects class members from such influence, and the perceptions of threat to one group's interests from the political and economic power of other classes. As noted earlier, the influence of dominant groups is particularly important for the outlook of peasants and the urban middle class; it has far less weight in the urban working class.

The working class varied in size and strength from country to country. Nowhere was it strong enough to achieve democracy by itself. It needed allies. The availability of allies depended on how urban middle-class groups and farmers were organized and how they perceived their own interests in the broader social and political situation. Where the working class was very weak, as in much of Latin America, the push for democracy often came from the middle class, with the working class as a junior partner, provided that the relationships of middle-class groups to the working class and bourgeoisie made this likely. As noted earlier, in a few countries the major breakthrough of democratization was achieved by independent farmers and middle-class groups before the industrial working class became a decisive social force.

The success of democratization also depended significantly on the coalitions formed by the dominant classes and their perceptions of threats to their interests. For instance, if the bourgeoisie allied itself with landed interests because of its perception of a strong socialist challenge from the working class, the chances of democratization and of stable democracy were significantly weakened. Thus, in an important sense, the interrelations among classes, rather than the typical class interests, shaped constitutional outcomes.

Looking beyond the complexities of class interaction, the shift in balance of class power as a consequence of capitalist development is still the best explanation for the link between capitalism and democracy. The conflicts and contradictions of capitalism account for its connection with democracy—not an inherent structural correspondence between capitalism and democracy, the rise of the bourgeoisie, or the growth of a vibrant and tolerant middle class.

The correlation between level of capitalist development and democracy is far from perfect. One explanation for this is found in the variations in class organization and class interaction. But the deviations from the overall trend point to other factors as well. On the premise that democracy is a matter of power, three other configurations of power seem of special importance: the structure of the state and of state-society relations, the impact of international power relations, and the patterns of ethnic fragmentation and conflict. All three are historically related to capitalist development, but the relationship is complex. These factors have an effect on the chances of democracy that is independent of the level of capitalist development in a country.

The impact of state structure on democracy can be clearly seen. A state's control over a territory has to be consolidated before democratic rule is possible. Beyond that, democracy requires a complex pattern of state autonomy: a state that lacks autonomy with regard to the landed or capitalist dominant classes is incompatible with democracy. Yet a state must not be so strong and autonomous as to overpower all of society. Centralized and direct state control of the economy, as well as a strong and autonomous military, are unfavorable conditions for democracy. More subtle but still significant effects come from historical relations between state offices and land-lords and from the role state churches play in the overall pattern of cultural influence and conflict.

The effect of international power relations is equally significant and must be analyzed in relation to the internal balance of class power. War affects this balance because it typically requires mass support, and in the case of defeat it discredits the dominant groups. Economic dependence on other countries and their dominant classes has been said to weaken the chances of democracy. The evidence suggests, however, that economic dependence is important only in conjunction with geopolitical relationships of dominance and dependence. In addition, the ways in which the interests of politically and economically dominant countries relate to democracy in dependent countries have varied historically.

Ethnic and cultural division and conflict can be major obstacles to democracy. Ethnic conflict may unsettle the established authority of the state as well as the minimal solidarity of the political society that is required to make majority decisions acceptable. Intense ethnic and national identification may also increase the influence of dominant groups that do not fully support democracy. Cross-national research has shown ethnic fragmentation to have a negative relationship to democracy. Quite a few culturally divided societies, however, have stable democratic politics, including Belgium, Spain, and Switzerland.

Is political culture a major factor shaping the chances of democracy? Arguments about political culture as a condition of constitutional development are often circular: the liberal culture of a country explains the survival of liberal politics. A better approach is to focus on how values and beliefs are grounded in different groups and institutions—and on how they persist or change because of this. Such an analysis largely reinforces what has been said here about the historical construction of the goals and beliefs in class-based organizations, the influence of dominant interests and defenses against it, and about the relationship of religion to the structure of the state. In this concept, political culture becomes the ensemble of beliefs and values, symbols and myths associated with diverse organizations and institutions that often are in conflict with each other.

Does Democracy Transform Capitalism?

If political democracy grew out of the conflicts and empowerment opportunities created by capitalism, did it in turn modify the structure of capitalism? Clearly, the fundamental democratization of social life, and in particular the new organizational opportunities of subordinate classes, that came about through capitalism helped to transform capitalism over time. This observation is true even where welfare-state measures and regulations of production and market exchange protecting workers and consumers were initiated by state managers and conservative political elites and perhaps opposed by working-class parties. This was the case in imperial Germany in the 1880s, where a conservative government used social policies as a political weapon against the socialist party. Yet these policies can be understood only against the background of the growing political power of subordinate classes.

Whether political democracy as such is associated with more extensive social policy programs and with the reduction of economic inequality is a more complicated question. Cross-national research has not found a clear correlation, although some results suggest that democratic rule may in the long run be associated with reductions of income differentials. The ambiguity of these research results is not astonishing. The distribution of income and wealth, as well as the state's social policies, is subject to struggles whose outcomes depend on constellations of economic and political power that vary considerably across democracies. In many countries, however, powerful unions and political parties based in the working class have achieved policies building strong welfare states and limiting the privileges of dominant classes. Democracy offers favorable conditions for the subordinate classes to use their strength to win policies that transform the system of inequality.

If history is any guide, political democracy is unlikely to transform capitalism toward similar patterns in all countries. Furthermore, the increasing globalization of capitalist production and exchange constrains political action in individual countries. Democracy will continue to make a difference, however. It is likely to create openings for egalitarian transformations of work and authority in production. It may also foster the political realization of public goods—for instance, in health, education, and the environment—where the play of private interests guided by profit yields unacceptable results.

See also *Class relations, Agrarian; Class relations, Industrial; Dahl, Robert A.; Development, Economic; Enlightenment, Scottish; Industrial democracy; Leninism; Markets, Regulation of; Marxism; Regulation; State growth and intervention; Tocqueville, Alexis de; Welfare, Promotion of.*

Dietrich Rueschemeyer

BIBLIOGRAPHY

Bollen, Kenneth A. "Political Democracy and the Timing of Development." *American Sociological Review* 44 (1979): 572–587.

Hayek, Friedrich A. von. *The Road to Serfdom.* Chicago: University of Chicago Press, 1944; London: Routledge, 1991.

Lipset, Seymour Martin. "Some Social Requisites of Democracy." *American Political Science Review* 53 (1959): 69–105. Reprinted in *Political Man.* Expanded and updated ed. Baltimore: Johns Hopkins University Press, 1981; Aldershot: Gower, 1983.

Marx, Karl. *Capital.* 3 vols. Moscow: Foreign Languages Publishers, 1959.

Moore, Barrington, Jr. *The Social Origins of Dictatorship and Democracy.* Boston: Beacon Press, 1966.

Muller, Edward N. "Democracy, Economic Development and Income Inequality." *American Sociological Review* 53 (1988): 50–68.

Rueschemeyer, Dietrich, Evelyne Huber Stephens, and John D. Stephens. *Capitalist Development and Democracy.* Cambridge: Polity Press; Chicago: University of Chicago Press, 1993.

Schumpeter, Joseph. *Capitalism, Socialism and Democracy.* New York: Harper and Brothers, 1942.

Therborn, Göran. "The Rule of Capital and the Rise of Democracy." *New Left Review* 103 (1977): 3–41.

Weber, Max. *Economy and Society.* 2 vols. Berkeley: University of California Press, 1978.

Caribbean, English

The independent countries and dependencies in the Caribbean that experienced British colonial rule; also called the Commonwealth Caribbean because the independent countries have remained members of the British Commonwealth of Nations. The independent countries (with the year of independence given in parentheses) are Antigua and Barbuda (1981), Bahamas (1973), Barbados (1966), Belize (1981), Dominica (1978), Grenada (1974), Guyana (1966), Jamaica (1962), St. Kitts and Nevis (1983), St. Lucia (1977), St. Vincent and the Grenadines (1979), and Trinidad and Tobago (1962). The dependencies include Anguilla, Bermuda, British Virgin Islands, Cayman Islands, Montserrat, and Turks and Caicos Islands.

Colonial Rule

Compared with their neighbors in the Spanish-speaking Caribbean and Central America, the countries of the English Caribbean have an impressive record of democratic rule. With the exceptions of Guyana and Grenada, all the independent countries have had democratic rule throughout their existence. They have achieved this in spite of a low level of economic development and a high degree of socioeconomic inequality. The surface of formal democratic institutions, though, has at times hidden some nondemocratic practices. Furthermore, political violence, corruption, and attempted coups have posed serious challenges to democratic stability.

The racial composition of most of these countries is primarily black and brown (that is, of mixed African and European descent), with East Indian and Chinese communities of varying size. Trinidad and Tobago and Guyana are exceptions: there the East Indian communities are, respectively, almost as large as or larger than the black and brown communities.

The original inhabitants of what came to be the English Carribean were Arawak and Carib Indians. The Arawaks were agriculturalists and not militaristic; thus they were vulnerable to their more warlike neighbors, the Caribs. This indigenous population was virtually wiped out by infectious diseases introduced through Spanish colonization. The first Spanish settlements were established on the island of Hispaniola shortly after the arrival of Columbus in 1492. Throughout the following century, Spanish colonization expanded to the other Caribbean islands. In the early seventeenth century the British, Dutch, and French challenged Spanish control over the area, first by establishing settlements in remote areas and finally by seizing control from the Spanish by military means.

All the English territories had experience with constitutional oligarchic rule. The earliest representative assemblies were established in Barbados, St. Kitts, Nevis, and Antigua, in the 1630s and 1640s. The right to vote was severely restricted, and these legislative assemblies were dominated by wealthy planters. Each assembly pushed local elite interests and defended them before the executive branch, headed by the British-appointed governor. The relationship between the two branches was characterized by frequent conflict.

By the mid-nineteenth century, social changes in the wake of the emancipation of slaves pointed toward the inclusion of nonelite groups under the old constitutional system. To forestall this threat, the local elites favored constitutional revisions to introduce Crown Colony government, under which the governor enjoyed virtually autocratic power. By 1878 the transition to the Crown Colony system had been completed, except in the Bahamas, Bermuda, and Barbados. As a result, power shifted decisively toward the governors, though local assemblies continued to exist. The surviving assemblies mostly had a mixture of appointed and elected members. There were property, income, and literacy qualifications for the franchise.

Nationalism and Independence

Significant progress toward responsible government and an expansion of the franchise began only in the 1930s. In that decade labor rebellions swept the English Caribbean as well as neighboring Spanish-speaking countries. This unrest gave rise to labor unions and political parties, which came to form the core of the nationalist movements. The local elites everywhere reacted to the situation with calls for repression. In the Spanish-speaking territories the state repressed the emerging labor and political organizations. In the English Caribbean, however, colonial rule served as a buffer for repressive tendencies. British troops were deployed to put down mass demonstrations and riots, and many leaders were imprisoned. Still, unions and political parties were allowed to organize and later to consolidate their organizations and alliances.

This difference between the English and Spanish Caribbean had lasting implications for the future trajectory of democracy in these places. In the Spanish-speaking areas, civil society and political parties remained weak, while in the English Caribbean civil society and political parties grew comparatively strong and became the driving forces for democratization and independence. After independence, unions and political parties continued to represent alliances between the middle and working classes. They became carriers and defenders of democratic institutions.

In response to the unrest of the 1930s, Britain appointed a royal commission, headed by Lord Moyne, to study social and economic conditions in the Caribbean colonies. Although the scope of the Moyne commission did not include questions of constitutional change, the commission recommended such changes in response to pressure from local political leaders. The speed of progress toward responsible government and constitutional decolonization varied among the English Caribbean territories. Jamaica, where local organizations and pressure were strongest, led the way, followed by the other large territories. The first parliamentary elections with universal suffrage were held in Jamaica in 1944, in Trinidad and Tobago in 1946, and in Barbados in 1951. Internal self-government followed later: it was introduced in Jamaica in 1957 and in Trinidad and

Tobago and Barbados in 1961. By the 1950s the British government was committed to progress toward self-government and eventual independence in the Caribbean. Early negotiations, particularly with Jamaica, had often moved slowly and only under pressure from the nationalist movement. Later reforms came more easily and even extended to territories where domestic pressures were very weak.

The British design for progress toward independence called for the formation of a Federation of the West Indies. In 1947 the secretary of state for the colonies convened a conference of West Indian political leaders to consider the idea of a federation and to draw up proposals to be submitted to the various legislatures. The leaders, however, put the interests of progress toward self-government in their individual territories above movement toward federation. Still, work on the federal constitution proceeded steadily. In 1958 the Federation of the West Indies was inaugurated. Immediately tensions erupted, particularly between Jamaica and the smaller territories of the eastern Caribbean, over the desirable degree of economic integration. The issue became entangled with domestic political competition in Jamaica. A popular majority rejected the federation in a referendum in 1961. Jamaica withdrew, and the federation collapsed. The various territories then pursued independence separately.

By the time independence was achieved, the infrastructure of democracy was well consolidated. With the exception of Guyana and Grenada, where political parties developed late, the English Caribbean had long-established parties. The middle and working classes were organized and could not be ignored by the local elites. Moreover, the repressive arms of the new states were comparatively small and not in a position to develop autonomy from civilian authority.

Challenges to Democracy

In the 1960s and 1970s economic growth helped to consolidate democratic rule. Governments could allocate resources for education and social services for the poor and the middle classes, as well as for economic projects to benefit economic elites. This use of resources, however, also generated a challenge to democracy in the form of political violence. Lower-class followers who were tied to the parties through patronage identified their material self-interest with the election victory of their party. Party leadership could incite them to resort to violent tactics. Challenges to democracy, such as coup attempts and riots, emerged in this period. With the support of all major organized forces, however, governments were in a strong position to restore the democratic order.

Less direct but still serious challenges to democracy emerged in the 1980s. These included the debt crisis and the reorientation of economic policy toward austerity and liberalization, as well as the spread of the drug trade. Living standards deteriorated, and politics seemed to lose its relevance for economic policy, as all parties began to adopt similar economic measures. The result was increased social tensions and a loss of popular confidence in political parties, visible in opinion polls and in declining participation rates in elections. Widespread corruption of officials because of the drug trade further damaged the legitimacy of the democratic state in many of the countries. Nevertheless, the commitment of political leaders to democracy and collaborative efforts in the region to defend democratic regimes against authoritarian attempts so far have managed to sustain democratic rule.

Jamaica

The struggle for self-government and independence in Jamaica was led by Norman W. Manley and the People's National Party. Manley was one of the founders of the People's National Party in 1938. He headed it until 1969, when he was succeeded by his son Michael Manley. Alexander Bustamante, the labor leader, broke with the party in 1942 and founded his own party, the Jamaica Labour Party. Bustamante, unlike Manley, was cool toward self-government. The Jamaica Labour Party won the 1944 and 1949 elections, which slowed progress toward the goal of self-government. The People's National Party won in 1955, and Jamaica finally achieved self-government in 1957. Jamaica joined the short-lived Federation of the West Indies in 1958 but withdrew after the federation was rejected in a 1961 referendum. Bustamante turned the withdrawal into the cornerstone of his opposition to the People's National Party government.

Britain granted Jamaica full independence in 1962. The democratic order in Jamaica was challenged by two riots with racial overtones in the 1960s. Political violence esca-lated in 1980 as a result of polarization over the democratic-socialist course of the 1972–1980 People's National Party government.

Trinidad and Tobago

In Trinidad and Tobago the parties that emerged in the 1930s were weaker than their Jamaican counterparts and less effective in promoting self-government and independence. Elections with universal suffrage were held in 1946 and 1950. The nationalist movement gained strength in 1956, with the founding of the People's National Movement under the leadership of Eric Williams. The People's National Movement attracted wide support in the black community, from the black middle and working classes and the trade union leadership. It thus represented an alliance of the middle and working classes, similar to the alliances formed by the two parties in Jamaica. The People's National Movement pressured the British Colonial Office for self-government, which was granted in 1961. Independence came a year later. Trinidad and Tobago experienced a major challenge to democracy in 1970 in the form of mass demonstrations led by black radicals, calling for an overthrow of the government. The People's National Movement, however, was able to restore order, consolidate its power, and stay in office until 1986. A renewed challenge emerged in 1990 with a coup attempt by the Jamaat-Al-Muslimeen, a black fundamentalist Muslim group.

Barbados

In Barbados the main protagonists in the struggle for democratization in the 1930s were the Barbados Progressive League, which later became the Barbados Labour Party, and its leader Grantley Adams. They constructed a middle class–working class alliance by founding the Barbados Workers Union in 1941. In the early 1950s a split in the party led its left wing to form the Democratic Labour Party. Both parties continued to press for self-government. Barbados had not become a Crown Colony, but its institutions remained far from democratic by the 1940s. The Barbados Progressive League made strong efforts to pass universal suffrage in 1940, but this goal was not accomplished until 1951. Self-government was achieved in 1961. A plan to form a smaller successor to the Federation of the West Indies, made up of Barbados and seven smaller islands, failed, and Barbados became independent in 1966. Barbados did not experience any significant challenges to the democratic order after independence.

Guyana

Democracy in Guyana was troubled from its beginnings. A labor rebellion in the 1930s did not give rise to a nationalist movement. The economy was characterized by dependence on sugar production and by concentration of this production in a small number of huge estates. Accordingly, the peasantry and the middle classes were weaker in Guyana than in the other English Caribbean colonies. The Sugar Producers Association managed to maintain control over labor through a combination of authoritarian and paternalistic practices. Progress toward self-government was a result of changing British policy.

Founded in 1950, the working-class People's Progressive Party rapidly became the dominant political force. Originally, the party was multiethnic. Among its leaders were the East Indian Cheddi Jagan and the African Forbes Burnham. The party attracted support from both the East Indian and the African communities. In the first elections under universal suffrage in 1953, the People's Progressive Party—led by Jagan, a Marxist-Leninist—won a large majority of the seats. It immediately embarked on a radical reformist course, pressing its still restricted constitutional powers to the limit. This activity caused alarm among the domestic elite and also in Washington and London. After only 133 days of the Jagan government, the British suspended the constitution.

In 1955 Burnham broke with the People's Progressive Party and formed the People's National Congress, a party based exclusively in the African community. This step institutionalized ethnic divisions in the party system and had a long-term negative effect on democracy in Guyana. New elections were held in 1957 and again were won by the People's Progressive Party. This time Jagan was allowed to serve out his term and to go on to win the 1961 elections. Politics took on clear racial overtones on both sides. Between 1962 and 1964 Jagan confronted large-scale opposition, general strikes, and riots. Most important, he lost control over the state apparatus, specifically the police, because state agencies were mostly staffed by people of African descent. Covert intervention by the United States, motivated by the determination not to let Jagan lead Guyana into independence, contributed to the turmoil. Finally, the combination of foreign and domestic pressures forced Jagan to accept an electoral system with proportional representation.

In 1964 Burnham and the People's National Congress came to power, in coalition with a business party. The party soon broke with its coalition partner. This break, in addition to the numerical superiority of the East Indian population, made it most unlikely that the People's National Congress could win the 1968 elections. Accordingly, the People's National Congress resorted to massive election fraud, a practice that continued for the next two decades. The first truly democratic elections in independent Guyana were held in 1992. They were won again by the People's Progressive Party under the leadership of Jagan.

Grenada

The history of democracy in Grenada has also been troubled. As in Guyana, there was no nationalist movement to promote democratization. Furthermore, two years before the first elections with universal suffrage in 1951, the degree of labor organization was much lower in Grenada than in other Caribbean territories. This situation provided the opportunity for the rise to power of the charismatic leader Eric M. Gairy. Gairy rapidly organized agricultural workers and won the 1951 elections with nearly two-thirds of the vote. His party, the Grenada United Labour Party, won fairly three of the five elections between 1952 and 1967.

After the election victory in 1967, while Grenada was under self-government, Gairy began to intensify the corruption of the political process. He used a personal police force, the Mongoose Gang, to suppress dissent and to ensure his election victories in 1972 and 1976. By the late 1970s there was widespread disaffection from his regime but no strong and well-organized democratic opposition. A small group of revolutionaries staged a successful insurrection, bringing the New Jewel Movement to power in 1979. The New Jewel Movement did not hold any elections before becoming engulfed in a deadly internal struggle in 1983 and being overthrown by a U.S. invasion in October of that year.

After the invasion the United States and other Caribbean actors maneuvered to reconstruct political parties and to influence the first elections. These activities further tainted the democratic quality of the political system. The formal democratic political institutions of Grenada have survived since 1984, in spite of the continued weakness of political parties, coalitions, and governments. Democracy has been strengthened by the closer integration of Grenada with the other countries of the Eastern Caribbean.

See also *Bustamante, Alexander; Caribbean, Spanish; Central America; Commonwealth, British; Williams, Eric.*

Evelyne Huber

BIBLIOGRAPHY

Beckles, Hilary M. *A History of Barbados: From Amerindian Society to Nation-State.* Cambridge and New York: Cambridge University Press, 1990.

Domínguez, Jorge I. "The Caribbean Question: Why Has Democracy (Surprisingly) Flourished?" In *Democracy in the Caribbean: Political, Economic, and Social Perspectives,* edited by Jorge I. Domínguez, Robert A. Pastor, and R. Delisle Worrell. Baltimore and Northampton: Johns Hopkins University Press, 1993.

Hintzen, Percy C. *The Costs of Regime Survival: Racial Mobilization, Elite Domination and Control of the State in Guyana and Trinidad.* Cambridge and New York: Cambridge University Press, 1989.

Knight, Franklin W. *The Caribbean: The Genesis of a Fragmented Nationalism.* 2d rev. ed. Oxford and New York: Oxford University Press, 1990.

Lewis, Gordon K. *Grenada: The Jewel Despoiled.* Baltimore: Johns Hopkins University Press, 1987.

———. *The Growth of the Modern West Indies.* New York: Monthly Review Press, 1968.

Rueschemeyer, Dietrich, Evelyne Huber Stephens, and John D. Stephens. *Capitalist Development and Democracy.* Chicago: University of Chicago Press; Oxford: Polity Press, 1992.

Ryan, Selwyn. *Revolution and Reaction: Parties and Politics in Trinidad and Tobago, 1970–1981.* St. Augustine, Trinidad: Institute of Social and Economic Research, 1989.

Stephens, Evelyne Huber, and John D. Stephens. *Democratic Socialism in Jamaica: The Political Movement and Social Transformation in Dependent Capitalism.* Princeton: Princeton University Press; London: Macmillan, 1986.

Stone, Carl. *Democracy and Clientelism in Jamaica.* New Brunswick, N.J.: Transaction, 1980.

Caribbean, Spanish

A set of societies in the Caribbean Sea, including Cuba, the Dominican Republic, and Puerto Rico, that were extensively shaped by Spanish colonial policy. The Dominican Republic achieved independence in 1844, and Cuba became independent in 1902. Puerto Rico assumed a unique status as a partially autonomous commonwealth of the United States in 1952.

Strivings toward democracy have a long history in the Spanish Caribbean, and both politicians and citizens have made sacrifices in pursuit of popular sovereignty. However, the quest for democracy in the region has faced several obstacles. The institutions and methods of Spanish rule were almost always hostile to popular participation and responsible government; colonial society in the region provided few models for civic competition. In addition, many political leaders in the Spanish Caribbean have perceived a conflict between national autonomy and the goals of democracy. As a result, popular government has at times been sacrificed in the name of nationalism. The United States, which has exerted great influence in the region, sometimes has assisted but often has undercut efforts for democracy there.

The Colonial Experience

Christopher Columbus reached the island he named La Española (Hispaniola) on Christmas Eve, in 1492. Within ten years Spanish colonial administration had been established at Santo Domingo on the island's south coast. Spain's rule in the island set many of the patterns for its domination of a large part of the Western Hemisphere over the next 300 years. Power centered in autocratic governors and viceroys, who were sent from Spain and who seldom remained more than a few years in any single colony. Backed by royal military and naval power, and in close cooperation with the Roman Catholic Church, the governors sought to organize both society and the economy to benefit the economic and security interests of the Spanish crown.

Town councils (*cabildos*) were primarily administrative, not consultative mechanisms, although open town meetings (*cabildos abiertos*) occasionally sought the advice of wealthy and influential citizens. A system of courts (*audiencias*) was established to purvey royal justice. Spanish colonial subjects did not have access even to the weak parliamentary bodies (*cortes*) that had existed in medieval Spain.

By 1525 Spain's primary attention in colonial matters had been drawn to the larger and richer territories in Mexico and South America. Spanish colonies in the Caribbean were used primarily to provision and protect the fleets that sailed to Europe laden with silver, gold, and agricultural produce. Harbors including San Juan in Puerto Rico, Havana in Cuba, and Santo Domingo were heavily fortified against British and French privateers and against pirates. In other respects the internal development of both Puerto Rico and Santo Domingo was neglected. In 1697 France established a flourishing plantation colony called Saint-Domingue in western Hispaniola. This action marked the decline of Spanish power, as did the loss of Jamaica to the British in 1655 and Spain's inability to extend its rule over the Lesser Antilles. Spain made greater, though still modest, investments in developing Cuba as a

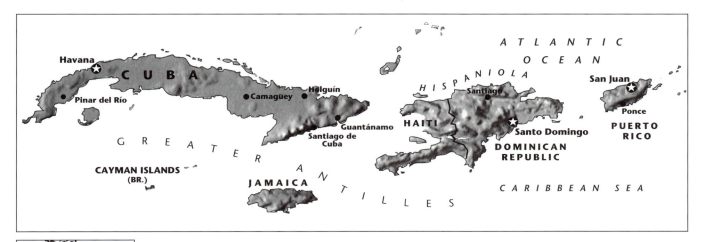

plantation colony, producing sugar for the European market.

Spain's military weakness at the start of the nineteenth century accelerated Santo Domingo's independence, but it delayed the end of Spanish rule in Cuba and Puerto Rico. In 1795 Spain ceded its section of Hispaniola to France. Almost immediately, France's hold on the whole island was challenged by a social revolution—centered in the western settlement, Saint-Domingue—which by 1804 created the independent nation of Haiti. Haiti dominated the Spanish portion of the island until 1844, when a rebellion led by Juan Pablo Duarte, Francisco del Rosario Sánchez, and Ramón Mella established the Dominican Republic as an independent country. The idealistic hopes of these three civilian leaders found little echo in the power struggles that dominated the new nation. National authority was weak in the poor and physically divided territory, and the central government was almost always in the hands of dictatorial presidents whose power rested on force.

Having lost Hispaniola and all its mainland possessions in the Western Hemisphere, Spain clung all the more tightly to Cuba and to Puerto Rico after 1825. These island colonies were less vulnerable to the multinational independence armies that had defeated Spain on the continent, and Spain made them profitable by rapidly modernizing their sugar production. Especially in Cuba, the new technology of steam power was applied successfully to the old task of producing refined sugar from raw cane. New networks of railways linked the cane fields directly with highly productive steam-driven mills that ground and re-fined the raw material. Cuba became the world's largest grower of cane sugar. The combination of this new prosperity with unyielding Spanish autocracy in the political realm bred rebellion. In 1868 young revolutionaries launched the *Grito de Yara* (Cry of Yara), a call for independence. In the Ten Years' War that followed, Cuban rebels pioneered anticolonial guerrilla tactics that came to be employed worldwide in the twentieth century.

Spanish repression prevailed after the war's end, but in 1895 a new uprising was launched by leaders including José Martí, a brilliant journalist and political organizer who had been exiled for fifteen years in the United States. Martí, whose political vision included a Cuban republic free of military rule or foreign dominance, was killed in battle in 1895. Three years later the United States intervened in Cuba's struggle for independence and expelled Spain. Although Washington disclaimed any desire to possess Cuba, it insisted on severely limiting the autonomy of the new Cuban government. The United States obliged Cuba to insert in its constitution a section that prohibited treaties without U.S. sanction, limited international borrowing by Cuba, and gave the United States the right to intervene militarily in Cuba whenever it wished. This imposition—to which Cuba objected strongly—came to be known as the Platt amendment, after the senator who introduced it in the U.S. Congress.

Spain lost Puerto Rico at the same time it relinquished Cuba, to a U.S. invasion that landed in 1898 at Guánica on the south coast and took the island with the loss of only three men. This conquest prolonged Puerto Rico's experience of full colonialism for more than fifty years. Spain's undemocratic rule was supplanted by that of the United States.

The Dominican Republic

Democracy could not become a viable option in the Dominican Republic until a stable national political community and government were established. Those necessary steps were completed, paradoxically, during the U.S. military occupation of the country that lasted from 1916 to 1924. Washington had intervened in the belief that European powers might take advantage of chronic Dominican political strife to advance their own interests. Direct rule by the U.S. marines was heartily resented by elites and masses alike, but the occupiers built the first all-weather roads to link Dominican cities and towns and created a durable national army for the first time. When the United States withdrew, the Dominican state could project increased power throughout the national territory.

These new political resources were almost immediately exploited and abused by Gen. Rafael Trujillo, commander of the new Dominican army. Trujillo seized the presidency in 1930 and ruled either directly or through puppet executives until 1961. Known by a string of grandiloquent titles including Benefactor of the Fatherland, Trujillo constructed a ruthless autocracy that approached totalitarian power. Those whose views showed any independence had to choose among servile submission, exile, or death. The Dominican economy did expand under this tyranny, however, and a new middle class was created. Trujillo also fostered a cult of Dominican nationalism, exalting the patriots of 1844 to nearly saintly status while scorning their democratic and civic hopes for the nation.

The "Benefactor" was assassinated in May 1961 by conspirators encouraged and partly armed by the United States. Washington feared that Trujillo's continued rule might spawn a revolutionary movement similar to that of Fidel Castro in Cuba. Although the plotters represented no coherent new political movement, the nation was fortunate that a group of exiles led by Juan Bosch Gaviño had long been planning for the aftermath of the Trujillo era. Bosch, an intellectual and accomplished writer, returned to Santo Domingo and in less than eighteen months organized the Dominican Republic's first modern mass political party, the Dominican Revolutionary Party. The new party, advocating a populist program that appealed especially to the poor both in the countryside and the growing cities, swamped its less change-oriented, upper-class rivals in elections held in December 1962.

The bastions of Dominican conservatism—landowners, the military, importers, and the Catholic Church—allied to overthrow Bosch after he had been in power barely seven months. These traditional interest groups could not compete with the Dominican Revolutionary Party electorally in the greatly broadened arena of postdictatorial politics. An urban popular rebellion in April 1965 sought to restore Bosch's government, and the United States once again sent troops to prevent "a second Cuba."

This sterile confrontation of military force with popular backing would probably have continued except for the political shrewdness of Joaquín Balaguer Ricardo, who had served as Trujillo's last puppet president in 1960–1961. Balaguer, exiled in New York, realized that a mass conservative party might compete in the civic arena against the Dominican Revolutionary Party. In 1964 he organized what is now the Social Christian Reformist Party. Balaguer won the presidency in relatively free elections in 1966, and military influence was steadily reduced during the unbroken series of elections held every four years through 1994.

Although the Dominican Republic maintains a relatively stable competition among modern mass political parties, and civil liberties have been observed for the most part since U.S. troops were withdrawn in 1966, democracy has not received adequate constitutional support. Democracy depends in part on effectively restraining government power, and there are few such checks in the constitution written under Balaguer's supervision. The Dominican presidency concentrates power unduly, facing no term limits and exerting great suasion over the judiciary and the Central Election Board. The Dominican Revolutionary Party did manage to win the presidency in 1978 and 1982, before Balaguer prevailed in the two subsequent elections. In 1994 the aged leader's effort to win a sixth full term as chief executive through election fraud was deflected by the growing international democratic consensus. The reports of outside election observers on voting irregularities induced Dominican leaders to negotiate a pact by which new elections are to be held in 1996.

Cuba

Between 1902 and 1959 democracy in independent Cuba was intermittent and partial. Some Cuban presidents, including Tomás Estrada Palma (1902–1906) and Ramón Grau San Martín (1933), were known for honesty and civic spirit; the constitution of 1940 provided for both civil liberties and social guarantees; and elections determined the formal holders of power in Cuba from 1934 until 1952. But these achievements were, for many Cubans, overshadowed by persistent corruption, militarism, and outside political influence. The Platt amendment probably encouraged Cuban political contenders who were anxious for U.S. intervention to create instability. Washington formally renounced its "right" to intervene in 1934, but its continuing capacity to use overwhelming force gave great weight to its preferences in Havana.

In 1952 Gen. Fulgencio Batista took over Cuba's government and canceled the planned elections, a step that the United States did not oppose and that radicalized Cuban politics. A young lawyer, Fidel Castro Ruz, emerged by 1957 as the primary focus of armed opposition to Batista's dictatorship. Leading a small guerrilla band in the Sierra Maestra range in eastern Cuba, Castro brilliantly exploited mass communications within Cuba and abroad to undercut the prestige and self-confidence of the corrupt regime. On December 31, 1958, Batista fled to the Dominican Republic. The Cuban revolution began January 1, 1959.

Although Castro's vague political program had promised restoration of the 1940 constitution, the new Cuban government focused its energies on land reform, massive expansion and improvement in education, and expropriation of most private enterprise, including foreign-owned firms. Deeply suspicious of the rulers in Havana, the U.S. government began plans to overthrow them as early as March 1959. Fidel Castro, his brother Raúl, Ernesto "Ché" Guevara, and other leaders in Cuba came to believe, in turn, that democracy was unnecessary and possibly dangerous at a time when they perceived Cuban nationhood to be at stake.

In 1961 the United States made an ineffective attempt to topple Castro by sponsoring an invasion by Cuban exiles at the Bay of Pigs. That same year Cuba formed a strong economic, diplomatic, and military alliance with the Soviet Union, which effectively deterred large-scale U.S. military interference. A reorganized Cuban Communist Party, led by Castro as a dominant charismatic figure and by scores of former guerrilla leaders, came to command all aspects of Cuban politics. A new constitution adopted in 1976 formalized Castro's autocratic power as head of both party and government. Popular participation was permitted only through mobilization in mass organizations, and limited choice among communist candidates was permitted only at the most local levels.

Intolerant of internal dissent, the government presided over the emigration of more than 900,000 Cubans from 1960 through 1980. Most settled in southern Florida in the United States, only a few hundred miles from Havana. Cuba's revolutionary policies advanced the cause of social equality and made great strides in education and health care. Cuban economic growth, however, was episodic and not robust. By the late 1980s the nation's political and economic reliance on Soviet backing revealed grave vulnerabilities. As communist power collapsed in Eastern Europe and Russia, Cuba was left with an autocratic regime in a hemisphere in which most states were democratizing and with a rickety economy in an era when growth required flexibility and openness.

Cuba's path to democracy in the future is far from clear. The Castro government hopes to attract foreign investment to reverse the nation's drastic drop in incomes since 1990, but it does not want to open the domestic political arena. Few exponents of democracy have been able to surface in Cuba. Those backers of democracy and human rights who have struggled bravely, such as María Elena Cruz Varela and Elizardo Sánchez, are not well known in Cuba because of government control of the media. Although fervently anti-Castro, many Cuban Americans do not fully grasp the social changes that have transformed Cuba's society since 1959. Committed and farseeing leadership will be needed for Cubans to enter once again on Martí's path to both nationhood and popular government.

Puerto Rico

The United States determined to rule Puerto Rico as a colony after 1898 because of the island's military value in the Caribbean and because of the U.S. view that the island was a poor candidate for self-government. The precise legal definition of this status proved awkward. The Foraker Act of 1900 characterized Puerto Rico as an "unincorporated territory" in which the U.S. Constitution did not apply but that was subject to the will of the U.S. Congress.

Fatefully, Puerto Rico was joined with the U.S. economy: all U.S. tariffs on Puerto Rican products were abolished and island residents were not required to pay taxes to the U.S. government. In 1917, in response to Puerto Rican protests, and perhaps to help justify the military draft of Puerto Rican men in the island for World War I, Congress and the president passed the Jones Act. The act granted Puerto Ricans U.S. citizenship and the right to elect an island Senate in addition to the elective House of Delegates created in 1900. However, the powerful governor, appointed by the president of the United States, could veto all insular legislation.

Deprived of meaningful self-government and largely forgotten by the U.S. administration, Puerto Rico languished in poverty and social backwardness, especially after the onset of the Great Depression in the 1930s. Political leaders in Puerto Rico were deeply divided. Traditional politicians vied for legislative seats and formed parties that promised to work for another political status: independence, statehood, or some form of autonomy. Nationalist sentiment had never been as strong in Puerto Rico as in Cuba, and from the mid-1920s until the 1950s the principal advocate of independence was Pedro Albizu Campos, a brilliant iconoclast who had been educated at Harvard. However, Albizu Campos's Nationalist Party and most statehood advocates did not focus squarely on the desperate poverty of most Puerto Ricans.

By the late 1930s Luís Muñoz Marín, a poet and politician, devised the formula for political organization that has done most to shape contemporary Puerto Rico. Muñoz combined an autonomist position in relation to Washington with a vigorous populist developmental and democratic program within Puerto Rico. He and a group of technocrats and experienced political organizers argued that the issue of ultimate political status should be postponed while the island utilized New Deal programs for relief and development. A new political party, the Popular Democratic Party, embodied this formula, and Muñoz and his followers won control of the legislature in 1940 and 1944. In 1947 an elective governorship was instituted for the first time. Muñoz was elected to this post the following year.

The level of popular backing for the Popular Democrats, in an era of worldwide decolonization, strengthened Muñoz's hand in negotiating with the U.S. government over Puerto Rico's status. In 1952 a new compact between Puerto Rico and the United States was negotiated and approved both by referendum on the island and by congressional vote. Puerto Rico became a "free associated state," controlling most internal policies through a competitive democratic system. Washington continues to direct all foreign and military policies and most aspects of trade and investment. Appeals from Puerto Rican courts are heard in U.S. circuit jurisdictions. Puerto Ricans have only a nonvoting representative in Congress, and only those resident on the U.S. mainland participate in presidential elections.

The 1952 commonwealth formula met with stunning success in the economic realm. The island government welcomed U.S. investors seeking low wages and tariff-free access to the U.S. market. Light industry spurred by this Operation Bootstrap policy, together with remittances from more than one million Puerto Rican migrants to the continental United States, made Puerto Rico far more affluent by the 1990s than the Dominican Republic or Cuba. Average yearly income per person in 1992 was $6,360, 40 percent of the average income in the fifty states of the United States.

The island's political status remains an unsettled and at times unsettling issue. As revealed in island-wide plebiscites in 1967 and 1993, most Puerto Ricans favor either commonwealth status or statehood. The commonwealth option prevailed over statehood by a slim 2 percent margin in 1993, with 48 percent of Puerto Ricans voting for commonwealth status and 46 percent favoring statehood. Only 4 percent favored independence in that referendum. These results, however, show that 50 percent of Puerto Ricans believed that "internal" democracy is incomplete without linking individual citizens to all the powers of a nation-state, either an independent Puerto Rico or a U.S. union including Puerto Rico as a fifty-first state. Muñoz's formula of limited democracy, full development, and very muted nationalism is still under vigorous debate in Puerto Rico.

See also *Caribbean, English; Dominican Republic.*

Christopher Mitchell

BIBLIOGRAPHY

Bosch, Juan. *The Unfinished Experiment: Democracy in the Dominican Republic.* London: Pall Mall Press, 1966.

Carr, Raymond. *Puerto Rico: A Colonial Experiment.* New York: New York University Press, 1984.

Domínguez, Jorge I., Robert A. Pastor, and R. Delisle Worrell, eds. *Democracy in the Caribbean: Political, Economic, and Social Perspectives.* Baltimore and Northampton: Johns Hopkins University Press, 1993.

Knight, Franklin W. *The Caribbean: The Genesis of a Fragmented Nationalism.* 2d rev. ed. Oxford and New York: Oxford University Press, 1990.

Lewis, Gordon K. *Puerto Rico: Freedom and Power in the Caribbean.* New York and Evanston, Ill.: Harper and Row, 1963.

Pérez-Stable, Marifeli. *The Cuban Revolution: Origins, Course, and Legacy.* New York and Oxford: Oxford University Press, 1993.

Thomas, Hugh. *Cuba: The Pursuit of Freedom.* New York: Harper and Row, 1971.

Catholicism, Roman

The body of beliefs and practices held by the members of the Christian church whose spiritual head is the pope, the bishop of Rome. A conventional view, particularly in Protestant-based cultures, regards Roman Catholicism and democracy as fundamentally opposed. An authoritarian church, hierarchically structured—and, at least since 1871, committed to a doctrine of papal infallibility in matters of faith and morals—seems to have little in common with political doctrines of majority rule and individual rights (including the rights of conscience and freedom of worship), and with the belief in pluralism and diversity that is found in democratic systems. Yet in the light of the history of the church, and its contemporary teaching and actions, this attitude is simplistic and inaccurate.

If we look at past Catholic political thought and organization, we find many elements that support democracy (as well as other forms of government such as monarchy). In recent years, especially since the Second Vatican Council (1962–1965), official Catholic doctrine has endorsed democracy as the form of government most in keeping with Christianity and has derived religious freedom and human rights from its understanding of the spiritual nature of the human person. Moreover, areas of predominantly Catholic culture, such as Latin America, Poland, Hungary, and Czechoslovakia, that in the past have been under authoritarian forms of government have now adopted constitutional democracy and rejected absolutisms of the left and the right.

Church Foundations

The early Christian church, which emerged in the first century in Palestine and spread throughout the Roman world, was neither a democracy nor a centralized hierarchical structure. The early Christian communities were self-governing bodies that saw themselves as direct recipients of the grace and inspiration of the Holy Spirit. There is continuing debate about the governance of the early church, but by the second century it included deacons (helpers), priests (elders), and bishops (overseers). In the New Testament Book of Acts the decision of the apostles and elders in the Council of Jerusalem as to whether circumcision was required for Gentiles seems to have been made by consensus. The apostle Peter was understood to have received a special commission from Christ. He be-

came the leader of the Christian communities in Jerusalem and Antioch and later was martyred in Rome. Peter's successors in the bishopric of Rome claimed, not always successfully, a general superintendence of the whole church. The other bishops also derived their authority from their succession to the apostles. The early church thus partook of elements of monarchy (the pope), aristocracy (the bishops), and democracy (the Christian community). When later Christians looked back to it as a model, they could find evidence of all three forms of government.

Also relevant to later ideas of limited government and constitutionalism was the early Christians' belief in religious obligations that transcended the political community. One's first loyalty was to God, whose will legitimized and set bounds on governmental authority. The claims of conscience and religious duty limited and sometimes overrode political, ethnic, and even family loyalties.

After centuries of persecution, the church was legalized by the emperor Constantine in A.D. 313 and soon became the established religion of the Roman Empire. Thereafter it made its most important doctrinal decisions through councils. The early ecumenical councils, usually held in the eastern Mediterranean, were made up of the bishops and patriarchs; although they were called by the eastern emperor in Constantinople, they usually included a representative of the pope. In western Europe and northern Africa councils of bishops enacted church legislation (canons) with or without the participation of temporal authorities. The popes demanded, but did not always receive, a special role in resolving disputes. Bishops most commonly were selected by a vote or consensus of the diocese or the priests of the cathedral. Often the strongest influence was the emperor or the local ruler. In theory, however (as argued explicitly by Pope Gelasius at the end of the fifth century), there was a duality of spiritual and temporal authority.

Doctrinal Development

The centralization that is associated with the modern Roman Catholic Church dates from the effort of the medieval popes to disentangle the church from the feudal system. In the twelfth and thirteenth centuries reforming popes created a separate system of law, courts, records, and church appointments that made Rome increasingly important in the government of the church and as an influence in the politics of western Europe. By 1302 Pope

Boniface VIII could argue that all power, both spiritual and temporal, flowed from the papacy.

Yet democratic elements also were present in the theory and practice of medieval Catholicism. In theory, bishops were still elected by their dioceses. New religious orders such as the Dominicans developed elaborate systems of election and representation for their internal governance. These systems, it has been argued, provided models for the parliamentary bodies that emerged in the thirteenth century. In the church-state controversies, defenders of both the pope and the emperor appealed to the role of the consent of the people to weaken the claims of the other side. Proponents of church councils drew on democratic elements in the church tradition (elections, consent to law, and natural law doctrines of equality) to argue that the council, as representative of all the members of the church, was superior to the pope.

Thomas Aquinas (1225–1274), an Italian theologian whose writings had a major effect on medieval church doctrine, favored monarchy but argued that all law must be community based; he endorsed a mixed constitution that included a popularly elected element. Human law ought to reflect the divine purpose as expressed in natural and divine law. An unjust law that violated the higher law was no law at all. Authoritarian, constitutionalist, and democratic conclusions can be drawn from Thomas's writings—and from the tradition of medieval Catholicism.

In the sixteenth century the Counter Reformation carried the process of papal centralization much further, with the imposition of a common liturgy, discipline, and greater Vatican control of appointments of bishops. In order to maintain the rights of the church—especially state support of Catholicism and church control over education and marriage—the popes gave Catholic monarchs a share in appointing bishops and concluded legal agreements that gave the monarchs extensive influence in the church. Jesuit and Dominican opponents of royal claims to govern by divine right, however, argued that royal authority came from God through a contract with the people. This argument contributed to the constitutional tradition that led ultimately to John Locke's *Second Treatise of Government* (1689), which argued that the ruler's authority was based on, and limited by, a social contract. Unlike Locke, however, the Catholic writers did not favor religious toleration but held that Catholic monarchs had a religious duty to repress heresy.

In the eighteenth century Vatican support for monar-chy and religious establishment was reinforced by the anticlericalism of the Enlightenment philosophers and the effort of the French Revolution to subordinate the clergy to civil authority. In the nineteenth century the Italian republican nationalists seized Rome and the Papal States in pursuit of their goal of Italian unification. As a result, Pope Pius IX imposed a ban on Catholic participation in Italian politics. His successor, Leo XIII, accepted democracy as one of several forms of government that could be supported by Catholics, but he continued to oppose freedom of worship except when it was necessary to avoid greater evils—when a significant part of the population was of a different religion. This position gave rise to a distinction made by Catholic theologians between the "thesis," or ideal situation of Catholicism as the established true religion, and the "hypothesis," or pragmatic compromise of religious toleration in a situation of religious pluralism.

After Germany was unified in 1871, the Catholic Center Party became one of the most important German parties. It was organized to resist the anti-Catholic *Kulturkampf* of Chancellor Otto von Bismarck, the Prussian who had carried out German unification. In Austria, Belgium, and Holland, Catholic parties began to participate in political life. In France and Italy parties of Catholic inspiration were not active because the Vatican opposed the republican legislation in those two countries separating church and state. After the ban on Catholic participation in Italian politics was lifted in 1919, the Catholic-inspired Popular Party had spectacular success, but it was dissolved by the Vatican in 1924 after Benito Mussolini and his fascist government came to power. In France most Catholics were monarchists. A small party of Christian democratic inspiration, the Popular Democratic Party, appeared only in the 1930s.

Maritain and Christian Democracy

The single person who did most to relate democracy and human rights to the Catholic tradition in the twentieth century was the French philosopher Jacques Maritain (1882–1973). Converted to Catholicism in 1906 and to Thomism (the philosophy of Thomas Aquinas) in 1912, Maritain only began to write about politics in the late 1920s. His political involvement came after Pope Pius XI had condemned Action Française, a right-wing movement with which Maritain had been sympathetic. In the late 1920s and early 1930s Maritain abandoned his earlier conservatism and embraced democracy. The best-known of his books applying Thomist principles to democracy are *Integral Humanism* (1936), *Scholasticism and Politics* (1940), *The Rights of Man and the Natural Law* (1943), and *Man and the State* (1951).

Arguing that the modern democratic state is the result of the leavening influence of the principles of the Gospel in human history, Maritain distinguished his religiously based and socially oriented "personalism" from what he considered to be the egoistic individualism of "bourgeois liberalism" and the statist collectivism of Marxism. Except for its emphasis on the religious roots of democracy, the pluralistic and socially concerned democratic state that he supported on Thomist grounds was almost indistinguishable from the contemporary liberal welfare states of Europe.

Along with other Catholic political thinkers of European background, such as Yves Simon *(The Philosophy of Democratic Government,* 1951) and Heinrich Rommen *(The State in Catholic Thought,* 1945), Maritain was responsible for a new development in Catholic thought: the endorsement of democracy not simply as one of several forms of government, all of which are acceptable to the degree that they promote the common good, but rather as the single political structure that is most in keeping with human nature and with Christian values. He also argued that the Thomist concept of the human person with an eternal destiny, and of the state as a "community of communities," provided a sounder basis for democracy and human rights than did the secularist individualism of liberalism.

Maritain's writings provided the ideological inspiration for the emergence of significant Christian Democratic parties in Europe in the 1940s and in Latin America in the 1950s and 1960s. After World War II the Popular Republican Movement was the largest party in postwar France, and the Christian Democratic Party dominated Italian politics from the 1940s until corruption scandals in 1994 led to its demise. The Christian Democratic Union in Germany included significant numbers of Protestants, but it saw itself as the successor to the Catholic Center Party and it based its ideology on Catholic social and political thought. Significant Christian Democratic parties emerged in Austria, Belgium, and Holland, and smaller parties appeared in other European countries. When direct elections to the European Parliament were established in 1979, representatives of Christian Democratic parties formed the largest party grouping. Similar parties were organized in most countries of Latin America. They continue to be important in Chile, Venezuela, and Central America.

The Christian Democratic parties, as the name implies, derived their belief in democracy from Christianity, and like Maritain, they attempted to distinguish their views from those of liberalism. At first they spoke of a third position, which was neither liberal nor socialist. They used expressions drawn from Maritain, such as *personalist* and *communitarian,* and propounded a more social and community-oriented view than what they saw as the exaggerated individualism of liberalism. In practice, the Christian Democrats have tended to support a combination of welfare state social legislation and free market economics—what the Germans call the "social market economy"—although in Latin America in the 1960s there was some Christian Democratic experimentation with worker-owned enterprises and programs of land redistribution.

The Church and Modern Politics

In his Christmas message of 1944, during the Second World War, Pope Pius XII had linked democracy and the Christian tradition, but the real breakthrough in papal thought did not take place until 1963. In that year Pope John XXIII argued in his encyclical *Peace on Earth* that every human being has by nature a right to freedom of worship in accordance with his or her conscience and that the dignity of the human person implies the right to participate in government and to be protected in the exercise of human rights. In 1965 the Second Vatican Council adopted two documents that formally committed the Roman Catholic Church to democracy and religious freedom. First, the Pastoral Constitution on the Church in the Modern World endorsed legal and constitutional protections for human rights, including freedom of assembly, speech, and the free exercise of religion, both in public and in private. It also described political participation, constitutional government, and regular elections as fully in accord with the nature of man. This was followed by the Declaration on Religious Liberty, which based the right to religious freedom on the dignity of the human person.

Although in many ways the council's action was simply a recognition of ideological and political changes that had taken place at the grass roots and in the national communities, the fact that democracy and religious freedom had been formally endorsed at the highest level had an important effect on the conduct of church leaders and clergy in

Pope John XXIII

subsequent decades. The bishops themselves had received a political and moral education as a result of their participation in the council. In Latin America in particular the council reoriented the church toward the defense of human rights and democracy.

The council's actions accelerated the movement by the Latin American hierarchy away from its earlier alliance with landowners, the upper classes, and the conservative parties. Christian Democratic parties, with tacit church support, came to power in several countries. Some members of the clergy and Catholic intellectuals became radicalized. The door was opened for the liberation theology movement, which criticized "bourgeois" democracy and called for a grassroots approach, oriented toward the poor. Most important, the council's endorsement of democracy and human rights led the Latin American church to defend democracy and to provide a haven for persecuted human rights groups in the 1960s and 1970s,

when the military seized power and engaged in torture and repression in many countries of Latin America. In the 1980s, as a continentwide transition to democracy began, the Catholic hierarchy acted as both a mediator and a proponent of the acceleration of the process. In the 1990s, with the return to democracy almost everywhere in Latin America, the church's support for democracy and human rights was less crucial. The bishops returned to more directly ecclesiastical concerns, although various church conferences continued to publish statements supporting democracy and social justice.

In the United States the relationship between Catholicism and American democracy has been an issue at various times. In 1928 fear of the antidemocratic tendencies of Catholicism was cited by Protestants who opposed the election of a Catholic candidate, Al Smith, as president. In the 1940s the writer Paul Blanshard quoted the nineteenth-century popes to demonstrate that Catholicism was an enemy of democracy and religious freedom. The election of John Kennedy, a Catholic, as president in 1960, and the changes in the church's official position at the time of the Second Vatican Council seemed to lay this issue to rest. Roman Catholic opposition to birth control and divorce was no longer seen as a threat, since the church no longer argued that its position on these issues should be put into law. The controversies over the legal status of abortion, pornography, and homosexuality, however, which many Catholics, along with conservative Protestants and Jews, saw as issues affecting the moral health of society, led to calls for restrictive legislation and efforts to secure a constitutional amendment reversing the U.S. Supreme Court decision permitting abortion. Some secular liberals criticized the church hierarchy for using its position to push for such legislation; they saw the church's stance on these issues as the sectarian point of view of a nonelected and undemocratic authority.

In the traditionally Catholic areas of Eastern Europe, the church played a role similar to its role in Latin America. It provided a haven for dissidents and those resisting tyranny. In Poland it supported the Solidarity movement in its struggle against the Communist Party. In Czechoslovakia and Hungary it operated partly underground to counteract the efforts of the communist governments to control all aspects of life. After those countries were freed of communist domination in 1989, the church sought to achieve more specifically institutional goals, such as religious instruction, and to reassert its authority in areas of sexual morality. Catholic-influenced parties were represented in the parliaments of Poland, the Czech Republic, Slovakia, and Hungary, although none of them achieved the influence or size of their Western European counterparts.

Recommitment to Democracy

The *Catechism of the Catholic Church,* a summary of Catholic teaching published in English in 1994, reaffirmed the commitment of the church to democracy and human rights. It quoted the Second Vatican Council on the importance of citizen participation in public life and described the political community as based on the social nature of man. An essential element of the common good, the catechism declared, is respect for, and promotion of, fundamental human rights. Reflecting a shift in papal teaching on free markets that had become evident only in the decade before the publication of the catechism, it included among those rights the right of free initiative in economic matters.

Although the Roman Catholic Church has endorsed democracy as the best form of government in temporal affairs, within the church the structure of authority and decision making is not democratic. It is true that the Second Vatican Council involved the bishops and the laity in church governance to a greater degree than before and that there has been a partial decentralization in the church. Consultative bodies such as the universal synod of bishops have been established, and lay people are involved in parish councils and advisory groups. The church, however, has not become a democracy, and those like the Brazilian theologian Leonardo Boff who have argued for an increase in internal democratization, have had difficulties with the Vatican.

There is still a tension between a hierarchical church that sees itself as the guardian and interpreter of divine revelation and a political system that decides public questions on the basis of majority rule. Yet, although there are limits to the acceptance of democracy in the internal structure of the church, it is now clear that in the political sphere Catholic thought endorses democracy and human rights as required by the nature of humankind as free moral beings, endowed by their Creator with the capacity as well as the duty to make the decisions necessary for self-government in an atmosphere of freedom.

See also *Christian democracy; Human rights; Maritain, Jacques; Protestantism.*

Paul E. Sigmund

BIBLIOGRAPHY

Abbott, Walter, ed. *Documents of Vatican II.* New York: Herder and Herder, 1966.
Blanshard, Paul. *American Freedom and Catholic Power.* Boston: Beacon Press, 1948; London: Greenwood, 1985.
Burtchaell, James. *From Synagogue to Church.* Cambridge and New York: Cambridge University Press, 1992.
Douglass, R. Bruce, and David Hollenbach, eds. *Catholicism and Liberalism.* Cambridge and New York: Cambridge University Press, 1994.
Fogarty, Michael. *Christian Democracy in Western Europe, 1820–1953.* London: Routledge, 1957; Westport, Conn.: Greenwood, 1974.
Hanson, Eric O. *The Catholic Church in World Politics.* Princeton: Princeton University Press, 1987.
Maritain, Jacques. *Man and the State.* Chicago: University of Chicago Press, 1951.
———. *The Rights of Man and the Natural Law.* New York: Scribner's, 1943.
Rommen, Heinrich. *The State in Catholic Thought.* St. Louis and London: B. Herder, 1945.
Thomas Aquinas. *St. Thomas Aquinas on Politics and Ethics.* Edited and translated by Paul E. Sigmund. New York: Norton, 1988.

Caucasus, The

The area, formerly part of the Soviet Union, in southeastern Europe between the Black Sea and the Caspian Sea. Within the Russian Federation the territories of Krasnodar and Stavropol and the republics of Adygey, Chechnya, Dagestan, Ingushetia, Kabardino-Balkaria, Karachay-Cherkessia, and North Ossetia are north of the Caucasus Mountains. South of the mountain range are Armenia, Azerbaijan, and Georgia. The boundaries of the Caucasus have been disputed for centuries. Ethnic and nationalist feelings—and economic hardship—have impeded the development of democracy in the region.

Historical Background

Until Russian conquests in the eighteenth and nineteenth centuries, the Caucasus was a region of constant struggle between nomads in the lowlands and farmers and herders in the highlands. The social structure of the highland people ranged from egalitarian tribal democracies to feudal principalities, but even the most authoritarian rulers had to tolerate and respect rights and customs in the peripheries of their domains, where their authority was recognized only nominally and conditionally. A few

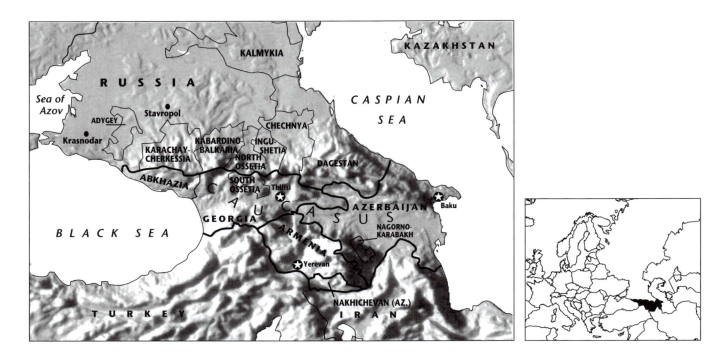

early attempts to restrict the absolute power of monarchs in the capitals of their kingdoms were unsuccessful. Centuries of invasions and civil wars prevented further democratic developments in the Caucasus until the 1980s.

In the late eighteenth century the Turks of the Ottoman Empire forced many Armenians to leave the area. During the Armenian diaspora ("dispersion"), when Armenians were scattered into the cities of Europe, Russia, and India, some attempts were made to devise a democratic British-style constitution for a future Armenian state. Although doomed to remain on paper, and little known even in Armenia, this effort nevertheless exerted some influence on the development of Armenian political thought and activity in the nineteenth century.

The Russians, who first invaded the Caucasus in 1763, finished absorbing it into the Russian empire in 1864. The institution of limited reforms in the early 1860s influenced later political thinking in Russia generally and in the Caucasus in particular. The Russian revolution of 1905 led to the creation of a number of political parties in the Caucasus. The main division lay between social democrats, who insisted on a socialist transformation of the whole empire, and various nationalists, who were concerned with the social and cultural development of their respective ethnic groups.

In April 1918 the Transcaucasian Provisional Congress declared the independence of the Caucasus as a whole. Several events prompted this declaration: the Bolshevik revolution in Russia in 1917; the Treaty of Brest-Litovsk in 1918, which ended Russian participation in World War I; and the retreat of demoralized Russian troops from eastern Turkey, which Russia had occupied during the war. The leaders of the various ethnic groups could not coordinate their efforts, however, and in late May the Democratic Republic of Georgia, the Armenian Democratic Republic, and the Republic of Azerbaijan declared their independence separately.

Three Independent Republics and the Soviet Period

Armenia, which was in the weakest position of the three, immediately became embroiled in conflict with Turkey; an unfavorable peace was followed by renewed war. The Armenian Dashnak (Socialist Federalist Party) government declared a number of democratic administrative reforms, but after facing economic and social disaster, the government surrendered to an invasion by the Russian Federation at the end of 1920. Similar events took place in Azerbaijan, where the liberal-democratic Moussavat (Party of Equality) government was overthrown by the Soviets in April 1920. Armenia and Azerbaijan were incorporated into the Union of Soviet Socialist Republics in 1922.

Georgia also faced difficult economic and military problems but was aided by the British, who occupied Georgia at the end of 1918, after the Germans retreated. The British left in 1919. The Georgian government, under the leadership of the Mensheviks (a social democratic party), was able to conduct municipal elections in 1918 and national elections in 1919. More than 70 percent of the eligible voters cast ballots. The Mensheviks, who enjoyed the support of peasants and workers, won most of the seats in the Constituent Assembly. Several democratic reforms, including land reform, were carried out. On May 7, 1920, the Soviet Union signed a treaty renouncing all claims to Georgian territory. But in February 1921, on the pretext of unrest in the disputed district of Lori (the northernmost part of present-day Armenia), the Soviet army invaded Georgia. Within a couple of months the Menshevik government had to flee abroad. Georgia was absorbed into the Soviet Union, first as part of the Transcaucasian Federation in 1922; it became a separate Soviet Socialist Republic in 1936.

Despite their democratic vocabulary and serious attempts at reforms, these three governments were motivated chiefly by nationalist objectives. Armenia and Azerbaijan fought over the territories of Nakhichevan, a predominantly Azeri district within Armenia, and Nagorno-Karabakh, a largely Armenian district within Azerbaijan. The conflict was marked by atrocities on both sides clearly aimed at "ethnic cleansing." The Georgian government behaved equally brutally in suppressing any attempts at self-determination among ethnic Abkhazians and Ossetians. Its social reforms were arranged so as not to injure the property rights of ethnic Georgians but to take as much property as possible from rich farmers and urban bourgeoisie (mostly Armenians).

Prospects for democracy disappeared after the Soviets invaded the Caucasus. Dissidents who dared to mention the notion were arrested and sent to prisons or mental asylums. Although the reform efforts made by Soviet leader Mikhail Gorbachev in the 1980s should not be underestimated, the collapse of the Soviet Union in 1991—and the emergence of fifteen independent states and the end of communist rule—had never been his aim. True democratization came not from Gorbachev's reforms but from continuous popular pressure, especially from the intelligentsia. This pressure had been present long before Gorbachev, and it bore some early fruit in spite of repression. Popular demonstrations in Armenia in 1965, for instance,

publicized the fiftieth anniversary of genocide by Ottoman Turks in western Armenia in 1915. And student demonstrations in Tbilisi, Georgia, in 1977 forced the inclusion of national language rights in the constitutions of all three Transcaucasian republics. These actions paved the way for subsequent democratic developments.

Nationalism and Democratic Prospects

Since 1923 Nagorno-Karabakh had been an autonomous district within Azerbaijan; 75 percent of its people were Armenians and they wanted to be part of Armenia. In February 1988 Nagorno-Karabakh was declared separate from Azerbaijan. Azerbaijan responded by blockading Nagorno-Karabakh, starving it of food and fuel. Moscow was unable to control the situation; violence erupted, and many were killed or became refugees. In 1991, after mass rallies and strikes, Armenia proclaimed independence, though Nagorno-Karabakh remains disputed. Armenia's situation is difficult economically and politically. (It is blockaded by Azerbaijan and Turkey and is facing famine.) Not all the actions of its present government are democratic, but further democratic elections and reforms are possible, especially if tensions with Azerbaijan abate.

In Azerbaijan political developments still are motivated chiefly by nationalism. The National Front of Azerbaijan unified many factions ranging from neofascists to a tiny liberal Social Democratic Party. After many coup attempts, Azerbaijan finally had a democratically elected president, when Abulfaz Elchibey was elected in June 1992. But Elchibey's government failed to carry out any consistently democratic reform, and in June 1993 it was overthrown by military commanders, allegedly for inconsistency in carrying out the anti-Armenian policy in the war for Nagorno-Karabakh. The Azerbaijanis then elected as their president Heydar Aliyev. It would be naïve to expect any democratic action to be undertaken by Aliyev, the former first secretary of the Communist Party and chief of the KGB in Azerbaijan.

The most dramatic movement toward democracy in the early years of Gorbachev's tenure came in Georgia, where memories of a democratic past were stronger, the Social Democrats were less discredited in public opinion than were the Socialist Federalists, and democratic leanings among the intelligentsia were more robust. Various dissident groups gained momentum, and a number of political organizations opposing the Soviet government were created. In April 1989 demonstrations in Tbilisi, which began as a protest against Abkhazian separatism, turned into massive rallies for independence. In dispersing the protesters, special troops using toxic gas and tanks killed more than twenty people, mostly young women. From that moment on communism was doomed in Georgia. Two years later independence was proclaimed, and the collapse of the Soviet Union made it a reality.

Zviad Gamsakhurdia was elected president of Georgia, but he behaved inconsistently and often dictatorially and was overthrown. His main political opponent, former first secretary Eduard Shevardnadze, was then elected president of the parliament and head of state. Real power, however, was held by a junta of military commanders, who in August 1992 launched a military invasion of Abkhazia, which sought independence from Georgia. With the aid of volunteers from the northern Caucasus (mostly Kabardinian and Chechen), the Abkhazians threw the Georgian armed forces out of Abkhazia. Nearly 200,000 ethnic Georgian civilians fled Abkhazia in fear of mass murders. As long as the armistice between Abkhazia and Georgia remains shaky, and the authority of the central government in Georgia is disputed in nearly every town by local warlords, it is futile to talk about democratic progress in Georgia. Russian peacekeeping forces introduced in 1994 may change the situation.

In most of the republics of the northern Caucasus, which are now part of the Russian Federation, the ruling groups are by and large the same party leaders as before. No opposing organization is strong or politically mature enough to challenge an establishment that shrewdly manipulates nationalist feelings and fears. Chechnya, which has proclaimed independence but is not recognized by other states, and Ingushetia, which willingly signed the treaty establishing the Russian Federation, are the exceptions: their presidents, Dzhokhar Dudayev of Chechnya and Ruslan Aushev of Ingushetia, were both elected with true popular support. Both nations, however, must struggle with rivalry between various clans.

There is thus little real prospect for democratic development in the Caucasus. Only Armenia holds some slight promise. Three groups of leaders are found in these societies: former party elites, military officers, and intellectuals. Before we can seriously talk about democracy in the region, we will have to wait for entrepreneurs, managers, lawyers, and economists to appear.

See also *Armenia; Europe, East Central; Union of Soviet Socialist Republics.*

Sergei A. Arutiunov

BIBLIOGRAPHY

Batalden, Stephen K., and Sandra L. Batalden. *The Newly Independent States of Eurasia: A Handbook of Former Soviet Republics.* Phoenix, Ariz.: Oryx Press, 1993.

Bremmer, Ian, and Ray Taras, eds. *Nations and Politics in the Soviet Successor States.* Cambridge and New York: Cambridge University Press, 1993.

Libaridian, Gerard, ed. *The Karabagh File.* Watertown, Mass.: Zoryan Institute, 1988.

Suny, Ronald Grigor. *Looking toward Ararat: Armenia in Modern History.* Bloomington: Indiana University Press, 1993.

———. *The Making of the Georgian Nation.* Bloomington: Indiana University Press, 1988; London: I. B. Tauris, 1988.

———. *The Revenge of the Past: Nationalism, Revolution, and the Collapse of the Soviet Union.* Stanford, Calif.: Stanford University Press, 1993.

Walker, Christopher. *Armenia and Karabagh: The Struggle for Unity.* London: Minority Rights Publications, 1991.

Censorship

The review of publications, plays, visual media, proposed public demonstrations, and the like for the purpose of prohibiting their dissemination or punishing their purveyors if they are deemed harmful to the morality or safety of society. The decline of censorship historically has accompanied the march toward democracy. In his famous funeral oration for the first soldiers killed in the Peloponnesian War in the fifth century B.C., the great Athenian leader Pericles declared that Athens differed fundamentally from Sparta because it tolerated much more freedom of thought and speech. Today, no political order may lay claim to democratic status without sufficient legal protections of freedom of expression.

Reasons for Censorship

Censorship in one form or another is as old as organized society. And while it is relatively limited in modern societies, unbridled freedom of expression has never prevailed. Authorities have used censorship for several reasons: to protect society and political and religious authority from perceived threats to their security or reputation; to defend traditional values and sensibilities; to protect individuals or discrete groups from harm to their dignity, security, or reputations; to promote a vision of virtue held by a society or a powerful group. Today democracies also limit some forms of expression in the name of promoting democratic and progressive values.

Censorship policy also reflects a vision of citizenship held by a particular society or political group. Friedrich Nietzsche observed that strong societies can afford to be tolerant of dissent (*Genealogy of Morals,* 1886); thus lack of censorship can reflect social strength. But other famous political philosophers have championed censorship as a means to foster social health and justice. In the *Republic* (written about 380 B.C.), Plato maintained that justice needed censorship of the arts and unworthy political opinions. Jean-Jacques Rousseau, in his *Politics and the Arts* (1758), advocated the total ban of the theater in Geneva because he thought such expression would corrupt Geneva's Spartan qualities and the Calvinist virtues of simplicity and hard work. Like Montesquieu and other political theorists, Rousseau believed that political liberty could not prevail unless it was buttressed by civic virtue. But history shows that censorship may prevent just social change (as in the early civil rights movement in the United States) or further the ends of factions that have captured political power in situations of cultural and ideological conflict.

Societies have deployed several types of legal tools to censor their citizens. First, laws have prohibited "seditious libel," which is harsh and threatening criticism of the government. The status of seditious libel law is important because the very notion of democracy implies the right to criticize the government. China's bloody suppression of dissent in Tiananmen Square in 1989 provides a telling example of how the logic of seditious libel thwarts democratic aspirations. Many Asian countries today outside Japan maintain tight restrictions on political commentary.

The historical decline of seditious libel laws corresponds to the growth of modern democracy. In 1275 the English Parliament made it a crime to spread disorder by stories that cast a critical light on the king or other important men of the country. In seventeenth-century England and early-twentieth-century Japan it was a capital offense even to imagine the death of the ruler. But as England and Japan grew more democratic in the nineteenth and twentieth centuries, respectively, prosecution for seditious libel declined significantly.

Second, governments have prosecuted people for "blasphemy," which is a malicious reproach cast upon God or other sacred authority. European countries punished individuals for heretical beliefs when the Roman Catholic Church enjoyed political clout (before the mid-sixteenth century in England). In England the government used licensing to protect the authority of political and religious institutions during the sixteenth and seventeenth centuries. In the United States the governor of the state of Virginia, Thomas Dale, proclaimed in 1612 that impiety was punishable by death. And in 1646 the Puritans in Massachusetts passed the Act against Heresy, by which individuals who did not accept such basic religious doctrine as the immortality of the soul were punished. As recently as 1925 the state of Tennessee prosecuted John T. Scopes for teaching Darwinism in the famous Scopes trial. Not surprisingly, legal restrictions against blasphemy have waned as theocratic orders have given way to the more secular democracies of today. Still, the crime of blasphemy survives in some Muslim countries, as seen in Iran in 1989, when Ayatollah Ruhollah Khomeini issued a death order against Salman Rushdie for publishing *The Satanic Verses.*

Third, laws proscribe "obscene libel," which is expression that threatens or undermines sexual morality. The Catholic Church's famous *Index* of banned books, first published in 1564, dealt with obscene works. Most early prosecutions of obscene works were tied to seditious libel concerns, but by the eighteenth century social morality had gained status as an entity meriting protection in its own right. Virtually all democracies maintain laws against obscenity (Denmark is a famous exception), but legal standards protect freedom of expression in this area much more than in the past.

Fourth, governments prohibit expression that threatens more concrete social interests, such as personal security, social peace, and property. Laws against disorderly conduct or disturbance of the peace (by speakers or their audiences) exist in every society. Through the "heckler's veto" doctrine, however, the United States has special constitutional protections that require police to attempt to control crowds before compromising the rights of speakers. In the famous *Skokie* case of 1978, the First Amendment required state and local officials to supply the largely Jewish community of Skokie, Illinois, the home of more than a thousand Holocaust survivors, with hundreds of police officers and National Guardsmen to protect a small group of Nazis who planned to demonstrate.

Types of Censorship

Censorship takes many forms, overt and subtle. The major overt forms include "prior restraint" and punishment for engaging in prohibited expression. Governments

London police hold back a crowd of several thousand Muslims demonstrating against Salman Rushdie's 1988 novel, *The Satanic Verses*.

exercise prior restraint through such mechanisms as licensing and judicial injunctions. In 1644 John Milton published his famous *Areopagitica* illegally to protest England's licensing law, which Parliament eventually refused to renew in 1694. In the fourth volume of his *Commentaries on the Law of England* (1769), William Blackstone propounded the doctrine that freedom of expression meant simply an absence of prior restraint. A more libertarian logic emerged by the end of the eighteenth century in the United States. Today licensing prevails mainly in special domains such as broadcasting and authorization for public demonstrations. Subsequent punishment for engaging in unlawful expression also amounts to censorship because the exaction of criminal penalties deters people from publishing or speaking their thoughts.

More subtle forms of censorship include civil lawsuits and social pressures. Libel and defamation may injure one's reputation and possibly one's financial status; so even democratic societies provide reasonable civil and even criminal remedies. But such suits can seriously deter the press and others from engaging in political debate and criticism. Consequently, newspapers and individuals in the United States enjoy unrivaled legal protections against libel suits when they are engaged in debating public matters.

Along similar lines, laws making it a crime to engage in group libel (damaging the reputations or esteem of groups, normally defined in terms of race, ethnicity, or religion) and laws against "hate speech" are constitutionally suspect in the United States. In contrast, such laws are sanctioned in most other modern democracies, including Canada, England, France, Germany, and Israel. These policy differences reflect America's greater emphasis on individualism and libertarianism.

There is one covert form of censorship that can be more insidious than legal proscription: social pressure. Alexis de Tocqueville (*Democracy in America*, 1835–1840) and John Stuart Mill (*On Liberty*, 1859) feared that modern democracy's penchant for equality of condition encouraged intellectual conformity and a "tyranny of the majority" that jeopardized liberty and independent thought without resort to legal sanctions. Restrictive speech codes and associated pressures of recent vintage on American campuses and elsewhere in the name of "political correctness" and egalitarianism represent contemporary examples of the tensions between liberty and equality that Tocqueville divined at the heart of modern democracy.

Recurrent conflicts surrounding textbook selection, library book selection, and curriculums in American public schools bear witness to similar political and social pressures. Religious and political activist groups on both the left and the right in major states such as California and Texas have pressured publishers or school boards to include or exclude material for their own religious and political reasons. Such influences are tantamount to broader covert censorship because publishers are very sensitive to the needs of these major markets.

Censorship and Democracy

The expansion of freedom of expression and the concomitant restriction of censorship have contributed to the spread of democracy. Today the global information revolution has furthered the rise of democracy in Eastern Europe and elsewhere, echoing the opening of society that followed the advent of Johannes Gutenberg's printing press in 1450. (The old English licensing laws were restrictive responses to Gutenberg's great discovery.) The right of freedom of expression is also associated with the extension of other civil rights and liberties. In the United States, for example, the Supreme Court expanded civil liberties in the 1960s and 1970s at the same time that it significantly broadened freedom of expression.

In England the writ of habeas corpus was established, in significant part, by claims brought by writers imprisoned for offending or threatening the state during the seventeenth century. Then the English Bill of Rights of 1689 extended freedom of speech to Parliament in its official capacity. Charles James Fox's Libel Act of 1792 made it more difficult to prosecute individuals for seditious libel. The Reform Bill of 1832 expanded the franchise and citizenship, leading ultimately to more freedom of speech for all citizens. In the United States the Jeffersonian Democrats rescinded the Sedition Act in 1801, after assuming power in the name of furthering democracy.

Until recent times most of the intellectual debate about free speech has pitted the advocates of democratic progress against the advocates of tradition. But new arguments for censorship of sexist, racist, and other oppressive forms of speech today are often motivated by the democratic values of equality and individual dignity. The philosopher Herbert Marcuse supported such censorship in his famous essay "Repressive Tolerance," published in 1965. Canadian courts have accepted new feminist-inspired restrictions on pornography, but similar laws have met with constitutional suspicion in the United States. Debate currently rages over whether such censorship promotes or threatens democratic values.

The International Covenant on Civil and Political Rights of 1966 endorses freedom of speech but calls for the legal prohibition of speech that advocates national, racial, or religious hatred and constitutes incitement to discrimination, hostility, or violence. Dozens of countries, including Denmark, England, France, and Germany, have ratified the covenant and passed laws consistent with its logic. In these and other democracies, hate speech enjoys less legal protection than it is afforded in the United States under the First Amendment. The United States ratified the covenant in 1992, but it attached a set of exceptions, including the assertion that signing in no way compromised the status of First Amendment rights in the United States.

See also *Freedom of assembly; Freedom of speech; Montesquieu; Rousseau, Jean-Jacques; Virtue, Civic.* In Documents section, see *Pericles' Funeral Oration (431 B.C.).*

Donald A. Downs and Samual Nelson

BIBLIOGRAPHY

Greenspan, Louis, and Cyril Levitt, eds. *Under the Shadow of Weimar: Democracy, Law, and Racial Incitement in Six Countries.* New York: Praeger, 1993.

Levy, Leonard. *Freedom of Speech and Press in Early American History: Legacy of Suppression.* New York: Harper and Row, 1963.

Marcuse, Herbert. "Repressive Tolerance." In *A Critique of Pure Tolerance,* by Robert Paul Wolff, Barrington Moore, Jr., and Herbert Marcuse. Boston: Beacon Press, 1965.

Meiklejohn, Alexander. "Free Speech and Its Relation to Self-Government." In *Political Freedom.* New York: Oxford University Press, 1965.

Mill, John Stuart. "On Liberty." In *The Essential Works of John Stuart Mill.* Edited by Peter Laslett. New York: Bantam Books, 1961.

Milton, John. "Areopagitica." In *The Portable Milton.* Edited by Douglas Bush. Harmondsworth, England, and New York: Penguin Books, 1976.

Rousseau, Jean-Jacques. *Politics and the Arts.* Translated by Allan Bloom. Ithaca, N.Y.: Cornell University Press, 1968.

Tocqueville, Alexis de. *Democracy in America.* 2 vols. Translated by Henry Reeve. New York: Schocken Books, 1961.

Central African Republic

See *Africa, Subsaharan*

Central America

A slender isthmus bridging North and South America that includes the countries of Belize, Costa Rica, El Salvador, Guatemala, Honduras, Nicaragua, and Panama. This small region has been the scene of some of Latin America's most destructive civil wars, revolutions, and foreign invasions as well as some of its most brutal military dictatorships.

Historically, the region of Central America referred to Costa Rica, El Salvador, Guatemala, Honduras, and Nicaragua—the five countries that after gaining independence from Spain in 1821 formed the United Provinces of Central America, which broke up in 1838. More recently, Panama, which separated from Colombia in 1903, has been considered a part of Central America. Belize, the only English-speaking country in the area, has a different history because of its colonization by the British and is not discussed here.

Historical Background

For thousands of years before its conquest by Spain, this land was occupied by a succession of indigenous Amerindian people of various cultures and linguistic groups, most notably the Mayans of Guatemala. Spanish colonial rule disrupted these civilizations. The colonizing oligarchs dispossessed peasants of their lands and subjugated them through repressive labor policies.

The same processes continued throughout Central America's history. After the dissolution of the United Provinces of Central America, each of the five provinces became an independent country. Independence did not bode well for democratization, however. Unrestricted democracy has never been established in any Latin American country in which agriculture was the crucial source of exports, agricultural production was generally labor-intensive and coercive, and land was primarily domestically owned.

Landlords have been the most intransigent actors blocking democratic rule. Believing that the effective enfranchisement of rural lower classes threatened their control over a cheap labor supply, the landed elite traditionally have become partners in an authoritarian alliance with their own countries' militaries and with the United States. This alliance has permitted them to pursue economic policies that redistributed wealth to them and away from the poor. Although their authoritarian rule had a liberal democratic guise, it is best described as "reactionary despotism."

Since independence, Central America has had the dubious honor of having the most constitutions and frustrated constitutional projects in Latin America. Where political parties existed and were permitted to function, they were either elite clubs associated with a faction of the oligarchy, weak organizations linked to competing foreign companies, or adjuncts of local militaries. Although elections were scheduled regularly, they were routinely won by generals and dictators using coercion and fraud. As a consequence, popular distrust in the promise of elections was widespread.

This pattern of reactionary despotic rule was typical of most of the countries of the region. In Guatemala, which, with 9.5 million people, is the most populous and ethnically diverse Central American nation, a series of strong dictators defended an agricultural economy based on the export of coffee, sugar, bananas, and, later, cotton and petroleum. Only occasionally interrupted by moments of constitutional government, Guatemala's authoritarian rulers became known for their especially brutal policies toward indigenous peoples. The period from 1944 to 1954 seemed to mark the beginning of democratization linked to agrarian reform, but these developments were ended abruptly by a U.S.-backed military coup supported by the country's leading landowners, the largest of which was United Fruit Company. From the 1960s on, a series of military-dominated governments and an almost feudal form of land ownership encouraged the formation of a guerrilla-based opposition, on the one hand, and a heightening of state terror, on the other.

The situation has been similar in El Salvador, the smallest and most densely populated (5.3 million) country in the region. Beginning in the middle of the nineteenth century, a small group of local landowners transformed El Salvador into a specialized producer of agricultural exports. But the introduction of coffee and, later, sugar, cotton, and cattle was achieved at the expense of traditional systems of food production. Three-quarters of the land was concentrated in the hands of only 2 percent of the population, and the majority of laborers were displaced from their lands.

Landowners held tight control of political power as a means to guarantee their privileges until a large-scale peasant uprising in 1932, which was led by the Communist Party of El Salvador under the leadership of Agustin Farabundo Martí. Its violent suppression by the military

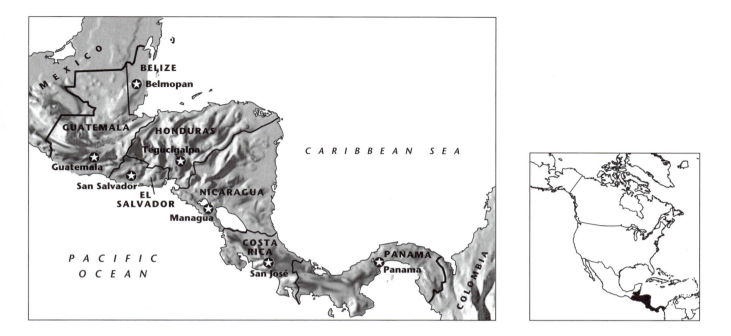

forced the landowning oligarchy to share power with the armed forces. For the next fifty years, this authoritarian alliance vetoed all reform and manipulated elections to its advantage. As in Guatemala, this manipulation led to the emergence in the 1960s and 1970s of a strong opposition to the government, much of it religion-based, ranging from the Christian Democratic Party and Christian communities to powerful armed guerrilla movements united in the Farabundo Martí National Liberation Front. It also produced a civil war in 1980.

Nicaragua, the largest country in Central America, has a population of only 4 million. It followed the region's general pattern but was unique in that it faced external involvement in its affairs. When neither the liberal nor the conservative faction could achieve dominance after independence, each sought support from foreigners to buttress its position. Foreigners intervened repeatedly as interest grew in Nicaragua as a possible site for a transisthmian canal, culminating in 1855 in a U.S.-sponsored invasion led by William Walker. In 1909 the U.S. intervened again, introducing three decades of a foreign military presence.

The U.S. government withdrew its marines from Nicaragua after they failed to defeat a guerrilla band led by Augusto César Sandino that was aimed at driving them out. But before leaving, the U.S. government established the Nicaraguan National Guard and installed the Anastasio Somoza family in power, thus initiating forty years of dictatorial rule. The Somoza dynasty, which ultimately

seized almost 10 percent of the country's arable land and some of its most profitable industry, governed until 1979. It was overthrown by the Sandinista National Liberation Front and a broad coalition of groups seeking democratic rule. But as the victors fought over the type of government they would establish, the United States intervened once more, this time supporting the formation of a "contra" army to fight Sandinista domination. Again, Nicaragua was plunged into armed conflict.

Because the class systems of Honduras and Costa Rica do not fit this same mold, these two countries had different political trajectories. Costa Rica, a country with a population of 2.8 million, suffered less zero-sum conflict, thanks to the paucity of Indians who could be subjugated for coerced labor. Because of the acute shortage of workers, coffee production, when it was introduced, spread to small landholders rather than to haciendas, or plantations; it was based on family labor rather than on coerced labor. This landholding structure contributed to the process of democratization.

In Honduras, a country with a population of 5 million, authoritarian rule was linked to the development of the country's principal export product, bananas. But unlike its neighbors, Honduras never developed a reactionary national landowning class. Instead, U.S. companies, especially United Fruit Company, were granted vast tracts of land, displacing local ownership. The predominance of the foreign-owned fruit companies gave rise to a strong independent labor movement, which gradually helped to divide local urban elites from the multinationals and encouraged more accommodationist policies. For seventy years after 1910, when President Miguel Dávila's attempt to halt these drastic land concessions led to his overthrow, the military ruled, interrupted only occasionally by civilian presidents. But army rule was generally more moderate and flexible than elsewhere in the region, with the exception of a brief period in the 1980s, and the country avoided the wars that wracked the rest of the region.

Panama, the southernmost country on the isthmus, has stood completely apart from its neighbors in its development pattern. Formerly a province of Colombia, Panama never belonged to the Central American federation. Its periods of military rule were not linked to a model of export agriculture. Instead, Panama was defined by its special character as a country created solely in order to establish a new international crossroad, the Panama Canal.

A nationalist battle to define itself in regard to the United States, which built and controlled the Canal Zone, has been Panama's central effort since independence in 1903. This special relationship with the United States brought Panama the region's highest per capita income, highest rate of foreign investment, and most highly developed economic infrastructure. But it also led to repeated interventions by U.S. troops, constant conflicts over control of the canal until the signing of the Panama Canal treaties in 1977, and domination of political life by the U.S.-created Panamanian National Guard (later renamed the Panama Defense Forces).

Reform and Reconciliation

This pattern of almost constant authoritarian rule throughout Central America was reversed during the 1980s. The threat of widespread regional war, the destruction wrought by seemingly endless and stalemated local conflicts, and a gradual transformation in agrarian relations that began in the 1970s altered the social basis for the reactionary despotic alliance between landlords, militaries, and foreigners. Throughout most of Central America, with the notable exception of Guatemala, the power of large landowners was weakened. Divisions grew between economic elites and the military as businessmen became increasingly resentful of the military's corruption and its preponderant role in the economy. At the same time, the proliferation of peasant, worker, student, religious, and women's organizations combined with the rise of the Christian democratic, social democratic, and communist

parties to encourage a process of reform. Finally, international condemnation of abusive military rule grew, often linked to the threat of economic sanctions.

By 1990, for the first time in their collective history, all Central American countries were governed by civilian presidents who had assumed office as the result of elections. All had experienced some rotation of power; in each case a president of one party voluntarily relinquished power to an elected successor of a rival party. Even more significant, by 1994 efforts toward national reconciliation were taking place in the three countries of the region that had been the primary site of civil war or armed conflict: El Salvador, Guatemala, and Nicaragua.

In Nicaragua a peaceful transition of power from governing to opposition forces occurred in 1990—for the first time since the founding of the republic. This historic moment accompanied the end of the U.S.–sponsored war against the country's Sandinista government and the demobilization of the contras. It was marked by the establishment of an elaborate set of institutions, which included a new electoral code and political party law and the separation of party and army.

In El Salvador a similar transfer of power from one party to another took place in 1989—for the first time since 1931. The subsequent United Nations–sponsored peace accords between the government and the Farabundo Martí National Liberation Front were so wide ranging that they have been called a "negotiated revolution." The accords eventually led to internationally supervised elections in March 1994, in which the leftist opposition won a substantial portion of legislative power for the first time in the country's history.

In Guatemala, where power traditionally shifted through military coups or "façade" elections, a new constitution was formulated in 1984. Elections followed in which the presidency was transferred from the center-right Christian Democratic Party to the right-wing Movement of Solidarity Action—the first peaceful transfer of power since 1951. Despite consistent high levels of repression, the May 1993 ascension to the presidency of human rights ombudsman Ramiro de Léon Carpio, and the March 1994 announcement of a U.N.–mediated human rights accord between the government and leading elements of the armed opposition, appeared to reinforce the claims that Latin America's longest and bloodiest civil war was coming to an end.

Those countries less affected by internal warfare also showed some positive signs of democratization. In Honduras the first direct elections for president in more than twenty-five years were held in 1981. Peaceful transfers of power between the Liberal Party and the National Party followed in 1989 and 1993. Like its neighbors, Honduras took steps toward national reconciliation. A new electoral law, the offer of unconditional amnesty for guerrilla organizations that had been fighting for thirty years, and the 1993 legalization of leftist parties seemed to pave the way for a deepening of democratic trends.

Panama again proved to be the odd country out. Civilian president Guillermo Endara was sworn in on a U.S. military base on December 20, 1989, following a U.S. invasion of Panama. His swearing in represented the rupture of a two-decade tradition of authoritarian rule as well as a validation of his previous electoral victory, which had been nullified by the commander of the Panama Defense Forces, Gen. Manuel Antonio Noriega. It also meant that the U.S. military resumed its historical role as the chief arbiter and guarantor of political power in Panama.

More predictably, elsewhere in the region the February 1994 elections in Costa Rica restored the National Liberation Party to office. These elections confirmed that country's tradition of determining power holders through peaceful and competitive elections.

Economic Constraints on Democratization

These achievements in little more than a decade are remarkable, especially because they occurred in some of the continent's poorest countries. But the experience of Central America has demonstrated that elections and even civilian governments do not necessarily lead to democracy. It remains to be seen whether these achievements mark a major step forward in a broader process of expansion of civic rights, political equality, participation, contestation, accountability, and governability or simply a new cycle of liberalization followed by repression—a pattern that has repeatedly plagued the countries of the region.

Established scholarly wisdom emphasizes the extreme difficulty of building democracies where certain basic requisites do not exist. With the exception of Costa Rica, the countries of Central America lack most, if not all, of the social, economic, cultural, and institutional conditions that have been identified as prerequisites to democracy: high levels of literacy and education, cultural homogeneity, an established party system, a professional bureaucracy, a tradition of tolerance, an independent and secure place in the world economic system, an equitable distribution of wealth, a modern and productive agrarian struc-

ture, and a certain degree of prosperity. Consequently, they are considered unlikely to succeed in their transitions to democracy.

The poor performance of Central American economies today makes their democratic prospects look especially bleak: 75 percent of the region's people live in conditions of poverty, almost 40 percent live in extreme poverty, and 23 percent cannot satisfy their minimal needs. Except for Costa Ricans, Central Americans live in conditions that are notably worse than those of South America.

In virtually every economic category, the facts are even harsher for Central America than for Latin America as a whole. Although per capita real gross domestic product declined during the 1980s throughout the hemisphere, the decline in Central America was greater, and its growth rates in the preceding decade were smaller—despite a substantial outmigration that should have improved its performance. Food production, exports of goods and services, and the purchasing power of exports shrunk in the region even as they grew in the rest of Latin America, and Central American debt service ratios and unemployment were greater. In sum, an economic crisis of major proportions subverts the decision-making space of fragile new democracies in Central America.

Moreover, the region's less diversified economies are more vulnerable than those of most Latin American countries to the fluctuations and unfavorable development trends that characterize dependence on commodity exports. Because their economies are so small, so open to wealthier ones, and so inequitable, a world economic downturn or shifts in commodity prices can trigger a cycle of destabilizing forces, with adverse consequences for long-term political stability and democratization. Indeed, during periods of world economic crisis, Central American countries have seen more changes of presidents than the rest of Latin America. Downturns have also been associated with changes in governments because of coups or resignations.

Political and Military Constraints

Central America's political inheritance adds fuel to a pessimistic vision. In El Salvador, Guatemala, and Nicaragua, the three countries in which the heritage of especially brutal autocratic regimes is combined with the aftermath of war, the historical legacy is particularly grim. It includes the deaths of almost 200,000 civilians and 100,000 military during the 1980s alone, the displacement of more than 2.5 million refugees, the systematic practice of torture and arbitrary detention, the destruction of centrist and leftist forces, the radicalization of popular movements, and the proliferation of uncontrolled armed groups. If the time frame is extended, these numbers increase. Amnesty International estimates that more than 100,000 people were murdered and 38,000 disappeared in Guatemala alone between 1970 and 1990. The infrastructure, environment, and productive apparatus of these countries have been ravaged by war at a cost of more than $30 billion. Not surprisingly in this setting, drug trafficking has exploded, especially in Guatemala, as narcotics are shipped between South America and the United States.

The most worrisome legacy is the disproportionate power of the Central American armed services. Wars in El Salvador, Guatemala, and Nicaragua resulted in the greatest and most rapid military buildup in the history of the region. The armed forces quintupled in size from 1970 to 1990. The 120 percent change in the numbers of the armed forces in Central America between 1980 and 1990 is especially impressive when compared with the 13 percent decline in the rest of Latin America during the same period. In addition, the value of arms imports soared 993 percent in Central America, but it rose 159 percent in Latin America as a whole. The single greatest impact of this buildup has been to strengthen military forces over civilian governments and organizations. Even though the armed forces have withdrawn from the direct exercise of political power, they still dominate almost every government in Central America; indeed, superpower largess during the 1980s permitted the armed forces to become more sophisticated, more resistant to restrictions on their autonomy, and wealthier than ever.

The disproportionate role of the military in Central America has been accompanied by the militarization of civil society. Running throughout these countries is a common thread of fear, the product of years of authoritarian rule, war, and state terror. To an extent not seen elsewhere in contemporary South America, even in Argentina, most Central Americans have become accustomed in their daily lives to extraordinarily abnormal conditions, in which fear, pain, insecurity, and suspicion predominate. Especially in rural areas, a culture of repression and passivity has emerged, which is the antithesis of democratic citizenship.

Influence of the United States

A final constraint, which stands in sharp contrast to the rest of South America, is the profound impact of the Unit-

ed States. No other area of the world has been more tightly and asymmetrically integrated into the U.S. political and economic system than has Central America, and, except for the Caribbean, no other area is more dependent on the United States. The region's main trading partner for both imports and exports is the United States, and its leading creditors are U.S. banks. Moreover, official U.S. development assistance has played a significantly larger role in Central America than in the rest of Latin America. In 1989, for example, the U.S. spent an average of $10 per capita in official development assistance to Latin America, compared with $87 per capita in Honduras, $82 in Nicaragua, $76 in Costa Rica, $65 in El Salvador, and $21 in Guatemala. At the same time, no other area has been so thoroughly targeted for military intervention; indeed, every twentieth-century intervention by U.S. troops in the hemisphere has occurred either in Central America or in the Caribbean.

Proximity to the United States, coupled with the extreme economic underdevelopment of the region, has resulted in a disproportionately large and decisive foreign role in domestic affairs. Occasional (and generally unsuccessful) efforts by the United States to promote democracy notwithstanding, this intervention has left an unfortunate political legacy. On the one hand, it has created solid historical ties between an external power and traditional antidemocratic domestic forces as well as strong traditions of foreign imposition that have proved difficult to break—even in a post–cold war setting. On the other hand, to varying degrees in each country, it has sharply restricted both the development and the room to maneuver domestic forces, often leaving them unaccustomed to defining their own interests, organizing into autonomous parties, or establishing the leadership credentials so essential in moments of transition.

Prospects for Democracy

Despite the democratic progress that has been made in Central America, these constraints, along with the unfortunate patterns inherited from the past, have created some grim realities. Nicaragua has been virtually ungovernable since the 1990 defeat of the Sandinistas. It suffers from legislative paralysis, fragmented political parties, repeated outbreaks of armed violence between government and "recontra" forces that threaten its fragile political balance, and an economic crisis that has left the majority of its people worse off than they were even during the Somoza dictatorship and the worst years of the war. Although

Nicaragua's devastated economy remains far from recovery, international assistance has fallen short of the sums originally anticipated.

In neighboring El Salvador the peace settlement ending the civil war and establishing the broad parameters of democracy has been undermined by half-hearted compliance, especially in the areas of judicial and electoral reform, the formation of a new civilian police, and the regulation of conflicts over land. At the same time, international pressures for economic stabilization have subverted the settlement by undercutting the financial commitments necessary to sustain the accords.

Prospects for democratization look even worse in Guatemala. Since the introduction of competitive elections, the country has suffered from a failed coup d'état attempt, a dramatic rise in human rights violations, a series of drug-related scandals in the cabinet and Congress, an institutional crisis in all branches of government, sharp increases in its concentration of wealth and its dismal poverty statistics, and a breakdown in peace negotiations with the Guatemalan National Revolutionary Unity.

In Honduras only minimal inroads have been made against military power, while elected governments have presided over a sharp increase in economic difficulties, riots and protests, and repression. In Panama the elections that followed the U.S. ouster of Gen. Manuel Noriega returned his political party to power. Even generally peaceful Costa Rica experienced in 1994 what is widely regarded as the dirtiest campaign in its democratic history.

Such inauspicious signs cast doubt on the prospects for rapid democratization of the region. Yet, clearly, Central American political organizations are characterized by more contestation and inclusion today than ever. The regimes that have appeared in the 1990s represent not the reconstitution of a previous authoritarian coalition in another guise but a hybrid form that has the potential to mobilize mass pressures for institutionalizing contestation and broadening political inclusion.

Moreover, the probability of regression to the "reactionary despotic" regimes of the past is low, although prospects vary among countries. In Honduras, Panama, and Costa Rica, where patterns of compromise have historical roots and where such regimes have never existed, and in Nicaragua and El Salvador, where social forces have been most profoundly transformed and where both progressive and conservative forces have demonstrated their capacity to create a stalemate, such regimes are unlikely. However, this is not the case for Guatemala, where politi-

cal-military stalemates have never been established, ethnic conflict profoundly complicates negotiations between opposing sides, and compromise has not become part of the dominant political style.

But the likelihood that fragile democratic processes will deepen, consolidate, and be able to deliver long-deferred public goods to their populations is also low. Democracies are built in phases and over time. In Central America, where conditions are especially unfavorable, progress will have to be measured in small increments of empowerment of the previously disempowered, coupled with gradual curbs on the authority of traditional rulers.

More plausible in the medium term is the establishment of "hybrid regimes" that mix authoritarian and democratic practices. Contemporary Central American polities are characterized by the uneven acquisition of the procedural requisites of democracy. They show gains in the electoral arena, but without civilian control over the military or the rule of law. Elections that once were openly fraudulent are fairer than they once were, yet important sectors remain politically and economically disenfranchised. Armies that once ruled now support civilian presidents, but they resist any efforts by civilians to control internal military affairs, dictate security policy, make officers subject to the judgment of civil courts, or diminish their role as the ultimate arbiter of politics. Absolute power is condemned, yet judiciaries remain weak, rights are violated, and contracts are broken.

These polities are also distinguished by the uneven distribution of citizenship across the national territory. Depending on the outcome of particular localized struggles, different mixes of authoritarianism, patronage, and pluralism coexist under the same national regime. Thus, within the same polity, bargaining relations can be based on collective action in one place and the political subordination of clients, reinforced by coercion, in another. This is especially evident in rural municipalities, where local notables can interfere in the electoral process in a manner that systematically biases the outcome, distribute favors based on political loyalties, and actively encourage or discourage mass mobilization.

Aptly referred to elsewhere in Latin America as "democraduras," a label that captures their persistently authoritarian qualities, these hybrid regimes are not mere façade democracies. Given Central America's authoritarian history, they represent a very real advance over the past. But whether these hybrids have the capacity to govern their territories at all, and whether they will develop in a more open and participatory direction, will depend on the extent and direction of organized pressure from below, the presence of reformers in government, the degree of elite competition and flexibility, and the extent of international support—an unpredictable mix at best.

See also *Caribbean, English; Caribbean, Spanish; Christian democracy; Colonialism; Costa Rica; Dominican Republic; War and civil conflict.*

Terry Lynn Karl

BIBLIOGRAPHY

Baloyrn-Herp, Enrique. "Reactionary Despotism in Central America." *Journal of Latin American Studies* 15 (November 1983): 295–319.

Barry, Tom. *Central America inside Out.* New York: Grove Weidenfeld, 1991.

Booth, John A. "Socioeconomic and Political Roots of National Revolts in Central America." *Latin America Research Review* 26 (1991): 33–73.

Garcia Laguardia, Jorgé Maria. "Constitutional Framework for Political Parties in Central America." In *Political Parties and Democracy in Central America,* edited by Louis Goodman, William M. LeoGrande, and Johanna Mendelson Forman. Boulder, Colo.: Westview Press, 1992.

Karl, Terry Lynn. "El Salvador's Negotiated Revolution." *Foreign Affairs* 71 (spring 1992): 147–164.

LaFeber, Walter. *Inevitable Revolutions: The United States in Central America.* New York: Norton, 1984.

Lindenberg, Marc. "World Economic Cycles and Central American Political Instability." *World Politics* 42 (April 1990): 397–421.

Moore, Barrington, Jr. *Social Origins of Dictatorship and Democracy.* Boston: Beacon Press, 1966.

Perez Brignoli, Hector. *Breve historia de Centroamerica.* Madrid: Alianza Editorial, 1985.

Stephens, Evelyne Huber. "Capitalist Development and Democracy in South America." *Politics and Society* 17 (1989): 281–352.

Weeks, John. "An Interpretation of the Central American Past." *Latin American Research Review* 21 (1986): 31–53.

Checks and balances

Constitutional devices by which each of the three branches of government (legislative, executive, and judicial) can check the others from upsetting the proper balance by invading its assigned sphere. Many analysts since the late nineteenth century have added that informal, extraconstitutional agencies such as political parties, mass communications media, and public opinion also check the actions of legislators, executives, administrators, and judges. Strictly speaking, however, informal checks are not equivalent to constitutional and legislative checks and balances.

Checks and balances are logical corollaries of the doctrine of separation of powers. That doctrine is premised on the belief that all governments exercise three distinct kinds of power: legislative (making laws), executive (enforcing laws), and judicial (interpreting and applying laws to individual cases). Tyrannical monarchies and oligarchies assign all three powers to the same rulers, but republics and democracies do not. As James Madison wrote, in *Federalist* No. 47, "the accumulation of all powers, legislative, executive, and judiciary, in the same hands, whether of one, a few, or many, and whether hereditary, self-appointed, or elective, may justly be pronounced the very definition of tyranny."

The Constitution of the United States not only uses separate articles to assign each power to a separate branch of government but also requires that the members of each branch be selected in different ways by different constituencies and gives each of the three branches of the federal government several checks to keep the others from encroaching on its allotted powers.

Separation of Personnel

The constitutions of most parliamentary democracies allow or require executive leaders to be chosen from among members of the parliament. Those chosen remain members of the parliament during their service as ministers or subministers. In the two-party British (Westminster) prototype, after a general election the monarch designates as prime minister the leader of the majority party in the House of Commons. The prime minister then chooses the ministers and chief subministers of the cabinet from the members of Parliament (most of them from the House of Commons). In the multiparty democracies with proportional representation, the head of state usually designates as premier the leader of the party with the plurality of seats in the parliament. The premier then puts together a coalition cabinet composed of members of the parliament belonging to the several parties that pledge to support the new cabinet in parliamentary votes.

Thus, in the parliamentary democracies, most executive officials must also be members of the legislature. The American prototype of presidential democracy has the opposite rule: a member of the legislature may not hold office in another branch, and, by extension, one who holds executive or judicial office may not concurrently hold office in another branch.

Moreover, the members of each branch are selected in distinctive ways and for distinctive terms, and thus they represent somewhat different constituencies. In the United States all members of the House of Representatives are elected for two-year terms from 435 single-member districts apportioned roughly according to population. Members of the Senate are elected for six-year terms, two from each state regardless of its population, with the elections staggered so that one-third of the senators are elected every two years. The president is elected by a majority of the 538 votes cast by the members of the electoral college, who are selected by the voters in each state and the District of Columbia from one or another of the slates nominated by political parties. Federal judges, including Supreme Court justices, are appointed for life on the nomination of the president and the consent of the Senate.

Mechanisms in the United States

In the United States, Congress checks the president by holding the final word on making laws and appropriations (including the power, by a two-thirds vote of both chambers, to enact laws and appropriations vetoed by the president). The Senate is given special powers to "advise and consent" to the president's nominations for major executive offices and to foreign treaties negotiated and signed by the president. The House of Representatives counts the electoral votes and declares the winner of the presidential election. The president can be removed from office on being impeached by a two-thirds majority of the House of Representatives and convicted by a two-thirds majority of the Senate. Congress is also empowered to check the judiciary by establishing all federal courts other than the Supreme Court, by fixing the original jurisdiction of the lower courts, and by fixing the appellate jurisdiction of all federal courts, including the Supreme Court.

The president checks Congress mainly by the veto power: nearly all actions of Congress must be submitted to the president. If he signs a measure, it becomes law; if he refuses to sign, he returns it to Congress with the reasons for his veto. Then the measure can become law only if it is passed again by a two-thirds majority in both chambers. In practice the veto has been a formidable check on Congress: since 1789 less than 10 percent of all presidential vetoes have been overridden. In many cases, presidents have used the threat of a veto to shape legisla-

tion as it passes through Congress. A president can let it be known through friends in Congress that, if certain objectionable provisions remain in a particular bill, he is prepared to veto the bill. Members of Congress often decide that enacting the bill's other provisions is worth the price of dropping the parts the president opposes.

The president's veto is significantly restricted by the limitation that he can veto only entire bills, not parts of bills. Consequently, Congress often adds riders (provisions that the president would veto if they were submitted independently) to bills (notably, appropriations bills) that the president has little option but to accept. Many presidents have urged Congress to give them a power enjoyed by the governors of many states: a line-item veto that would enable them to approve parts of a bill while disapproving other parts. Such a power would considerably increase the president's influence over legislation, and so it is not surprising that no Congress has ever enacted a line-item veto.

The president checks the judiciary mainly by his power to nominate all federal judges, including the chief justice of the United States and the other Supreme Court justices. Most presidents have tried to nominate only persons with judicial philosophies close to their own, though some judges' subsequent rulings have been unpleasant surprises. The Senate can reject any of the president's nominees by a simple majority vote, but no person can become a federal judge without first being nominated by the president.

The Constitution of the United States does not give the Supreme Court explicit power to check the actions of Congress or the president. In the case of *Marbury v. Madison* (1803), however, the Supreme Court established its own check on both other branches by asserting the doctrine of judicial review—the power and duty of the courts to annul legislative and executive acts that they find incompatible with the Constitution. Many Congresses and presidents have chafed under this claim of judicial power, but they have nevertheless accepted it, and the Court's exercise of judicial review has been one of its most powerful checks on the legislative and executive branches.

The Framers of the Constitution evidently assumed that each branch would use its constitutional checks largely or solely to keep the others from invading its constitutionally assigned sphere of power. Since 1789, however, each branch has used its checks much more to keep the others from making unwise policies than to preserve a proper balance with the other branches.

See also *Constitutionalism; Electoral college; Impeachment; Presidential government; Separation of powers; United States Constitution.* In Documents section, see *Constitution of the United States (1787).*

Austin Ranney

BIBLIOGRAPHY

Bryce, James. *The American Commonwealth.* 2 vols. London and New York: Macmillan, 1914.

Crozier, Michel. *The Trouble with America: Why the Social System is Breaking Down.* Translated by Peter Heinegg. Berkeley: University of California Press, 1984.

Goldwin, Robert A., and Art Kaufman, eds. *Separation of Powers: Does It Still Work?* Washington, D.C.: American Enterprise Institute, 1986.

Heren, Louis. *The New American Commonwealth.* New York: Harper and Row, 1968.

Lijphart, Arend. *Democracies: Patterns of Majoritarian and Consensus Government in Twenty-one Countries.* New Haven and London: Yale University Press, 1984.

Nicholas, H. G. *The Nature of American Politics.* 2d ed. Oxford and New York: Oxford University Press, 1986.

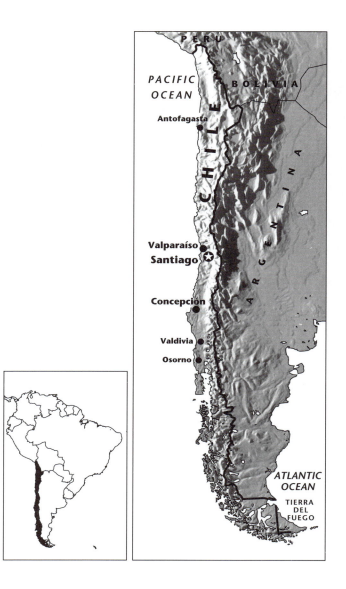

Chile

A country of 13 million people situated on the western and southern extremes of South America's Southern Cone between the Andes Mountains and the Pacific Ocean. With the exception of the decade of the 1920s and the period of military rule from September 1973 to March 1990, Chile has had democratic civilian rule under constitutions embodying separation of powers, regular elections, and the orderly transfer of power since it became an independent republic in 1818.

Historical Background

Unlike its neighbors, Chile succeeded after its independence from Spain in establishing a stable political system, embodied in its constitution of 1833. In this early period the government was shaped largely by the conservative aristocracy as a republican system with a strong president.

Toward the end of the nineteenth century, several liberal reforms were enacted that introduced a parliamentary-like government that lasted until 1925. Throughout the period, ideological conflicts dominated politics. Conflicts between the Conservative and Liberal Parties were later joined by newly formed parties, which sprang up to represent the emerging middle class. Growing industrialization and urbanization in the early twentieth century created new social cleavages in the country and led to the emergence of a new middle class and working class (mainly miners), which began to exert political pressure and demand social legislation to protect their interests. To give political voice to these rapidly growing groups, new political parties arose, ranging from the Communist Party in 1922 to the Socialist Party in 1933 and the National Falange Party in 1935 (a splinter group of the Conservative Party that became the Christian Democratic Party in the 1950s).

The period 1920–1932 was one of instability and military interventions. A new constitution was promulgated in 1925, embodying the reality of the new social order, but it was not implemented until 1932, when the first of a series of elected governments came to power and ushered in four decades of democratic stability. From the 1930s to 1973 Chileans elected governments from across the political spectrum. In 1973 a military junta took control, and democracy in Chile broke down.

Breakdown of Civilian Rule

The Chilean polity was a restricted democracy until the 1960s. Women did not get the right to vote until the 1950s, and peasants and the urban poor were politically excluded or manipulated until the 1960s. But despite these limits on real political participation, multiple parties—from the extreme right to the extreme left—gave voice to all ideological views. Negotiation among the parties was a necessity, since no party could win a majority on its own. Both these features were crucial for integrating the population into modern society and for reaching agreements on institutional rules of behavior that held the military at bay and kept it from interfering directly in political affairs until 1973.

The relative weakness of civil society compared with political forces allowed considerable autonomy for the political class. Its ideological polarization was tempered until the 1960s by the pragmatism of the Radical Party, which routinely forged alliances with other parties across the political spectrum. Although every political group that aspired to the presidency played by democratic rules and built up political alliances in order to win elections and push through its legislative agenda, there were no incentives for broad, majority-based governing alliances because so much power was in the hands of the president. The outcome was a series of governments that pushed their radical agendas of social change without majoritarian legislative support for their programs. Thus the legitimacy of these democratically elected regimes was weakened at times of crisis.

In the 1960s political participation was extended to peasants and the urban poor, and the party system became more rigid and polarized. An authoritarian right wing unified around the National Party, an ideological center was led by the Christian Democrats, and a radical left wing was formed by the Socialist and Communist Parties. It was commonly believed that capitalist development and social democratization were in conflict with

each other and had reached an impasse. The last attempt to make the two compatible was the "Revolution in Liberty" led by President Eduardo Frei, whose Christian Democratic Party governed from 1964 to 1970, caught between a right-wing opposition that was deeply affected by agrarian reform and a left-wing opposition that criticized these same reforms as merely an attempt to prolong capitalism.

At the end of the 1960s the political class was sharply split between those who favored greater democratization and social integration by reversing the course of capitalist development and those who wanted to strengthen capitalism by reversing the process of social democratization and income redistribution. These two views were represented by the candidates for president in 1970.

On one side, the candidate put forward by the right presented a more authoritarian program. On the other side, the Christian Democrats' candidate favored pressing forward with the social reforms initiated under the Frei government, and the candidate nominated by Popular Unity, a coalition of Socialist, Communist, and other center and leftist groups, stressed anticapitalist measures, social reform, and popular participation, along with continued democratic rule.

Because none of the candidates won an absolute majority of the popular vote, the president was selected by the congress. It elected Salvador Allende, who had the most votes. Allende, a Socialist senator and the Popular Unity coalition's candidate, was sworn in as president in November 1970.

From Military Coup to the Return to Democracy

The escalating political conflict from 1970 to 1973 revealed the polarization of Chilean democracy and led to a crisis of legitimacy. The rightist opposition, with the support of the U.S. government, resorted to both legal and extralegal means to overthrow Allende. The Popular Unity government was unable to create a consensus for its program. The Christian Democrats became trapped in the insurrectional strategy of the right. By the end of 1973 the deepening economic crisis, the antagonism among all political forces, and the institutional crisis of legitimacy combined to create the opportunity for a successful military insurrection.

The military coup of September 11, 1973, began seventeen years of harshly repressive rule by a rightist military regime, led by Gen. Augusto Pinochet. Pinochet attempted to establish a new social order through economic and institutional reform. He imposed a new constitution in 1980 that institutionalized military rule until 1988 and conferred authoritarian power on him. Pinochet's social and political opposition, however, won a constitutionally imposed plebiscite in 1988 by a large margin and paved the way for the return to democracy. This coalition, organized as the Coalition of Parties for Democracy, was composed of centrist forces (mainly the Christian Democrats) and leftist forces (mainly the Socialist Party and a newly formed Party for Democracy). In 1989 the coalition won the presidential election. The elected president, Patricio Aylwin, leader of the Christian Democratic Party, took office in March 1990.

The new democratic government was restricted in its actions by the institutional structure inherited from the military and its constitution of 1980. Aylwin's government focused on political reforms to eliminate the remnants of the former regime and to consolidate its own institutions and legitimacy. It also passed measures to overcome poverty and inequalities and to promote modernization.

The breakdown of Chilean democracy was in large part due to the absence of a majoritarian political coalition that supported democracy and social change. Redemocratization was possible in Chile because a broad social, political, and electoral alliance supported a stable majoritarian government for the first time in the twentieth century. This was the principal lesson learned during the military dictatorship.

See also *Aylwin, Patricio; Frei, Eduardo; Military rule and transition to democracy.*

Manuel Antonio Garretón M.

BIBLIOGRAPHY

Aylwin, Mariana, et al. *Chile en el siglo XX.* Santiago: Editorial Emisión, 1985.

Bethell, Leslie. *Chile since Independence.* Cambridge and New York: Cambridge University Press, 1993.

Drake, Paul, and Iván Jaksic, eds. *The Struggle for Democracy in Chile: 1982–1990.* Lincoln: University of Nebraska Press, 1991.

Garretón, Manuel Antonio. *The Chilean Political Process.* Boston: Unwin and Hyman, 1989.

———. *Una nueva era política: estudio de las democratizaciones.* Santiago: Fondo de Cultura Económica, 1995.

Heise, Julio. *150 años de evolución institucional.* Santiago: Editorial Andrés Bello, 1979.

Loveman, Brian. *Chile: The Legacy of Hispanic Capitalism.* 2d ed. New York: Oxford University Press, 1988.

Tagle, Matías, ed. *La crisis de la democracia en Chile: antecedentes y causas.* Santiago: Editorial Andrés Bello, 1992.

Valenzuela, Arturo. "Chile: Origins, Consolidation, and Breakdown of a Democratic Regime." In *Democracy in Developing Countries: Latin America,* edited by Larry Diamond, Juan J. Linz, and Seymour Martin Lipset. Boulder, Colo.: Lynne Rienner; London: Adamantine Press, 1989.

China

An East Asian nation formally known as the People's Republic of China since the advent of Communist rule in 1949. The Chinese tradition of democracy differs in both concept and form from the Western tradition. Whereas the Western tradition has placed a premium on individual rights, the Chinese tradition has sought harmony between the ruler and the ruled, placing a premium on the welfare of the people and the ability of the people to communicate their needs to the ruler without interference.

China's Confucian Tradition

Within this Confucian tradition, the right—indeed the obligation—of the moral person to remonstrate against corruption and misgovernment is enshrined in the story of Qu Yuan, a government minister of the fourth century B.C. who drowned himself when his entreaties were rejected by his king and disaster ensued. Yet this call to individual conscience was an appeal to the superior person as guardian of the kingly way, not to the articulation of individual, partial interests. Whereas the Western liberal tradition has assumed that a greater good will emerge from the competition of partial interests, the Chinese tradition has assumed harmony between the part and the whole. Just as the Confucian classic the *Great Learning,* written in the third century B.C., locates the basis of universal peace in the superior person's efforts to rectify his heart, the Confucian tradition has sought to harmonize the interests of the people under virtuous rulership.

In the late nineteenth and early twentieth centuries China was still under the sway of the Qing dynasty. Established in the mid-seventeenth century after the Manchu conquest of China, the Qing was suffering from both a demographic revolution and dynastic decline as the West began to assert its demands aggressively in the mid-nineteenth century. Forceful leadership was not forthcoming

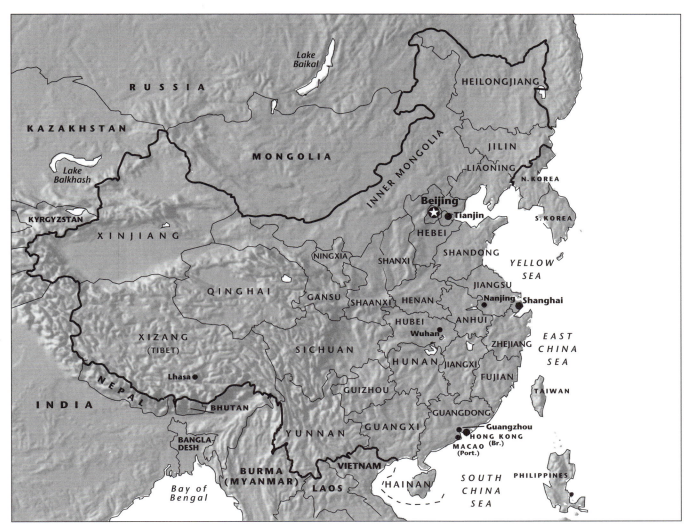

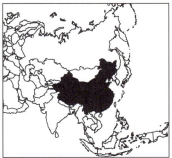

under the rule of the Empress Dowager Cixi, who died in 1908 after dominating Chinese politics for nearly half a century.

As democratic thought from the West began to enter China in the late years of the Qing dynasty, Chinese liberals responded largely within the constraints of their Confucian tradition, with two important exceptions. One was that Chinese liberals firmly located sovereignty in the people, thereby destroying the doctrinal basis of the monarchical system, which was so intertwined with Confucianism that the fall of China's last dynasty largely discredited Confucianism. The other was that Chinese liberals responded to the Western democratic message out of a sense of weakness and vulnerability; hence, nationalism and state building were an inherent part of the democratic enterprise. China had lost a series of wars with the Western powers, had been forced to sign unequal treaties, and appeared under imminent threat of dismemberment. Thus Chinese liberals looked to Western democracy as a key to understanding the source of Western wealth and power; their goal was not to promote individual rights and liberty but to restore Chinese greatness. Whereas Western democracy emerged as a response to absolutism, the modern Chinese democratic tradition looked to democracy as a way to enhance the strength of the state.

The Emergence of Modern Democratic Thought

Modern democratic thought in China emerged in large part as a reaction to China's defeat in the Sino-Japanese war of 1894–1895. This defeat by a nation that China had always regarded as inferior, and that had only begun its own reform efforts some seventeen years earlier, dispelled any illusions that the half measures that China had adopted to strengthen itself in the latter half of the nineteenth century would be sufficient.

The sense of imminent national disaster was captured by Kang Youwei, a brilliant and eccentric interpreter of the Confucian tradition. He organized some 800 of his fellow provincial degree holders, then in Beijing to take the metropolitan exam (the highest level of China's three-tiered traditional examination system), to sign a memorial to the throne demanding that the treaty with Japan be rejected and institutional reforms be implemented immediately. Three years later, in 1898, Kang and his precocious follower Liang Qichao were named advisers to the emperor. From this position they oversaw a radical reform effort aimed at transforming China's traditional monarchical system into a constitutional monarchy complete with a division of power between an executive, a legislature, and a judiciary.

The radical reform program of 1898 lasted only a hundred days before a coup d'état by the Empress Dowager sent Kang and Liang fleeing to Japan. In the ensuing years Liang overtook his mentor and became the undisputed leader of the reform movement. Liang, more than any other single person, defined modern democratic thought in China. He excoriated the monarchy for regarding affairs of state as personal and private; instead, he identified sovereignty as residing in the people. Liang also urged the formation of such institutions as chambers of commerce and scholarly associations to enhance the flow of information between state and society and thereby improve policy formation.

Liang's thought, however, differed significantly from Western democratic ideas and often led him to misunderstand the writings of the Western democratic thinkers he so avidly introduced into China. In particular, Liang never understood one of the basic underpinnings of Western democratic thought—namely, that the pursuit of private, indeed selfish, interests could result in the common good. Such a notion of the "hidden hand"—the idea that the pull and haul of individual interests can result in the greatest good for society—was completely alien to the Chinese tradition, which placed a premium on the harmony of social interests. For a scholar such as Liang, bred in the tradition of the *Great Learning,* interests were to be reconciled on the basis of a higher good, not pursued at the expense of other interests. One searches Liang's work in vain for institutional mechanisms to reconcile divergent interests, for the assumption underlying such a need was simply alien to Liang's mental world.

Constitutionalists and Revolutionaries

If China's modern democratic ideas are inextricably linked with Liang Qichao, democratic practice finds its origins in the Constitutionalist Movement, which was closely linked with Liang. Following the antiforeign Boxer Rebellion of 1900 and the Qing dynasty's subsequent humiliation at the hands of an expeditionary force formed by eight foreign powers, the Empress Dowager finally agreed to a reform program. To win support from increasingly disaffected local gentry, the Qing court in 1905 yielded to pressures to move toward constitutional rule and sent a five-person observation team abroad to study the constitutions of other nations. After the mission returned the following year, the court announced a nine-year program to prepare for constitutional rule. This program included a call for the establishment of provincial assemblies as a first step toward full constitutional rule.

As a result, China held its first elections from February through June 1909. Only those with significant wealth or holders of higher education degrees were eligible to vote—requirements that restricted the electorate to less than one-half of 1 percent of the population. Moreover, the elections were indirect. The electorate chose an electoral college, which in turn elected members of the provincial assemblies.

Despite evidence of indifference and corruption in the election, some of the provincial assemblies boasted highly qualified members, and the assemblies quickly became forums for promoting local interests as well as for demanding more rapid reform and democratization from the Qing court. Since many began to feel that China was in imminent danger of partition, the provincial assemblies organized for joint action. In 1910 representatives from the provincial assemblies organized three petition drives—the last one allegedly collecting 25 million signatures—demanding an early convening of the parliament.

The representatives who made up the provincial assemblies were the last generation of China's traditional gentry. Met by resistance from the court, they turned toward revolution, and their support was one of the major reasons that the Revolution of 1911 succeeded quickly and without social turmoil.

As Liang was charting a reformist path and the Constitutionalist Movement was pushing for a constitutional monarchy, a revolutionary movement that rejected the Qing dynasty as beyond redemption was developing. Sun Yat-sen (Sun Zhangshan) established the Revive China Society in November 1894 to overthrow Manchu imperial rule, restore Chinese rule, and establish a federal republic. By the time Sun joined with other revolutionaries to establish the Chinese United League in 1905, he had formulated the ideas embodied in his famous Three People's Principles—nationalism, democracy (sometimes translated as the "people's rights"), and the people's livelihood.

Sun's revolutionary aspirations met with success in 1911, when the tottering Qing dynasty responded ineptly to a prematurely launched revolutionary uprising in the central Chinese city of Wuchang. Most of the southern provinces, whose disgust with the central government had risen in the course of efforts to promote constitutionalism, responded by declaring their independence from the Qing and supporting the establishment of a republic.

This first effort at republican government was handicapped from the outset by the weakness of the democratic impulse that underlay the revolutionary movement. Anti-Manchu nationalism and local distrust of the corrupt Qing court contributed more to the overthrow of the dynasty than did the demand for democracy. Nevertheless, Sun and many other revolutionaries had been impressed by the combination of national strength and democratic institutions in Western nations, and they hoped that republican institutions would be the key to national strength and prosperity for China. Fear of foreign intervention, divisions within the revolutionary ranks, and the strong showing of northern military leader Yuan Shikai, however, led Sun and the revolutionaries to yield power to Yuan, who became the first president of the new republic.

Chinese hopes for democracy following the revolution thus centered on the reorganization of the United League as an open political party under the name Kuomintang (Guomindang), or Nationalist Party, and the development of an effective parliament to balance Yuan Shikai's authority. Largely through the efforts of Song Jiaoren, a young and articulate advocate of democracy and parliamentary

government, the Kuomintang (KMT) emerged as the dominant party in the elections of 1912.

This optimistic beginning soured quickly, however, as the ambitious Yuan abandoned all pretense to democratic ideals, handily defeated the "Second Revolution" launched in 1913 to oppose him, and finally moved to make himself emperor. Widespread resistance quickly doomed Yuan's efforts as one province after another announced its independence. Yuan's monarchical ambitions collapsed, and he died in June 1916.

Warlordism became Yuan's legacy to China, as military commanders, many of them Yuan's former subordinates, carved out fiefdoms of their own and struggled for control of Beijing, the capital. Warlordism not only destroyed what little remained of constitutionalism but also undermined the belief that democracy could be achieved either quickly or directly through constitutional means. It also fueled the rise of the two revolutionary movements—the Nationalist and the Communist—that would dominate twentieth-century Chinese politics.

The May Fourth Movement

Although the period of warlordism marked the nadir of Chinese political development, it was nevertheless a period of remarkable social and intellectual ferment. In this period, while the West was embroiled in World War I, the Chinese economy expanded rapidly, even as Japanese pressures on China escalated at the same time. Both developments provided the impetus for popular nationalism, while the democratic ideals espoused by U.S. president Woodrow Wilson during World War I ignited hope and idealism among Chinese intellectuals.

Democratic ideals and nationalistic passion came together in the May Fourth demonstration of 1919, which was provoked by the news that the Versailles peace conference at the end of World War I had, contrary to Chinese popular hopes and expectations, awarded Germany's rights in Shandong province to Japan. Outraged students and faculty took to the streets to protest the decision as well as the news that the warlord government had betrayed China's national interests by agreeing to the transfer.

The protest movement that ensued combined the Chinese tradition of remonstration by the scholarly upholders of public morality with mass nationalism and an iconoclastic critique of Chinese tradition based on an ideal of enlightenment. It thus went beyond the visions of Liang

Qichao, who never conceived of politics in anything but elite terms, by linking democratic demands with popular protest and cultural critique. Moreover, the sense of democracy held by many May Fourth intellectuals, especially those who had studied abroad, was more sophisticated than that of Liang Qichao.

Nevertheless, the driving force of the May Fourth Movement was nationalism, a passion that soon led to the revitalization of the Nationalist Party on the one hand and the founding of the Chinese Communist Party (in 1921) on the other. The ideal of enlightenment might in time have led to a more sophisticated understanding of democracy, but it was soon overwhelmed by nationalistic passions.

The Federalist Movement

A brief interlude that has generally received insufficient attention in Western and Chinese literature alike was China's federalist movement of 1920–1923. The federalist movement had its origins in the expansion of local authority in the late Qing period and in efforts to reform or overthrow the Qing. Sun Yat-sen, strongly influenced by the American example, appears to have been the first to advocate federalism, although he later denounced it as undermining nationalism. Participants in the constitutionalist movement, including Liang Qichao and others, looked to federalism as a way of resolving the conflicts between local and central interests. Federalist ideas grew in the aftermath of the 1911 Revolution, particularly in the southern provinces, which hoped to ward off a recentralization of authority in the hands of Yuan Shikai. Federalist ideas waned in the aftermath of the unsuccessful Second Revolution (1913) but revived after the collapse of Yuan's imperial ambitions, his death shortly thereafter, and the emergence of local warlords.

Federalist ideas in China also received a boost from Woodrow Wilson's proposal of a League of Nations and from the visit of John Dewey, the American philosopher of pragmatism, whose ideas bolstered those looking for ways to build democracy from the ground up and realistically address China's problems in a period of warlord division. American freedoms were widely perceived in China to be protected by its federalist system. At the same time, intellectuals looking for ways to end the fighting among warlords began calling for a constitutional convention.

The idealism and political activism unleashed by the May Fourth Movement contributed to this effort to convene a constitutional convention, but as the passions released by the movement began to wane, intellectuals began to look for ways to put their ideas into practice. Some of them turned to federalism. Perhaps no one better exemplified the convergence of these trends than Hu Shi, a May Fourth intellectual luminary and student of John Dewey, who became a strong advocate of federalism.

Federalism grew in opposition to militarism and in support of democracy, but ultimately it fell victim to continued militarism on the one hand and revolution on the other. The first and most important bastion of self-government and federalism was Hunan province, where local generals took advantage of shifts in warlord power to drive out the local warlord and invited prominent intellectuals to draw up a provincial constitution. Promulgated on January 1, 1922, Hunan's constitution was revised and diluted in 1923 and then set aside in 1924 amidst renewed warlord battles.

Other provinces also adopted federalist plans, but the conflict between provincialism, which was a necessary foundation of federalism, and nationalism became clear when Chen Jiongming, the Guangdong warlord who supported federalism and hoped to make Guangdong a model province, rebelled against Sun, driving him from the province. The following year, however, Sun and his followers returned to Guangdong, defeating Chen and establishing their own revolutionary government. When the reorganized Kuomintang held its first congress in January 1924, supporters of provincial autonomy and federalism were scolded as presenting obstacles to national unification. The day of federalism had passed.

The Nationalist Government

Despite the corruption and ineffectiveness of parliamentary politics in the early republic and the deprivations of warlord politics, democracy remained a good word in China's political lexicon as well as one of Sun's Three People's Principles. The failed experiment with democratic politics, however, and the changing international climate (particularly with the Great Depression, which began in 1929, and the rise of authoritarian governments in much of Europe) made many think of democracy as a distant goal. The Kuomintang, reorganized with Soviet assistance in 1923, began to place greater stress on Sun's three-stage program for the realization of democracy: military conquest, political tutelage, and constitutional democracy.

The Kuomintang announced in 1928 that the stage of political tutelage would last six years, but even many supporters of democratic politics soon began to view this goal as unrealistically optimistic.

The drift toward more authoritarian solutions was reinforced by the rise of Chiang Kai-shek (Jiang Jieshi), the former commandant of the Whampoa Military Academy, who had successfully outmaneuvered more senior members of the Kuomintang to become the successor to Sun following Sun's death in 1925. The success of the Kuomintang's Northern Expedition in 1926–1928 nominally reunified the country, although Nationalist authority was initially effective only in five provinces of eastern China. Chiang also faced challenges to his authority from members of the Kuomintang, from warlords who were nominally allied to the KMT, and later from an increasingly effective Communist movement based in the south-central province of Jiangxi. Given these challenges and his own predilection to rely primarily on military force, Chiang turned readily to authoritarian approaches and repeatedly postponed the stage of constitutional democracy.

Influenced by the rise of fascism and militarism in such countries as Germany, Italy, Spain, and Japan, at least some elements of the Kuomintang became quite attracted to fascist doctrines, although the party never developed the fascination with violence that characterized European fascist movements. At a minimum the theories of organic unity between state and society propounded by such movements resonated with Chinese concepts of societal harmony as well as with the needs of the Nationalist government.

Under such conditions, even longstanding proponents of democratic rule seem to have developed doubts about democracy, or at least about its applicability to China. Even Hu Shi, China's leading exponent of Western liberalism, defended democracy with the weak and convoluted argument that China could adopt democracy only because it was not yet ready for enlightened despotism—a form of government that Hu argued required more leaders of knowledge and ability than did democracy.

Given the government's increasing predilection for authoritarian solutions and the liberals' faltering defense of democratic ideals, the demand for democracy fell by default to the leaders of student movements, who repeatedly challenged the authority and authoritarianism of the government. The factor that lent passion and legitimacy to these student movements, however, was not so much the yearning for democracy as it was nationalism. Student movements were expressing the nationalistic feelings of Chinese frustrated by the government's corruption, inefficiency, and unwillingness to resist Japan's increasing encroachments on Chinese territory.

The Communist Movement

At the same time that a factionalized Kuomintang tried to exert effective control over China, the Chinese Communist movement capitalized on local grievances and nationalistic frustrations to build a highly organized and effective political movement. Though driven from their base in Jiangxi to the plains of the far northwest in the mid-1930s, the leaders of the Chinese Communist movement used its organizational abilities and appeals to nationalism to expand rapidly following the outbreak of the Sino-Japanese war in 1937 and the declaration of a second United Front with the Kuomintang.

Although the Communist Party rejected "bourgeois democracy" as a sham, democratic aspirations of a sort were recognized in the party's call for developing a higher level of democracy, one that was more "substantive" than its bourgeois counterpart. Moreover, in the course of the revolutionary movement, the Communists adopted a mobilizing technique known as the "mass line," which tried to combine the demands of a local population with the overall line of the party. At its best, the mass line mitigated the party's ideological rigidity and increased its popular support.

At the same time, the party developed the "unity-struggle-unity" formula for conducting intraparty struggle, an approach that rejected the wholesale use of secret police in purging party dissidents and placed a premium on forging group unity. Finally, in the course of the war years, the Communist Party cooperated with noncommunist forces in the areas it controlled, forming coalition governments through the so-called three-thirds system, in which party members would not occupy more than one-third of the government positions.

At their best, these organizational methods of the Communist Party greatly widened political participation, took into account local realities and divergent views, and forged solidarity both among participants and between the population and the party. In this sense, they marked a radical version of the late Qing and early Republican democratic ideal of a community of interests between state and society that would "awaken the people" on the one hand and make government responsive to the needs of the people on the other. The energies of the people could be mobilized, the state strengthened, and societal unity forged.

Following a devastating eight-year war against Japan, the Nationalist government squared off against a much enlarged Chinese Communist Party. In this fight, the Communists effectively utilized nationalist and democratic appeals, as well as superior organization and military tactics, to gain victory over the Kuomintang. The KMT, increasingly demoralized, collapsed rapidly and fled to Taiwan, as the Communists came to power in 1949.

Because the victory of the Communist Party was total and its dominance over society complete, the new government no longer had to compromise with other sources of power. At the same time, it placed emphasis on what it conceived to be overriding national priorities—strengthening socialist ideology, heavy industry, and national defense. These goals demanded ideological conformity and material sacrifice from the population, however, and thus undermined support for the party.

In 1957 Mao Zedong, chairman of the Chinese Communist Party, led an attempt to recapture the sense of unity between party and society when he launched the ill-fated Hundred Flowers Movement. Calling for the forthright expression of criticisms, Mao soon found himself beset with harsh criticism from China's intellectuals and a burgeoning student movement. The democratic expression of criticism, which resonated with China's longstanding tradition of remonstrance, outraged Mao and other party leaders. The Anti-Rightist campaign that followed sent more than 500,000 intellectuals to the countryside and ended the party's willingness to open itself to societal criticism until after Mao's death. Nevertheless, many of the intellectuals affected by this movement would emerge in the late 1970s and early 1980s as forceful advocates of democratization within the party.

New Pressures for Democracy

Two decades later, in its quest for a more democratic polity, the generation of intellectuals affected by the Anti-Rightist campaign was joined by a new generation of youth whose formative experience was the Cultural Revolution. The Great Proletarian Cultural Revolution (as it was known formally), launched in 1966, was anything but democratic in its inspiration and practice. It did, however, resonate with one longstanding tenet of democratic

thought in China—antibureaucratism. For at least the past century, Chinese democrats had railed against a bureaucracy that stifled popular expression and hindered social mobilization on behalf of a stronger state. The Cultural Revolution unleashed a torrent of idealistic youth, most of whom had absolute faith in Mao and were convinced that he wanted them to break down the bureaucracy that had prevented unity between state and society.

Far from bringing about the utopian society the Red Guards thought they were called upon to build, the Cultural Revolution resulted in rampant factionalism, social chaos, and countless incidents of torture, murder, and suicide. Seeking to restore order, Mao turned to the People's Liberation Army in the summer of 1968. Millions of Red Guards were soon disbanded and sent to the countryside to "learn from the peasants." This action, which many viewed as a betrayal, was followed in 1971 by the report that China's minister of defense, Lin Biao, had died while trying to flee China after an abortive attempt to assassinate Mao. These events forced the once idealistic Cultural Revolution activists to rethink their ideological commitments and their understanding of Chinese politics. Thus did the Red Guard generation of Chinese youth become known as the thinking generation.

This reevaluation of politics marked an important new phase that would provide the shock troops of China's contemporary democratic movement. An important expression of this change can be seen in the famous "Li Yizhe" posters pasted on Guangzhou's city walls. In April 1974 a long essay entitled "What Is to Be Done in Guangdong?"—written under the pseudonym Li Yizhe—argued that only by restoring the democratic rights of the people could China repudiate Lin Biao and prevent a fascist dictatorship from recurring. Later that year another manifesto, on socialist democracy and the legal system, was posted. These protests skillfully skirted the border of permissible policy. While the posting of the original poster had violated party policy (a policy that was soon changed), it also led Zhao Ziyang, then Guangdong's party leader and later the general secretary of China's Communist Party, to consult secretly with the group in an effort to hitch its activities to the goals of the party's moderate faction.

The next major expression of democratic aspirations came in April 1976, when thousands of people took advantage of China's traditional day of mourning to pay honor to the country's recently deceased premier, Zhou Enlai. Mourners posted poems and essays in Beijing's

Tiananmen Square that were sharply critical of the radical faction within the party, later known as the Gang of Four. The April Fifth Movement, as it was called, attracted thousands to Tiananmen Square, but the leaders appear to have been mostly disillusioned Red Guards like those who had participated in the 1974 movement in Guangzhou.

The death of Mao in September 1976 and the subsequent arrest of the Gang of Four ushered in—although not without considerable resistance—a more moderate phase in Chinese politics. In the spring of 1978, Hu Yaobang, who was later to become general secretary of the Communist Party, orchestrated a discussion on "practice as the sole criterion of truth," which was designed to loosen the ideological strictures of the party and pave the way for more pragmatic leaders, led by Deng Xiaoping, to return to power.

In this more relaxed ideological atmosphere, the democracy movement reemerged in the fall of 1978, not long before the party was to convene for a crucial work conference that would precede the historic Third Plenum in December 1978. Posters were pasted on a wall, which soon became known as Democracy Wall, near the heart of Beijing. Democratic activists began exploring heretofore forbidden topics in a variety of new journals. Such journals, while not strictly illegal (until later), circumvented China's publishing laws and opened up a new realm of public discourse.

Again, people inside the party aided people outside the party, the former providing inside information and appropriate themes while the latter provided the pressure of public opinion. Even Deng Xiaoping, in the heady days prior to convening the Third Plenum, declared that the posting of handwritten signs ("big-character posters") was normal and demonstrated the stability of China. However, as some within the democratic movement, most notably Wei Jingsheng, moved beyond the limits set by the regime, and as Deng successfully ousted his major rivals and consolidated power, the party moved first to curtail and then to suppress the movement. The new state constitution adopted in 1982 forbade the display of big-character posters.

As the regime began to pressure the democratic movement, participants frequently were forced to choose whether to work within the regime, sometimes accepting important advisorial jobs, or to remain on the outside. Some democratic activists called for cooperation between reformers within the regime and those on the outside;

Mao Zedong

only thus, they believed, could democratic reform be achieved.

The structure of Chinese politics made that hope impossible to achieve. For instance, Yan Jiaqi, perhaps China's foremost political scientist, comments in his intellectual autobiography that he worked with democracy activists Wang Juntao and Chen Ziming in 1978 but ceased such activities after accepting an invitation to participate in the party's 1979 theory conference. Yan's predicament was understandable; contact with democratic activists outside the party naturally jeopardized the position and influence of reformers working within the party. In addition, many reformers in the party believed that the demands of democratic activists were excessive and that democracy in China could come only from the top down.

Calls for Democracy in the 1980s and 1990s

In the mid- and late 1980s demands for democracy in both the party and society reemerged with unprecedented

On June 4, 1989, after the Chinese army recaptured Tiananmen Square from protesters, a Peking citizen resisted by standing in front of a convoy of tanks. The tanks did not slow down but turned around him, and he was not injured.

force. Some party intellectuals tried to reinterpret Marxism in terms of humanism, while others began exploring democratic theory and institutions. At the same time, reforms released societal expectations and anxieties and stimulated a new generation of students to take the lead in demanding more freedoms. In the fall of 1985 students took to the streets to protest what they saw as Japan's economic invasion of China. The following year a student movement started in the east-central province of Anhui and quickly spread to other locations, including Shanghai, where more than 50,000 students took to the streets. In the ensuing crackdown, Hu Yaobang was removed from the nation's top party position and three prominent intellectuals—Fang Lizhi, Liu Binyan, and Wang Ruowang—were ousted from the party and criticized in a campaign as exemplars of bourgeois liberalization.

Such movements proved to be a prelude to the much larger protest movement of 1989, which had its origins in the confluence of many factors: rising expectations and frustration over rising costs, corruption, and fears of layoffs; a clash of generations with widely varying views of China's achievements and prospects; and elite conflict that pitted different visions of economic, social, and political development against each other. Although the movement demanded democracy, the content of its demands differed

significantly from the aims of the democratic movements in Eastern Europe and elsewhere as well as from Western, particularly American, understandings of democracy. Students demanded that the regime recognize an independent, autonomous student organization and hold a dialogue on an equal basis with the student leaders. Such demands were difficult to accept explicitly, since they challenged the Communist Party's monopoly over political affairs and social organization.

In keeping with China's democratic tradition, the 1989 movement protested the corruption and bureaucracy that made the regime unresponsive to public opinion, rather than pushing demands for individual rights, which are usually seen as the basis for Western democracy. Moreover, the continuing force of China's tradition of moral remonstrance was palpable in the movement's use of moral symbols to present its demands. For instance, during the memorial service for deceased party chief Hu Yaobang, three students knelt for hours on the steps of the Great Hall of the People, waiting for one of the leaders to come out. (No one ever did.)

Critics of the students have pointed out that their unwillingness to compromise mirrored the government's own intransigence. For about a month, moderates on both sides searched for a way out, but various factors prolonged the protests: the glare of international media, the prospect of Soviet leader Mikhail Gorbachev's visit (on May 15, a month after the protests started), and severe division within the Communist Party. As the protests continued and even escalated, prospects for compromise dimmed. Students demanded explicit concessions from the government, while the government saw the movement as a challenge to its very existence. Finally, martial law was declared on May 20. On the night of June 3–4 the People's Liberation Army shot its way into the center of the city to recover Tiananmen Square, the site of mass demonstrations, killing hundreds.

The demand for democracy has been a constant element of modern China's effort to reconcile its traditions, its national aspirations, and its hopes for a government that truly serves the people. Chinese society, however, has been reluctant to recognize a genuinely private sphere, the force of law, and the legitimacy of interest group politics. Moreover, China's traditional political culture has depicted political power as monistic, unified, and indivisible. This conception has been reinforced continuously throughout modern Chinese history; most recently it contributed to the tragedy of Tiananmen. To date, this

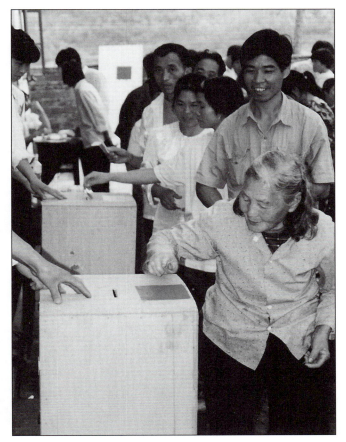

An elderly woman from a village in Fujian Province casts her first vote in 1994. Local elections began to make a comeback in the early 1990s after being suppressed following the 1989 democracy movement.

tradition has prevented the emergence of the type of politics of compromise necessary for democratic governance.

Some speculate that the societal changes currently under way—the growing strength of the provinces, the country's increasing economic and social diversity, and the increasing wealth and educational levels of many areas, especially in the east and southeast—will bring new pressures for democracy. These tendencies have been reinforced by the increasing integration of Hong Kong's economy and society with that of south China, a trend that will only increase with the return of Hong Kong to China in 1997. In addition, the efforts of other Confucian societies, particularly South Korea and Taiwan, to pioneer democratic transformations are certain to influence China. At the same time, however, other social issues and changes—the migration of peasants into cities, questions of law and order, the decline of state-owned enterprises,

and the threat to Beijing's authority—are generating antidemocratic pressures.

Ultimately, the question is whether China's political traditions can be reconciled with democratic governance. Although the demand for democracy has been a major force throughout the twentieth century, even those demanding democracy have generally placed greater stress on unity between state and society, strong and effective rule, and antibureaucratism than on such requisites for democratic rule as institutionalization, procedure, law, division of power, and the willingness to compromise.

See also *Confucianism; Dewey, John; May Fourth Movement; Sun Yat-sen; Taiwan; Three People's Principles.*

Joseph Fewsmith

BIBLIOGRAPHY

Chan, Anita, Stanley Rosen, and Jonathan Unger, eds. *On Socialist Democracy and the Chinese Legal System: The Li Yizhe Debates.* Armonk, N.Y.: M. E. Sharpe, 1985.

Chang, Carson. *The Third Force in China.* New York: Bookman Associates, 1952.

Chesneaux, Jean. "The Federalist Movement in China, 1920–23." In *Modern China's Search for a Political Form,* edited by Jack Gray. London and New York: Oxford University Press, 1969.

Des Forges, Roger V., Ning Luo, and Wu Yen-bo, eds. *Chinese Democracy and the Crisis of 1989: Chinese and American Reflections.* Albany: State University of New York Press, 1993.

Eastman, Lloyd. *The Abortive Revolution: China under Nationalist Rule, 1927–1937.* Cambridge, Mass., and London: Harvard University Press, 1974.

Goldman, Merle. *China's Intellectuals: Advise and Dissent.* Cambridge, Mass., and London: Harvard University Press, 1981.

Grieder, Jerome B. *Intellectuals and the State in Modern China.* New York: Free Press, 1981.

Hsu, Immanuel C. Y. *The Rise of Modern China.* 4th ed. Oxford and New York: Oxford University Press, 1990.

Liew, K. S. *Struggle for Democracy: Sung Chiao-jen and the 1911 Chinese Revolution.* Canberra: Australian National University Press, 1971.

Nathan, Andrew J. *Chinese Democracy.* New York: Knopf, 1985; London: I. B. Tauris, 1986.

Seymour, James D., ed. *The Fifth Modernization: China's Human Rights Movement, 1978–1979.* Stanfordville, N.Y.: Earl M. Coleman, 1980.

Tsou, Tang. "The Tragedy of Tiananmen." In *Contemporary Chinese Politics in Historical Perspective,* edited by Brantly Womack. Cambridge: Cambridge University Press, 1991.

Womack, Brantly. "In Search of Democracy: Public Authority and Popular Power in China." In *Contemporary Chinese Politics in Historical Perspective,* edited by Brantly Womack. Cambridge: Cambridge University Press, 1991.

Yan, Jiaqi. *Toward a Democratic China: The Intellectual Autobiography of Yan Jiaqi.* Translated by David S. K. Hong and Denis C. Mair. Honolulu: University of Hawaii Press, 1992.

Christian democracy

The political philosophy, and the movements and parties based upon it, that derives its belief in democracy and human rights from the principles of Christianity. Although Christian democracy is a worldwide movement, its greatest influence is in Europe and Latin America, especially but not exclusively in Roman Catholic countries.

European Origins of the Movement

Christian democratic parties and movements (trade unions, employers organizations, youth groups, and so forth) trace their ideological origins to the responses of Catholics in Italy, Germany, and France to nineteenth-century liberalism, nationalism, and socialism. Liberalism in France and Italy had a strongly anticlerical strain, attacking the prerogatives of the Catholic Church in areas such as education, marriage, and official state recognition. In Italy liberals opposed the existence of the Papal States as an obstacle to Italian unification. German unification was carried out in 1871 under the auspices of a Protestant state, Prussia. Otto von Bismarck, the German chancellor, initiated the *Kulturkampf,* a campaign against Catholicism, which forced Catholics to unite to defend the church. In all three countries socialist movements made inroads among the working classes, appealing to Marxist doctrines of dialectical materialism that were hostile to religion.

The Vatican at first condemned the doctrines of liberal democracy in such documents as *The Syllabus of Errors* (1864) of Pope Pius IX. Some French Catholic clergymen, for example, Felicité de Lamennais, however, argued for universal suffrage and liberal freedoms, decentralization of political authority, and separation of church and state as most appropriate for modern conditions. Lamennais's views and his newspaper, *L'Avenir,* were condemned by the papacy. A few Catholic political leaders, such as Count Charles de Montalembert, continued to articulate his views, although most French Catholics in the nineteenth century favored monarchy and state support for Catholicism. In early twentieth-century France, similar views were put forward by Marc Sangnier, founder of *Le Sillon,* a youth movement with Christian democratic views. The movement was dissolved by the hierarchy in 1910. It was only with the founding of the Popular Democratic Party in the 1930s that French Christian democracy received organizational expression. After World War II, the leaders of the Popular Democratic Party helped to create the Christian democratic Popular Republican Movement, one of the most important parties of the postwar Fourth Republic.

In Germany the most influential nineteenth-century representative of Christian democratic thinking was Wilhelm von Ketteler, the bishop of Mainz. In his sermons and writings Ketteler criticized liberalism for reducing labor to a commodity and ignoring the social responsibilities of property. He also attacked socialism for placing too much power in the state and ignoring the advantages of widespread distribution of property. Calling for the formation of cooperatives and workers associations, Ketteler urged Catholics to give special attention to the problems of the working class. In response to Bismarck's *Kulturkampf,* Catholics organized the Center Party, which was intended to be interconfessional but in fact was almost wholly Catholic. The Center Party took up Ketteler's social program and added a defense of democracy. It became a major party, with ninety to a hundred seats in the legislature (the Reichstag) from 1874 until Hitler's accession to power in 1933.

In Italy the seizure of the Papal States and the occupation of Rome in 1871 led Pope Pius IX to withdraw into the Vatican palace and to forbid Catholics to participate in Italian politics. His successor, Leo XIII (1878–1903), recognized in his encyclical *Immortale Dei* (1885) that democracy could be a legitimate form of government, but he continued to insist on the desirability of the recognition of Catholicism as the state religion. Leo's principal contribution to Christian democratic thought was his encyclical *Rerum Novarum* (1891), which criticized both liberalism and socialism and endorsed the rights of workers to organize—preferably in Catholic trade unions.

The ban on Catholic political participation in Italian politics was lifted only in 1918. Luigi Sturzo, a priest and political activist, then founded the Popular Party, which had considerable electoral success until it was dissolved by the Vatican; Sturzo went into exile in 1924 after Benito Mussolini's triumph. Like its French counterpart, the Popular Party prepared the ideological terrain for the emergence of the Italian Christian Democratic Party after World War II.

Pope Pius XI (1922–1939) reinforced the tradition of Catholic social thought with the publication of *Quadragesimo Anno* (1931). The encyclical repeated the criticism made by Leo XIII of liberal individualism and socialist collectivism and confirmed Leo's endorsement of the right of workers to organize. Its most influential passage was the pope's argument for the principle of subsidiarity, which called for the state to decentralize social functions and to promote lower-level associations such as the family, professional groups, and local governing bodies. The pope did not endorse democracy as such, however; he seemed to prefer a decentralized corporate state as a middle way between liberalism and socialism. He attacked both socialism and capitalism as economic systems, criticizing the latter for promoting the "international imperialism of money" and the former for contradicting Christian principles.

Jacques Maritain and Postwar Europe

The single writer who did most to articulate the principles of Christian democracy was the French Catholic philosopher, Jacques Maritain (1882–1973). Maritain was already well known for his writings on the philosophy of Thomas Aquinas when he began to write on political thought in the late 1920s. His best-known works on the subject, *Integral Humanism* (1936), *Christianity and Democracy* (1942), *The Rights of Man and the Natural Law* (1943), and *Man and the State* (1951), advocate what he called a personalist, communitarian, and pluralist political and social philosophy, which is grounded in the basic principles of Christianity as the soundest foundation for human freedom.

The personalist conception of human nature, Maritain argued, is based on a view of the human person that is superior to the individualism of liberalism and the collectivism of socialism. The communitarian and pluralist aspects of his thought support the promotion of a multiplicity of human associations and organized groups ranging from the family to the world community. Democracy is the political structure most in keeping with human dignity and freedom, and it is more likely than other forms of government to promote the temporal common good. That common good includes religious pluralism and governmental neutrality toward the various creeds held by the citizens, as well as freedom of thought, expression, and assembly, which are a reflection of the God-given freedom with which human beings are endowed. Following Aristotle and Thomas Aquinas, Maritain argued that private property is a natural right but subject to social obligations.

Maritain's wartime writings on politics from exile in New York were translated into many languages and in the immediate postwar period were a source of inspiration for the newly emerging Christian democratic parties of Europe. These parties were instrumental in creating and supporting democracy in Europe after the war.

In France, Catholic members of the Resistance, some of them former adherents of the Popular Democratic Party, formed the Popular Republican Movement (MRP), which for a time received the most votes of any French party. The MRP supported Charles de Gaulle until he withdrew from politics in 1946. It continued to participate in Fourth Republic politics, providing continuity to the Foreign Ministry, which under the guidance of MRP members Robert Schuman and Georges Bidault promoted European unification and Franco-German cooperation. De Gaulle's reentry into French politics in 1951 at the head of his own movement weakened the Popular Republican Movement by cutting into its voting base. This erosion continued into the Fifth Republic after 1958, leading finally to the party's dissolution in 1969. Today the Democratic and Social Center, a small group loosely identified with the center right, continues to represent the Christian democratic tradition.

In Italy the Christian Democratic Party was the principal governing party from the end of World War II until 1994. Like many Christian democratic parties, the party drew its support from practicing Catholics, women, intellectuals, the peasantry in the South, and organized workers in the North. Alcide De Gasperi, its most important leader, was prime minister from 1945 until 1953. The party's powerful electoral organization received significant support in the 1940s from the Roman Catholic Church, which considered it best able to oppose the Italian Communist Party, the largest in Western Europe. De Gasperi's government was followed by more than thirty other governments headed by Christian Democrats. In addition, half the Italian presidents and most of the heads of the Chamber of Deputies and the Senate have been Christian Democrats. The close links between the party and the church were weakened in the 1970s and 1980s, although the party supported the Vatican in its opposition to divorce and abortion—positions that were defeated in referendums in 1974 and 1981. After revelations in 1993 of massive corruption involving its leaders, the party was reorganized and rechristened itself the Italian Popular Party, recalling its predecessor of the 1920s.

In Germany the Christian Democratic Party became, along with the Social Democrats, one of the mainstays of postwar German politics. Although some of its leaders, notably Chancellor Konrad Adenauer, had been affiliated with the Catholic Center in the days of the Weimar Republic (1919–1933), it also has had significant Protestant participation and leadership. Among its Protestant leaders was Ludwig Erhard, the architect of the German "economic miracle" in the late 1940s. It was Erhard who coined the term "social market economy" to describe the mixture of capitalist economics and governmental social welfare programs that characterized the Bonn Republic. Adenauer, though at first critical of capitalism, soon abandoned the search for a third position in economics (just as the Social Democrats discarded their belief in social—that is, state—ownership of the means of production). Adenauer's ardent Europeanism was related to his Christian Democratic ideology, as was his support for *Mitbestimmungsrecht,* the legal guarantee of worker representation on the boards of directors of medium and large enterprises. The German Christian Democrats have led most of the governments of postwar Germany, although the Social Democrats have also governed for a time.

Significant Christian democratic parties also exist in Austria, Belgium, Holland, and Luxembourg. Like those in France, Italy, and Germany, they are descendants of earlier parties organized to defend the church. These parties now see themselves as nonconfessional but Christian-inspired defenders of democracy, human rights, and social welfare; they advocate a mixed but basically capitalist economy and European integration.

With the fall of communism in 1989, Christian democratic parties appeared in Russia and several Eastern European countries, notably in the Czech Republic, Hungary, and Slovakia. After the reunification of Germany the Christian Democrats secured significant electoral support in the former German Democratic Republic, thus enlarging the Protestant presence in the German party.

The Christian Democrats, formally organized as the Popular Parties of Europe, have formed the largest voting bloc in the European Parliament at Strasbourg. An international trade union of Christian democratic orientation, headquartered in Brussels, has changed its name from the International Federation of Christian Trade Unions to the World Confederation of Labor, but it continues with the same membership. There is also a world organization of Christian democratic parties, as well as an international Christian employers association.

Latin America and Developing Nations

Small parties of Christian democratic orientation and a continentwide organization were founded in the 1940s in Latin America, but Christian democracy did not become a significant force there until the late 1950s. In 1958 the Social Christian Party in Venezuela, led by Rafael Caldera, joined the social democratic Democratic Action Party to form a democratic government following the overthrow of the dictator, Marcos Pérez Jiménez. In the same year in Chile, the Falange, a small party founded in 1935 by reformist Catholic students, fused with the Social Christian wing of the Conservative Party to form the Christian Democratic Party of Chile and to run its leader, Eduardo Frei, as a presidential candidate. Both Caldera and Frei had been active in Catholic student movements in the 1930s, and Frei had been strongly influenced by Maritain during a visit to Europe in 1934. (Maritain had also lectured in Rio de Janeiro and Buenos Aires in 1936, and his *Letter on Independence,* calling for the creation of democratic movements of Christian inspiration that transcended the divisions of left and right, had been widely distributed and reprinted at that time.)

By the early 1960s Christian democratic parties were becoming active throughout the continent, but the largest and most significant ones were those in Venezuela and Chile. In the 1980s Christian democratic parties also won elections in El Salvador, Costa Rica, and Guatemala.

The Latin American parties shared their European counterparts' commitment to democracy and human rights as well as their interest in Maritain's political writings. They organized seminars, think tanks, and institutes on Christian democratic thought, and promoted contact among the Latin American and European parties. Some received financial support from the German Christian Democratic Party. The Christian democratic parties in Latin America offered a reformist alternative to the Marxist left; along with the social democratic parties, they were viewed favorably by the Alliance for Progress, sponsored by the United States. In the economic arena, they generally took a position to the left of the Europeans, particularly in their support for agrarian reform (citing Catholic teaching on the social function of property) and greater control over national mineral resources (copper in Chile, petroleum in Venezuela).

In the 1970s, a decade in which military rule and repression prevailed in many Latin American countries, Christian democratic leaders organized and led human rights movements. After the return of democracy in the middle and late 1980s, Christian democrats endorsed the market as the most efficient allocator of resources, but they continued to support social welfare legislation in the areas of health, education, housing, and job training, and they criticized the continentwide movement to laissez-faire economics. Like their counterparts in Europe, they favored economic integration; now they sought to include the entire hemisphere rather than only Latin America, as they had done in the 1960s.

Nascent Christian democratic movements have emerged in other developing nations with large Catholic populations, such as Uganda and the Philippines. The principal Christian democratic parties, however, are in Europe and Latin America.

The Future: From Mystique to Politique

The Christian democratic movement began as a protest against liberalism, socialism, and nationalism. Its proponents argued that the Christian tradition supported a middle position that was superior to liberalism in its concern for the working classes and the poor, to socialism in its emphasis on the "subsidiary" role of the state and in promoting intermediate groups, and to nationalism in encouraging wider international affiliations. Particularly in areas where Catholic culture and educational institutions dominated, this movement appealed to students and intellectuals as a creative response to modernity that still maintained links with Western religious and philosophical traditions. Where there were political openings on the center right and center left after World War II in Europe and in Latin America, Christian democracy often provided the ideological and organizational basis for significant mass parties that were committed to democracy, pluralism, and human rights.

With the opening of the Catholic subculture to other religious and philosophical currents after the Second Vatican Council (1962–1965), and with increasing secularization and a decline in religious belief and practice, Christian democracy's idealistic component has diminished. Once in power, Christian democratic parties have not been able to deliver on their promises to establish an alternative to contemporary capitalism and the welfare state; however, they have promoted worker organization, family legislation, regional decentralization, and broader economic and political groupings beyond the nation-state. In many countries in Europe and Latin America, they have helped to bring democratic stability and have counteracted extremism of the left and the right. Where authoritarian governments have emerged, Christian democrats have been stalwart defenders of democracy and human rights.

The leaders and activists of the Christian democratic parties today do not confront the same threats that earlier leaders encountered, but those who ground their commitment to democracy and human rights in the Christian tradition continue to provide important support for free government in the contemporary world.

See also *Adenauer, Konrad; Catholicism, Roman; De Gasperi, Alcide; Frei, Eduardo; Maritain, Jacques; Reformation.*

Paul E. Sigmund

BIBLIOGRAPHY

Einaudi, Mario, and François Goguel. *Christian Democracy in Italy and France.* Notre Dame, Ind.: University of Notre Dame Press, 1952.

Fogarty, Michael P. *Christian Democracy in Western Europe, 1820–1953.* Notre Dame, Ind.: University of Notre Dame Press, 1957.

Herman, Donald L. *Christian Democracy in Venezuela.* Chapel Hill: University of North Carolina Press, 1980.

Leonardi, Robert, and Douglas Wertman. *Italian Christian Democracy.* London: Macmillan; New York: St. Martin's, 1989.

Lynch, Edward A. *Latin America's Christian Democratic Parties.* Westport, Conn.: Praeger, 1993.

Maritain, Jacques. *Man and the State.* Chicago: University of Chicago Press, 1951.

Williams, Edward J. *Latin American Christian Democratic Parties.* Knoxville: University of Tennessee Press, 1967.

Churchill, Winston

Prime minister of Great Britain during and after World War II. As prime minister, Winston Leonard Spencer Churchill (1874–1965) led Great Britain from the dark hours of 1940, when it was the only major country fighting Nazi Germany, to triumph in 1945. His career as a member of Parliament began in 1900 and ended in 1964. In that time Britain moved from government by an elected aristocratic oligarchy to government by popularly elected politicians promoting the mixed-economy welfare state. As the grandson of a duke and an early proponent of welfare-state measures, Churchill was himself a transitional figure. He supported reform when young but turned conservative later. Knighted in 1953, he was thereafter known as Sir Winston Churchill.

Winston Churchill

In the spring of 1940 the armies of Adolf Hitler conquered Western Europe. The collapse of France brought German troops to the English Channel; from there it was a short bombing run to London and industrial cities. The United States and the Soviet Union were both neutral, and the British defense forces were much less prepared than the forces of the German blitzkrieg. The British had two choices: to negotiate peace with Hitler, as the French government had done, or to continue the war.

In May 1940 Churchill became prime minister. He had been warning the British of the military threat of Nazi Germany for years. Known as a great orator, he made one of his best-known speeches, telling the House of Commons, "I have nothing to offer but blood, toil, tears and sweat."

World War II was a total war for Britain, in which everyone was subject to rationing and conscription for the war effort and everyone was vulnerable to bombing. Fighting the war required massive popular support under conditions of hardship and danger. Churchill was superb in inspiring civilian morale. A former soldier and defense minister, he was adept at managing competing claims for scarce resources from the army, navy, and air force. He was also a diplomat, cultivating material support from U.S. president Franklin Delano Roosevelt before the United States became a belligerent nation in December 1941. Although no one individual or country can claim credit for victory, Churchill undoubtedly made a unique contribution to the downfall of the Nazi regime, which threatened to replace democracy with totalitarianism as the prevailing form of government in Europe.

Churchill's peacetime career was erratic. He was elected to the House of Commons in 1900 as a Conservative. By 1904 he had switched to the Liberal Party and was an active member of the Liberal government, which from 1906 to 1914 laid foundations for the British welfare state. By 1924 he was once again a Conservative cabinet minister, advocating economic policies so far to the right that the liberal economist John Maynard Keynes wrote a famous pamphlet decrying the economic consequences of Churchill's policies. In the 1930s his imperialist opposition to self-government in India prevented him from gaining office in Conservative governments.

The British electorate discriminated between Churchill as a national leader in wartime and as a party leader in peacetime. In a general election held two months after victory in Europe in 1945, the Churchill-led Conservative Party was resoundingly defeated by the Labour Party, which promised to promote social democratic reforms. In 1950 the Conservatives were again defeated. Churchill used the time in opposition to warn against the dangers to democracy in Europe arising from an iron curtain imposed by the Soviet Union. He returned as prime minister in 1951 but soon began to suffer health problems that led to his retirement in 1955.

See also *Commonwealth, British; United Kingdom; World War II.*

Richard Rose

BIBLIOGRAPHY

Churchill, Winston. *The Second World War.* London: Cassell, 1948.

Kavanagh, Dennis. *Crisis, Charisma, and British Political Leadership: Winston Churchill as the Outsider.* Beverly Hills, Calif.: Sage Publications, 1975.

racy, or oligarchy) and praises the liberty characteristic of the regime in which no power is greater than the people. He distinguishes between regimes in which the people choose their leaders and those, like Athens, where the people themselves hold political office. He praises the former. In aristocracies and in kingships the people will be ruled by the "better" or more virtuous and will benefit when their concerns are addressed by those most capable of attending to their interests.

Of the three regimes, Cicero favors the kingship of the most virtuous man, but he argues against any pure regime. Instead, a mixed regime provides security against the injustice of one man, the arrogance of the few, and, quoting from Plato's *Republic,* the unbridled power of the many found in democracies. The best model for the stable mixed regime appears in the Roman Republic of the second century B.C.

In *De legibus,* Cicero tries to balance tendencies toward both democracy and aristocracy by proposing laws that would moderate the excesses of too much power among the people. Although eager to retain the institutions that gave Rome its democratic aspects, Cicero worried about democracy's potential for corruption and disorder. The virtuous are by nature obliged to provide leadership for the state, which will benefit by accepting their rule.

See also *Classical Greece and Rome.*

Arlene W. Saxonhouse

Cicero, Marcus Tullius

Statesman, orator, and writer during the late Roman Republic. Cicero (106–43 B.C.) overcame the traditional boundaries that reserved high political office to patricians. In 63 B.C. he became the first nonaristocrat in thirty years to attain the highest political office in the Roman Republic, the office of consul. While consul, he successfully defended Rome from conspiracy, but he may have acted illegally by condemning the conspirators to death. This action limited his subsequent involvement in politics, though after Julius Caesar was assassinated in 44 B.C., Cicero eloquently warned against Mark Antony's designs on the republic. When Antony came to power, he arranged for Cicero's assassination.

While removed from active public life, Cicero drew on Plato's primary political works to write his own *De republica* and *De legibis* (on laws). Cicero did not favor a widespread democratic regime. In *De republica,* he asks which is the best form of government (monarchy, aristoc-

Citizenship

The condition of being a citizen and the responsibilities and rights this status entails. Citizenship is a key notion in democratic thought and practice. Citizens are full and equal members of a democratic political community; their identity is shaped by the rights and obligations that define that community. There are many different interpretations of the nature of citizenship, and disputes over those interpretations have played an important part in the evolution of democracy.

Ancient and Classical Citizenship

Emerging jointly with the democracy of the Greek city-states, the notion of citizenship derives from the classical

Greco-Roman concept of the self-governing political community. Ancient citizenship implied equality in rights and obligations before the law and active political participation. To be a citizen was to be capable of governing and being governed. In the Greek democratic city-states, however, citizenship was restricted to free, native-born men, which meant that citizens constituted a minority of the population, even in Athens. Their participation in public life was made possible by the existence of slaves, who were responsible for performing the principal economic functions.

During the Roman Empire the extension of citizenship first to lower classes and then to conquered foreigners produced a much more heterogeneous group of citizens. The term began to refer more to equal protection under the law than to active participation in the making and implementing of laws. Initially, the assertion of a political identity indicating allegiance to and active participation in a political community, citizenship came to signify a particular legal and juridical status. At the height of the Roman Empire the emperor Caracalla issued an edict (A.D. 212) granting citizenship to the great majority of Rome's male subjects; only the very lowest classes were excluded.

After a long eclipse during the Middle Ages, Greek and Roman notions of republicanism and citizenship were revived in the city-states of the Italian Renaissance. In the sixteenth century Niccolò Machiavelli, especially in his *Discourses on Livy,* championed a concept of politics generally referred to as "civic republicanism" or "civic humanism," the main tenet of which is that human potential can be realized only if one is a citizen of a free and self-governing political community. Machiavelli's ideas acquired an English pedigree when they were reformulated and reasserted by John Milton and others during the constitutional revolution of the seventeenth century. By synthesizing Aristotelian and Machiavellian elements, the English version of civic republicanism provided a political language organized around the notions of the common good, civic virtue, and corruption.

That language later traveled to the New World, where it played an important role in the revolutions in North America and Latin America. Several historians have contested the idea that the American Revolution represented a rupture with the old world inspired principally by the ideas of the English philosopher John Locke. These historians stress the centrality of the idea of "corruption" in the vocabulary of the American patriots, an idea profoundly influenced by the culture and theory of civic humanism.

The ideal of citizenship, however, found its culmination in the French Revolution with the Declaration of the Rights of Man and the Citizen (1789). In *The Social Contract* (1762), Jean-Jacques Rousseau established the basis for the modern concept of the role of citizen by connecting it to the theory of consent. The citizen, in Rousseau's view, is a free and autonomous individual entitled to participate in making decisions that all are required to obey. This concept of citizenship draws both on the classical tradition and on modern contractualism by linking the republican concept of the political community with the premises of individualism. Writing in the context of an emerging commercial society, Rousseau was aware of the tension between the common good and private interests and considered that tension to be the main threat to the well-being of the body politic. To be a true republican citizen, Rousseau believed, was to place the common good before one's individual self-interest.

Modern Citizenship

With the development of market relations and the growing influence of liberalism during the nineteenth century, the republican concept of the active citizen was gradually displaced by another view expressed in the language of natural rights. The classical concept of politics, in which individuals participate actively in the *res publica,* was replaced by a new paradigm in which people were no longer thought to be connected by their common identity as citizens but were regarded as individuals with conflicting interests. The insistence on public virtue and the common good disappeared. As direct democracy was rejected in favor of representative democracy, liberal writers came to view the idea of political participation in a community of equals as a relic of the past. They argued that in order to defend the "liberties of the moderns" it was necessary to renounce the "liberties of the ancients."

Although it took time to overcome many forms of discrimination, liberalism undeniably contributed to the idea of universal citizenship based on the argument that all individuals are born formally free and equal. However, it also reduced this condition to a mere legal status, based on the possession of individual rights against arbitrary actions by the state. How those rights are exercised is irrelevant as long as citizens do not break the law or interfere with the rights of others. In such a view, cooperation is justified to the extent that it promotes individual prosperity, not by its contribution to the common good.

Citizenship and Rights

The notion of citizenship that became prevalent in the nineteenth century should be understood as the set of rights and obligations that defines the relationship between nation-states and their individual members. Its origins are clearly Western, but its principles have now been adopted by many other societies.

According to T. H. Marshall's celebrated model of citizenship, civil rights developed first in the eighteenth century. The rights in question were freedom of speech, right to a fair trial, and equal access to the legal system. At the time, many people were refused those rights on grounds of class, gender, race, and other factors. During the nineteenth century, as an outcome of working-class struggles for political equality, important advances in political rights provided wider access to the electoral process. In the twentieth century the idea of "social rights" emerged. These involved access to an expanding set of public benefits provided by the state in such fields as health, education, insurance, and retirement benefits. With the creation of the welfare state following World War II, citizens became "entitled" to social security payments in periods of unemployment, sickness, and distress. In Marshall's view, the expansion of citizenship served to contain the socially divisive effects of class conflict and to limit the social and economic inequalities generated by capitalism. He considered that a necessary tension existed between capitalism and its class system, on the one hand, and citizenship as a status involving a fundamental equality of rights, on the other.

Although influential in the work of American sociologists such as Talcott Parsons, Reinhard Bendix, and Seymour Martin Lipset, Marshall's account of citizenship has been criticized for its ethnocentric assumptions and evolutionary bias. Michael Mann has argued that Marshall's argument applies only to Great Britain and is inappropriate for other societies. Bryan Turner faults Marshall's failure to recognize the extent to which the growth of social citizenship had been the outcome of struggles that brought the state into the social arena as a stabilizer of the social system. Turner also stresses the shortcomings of approaching citizenship exclusively in terms of class relations. An adequate theory of citizenship, he argues, should

not overlook the violent "modernization" of aboriginal communities that has accompanied the development of citizenship in countries like the United States, Canada, and Australia.

Liberal Versus Communitarian Citizenship

Thinkers have also debated the question of what type of democracy best corresponds to the exercise of citizenship. A school of "communitarians" emerged in the 1970s to denounce the individualistic bias of the liberal understanding of citizenship dominant in Western democracies. In their view, liberal individualism has eroded social cohesion in those societies; the rejection of notions like the common good and civic virtue in liberal thought has destroyed feelings of common purpose and obligation as well as community values.

Whether individual rights can exist independently, without reference to the community, is a question that lies at the heart of the controversy between communitarians and liberals. John Rawls, in *A Theory of Justice* (1971), describes the citizen in terms of equal rights. Once citizens see themselves as free and equal persons, they should recognize that if they are to pursue their different concepts of the good, they will need the same primary goods—that is, the same basic rights, liberties, and opportunities, the same means (wealth), and the same social bases of self-respect. According to that liberal view, citizenship is the capacity of persons to form, revise, and rationally pursue their personal definition of the good. Citizens use their rights to promote their self-interest within certain constraints, notably respect for the rights of others.

Communitarians object that Rawls's formulation precludes the notion that it is natural for the citizen to join in common action with others to pursue the common good. The communitarian alternative, which rests on the revival of civic republicanism, strongly emphasizes the notion of a public good that exists prior to and independent of individual desires and interests. Advocating a more participatory form of democracy, communitarians define democratic citizenship as active participation in a political community unified by shared values and respect for the common good.

Liberals retort that communitarianism is incompatible with the pluralism of modern democracy. To them, assumptions about the common good have totalitarian implications. It is not possible to combine modern democratic institutions with the same sense of singular purpose that premodern societies enjoyed. Citizenship as active political participation is antithetical to the contemporary idea of liberty understood as the absence of coercion.

Quentin Skinner, a leading British political theorist, denies that there is a basic incompatibility between the classical republican concept of citizenship and modern democracy. Several forms of republican thought—for instance, that of Machiavelli—conceived of liberty in terms of the absence of coercion or oppression but also included political participation and civic virtue. In such thought, liberty is seen as the absence of impediments to the realization of chosen ends. But individual liberty can be guaranteed only in a "free state," a community whose members participate actively in government and pursue the common good. The idea of a common good transcending private interests becomes a necessary condition for enjoying individual liberty in this concept of citizenship.

Citizenship and Recognition of Differences

Just as there are serious problems with the liberal concept of citizenship, the civic republican solution has shortcomings. Some of its advocates would renounce pluralism in the name of a fabricated vision of the common good. Although the ideas of shared purpose and active participation play an important role in political thought, a modern democratic community cannot be organized around a single idea of the common good. The emergence of the individual, the development of civil society, and the separation of the public and the private are valuable and unavoidable components of modern democracy. The recovery of a more participatory notion of citizenship must acknowledge the tension that necessarily exists between the identity of persons as citizens and as individuals.

A revised concept of citizenship should also take account of feminist critiques. Several feminists have argued that ancient and modern concepts of citizenship have been inimical to women. Carole Pateman has shown that the ideal of the universal citizen was based on the exclusion of women. Women were confined to the private sphere because they were seen as lacking the qualities of independence required for responsible citizenship. Centuries later, after bitter struggles, women were finally awarded their formal rights of citizenship, but the conditions for their full exercise are still far from being attained. Feminists declare that as long as women are not equal to men in all respects, they cannot be complete citizens. Full incorporation of women would require a radical transfor-

mation of the public-private distinction. Difference, diversity, and plurality ought not to be relegated to the private sphere. The idea of a homogeneous public sphere where universality reigns in opposition to the particular should be abandoned.

This feminist debunking of "abstract universalism" echoes demands from many other quarters to reformulate the concept of citizenship so as to take in account the significance of differences. Whatever crucial role the universalistic idea of citizenship might have played in the emergence of modern democracy, it has become an obstacle to the expansion of democracy. Many of the new rights being claimed by women, ethnic groups, and sociocultural minorities cannot be universalized and extended equally to all. As expressions of specific needs, such rights apply only to particular groups or constituencies. Only such a pluralistic concept can accommodate the specificity and diversity of contemporary demands and take into consideration the proliferation of political identities.

Such a revised concept of citizenship might draw inspiration from both the civic republican and the liberal approaches, but it would have to go beyond them and tackle the problem of how to make belonging to different communities of values, language, culture, and interests compatible with membership in a single political community whose overarching rules must be accepted.

Contemporary Problems of Citizenship

Although it has become increasingly controversial in Western democracies, the liberal model has gained new momentum in postcommunist countries, where the main task is to establish the basic conditions for civil society and pluralistic democracy. This effort has raised serious questions concerning the relationship between citizenship and nationality. With the upsurge of competing nationalisms, the very conditions of membership in a political community are strongly contested in many places. The growth of ethnic nationalism constitutes a serious threat to modern ideas of democratic citizenship.

Many of the Western democracies are facing similar problems because of the increasingly multiethnic and multicultural character of their populations. In both East and West, the question of how to maintain the political community as a space for creating unity without denying specificity is hotly contested. Several solutions have been proposed that suggest separating nationality from citizenship and establishing criteria for granting citizenship rights that do not depend on nationality. The ideal of "European citizenship" is one step in that direction: nationals of the member states of the European Union will have certain, albeit limited, rights in all other member states.

The notion of "constitutional patriotism" defended by Jürgen Habermas is another attempt to break the connection between ethnicity and citizen identity by linking the granting of citizenship to allegiance to certain universalistic principles. The danger in approaches of this sort is that, in postulating the availability of so-called postconventional identities, theorists tend to ignore the important emotions and passions that are roused by existing symbols of nationhood. Their incapacity to understand the strength of these sources of identification leaves them unable to offer a real alternative to the forces of ethnic nationalism. It would be more promising to counter such forces by fostering a form of "civic nationalism," one that would not only acknowledge the need for belonging and for acquiring a national identity but would also try to satisfy that need by mobilizing the common values of a shared democratic tradition.

With the collapse of the communist model, many movements aiming at a radicalization of democracy are increasingly trying to formulate their goals within the framework of pluralism. Instead of challenging the basic institutions of the political regime, they struggle for an increased democratization of both the state and the civil society within that regime. The idea of democratic citizenship is at the center of this effort by the left to extend democracy. Long used to challenge the antidemocratic practices of neoliberalism or to revive a more participatory form of political community, the theme of citizenship is becoming central to the task of promoting awareness of individual and collective rights.

One interesting proposal would involve a "universal grant" to every adult male or female to cover basic needs. The idea is to shift the meaning of welfare benefits from the domain of assistance to that of the rights of citizens. To be sure, in many Western countries several such rights are already granted in practice, but they have never been adequately theorized and justified. That omission has left them exposed to the neoliberal campaign to restrict them.

Another set of questions is linked to the increasing globalization of socioeconomic relations and the limits of nation-states in coping with this phenomenon. The present territorial model of citizenship creates difficulties that are not easy to overcome. Some argue that in a world subject to globalization, the idea of citizenship should be shaped by a new discourse on human rights. But the prac-

tical implementation and enforcement of such rights remain unresolved and extremely intricate issues.

Linked as it is to the idea of democracy, the notion of citizenship is inevitably complex. Different concepts of democracy construct the role of the citizen and the rights and obligations of citizenship in quite diverse ways. The nature of democratic citizenship will remain as contested as the idea of democracy itself.

See also *City-states, communes, and republics; Civil rights; Civil society; Classical Greece and Rome; Communitarianism; Liberalism; Machiavelli, Niccolò; Multiethnic democracy; Republicanism; Revolution, French; Rousseau, Jean-Jacques; Socialization, Political; Virtue, Civic; Women's suffrage in the United States.* In Documents section, see *Declaration of the Rights of Man and of the Citizen (1789).*

Chantal Mouffe

BIBLIOGRAPHY

Bendix, Reinhard. *Nation-Building and Citizenship: Studies of Our Changing Social Order.* New York: Wiley, 1964.

Finley, M. I. *Politics in the Ancient World.* Cambridge: Cambridge University Press, 1983.

Habermas, Jürgen. "Citizenship and National Identity: Some Reflections on the Future of Europe." *Praxis International* 12 (1992): 1–19.

Mann, Michael. "Ruling Class Strategies and Citizenship." *Sociology* 21 (August 1987): 339–354.

Marshall, T. H. *Citizenship and Social Class.* Cambridge: Cambridge University Press, 1950.

Mulhall, Stephen, and Adam Swift. *Liberals and Communitarians.* Oxford: Blackwell, 1992.

Pateman, Carole. *The Sexual Social Contract.* Cambridge: Polity Press, 1988.

Skinner, Quentin. "On Justice, the Common Good and the Priority of Liberty." In *Dimensions of Radical Democracy: Pluralism, Citizenship, Community,* edited by Chantal Mouffe. London: Verso, 1992.

Turner, Bryan S. *Citizenship and Capitalism: The Debate over Reformism.* London: Allen and Unwin, 1986.

City-states, communes, and republics

Forms of government in medieval and early modern Europe, from the eleventh through the seventeenth centuries, that played an important role in the development of modern democratic theory and institutions. Notable among these were the city-states of northern Italy, particularly Florence and Venice; the Swiss Confederation; and the Dutch republic. These communal and republican regimes applied doctrines of popular sovereignty and created representative systems of government that have been fundamental to modern democracy. But few of them can be called democratic by modern standards. They were oligarchies (systems of rule by the few) controlled by the landed aristocracy or prosperous merchants.

Beginning in the eleventh century the towns and cities of Europe assumed increasing economic and political importance. Some became centers of regional trade, while others took a leading role in international commerce. In relatively strong kingdoms, such as England and France, towns were incorporated as privileged members of the commonwealth, with certain fiscal responsibilities and a limited ability to regulate themselves internally. In other parts of Europe, especially where political authority was not very stable, as in northern Italy, the Rhineland, and the Low Countries (Belgium, Luxembourg, and the Netherlands), towns and cities became much more independent, treating neighboring principalities and lordships as their political equals. Especially in northern Italy, where a strong tradition of Roman law survived, towns refined a series of legal and theoretical justifications of their independence.

Italian City-states and Communes

The word that towns used to describe themselves was *commune*. The commune was "the thing held in common" by the citizens of a town. Governments known as communes were formed in various Italian urban centers in the late eleventh and twelfth centuries, for instance at Pisa (1081–1085), Arezzo (1098), Genoa (1099), Pistoia (1105), and Bologna (1123). Although all residents of a city were subject to the commune, participation in government was initially restricted to a fairly limited number of citizens defined principally by property qualifications.

To ensure impartial administration of justice and to curb factionalism, an officer known as the *podestà* was invited from another city for what was generally a six-month term as judge and chief magistrate. In the thirteenth century guild-based movements arose in the Italian communes and sought to place control in the hands of the merchant and artisan classes, who were together known as the *popolo*. The *popolo* generally seized power by force. It created executive officers known as "captains of the people," who served alongside the *podestà* and were charged with protecting the interests of the *popolo*.

The success of the Italian popular regimes even resulted in a few rare instances in which the word *democracy* was used in a positive sense, rather than to signify the debased, tyrannical regime of Aristotelian political theory. The German scholar Albertus Magnus (1206–1280) inverted traditional expectations when he criticized timocracy, the rule of the honorable, as a corrupt regime and praised democracy as "not a deviant constitution but a polity." On the whole, however, the weight of the Aristotelian tradition was such that writers avoided the negative implications of the word *democracy,* preferring to use *polity* and *republic* even when describing the most democratic of contemporary regimes. Not until the Enlightenment in the eighteenth century would political theorists offer general endorsements of regimes they dared to call *democratic.*

The idea of popular sovereignty that would prove so important in the free republics of Europe actually had its origin not in republican but in imperial practice. Various Roman emperors had asserted that their absolute power rested on a cession of sovereignty by the Roman people. In the Middle Ages, during the conflicts between the popes and the emperors of the Holy Roman Empire, jurists in Roman civil law argued that the sovereignty of the Holy Roman Empire was independent of the papacy since it was derived from this original popular cession of sovereignty. With the decline of the empire as a political force, princes and city-state governments looked for ways to justify the establishment of their own laws and statutes. The civil lawyer Bartolus of Sassoferrato (1314–1357) was the most important of the legal theorists who established the principle that sovereignty did not belong to the emperor alone, but that it might be possessed by a particular association of people acting as the government of a city-state.

The percentage of the population that actually was able to participate in the affairs of these governments was quite small. In Venice, with a population of roughly 120,000 at the beginning of the fourteenth century and 115,000 in 1509, office holding from 1297 on was limited to the members of the roughly 200 patrician families that belonged to the Great Council. When the Florentine republic was at its most democratic (during the period 1494–1512), it had an officeholding class of about 3,500 male citizens in a total population of about 60,000.

Electoral procedures in the Italian city-states were generally devised with the aim of preventing domination by any single group or faction. A list of persons eligible to

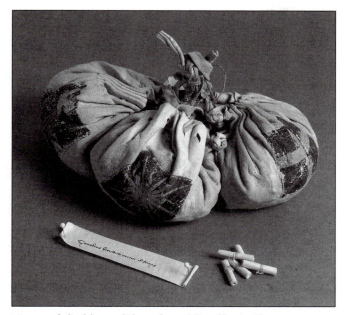

Names of eligible candidates for public office in Florence were written on parchment strips and placed in electoral purses. Names were then drawn at random. Here, fifteenth-century purses are shown with the name strips.

hold office, periodically revised and presided over by an electoral commission, served in each commune as the basis for an often complicated process involving nomination, majority approval, and selection by lot. In Florence, beginning in 1291, election took place through a procedure called *imbursation*. Small parchment strips bearing the names of eligible candidates were placed in leather purses (see photo). Those whose names were drawn at random from the purses would become officeholders. Much political struggle surrounded the composition of electoral commissions, since they decided which names would be placed in the purses. Only at the final electoral stage, when names were drawn from the bags, did a strong element of chance exist. By controlling appointments to electoral commissions, the Medici family was able to exercise unofficial control over Florentine politics for much of the fifteenth century.

In the course of the fourteenth century many independent communes were taken over by more powerful neighbors; others came under the control of princes or tyrants. The Florentine republic became increasingly oligarchical, notwithstanding two episodes of renewed popular government, in the years 1494–1512 and 1527–1530. In 1530 the city became a principate ruled by the Medici family. Free

republics such as Venice, Genoa, and Lucca, which maintained their independence down to Napoleonic times in the early nineteenth century, survived as fairly rigid patrician oligarchies.

The Swiss Confederation

Switzerland—whose republicanism fascinated intellectuals from Niccolò Machiavelli, the sixteenth-century Florentine political theorist, to Jean-Jacques Rousseau, the eighteenth-century Geneva-born philosopher—also owed its independence to an inability of greater European states to assert their sovereignty successfully. The earliest documentary evidence for the existence of a Swiss Confederation dates from 1291, when the cantons (or states) of Uri, Schwyz, and Unterwalden allied to protect their independence from the Hapsburg monarchs. The treaty of 1291 governed relations among the cantons until 1798.

In contrast with the urban world of the Italian communes, the Swiss cantons comprised many small rural communities along with a few cities. Peasants and city dwellers were considered citizens of equal status. During the fifteenth and early sixteenth centuries, when (thanks to their infantry) the Swiss were one of the most important and successful military powers in Europe, cantonal institutions seem to have been especially democratic, both in practice and in spirit. Not without reason does Switzerland consider itself the world's oldest continuous democracy.

But the "democracy" of Switzerland in the medieval and early modern period was fundamentally local. Legislative powers rested with each canton, each of which was governed according to its own customs and statutes. The confederation was a largely ineffectual body, unable to impose its decisions on recalcitrant cantons. Moreover, from the sixteenth century on, the Swiss were riven by religious disputes. In the sixteenth and seventeenth centuries an awareness that disagreements over foreign policy could sunder the confederation led Switzerland to develop its stance of defensive neutrality toward all foreign powers. By the mid-sixteenth century, as the cantons turned increasingly inward, provincial aristocracies of wealth and blood asserted themselves, dominating local elections. Reform was impeded at both the national and cantonal levels down to the time of the French Revolution.

The Dutch Republic

The Dutch republic, established in 1579, was born of the resistance of the northern provinces of the Low Countries to Spanish rule. Although writers such as the Dutch scholar and jurist Hugo Grotius (1583–1645) attempted to present the Dutch political system as largely unchanged since Roman times, and the myth of Dutch traditionalism would act as a powerful deterrent to further social and institutional change, the republic that emerged from the Dutch revolt was novel in many respects.

Once the Dutch were rid of the Spanish, the republic that they structured around several fiercely defended tiers of autonomy maintained a remarkably durable equilibrium. Sovereignty resided in the seven United Provinces, which met in an assembly known as the States General. The States General was supposed to act "as one province," so most decisions regarding war, peace, and taxation were made unanimously. Because Holland was by far the wealthiest and most populous of the provinces, it tended to control the decisions of this assembly.

Often opposed to the States General—and thus to the province of Holland—was the princely House of Orange. Each province appointed an officer known as a *stadhouder,* who was responsible for commanding local troops and preserving public order. Beginning with William the Silent, prince of Orange (1572–1584), it became common for the prince of Orange to be joint *stadhouder* of most of the provinces. This arrangement provided the republic with effective leaders during military crises, but members of the House of Orange were ambitious to establish themselves as monarchs. A rivalry between Orangists and republicans lasted until 1702, when William III of Orange died without direct heirs, and republican forces remained in control.

There was little that was democratic about the Dutch republic. Office holding was available only to a relatively small noble or propertied elite. A few writers, such as Pieter de la Court (1618–1685), argued for increasing political participation among the propertied classes, but their aim was to restrain the unpredictable masses. What later English and American theorists found most interesting in the Dutch model was its largely successful accommodation of competing power interests—including the *stadhouder* as a kind of "tamed prince."

The eighteenth-century writers and statesmen who established the modern democracies of America and Europe spent much time studying the histories of medieval and early modern republics, but they were not just seeking lines of evolutionary descent. As John Adams, second president of the United States, once noted, the imperfec-tions of these regimes are "full of excellent warning for the people of America."

See also *Italy; Low Countries; Small island states; Switzerland.*

William J. Connell

BIBLIOGRAPHY

Barber, Benjamin R. *The Death of Communal Liberty: A History of Freedom in a Swiss Mountain Canton.* Princeton: Princeton University Press, 1973.

Bertelli, Sergio. *Il potere oligarchico nello stato-città medievale.* Florence: La Nuova Italia, 1978.

Black, Antony. *Political Thought in Europe, 1250–1450.* Cambridge and New York: Cambridge University Press, 1992.

Handbuch der Schweizer Geschichte. 2 vols. Zürich: Verlag Berichthaus, 1972.

Price, John Leslie. *Holland and the Dutch Republic in the Seventeenth Century: The Politics of Particularism.* Oxford and New York: Oxford University Press, 1994.

Riesenberg, Peter. *Citizenship in the Western Tradition: Plato to Rousseau.* Chapel Hill: University of North Carolina Press, 1992.

Skinner, Quentin. "The Italian City-Republics." In *Democracy: The Unfinished Journey,* edited by John Dunn. Oxford and New York: Oxford University Press, 1992.

Civil disobedience

The deliberate disobeying of law or government by citizens in order to publicize or advance a political cause or argument. Civil disobedience differs from crime or ordinary lawbreaking, in that those who carry it out seek no personal advantage, nor do they expect to avoid the penalties of disobedience. On the contrary, a part of the public character of what they do depends on the government acting against them in response to their disobedience. By breaking the law they seek to attract the attention of both the government and other citizens.

The term *civil disobedience* covers a range of political conduct. It is often applied to what is otherwise known as "conscientious disobedience," "conscientious objection," or "conscientious refusal." The most familiar example is the refusal to fight or bear arms. The action is normally based on a moral or religious objection to either violence, war, or killing in general or to the particular war for which the person is being called up or conscripted. It is a personal rather than a public act, in that the objector is not necessarily attempting to make a wider political point, to in-

The anti–nuclear weapons movement was invigorated in the fall of 1981, when the North Atlantic Treaty Organization reaffirmed its 1979 commitment to deploy a new generation of medium-range nuclear weapons in Western Europe. As many as 100,000 protesters took to the streets in London's West End October 24, 1981. Similar marches were held in other parts of Europe.

fluence policy, or to persuade others. Thus there were those who refused to fight or to participate in military activity in Europe during the First and Second World Wars or in the United States during the Vietnam War. Many who did so sought to follow in their own conduct what they took to be the dictates of conscience or morality.

Civil disobedience narrowly or properly defined is, unlike conscientious disobedience, intended to be part of a civil, public, or political process. It is an attempt either to alter the circumstances in which government acts or to introduce into the public debate dimensions, points of view, or values that previously had been absent or neglected. The best-known examples of such political disobedience occurred in the United States during the civil rights campaign of the 1950s and early 1960s and in both North America and Western Europe during the campaigns against the possession of nuclear weapons from the 1960s into the 1990s. Although campaigns like these do place small obstacles in the way of a government's policy—for instance, by briefly blocking the entrance to a nuclear missile site with a human chain—the principal intention is to extend the dimensions of debate. In the United Kingdom women demonstrators at the Greenham Common missile base climbed over the wire and, dressed as teddy bears and Easter rabbits, held picnics on the missile silos. Their in-

tention was not to obstruct official policy but to ridicule its belligerent masculinism: "take the toys from the boys."

Citizens who engage in conscientious lawbreaking do not claim that laws do not apply to them. The pacifist who refuses to fight accepts the penalties that the law lays down for such refusal. The equal rights campaigner who continues to sit on a bus when it crosses the state line into segregated territory, or who sits at a racially segregated lunch counter in defiance of laws that separate the races, is not saying that the laws do not apply. On the contrary, by creating dramatic circumstances in which the law has to be applied, but applied with great publicity, the citizen accepts the consequences of lawbreaking but uses them either to bring pressure on the government or to heighten debate among the citizens.

It is sometimes suggested that civil disobedience is an attack on democracy or a departure from democratic methods. If democracy is rule by the people or by a majority of them, then democratic decisions ought to be accepted, and all citizens, whether or not they agree with a policy, ought to put up with it. One obvious flaw in this objection is that, taken to extremes, it leads to what has become known as the Eichmann defense. Adolf Eichmann, the former administrator of Nazi extermination camps, when kidnapped and put on trial in Israel in the early 1960s, claimed that he was doing no more than obeying lawful orders. Acceptance of this justification would rest on a belief that laws—however oppressive, unjust, or murderous—should be obeyed if they have been passed in due manner by a majority. Once democratic decisions have been reached, the duty of the citizen is at an end, and the moral responsibilities of citizens are overridden by whatever public policy happens to be.

If democracy is defined, however, not as government by a majority of the people but as government by the people, then the widest possible discussion, on a continuous basis, is one of its conditions. Looked at in this way, civil disobedience, far from being a threat to democracy, is one of its defenses of last resort. Moreover, it is frequently argued that the extension of democracy has often depended on civil disobedience. When women in the United Kingdom were denied the vote in parliamentary elections in the early part of the twentieth century, one of the tactics they used to draw attention to their case and to undermine male stereotypes of women as vulnerable, dependent, second-class citizens was a campaign of token offenses against property and breaches of the law governing demonstrations.

A form of political resistance related both to civil disobedience and to conscientious refusal, yet distinct from both, is passive resistance. People may feel that laws or politics are wrong but that they are denied any means of political redress—for example, because of foreign occupation or rule by those who are considered alien. In these circumstances they may attempt to resist in a nonviolent manner, as did the opponents of British rule in India and some of the original members of Sinn Féin, which was founded to promote independence for Ireland.

Civil disobedience must be distinguished from coercion or terrorism. Those among the opponents of abortion or vivisection who pursue their goals not by persuasion or propaganda, but by burning down women's clinics or abortion centers or by making arson attacks on animal research laboratories, are not generally accepting the consequences of lawbreaking. On the contrary, they seek to avoid those consequences by acting secretly. They are not trying to persuade their fellow citizens but to coerce them. They are therefore seeking to play a part not in politics, which is characterized by negotiation and argument, but in government, whose methods in the last resort rely on compulsion.

Civil disobedience is probably possible or effective only in democracies. It assumes that governments will apply the law, not repress the lawbreaker. It assumes free public discussion. Neither of these conditions applies in despotisms, one-party regimes, or military dictatorships. In such systems, people may and do engage in conscientious refusal, but there is hardly any serious possibility of civil disobedience as an extension of democratic politics.

See also *Freedom of assembly; Gandhi, Mohandas Karamchand; King, Martin Luther, Jr.; Pankhurst, Emmeline; Theory, Postwar Anglo-American.*

Rodney Barker

BIBLIOGRAPHY

Barker, Rodney. "Civil Disobedience as Persuasion: Dworkin and Greenham Common." *Political Studies* 40 (June 1992): 290–298.
Bedau, Hugo Adam. *Civil Disobedience in Focus.* London and New York: Routledge, 1991.
———, ed. *Civil Disobedience: Theory and Practice.* 3d ed. New York: Pegasus, 1969.
Dworkin, Ronald. "Civil Disobedience and Nuclear Protest." In *A Matter of Principle,* by Ronald Dworkin. Cambridge: Harvard University Press, 1985; Oxford: Oxford University Press, 1986.
Gandhi, M. K. *Non-Violent Resistance.* New York: Schocken Books, 1961.
Rawls, John. *A Theory of Justice.* Cambridge: Harvard University Press, Belknap Press; Oxford: Oxford University Press, 1971.
Thoreau, Henry D. "Civil Disobedience." In *Civil Disobedience: Theory and Practice,* edited by H. A. Bedau. 3d ed. New York: Pegasus, 1969.
Walzer, Michael. *Obligations: Essays on Disobedience, War, and Citizenship.* Cambridge: Harvard University Press, 1970.

Civil-military relations

The relationship between civil society and the armed forces is an essential part of any polity, democratic or otherwise, since a military force is an almost universal feature of social systems above a minimum size. If all those under arms held the same opinions and had the same interests, and if their opinions and interests differed from those of the rest of society, they presumably would always be able to impose their will, given the superiority of their capacity for applying violence. The normal state of any community should therefore be its domination by the armed forces. In fact, military domination was the state of affairs in most primitive societies. A similar situation prevailed in Europe in the Middle Ages, when a land-owning nobility held both economic and military power.

Even in such cases, however, the fit between military force and economic privilege or social prestige was never complete. There were other sources of wealth—commercial, financial, agrarian, and later industrial—that were not directly accompanied by or dependent on the exercise of armed might. Moreover, the clergy, by appealing to divine sanctions or popular beliefs, could exercise considerable power without the use of weapons. And, in moments of crisis, the mass of the population could rebel and arm itself with sufficient weapons to become a match for most military units. The basis for an equilibrium between civilian and military power was thus created.

With economic and technological development, and the consolidation of the nation-state, the armed forces became more professionalized, forming a corporate body distinct from the nobility, from which they usually emerged. In many societies a link remained between the upper classes and the top military positions, to which the nobility had special access. These semiprofessional armed forces were relatively easily controlled by the dominant socioeconomic class, with the monarchy functioning as an important link between the two.

The eighteenth-century French political philosopher Montesquieu, in his famous chapter on the English constitution in *The Spirit of the Laws* (1748), described a free political system as one based on a division of powers. This division was not only the classical one differentiating the legislature from the executive and the judiciary but also the underlying confrontation between three social forces: the aristocracy, represented by the House of Lords; the commoners, whose opinions were reflected in the Commons; and, finally, the armed forces, whose confidence rested in the monarchy.

Political liberalization and constitutional experimentation led to theories about shared sovereignty between the king and the people. In countries peripheral to the main centers of social and economic development, however, the armed forces became less reliable in their allegiance to the king and therefore to the dominant class. New ideologies, especially liberalism, began to influence wide sectors of the military. This liberalism was not incompatible with a predisposition to authoritarian forms of government and could even be mixed with personal allegiances to individual leaders, thus creating crisscrossing political cleavages.

In Eastern Europe this situation persisted into relatively recent times, notably in Poland, where Józef Piłsudski, a man who had a socialist past and experience leading irregular forces during the First World War, staged a coup d'état against the prevailing conservative government in 1926. Piłsudski had popular support and the acquiescence of large parts of the parties on the left.

Latin America, from its independence in the early nineteenth century, has witnessed a complex political role for its military institutions. Social tensions created by economic turmoil and by sharp divisions among the ruling classes—or between them and the middle strata—diminished the prospects for orderly conservative civilian rule. Liberated from the control of the local establishment, the military tended to form populist alliances, basing their access to power not only on superior armed force but also on their capacity to mobilize the people.

In some countries, for example, Brazil and Cuba, where the menace of a slave revolt was especially strong, the solidarity of the upper and middle classes was greater. The tendency of aspiring politicians to appeal to the masses and the ability of military officers to act independently were more severely controlled, and a peculiar type of conservative civil-military relations was frozen in place until the 1930s.

Social Origins of the Military

In many parts of the developing world, the military have performed vital roles in economic and political development since decolonization, substituting for a weak or nonexistent bourgeoisie and acting as the nucleus of a new bureaucratic class. In most of Asia and Africa ethnicity and religion generated attitudes of opposition to the colonial powers. These two powerful social forces, which in the West historically have interacted to produce a basically conservative outcome, pushed important sectors of the dominant class of developing countries toward radical forms of anti-imperialism. The resulting polarization could lead them to adopt some form of leftist ideology or to support a nationalist and populist regime. The ideological allegiance of such elites is quite unpredictable, however, so conservative outcomes are also possible.

In most of the Arab world the first type of reaction emerged earlier, giving rise to Egyptian president Gamal Abdel Nasser's defiance of the West in the 1950s over the Suez Canal and the rise of "Nasserism," the Pan-Arabic Ba'ath Party, and what has been called Arab socialism, all of which had important military support. In more recent times, religious fundamentalism has been on the rise, obviously among clerics, but with a significant appeal to other sectors and the people as a whole. The fundamentalist appeal is particularly strong in countries in which the first wave of independent regimes proved ineffective in solving national problems.

Military socialist and religious fundamentalist regimes can be seen as alternatives to the growth of a strong communist movement. Both are based not on worker and peasant support but on the organizing efforts of the petty bourgeoisie.

In Latin America neither religion nor ethnicity has motivated the upper and middle classes to oppose the domination of the Western powers. The contrast between Roman Catholicism and Protestantism is not strong enough to inspire fanaticism. As for ethnicity, there is great potential for confrontation in Latin America among the lower middle and popular classes, where the native Indian and African component is much stronger than among the upper classes. Ethnic differences among the upper classes are practically absent, and they are present only to a slight degree among clerics and the military. Within the military, however, there is a certain form of nationalism with ethnic roots, even if its intensity is much weaker in Latin America than in the rest of the developing world. The impoverished middle class and intellectuals are more open to varieties of socialism or of nonethnically based populist ideologies.

The social origins of military officers, and the patterns of social mobility for noncommissioned officers, are radically different in developed and less developed countries. In developed countries, recruitment to officer status is similar to recruitment processes in the other professions, drawing aspirants principally from the middle and upper classes, along with some able individuals from the popular strata. Training and promotion, which have become highly professionalized, convert the military into a disciplined corps that accepts its role as an armed bureaucracy—equivalent to the civil service—giving and receiving orders according to a set of rules. The fact that social conflict is not very intense in developed countries helps to instill within those in the armed forces attitudes of discipline and obedience to civilian authorities.

In countries that are undergoing the early stages of industrialization or economic development, and passing through the revolution of rising expectations, the patterns of recruitment to the armed forces, as well as to the civil service and the professions, are quite different. To begin with, military salaries are often low compared with the salaries of most entrepreneurs and professionals. "Military families," which preserve standards of behavior inherited from earlier historical periods, are quite common. But most young men from the better-off elements of the middle classes avoid the military profession, leaving it open to people of more modest origins. In some Latin American countries, these are people of different ethnic origins.

Social discontent among the military is likely to be high. A chasm opens between the minority, who are well-off through inherited family wealth or illegitimate access to influence and corruption, and the middle ranks, who feel unjustly treated—thus creating the preconditions for the growth of nonconformist ideas among recruits to the officer corps. These ideas can follow leftist channels (through some variety of popular nationalism or military socialism), or they can contribute to authoritarian ideologies of the right or to clerical fundamentalism.

The Role of the Armed Forces in Society

Sociological analysis of the role of the armed forces in civilian society tends to oscillate between reductionism and autonomy. A certain form of reductionism, of Marxist origins, regards the armed forces as executors of the interests of the dominant classes. If the state is the "executive committee" of the dominant classes, the military is their "subcommittee," even when there is antagonism between the upper classes and the military or when a prominent figure among them is ruling. (Such was the case of Louis Napoleon, king of France from 1830 to 1848.)

Karl Marx, in his essay on the coup d'état of 18 Brumaire (November 9–10) 1799, in which Napoleon Bonaparte became first consul of France, suggested that when social conflict is intense, and the capacity of the bourgeoisie to establish its hegemony in a legitimate form has been eroded, the field of action opens up for an independent political leader—often from the military—to mobilize the masses. Although this new leader justifies his actions as an effort to overcome conservative or moderate forces, the desire to control the masses through personal leadership, charisma, or dictatorship is the true motive. According to Marx, this scenario was typical of the last stages of the capitalist system, when the impending revolutionary conditions made business as usual impracticable in the political sphere.

Historical experience has shown the limits of this analysis, even if several of the more specific hypotheses derived from it have proved worth considering. These concentrate on the kinds of contradictions among the upper sectors of the social pyramid that may increase the likelihood of independent military action. One can also argue that military interventions do not derive from the prevalence of authoritarian attitudes among officials of the armed forces but from unresolved contradictions between civilian groups. Civilian groups appeal to the military and thereby encourage them to take the path to power.

The antireductionist approach treats the military like any other social group—with its own interests, attitudes, and culture—vying for power with the rest of society. This group may be united or divided into factions. Democratic or authoritarian attitudes may prevail within it, either enabling a free polity to thrive or destabilizing its institutions.

It is also necessary to consider the difference between conscription-based and fully professional armed forces, since this difference can affect the relationship between the civilian and military sectors of society and the prospects for the consolidation of democracy. Universal conscription has been a requirement of modern warfare, both during a war and in preparation for it. Since the French Revolution, one theme in democratic thought has been that military service by the mass of the (male) population creates an element of democratic control. This assumption is highly debatable; in many less developed countries, periodic authoritarian rule and a succession of coups d'état have been compatible with universal male conscription for a long time.

It seems plausible that if the majority of the soldiers in a military organization are recent recruits, influenced by opinions prevalent among the general population, it may be more difficult to employ them against that population. However, most recruits are quite helpless to resist orders; they tend to follow passively the orders of their officers. The presence of recruits may place some limits on the use of the armed forces for purposes of repression, but those limits are very wide. There may be extreme situations, for example, after the loss of a war, when the presence of conscripts becomes an important factor in limiting the internal political role of an army.

Most consolidated democracies have professional armed forces. Many less consolidated democracies, and actual dictatorships, are based on conscription. But opponents of professionalization argue that in the absence of universal conscription, the prospects for democracy would be even worse. Other matters that should be considered include the waste of conscripts' time and resources, the interruption of their early work careers or studies, and the effect on their personalities of a year or more of authoritarian and often abusive training. More important in terms of the effects on the political system is the existence of frequent and close social interaction between military officers and their peers in civilian occupations. In societies suffering continued military intervention and violence, these contacts are usually reduced, creating patterns of self-recruitment and a mutual lack of confidence that breeds intolerant attitudes on both sides.

Some civilian groups inevitably have close connections with the military because of the nature of their work. These are industrialists, especially the providers of arms, and, in less developed countries, trade unionists, who form one of the two bases of support for a national-populist alliance. At the height of the cold war, the existence of a "military-industrial complex," controlling enough sources of power and money to be dangerous to the democratic process, was mentioned as a threat in the United States. In Argentina the existence of a military–trade union pact—referring to the determination of those two groups to share power among themselves to the detriment of the rest of society—has been suggested for decades.

Patterns of Military Intervention in Politics

In economically developed and consolidated democracies, the armed forces, through professionalization and the spread of a civic culture, have accepted a role subordinate to the constitutional government. But this subordinate role does not mean that they have no political opinions. In times of serious civic strife, the military may act either independently or in association with a conservative group within the establishment. When the French had to confront the Algerian bid for independence in the 1950s (because of the ineffectiveness of the parliaments of the Third and Fourth Republics), a semi–coup d'état opened the way for the presidency of Charles de Gaulle in 1958. Civilian institutions soon resolidified, however, even if the first few years of de Gaulle's presidency saw greater authoritarianism in government than has been the case since then.

It is significant that the Nazis came to power in Germany not through military intervention but through the emergence of a mass movement stimulated by unbearable economic conditions. Germany's dire economic situation was generated by reparation payments after World War I and the worldwide depression of the late 1920s. Although the military was not directly involved in the Nazi movement, it was permissive about its rise. Once Adolf Hitler was in power—and had established a totalitarian system in very short order—the armed forces were rather helpless against him. Totalitarian sentiments infiltrated the ranks of the armed forces, rendering them incapable of a unified reaction. What would have happened, in time, if the Nazi regime had been consolidated through victory in the Second World War is far from clear. Bureaucratization might have rendered Nazism more vulnerable either to slow processes of liberalization or to an eventual army coup. Spain under Francisco Franco, admittedly a very pale copy of the German behemoth, evolved in the first of these directions, aided by peaceful international conditions and economic prosperity.

Iran's "Islamic revolution," which began in the late 1970s, was also the result of a mass movement, independent of the military. The military, overwhelmed by a popular mobilization, received little or no support from abroad and has been incapable of offering effective resistance to the new regime. The dictatorships of Fulgencio Batista in Cuba and Anastasio Somoza in Nicaragua, both supported by the military, were incapable of overcoming widespread armed insurrection. Under conditions of defeat in international warfare, as in Russia toward the end of the First World War, such incapacity has been even more evident.

The armed forces in communist countries have usually been under party control, probably for the same reasons as in Nazi Germany. There is further evidence, however, of what may happen after decades of party rule have extinguished the early enthusiasm of the creators of such regimes. By the 1980s it was evident that communism, in both the Soviet Union and Eastern Europe, had lost much of its totalitarian character and had degenerated into a more traditional form of dictatorship. The military had become an important element in the system of social control and hence was capable of assuming an independent position in the complex struggle for power.

This capability was demonstrated in Poland during the crisis generated by the Solidarity movement in 1980. The regime, facing an increasing rebellion by civil society, had to rely more and more on the armed forces, which were capable of dictating their own conditions for intervention. In 1981 Gen. Wojciech Jaruzelski, a moderate communist, decided that it was necessary to jettison the old party structure. He forced the system to grant him paramount powers—in effect staging a coup d'état. The aims of this coup were first to control the rebel Solidarity union and second, but equally important, to remove the hard-core communist leadership.

During the democratization wave in Eastern Europe in 1989–1990, the armed forces played a critical political role. Given the decline of external Soviet power, the local armed forces inevitably became the arbiters of the political system. Their help was necessary to quell the popular revolts, which had occurred periodically in Eastern Europe since the Second World War, but their loyalty was no longer evident. Romanian dictator Nicolae Ceausescu, facing widespread popular protest, proved the weakness of a local communist regime bent on rejecting reform. The regime fell, not as a direct result of popular revolt, but as the consequence of a military intervention intent on preventing a popular upheaval.

As history has shown time and again, civil-military relations depend not only on the culture and attitudes that are prevalent among the armed forces but also on the intensity and violence of the major conflicts dividing civil society.

See also *De Gaulle, Charles; Military rule and transition to democracy; Populism; Solidarity.*

Torcuato S. Di Tella

BIBLIOGRAPHY

Abrahamson, Bengt. *Military Professionalization and Political Power.* Beverly Hills, Calif.: Sage Publications, 1972.

Christiansen, E. *The Origins of Military Power in Spain, 1800–1854.* London: Oxford University Press, 1967.

Corradi, Juan, Patricia Weiss Fagen, and Manuel Antonio Garretón, eds. *Fear at the Edge: State Terror and Resistance in Latin America.* Berkeley: University of California Press, 1992.

Decalo, Samuel. *Coups and Army Rule in Africa: Motivations and Constraints.* New Haven and London: Yale University Press, 1990.

Finer, S. E. *The Man on Horseback: The Role of the Military in Politics.* 2d ed. Boulder, Colo.: Westview Press; London: Pinter, 1988.

Janowitz, Morris. *The Military in the Political Development of New Nations.* Chicago: University of Chicago Press, 1964.

Stepan, Alfred. *The Military in Politics: Changing Patterns in Brazil.* Princeton: Princeton University Press, 1971.

Volgyes, Ivan, and Dale R. Herspring, eds. *Civil-Military Relations in Communist Systems.* Boulder, Colo.: Westview Press, 1978.

Wiatr, Jerzy. *The Soldier and the Nation: The Role of the Military in Polish Politics, 1918–1985.* Boulder, Colo.: Westview Press, 1988.

Widner, Jennifer A., ed. *Economic Change and Political Liberalization in Sub-Saharan Africa.* Baltimore: Johns Hopkins University Press, 1994.

Civil rights

The rights that are guaranteed to citizens by a constitution or by legislation. Civil rights legislation has come to mean government acts that are intended to guarantee constitutional rights for particular groups and to protect them against discrimination. Two notable civil rights movements have been the struggle to secure civil rights on behalf of African Americans in the United States and the efforts to ensure equal application of the laws on behalf of black Africans in South Africa.

In this essay we examine the quest for civil rights mainly from the perspective of African Americans. Their history can be viewed as a continual social movement to achieve civil rights based on the principles of American democracy. Insofar as democracy—by any definition—includes equal rights for all citizens, the American civil rights movement has been geared toward that end.

Civil rights are one component of a threefold set of rights that also includes human rights and political rights. Human rights are the basic rights each individual has by virtue of being human—freedom from violence, coercion, terror, torture, or murder. Struggles for human rights include the eighteenth-century revolutions for freedom and well-being in England, France, and America. A worldwide commitment to inalienable human rights is found in the Universal Declaration of Human Rights that the United Nations adopted in 1948.

Political rights—or civil liberties—are concerned with individual rights and personal freedoms. Generally, they are applicable to connections between citizens and their governments. Civil liberties permit citizens to confront the government, publish in opposition to the government, and vote against the ruling government. Political rights allow citizens to use democratic procedures and to help determine who should govern. The Bill of Rights was added to the U.S. Constitution in 1791 to set forth individual rights.

Finally, civil rights are concerned with questions of equality; they attempt to ensure full citizenship for all citizens. They can be found in legal statutes, but most frequently they have a constitutional source. The General Assembly of the United Nations adopted an International Covenant on Civil and Political Rights on December 16, 1966; it went into effect on March 23, 1976.

The civil rights movement in the United States has a human rights foundation. The report of a committee on civil rights issued in 1947 during President Harry S. Truman's administration documented murder, lynchings, and police brutality toward African Americans, as well as unequal application of laws and denial of opportunities to participate in democratic governance.

Historical Background

When the United States became a nation, slavery was legal. In 1650 most of the 300 Africans in the American colonies were indentured servants—contract laborers who worked to pay off the price of their passage or purchase and thus secure their freedom. Subsequently, however, Africans commonly were sold for life. Of the nearly 400,000 blacks in the colonies in 1765, all but a handful were slaves. After their military service in the American War of Independence (1775–1783), approximately 5,000 Africans were emancipated. But slavery was condoned by the Framers of the Constitution and by all local governments in existence at the time.

The Civil War (1861–1865) ended American support for slavery. Three amendments to the Constitution laid the foundation for the rights of the former slaves: the Thirteenth Amendment, ratified in 1865, freed the black slaves; the Fourteenth Amendment (1868) granted them citizenship; and the Fifteenth Amendment (1870) protected their right to vote. African Americans were thereby included in the rhetoric of American democracy, but the reality was another matter. At first, Congress supported black Americans' civil rights. In an effort to assist newly freed slaves and to extend the provisions of the Constitution to them, Congress created the Freedmen's Bureau in 1865. In the law establishing the bureau, Congress declared that civil rights and immunities were identical for whites and blacks.

Congress also passed seven civil rights acts during the Reconstruction era after the Civil War. The first, the Civil Rights (or Enforcement) Act of 1866, was passed over the veto of President Andrew Johnson. It overturned the Supreme Court's *Dred Scott* decision of 1857, which ruled that Congress did not have the authority to limit the expansion of slavery and declared Africans and their descendants ineligible for U.S. citizenship.

The Slave and Kidnapping Act of 1866 made it a crime to kidnap people for the purpose of selling them into slavery. The Peonage Abolition Act of 1867 was passed with the intent of stopping the practice of forcing debtors into servitude. (Despite the act, such practices continued in the United States into the twentieth century.)

The fourth and fifth pieces of civil rights legislation imposed criminal sanctions on those who interfered with others' right to vote as granted in the Fifteenth Amendment, and the sixth act, the antilynching Ku Klux Klan Act of 1871, made it a crime to use force or intimidation to deny any citizen the equal protection of the laws. The Public Accommodations Act of 1875 was the final and strongest civil rights act during the Reconstruction period. Its provisions were aimed at giving black Americans full and equal access to a wide range of public conveyances and facilities.

The Reconstruction acts were offset by legislation that excluded immigrants because of race. In 1882, for the first time, federal legislation barred a group of immigrants from becoming citizens because of race. The Chinese Exclusion Act of 1882 barred Chinese immigrants from entering the United States. The Chinese were not treated as welcome immigrants, especially in California and particularly by organized labor. Throughout the 1850s and 1860s Chinese immigrants were sporadically subject to mass violence, which intensified during the economic depression of the 1870s.

Finally, the Supreme Court began to dismantle the massive array of statutory civil rights protections. The Court invalidated the power and authority of the Reconstruction legislation in a series of rulings that relied principally on arguments that Congress had violated the principle of federalism and had attempted to interfere with the power of the states. The Court maintained that neither the Thirteenth nor the Fourteenth Amendment empowered Congress to enact legislation that would apply to private or social actions of citizens or that could prohibit discrimination against black Americans in privately owned public accommodations. These rulings were a major setback for an isolated African American minority seeking inclusion, fairness, and equality in accordance with the democratic ideal.

The decisions of the Court, which tended to legitimize social discrimination, were especially damaging because separation of the races at the time had been achieved through private action, rather than by law. Subsequently, the Court spelled out the status of black Americans quite clearly in *Plessy v. Ferguson* (1896). In this decision the Court ruled that the Thirteenth Amendment, which abolished slavery, was not intended to abolish distinctions based on color. Furthermore, the Court ruled, laws that required or permitted separation of the races were valid and reasonable exercises of the police power of the states.

The Court concluded that the Fourteenth Amendment could not have been intended to enforce social, as distinct from political, equality.

The situation remained basically unchanged for nearly sixty years. Legal segregation between blacks and whites became the norm, particularly in the South.

Fighting Segregation

The National Association for the Advancement of Colored People (NAACP) was launched in 1909. Its founders held diverse views about the best strategy for black Americans, but they were united in their disagreement with black educator Booker T. Washington, founder of the Tuskegee Institute in Alabama, who argued that blacks must rise to white economic and social standards before they could expect equality. Educator and writer W. E. B. Du Bois, the leading theoretician of the NAACP, maintained instead that race was not a black problem but a white problem, that equality was the right of blacks as well as whites, and that blacks should oppose segregation through political activity. The NAACP chose to fight discrimination primarily through the use of litigation.

For decades the NAACP attempted unsuccessfully to convince Congress to pass antilynching legislation. During the early years of the twentieth century, many black Americans were victims of lynchings or of race riots, notably in East St. Louis, Missouri, in 1917 and in Chicago in 1919. Violence against blacks occurred most frequently in the deep South, where brutality, lynchings, and pogroms against African American sections of towns took place.

During the two world wars, black Americans were segregated in their own military units. In the First World War (1914–1918), 400,000 African Americans served, but only about 10 percent were assigned to combat duty. The others served in stevedore units or in quartermaster units as laborers. By the end of the Second World War in 1945, more than 10 million Americans had been inducted into service; of these, more than one million—10.7 percent—were African Americans. The United States had emphasized in its war propaganda the links between fascism and racism and had associated the democratic ideal of freedom with racial equality. War against the fascist regimes of Germany and Japan suggested to many Americans a fundamental paradox in their attitudes toward, and treatment of, blacks.

Moreover, a massive movement of the black population from the South to the North, which started after the Civil War, peaked between 1940 and 1960. From 1910 through

1940, some 4,600,000 African Americans migrated north. With this population shift, new organizations appeared, aimed at resolving the problems of blacks in cities and emerging ghettos. The Nation of Islam, founded in 1930 by Wali D. Fard, later became known as the Black Muslims. The Congress of Racial Equality (CORE) was founded in 1942; the Southern Christian Leadership Conference, founded by Martin Luther King, Jr., appeared in 1957; and the Student Nonviolent Coordinating Committee (SNCC) was established in 1960. Each of these organizations played a significant role in the civil rights struggle, although their views became increasingly divergent after 1966.

Other progress had come in the 1947 recommendation by the Truman committee that a Commission on Civil Rights be established; that commission was created a decade later. Also in 1947 an executive order of the president abolished segregation in the armed services. Legislative achievements that followed included acts to protect civil rights through federal law enforcement and to penalize obstruction of court orders promoting civil rights.

In 1954 the NAACP's legal activity led to a major success in *Brown v. Board of Education.* In this case a team of African American lawyers led by Thurgood Marshall (who later became the first black justice on the Supreme Court) convinced the Court that segregation had no place in the public schools.

Under Chief Justice Earl Warren and to a lesser extent later under Chief Justice Warren E. Burger, the Supreme Court ruled in favor of the civil rights movement. The Equal Pay Act of 1963 promised equal pay for men and women doing equal work; the landmark Civil Rights Act of 1964 ensured African Americans access to public accommodations and equal employment opportunity; and the Voting Rights Act of 1965 protected the voting rights of black and other minority Americans. The Court also ruled that discriminatory housing practices were in violation of the Constitution. All these laws and decisions were significant in making true democracy available for all African Americans. During the 1960s women also began to organize for their civil rights.

Martin Luther King, Jr., was a major figure in the civil rights movement. He came into national prominence when he directed the Montgomery, Alabama, bus boycott in 1955. King was the symbolic leader of the movement until his assassination in 1968. His use of nonviolent, direct action against segregation gave the movement its tactical advantage, morality, and symbolic strength. Of par-

ticular note is the dramatic conflict of opinion between King and Malcolm X, a leading figure in the Black Muslim movement. Malcolm X, a proponent of separation, argued for the establishment of an all-black state because he did not believe white Americans would extend democracy to blacks.

Between 1954 and 1968 there were repeated civil rights demonstrations throughout the country. Between 1965 and 1968 urban riots and other disturbances took place as well. In 1967 alone 150 urban riots took place, including major upheavals in Newark, New Jersey, and Detroit, Michigan.

Although the civil rights movement peaked in the late 1960s, four later pieces of legislation deserve mention. They reflect the desire of Congress to protect and enforce civil rights for black citizens and to support democratic justice. In 1976 Congress enacted legislation that allowed the winning party in civil rights litigation, at the discretion of the Court, to apply for reimbursement of attorney fees. The Civil Rights Commission Authorization Act, also passed in 1976, made it easier to investigate allegations of discrimination. Later acts promoted equal employment opportunity in federally assisted programs and activities and established equal rights under the law in public accommodations, education, and employment.

Equal Protection

The Supreme Court more recently has interpreted these and subsequent measures in light of the equal protection clause of the Fourteenth Amendment. With greater frequency the Court has balanced concepts of equal justice against requests based on reverse discrimination and compensatory justice. Chief Justice William H. Rehnquist's position on litigation over equal protection of the laws captures the present thinking of the Court. He does not accept a "spirit" of equal protection; rather, he believes the Constitution and legislation must be strictly observed and narrowly applied. The key issue for the Court is to decide cases in a racially neutral manner. According to Rehnquist, there is no affirmative guarantee of equality embodied in the Fourteenth Amendment, there is no implicit remedy for past wrongs, and any claim must demonstrate official involvement with a clear intent to discriminate.

In 1988 Congress acknowledged the clear intent to discriminate in regard to violations of the rights of persons of Japanese ancestry carried out under the Wartime Relocation of Asians Act. The purpose of the 1988 legislation was to provide reparations to those who had been sent to relocation centers during World War II. Federal entitlement funds of $20,000 per person were to be paid to those detained and deprived of the equal protection of American laws.

Native Americans

The experiences of black Americans have long presented questions about the definition and application of the rights of U.S. citizenship. Similarly, the status of Native Americans has been in flux and continues to be ambiguous. Issues and conflicts pertaining to the civil status of indigenous peoples in America encompass questions of the recognition, status, and allegiance of Native Americans as well as of the sovereignty and jurisdiction of tribes. Beginning about 1815, federal government policy supported the removal of Native Americans from their traditional territories to isolated reserved areas that were administered as trusts by the federal government. Between 1830 and 1840 more than 60,000 were forced to move to the newly established Indian Territory in what later became Oklahoma. That territory was already in use by other Native Americans.

The Citizenship Act of 1924 extended citizenship to all indigenous people born within the territorial limits of the United States. But given the unique social and political status of Native Americans, matters of citizenship and political and civil rights are not easy to determine. Native Americans frequently have not only a tribal identification but also a band or clan (sometimes reservation) identification. They also are citizens of the United States and of the individual state in which they reside. The rights, duties, and obligations that correspond to each of these attachments are constantly in a state of contention.

The Future

In an effort to create a colorblind society, the U.S. Supreme Court has articulated a theoretical ideal for democracy that confronts persistent discrimination. Race relations and the quest for civil rights remain among the most pressing matters on the nation's political and legal agendas. The struggle poses a challenge for democracy.

From an international perspective, transitions from military or authoritarian governments to civilian and elected governments in Latin America and Eastern Europe represent opportunities to expand human, political, and civil rights. South Africa codified racism and separation into law with the implementation of apartheid in 1948.

However, black South Africans struggled against oppressive racist governments and won a major victory when democratic elections took place in April 1994.

Human rights are now viewed globally as fundamental entitlements for all persons. These rights, advanced as universal in character and codified in international law, are receiving international attention and greater formal recognition by nation-states.

See also *Abolitionism; Americans, Ethnic; Human rights; King, Martin Luther, Jr.; Majority rule, minority rights; Racism; Slavery; Social movements; Theory, African American.* In Documents section, see *Constitution of the United States (1787); Universal Declaration of Human Rights (1948).*

William J. Daniels

BIBLIOGRAPHY

Blumberg, Rhoda Lois. *Civil Rights: The 1960s Freedom Struggle.* Boston: Twayne, 1984.
Cashman, Sean Dennis. *African-Americans and the Quest for Civil Rights.* New York: New York University Press, 1991.
Lomax, Louis E. *The Negro Revolt.* New York: Harper and Row, 1962.
Moreland, Lois B. *White Racism and the Law.* Columbus, Ohio: Merrill, 1970.
Muse, Benjamin. *The American Negro Revolution: From Nonviolence to Black Power.* Bloomington: University of Indiana Press, 1968.
Nelson, Bernard Hamilton. *The Fourteenth Amendment and the Negro since 1920.* New York: Russell and Russell, 1967.
Revolution in Civil Rights. 4th ed. Washington, D.C.: Congressional Quarterly, 1968.

Civil service

The organization and personnel of the executive branch of contemporary government. Every contemporary state, democratic or not, has some kind of civil service, however small or large, occupied with the execution of public policies and the implementation of laws. Civil service originates in the European tradition of public administration. It is not the same as public service or bureaucracy.

Public service is a broad concept that comes out of the tradition of French administrative law. It is a wider notion than civil service in the sense that it refers to various kinds of services offered by the state to its citizens through a multitude of agencies and organizations of the wider public sector. In more philosophical language, public service is also associated with public interest as a criterion of the actions of state authorities.

Bureaucracy, on the other hand, is a system of hierarchically related positions. These offices are occupied by trained, full-time employees who have jurisdiction over an officially delimited area and process written documents. They are supervised by superiors who must comply with technical rules sanctioned by law. This classic conception of bureaucracy draws on the thought of the German sociologist and historian Max Weber (1864–1920). Although Weber's idea of bureaucracy stemmed from the Prussian state (the predecessor of modern Germany), it has also been used for the study of large private and nonprofit organizations.

Role of the Civil Service in Democracy

The role of civil servants in democracy is a long debated question, which was lucidly considered by Weber in his discussion of the bureaucratization of the contemporary state. On the one hand, Weber perceived bureaucracy as a correlate of democracy in the sense that the existence of a civil service, staffed on the basis of merit, contributes to the realization of the principle of equality before the law in the day-to-day contact between citizens and the bureaucracy. More specifically, the selection and promotion of civil servants according to achievement criteria is a guarantee of the application of universal criteria in the distribution of goods and services by the state to its citizens.

On the other hand, the execution of laws, typically formulated by the government and passed by the legislature in modern democracies, is left to the civil servants. These individuals' interests, related to their personal, ideological, and corporate biases, may find their way into the implementation of the policies of the political elites that have won the confidence of the electorate. In other words, the strategic position of civil servants in democratic political systems, and the leeway they enjoy in the interpretation of laws—particularly in novel situations or when there are conflicts of interest—may allow them to deflect the import of policies initiated by legitimate governments. In short, politicians can carry out the will of the electorate only with the help of the civil service; civil servants, who are not periodically evaluated by the electorate as politicians are, may be able to circumscribe the options of the electorate.

The civil service, then, can be perceived as a potential threat to democracy. The sources of the threat can be found in the growing size of the modern state, the accelerating intervention of government in the economy, and the secrecy and increasing technicality of state activities, which together may remove bureaucratic activities from the reach of democratic control. In particular, the growth of bureaucracy, evident in the rise of the numbers of civil servants over time, has long and justifiably been considered a factor that can lead to a relapse to nondemocratic government. The legislature and the judiciary, let alone individual citizens, have difficulties monitoring decisions made in the silent corridors of the civil service.

A relevant question concerns the extent to which the civil service is responsive, reliable, and responsible, as part of the executive branch of government in a democratic regime. A responsive civil service caters more to the needs of the citizens than to its own tendencies to reproduce and grow. A reliable civil service delivers services that measure up to the standards of international economic competition and diplomacy and to the expectations of the democratic government in power as to the thorough implementation of its policies. A responsible civil service is held accountable by the majority of the electorate through the exercise of the right to vote and other forms of political participation. Furthermore, a responsible civil service refrains from discriminating against the parliamentary minority and against social groups who traditionally possess fewer resources, such as social status (racial or ethnic minorities) or political pull (women or the poor), than others.

Patterns of Organization

The organization of the civil service involves the recruitment, training, promotion, and transfer of civil servants. Basically, there are two paths along which civil services of the contemporary world are structured: the career system and the system of positions.

In the career system, employees are recruited to the civil service through competitive entrance examinations. Once accepted in the civil service, new employees enjoy tenure. After an initial probationary stage, they expect to pass the whole of their professional life in the bureaucracy, more often than not in the particular sector of the bureaucracy where they began. In some cases, they are trained in schools set up to prepare the newly recruited employees for the requirements of civil service. In other cases, civil servants receive in-service training in new fields of interest, such as modern public management, public finance, and computers.

In-service training is usually a prerequisite for the advancement of civil servants. The career ladder is a grade scale, consisting of several categories with different entry levels depending on educational credentials. The career path up this grade scale is closely linked to, but not identical with, promotion in the hierarchy of supervising positions—typically, head of bureau, head of section, and head of division of a ministry (or "department" in the United States, "office" in the United Kingdom).

In the career system, civil servants who have comparable formal qualifications and specialties form homogeneous groups or bodies—known as *grands corps* in France or *cuerpos* in Spain—that monopolize the management of the ministries and agencies related to their areas of specialization. For example, specialists in public finance may populate as a group the often powerful ministry of finance. These groups are officially recognized by law, and, in practice, they limit the freedom of the political masters of the civil service (that is, the elected governments) to transfer civil servants from one domain of public administration to another. The *corps* or *cuerpos*, which consist of high-ranking employees, enjoy prestige, constitute the informal networks inside the bureaucracy, and usually compete among themselves and with political appointees and cabinet ministries for power in the bureaucracy. The phenomenon has led to strife and fragmentation in some civil services.

The Career System

The career system is influenced by the intellectual tradition of German idealism and the concept of the state of the philosopher G. W. F. Hegel (1770–1831). Hegel declared that universal standards should apply to the selection, training, and promotion of civil servants. Appointments to state jobs should be made only on the basis of objective evaluation of the candidates' knowledge and ability.

In the German idealist tradition the state is conceived as separate from society, which it oversees with the aim of protecting the general interest against individual interests. The theoretical separation of state and society is complemented by the division of tasks between the government, which formulates policies, and the civil service, which executes them. The career system, by establishing a lifelong professional relationship between the civil servant and the state, and by subordinating the civil servant to legitimate political authorities, satisfies the mission of the Hegelian state to function as an ideal, impartial arbiter of conflicting societal interests. The civil servant does not have the same status as employees in the private sector but has a special relation to the state, which brings additional duties and fewer freedoms, such as the duty of subordination to the political will of the government and, commonly, limitations on the freedom to strike. The additional burden of obligations imposed on civil servants is—theoretically, at least—balanced by increased job security and a respectable salary.

The career system is applied in the public administrations of most Western European states (including France and the United Kingdom) and many postcolonial, independent states on other continents. In the United Kingdom civil servants are recruited on the basis of examinations among university graduates. There is a long tradition of hiring graduates of Oxford and Cambridge Universities with nontechnical education; they reach the top echelons of civil service through a "fast stream" of promotions. Civil servants generally advance in their careers by acquiring experience on the job.

The British career system was solidified after the Northcote-Trevelyan report of 1854, which helped to extinguish the particularism and clientelism that had been evident in the British administration. Later, the British civil service developed into a polymorphous and fragmented set of bodies of civil servants, known as *classes*. The Fulton report, published in 1968, contributed to the reshaping of the career system by recommending a decrease in the number of classes, a wider pool of candidates for the top positions in the civil service hierarchy, and more specialized in-service training through the establishment of the Civil Service College. However, despite the Fulton committee recommendations, the British civil service was not thoroughly reformed; it remained deficient in openness and accountability.

In France civil servants are also recruited on the basis of examinations. Prospective high-level civil servants are trained in an elite school, the Ecole Nationale d'Administration. The school, founded in 1945, administers highly competitive entrance examinations, offers courses leading to specialization, and ranks the members of the graduating class. Under the ranking system, civil servants are assigned to different *grands corps* and to the levels of positions they will occupy in the bureaucracy. Differentiation along the grade scale provides for greater mobility of civil servants in the hierarchy of positions.

In Germany civil servants are recruited on the basis of

competition; initially, they are appointed for a probationary period. After successful completion of the probationary stage, they become career civil servants. Depending on their formal qualifications and the type of job, civil servants are classified into several categories, forming a hierarchy. There is a long tradition of legal education among German civil servants. Not all public employees have the same legal status: the German state has a federal structure, and the component states *(Länder)* hire some employees on a contract basis. Civil servants have a special relationship to the state, regulated by provisions of the public law, including the obligation of loyalty to the public interest.

The System of Positions

The system of positions is an alternative to the career system, but it is sometimes applied along with it. In the position system the needs of ministries and public agencies for new personnel are registered. Job openings are outlined, with descriptions of the duties and qualifications of each position. Public employees are hired on a limited contract; when their contract expires, they may be rehired or let go.

The civil servant in the position system does not have the special relationship with the state that the career civil servant does. Although the uncertainty of employment and advancement may be a drawback for the position system, there are advantages. The position system is superior to the career system in that recruited employees have specialized skills, and the government enjoys a flexibility in hiring similar to that of private enterprises (which hire by position). In the position system, civil servants are recruited not to begin a career in the bureaucracy but to fill an opening for a certain period of time, under a contract comparable to those in the private sector. The position system is found in the United States and, in a particular sense, was used in the Soviet Union and Eastern Europe.

A strong anti-elitist sentiment has permeated the organization of the civil service in the United States almost from the country's beginning. In the nineteenth century the American federal bureaucracy was highly politicized: civil service positions were handed out in exchange for political support, an allocation system known as the "spoils system." The abolition of the spoils system was accomplished gradually, beginning with the Pendleton Act of 1883.

In the United States today, job openings are announced in conjunction with job descriptions. Applicants pass through a selection process, based on merit; successful candidates are offered a contract that binds the administration to keep the employee in the same position. The employee may be transferred to other posts after the contract expires. Top positions are also open to competition, but in the late 1970s there was an effort to create an administrative elite, the Senior Executive Service, which included approximately the 6,000 highest officials in the civil service. Still, incoming presidents of the United States can make a wide sweep of appointments, staffing the top layers of the federal administration with temporary advisers. Some degree of politicization characterizes state- and local-level administrations as well.

In Canada civil servants are appointed on the basis of merit; they are selected from an inventory of candidates who have successfully passed examinations and interviews in career areas of their choice. Having entered the civil service, Canadians may develop their career through promotion and transfer among several dozen departments and agencies. Recruitment to new positions is accomplished through competitions, first within public service and then outside public service.

Compared with the career system, the system of positions, as applied in Canada and the United States, allows for more personnel mobility and perhaps a better match of person to task. Yet the position system offers less prestige for the high and middle ranks of the civil service and is vulnerable to wider politicization of the top echelons of the bureaucracy.

With significant variations the system of positions was also applied in Eastern Europe and the Soviet Union under communism. Officially, employment in the communist public administration did not entail a special labor relationship, like the relationship between the civil servant and the state in the West.

In the Soviet Union, in particular, civil servants did not formally enjoy the guarantee of tenure or the prospect of a career in the administration. Once hired, civil servants could be fired or transferred, but in practice they occupied the same position for long periods of time. The content and development of a civil servant's job was not specified in advance, but civil servants who showed competence and loyalty to the Communist Party were compensated with higher-ranking positions. On the whole, because of their access to better goods and services, Soviet civil servants enjoyed higher living standards than the majority of the population, and top bureaucrats had considerable privileges.

Change and Reform

The tasks of civil service have changed over the past two centuries, adapting to the changing role of the state in the economy and society. In the beginning of the modern era the role of the state was limited to waging wars and collecting taxes. Gradually, the state took up more functions, such as monitoring the national economy and providing welfare services. The expansion of state activity led to the growth and differentiation of the civil service. For some time now, particularly in developed societies of the post–World War II era, central government institutions have felt the need for more and increasingly specialized civil servants to deal with increasingly complicated problems that require expert knowledge and technology.

In some developing and undeveloped societies, however, the growth of the civil service was not commensurate with the need to adapt to economic development and the complexity of available technology. Instead, expansions in the civil service were motivated by the need to absorb excess labor from among internal migrants, the young, and the unemployed and to preserve the leverage exercised by political elites through patronage. The more visible presence of the state in the economy and society then gave rise to demands for new and better services by the state. The new demands on the state were nourished by the labor struggles and the wider participation of the working class in the democratic politics of Western Europe and North America.

Recent debates on the socioeconomic role of the state concern not only the extent of its intervention but also the efficiency with which political and civil service elites steer the economy in an antagonistic international environment and the quality of the services offered by civil servants to the citizens. Whereas some earlier transformations of the civil service were prompted by changes in the relations between state and society, some recent changes can be accounted for by administrative reform in the direction of increased efficiency and improved services.

The call for greater efficiency has often meant that the size of the civil service is trimmed, as governments—particularly in Europe—privatize services previously offered by large state monopolies (for example, national airlines and telephone companies). Alternatively, contemporary governments seek to modernize the organization and methods of public administration. Such modernization involves training civil servants in new technologies, especially the use of computers, and teaching new skills related to better planning and evaluation of civil service activities. Governments have responded to the demand for higher quality services by attempting to change the attitude prevailing in the civil service from inertia and aloofness to flexibility, attention to quality work, and sensitivity to the needs of citizens. They are also attempting to inform citizens about the services to which they are entitled.

Role in the Transition to Democracy

The wave of democratization that swept southern Europe, Latin America, and Eastern Europe in the mid-1970s and in the late 1980s brought to the fore the relationship between bureaucracy and democracy. In the democracies that have emerged in the last quarter of the twentieth century, the civil service may be far from responsive, reliable, and responsible. A civil service that has been associated with an authoritarian regime can easily be considered illegitimate after the transition to democracy takes place. To prove itself legitimate, the civil service must submit to the leadership of new democratic governments. Such governments often begin their terms in office by "cleansing" the ranks of the civil service of authoritarian elements. Thus the civil service in a new democracy is vulnerable, more so if it has traditionally proved to be inefficient.

Nevertheless, new democracies put a difficult double task to their civil service: to remain weak and pose no threat to democratic government and, simultaneously, to help legitimate the democratic regime by improving its economic performance over that of the previous, authoritarian regime. The evaluation of the performance of the civil service in a new democracy is based on a trade-off between these two demands.

In fact, additional conflicting pressures may be exerted on the civil service of a new democracy. The democratic state needs a civil service that is to a certain extent resistant to all governments in order to safeguard the well-being, the security, and the defense of the people living within its territorial boundaries. This demand clashes with the drive of the governing party (or coalition of parties) to use the capacities of the civil service freely to fulfill their election promises. For instance, nationalist governments may want to expand the state beyond its boundaries, socialist ones to reform it, neoliberal ones to reduce its economic functions to a minimum. Political parties that govern in new democracies may use the civil service for any of these purposes, depending on their profile and the constraints they face once in power.

The removal of elements of the previous authoritarian regime from political institutions is part of the transition to democracy, and its extent is heavily debated in young democracies. Still, if the democratic government dominates political institutions, like the legislature and the judiciary, and also permeates the civil service, democracy suffers from the reduction of multiple centers of power into a single one—that is, the governing elite. If, as is often the case after the transition from authoritarian rule, the political party in power happens to be run autocratically by its leader or by a party oligarchy, power in the new democracy is even more concentrated. Chances are that the civil service will become responsive only to the needs of the leadership of the governing party. Democratic consolidation, which follows the initial transition to democracy, leaves much to be desired in such circumstances.

Yet the permeation of the civil service by the governing democratic party (or coalition of parties) does not necessarily undermine the legitimacy of postauthoritarian democracy. In postauthoritarian democracies, civil servants cannot be fired all at once, even if they have been politically socialized to serve authoritarian governments. The recruitment of new civil service personnel, with records of resistance against the deposed dictatorship, may serve as an injection of democratic legitimacy into a suspect body of civil servants. Otherwise, the existence of an intact civil service that is known to have collaborated with nondemocratic rulers may compromise any efforts to deepen and expand democracy. It should be kept in mind, however, that the deepening and expansion of democracy is often pursued by political elites only to the extent that they can control the outcome of opening up institutions, such as the civil service, to democratic participation from below.

In the early phases of the transition to and consolidation of democracy, a state needs a strong government aided by a competent civil service for a number of reasons. During that time a competent civil service is instrumental in keeping at bay military and security forces and countering pockets of supporters of authoritarian rule in other institutions. Moreover, rarely do new democracies emerge amidst economic prosperity. New democratic governments often must grapple with economic stagnation or decline as they strive to consolidate democratic rule. Again, an efficient civil service may play a strategic role in economic recovery and thus contribute indirectly to the legitimation of the democratic regime.

In conclusion, a civil service, which in a new, unstable democracy must be weak in the face of alternating democratic governments and strong in the face of undemocratic challenges and economic adversity, feels strongly the difficulties of democratic consolidation. A young democracy that counts on competing democratic parties to consolidate its existence may find aspects of its new, faction-ridden life disagreeable and resort to the civil service as a pillar of democratic stability. The quest for democracy involves, among other things, striking a delicate balance between the elected government and the civil service.

See also *Bureaucracy; Government, Levels of; Idealism, German; Legitimacy; Spoils system; Weber, Max.*

Dimitrios A. Sotiropoulos

BIBLIOGRAPHY

Aberbach, Joel D., Robert D. Putnam, and Bert A. Rockman. *Bureaucrats and Politicians in Western Democracies.* Cambridge, Mass., and London: Harvard University Press, 1981.

Armstrong, John A. *The European Administrative Elite.* Princeton: Princeton University Press, 1973.

Chapman, Brian. *The Profession of Government.* London: Allen and Unwin, 1959.

Crozier, Michael. *The Bureaucratic Phenomenon.* Chicago: University of Chicago Press, 1964.

Dogan, Mattei, ed. *The Mandarins of Western Europe.* New York: Wiley, 1975.

Etzioni-Halevy, Eva. *Bureaucracy and Democracy: A Political Dilemma.* Rev. ed. London: Routledge and Kegan Paul, 1983.

Heady, Ferrel. *Public Administration: A Comparative Perspective.* 2d ed. New York: Marcel Dekker, 1979.

Lipset, Seymour Martin. *Political Man: The Social Bases of Politics.* Expanded and updated ed. Baltimore: Johns Hopkins University Press, 1981; Aldershot: Gower, 1983.

Mouzelis, Nicos P. *Organization and Bureaucracy.* London: Routledge and Kegan Paul, 1975.

Peters, Guy B. *The Politics of Bureaucracy: A Comparative Perspective.* 2d ed. New York: Longman, 1984.

Suleiman, Ezra N., ed. *Bureaucrats and Policy Making: A Comparative Review.* Princeton: Princeton University Press, 1974.

Timsit, Gerard. *Administrations et états: Etude comparée.* Paris: Presses Universitaires de France, 1987.

Weber, Max. *From Max Weber: Essays in Sociology.* Edited by Hans H. Gerth and C. Wright Mills. New York: Oxford University Press, 1946; London: Routledge, 1991.

Civil society

A specific mode of relations between the state and social groups such as families, business firms, associations, and movements that exist independent of the state. This mode of relations developed above all in modern societies, although its seeds can be found in earlier periods. Several components of civil society are necessary for the persistence of modern democracies and are helpful for the transition from an authoritarian or totalitarian regime to a democratic one.

Components of Civil Society

The first, most obvious, and indispensable component is autonomy from the state. The second involves the access of different sectors of society to the agencies of the state and their acceptance of a certain commitment to the political community and the rules of the state. The third aspect rests on the development of a multiplicity of autonomous public arenas within which various associations regulate their own activities and govern their own members, thereby preventing society from becoming a shapeless mass. Fourth, these arenas must be accessible to citizens and open to public deliberation—not embedded in exclusive, secretive, or corporate settings.

Thus one necessary, but not sufficient, condition for a viable democracy is the existence of many private arenas of social life that are independent of the arena of public authority or private coercion. At the same time, these self-organized groups must offer access to the major political arena and have a relatively high degree of acceptance of the basic rules of the political game.

No social group or institution should effectively monopolize the society's bases of power and resources so as to deny other groups access to power. Such monopolization has occurred at various historical periods in many oligarchic societies that have formally adopted democratic constitutions but in which access to power has been limited to very narrow groups.

It is not just the existence of multiple autonomous social sectors, then, that is of crucial importance for the foundation and continuous functioning of democracies. Rather, it is the existence of institutional and ideological links between these sectors and the state. The most important among these links have been the major institutionalized networks of political representation (legislatures and political parties), the major judicial institutions, and the multiple channels of public discourse that collectively determine how politically relevant information is communicated and who has access to these communications. The extent to which these links are not controlled by the public authorities, or monopolized by any dominant class or sector, and the extent to which they foster the accountability of the rulers, are of crucial importance for democracy.

The structure of civil society—and above all of public arenas and the paths of access of various sectors of society to the political arena—varies greatly between different countries and within them at different periods in their history. That structure is affected by social and economic forces, such as the extent of division of labor and the type of political economy in a society. It is also affected by cultural and institutional factors. Among them are the major symbols of collective identity, especially the relative importance of primordial (tribal, ethnic, national), religious, and ideological components among those symbols; the prevailing conceptions of the arena of political action, the scope of the state, the nature of statehood, and the desirable relationship between state and society; the conceptions of public authority and accountability prevailing in the principal sectors of society; the place of law in political discourse and activity; the concept and practice of citizenship; the pattern of interaction between central and peripheral institutions and sectors; the structure of social hierarchies and classes, the level of their collective consciousness, and their modes of political expression; and, finally, the basic characteristics of protest movements and other challenges to political authority.

The way in which these cultural and institutional factors are promulgated and implemented by a society's elites—in interaction with broad sectors of the society—greatly influences the way in which various components of civil society come together, the way in which different social groups relate to each other, and whether they share a vision of the common good for the society.

Early Forms of Civil Society

The first full-fledged civil society emerged in Europe in the seventeenth and eighteenth centuries. It was built on several basic institutional characteristics and cultural premises of European civilization. The most important of these were the presence of several competing centers of society (for example, state, church, and cities) and a pattern of interdependence, as well as competition, between the centers and their respective peripheries. Class, sectoral, ethnic, religious, professional, and ideological groups were largely separated—from each other and from the state. Often, they changed their structure while maintaining their autonomy and their ease of access to the centers of society. Various elites (cultural and economic or professional) were so closely related that they often overlapped and frequently engaged in political activity on a nationwide basis. Finally, the legal system was highly autonomous, as were many cities, which served as centers of social and cultural creativity and as sources of collective identity—for example, with respect to the group's ideas of the meaning of citizenship. A good example is provided by the Italian cities of the Renaissance.

These cultural and institutional features greatly influenced the development of civil society in modern Europe. In particular, they influenced the processes of competition and confrontation between rival national, regional, and local centers and between various groups and elites with regard to access to the centers and influence over their policies.

The same cultural and institutional features have also greatly influenced the major movements of protest that developed in Europe, especially those that demanded the transformation of the centers in the name of an ideology such as socialism or nationalism. This confrontational style was to no small extent rooted in the heritage of the great revolutions of the seventeenth and eighteenth centuries, especially the French Revolution of 1789.

In western and central Europe during this period there developed some very important variations in the structure of civil society and in the links between civil society and the state. These differences were influenced by a variety of historical and structural conditions as well as by cultural factors. Among these were the relative emphasis on equality or hierarchy, differing conceptions of the political arena, and the relative importance of ideological and civil components in the construction of collective identities. They also were influenced by the prior existence of a common political community or, conversely, the extent to which the struggle for access to the political center was interwoven with struggles over collective boundaries—especially territorial boundaries—and identities.

In England, for example, a common political community developed early, and the confrontation between state and society was relatively muted. In Germany and Italy a common political community did not develop until the middle of the eighteenth century. Its very construction was a focus of protest, and the resulting society was greatly fragmented. Constant confrontations, which occurred between the state and those fragmented societies, contributed to the breakdown of constitutional democratic regimes in the 1920s and 1930s.

The crystallization of a distinct American civilization with its strong emphasis on equality, its weak conception of the state, its collective identity based on ideological (more than historical) components, and its strong moralistic principle of the accountability of rulers gave rise to yet another distinct type of civil society. Society generally was seen as relatively more important than the political and administrative center. Earlier movements of protest had been oriented to the ideological reconstruction of the center, as in Europe, or to the construction of distinctive collective political identity. Protest movements in the United States were much more oriented toward moral purification or the enhancement of the national social community.

The Expansion of the Western Model

The expansion of modern European civilization beyond the Western world has transplanted modern political institutions and ideologies, including democratic ones, to civilizations that did not share the basic premises and institutional characteristics that shaped the first modern constitutional regimes and the initial forms of civil society. Non-Western countries have been able to adopt or adapt these institutions and ideologies in many cases. Some components of non-Western traditions—such as the accountability of rulers to a higher law or order, the existence of groups and professions autonomous from the state, and even the caste system of India—have aided democratization, or at least the operation of constitutional systems. In addition, international pressures for democratization have been felt in many countries. The combinations of these factors in different countries has generated far-reaching developments in the structure of civil society and has influenced the ways in which modern political institutions have been incorporated into non-Western civilizations.

The various formats of civil society—European, American, Latin American, and Asian alike—have changed continuously in response to structural changes and new cultural and ideological ideas. A major example of this kind of change is the institutionalization of welfare-state programs.

All societies have redefined the boundaries of the political arena. They have modified conceptions of the appropriate range of activities of the state, the degree of access that different sectors of society should have to political power, the nature of the links between the sectors, and the kinds of benefits that different sectors of society should receive. Whether a country moves from a nondemocratic to a democratic regime, or whether it evolves within a consistent constitutional framework, changes in civil society have involved struggles over competing conceptions of good social order. During transitions, civil society may develop in one of several directions. Some sectors may become more autonomous from the state or more politically active than they have been before. New sectors may emerge and assert their independence.

There is always the danger that changes may undermine those characteristics of civil society that are most conducive to the development and continuity of democratic regimes. First of all, social and economic transformations may cause a redistribution of power within the social sectors and erode existing centers of power. Often policies initially intended to weaken existing centers of power (for instance, policies connected with the welfare state) can increase the power of the state to such an extent that they obliterate independent bases of power.

Furthermore, during periods of transition, existing groups within civil society may fight the changes. There may develop within them tendencies to represent narrow interests based on race, class, ethnicity, or economic status at the expense of acceptance of a common social framework of rules and distribution of power. Thus they can become impediments to the restructuring of the relations between civil society and the state, even to the extent of jeopardizing the continuity of constitutional-democratic regimes.

Finally, the emergence of new sectors within civil society may give rise to the formation of volatile mass movements that define themselves in opposition to other sectors or to the center of political and administrative authority.

In many cases—for example, in Germany and Italy in Europe and even more so in Asian and African societies—these problems have been aggravated by becoming closely entwined with the processes of constructing new national and ethnic communities.

See also *Associations; Authoritarianism; Autonomy; Decentralization; Interest groups; Liberalism; Majority rule; minority rights; Markets, Regulation of; Mass society; Protest movements; Social movements; Unitary state.*

S. N. Eisenstadt

BIBLIOGRAPHY

Bobbio, Norberto, ed. *Democracy and Dictatorship.* Minneapolis: University of Minnesota Press, 1988; London: Polity Press, 1989.

Calhoun, Craig, ed. *Habermas and the Public Sphere.* Cambridge, Mass.: MIT Press, 1992.

Ferguson, Adam. *An Essay on the History of Civil Society.* With a new introduction by Louis Schneider. New Brunswick, N.J.: Transaction Books, 1980.

Hegel, G. W. F. *Hegel's Philosophy of Rights.* Translated by T. M. Knox. London: Oxford University Press, 1967.

Keane, John, ed. *Civil Society and the State: New European Perspectives.* New York and London: Verso Books, 1988.

Maser, Charles S., ed. *Changing Boundaries of the Political: Essays on the Evolving Balance between State and Society, Public and Private, in Europe.* Cambridge and New York: Cambridge University Press, 1987.

Perez-Diaz, Victor M. *The Return of Civil Society: The Emergence of Democratic Spain.* Cambridge, Mass., and London: Harvard University Press, 1993.

Class

A grouping or positioning within a social hierarchy in which divisions are derived from a society's economic relations. Although people often refer to classes as rich or poor, class divisions, in precise usage, stem from differences in types of economic ownership, not simply in amounts of wealth. Karl Marx, the nineteenth-century founder of contemporary work on class, proposed that with industrialization, two main classes would emerge: the bourgeoisie, or capitalists, who employ individuals and own economic profits, and the proletariat, or propertyless workers.

Debate about class often revolves around three core issues: social opportunities, identities, and politics. First, do members of different classes face unequal opportunities to advance in society (for example, in educational institutions or in the job world), or do they confront unequal, discriminatory treatment in day-to-day social encounters? Second, do class members share common personal identities (for example, common self-conceptions, cultural outlooks, leisure interests, or communication styles)? And, third, do class members share common political interests, and do they act together to work for political change?

Marx answered all three questions in the affirmative. He believed that the everyday work experiences of those in the same class generate in them a wide range of common personal and political identities. A society's dominant class—for example, the capitalists in industrialized societies—attempts to suppress the rise of common identities among subordinate class members by using ideological coercion; an example is using schools to instruct the young of subordinate classes to accept ideas favorable to dominant class interests. Marx, however, maintained that subordinate classes would eventually attain a consciousness of their oppressed status (class consciousness) and would then initiate open conflict.

At the turn of the century the German social scientist Max Weber offered three influential objections to Marx's ideas. First, Weber disagreed that capitalists and workers alone are the main classes in industrialized societies. In addition to the labor market or job world, which divides capitalists from workers, important economic relations could also exist in the credit market, which divides lenders from borrowers, or in the commodity market, which divides sellers from consumers. Second, Weber disputed Marx's position that the objective fact of class divisions in regard to socioeconomic opportunities always spawns the formation of subjective class identities and political movements. Weber countered that status groups, defined solely by a shared cultural style of life (for example, among members of an ethnic enclave or hereditary social elite) could sometimes exert a stronger influence than classes over subjective affiliations. Third, Weber included the state—its administrators and the political parties that fight for power within it—as an active social force. For Marx, the state was a neutral site where class conflict plays out.

Twentieth-century developments have compelled further revisions of these views. For instance, the rise of finance, computer, and related high-technology industries in the private sector, and the increase of administrative offices in the public sector, have caused a better paid, mental-laboring "middle class" to grow, while the classic, manual-laboring working class (to which Marx typically referred) has diminished. Aristotle in the fourth century B.C. observed that a large middle class can buffer the competition and conflict that otherwise develop between upper and lower classes. This role of the middle class is especially important in ensuring the political stability of a democracy. Its rise has contributed to the decline of class conflict during the twentieth century.

In addition to the classic division of capitalist and working classes, several intermediate classes, such as professionals, middle managers, and small-business owners, are now commonly identified. Members of these intermediate classes have distinct labor market experiences and locations in the economy, but the differences are not as encompassing of social existence as the differences between capitalists and workers. Consequently, it is now less plausible for the members of any one class to share a fundamentally distinct personal or political identity or, without forming a cross-class alliance, to engage in meaningful political action.

In democracies the effect of class on politics can be seen by the extent to which members of a particular class vote for the same political parties. Most contemporary parties were formed to appeal to particular classes. Recent research, however, shows that in some democracies, class voting has declined since World War II. Blue-collar workers, for example, vote for left-leaning parties less often than they did formerly.

Broadening the focus beyond class, some researchers propose that ideological and political domination along intersecting hierarchies of class, race, and gender combine to affect social opportunities, personal identities, and politics. Therefore, reference to just one of these three hierarchies is inadequate to explain the true complexity of modern social and political life. For example, some American researchers on urban poverty identify a predominantly African American and Latino "underclass," characterized by the severe conditions of social isolation and institutional abandonment now prevalent in the urban ghettos of the United States. Although this view focuses on class-based social isolation in the present, those proposing it typically emphasize the factors of race or ethnicity as having a major subordinating influence historically.

Other researchers suggest abandoning the use of class terminology altogether. The contemporary sociologist Bryan Turner, for instance, suggests that conflict now exists among several single-issue status blocs, ranging from consumer advocates to gay rights activists to welfare recipients. These groups more often are concerned with consumption or lifestyle issues than with traditional class issues, such as working conditions or unemployment. Furthermore, Turner maintains, instead of competing with each other directly, these status blocs approach the state with their demands, affirming Weber's point that the state plays a vital adjudicating role in social conflict.

Although Turner freely uses Weberian terminology, his status blocs are more confined groups, which come together around specific issues, than are Weber's status groups, whose ideological bonds subsume entire cultural styles of life. Moving further in Turner's direction, we might conclude that the greatest challenge to class—and the combined hierarchies of race, class, and gender—and modern status-based concepts is the radical position that we live in a postmodern world, characterized by a fragmented hodgepodge of competing values, identities, and political groupings. If this position is valid—which remains heavily debated—class and status distinctions may have declined irrevocably in social and political significance.

See also *Class relations, Agrarian; Class relations, Industrial; Critiques of democracy; Marxism; Weber, Max.*

Michael Rempel and Terry Nichols Clark

BIBLIOGRAPHY

Clark, Terry Nichols, Seymour Martin Lipset, and Michael Rempel. "The Declining Political Significance of Social Class." *International Sociology* 8 (December 1993): 293–316.

Lipset, Seymour Martin, and Stein Rokkan. "Cleavage Structures, Party Systems, and Voter Alignments: An Introduction." In *Party Systems and Voter Alignments,* edited by Seymour Martin Lipset and Stein Rokkan. New York: Free Press, 1967.

Marx, Karl. *Karl Marx: Selected Writings.* Edited by David McLellan. Oxford and New York: Oxford University Press, 1977.

Turner, Bryan S. *Status.* Minneapolis: University of Minnesota Press; Ballmoor, Bucks.: Open University Press, 1988.

Weber, Max. *From Max Weber: Essays in Sociology.* Edited by Hans H. Gerth and C. Wright Mills. New York: Oxford University Press, 1946; London: Routledge, 1991.

Wilson, William Julius. *The Truly Disadvantaged: Inner City, the Underclass, and Public Policy.* Chicago: University of Chicago Press, 1987.

Wright, Erik Olin. *Classes.* New York and London: Verso, 1985.

Class relations, Agrarian

Agrarian class relations are the relationships of domination and subordination in rural areas that determine access to land and control over labor. Historically, rural areas in many countries have been characterized by extreme inequalities in economic and political power. Many countries with large rural populations and economies based on the production of primary products have continued to demonstrate such inequalities. These inequalities have consequences for democracy because they can affect the political demands of rural inhabitants and the incorporation of agrarian interests into national political systems.

Agrarian class relations affect how land and labor are used in economic production. It is often argued, for example, that agrarian systems that minimize inequalities lead to more efficient agricultural development, which in turn provides an important basis for industrialization. In addition, class relations have been linked to specific forms of political conflict and to differences among political systems. Barrington Moore, Jr., for example, argued in a classic historical analysis of development that certain types of agrarian class relationships are identified with the emergence of democratic and authoritarian political regimes and with the nature of rural rebellion and political movements. The factors that determine access to land and control over labor have become increasingly complex and diverse, and their probable economic and political links have also become more difficult to anticipate.

Agrarian Classes and Political Conflict

There are several general categories of agrarian class systems. Slavery, as it existed in the United States in the pre–Civil War era, is the most extreme system, because it fully limits access to land to a dominant class and provides for total control of the labor of a subordinate class. A second category, found in medieval Europe and colonial Latin America, is feudal systems. In such systems landlords seek to accumulate land primarily to enhance their status and power. They ensure a stable and dependent labor force through a monopoly over land and through various forms of serfdom, peonage, sharecropping, or renting arrangements that limit the options available to smallholders. The landowners use indebtedness, overt coercion, and traditional social obligations and deference to maintain control over land and labor. Agrarian capitalism, as developed in colonial areas of Southeast Asia in the late nineteenth century, is a third category. It is characterized by plantation production and relies on a monopoly over land and on slave, debt-bound, or wage labor to maintain domination over subordinate classes. Where large-scale capitalist farming has developed, as in parts of Mexico and Brazil, productive land has been monopolized by large landowners, and wage labor has replaced tenancy. Where small-scale capitalist farms have emerged, land and labor markets have been more open and less subject to coercion.

These characteristic types of agrarian class relations have been linked to certain forms of political conflict. Violent revolt or desertion is anticipated in systems of enslaved labor, in which slave owners use extreme forms of coercion to ensure their dominance. In societies under feudal conditions, scholars have generally predicted, political conflict will focus on rights to land and expectations about reciprocal relationships between peasants (or sharecroppers or renters) and landlords. Peasants are considered likely to rebel against landlords only when traditional social conventions have eroded or have been violated by landlords or their class allies. Some analysts argue that peasants become politically active when objective economic conditions favor a changed relationship to the dominant class. Where capitalist development has favored the expansion of large landholdings and wage labor, rural political relations are expected to be polarized and unstable. Capitalist production based on smallholdings is thought to be important as a basis for creating stable democratic systems.

More generally, the political struggles of smallholders, tenants, and sharecroppers are expected to focus on the terms of access to land and the bargains that are struck over rents, rights to water, crop shares, or conditions of labor service. Landless wage laborers are expected to focus their demands on improved wages and working conditions; they provide the base for more radical political movements. Such laborers would likely be the prime movers in efforts to form rural unions, syndicates, and armed revolts to alter existing inequalities. Communally based peasants are expected to conform to communal, ethnic, or regional political loyalties and to be mobilized into political action primarily when traditional rights to land are challenged or threatened. These assumptions concerning class relations are relevant to analyses of how and why rural interests are likely to be mobilized into national political systems.

Rural Realities

Among scholars there is considerable interest in assessing how well these predictions reflect rural realities, particularly in countries with large agricultural sectors. Analysts agree that capitalism has become the dominant mode of production in agriculture in most regions. Capitalist producers have become increasingly incorporated into national and international markets and have sought to take advantage of economic opportunities by modernizing their productive systems. In so doing they have accumulated larger holdings of productive land, replaced labor through mechanization and other technological advancements, and simplified their obligations to laborers by hiring only for peak work periods, rather than maintaining a settled work force. This process has had several consequences. Productive land has become scarcer for smallholders, traditional dependence relationships between dominant and subordinate classes have become less important, landlessness among the rural poor has increased, and wage labor has become more mobile and insecure.

Analysts anticipated that the expansion of capitalist agriculture would simplify agrarian class relations, as landlords accumulated land and turned to wage labor as the principal means for exploiting it. Correspondingly, many expected that smallholders and peasant communities would eventually disappear, forced off the land and absorbed into a rural or urban labor force whose numbers and insecurity would keep wages extremely low. Considerable evidence, however, shows that smallholders and peasant communities have great capacity to persist and to survive the expansion of capitalism. At the level of the household, these survivors have diversified their sources of income as a way of hanging onto small plots of land. Others have resisted the incursions of large landowners, particularly on land that traditionally has been held communally. By joining together for production or marketing, some have been able to compete with capitalist producers. Others have retreated into subsistence production to protect themselves from an expanding cash economy.

Complicating Factors

The means that peasants and smallholders have adopted to persist as households and communities have called into question theoretical assumptions about the political correlates of class relationships. One of the most significant results of increasing economic pressure on smallholders, tenants, sharecroppers, and communally based peasants has been the economic diversification of rural households. A smallholding household, for example, may be composed of those who work a family plot, along with seasonal agricultural wage laborers, wage laborers in the nonfarm informal sector, and temporary urban labor migrants. The members of the household may also sharecrop or rent their own or other people's land. An individual within the household may, over the course of a year or a lifetime, engage in several income-generating activities, each of which is characterized by distinct relationships to the land and to employers.

The expansion of capitalist modes of production has also frequently implied specialization within the household. Some members are responsible for subsistence crops, while others plant cash crops or become labor migrants to earn income to enable the family to survive in a cash economy. In other cases, rural producers have formed cooperatives or associations that allow them to compete with large landowners for markets.

This diversification makes it difficult to predict the political behavior of rural classes and their links to democratic political regimes, based on an assessment of their economic interests. Within households, economic interests—and political concerns—may be diverse and even contradictory. This also holds true for large modern commercial farmers, who may align themselves with urban and industrial classes to support policies that promote further modernization and access to domestic and international markets.

The link between economic relationships and political behavior is open to question in other respects. For example, class relations may not be the most salient factor defining political or social identities in many rural areas. In many parts of Africa, for example, relationships to land and labor are frequently defined in terms of gender, age, and kinship. Political divisions are often based on issues related to ethnolinguistic community, clan, and kinship. Such factors, in addition to the diversification of economic relationships at the household level, have prompted analysts to look beyond relationships to land and labor to explain the economic and political behavior of rural inhabitants and the underpinnings of stable democratic systems.

Another development complicating earlier insights into agrarian class relations is the expansion of the state in the decades since World War II. In many countries the state has assumed a large role in promoting economic and social development. The state is present in rural areas in the guise of the local agricultural research station, the marketing agency, the rural credit bank, the fair-price store, the school, the health dispensary, the public works office, and other institutions. In many countries agrarian reform initiatives have increased the state's legal capacity to determine rural property rights. State-led development initiatives have in many cases enabled the state to replace the landlord as the principal determinant of rural economic conditions.

Given the increased role of the state in the rural economy, rural protest has focused increasingly on access to state-provided goods and services, including legal rights to land, rather than on the landlords and other local economic agents. Much state intervention in rural areas comes in the form of goods and services that can be provided selectively to individuals, groups, or communities. As a result, state leaders have frequently used rural investments to develop clientele linkages or to reward particular areas or groups for political conformity and support. Although the developmental state has in some cases been able to assert its autonomy from landowning groups, it has also increased its potential to manipulate the rural poor politically. The activities of developmental states also show the extent to which the state itself may be divided by competing interests, objectives, and political voices over agrarian issues.

The increasing variety of forms of association among rural groups is another complicating factor in the assessment of agrarian class relations. Smallholders and others have continued to organize around issues of land and working conditions, but they have also become mobilized as producers of particular crops or as consumers pressing for more responsive government policies. They have associated to gain access to domestic and international markets for their crops. Various forms of association—unions, syndicates, cooperatives, parties, and producer associations—have also allowed peasants to make demands on regional and national governments. Similarly, large landowners have associated in formal ways to lobby for certain policies and to resist those they see as harmful to their interests.

Party systems and elections in some countries have also altered rural politics. In cases of open and democratic party competition, national politicians have at times competed for the support of rural groups by promising or promoting policies of agrarian reform and rural development. In other cases, rural groups have been incorporated into clientelist networks that extend from national government or party offices rather than from the local landlord. Even in these situations, rural inhabitants have been able to develop a more independent political voice. At the least they have been able to diversify the sources of their dependence in a way that has allowed them to become less dependent on local landowners. Consequently, rural class relations are now seen to be determined by more than patterns of land ownership and labor use. They also depend on relative power relationships between rural land-owners and the developmental state and on the ways in which subordinate classes have been incorporated into national political systems.

Increased insight into the dynamics of rural economic and political life has made it more difficult to generalize about agrarian class relations and the links to democratic government. Nevertheless, these relations remain important to the analysis of the economic and political behavior of rural groups. Key issues still generate lively debate: the dynamics of agrarian revolts; the viability of peasant forms of production; the importance of nonclass factors, such as gender, ethnicity, and community, in rural identities; the analysis of household-based systems of production and accumulation; and the forms of incorporation into party and representational systems. In all these debates a central theme is the extent to which changing local, national, and international conditions have confounded earlier assumptions about the economic and political behavior of rural inhabitants.

See also *Class; Class relations, Industrial.*

Merilee S. Grindle

BIBLIOGRAPHY

Bates, Robert H. *Markets and States in Tropical Africa: The Political Basis of Agricultural Policies.* Berkeley: University of California Press, 1981.

Berry, Sarah. *No Condition Is Permanent: The Social Dynamics of Agrarian Change in Sub-Saharan Africa.* Madison: University of Wisconsin Press, 1993.

Chayanov, A. V. *The Theory of Peasant Economy.* Edited by Daniel Thorner, Basile Kerblay, and R. E. F. Smith. Homewood, Ill.: Richard D. Irwin, 1966.

Grindle, Merilee S. *State and Countryside: Development Policy and Agrarian Politics in Latin America.* Baltimore and Northampton: Johns Hopkins University Press, 1986.

Moore, Barrington, Jr. *Social Origins of Dictatorship and Democracy: Lord and Peasant in the Making of the Modern World.* Boston: Beacon Press, 1966.

Popkin, Samuel. *The Rational Peasant: The Political Economy of Rural Society in Vietnam.* Berkeley: University of California Press, 1979.

Scott, James C. *The Moral Economy of the Peasant: Rebellion and Subsistence in Southeast Asia.* New Haven and London: Yale University Press, 1976.

Tomich, Thomas P., Peter Kilby, and Bruce F. Johnston. *Transforming Agrarian Economies: Opportunities Seized, Opportunities Missed.* Ithaca, N.Y.: Cornell University Press, 1995.

Class relations, Industrial

Industrial class relations are the relations among aggregates of individuals, or classes, with each person's class membership defined by his or her position in the productive system of industrial society. Although the concept of social class goes back to Plato and Aristotle, the analysis of industrial class relations is rooted in the writings of Karl Marx.

In *Capital* (1867), Marx argued that individuals performing similar productive functions would come to have similar collective interests. According to Marx, the basic conflict in the birth of capitalist society was between feudal landowners and a rising class of capitalists who owned the bulk of the means of production. The basic conflict in mature capitalist society was between capitalists and wage workers. Marx viewed liberal freedoms and representative institutions based on property suffrage from the standpoint of class struggle, as the means by which capitalists attained and sustained their political hegemony. Marx believed that capitalist democracy could never accommodate the ultimate conflict between workers and capitalists, and he argued that systemic change to socialism was inevitable. Still, he did suggest that in some circumstances, particularly in England, Holland, and the United States, workers might find it possible to operate within democratic institutions to achieve their revolutionary goals.

Theory After Marx

The link between industrial class relations and the development of democracy has been elaborated by many social scientists since Marx. In the 1960s Barrington Moore, Jr., argued (in *Social Origins of Dictatorship and Democracy,* 1966) that one of the basic conditions of democracy in postfeudal Europe was an autonomous urban middle class, which could serve as a useful ally for the landed upper classes opposed to the monarchy. Moore summarized his argument as "no bourgeoisie, no democracy." The importance of a strong and independent middle class for stable democracy is attested by many historical and contemporary surveys of Western and non-Western societies. These surveys reveal strong positive relationships between democracy and a variety of socioeconomic indicators, such as level of economic development, education, literacy, and communication, all of which are associated with the development of an urban society and a large middle class.

Just as industrial class relations influence the chances for democracy, democracy in turn shapes class relations. Historically, liberal freedoms and representative institutions have been associated with a reduction of violent class conflict and the creation of incentives for nonviolent democratic class struggle. In the late nineteenth and early twentieth centuries the most intense class conflict took place in the most authoritarian societies, such as Russia, Finland, and Germany, where elites attempted to consolidate their hold on power by suppressing opposition.

By contrast, class conflict was less violent in countries with established liberal freedoms and effective representative institutions, such as England and Switzerland. In these countries, the extension of the vote to workers gave them a greater sense of social and political inclusion. The vote offered workers' parties the opportunity to strive for reform under capitalism. Moreover, where a competitive party system was established, existing liberal or left-wing bourgeois parties often tried to gain votes by meeting working-class demands. When these parties were unable to gain parliamentary majorities on their own, they were induced to build governing coalitions with socialist or labor parties, thereby further integrating workers into the democratic process.

Similarly, freedom of political association and expression gave workers the chance to press their group demands through legitimate channels. Freedom to combine in the labor market, to strike and to picket, gave groups of workers the ability to press a range of demands immediately through trade unions. The earlier the union movement was established and the stronger it became, the more difficult it was for socialists to encompass unions and their members in a revolutionary movement that aimed to abolish, rather than reform, capitalism.

The Post–World War II Era

After the period between the two world wars, which saw the breakdown of democracies and the establishment in some countries of fascist dictatorships, class struggle was moderated in Western society in the post–World War II era. Successful economic reconstruction and high levels of economic growth contributed to what was described as a postwar social contract in which previously radical working-class organizations moderated their ideological opposition to capitalism as they were integrated into the body politic. Trade unions, the largest and most powerful working-class organizations, became quasi-public institutions with diverse opportunities for participation in economic policy making, often at the highest levels.

As a result of improved working conditions and political integration, most Western societies saw a significant reduction of industrial conflict. Socialist parties adopted catchall electoral strategies, appealing to uncommitted voters by dropping demands for the reconstitution of capitalism in favor of reforming and fine-tuning it. Reforms included Keynesian "demand management" (from the English economist John Maynard Keynes, 1883–1946), new and expanded welfare programs, and consensual policies designed to constrain wage demands and inflation.

Beginning in the late 1950s several observers described this new situation as an "end of ideology." The dominant ideologies of the nineteenth century, Marxism and laissez-faire capitalism, had apparently lost their mass followings and their relevance in guiding complex policy choices in the modern world. Traditional class-based ideologies seemed to be giving way to technocratic, more pragmatic approaches to achieve common goals of economic growth, full employment, and economic security for those unable to compete in the labor market.

Countries varied widely, however, in the extent to which the postwar social contract was institutionalized. Class compromise was strongest in northern and central Europe and weakest in southern Europe and the Anglo-American democracies. Until the late 1970s in northern and central Europe, and particularly in Sweden, Norway, Austria, and the Low Countries (Belgium, Luxembourg, and the Netherlands), the working class was strongly organized both in politics and in the labor market. In these countries, socialist parties were able to participate in governments on a regular basis. This participation opened a political channel for trade unions to exchange moderation of their labor-market demands for favorable state action, including legal protection of unions, economic policies for full employment, and welfare and egalitarian social policies. Where unions were strong and centralized, they were best able to provide the collective restraint in the labor market (reflected in low strike levels) that allowed them to carry out their side of the bargain. Cross-national research has found the lowest levels of unemployment, the lowest strike levels, and the most egalitarian social policies in societies where employees are highly organized in trade unions, where those unions are highly centralized, and where socialist or social democratic parties have consistently participated in government.

In terms of organizational structure, societies characterized by "societal corporatism," as conceptualized by Philippe Schmitter, were best placed to institutionalize democratic class compromise. Under societal corporatism, interest groups resemble a set of pyramids: they are hierarchical organizations clearly differentiated from neighboring interest groups at the base as well as the top (that is, they are noncompeting). Such a structure promotes policy bargaining at the national level because constituencies are clearly defined and uniquely represented; the interests of each constituency are gathered within the interest group before, not during, the process of national negotiation; and interest group leaders are secure in their leadership. Bargains made by leaders will not be undercut by competing interest groups bidding for the support of that constituency. Moreover, as Mancur Olson has argued, the broader the scope of an interest group, the more likely it is that interest group leaders will take into consideration the wider social consequences of their actions. This is true for the simple reason that the constituency of a broad-based interest group includes a significant part of the entire society.

Under the postwar social contract, class relations assumed a new guise, as means by which conflicts about the distribution of economic rewards could be channeled into a structured bargaining process. Where the working class was organizationally strong and coherent, it could enter into national bargains. Conversely, where the working class was organizationally incoherent (as in Britain), or split along political or religious lines (as in France or Italy), national bargains exchanging wage restraint for full employment and greater economic equality were either impossible to make or impossible to implement. In the postwar decades, instead of fomenting intense political conflict that might blow society apart, class solidarity was transformed into a force for political stability and democratic effectiveness.

Postindustrial Society

Just as classes and class relations were transformed in the shift from agrarian to industrial society (some social analysts believe), the shift from industrial to postindustrial society will see the rise of a new class based on the new productive forces. This view, developed by Daniel Bell, John Goldthorpe, and Alain Touraine, shares with Marxist philosophy the supposition that individuals' interests are shaped mainly by their position in the process of production. But these analysts diagnose fundamental changes in the productive process—changes of which Marx was only dimly aware—such as the growth of the "knowledge and professional" sector, which includes educators, scientists, professionals, administrators, and managers. The rapid growth of this sector arguably has created the conditions for a new "service" or "knowledge" class. Conceptions of how this class will define, organize, and express its political interests vary. Touraine has argued that this new class may forge an alliance with the old working class, while Goldthorpe emphasizes that the interests of individuals in this new class are oriented around their autonomy in the productive process and therefore are opposed to the interests of blue-collar workers. Despite their differences, both conceptions assume the growth of a coherent class with clearly defined interests.

The evidence of the 1980s and early 1990s indicates, however, that postindustrialism is actually creating diverse new groups with diverse interests, loosening class ties generally, and undermining the industrial class cleavage without replacing it with a new dominant cleavage. As Seymour Martin Lipset stressed in the second edition of his classic comparative analysis, *Political Man* (1981), postindustrialism has split the left into a traditional left, appealing mainly to blue-collar workers on issues relating to economic equality, and a new left, oriented to environmental and lifestyle issues. Whereas the new left is relatively conservative on state action to reduce inequality, the old left is conservative on environmental and lifestyle issues.

The effect of this split is to reduce the class nature of party appeal. In the first edition of *Political Man*, published in 1960, Lipset emphasized that party competition across industrialized societies reflected the class divide more than any other influence; in the second edition he noted that the correlation between class position and voting has eroded across Western society.

Several influences appear to have contributed to the weakening class basis of politics in postindustrial societies. Not only has the emergence of new occupations created a more complex class structure, but a variety of economic and social developments have weakened the influence of class position for those individuals who still fit unambiguously in traditional working-class and middle-class categories. With the decline of heavy industry and coal mining across Western societies, working-class communities that formerly were the core of the socialist movement have shrunk. Those that remain are less insulated from diverse influences of the wider society. Commuting has weakened the link between work and home; increased geographical mobility has eroded the sense of collective identity within working-class communities built over generations; the growth of mass media, particularly television, has weakened socialist and working-class parties as purveyors of political information. These developments have given people a greater sense of choice of lifestyles—and of political opinions. They have reduced the solidarity of working-class communities and the political cues they offer; as a consequence they have undermined the cultural importance of working-class movements.

Trade unions, the largest working-class organizations in every Western society, have become noticeably more heterogeneous in membership, more organizationally incoherent, and more politically fragmented in the past two decades. The chief reason for these developments is that the old core of union movements—blue-collar male workers in heavy industry and mineral extraction—has lost its predominance as the proportion of organized white-collar, professional, and female employees has grown.

Generally speaking, the mobilization of non–blue-collar workers has created the greatest fragmentation in union movements that were formerly the most cohesive. In Britain, for example, where the union federation, the Trades Union Congress, was never centralized or coherent, white-collar unions have been encompassed within the organization. But in Sweden, where unions developed along socialist industrial lines, with the goal of one and only one union for any particular industry, the organization of white-collar and professional workers has drastically reduced the coherence of the union movement. The main blue-collar–dominated federation, the *Landsorganisationen,* which is the industrial wing of the Swedish Social Democratic Party, faces rapidly growing, autonomous white-collar union federations. Swedish unions remain large and powerful organizations, but they are becoming noticeably less coherent.

When we turn to the level of union membership in advanced industrial democracies, the overall trend has been downward. In the 1980s the level of union organization fell one-fifth, from 35 percent to 28 percent. This average conceals wide variations across individual countries. Union membership actually increased in this period in Finland, Norway, and especially in Sweden, while it fell sharply in France, the Netherlands, Spain, and the United States.

The changes in the class basis of Western society described here have weakened or undermined social contracts even in societies where they were formerly entrenched. The relevance of class for voting has declined, and party competition is less and less dominated by the divide between employees and employers. Strong social democratic parties persist across Western Europe, but socialists no longer monopolize the discourse of dissent. They must compete with a variety of new left groups, including environmentalists, women's groups, antinuclear groups, and greens. These groups raise issues concerning the quality of life, the role of gender, participation, and decentralization that cut across traditional socialist issues and divide the socialist electorate. Although their aggregate electoral support remains high, for the first time socialist parties are losing support among young people to radical parties that reject socialism.

Instead of transforming the class system to one in which a new class based in the growing knowledge and professional sector is pitted against a traditional middle class and an industrial working class, the changes associated with postindustrial society are diminishing the extent to which class shapes political conflict. In short, contemporary changes in Western society challenge the usefulness of concepts, such as class and class relations, that were developed to analyze industrial society.

See also *Class; Class relations, Agrarian; Corporatism; Industrial relations; Interest groups; Lipset, Seymour Martin; Marxism; Mill, John Stuart; Socialism.*

Gary Marks

BIBLIOGRAPHY

Bell, Daniel. *The Coming of Post-Industrial Society.* New York: Basic Books, 1973.

Goldthorpe, John H. "On the Service Class, Its Formation and Future." In *Social Class and the Division of Labour,* edited by Anthony Giddens and Gavin Mackenzie. Cambridge: Cambridge University Press, 1982.

———, ed. *Order and Conflict in Contemporary Capitalism.* Oxford and New York: Oxford University Press, 1984.

Lemke, Christiane, and Gary Marks. "From Decline to Demise? The Fate of Socialism in Europe." In *The Crisis of Socialism in Europe,* edited by Christiane Lemke and Gary Marks. Durham, N.C.: Duke University Press, 1992.

Lipset, Seymour Martin. *Political Man: The Social Bases of Politics.* Expanded and updated ed. Baltimore: Johns Hopkins University Press, 1981; Aldershot: Gower, 1983.

———. "Radicalism or Reformism: The Sources of Working-Class Politics." *American Political Science Review* 77 (March 1983): 1–18.

Marks, Gary. *Unions in Politics: Britain, Germany, and the United States in the Nineteenth and Early Twentieth Centuries.* Princeton: Princeton University Press, 1989.

Olson, Mancur. *The Rise and Decline of Nations.* New Haven and London: Yale University Press, 1972.

Schmitter, Philippe C., and Gerhard Lehmbruch, eds. *Trends towards Corporatist Intermediation.* London: Sage Publications, 1979.

Touraine, Alain. *The Post-Industrial Society.* New York: Random House, 1971.

Athena, the patron goddess of Athens, appears on a silver coin from the fifth century B.C.—the high point of Athenian culture.

Classical Greece and Rome

The sites of the earliest democratic institutions. The first theoretical reflections on democracy and democratic institutions are found in the Greek city-states and the Roman Republic. Classical Greece and Rome were also models for later political regimes.

Niccolò Machiavelli, the Florentine political practitioner and theorist of the early sixteenth century, in his *Discourses on Livy* urges his readers to learn from and imitate the political regimes and noble actions of antiquity. In particular, he turns back to the regime of republican Rome, a sharp contrast to the Rome of his own time. Although he recognizes that republican Rome can never be re-created in the modern world, Machiavelli praises the political institutions and heroic values of a pre-Christian era, when men sought public glory for themselves and for the city in which they lived. The lessons of Machiavelli's *Prince* earned him ignominy, but his exhortations to imitate the republicanism of ancient Rome spawned interest among political theorists in the institutions of the Roman Republic.

From the sixteenth century on, Roman republicanism enjoyed a renaissance in the writings of political theorists and in political movements toward more popular participation, but it was not until the nineteenth century that the institutions and principles of Athenian democracy won favor among political theorists and practitioners. Until then Athenian democracy symbolized a regime to be avoided; it showed the dangers of allowing the many to rule, a practice that would lead to chaos. Nineteenth- and twentieth-century authors reversed this focus by finding in Athenian democracy, whether accurately or not, freedom for the individual and a model of participatory government for the modern world to admire, if not to emulate.

Athenian Democracy

Discussions of ancient democracy today usually refer to the institutions of Athens from 508/507 B.C. to 338 B.C. Athens was the largest of the classical Greek city-states, the most powerful of the democratic cities, and the only one to leave a sufficient written record by which we can understand how it functioned and how its citizens viewed it. From Thucydides, the fifth-century B.C. historian of the Peloponnesian War between Sparta and Athens, we first learn of the dominant categories for the governments of the ancient Greek world: oligarchy and democracy. Both oligarchies and democracies might have assemblies at which major decisions concerning the public life of the community would be made, but oligarchies opened political participation to a fraction of their populations, usually the wealthy. Democracies gave power to the *demos,* the people, allowing large numbers of their populations (though certainly not all, since women and slaves were excluded) to be citizens and engage in political self-rule.

Sparta led the oligarchies and Athens the democracies. Thucydides' history presents a conflict between democracy and oligarchy, the disorder but vitality of the former and the order and immobility of the other. From Aristotle's *Politics* we learn that there were many different forms of democracy, depending on who "the people" were (farmers, fishermen, merchants), what limits laws set on the decisions of the assembly, and what offices were filled by lot or by election. Despite the great variety of regimes Aristotle describes, Athens remains the one we know best and the one to which subsequent generations have turned for their vision of ancient democracy.

The political transformation of Athens from a landed aristocracy to a democracy began in the early sixth century B.C., with the reforms of Solon, the elected leader of Athens in 594 B.C. Faced with social unrest, Solon tried to balance the conflicts between the rich and poor by enacting laws controlling consumption and display, freeing those men who had sold themselves into bondage, and opening political offices to a wider portion of the population. In poems describing his reforms he emphasized that all members of the city, not the gods, are responsible for saving the city and maintaining the principles of justice. Although Solon did not institutionalize democracy in Athens, and his reforms were almost immediately replaced by the tyranny of Peisistratus, he articulated the principles of community action and responsibility central to the emergence of a democratic regime.

Cleisthenes, who lived at the end of the sixth century, is credited with creating the institutions associated with Athenian democracy. In the early years, at least, the Athenians referred to their regime as an *isonomia* (equality before the law) rather than a *demokratia* (power of the people). In an appeal for political power to the people, Cleisthenes "founded" democracy by reorganizing the city. He replaced the four ancient patrilineal tribes with ten artificially created tribes, composed of locally based administrative units, or *demes,* which were themselves divided into three subunits. Each of the tribes contained demes from three distinct geographic areas, thus ensuring that tribes had an administrative, but not political, role in Athens.

Following Cleisthenes' reorganization, Athens in the fifth century B.C. developed its major democratic institutions. The Assembly replaced the aristocratically dominated Areopagus as the center of the city's decision making. Participation was open to all citizens. Citizenship at first required an Athenian father, with confirmation of parentage and age at a local inscription ceremony. In the middle of the century, citizenship required that the mother as well as the father be Athenian (though women did not participate as citizens in the political life of the city). An executive council determined the agenda for each meeting of the assembly and formulated draft proposals. The assembly met about forty times each year. Membership on the executive council, which was determined by lot, changed each month, while the chair, also chosen by lot, changed each day. The courts were also open to all citizens, and service was determined by lot. All offices in the city, from port authority officials to market and treasury supervisors, were likewise assigned by lot. It is estimated that close to 1,000 positions were filled this way each year.

At the end of a year of service, all public officers were subjected to scrutiny to ensure that no untoward actions, particularly embezzlements, marred their service. Toward the end of the fifth century, officers received modest remuneration for their service, as did those attending the assembly. The major elected officials were ten military commanders. Pericles (c. 495–429 B.C.), the renowned leader of Athenian democracy, derived his political power from his repeated yearly election as commander for almost twenty years. While Pericles was in power Athens asserted its dominion over the islands of the Aegean Sea, forcing them to become revenue-paying subjects and bringing great wealth to Athens.

Scholars debate the degree to which Athenians participated in the processes of self-government and the different levels of participation during the 170 years of Athenian democracy. There can be no doubt that the system depended on the engagement of large numbers of citizens. Recent archaeological work suggests that the site where the assembly met had space for only 6,000 individuals, and, though that number is large, it is a fraction of the 20,000–30,000 Athenian citizens eligible to attend. Participation in the life of the city, however, did not depend only on the assembly. There were many offices to be filled at the city and deme levels. Calculations of the number of citizens and of offices to be filled suggest that few citizens could have avoided serving in an office during their lifetimes.

Athenian democracy, and with it Greek democracy, disappeared with the Battle of Chaeronea in 338 B.C. when Philip of Macedon conquered Greece and subjected the Greek city-states to Macedonian rule.

Theoretical assessments of Athenian democracy suffer because there are no authors who we might consider democratic theorists. The Sophist Protagoras, appearing in Plato's dialogue of the same name, is the most promising spokesman of democratic principles. He claims that all participate in self-government because Zeus, the supreme divinity, has given all a sense of justice and a sense of shame. It is not an argument of equality but of shared qualities that enable humans to survive because they can live together and rule themselves. Characters in the tragedies of the fifth century often indicate pride in the self-rule of the Athenian regime. Aeschylus, the tragedian of the early fifth century, has a character in his *Persians* describe the Athenians as "slaves of no man, not listening to any one person." In his *Suppliant Women* he portrays the Athenian rulers as making no decisions without consulting the people, but he offers little analysis of the structure and virtues of the democracy. Herodotus, the historian writing in the mid-fifth century of the conflict between the Greeks and Persians, portrays the Greek city-states under the leadership of the Athenians as autonomous in contrast to the despotically ruled Persians. Herodotus attributes Athenian success in battle to self-government and an independent spirit. In Thucydides' history, Pericles in his funeral oration for the first Athenian soldiers killed in the Peloponnesian War, vividly expresses the Athenians' pride in a regime that favors the many rather than the few, affords equal justice, and attends to individual qualities rather than family or economic background. Although one may debate whether the funeral oration idealizes the regime, Pericles articulates the principles on which the Athenians built their democracy.

From most other authors there is criticism of the democracy. In a work attributed to an unidentified "Old Oligarch," the author, while critical of the rule of the "worse" over the "better," describes Athenian success at institutionalizing through their assemblies, courts, and the rotation of offices a system that enables the poor to control the wealthy. Plato's criticisms are more serious. He focuses on the incapacity of the many to have a true science of politics and says that rhetoric, based on the manipulation of opinion, controls the many and corrupts the young men who might have the capacity for philosophy. Aristotle's analysis of politics draws heavily on the experiences of Athens. His definition of the citizen as one who participates in the offices and judgments of the city derives from Athenian practice, but he worries about democracy's potential for turning the people into a tyrant and for limiting the role of the truly good man.

Until the nineteenth century Athenian democracy was considered a regime to be avoided. The political turbulence in Athens supposedly illustrated the dangers of allowing the people—especially the poor—excessive power. The *Federalist Papers,* written to support the adoption of the U.S. Constitution, warned against adopting the political institutions of the Greek city-states and instead urged adoption of those institutions that would restrain the excessive effects of a popular democracy. In the nineteenth century this attitude changed. In the 1830s, with Andrew Jackson in the White House, Jacksonian democracy emerged as a potent political force, Hellenism swept America, and in England such authors as George Grote, the historian of Greece, rejected earlier histories that condemned Athenian political life and turned to Athenian democracy as the true source of greatness—political, moral, and cultural. This exaltation of the democratic political life of the ancient world continues in the thought of recent political theorists such as Hannah Arendt, who harks back to the Athenian citizen engaged in debate, seeking an immortality of action rather than involvement in the daily necessities of economic life that engage the modern citizen. Arendt is one of many writers who find in the ancient democracy a model of political participation that reveals the inadequacies of the individualistic liberal democracies of today.

The Roman Republic

The Roman Republic grew from a small city by the Tiber River to a massive empire controlling much of the known world for almost 500 years. During that time numerous changes took place in its political organization as a series of concessions were made to the poorer classes and to newly conquered cities of the Italian peninsula.

Polybius, a Greek who came to Rome in the middle of the second century B.C. as a political exile, wrote an extensive history of Rome in which he commented favorably on the Roman constitution. He described the regime as successfully mixing the elements of kingship, aristocracy, and democracy to ensure a permanence impossible for any of the pure regimes. Although the accuracy of the details of Polybius's description may be doubted and his assurance of Rome's imperviousness to change was shortly shown to be false, his classification captured the central elements of the Roman Republic.

Once the kings were overthrown, about 509 B.C., the Roman Senate became the primary locus of political power. Elected magistrates became lifelong members of the Senate, thus giving the Senate a flavor of popular or democratic origins. But membership in the Senate was confined to a small number of wealthy families with the funds to secure the magisterial election. Until the first century B.C. the Senate predominated, despite the creation and increasing influence of the more popularly constituted assemblies of the people and the institution of tribunes as the official defenders of the people.

All the officers of the state, including the consuls and the tribunes, were elected for one-year terms in one of the assemblies of the *plebs,* or common people. The consuls, whom Polybius identified as the monarchical element of the Roman constitution, had primary authority as the conveners of the Senate and representatives of the state to foreign powers, but they did not control the decisions taken in the Senate. At times of extreme danger the consuls could recommend that all power be turned over to a dictator for a period of six months. The tribunes had the power to veto laws decreed by other magistrates that they judged harmful to the people. At first the tribunes had no authority for positive actions. They could call the assemblies and ask for views, leading to the advisory, but not binding, *plebi scita* (resolved by the people). After the Lex Hortensia of 287 B.C. such *plebi scita* could become binding laws without approval of the Senate.

There was a division of responsibility between the popular assemblies. The *comitia centuriata,* whose complicated structure was originally based in part on what sort of armor a citizen was able to provide, thereby ensuring the continued influence of the wealthier sections of the society, elected the magistrates, authorized declarations of war, and voted on proposals submitted by the consuls. No opportunity was provided for discussion, and voting was so structured that the wealthy groups voted first, with voting ceasing once a majority was attained. Progressively the *comitia tributa* became the more significant assembly. It could pass laws and elected a number of officials. Its voting structure was not nearly so complicated as that of the *comitia centuriata,* and with the expansion of citizenship to the Italians perhaps close to one million people had the right to vote by tribes in the *comitia tributa.* The structure of these assemblies, however, made them susceptible to bribery. Bribery became more of a problem as the institutions of the republic deteriorated at the end of the second century B.C. with the emergence of opposing political parties, the senatorial Optimates and the more popularly focused Populares. Attempts at economic reforms by Tiberius and Gaius Gracchus led to divisions among the traditional senatorial leadership and diminished the Senate's unified control over the activities of the state.

In the first century B.C. the conflicts escalated, and individual leaders acquired armies of men loyal to them. The result was open battles on the street, conspiracies against the republic, and individual leaders such as Sulla and Marius gaining dictatorial power for brief periods. Julius Caesar, the successful military leader, was assassinated in 44 B.C. for fear that he would diminish further the power of the Senate and establish an autocracy. After the battle of Actium in 31 B.C., in which Octavian, the adopted son of Caesar, defeated Mark Antony, the republic with its powerful Senate and assemblies of the people was replaced with a principate, rule by one man. Octavian, now called Augustus, was the prince.

Unlike Athens, Rome did not produce a large number of authors who reflected on the political life of the city. Polybius (who was Greek) wrote the most serious analysis of the political experiences of the Roman Republic before Cicero. The writings of Cicero, while drawing inspiration from Plato, praise Rome of the second century B.C. before the decline of senatorial authority. Sallust, a historian writing in the first century B.C., found much to criticize as he looked at contemporary signs of corruption and much to long for from the early days of the republic when, according to report, men loved their country and were virtuous by instinct rather than because of law. Writers focused on an idealized vision of patriotic heroes who devoted themselves to the state's welfare rather than to their private interests. They did not focus on the participation of the many in the political regime.

The word used to describe the Roman state captures the difference between the participatory democracy of the Athenian city-state and the aristocratic governance of Rome: *res publica* means the "public thing." The state belonged to the public, and those who served Rome could protect that which belonged to the whole. Care for the public thing did not mean that all needed to participate in public life. Responsibility for care fell on those who had positions of authority. This concept of responsibility for those who needed protection characterized Roman thought within the state and served as a justification for the wide expansion of the empire while republican institutions developed at home. The state, however, was continuously shaken by challenges to this vision of aristocratic benevolence as the people demanded more control over the political agenda.

Rediscovery of Ancient Models

During the Renaissance, Roman republicanism and Cicero's activity as a major participant in that republic enchanted those rediscovering ancient models. Machiavelli looked to the glory of the Roman Republic for his presentation of how political men behaved before they were corrupted by Christianity. The conflicts between the patricians and plebeians represented for him the engagement of a people in their public life and a commitment to a glory that was worldly rather than otherworldy. J. G. A.

Pocock has traced the influence of Machiavelli's thought through a tradition of republicanism in Europe and America. In the *Federalist Papers* the early defenders of the American Constitution recalled the nobility of Roman statesmen as the model for their own behavior. The structure of the Roman state offered a paradigm for their radically new political system. They turned to the language of the Roman state to name the central body of the American political system, the Senate. Jean-Jacques Rousseau, the first great modern democratic theorist, arguing for the feasibility of combining freedom and equality in his *Social Contract* (1762), suggested studying the Roman popular assemblies to see how this approach might be possible. And the leaders of the French Revolution, following Rousseau's suggestion, looked to the Roman Republic for their inspiration as they, like the Romans, instituted a republic upon the overthrow of a monarchy.

Today we often find a conflation of the republican model of Rome and the participatory model of Athens as theorists hark back to a classical age for earlier examples of democratically constituted regimes; the two, however, are distinct in their underlying principles and structure.

See also *Aristotle; Cicero; Communitarianism; Dictatorship; Machiavelli, Niccolò; Participatory democracy; Plato; Popular sovereignty; Revolution, French; Rousseau, Jean-Jacques; Theory, Ancient; United States Constitution; Virtue, Civic.* In Documents section, see *Pericles' Funeral Oration (431 B.C.); Constitution of the United States (1787).*

Arlene W. Saxonhouse

BIBLIOGRAPHY

Arendt, Hannah. *The Human Condition.* Chicago: University of Chicago Press, 1958.

Cowell, F. R. *Cicero and the Roman Republic.* Baltimore: Penguin Books, 1967.

Finley, M. I. *Democracy: Ancient and Modern.* Rev. ed. New Brunswick, N.J.: Rutgers University Press, 1985.

Grote, George A. *A History of Greece.* 12 vols. London: J. Murray, 1851–1856.

Hansen, Mogens Herman. *The Athenian Democracy in the Age of Demosthenes: Structures, Principles and Ideology.* Oxford and Cambridge, Mass.: Blackwell, 1991.

Nicolet, Claude. *The World of the Citizen in Republican Rome.* Translated by P. S. Falla. Berkeley: University of California Press, 1980.

Ober, Josiah. *Mass and Elite in Democratic Athens: Rhetoric, Ideology, and the Power of the People.* Princeton: Princeton University Press, 1989.

Pocock, J. G. A. *The Machiavellian Moment: Florentine Political Thought and the Atlantic Republican Tradition.* Princeton: Princeton University Press, 1975.

Stockton, David. *The Classical Athenian Democracy.* Oxford and New York: Oxford University Press, 1990.

Taylor, Lily Ross. *Party Politics in the Age of Caesar.* Berkeley: University of California Press, 1971.

Coalition building

The process of uniting different political actors or organizations in the pursuit of some common goal. Organizing individuals and groups for collective action is a fundamental political problem. The problem is sometimes described as building political coalitions. A coalition is a set of actors or "players" who agree to pursue a common goal or set of goals, pool their resources in pursuit of this goal, communicate about and form binding commitments concerning their goal, and distribute what they receive when they reach their goal.

Coalitions thus consist of distinct players or actors (which may be individuals, groups, or organizations) with their own respective resources and goals. Political coalitions may, for example, be made up of individual legislators, political parties seeking to control the executive branch, or states engaged in joint international action (such as the United States and its allies during the Persian Gulf war in 1991). Actors who participate in coalitions commit resources, such as votes, money, or soldiers, to goals that may not be entirely their own. Senators who take action together to pass welfare reform legislation or states that join forces to resist Iraqi aggression may disagree substantially over what result they want. The fundamental question confronting the student of political coalitions is therefore why and under what conditions such coalitions form and survive.

Coalitions form in countless political situations. Political scientists have paid particular attention to coalitions in legislatures, courts, and other multimember decision-making bodies; to party coalitions in cabinets; and to the alliances of states in the international system. Although these are not the only important examples of political coalitions, they have helped to motivate the formal study of coalitions. This article pays particular attention to interparty executive coalitions in parliamentary democracies—that is, to agreements between political parties that seek to control a cabinet that is responsible to a parliamentary (or legislative) majority. Cabinet coalition building is very important in parliamentary democracies, and many distinguished scholars have studied how they form and survive.

Building Executive Coalitions

In multiparty parliamentary democracies, such as most European nations, Japan, and most former British colonies, political parties play a powerful intermediary role in deciding who will control the executive branch and formulate public policy. In some parliamentary systems that have two dominant parties (Conservatives and Labour in Britain; Liberals and Labor in Australia), one party or the other will normally hold a majority of the seats in the legislature (for example, the House of Commons). In such situations the majority party typically can control the legislature by itself and need not build coalitions with any other party. Similarly, in the United States one of the two major parties normally controls the Senate or the House of Representatives. In such circumstances, parties do not need to build coalitions with one another. Instead, we often speak of coalitions within the dominant parties, for example, between northern and southern Democrats or between liberals and moderates.

Things get more complicated when there is no majority party. Parliamentary democracy requires that a majority of the members of the legislature support the prime minister and his or her cabinet. If no party has a majority, the supporters of the cabinet must necessarily be a coalition of more than one party's representatives. Sometimes the cabinet consists of representatives of one party only, although members of other parties (or independents) support the cabinet members in parliamentary debates and votes. Coalitions that do not share cabinet responsibilities are called *legislative coalitions*. More commonly in parliamentary democracies, the parties that support the cabinet in parliament also agree to share control of the executive branch. Such alliances are known as *cabinet coalitions* or *executive coalitions*.

Coalition formation is a part of the larger process of government formation. The first step of that process is the naming of a head of government, that is, a prime minister or premier. Typically, the head of state (monarch or president) will officially take this step. The prime minister will then begin to assemble a team of ministers and prepare a government policy program. The legislature may have to approve of these choices. In most cases the critical players in cabinet bargaining are the parties' leaders in the parliament, and only a few of them are directly involved. After the head of state has designated a prime ministerial candidate, the coalition formation process is almost entirely in the hands of these parliamentarians. Although party leaders are ultimately accountable to their rank and file, it is very difficult and costly to overturn top-level agreements.

Institutional rules can limit the range of feasible coalitions, as can players outside the parliament, such as foreign powers or influential interest groups. For example, if the largest party always gets the first opportunity to form a government, the party's chances of participating in the cabinet coalition are good. If parties bargain under strict deadlines, they may be less likely to form previously untried coalitions. Investiture requirements—the need for parliamentary approval before a coalition can take office—restrict bargaining by placing a hurdle at the end of the negotiations.

In multiparty systems, particularly when there are more than four or five parliamentary parties, the number of possible coalitions is greater. Structural constraints, such as constitutional requirements that the cabinet include certain social groups, may reduce the number of feasible coalitions, but typically the reduction is only moderate.

Particularly in countries with many political parties, executive coalition negotiations often proceed sequentially. A set of parties that seek to control the government form a protocoalition. If this emerging coalition does not control enough votes, it may decide to include additional parties. Initially, the "coalition" may consist only of the party of the premier-designate. Even if this party does not command majority support, it may decide to try to form a cabinet alone, for example through ad hoc (shifting) legislative coalitions.

When the primary party invites one or more parties to join, the latter may accept or decline that invitation. In the next stage the members of the new protocoalition may then decide to invite other parties; these invitations continue until the members of the protocoalition do not wish to expand any further or until no additional members can be found. Any existing member of a protocoalition commonly has veto power over the admission of additional members. Deviations from this pattern do occur, as when the head of state explicitly gives the official task of forming a government to a coalition of parties (for example, a coalition that agreed in advance to join forces).

Types of Executive Coalitions

There are many different types of executive coalitions. First, governments may be either true coalitions of two or more parties or single-party cabinets. Second, executive alliances may be majority or minority coalitions. The former can count on the support of a majority in parliament, whereas the latter cannot.

Minority coalitions are particularly common in Scandinavia (Denmark, Norway, and Sweden), in some countries that have been strongly influenced by the British parliamentary tradition (Canada and Ireland), and in several southern European nations (such as France, Italy, and Spain). In some countries, especially Denmark, minority coalitions have been more common than majority governments.

Parliamentary democracy would seem to require that all cabinet coalitions be majority coalitions. Indeed, all viable cabinets must be able to summon a legislative majority when challenged through a motion of no confidence. Occasionally, however, one or more parties may agree to support the government in parliament without getting cabinet representation. We commonly refer to such parties as *support parties*. Their existence implies that some coalitions that seem to be minority coalitions may in fact be able to count on majority support in parliament. Legislative support coalitions need not include the same parties across all issue areas. Such shifting legislative coalitions have been particularly common in multiparty systems such as Denmark, Israel, and Italy.

Minority governments, whether they rely on stable or shifting legislative coalitions, tend to be less stable than majority cabinets. The conventional view is that they are also less effective in policy making. Yet minority governments are quite common in stable and well-functioning democracies such as Canada, Ireland, and the Scandinavian countries, where they often alternate with single-party majority governments.

We also distinguish among minimal winning, oversized, and undersized coalitions. Minimal winning coalitions are coalitions that have no unnecessary members—that is, members whose defection would not cause the coalition to be defeated. Oversized coalitions have one or more unnecessary members, whereas undersized coalitions have fewer members than are necessary to win. William Riker introduced these concepts to the study of executive coalitions in his seminal book *The Theory of Political Coalitions* (1962). According to Riker, in many social situations similar to particular games, only minimal winning coalitions will form. Executive coalition bargaining, Riker argued, is among these social situations. Because Riker's theory establishes a size criterion for

coalitions, we commonly call its prediction the *size principle*.

Only recently have political scientists begun seriously to discuss what it means to win in coalition bargaining. Clearly this depends in large part on the rules by which politicians play. In bargaining over cabinet coalitions, the meaning of winning depends on the parliamentary decision (voting) rules. If all important decisions require a two-thirds majority, it takes at least a two-thirds majority to win. Because most legislatures make decisions by simple majority vote, most students of cabinet coalitions have equated winning with majority status. By that measure, all minority governments are undersized, and oversized coalitions are any that could lose a member and still retain their majorities. Oversized coalitions are particularly common in some countries where the population consists of several distinct ethnic, linguistic, or religious groups. Examples are Belgium, Italy, the Netherlands, and Lebanon before the civil war broke out.

We call coalitions that involve all, or almost all, significant parliamentary parties *grand coalitions*. Such governments are particularly common during wartime and other emergency situations. They are also a feature of everyday politics in some societies, such as Switzerland and, in some periods, Belgium and Finland.

Riker's size principle builds on several critical, and sometimes controversial, assumptions. Like all game theory, his argument assumes that parties act rationally. Riker's theory also assumes that parties have full information when they bargain; that the "prize" for the winning coalition is the same regardless of who its members are; and that each case of coalition bargaining is an independent event, in which the parties pay no attention to what has happened in the past or what they expect to happen in the future. Critics have challenged many of the assumptions of Riker's approach, among them the assumption that, apart from considerations of size, parties are totally indiscriminate in their search for partners. Conservatives looking for a coalition partner would, for example, be indifferent between choosing Communists or Christian Democrats if both parties controlled the same number of legislative seats.

Because it depends on radical simplifications, the size principle does not explain real-world cabinet coalitions very successfully. Its predictions are often inaccurate and even wildly implausible, and it cannot explain either minority or surplus majority governments, both of which are common.

Policy-based coalition theory emerged as a critique of "policy blind" models such as the size principle. It assumes that policy considerations are foremost in the minds of the actors and that the parliamentary game is about the determination of government policy. Policy-based coalition theory has gradually gained the support of most students of multiparty democracy. Policy-based coalition theory predicts minimal connected winning or minimal range coalitions.

Connectedness requires that coalitions consist of parties that are adjacent (connected) along a left-right (or liberal-conservative) scale or any other important policy dimension. It also means that all the parties within the coalition's policy range participate. The policy range is that part of the policy spectrum that lies between the most extreme members of the coalition, for example the farthest left party (say, Social Democratic) and the farthest right party (say, Christian Democratic). If a coalition is connected, it leaves no gaps in this range but includes all the parties within it. A minimal range coalition makes this range as small as possible.

In recent years, some coalition theorists have rejected the size (majority) criterion. If parties truly have strictly policy objectives, they argue, all coalitions that cannot be defeated on policy grounds should be feasible. A policy-viable coalition is one that cannot be defeated by those in the legislature who prefer different policies. Policy-viable coalitions will always include the "core" party. In a one-dimensional policy space, such as the left-right scale, the core party is the one with the median legislator, that is, the person who has as many members to the right as to the left. If parties care only about policy, no majority can rationally agree to shift the policy position away from that of the median party. Consequently, the core party can prevail even if it controls far less than a parliamentary majority. It should always be in the governing coalition.

Although the policy core is a simple and elegant theory of coalition formation, it contains many assumptions and does not always make successful predictions. Other coalition theorists have therefore tried to capture the effects of various institutions on coalition bargaining. Election laws, parliamentary procedure, and the rules of cabinet decision making all affect the coalitions that parties make. Thus students of coalition politics increasingly recognize the importance of the broader rules of democratic governance. Many of the insights gained through the study of cabinet coalitions have improved our understanding of other types of coalitions as well.

See also *Cabinets; Government formation; Types of democracy.*

Kaare Strøm

BIBLIOGRAPHY

Axelrod, Robert. *Conflict of Interest.* Chicago: Markham, 1970.

De Swaan, Abram. *Coalition Theories and Cabinet Formation.* Amsterdam: Elsevier, 1973.

Dodd, Lawrence C. *Coalitions in Parliamentary Government.* Princeton: Princeton University Press, 1976.

Laver, Michael J., and Norman Schofield. *Multiparty Government: The Politics of Coalition in Europe.* Oxford: Oxford University Press, 1990.

Ordeshook, Peter C. *Game Theory and Political Theory: An Introduction.* Cambridge: Cambridge University Press, 1986.

Riker, William H. *The Theory of Political Coalitions.* New Haven: Yale University Press, 1962.

Von Neumann, John, and Oskar Morgenstern. *The Theory of Games and Economic Behavior.* Princeton: Princeton University Press, 1945.

Colombia

A nation situated in northwestern South America, in which periods of political violence have alternated with long periods of constitutional civilian rule. The northern coast of Colombia borders the Caribbean Sea, and its western coast faces the Pacific Ocean. With approximately 33 million people in 1990, Colombia is the third most populous country in Latin America (behind Brazil and Mexico, and just ahead of Argentina) and has the fifth largest economy in the region (behind those three countries and Venezuela). In 1990 it had a gross domestic product of $1,425 per capita, lagging behind nine other Latin American countries.

Colombia's geography is marked by extremes. Three Andean mountain ranges traverse the western half of the country, though the country's highest peaks are located off the Caribbean coast in the Sierra Nevada. In the east are plains, and to the south and east from the plains are the scarcely populated Amazon territories. The country's geography fostered and protected regional centers and hindered national integration. It has also hampered efforts to control guerrilla groups, smuggling, and drug trafficking.

From the perspective of democratic politics, Colombia is difficult to categorize. Throughout its history, it has alternated between political violence and constitutional civilian rule. Since 1958 the country has had a civilian regime and has consistently held elections for all major political offices, though for much of this time elections took place under a restrictive political arrangement. In the mid-1990s Colombia's democracy persisted, although with significant restraints.

Paradoxically, the preceding decade saw changes both in more democratic and in less democratic directions. Democracy was strengthened by the enactment in 1991 of a democratizing constitution and other political reforms and by the incorporation of demobilized guerrilla groups into electoral politics. But basic civil and human rights were threatened by growing violence from several sources and by the collapse of a functioning judiciary and thus of an effective rule of law. Disruptive elements included drug traffickers, radical guerrillas (whose ideology and goals have become more difficult to categorize in the post–cold war era), and reactionaries (especially state security agents and landowners). Political violence included the targeted killings of leftist politicians and activists, as well as the assassination of high government officials, mainstream politicians, leading journalists, and judges. The country was also experiencing unparalleled levels of crime in general and of homicide in particular.

Historical and Political Development

Colombia's development has been deeply marked by its history. At the time of Spanish colonization, the people of the indigenous cultures in what is now Colombia numbered from 3 to 4 million, considerably fewer than in Mexico and Peru but significantly more than in Venezuela, Argentina, and Brazil. Exploitation, disease, and the growing number of *mestizos* (people of mixed parentage) led to a sharp reduction in this Indian population, which had dropped to about 130,000 at the time of independence in 1819. This decrease helps explain the limited indigenous influence in Colombia in the postindependence period. In contrast, since the colonial period the Catholic Church has played a powerful role in Colombian history. The country's vastly unequal land-tenure patterns were also established in the colonial era.

One factor that sets Colombia apart from its neighbors is the nature and strength of its two major political parties, which emerged in the mid-nineteenth century. The federation of Gran Colombia, which gained independence

from Spain, included what are now Venezuela, Ecuador, and Panama as well as Colombia. The federation lasted little more than a decade, until 1830, when what are now Venezuela and Ecuador broke away. Panama gained its independence in 1903. By the 1850s the Liberal and Conservative Parties had been established and were capable of mobilizing the population both for elections and for violence. The importance of the parties was increased by the weakness of the central state and the military. The parties, rather than the state, became the agents of national integration.

The history of the two parties includes periods of one-party rule, civil war, and coalition government. In the second half of the nineteenth century, seven major civil confrontations took place. As a consequence of this turmoil, the people of Colombia came to identify themselves with one party or the other. Liberals dominated the national political arena from 1863 to 1885, enacting antichurch reforms and adopting federalist, secular, and politically liberal constitutions. Economic and political crises during this period finally led to a centralizing tendency with bipartisan support, which ultimately came to be controlled by the Conservatives. This shift in power led to adoption of the 1886 constitution and to an 1887 agreement with the Vatican that reestablished the centrality of the church.

Economic development in the nineteenth century was hampered by fluctuating world prices, leading to boom-and-bust cycles for Colombia's major export products. Only when coffee became the major export product toward the end of the century did Colombia enter into a period of relatively expansive international trade. The dependence on agricultural export products enhanced the political power of landowners and merchants.

By 1910 the country had evolved into an oligarchy, which lasted until 1949. Conservatives controlled national politics until 1930, when the effects of the Great Depression and division within the party contributed to a Liberal victory. An unprecedented constitutional transfer of power between the political parties took place; it was aided by the willingness of the Liberals to form a bipartisan cabinet. A "Liberal republic" emerged in the mid-1930s. In his first term, Liberal president Alfonso López Pumarejo (1934–1938; 1942–1945) enacted ambitious constitutional, administrative, electoral, fiscal, and agrarian reforms, collectively known as the Revolution on the March. The reforms were an essential step in adjusting the country's institutions to changing economic realities. The measures also consolidated the position of the Liberals as Colombia's majority party by limiting the influence of the church, expanding the electorate in urban areas, and increasing the party's support base within labor as industrialization progressed.

Unlike other Latin American countries, Colombia had little experience with populism. This was due in part to its multiparty structure and in part to the absence of other factors that could foster nationalist and populist politics. For example, there was little foreign investment, and low levels of immigration (particularly in contrast to such countries as Argentina, Uruguay, or Chile) limited outside influences on the incipient working-class movements. Furthermore, conflict between industrial and agricultural sectors was muted because of the role of coffee exporters in Colombia's industrialization. The process of industrialization was bipartisan. So were the organization of workers into labor confederations and their incorporation into politics, although the Liberals initiated these measures.

In 1946 divisions within the Liberal Party granted the Conservatives a narrow victory in the presidential elections, though the Liberals retained control of Congress. Local violence associated with the forced turnover of government personnel exploded into a national conflagration after the acclaimed populist Liberal leader Jorge Eliécer Gaitán was assassinated in 1948. Democracy broke down a year later when the Conservative president, Mariano Ospina Pérez, closed Congress and declared a state of siege. The country descended into an undeclared civil war between adherents of the two parties. The war took the lives of some 200,000 people and helped usher in the military government of Gen. Gustavo Rojas Pinilla (1953–1957).

Coalition Government and Afterward

Since 1958 Colombia has been ruled continuously by elected civilian presidents. In 1957–1958 leaders of the two parties reached agreement on coalition rule and a complex web of mutual guarantees, forming the National Front. This arrangement was similar to consociational arrangements in other countries. It was intended to facilitate the parties' return to power while bringing an end to interparty violence. This was the most formal, rigid, and long lasting of the various agreements between the parties. In its final form, the agreement gave both parties equal representation in all legislative and judicial posts and in non–civil service executive positions. It also specified that the presidency would alternate between parties from 1958 to 1974. In 1968 a reform partially dismantled the National Front. Nonetheless, until 1986 all governments in Colombia consisted of bipartisan coalitions. Since then, decentralizing and democratizing reforms have gradually done away with all remaining legal requirements for rule by coalition.

The National Front governments oversaw Colombia's socioeconomic transformation. The country's population doubled from the late 1950s to the mid-1970s, becoming more urbanized and more educated. At the same time the strong party identities that had justified coalition rule gradually disappeared. Most of the National Front governments ruled under state-of-siege regulations, however—in part because the restrictive National Front rules made change difficult and in part out of fear of popular protests. They did not enact significant reforms in the unequal distribution of income, land, or other forms of wealth. There was no dramatic strengthening of popular organizations in response to the weakening of party identities.

Many incentives to retain coalition rule remained. For regional political leaders, especially those of the minority Conservative Party, it meant access to patronage. For major economic groups it gave access to policy making, and for international interests it meant that decision making was at least partially insulated from popular and narrow partisan pressures. Extended coalition rule, the narrow differences between the country's two major parties, and the influence of powerful societal and international actors all played a role in ensuring a basic continuity in Colombia's economic policies, with careful attention to variables such as inflation, fiscal deficits, and growth. At the same time, these factors also help explain why the political regime has been so slow in opening up to new movements and demands.

The centrality of the two parties to the political life of Colombia declined, although they retained a near monopoly in elections. The post–National Front governments of the Liberal Alfonso López Michelsen (1974–1978) and of Julio César Turbay Ayala (1978–1982) met with growing nonelectoral opposition—from labor confederations independent of the two parties, civic protest movements, and guerrilla violence. The administrations of the Conservative Belisario Betancur Cuartas (1982–1986) and of the Liberals Virgilio Barco Vargas (1986–1990) and César Gaviria Trujillo (1990–1994) sought to combine military strategies with political reforms and negotiation. Several reincorporated guerrilla groups formed new political parties. Among these was the M-19 group, which took its name from the April 19, 1970, elections that members believed fraudulently kept the presidential victory from General Rojas. Other guerrilla groups continued their violent actions. The AD-M19 Party (formerly the M-19 group) gained significant representation in the 1991 Constitutional Convention and played a central role in drafting the new constitution. It did less well in the two subsequent elections.

Efforts to govern and to enact change in Colombia have been impeded by widespread drug trafficking, which has vastly weakened the state, particularly its legal system. The drug trade has emboldened guerrilla groups as well as elements of the national security forces. It has led to the assassination of popular leaders, leftist party activists, journalists, and high government officials. It has aroused widespread cynicism, despair, and embarrassment. Each year in the early 1990s some 15,000–20,000 Colombians met violent deaths, of which 10–15 percent were attributable to guerrilla activity, drug trafficking, or political conflict. The 1990 election campaign was marred by the assassination of the leading Liberal presidential contender and then by the killing of the presidential candidates of two different leftist movements.

Political Structure

Like the rest of Latin America, Colombia has had a strongly presidentialist democracy. Unlike many of its neighbors, however, Colombia has remained largely free of strongman rule, whether by *continuismo* (extension of a term in office) or military coup. The 1886 constitution—the country's basic document until 1991—created a unitary state, granting the central executive vast appointive powers (including the power to appoint mayors and departmental governors). Gradually these powers have been restricted. A constitutional reform in 1910, following a dictatorial period, decreed direct presidential elections for a four-year term with no immediate reelection. Selection of mayors by popular election was instituted in 1988, and the 1991 constitution introduced direct elections for governors while flatly prohibiting presidential reelection. The new constitution calls for a second electoral round if no presidential candidate receives an absolute majority.

From the 1930s on, a contrary trend increased executive authority. In Colombia, as elsewhere in the developed world, central governments were expanding their role as regulators, owners of productive enterprises, and providers of social welfare. The links between presidentialism, centralization of power, and the technocratic impulse to insulate economic decision making within the executive branch expanded during the National Front years. The 1991 constitution placed new limits on the president's powers, while seeking to ensure that key financial policies would be enacted by agencies free of short-term political pressures.

The Colombian Congress consists of a Senate and a Chamber of Deputies, whose members are elected to four-year terms. Until 1991 elections were based on closed-list proportional representation by departments; this meant that people voted for a list of predetermined names rather than for one or more individuals. The Senate is now chosen through a national district. Electoral procedures, particularly the ability to present multiple lists, have helped sustain the Liberal and Conservative Parties, while encouraging factionalism. Unlike many Latin American countries, Colombia has never had mandatory voting. This situation has encouraged clientelist practices, in which politicians sell votes in exchange for specific favors, such as funds for commercial projects or student scholarships. Colombia's voter abstention rates are among the highest in South America. Party discipline has been poor, forcing presidents continually to renegotiate governing legislative majorities. The judiciary system was overhauled in the 1991 constitution, but it remains weak as a result of budgetary neglect, personnel problems, and especially the intimidation and violence associated with drug trafficking.

The ingenious National Front arrangement highlights the difficulties of crafting consociational rule in presidential systems. More informal negotiated arrangements have been made to ease democratic transitions in other presidential systems, as in Venezuela in the late 1950s and in Chile in the late 1980s. In Colombia, however, widespread violence and the fear of continued mass mobilization led party leaders to prefer a rigid agreement set forth in a constitution. Political turmoil in the 1980s was almost inevitable, given the pressing need to move beyond the restrictive agreement and the difficulties in doing so. The conflicts were made more severe by the harmful effects of drug trafficking.

Ever since genuinely competitive presidential elections began again in 1974, the Liberal Party has consistently obtained a congressional majority and won the presidency, with the single exception of the 1982 election. Both the Liberals and the Conservatives are mainstream, catchall parties, but in the early 1990s the Conservatives were divided into two main factions, one led by Misael Pastrana Borrero and the other by Alvaro Gómez Hurtado. The strongest third party in the 1990s, the AD-M19 Party, was seeking to broaden its appeal. The Colombian Communist Party has always been weak electorally. It has close ties to the country's largest guerrilla organization, the Revolutionary Armed Forces of Colombia, created in 1964. After signing a truce with the government in 1984, the Revolutionary Armed Forces created a political arm, the Patriotic Union, which soon overshadowed the Communist Party. The Patriotic Union has competed in elections since 1986, but many of its leaders, including two presidential candidates, have been assassinated.

In the 1990s Colombia's central challenges with regard to democratic governance remain rebuilding state institutions, extending the rule of law nationwide, and strengthening the organizational capabilities of all elements of society.

See also *Parliamentarism and presidentialism; Types of democracy.*

Jonathan Hartlyn

BIBLIOGRAPHY

Bergquist, Charles W., Ricardo Peñaranda, and Gonzalo G. Sánchez, eds. *Violence in Colombia: The Contemporary Crisis in Historical Perspective.* Wilmington, Del.: SR Books, 1992.

Berry, R. Albert, Ronald Hellman, and Mauricio Solaún, eds. *Politics of Compromise: Coalition Government in Colombia.* New Brunswick, N.J.: Transaction, 1980.

Bushnell, David. *The Making of Modern Colombia: A Nation in Spite of Itself.* Berkeley: University of California Press, 1993.

Dix, Robert H. *Colombia: The Political Dimensions of Change.* New Haven: Yale University Press, 1967.

Hartlyn, Jonathan. *The Politics of Coalition Rule in Colombia.* Cambridge: Cambridge University Press, 1988.

Leal Buitrago, Franciso, and León Zamosc, eds. *Al filo del caos: Crisis política en la Colombia de los años 80.* Bogotá: Tercer Mundo, 1990.

Pécaut, Daniel. *Crónica de dos décadas de política colombiana, 1968–1988.* Mexico: Siglo XXI, 1988.

Wilde, Alexander W. "Conversations among Gentlemen: Oligarchical Democracy in Colombia." In *The Breakdown of Democratic Regimes,* edited by Juan J. Linz and Alfred Stepan. Baltimore and Northampton: Johns Hopkins University Press, 1978.

Colonialism

The system in which countries maintain foreign colonies, which almost invariably are not democratic. Of the members of the United Nations (more than 180 in the mid-1990s), 115 were colonized for at least a decade by one of the Western European nations. Others have experienced colonial periods under non-European nations such as Japan. Yet despite this "common" heritage, the legacies of colonialism have differed tremendously across nations, and the prospects for stable democracy in postcolonial societies have been correspondingly varied.

The Colonial Experience

Several aspects of a country and its colonial experience affect the prospects of democracy. The first, often neglected, is the nature of the preexisting society. Except where the native population was virtually eliminated, as in certain settler colonies of the Americas, indigenous cultural traditions survive. These have complex, sometimes contradictory, and often still potent implications for the development of democracy. In Latin America, for example, authoritarian cultural legacies often attributed to the colonizers had roots in the precolonial societies, such as those of the Aztecs and the Incas.

Even within a single country, groups with different indigenous cultural legacies absorbed and reflected the colonial experience in politically divergent ways. This divergence was particularly so among the constituent nations of the British Empire, which emphasized "indirect rule." Thus, in the politically centralized, culturally authoritarian emirates of Nigeria's Islamic north, British rule actually reinforced the power of the emir as absolute ruler, while British administration of the more decentralized, participatory, and constitutional societies of southern Nigeria allowed for the emergence of their more democratic tendencies in modern politics. The other English-speaking foreign rulers—Australia (in Papua New Guinea) and the United States (in the Philippines and Puerto Rico)—and the Dutch (in Indonesia) apart, the imperial powers exercised "direct rule"—control by representatives of the overseas government. Hence the subject population usually lacked experience in self-government before obtaining independence.

Furthermore, the same colonizer could administer different societies differently, depending on what the prospective colony had to offer. Burma, unlike India, was governed directly by the British and has been more authoritarian since independence. Where mineral resources were particularly abundant and indigenous populations large, as in Peru and Mexico, or where slaves were imported for plantation agriculture, as in Brazil or the Dominican Republic, colonial rule by the Spanish and Portuguese was particularly intrusive and exploitative. In parts of the New World where both of these features were lacking, as in Uruguay, Argentina, or especially Costa Rica, Spanish control was less penetrating and authoritarian.

The timing of foreign invasion also affected what potential colonizers wanted and could use from their colonies, which in turn affected their legacy. The British pattern established in the 1600s and 1700s in India and the Americas differed from Britain's mode of operation in nineteenth-century Africa and in Burma. The later instances of colonization, which occurred after the beginning of the Industrial Revolution, concentrated much more on the control of production than did early colonization, which had focused on the control of trade.

More significant perhaps for democracy, the early British colonization of Asia and the Caribbean, along with certain other islands such as Mauritius, gave these countries much longer and deeper contact with British values and institutions as well as more time for the gradual emergence of indigenous representative institutions. With the British colonial presence dating back to the seventeenth century, both India and Jamaica, for example, had several centuries of contact with the British and many decades of experience with their own representative institutions, which gradually expanded to incorporate much of the population. By contrast, because Britain's colonization of Africa and Burma occurred later, and its withdrawal was more hurried, the colonizer's influence on postcolonial governments was weaker.

Finally, the most important aspect of colonialism and its legacy is the identity of the colonizer. One of the most widely recognized and powerful determinants of the likelihood of democracy among the new nations of the developing world is a simple, dichotomous, historical variable: whether or not the nation has been ruled by Britain. By no means have all of Britain's former colonies become stable democracies, but the developing countries with the most successful democratic experience since independence are, by and large, former British colonies—whether in Asia, Africa, or the Caribbean. Even in Africa, where experiences with democracy have generally been unsuccessful, the four countries where multiparty democracy has managed to persist—Botswana, Gambia, Mauritius, and (in its limited way) South Africa—all have experienced British domination. The reasons behind this striking pattern require closer examination.

British Colonial Practices

The imperial powers affected the subsequent democratic prospects of their dependencies in different ways. The positive impact of the British legacy can be seen among the older overseas colonies, as a comparison of the postindependence histories of Australia and British America with that of Spanish and Portuguese America indicates. The minor imperial powers Australia and the United States can roughly be classed with Britain (if the short-lived interventions in and occupations of Haiti, Nicaragua, Mexico, and other countries in Latin America by the United States are excluded).

French colonization gave rise to democratic traditions and values in some countries, but not to the same extent as British colonization. Quebec, as Pierre Trudeau noted in 1958, was much less democratic than English-speaking Canada until its "quiet revolution" of the 1960s. In Africa and Asia, Belgian, Dutch, and Portuguese rule (not to mention Japan's later entry into colonial domination) were almost completely devoid of any democratic legacy.

The Spanish and Portuguese legacy in Latin America is more difficult to assess, as nearly two centuries of independence have seen the colonial heritage recede in importance. Certainly, however, the newly independent states of Central and South America were notable mainly for their lack of democracy and political stability in the nineteenth century. The most significant, if limited, democratic ventures emerged in those states—Chile, Uruguay, and Costa Rica—where the Spanish colonial presence and influence had been weakest.

What accounts for the relative success of democracy after British colonial rule? Political scientist Myron Weiner cites two components of the British colonial model: the establishment of the rule of law through effective (and increasingly indigenous) bureaucratic and judicial institutions and the provision for some system of representation and election, which gave educated native elites experience in political leadership and limited governance. The resulting legacy, Weiner maintains, was not simply the presence of more effective political institutions at independence (in terms of both government administration and political party mobilization and competition), but also an enduring cultural commitment to the procedures of democratic politics and governance and to the rule of law as a constraint on government.

Where the British ruled for a long time, democratic institutions emerged gradually and expanded over time to incorporate larger segments of the population and to assume increasingly significant responsibilities. During its last eighty years under the British, India went through several phases of constitutional reform that opened government to indigenous representation and public scrutiny while successively broadening the basis of participation. The dramatic reforms of the Government of India Act of 1935 extended the franchise to only one-sixth of the population, but provisions for self-government in the provinces along with widespread electoral competition were to prove invaluable in preparing Indians and the Indian National Congress for the rigors of democratic politics. Of course, one cannot overemphasize the importance of the existence and growth of the Congress for Indian democracy. For six decades preceding independence in 1947, the Congress acted not just as a nationalist organization but as a political party, democratic in its procedures and goals, conciliatory in its approach to conflict, and increasingly incorporative of rural and urban mass groups. The contrast with Pakistan, where political parties were less active and where the process of obtaining separation from India stunted the development of party competition, suggests the usefulness of pre-independence development of democratic political institutions.

India was perhaps unique in the depth and complexity of its pre-independence democratic experience, though not in the fact of it. Indeed, Sri Lanka was the first country in the colonial world to win universal suffrage (in 1931), and its impressive democratic success in the decades following independence in 1948 had been prepared by seventeen years of limited self-government, during which the island colony held three general elections. In Malaysia under the British, the Philippines under the United States, and Papua New Guinea under the Australians, pre-independence electoral competition permitted the development of political parties and coalitions and the acquisition of democratic experience that clearly enhanced the capacity of democratic institutions after independence.

Jamaica—one of the most stable postcolonial democracies in recent decades—is another instructive example of the effect of long British control. During the nineteenth century the island evolved a very limited, exclusive parliamentary structure. Although Jamaica was long dominated by aristocratic white settlers and endured periods of revolt and repression, its governmental institutions gradually broadened to incorporate middle-class groups between 1884 and 1944, when the British granted the country universal adult suffrage and considerable self-governance. There followed eighteen years of two-party competition and gradual colonial withdrawal, leading to independence in 1962. The British handed over the administration of the colony to indigenous ministers in 1953 and granted full internal self-government in 1959. This staging was perhaps the ultimate expression of British colonial democratic design. Political scientist Carl Stone observes that the slow movement from British supervision to local leadership ensured that postindependence political structures would resemble the parliamentary democracy established in Great Britain.

A related strategy guided the British colonial project in Africa. Africanists Lewis Gann and Peter Duignan note that British-ruled Africans were more likely than black people in any other part of colonial Africa to have exercised executive power, and that power was transferred from London to local African governments by a constitutional machinery. The phased development of indigenous capacities for self-rule was a hallmark of the philosophy of indirect rule, which derived from a domestic political culture in Britain that distrusted rapid change and emphasized gradualism.

The Legacy of British Values

We have stressed so far the distinctive (although delayed, ambivalent, and paternalistic) British commitment to the transfer and development of representative institutions in the colonies. But other elements also made British rule more conducive than the rule of other colonial powers to the development of democracy.

Perhaps because of their own commitment to liberal, pluralist values, the British as rulers permitted significantly more free expression and open, autonomous associational life than did the other European colonizers (especially the Portuguese, Spanish, and Belgians). At the same time, the spread of education, transportation, and communication—although generally limited to urban elites among the native population—made possible higher levels of political consciousness and organization than ever before.

Decades of practice in the arts of independent reporting and political organization—even within the overall context of a generally undemocratic state that had become the target of nationalist demands—gave rise in many British colonies to a spirited civil society. Many of the lawyers, teachers, journalists, intellectuals, trade unionists, activists, entrepreneurs, and politicians in the making who composed this civil society internalized (sometimes directly from study in Britain) the democratic values of Great Britain. In addition, the domestic elites revealed and synthesized numerous continuities between British democratic principles and their own cultural traditions, thus giving democracy a deeper basis of legitimacy.

Again, the experience of India—the "jewel in the crown" and still in many ways the most important and surprising postcolonial democracy—is instructive. By the late nineteenth century, hundreds of newspapers and periodicals were in circulation, reporting on British and European politics as well as on the debates within the colonial administration in India. These media sources had an educational and unifying effect on the various regions of In-

dia as activities and matters of public interest were reviewed.

The British commitment to constitutional procedures and forms (as reflected in the successions of constitutional reforms and conferences) and to the rule of law was no doubt influential in the postcolonial governments. Ironically, a surviving concern with legalism has been apparent not only in the strength of the judiciary, the legal culture, and the legal profession in many former colonies, such as India, but even in actions that have temporarily curtailed free expression and choice. The suspension of democracy under the National Operations Council in Malaysia (1969–1971) followed appropriate legal and constitutional procedures; the council emphasized the temporary nature of the emergency, implying a return to democratic rights upon the restoration of law and order. Indira Gandhi's curtailment of democracy in India (1975–1977) was pursued and justified through the use of emergency powers in the constitution and was entrenched by laws and constitutional amendments duly passed in the parliament. One may speculate that the institutional and cultural legacies left by former rulers were important factors in limiting the duration and scope of these abridgments of democracy.

Along with a respect for constitutional law, the British conveyed a cultural commitment to democracy. Even in many of the former British dependencies that have not shown great success in maintaining democracy—such as Pakistan, Nigeria, and Ghana—a strong commitment to liberal principles, and to the eventual adoption of democracy, has persisted among segments of the political elite and general public. These values have preserved some space for political pluralism and autonomous organizations even during authoritarian regimes, while motivating citizens to press for a return to democracy.

The Australian and American experiences as colonizers in New Guinea and the Philippines, respectively, fit broadly with the British pattern. Even more explicitly and extensively than the British perhaps, American colonial rule in the Philippines during the first decades of the twentieth century set out to school the people in democratic citizenship. The United States left behind some important developmental and institutional legacies—including universal education, a high literacy rate, a politically active elite, and a free press. Unfortunately, these democratic legacies had to contend with the deeply rooted legacies of four centuries of autocratic Spanish colonial rule. The earlier background, Karl Jackson, a student of Filipino politics, suggests, may help to account for the stubborn persistence of oligarchical control and corrupt, clientelistic politics beneath the veneer of democratic commitment.

The French Colonial Legacy

Many of the characteristic differences between British and other colonial administrations resulted from governing arrangements. The French and most other colonizers chose to govern directly from their own capital; the British favored indirect rule and allowed the colonies some autonomy. In Africa, French administration was highly centralized, and local colonial officials were closely directed from Paris or from the regional headquarters at Dakar for French West Africa and Brazzaville for French Equatorial Africa. Traditional rulers were typically undermined rather than cultivated and incorporated into colonial government, and they were often replaced by "straw chiefs" who served at the bottom of the colonial administrative hierarchy.

In every respect the French colonies were much more strongly tied to France than the British colonies were to England. French colonial policy until the 1950s, according to Africanist J. Gus Liebenow, was to form "black Frenchmen" and to develop a French-speaking political community led by the French Republic and encompassing the African areas. Economically and politically, the local population remained dependent on France, and little attention was paid to the development of indigenous political and administrative abilities. Close economic links between the colonies and France were encouraged through practices such as direct subsidies from the French treasury and the establishment of common currency backed by the Bank of France. The British, in contrast, enforced as much budgetary independence as possible in individual colonies even before relinquishing political authority over them.

For the most part the French waited longer than the British to initiate indigenous political representation. Although the four communes in Dakar began electing a deputy to the French National Assembly in 1948, and a little later started electing members of municipal councils, the French did not introduce broadly elected indigenous assemblies into their African territories until reforms in 1956.

Britain and France often left behind political institutions that reflected their own constitutional models, an inheritance that led to differing democratic prospects in their colonies. The British transferred their parliamentary system; the French transferred the presidentialism of the Fifth Republic. The British embedded in their colonial constitutions emphasis on dispersed power and autonomous local government, which in some cases took the form of explicit federalism. France gave its colonies centralist and unitary constitutions. The stronger executives, weaker parliaments, and much more centralized governments of the former French colonies were more conducive to authoritarianism. This may be one reason why several former British colonies—Ghana, Tanzania (Tanganyika), Uganda—switched to presidential systems upon establishing dictatorial governments.

The British exported their electoral system of single-member districts (constituencies), while the French provided for election of assembly members from party lists. In British colonies the emphasis was more likely to be on the individual candidates in the district (with the ballot, as in Britain, sometimes lacking party identifications). Independents or small or local parties could win seats and survive politically. In the French colonies, where the multi-member candidate lists were identified by party name, voters had to choose a party rather than an individual candidate, and the leading party claimed all the district seats on a winner-take-all basis. As David Collier noted, the French system favored the emergence of a dominant party.

Thus, even within Africa, with its generally dismal record with regard to democracy, it may be suggested that the variations in colonial legacies have been of great significance in accounting for the more extended and frequent (if not ultimately much more successful) experimentation with democracy among former British as opposed to former French colonies, and for the greater level of electoral competition within dominant-party systems in English-speaking, as opposed to French-speaking, countries. Even setting aside the three former British colonies in Africa that have remained democratic, the countries that have made the most renewed attempts at democracy in the postcolonial period—such as Ghana, Nigeria, Sudan, and Uganda—have all been former British colonies.

When we turn to the other colonial legacies in Africa, however, we can appreciate the elements of democratic concern and potential for free institutions in the French colonial practice that were virtually absent in the rule of the Belgians and Portuguese. The French, in contrast to the Portuguese, Spanish, and Belgians, allowed some scope for the emergence of autonomous organizations. One former French African colony, Senegal, today has a functioning and relatively liberal semidemocracy, which can be traced in part to the lengthy exposure of the elite to political debate, organization, and competition. As Christian Coulan emphasizes, this exposure has made it difficult to restrict the activities of a people with more than a century of political experience.

Other Colonial Legacies in Africa and Asia

It is not by coincidence that the former African colonies of Belgium (Zaire, Burundi, and Rwanda) and Portugal (Angola, Mozambique, and Guinea-Bissau) have experienced some of the greatest repression, ethnic turmoil, instability, and bloodshed of all independent countries in Africa. The Belgian Congo, which would later become Zaire, was intensely exploited by King Leopold and later by the Belgian state for its extraordinary mineral resources. Belgium expected to hold on to the colony indefinitely, in contrast to the British goal of self-government and the French ideal of incorporation. Thus, although Belgium created a class of Westernized *évolués* (assimilated persons), who had education and training, they were prevented from developing associations, from obtaining postsecondary education (except for priests), and from holding responsible administrative positions. Representative institutions were not introduced in the Congo until 1957; even these consisted largely of a few indirectly elected urban councils on which Europeans were guaranteed parity. Subsequent reforms hastily enlarged the scope of elections, but these remained indirect, complex, and ineffectual. The 1959 inaugural elections for a territorial assembly were widely boycotted. After popular pressure and the experiences of other African states forced Belgium to grant independence in 1960, the Congo was left with virtually no preparation for self-government.

Portugal had the longest history of direct colonial domination in Africa, but it was the most repressive of all the European powers in Africa and did the least to prepare its colonies for independence. As a result of Portugal's intransigence, it alone experienced armed revolt in all its territories; ultimately, it had to be forced to withdraw, following a coup in April 1974 that ended dictatorship in Portugal itself.

Colonial experiences have shaped the subsequent democratic histories of nations in important ways, affecting cleavage structures (that is, class, ethic, religious, and comparable groupings), economic patterns, and institutional development. These factors, in turn, continue to influence the opportunities and obstacles for stable democracy. Any effort to understand the variations in postcolonial political systems therefore must deal with the colonial past.

See also *Africa, Lusophone; Africa, Subsaharan; African independence movements; Commonwealth, British; India; Political culture; Theory, African.*

Larry Diamond and Seymour Martin Lipset

BIBLIOGRAPHY

Diamond, Larry, ed. *The Democratic Revolution.* New York: Freedom House, 1992.

Fieldhouse, D. K. *The Colonial Empire: A Comparative Survey from the Eighteenth Century.* New York: Dell; Basingstoke: Macmillan, 1982.

Gann, Lewis, and Peter Duignan. *Burden of Empire: An Appraisal of Western Colonialism in Africa South of the Sahara.* Stanford, Calif.: Hoover Institution Press, 1967.

Huntington, Samuel. "Will More Countries Become Democratic?" *Political Science Quarterly* 99 (summer 1984): 193–218.

Lipset, Seymour Martin, Kyoung-Ryung Seong, and John Charles Torres. "A Comparative Analysis of the Social Requisites of Democracy." *International Social Science Journal* 45 (1993): 155–175.

Mazrui, Ali A. "Francophone Nations and English-Speaking States: Imperial Ethnicity and African Political Formations." In *States versus Ethnic Claims: African Policy Dilemmas,* edited by Donald Rothchild and Victor A. Olornsol. Boulder, Colo.: Westview Press, 1983.

Morse, Richard M. "The Heritage of Latin America: The Distinct Tradition." In *Politics and Social Change in Latin America,* edited by H. J. Wiarda. Amherst: University of Massachusetts Press, 1973.

Mouzelis, Nicos P. *Politics in the Semi-Periphery: Early Parliamentarism and Late Industrialization in the Balkans and South America.* New York: St. Martin's; London: Macmillan, 1986.

Smith, Tony. "A Comparative Study of French and British Decolonization." *Comparative Studies in Society and History* 20 (1978): 70–102.

Stein, Stanley J., and Barbara H. Stein. *The Colonial Heritage of Latin America: Essays on Economic Dependence in Perspective.* New York: Oxford University Press, 1970.

Weiner, Myron. "Empirical Democratic Theory." In *Competitive Elections in Developing Countries,* edited by Myron Weiner and Ergun Ozbundun. Durham, N.C.: Duke University Press, 1987.

Commonwealth, British

The British Commonwealth of Nations is an association of nations and dependencies that once formed the British Empire. The Commonwealth includes one-quarter of the world's population. It is the largest organized grouping of nations extant, although it has little central power or institutional structure.

The British Empire had its roots in the sixteenth century with trading links in India and colonial settlements in North America and the Caribbean. At the end of the eighteenth century Australia began to be settled, followed fifty years later by New Zealand. Toward the end of the nineteenth century Britain led the race to colonize Africa. By 1900 the British Empire covered a quarter of the world's land mass, and the British people delighted in being at the heart of an empire on which the sun never set.

The civilized evolution from British Empire to British Commonwealth is a notable feature of twentieth-century history, in large part because former British colonies were more likely to be democratic than any other country's former colonies. In fact, many colonies (such as Canada, India, and Nigeria) had elections before they became independent. British colonization, however, often involved deals with local rulers and was never as centralized in style as German, Italian, or French colonization. Indeed, the concept of *France d'outremer*, in which overseas colonies were considered part of metropolitan France, was never matched in British policy.

From Empire to Commonwealth

The term *commonwealth* can be traced back to David Williams, a friend of Benjamin Franklin, in 1778. Indeed, before the Declaration of Independence in 1776, North Carolinian James Iredell and other American thinkers had envisaged autonomy under the Crown. As for Britain, the American War of Independence served as a painful lesson that it was not easy to govern distant parts of the world from London. In fact, in 1839 the Earl of Durham, governor general of Canada, issued a report on the government of Canada that recognized the desirability of offering mature settlements autonomy in everything but foreign affairs and defense. The Durham report led ultimately to the establishment in 1867 of the Dominion of Canada, independent in almost every respect except the amendment of its own constitution.

In 1884 the term *commonwealth* again found favor when it was used by the Earl of Rosebery, later foreign secretary under William Gladstone, as he proclaimed in Adelaide that the British Empire was a commonwealth of nations. In 1897, at the Second Colonial Conference during Queen Victoria's Diamond Jubilee (the first had been held during the Golden Jubilee in 1887), Joseph Chamberlain,

then colonial secretary, spoke of a commonwealth as he strove, against Canadian skepticism, for closer connections among the nations of the empire.

A conscious policy of imperialism developed at the end of the Victorian period, and much thought was given to the relationship of the territories under British rule. The industrially successful Britain of the 1850s had regarded the governing of overseas territories as a burden, but as Germany and the United States overtook Britain economically toward the end of the century, the appeal of expanding and consolidating the empire grew. Rudyard Kipling and other writers romanticized the imperial dream to appeal to an increasingly jingoistic and nationalist public.

At the turn of the century Chamberlain articulated the goals of imperial preference in trade (the preference in tariffs given to British territories) and even imperial federation in government (establishment of a federal institutional structure). Viscount Milner—together with the "Kindergarten" who went out to help him in the reconstruction of South Africa after the Boer War (1899–1902)—provided an intellectual basis for policies of imperial integration through the pages of the quarterly *Round Table*, under the messianic political writer Lionel Curtis. Curtis's 1916 books, *The Problem of the Commonwealth* and the *Commonwealth of Nations*, outlined his vision of an expanding association of free but united countries.

In 1907, at the first Imperial Conference, it was agreed to use the term *dominions* for the self-governing, as distinct from the dependent, components of the empire. All the while the six colonies of Australia had rapidly developed full democratic self-government and, despite the distances involved, had opted by referendums to federate into the Commonwealth of Australia, which came into being in 1901. The settlers in New Zealand, largely self-governing from 1856 on, were granted dominion status in 1907. The Union of South Africa followed in 1910.

It was only the Imperial Conference of 1926 that formally defined *Commonwealth* as the group of "autonomous communities within the British Empire, equal in status, in no way subordinate to one another in any aspect of their domestic or external affairs, though united by a common allegiance to the Crown, and freely associated as members of the British Commonwealth of Nations." This formulation, devised by the Earl of Balfour, the former prime minister, was a compromise between Canada, South Africa, and Ireland, which wanted to emphasize freedom, and Australia, New Zealand, and Newfoundland, which wanted to stress association. The Statute of West-

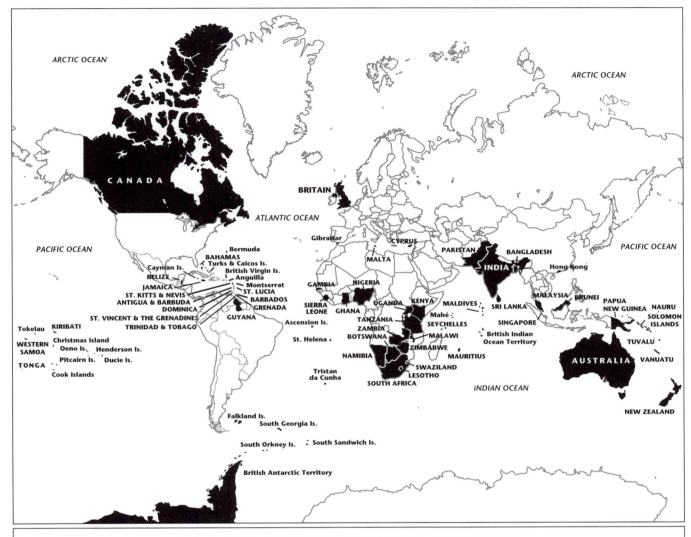

BRITISH COMMONWEALTH MEMBERS

(The date beside each country is the date the country entered the Commonwealth.)

Antigua and Barbuda (1981)	Ghana (1957)	Namibia (1990)	Solomon Islands (1978)
Australia (1931)	Grenada (1974)	Nauru (1968)	South Africa (1931)
Bahamas (1973)	Guyana (1966)	New Zealand (1931)	Sri Lanka (1948)
Bangladesh (1972)	India (1947)	Nigeria (1960)	Swaziland (1968)
Barbados (1966)	Jamaica (1962)	Pakistan (1947)	Tanzania (1964)
Belize (1981)	Kenya (1963)	Papua New Guinea (1975)	Tonga (1970)
Botswana (1966)	Kiribati (1979)	St. Kitts and Nevis (1983)	Trinidad and Tobago (1962)
Britain (1931)	Lesotho (1966)	St. Lucia (1979)	Tuvalu (1978)
Brunei (1984)	Malawi (1964)	St. Vincent and the Grenadines	Uganda (1962)
Canada (1931)	Malaysia (1957)	(1979)	Vanuatu (1980)
Cyprus (1961)	Maldives (1982)	Seychelles (1976)	Western Samoa (1970)
Dominica (1978)	Malta (1964)	Sierra Leone (1961)	Zambia (1964)
Gambia (1965)	Mauritius (1968)	Singapore (1965)	Zimbabwe (1980)

Commonwealth states are identified on the map in capital letters; British possessions are identified in lowercase letters.

Australia, Britain, Canada, the Irish Free State (Eire), Newfoundland, New Zealand, and South Africa were members of the Commonwealth formed under the Statute of Westminster in 1931. Eire left the Commonwealth in 1949 to become the Irish Republic. Newfoundland became a province of Canada in 1949. South Africa left the Commonwealth in 1961 and rejoined in 1994.

Pakistan left in 1972 but rejoined in 1989.

Fiji was a member of the Commonwealth from 1970 to 1987.

minster of 1931 formally defined the relationship, underlining the legislative autonomy of the dominions and requiring their assent to any decision over the succession to the throne. Some residual powers, mainly over constitutional change, were left in London and were only finally cleared away by the Canada Act of 1982 and the Australia Act of 1986. The statements of 1926 and 1931 did not mark a real change in relationships; they merely formalized the status quo.

In substantive terms the most important Commonwealth business during the period between World Wars I and II occurred at the Ottawa Conference of 1932, where, in response to the world depression, Joseph Chamberlain's dream of imperial preference was realized in a limited way. At a time when most nations, Britain included, were turning to protective tariffs, the Commonwealth countries agreed to some measures of reciprocal openness. However, Canada, which was dependent on the United States, could not let the process go very far. Australia and New Zealand were encouraged to gear their economies even more to supplying food and raw materials to Britain.

When India finally became a republic in 1950, the Commonwealth association ceased necessarily to involve loyalty to the Crown. The member countries accepted that, although India was no longer under the king-emperor, it would continue to be a full member of the Commonwealth and to accept the king as the symbol of the free association of the Commonwealth's independent member nations and as such the head of the Commonwealth. At the same time the term *dominion* was held to be obsolete, and the old dominions happily became members of the Commonwealth.

Other South Asian countries joining India after the Second World War in the rush toward independence were Pakistan and Burma in 1947 and Sri Lanka (Ceylon) in 1948. Between 1955 and 1970 almost all the major colonies in Africa and the West Indies followed the same path and became members of the Commonwealth. Rhodesia, now Zimbabwe (1980), and Hong Kong (1997) are the last substantial outposts of the empire to emerge from the suzerainty of London. In the mid-1990s fourteen overseas territories remained under British rule; Gibraltar, the Falkland Islands, and Bermuda are the best known.

Although a number of Commonwealth countries on attaining independence have continued with the British sovereign as head of state, a majority have become republics with presidents. Six states, however, have indigenous monarchies, including Malaysia and Western Samoa.

Yet almost all have chosen to remain members of the British Commonwealth. Among those countries once governed from London that are now outside the Commonwealth are the United States, Ireland, Burma, Fiji (expelled in 1987), Egypt, and Sudan, as well as the territories in the Middle East and Africa that Britain once governed under a League of Nations mandate (Palestine, Transjordan, Iraq, Aden, Somaliland, and Cameroon). Pakistan withdrew from the Commonwealth from 1972 to 1989 in protest of reactions to the breakaway of Bangladesh. South Africa, expelled from the Commonwealth on becoming a republic in 1961, was readmitted in 1994.

Commonwealth Relations

The Colonial Office in London regulated relations with the dominions and dependent territories until 1925, when the Dominions Office, under a separate cabinet minister, was established. Britain continued to organize the international relations of the dominions. Indeed, Canada did not appoint a minister to Washington, D.C., until 1927. Australia and New Zealand had virtually no overseas representation. At the conclusion of World War I in 1919 their interests had been represented at the Versailles peace conference by a notably harmonious British Empire delegation. It was not until the 1930s that Australia and New Zealand exchanged their first high commissioners with London. It was a significant advance when they sent independent representatives to the conferences that led to the establishment of the United Nations in 1945.

In 1947 the Dominions Office became the Commonwealth Relations Office, which was fused with the Colonial Office in 1966 to become the Commonwealth Office. In 1968 the merged department was absorbed into the Foreign Office. Since then the British foreign secretary has served as the "secretary of state for foreign and Commonwealth affairs."

A Commonwealth Secretariat was set up in 1965 to take over from Britain the management of inter-Commonwealth affairs. Although its headquarters is in London, it is answerable to the Commonwealth members as a whole. Under Arnold Smith of Canada (1965–1975), Shridath Ramphal of Guyana (1975–1990), and E. Chukwuemeka Anyaoku of Nigeria (1990–   ), the secretariat has grown in size and influence. Commonwealth Heads of Government Meetings have taken place every two years or so since 1944 (in London until 1971 and since then in different parts of the world). They replaced the old Imperial Conferences, which were held only seven times between 1911 and 1937.

As the number of Commonwealth nations has grown from five (United Kingdom, Canada, Australia, New Zealand, and South Africa) to fifty-one, the nature of these gatherings has changed. The United Kingdom used to be the dominant partner in the intimate meetings among the five members of the original "white Commonwealth," with a major role in organizing defense worldwide. But in the ever larger gatherings of the multiracial Commonwealth of the past thirty years, Britain has at times been under attack—notably from 1965 to 1980 over its policy toward Rhodesian independence and in the 1980s over its reluctance to join in the economic sanctions applied to South Africa in protest of that country's policy of apartheid.

At first some of the new members ostentatiously used Commonwealth meetings to prove their independence from Britain. But when Britain was isolated by Prime Minister Margaret Thatcher's stance over South Africa, no one talked of leaving the Commonwealth. Indeed, there were mutterings that if anyone left it would have to be Britain. On this and other occasions Queen Elizabeth II took pains to emphasize her quite separate roles and loyalties as head of the Commonwealth, on the one hand, and as queen of Great Britain, on the other. (She is also queen of Australia and of fifteen other countries.)

Commonwealth Linkages

Perhaps the most important role of the Commonwealth has been in channeling economic aid from its richer members to its poorer members. Ever since the Colombo Plan—a plan to promote economic development, which is headquartered in Colombo, Sri Lanka—was launched at a meeting of Commonwealth foreign ministers in 1950, successive schemes have been arranged through Commonwealth machinery to help the economies of African and South Asian states and of the Pacific and Caribbean islands. Caricom, a West Indies Common Market launched in 1973, is a notable example. On a wider scale, the Commonwealth Secretariat was active in formulating Commonwealth positions for the Uruguay Round of trade negotiations under the General Agreement on Tariffs and Trade (GATT), which culminated in 1993. In the 1980s it also tried to influence the Brandt Commission's work on North-South relations. (The commission was headed by the former West German chancellor, Willy Brandt.)

On the political front the Commonwealth Secretariat played a major role in ending Nigeria's Biafran conflict in 1968, when it sent a peacekeeping brigade to oversee the settlement. In the 1970s the Commonwealth cold-shouldered Gen. Idi Amin for his tyrannical regime in Uganda, and in 1987 it decided that Fiji's membership had lapsed, following Col. Sitiveni Rabuka's coup and declaration of a republic.

Immigration has become one of the Commonwealth's most contentious issues. Common citizenship was part of the original dream, and to this day any Commonwealth citizen is entitled to vote in Britain and in a few other countries. But since World War II, with the vast increase in international mobility, one country after another has felt forced to impose restrictions on immigration. In the 1950s the large influx into Britain of West Indians was at first welcomed as an answer to a shortage of unskilled labor. Social tensions soon developed, however, and when people from the Indian subcontinent began to arrive in large numbers, the government was impelled to pass the Commonwealth Immigrants Act of 1962. This act severely restricted the flow (although at least 5 percent of Britain's population now have "New Commonwealth" origins—that is, they are largely from the Caribbean and the Indian subcontinent). The act was supposed to be colorblind, but the barriers it set up gave much offense to second- and third-generation Australians and New Zealanders who still regarded Britain as home. The treatment of would-be immigrants from South Asia at the ports and in their home countries caused tension as well, as did sporadic outbursts of racial violence in Britain. Partly in retaliation and partly because they had their own problems, many countries imposed new visa and citizenship rules. At Commonwealth conferences and in bilateral discussions, issues of extradition and admission were raised frequently.

On a smaller scale, through its many associations the Commonwealth fosters special links among its members. For example, the Commonwealth Parliamentary Association (1911) does much to preserve common standards of practice within the countries that have maintained the Westminster (parliamentary) system of government, which includes the great majority of Commonwealth countries. Parliamentary clerks serve in the legislatures of other countries, and there are frequent consultations over Speakers' rulings and procedural matters.

The legal systems of most Commonwealth countries have their origins in Britain, and a few still use the Judicial Committee of the Privy Council, in London, as their ultimate court of appeal. London remains the prime source of training for lawyers in the New Commonwealth. The Commonwealth Press Union (1909), through its conferences and its exchange schemes for journalists, has contributed greatly to the flow of news and the maintenance of a free press within the Commonwealth. The Association of Commonwealth Universities (1913) acts as a clearinghouse for the recruitment of academic staff throughout the Commonwealth.

Since 1930 the quadrennial Commonwealth Games have attracted widespread publicity and come close behind the Olympics and the World Games as a popular event for athletes. Cricket, which is almost exclusive to the Commonwealth, has brought all the major countries (except Canada) together with the islands of the West Indies in regular and well-publicized "test matches."

A large number of professional groups—doctors, lawyers, engineers, and the like—have formed Commonwealth associations, which been active in setting professional standards and agreeing on the interchangeability of qualifications. Often these associations have been set up under the auspices of the semiautonomous Commonwealth Foundation, established in 1966 to coordinate nongovernmental organizations.

Britain's Role

The role of Britain at the center of the Commonwealth has declined by stages. The Second World War saw the emergence of the United States and the Soviet Union as interventionist superpowers. Britain, with its depleted resources, could no longer provide a worldwide defense shield. But even if it could have done so, any such act would not have been acceptable to a world in an anticolonialist mood. An attempt to regain control of the Suez Canal from Egypt in 1956 was seen as the last throes of imperialism, an attempt to safeguard by force Britain's traditional lifeline to the East. The old Commonwealth gave Britain some loyal support at the United Nations, but the failure of the Suez adventure produced disillusionment at home and abroad.

In 1967 the British withdrawal from Singapore and other eastern bases out of financial necessity signaled a recognition that Britain could no longer pose as a worldwide power. The withdrawal was regarded as a particular blow to Australia and New Zealand, which had long looked to Britain as a major contributor to their defense. To some extent Australia replaced Britain in both Singapore and (for a while) Malaysia.

A further blow to Britain's relationship with the Commonwealth came with the negotiations over Britain's entry into the European Common Market (now the European Union), which continued from 1961 to 1972. If Britain were to accept European tariff disciplines, it had to abandon longstanding commitments to Australia and New Zealand and to its former colonies, many of whom had geared their economies to supplying the British market. During the abortive talks with the original six members of the European Community in 1961–1962 and in 1966–1967, and during the successful negotiations in 1971–1972, Britain made great efforts to secure special concessions for Commonwealth imports, either on a permanent or a transitional basis. Nonetheless, the producers of lamb and butter in New Zealand and of sugar throughout the tropical islands expressed much bitterness at what they saw as Britain's betrayal of their interests.

The Commonwealth Today: A Mystical Entity?

The old imperial connections of Britain's former empire have largely disappeared, although many personal, educational, and commercial links remain. In varying degrees the members of the Commonwealth still find value in its organized patterns of cooperation. For the old dominions, particularly Australia and New Zealand, many ties of blood and family survive and indeed are continued through new immigration. For the developing countries, most of which accept English as a lingua franca, Britain remains a source of advice and aid and an alternative focus to the United States. For the British, the Commonwealth remains a mystical entity, comforting some of them for the loss of the empire. People who grew up taking satisfaction from being at the heart of the greatest empire the world had ever seen had to take pride in the relatively peaceful and civilized process of decolonization. Britain's legacy to global peace and order was a worldwide network linked under the Commonwealth label. The fact that this network was relatively impotent could be ignored.

Especially for the sixteen Commonwealth countries that have chosen to retain the monarchy—although with an indigenous governor general to act as head of state—royal visits and special treatment from London have helped to maintain solidarity within the Commonwealth. But the old loyalties that led to instant declarations of war by Australia, New Zealand, Canada, and South Africa in 1914, at the beginning of World War I, and again (although after rather fuller discussions) in 1939, when the Second World War began, no longer exist. Commonwealth countries largely go their own way when voting in the United Nations. Indeed, from time to time the Commonwealth has been mocked as no more than a tattered old boys' club. But, even though the special relationship among its members may be weakening, the Commonwealth remains far from a negligible force. And though it has British roots, it is very definitely no longer the *British* Commonwealth.

See also *Australia and New Zealand; Botswana; Canada; Colonialism; Federalism; Ghana; India; Ireland; Kenya; Malaysia; Namibia; Nigeria; Pakistan; South Africa; Sri Lanka; Uganda; United Kingdom; Zambia; Zimbabwe.*

David E. Butler

BIBLIOGRAPHY

Butler, David, and D. A. Low. *Sovereigns and Surrogates: Constitutional Heads of State in the Commonwealth.* London: Macmillan; New York: St. Martin's, 1991.

Dale, William. *The Modern Commonwealth.* London: Butterworth, 1981; New York: St. Martin's, 1983.

McIntyre, W. David. *The Significance of the Commonwealth, 1965–90.* London: Macmillan, 1991.

Mansergh, Nicholas. *The Commonwealth Experience.* London: Weidenfeld and Nicolson, 1968.

Smith, Arnold Cantwell. *Stitches in Time: The Commonwealth in World Politics.* London: Andre Deutsch, 1981.

United Kingdom Foreign and Commonwealth Office. *Commonwealth Year Book.* London: Her Majesty's Stationery Office, 1969– .

Wheare, K. C. *The Constitutional Structure of the Commonwealth.* Oxford: Clarendon Press, 1960.

Communism

A term that originated in the mid-1830s in secret revolutionary societies, first in Paris and then elsewhere in Western Europe. *Communism* referred at times to a form of society that would be brought about through the struggles of the working class and at other times to political movements of the working class within capitalist society.

Throughout most of the nineteenth century the terms *communism* and *socialism* were often used synonymously. But toward the end of the century, Karl Marx and Friedrich Engels defined communism as the final stage of the struggle between the working class and the oppressive capitalist class. The initial victory of the working class,

which Marx and Engels now called socialism, was thought still to show features of bourgeois class society and of modes and forms of human relations that were rooted in the past. On the other hand, under communism, classes would be abolished altogether and classless society would dawn as the final stage of the liberation of humankind from the enslavement and oppression that had characterized its previous history.

Marx and Engels theorized that only in classless communist society would people liberate themselves completely from the yoke of necessity and attain total freedom. Despite Marx's precise definitions, even in the latter part of the nineteenth century most Marxists and other working-class spokespersons used the terms *socialism* and *communism* interchangeably, generally with a strong preference for the former.

The early socialist circles in Russia were organized and attended largely by students and other intellectuals. One of the major problems that these early socialists faced was selecting a strategy and tactics that would link the intellectual and semi-intellectual members in these circles to the working class, about which, by and large, they knew very little.

A debate between evolutionary and revolutionary approaches to societal change led to a split in 1903 in the Russian Social Democratic Labor Party, a socialist party that had formed in 1898. The Bolsheviks (meaning "majoritarians") favored a revolutionary path led by a secretive cadre of professional revolutionaries. The Mensheviks (or "minoritarians") favored an evolutionary path. The Mensheviks argued that Russian society was still undeveloped and that it would need a fairly long time to reach the developmental stage of, say, Germany or England. The budding labor movement, therefore, could not yet aspire to gaining power but must await the maturation of bourgeois society.

In these circumstances the Mensheviks believed that the workers and their intellectual leaders should pursue limited goals and should fight for immediate gains. It would be foolish, they argued, to talk about a proletarian revolution when Russia had not even had its bourgeois revolution. The Bolshevik wing of the party, which was opposed to waiting for the maturation of bourgeois society, was led by Vladimir Ilich Lenin.

Leninism

In 1897 the young Lenin was arrested in St. Petersburg as a main organizer of the Union of Struggle, a militant circle made up largely of young intellectuals and students. When the first mass strike of St. Petersburg workers, centered mainly in the textile industry, broke out, these young men and women found that the workers were willing to accept their help and advice in technical matters, such as the printing of handbills, but that they were not interested in the intellectuals' argument that only a large-scale political upheaval would ameliorate the miserable condition of the workers. The workers were interested mainly in immediate economic improvement or, at best, in self-improvement, and they tended to look at their sympathizers in the Union of Struggle as hopeless windbags.

After his arrest, Lenin spent three years in exile in Siberia. He then emigrated to Europe, where he discussed the issues of the day with other socialist exiles. In Europe he went through a major political and spiritual crisis. He realized that the aims of labor and of the intelligentsia did not necessarily coincide, and he came to doubt the revolutionary potential of labor. If the workers were not at least potentially revolutionary, all Russian Marxist thought resting on the idea that the development of capitalism necessarily entailed the growth of proletarian class consciousness, even if only in the long run, was in jeopardy.

Lenin proceeded to recast Marxist doctrine. He argued that the workers could never spontaneously attain class consciousness. They could, at best, attain trade union consciousness. If that was the case, the working class would become a revolutionary force only if it accepted the leadership of trained professional revolutionaries who would inculcate class consciousness in the mass of politically inert workers.

In the years that followed, Lenin built a devoted cadre of militants, first within the general socialist movement, and later in the Bolsheviks. From 1903 on, although Bolsheviks and Mensheviks cooperated at times, most of the time they fought each other for the leadership of the struggle against oppressive czardom.

When World War I broke out in 1914, Lenin and his followers believed that the defeat of the belligerents would bring about the preconditions for a revolutionary thrust forward even in backward societies such as Russia's. Lenin's Bolsheviks hence not only opposed governmental policy but worked for the military defeat of the czarist regime, while the Mensheviks clung to a policy of loyal opposition.

The czarist regime collapsed in February 1917 and was succeeded by a coalition of liberals and centrists. Not only the Mensheviks but also most of the rank-and-file Bolsheviks, as well as many of the leaders of the Bolsheviks, prepared themselves for a long period of parliamentary and trade union struggle against the new government. Therefore, when Lenin arrived from exile in Switzerland at the Finland Station in St. Petersburg in April 1917, arguing with passionate intensity that the time had come to organize a second—socialist—revolution, even some of his own comrades thought he was mad. They argued that the working class made up only a small percentage of the population of Russia, and the Bolsheviks could be counted only in the hundreds. Yet Lenin managed within a few weeks to bring his own cadre to accept his position and to make serious inroads among the cadres of the Mensheviks as well.

At the time of the November 1917 revolution, the Bolsheviks did not have the support of the bulk of the working class or of the peasants, but they had managed to build revolutionary cadres at strategic points not only in the major cities but also in small towns and in the countryside. The professional revolutionaries and semirevolutionaries conquered Alexander Kerensky's provisional government, which had succeeded the czar, and filled the commanding heights of the revolutionary state.

The Bolsheviks at first collaborated in a new government with the Socialist Revolutionaries, a largely peasant, populist party, but they soon banned all rival socialist parties. Over time, non-Leninist factions were banned from within the Bolshevik Party itself. The Leninists justified this repression by citing the need to maintain unity in the civil war that tore Russia apart for what seemed endless months and years. But in reality the repression was largely rooted in the undemocratic Bolshevik doctrine that Lenin and his coworkers had elaborated long before the outbreak of the revolution.

Elections to the Constituent Assembly, which had taken place shortly before the outbreak of the November 1917 revolution, returned 420 Socialist Revolutionaries as against only 225 Bolsheviks. Red Army troops under Bolshevik control dispersed the assembly on the first day it met, January 18, 1918, arguing that it reflected the political thought of prerevolutionary days and hence was no longer representative of the orientations of the population.

Whenever critics—including the German socialists Rosa Luxemburg and Karl Kautsky—raised their voices in protest against the suppression of all democratic opposition, the Leninist answer was always the need to close ranks around those who had the mission to safeguard the existence of the first socialist workers' state.

Russian Communism After Lenin

Lenin was a sensitive intellectual steeped in Western culture. Whenever he succeeded in suppressing critical voices, especially among some of his old Menshevik comrades in arms, he apparently felt some guilt. His successor, Joseph Stalin, was not inclined to such "bourgeois" sentiment. He murdered his opponents and those he only suspected of opposition with no qualms whatsoever. Lenin, in his prerevolutionary writings, praised participatory democracy as he imagined it to have operated in the short-lived reign of the Paris Commune of 1871. It seems likely that he believed that working-class formations after the victory of communism would do away with the powers of the state, end the long history of bureaucracy, and do away with all distinctions based on the division of labor. But none of these ideals could be pursued, Lenin believed, as long as domestic and foreign adversaries still threatened the young Soviet revolution.

Socialists and social scientists have debated for many decades whether Russian developments would have taken a different course had Lenin lived longer and had Stalin not taken power. It would seem that a post-Leninist regime under Leon Trotsky or Nikolai Bukharin might have been less draconian and more humane than Stalin's regime turned out to be. Trotsky and Bukharin probably would not have murdered the majority of their former comrades, nor would they have endorsed a policy of extermination in the countryside. But a Soviet Union under the guidance of another Bolshevik probably would not have been different from what it turned out to be under Stalin. The isolation of the Soviet Union in a sea of basically hostile states, combined with the rule of men and women trained over years to believe that they belonged to a chosen elite that was entrusted by history to guide Russia toward a blissful future and to make the country a beacon to the unenlightened, would most likely have led to a regime only marginally less horrifying than Stalin's.

Lenin seems to have believed that one could postpone the emergence of a democratic regime to a time less stressful and dangerous than the 1920s in the Soviet Union. That idea was ultimately his major failing. One cannot turn on a democratic course of action as one turns on a faucet. The ultimate fate of the Soviet body politic was already sealed in the first few years of its existence, as Rosa Luxemburg saw with exemplary lucidity. There are exceptions to the rule that political regimes tend to follow the course in which they have been set at the beginning—but such exceptions are few.

Lenin had already broken with traditional Marxism when he set the course of his party in the direction that ultimately submitted the working class to the heavy hand of the dictatorship of the Bolshevik Party. Neither Bukharin nor Trotsky would have broken this initial deadly political mold.

The International Movement Between the World Wars

By the early 1920s it was clear to the Russian communists that the international revolution Lenin had prophesied would not occur. This failure left the Soviet Union in a precarious position. Industrially underdeveloped, exhausted from world war and civil war, and surrounded by capitalist states, the Soviet Union sought moral and political help from its sympathizers around the world. One of the major aims of the Russian communist leaders in the post–World War I period was to create in all capitalist and colonial countries communist parties that would compete with and eventually supplant the local socialist parties. In 1919 the Russian communists created the Communist International (the Comintern), which sought to displace all existing socialist parties that were unwilling to become their instruments. They never succeeded in replacing the European socialist parties that were reconstructed after the war, but they succeeded in creating almost everywhere rival organizations subservient to the Kremlin and willing to follow every twist and strategic turn that the Russians demanded.

Throughout the 1920s and 1930s the various national communist parties that belonged to the Comintern changed their platforms, policies, and tactics at the behest of the Russian heads of the Comintern—even if those changes made no sense in the local context. The choice of strategies was made in Moscow and not in the home countries, and the shifts in the party line did not result from assessments or reassessments of the local scene but from calculations as to what political line was most advantageous for the Soviet Union. No matter how absurd were the policy guidelines that the Comintern imposed on the national parties, they invariably were followed.

The effects of Comintern vacillation on the national

parties and on the European labor movement as a whole were devastating. Many old-time radicals and labor leaders with local roots and deep loyalties in the labor movements of their respective nations left the parties in disgust. As the "Stalinization" of the communist parties continued, all leaders who could still distinguish between their loyalty to the Russian dictatorship and to the working class of their own country were eliminated. A new kind of leader began to appear, the "apparatus man" (apparatchik), whose chief talent was the justification and carrying out of Moscow's orders. The professional revolutionaries of the Leninist period were, in Trotsky's phrase, "domesticated and then destroyed." Their place was taken by bureaucratic careerists whose fundamental means of judging their success in office was their standing in the eyes of Moscow.

Factional struggles broke out from time to time within the national communist parties, as in France, Italy, and the United States, but these struggles had almost nothing to do with normal political disputes. They resembled instead the jockeying for power of cliques on top of a bureaucratic structure. Rather than reflecting different assessments of the political arena at home, the factional struggles were all directed at winning the favor of the highest Russian authorities in the communist world.

In part because of vacillations in Comintern policies and in part because of philosophical disagreements that had been percolating in the communist movement since the early years of the century, the history of the European labor movement between the world wars was one of fratricide and mutual contempt. The socialist and communist parties in each European nation seldom agreed on major issues of strategy or tactics. For these reasons the European labor movement as a whole never regained the strength that it had shown before World War I. Deeply divided within itself, it went from defeat to defeat.

Some comment on the structure and function of the communist parties worldwide is in order. The basic organizational unit of the party was the cell. It was made up of not more than fifty members, often considerably fewer. The cell was connected to the next higher organizational unit by its leading cadres. The next higher organizational unit was linked through its officers to the unit above it, and so on. Because all connections were vertical, cells had no contact whatsoever with neighboring cells on their level. Furthermore, officers were "elected" by their constituency upon submission of their names by higher bureaucrats. Factions were strictly forbidden. A person who opposed party policy in any way was subject to ra-

pid expulsion. The communists held democracy in contempt.

Given the extreme rigidity of such a structure, the only course of action open for a party member who had grown skeptical and disaffected was to leave the party. Indeed, massive fluctuation in membership was the rule in all national parties. The bureaucrats stayed on, but the rank-and-file members usually stayed only a fairly short time. Nevertheless, it would be a mistake to believe that the parties consisted only of members who would leave after a short period of disillusionment. Stalinism, though a corrupt and deadly movement, managed all the same to infuse vast numbers of members and fellow travelers with sincere devotion and readiness to sacrifice.

International Communism After World War II

When the Soviet Union was attacked by Nazi Germany in 1941, European communists in many cases became the vanguard in their respective nations' resistance movements. Their heroic deeds became legend. Their martyrs often became the best means for the party to advertise its message and to attract a new generation of converts. The communists often provided the only message of hope for those who were disillusioned by the postwar governments.

Stalinist communists thrived whenever and wherever the traditional parties of the center or of the left failed to deliver on their electoral promises. The communists profited from the decline of those parties that had previously dominated the left. Wherever the labor movement had tasted defeat and humiliation, the typical Stalinist militant "knew" that the door to a better future was largely barred within the national borders. Only total devotion to the Soviet Union would assure a brighter tomorrow.

But when the Soviet monolith began to be shaken, when even total devotion could no longer ignore its fissures, the Western communist parties began to decline at a rapid pace. Either they became indistinguishable from social democratic parties, as in Italy, or they shrunk into politically impotent sects.

Moreover, the image of the Soviet Union suffered by comparison with the welfare state that had come into existence in all Western European countries. The welfare state was far from a communist utopia, but it did diminish the sense of alienation of the working class. Although still deprived of equal access to the material goods that came as a matter of course to the members of other classes, the working class had managed to break out of the ghetto to which it had been relegated since the beginning of the Industrial Revolution. When the golden image of the Soviet Union became tarnished, and when the welfare state began to make good on at least some of its promises, the communist myth and the communist messages lost their potent appeal, and the communist movement, which for decades had seemed to be a threat to the democratic West, began to fade.

If the communist parties of Europe continue on their present course, their chances of attracting new members and voters are very small indeed. Only a revived democratic socialist movement that tempers realistic policies with a renewal of social idealism and utopian vision can hope to profit from the disillusionment of former communist party members, followers, and sympathizers.

See also *Engels, Friedrich; Leninism; Luxemburg, Rosa; Marx, Karl; Marxism; Socialism; Union of Soviet Socialist Republics.*

Lewis A. Coser

BIBLIOGRAPHY

Arendt, Hannah. *The Origin of Totalitarianism.* New York: Meridian, 1954.

Billington, James H. *Fire in the Minds of Men: Origins of the Revolutionary Faith.* New York: Basic Books; Aldershot: M. T. Smith, 1980.

Borkenau, Franz. *World Communism.* Ann Arbor: University of Michigan Press, 1962.

Cohen, Stephen. *Bukharin and the Bolshevik Revolution.* New York: Knopf, 1973.

Coser, Lewis A. "Death Throes of Western Communism." *Dissent* (spring 1989).

———. "Marxist Thought in the First Quarter of the 20th Century." In *A Handful of Thistles.* New Brunswick, N.J.: Transaction, 1988.

Howe, Irving, and Lewis A. Coser. *The American Communist Party: A Critical History (1919–1957).* 2d ed. New York: Praeger, 1962.

Lenin, V. I. "One Step Forward, Two Steps Backward," and "What Is to Be Done?" In *Selected Works.* Vol. 2. New York: International Publishers, 1969.

Lichtheim, George. *A Short History of Socialism.* New York: Praeger, 1970.

Lipset, Seymour Martin. *Political Man: The Social Bases of Politics.* Expanded and updated ed. Baltimore: Johns Hopkins University Press, 1981; Aldershot: Gower, 1983.

Pipes, Richard. *Social Democracy and the St. Petersburg Labor Movement.* Cambridge: Harvard University Press, 1968.

Schapiro, Leonard. *The Origin of the Communist Autocracy.* New York: Cambridge University Press, 1955.

Tucker, Robert. *Stalin in Power: The Revolution from Above.* New York and London: Norton, 1992.

Wilson, Edmund. *To the Finland Station.* Garden City, N.Y.: Doubleday, 1953; Harmondsworth, England: Penguin Books, 1991.

Wolfe, Bertram D. *Three Who Made a Revolution.* Boston: Beacon Press, 1955.

Communitarianism

An antiliberal political theory whose advocates seek to establish a democratic politics of the common good and thereby to tame or even to supplant the prevailing liberal politics of individual rights. The communitarian movement rose to prominence in the 1980s, in the political world as well as in the academy. This revival of the idea of community has taken a remarkable variety of forms, from traditional conservative to social democratic to radical postmodernist. As a result, it is difficult to state with precision the distinctive features of a communitarian political theory.

But communitarians at least are united by a shared hostility to the pervasive individualism of contemporary liberal democratic politics. They are critics of liberal democracy founded on individual rights and partisans of more robust forms of democratic politics founded on common deliberation about the common good. Communitarians thus raise again a question that for a time had been closed by the theoretical and practical successes of liberal democracy: the nature of a just and healthy democratic polity.

Liberty, Virtue, and Equality

It is evident that there are several forms of democracy. These forms differ substantially according to the weight that each assigns to certain basic political goods—especially liberty, virtue, and equality.

First, a liberal democracy is founded on the idea that liberty (and not, say, salvation or virtue or equality) is more fundamental than all other political goods. The liberal democrat affirms, in addition, that a democratic polity is most likely to respect the rights of individuals, to secure the blessings of liberty. But because democracy itself can sometimes be a threat to liberty (what Alexis de Tocqueville called the "tyranny of the majority"), liberals are rarely unqualified partisans of democracy. Indeed, as the American Declaration of Independence makes clear, the rights of individuals might in some circumstances be made more secure through the establishment of forms of government that are only qualifiedly democratic, or not democratic at all. For this reason, more wholehearted partisans of democracy suspect that there is an antidemocratic impulse hidden at the heart of liberal philosophy. In any case, for the liberal democrat, democracy is a means to secure liberty.

Next, the foundation of a democratic republic is virtue. According to the republican argument, democracy depends on virtue to ensure good citizenship. Because the same human beings are, in a democratic republic, both rulers and subjects, as Montesquieu argues, such democratic communities cannot rely on force employed by rulers to ensure civility among the subjects. Citizens must learn to govern themselves, since there are no rulers to govern them. Democratic citizens must freely choose to serve the community, animated by patriotism or public spirit, or they will not be found to serve the community at all. According to the most formidable partisan of the democratic republic founded on virtue, Jean-Jacques Rousseau, virtue is a passionate identification with one's community, a wholehearted love of the democratic republic. Good citizens are happy to participate in the common life of the community, working for the common good even at the expense of private pursuits of happiness and somehow identifying their own happiness with the common good.

Virtue is thus utterly incompatible with liberal privacy, much less with the self-absorption that marks the ways of life of individualists today. Rousseau's democratic republic is an illiberal democracy: rights are not respected and commerce is despised, since these liberal goods invariably give rise to disharmony between public and private interest in the souls of citizens. It is also an egalitarian and homogeneous community, since inequality and diversity would undermine the love of the republic that alone makes virtue possible. The democratic republic is thus less tolerant than liberal democracy.

Finally, the foundation of pure or participatory democracy is equality. Strictly speaking, democracy is (as Aristotle says) the rule of the people, wherein each citizen has an equal share in politics and no quality distinguishes those who are fit for citizenship from those who are not. Thus the purest form of democratic argument is the argument for direct or participatory democracy: justice demands that each citizen should share equally in the goods that belong to the political community. Equality can be achieved only where the people act collectively to defend this claim (in assembly or by means of plebiscites and similar tools of direct popular action). Furthermore, egalitarian justice requires not only equality of political power but also some measure of economic equality. This form of democracy is often associated with ancient Greece; in the modern world, the cause of egalitarian democracy has been advanced primarily by social democrats.

Whether or not this democratic argument from justice succeeds, it is widely admitted that a purely democratic politics is indefensible on prudential grounds: the people are often foolish—fickle and fanatical by turns. Especially in modern societies based on mass politics and faced with problems of unprecedented complexity, partisans of democratic politics have often found it necessary to embrace various liberal and republican principles and practices designed to tame popular vices and to refine popular judgment.

The Idea of Community

The communitarian revival of the idea of community might be understood as a revival of these old republican and democratic arguments in a somewhat hybrid form: marrying the older concerns about equality and virtue yields the more or less novel idea of community. This revival comes at a time when the case for a democratic politics dedicated to securing liberty is no longer satisfying, for both political and philosophical reasons that are outlined below. For this reason, communitarianism is somewhat difficult to classify as a movement of either the right or the left: the language of community seems conservative at times and social democratic at times, depending on whether the republican (virtue) or democratic (equality) aspect of the idea of community dominates.

Communitarianism is in some sense the newest replacement for failed Marxism. Yet it lacks the moral rigor, the love of justice understood as equality, of socialism and social democracy. If communitarians are less than wholehearted in their commitment to equality, they are even more ambivalent in their praise of virtue. Thus the republicanism of today's communitarians also lacks the moral rigor of Rousseau's republicanism, which is marked by moralism, the abolition of privacy, and the unremitting self-sacrifice of citizens.

In republican moments, communitarians are tempted to excuse this or that (mild) policy of censorship, to praise "family values," or to call for a renewal of moral education in the schools—but not, they invariably add, at the expense of toleration and the rights of individuals. In democratic moments, which are perhaps somewhat more frequent than the republican ones, communitarians are tempted to seek policies that redistribute wealth (designed to secure greater economic equality) and to call for the establishment of participatory institutions, for example, "teledemocracy" (designed to ensure a greater voice for the people in their collective capacity). But there is no question of abandoning liberal (free market) economics, much less of withdrawing from the goal of private prosperity. And there is no question of abolishing representation (as Rousseau suggested) or any of the other liberal political institutions that filter the judgment of the people and so diminish the likelihood of folly or fanaticism. In short, communitarians remain liberal democrats at bottom, in spite of the occasional immoderation of their attacks on liberal individualism. Let us turn to this more critical aspect of communitarianism, beginning with a review of the classical liberal portrait of the community.

The Liberal Community

Classical liberalism (for example, the liberalism of John Locke) is a doctrine of acquisitive individualism. It maintains that human beings are by nature solitary and selfish, not political or communal. We are not friends by nature but enemies who are driven by our most potent natural passions and needs to compete, and so to quarrel, in order to provide for our security and comfort. Thus the natural condition of human beings is a state of war, a terrible condition from which any reasonable human being seeks to escape.

Classical liberalism therefore contains an account of the nature and purpose of political community (as a means of escape from the hardships of our natural condition of war and scarcity) as well as an idea of the common good and even an account of moral and political virtue. But the liberal community is an austere one, founded only on the basis of a social contract among naturally hostile individuals, and not on the basis of any more robust common opinions about justice. For the liberal the only truly common goods are peace and the means to peace, since peace is the almost necessary condition of security in the possession of all private goods. And the liberal virtues are simply those habits of reasonable self-restraint that enable human beings to establish and to sustain such communities (Tocqueville's idea of "self-interest rightly understood").

For the classical liberal, then, community is not at all warm and cozy. The liberal community is not a home, and liberal citizens do not regard each other as lovable and trustworthy companions in a kind of extended family (or even in a common moral enterprise). Indeed, the political community is not quite natural. It has no moral authority beyond that derived from the consent of the governed, who build liberal communities in order to secure certain private goods that are naturally insecure. That is, liberal politics is a politics of fearful accommodation among natural foes who have somehow learned to transform themselves into civil friends. And so the liberal community is marked in the best case by mutual respect for individual rights (life, liberty, and the pursuit of happiness); by tolerance of a rather wide variety of ways of life and opinions (free exercise of religion); and by the moderation of parties and sects whose members refrain from seeking the community's endorsement of contentious moral, religious, and ideological opinions (no establishment of religion).

Thus liberal communities are not communities of moral opinion. There is no liberal orthodoxy regarding justice or salvation or virtue or the good life, since common deliberation about such common goods too often disturbs the peace and in any case renders private pursuits of happiness vulnerable to prejudice and authority. And the idea of a community that somehow possesses a natural moral authority independent of the consent of those individuals who establish it is always suspect for liberals, who are inclined to view partisans of such a community as romantic utopians or dangerous authoritarians. If there is no natural common good beyond peace or security, invocations of the spirit of community are either foolish or fraudulent, impossible dreams or wicked ideologies.

But this austere vision of the liberal community has proved to be unsatisfying to many critics who hope for more from community—more warmth, more justice, more nobility. We turn next to these communitarian criticisms of liberal community.

The Communitarian Critique

A variety of prominent contemporary critics of liberal individualism and the liberal democratic polity are now called communitarians (although not every so-called communitarian is eager to embrace the name). Any list of communitarian theorists would surely include the following thinkers: Benjamin Barber, Robert Bellah, Jean Bethke Elshtain, Amitai Etzioni, Mary Ann Glendon, Stanley Hauerwas, Alasdair MacIntyre, Michael Sandel, William Sullivan, and Michael Walzer. These theorists evidently disagree about many important matters, more than is common in a movement (as communitarianism is sometimes said to be). Participatory democrats, classical republicans, feminists, socialists, theologians, postmodernists, and others now raise their voices, but not altogether in unison, in praise of community. That is, they are more united in their diagnosis of the disease than in their prescriptions for a cure.

It has proved to be far easier to say why we now miss community than to say what form (democratic, republican, or something altogether new) a renewal of community might take. The communitarian criticism of liberal individualism has several dimensions. Here, we look at three arguments: political, moral, and philosophical.

According to the political argument (advanced by Barber and Walzer, among others), liberal individualism destroys citizenship and undermines civic virtue. It is incapable of providing an adequate foundation for a truly democratic community of free and equal citizens. As we have wholeheartedly embraced private life, we have also neglected to cultivate the virtues and other habits of citizenship that even a liberal community must sometimes summon. Thus we now find ourselves disempowered in face of the various impersonal modes of authority that are present in a modern bureaucratic state with a capitalist economy. What is more, we have lost the capacity to exercise even the most modest forms of self-restraint or public-spiritedness, much less to nurture old-fashioned republican virtue.

This combination of slavishness and selfishness makes possible a contemptible mode of liberal politics. We are the (happy) slaves of paternalistic elites who purchase public passivity and conformity by base appeals to selfishness—"bread and circuses" administered efficiently and rationally by hidden authorities who serve the bureaucratic state and capitalist economy. This is far from the liberal imagination of autonomous individuals capable of reasonable self-government. Only the revival of truly democratic citizenship, which teaches human beings to consider the common good and not merely their private rights and interests, can generate the civic virtues and political judgment that might enable contemporary men and women to take control of their common life once again and to throw off their new masters.

The communitarian moral critique of liberal individualism is somewhat more difficult to summarize because the communitarians are (in terms of moral psychology) a diverse lot. Nevertheless, a number of common accusations can be discerned. According to the moral argument (advanced by MacIntyre, Sandel, and Walzer, among others), prevailing liberal ways of life are morally impoverished. Thus communitarians argue not only that we are not good citizens but also that the vaunted privacy of liberal individualists is itself a fraud. In a way, this moral assault on liberal individualism is more devastating than the political criticism (at least for partisans of liberalism), since the case for liberalism rests above all on the claim that liberal polities protect a variety of dignified private ways of life from clumsy and benighted political judgment. But what if these ways of life are often contemptible? And what if the now liberated human beings who inhabit liberal communities are often miserable? Perhaps our individualism has gone too far. It has, to be sure, liberated us from tyrants and priests, as was its aim, but that same individualism has also made it more difficult for us even to imagine a genuine common life with fellow citizens, or even with family and friends.

Liberal moral psychology reduces the primitive or natural self-knowledge that makes manifest the importance of such moral attachments in a complete human life. We have learned to think of ourselves as free individuals above all, thereby forgetting that our selves are embedded in particular communities (families, religions, peoples, republics) that at least in part constitute our identities. Moreover, we have loyalties and duties toward our companions in those communities that are not acquired through our free acts as individuals. An individual who does not recognize the moral force of such attachments is shallow and pitiable. Liberation has left us lonely and helpless. Our private ways of life are no longer marked by the proud practice of freedom but by grim dissipation, careless self-satisfaction, mindless conformity, or quiet desperation. Only a restoration of the moral authority of community can enable contemporary men and women to attribute moral meaning to their ways of life.

This moral critique of liberal individualism gives rise, finally, to a philosophical critique that is less important for present purposes than the political and moral arguments. Liberal individualism is now said to be philosophically defective insofar as it rests on an incoherent account of moral reasoning and the nature of the self. According to many communitarians (and others), the liberal quest for universal and objective principles of political right, against which one might measure the justice of the principles and practices of any particular community, is misguided. If there are any universal moral principles, they are too minimal and abstract to provide more than the framework for a moral life. Liberal philosophy is incapable of constituting communities. The proper task of philosophy therefore is poetic or creative: evocative interpretation of a shared moral horizon, not liberation from such horizons.

Against the liberal, the communitarian insists that human beings are wholly constituted by particular histories, that there is no escape from contingency (and so, no escape from community). Thus the aspiration to liberate oneself from the bonds of particularism is founded on a misguided metaphysical hope. The philosophic quest for a metaphysical comfort (that the world should be intelligible) must now give way to a communitarian quest for a certain moral comfort (that we should have a "home"). Here is the moral meaning of the new idea of philosophy: community can serve as a bulwark against the dislocating and disorienting qualities of modernity—against nihilism, meaninglessness, alienation, and the rest.

It is worth remarking that the posture of many communitarians toward liberal individualism is more ambivalent than that described here. Most such critics acknowledge that liberalism has proved to be an admirably liberating doctrine and that liberal polities have begun to reveal a notable capacity to accommodate the just claims of the formerly disadvantaged. The communitarian critique of liberalism thus lacks the radicalism of earlier antiliberal doctrines, although it is sometimes expressed in rather feverish language. As a result, some critics accuse the communitarians of taking the achievements of liberalism for granted, of forgetting that liberty is a historically precarious possession and that it may come at a high moral and political price (including the decline of virtue and the rise of inequality) that is yet worth paying. Perhaps this is the quality that most distinguishes today's communitarians: the desire to have it all, to revive virtue and to establish equality, but without diminishing the liberty achieved by the liberal democratic politics of individualism.

See also *Declaration of Independence; Liberalism; Locke, John; Montesquieu; Participatory democracy; Rousseau, Jean-Jacques; Theory, Ancient; Tocqueville, Alexis de; Virtue, Civic.* In Documents section, see *American Declaration of Independence (1776).*

Steven Kautz

BIBLIOGRAPHY

Barber, Benjamin. *Strong Democracy: Participatory Politics for a New Age.* Berkeley: University of California Press, 1984.

Elshtain, Jean Bethke. *Public Man, Private Woman: Women in Social and Political Thought.* Princeton: Princeton University Press, 1981.

Fowler, Robert Booth. *The Dance with Community: The Contemporary Debate in American Political Thought.* Lawrence: University Press of Kansas, 1991.

Glendon, Mary Ann. *Rights Talk.* Cambridge: Harvard University Press, 1991.

Holmes, Stephen. *The Anatomy of Antiliberalism.* Chicago: University of Chicago Press, 1993.

MacIntyre, Alasdair. *After Virtue: A Study in Moral Theory.* Notre Dame, Ind.: University of Notre Dame Press, 1981; London: Duckworth, 1982.

McWilliams, Wilson Carey. *The Idea of Fraternity in America.* Berkeley: University of California Press, 1973.

Rorty, Richard M. *Contingency, Irony, and Solidarity.* Cambridge and New York: Cambridge University Press, 1989.

Sandel, Michael J. *Liberalism and the Limits of Justice.* Cambridge and New York: Cambridge University Press, 1982.

Walzer, Michael. *Spheres of Justice: A Defense of Pluralism and Equality.* New York: Basic Books, 1983; Oxford: Blackwell, 1985.

Comoros

See *Africa, Subsaharan*

Complexity

A core characteristic of the modern democratic state, arising from the massive expansion in the functions of the state and the number of bodies of which it is composed. Can citizens participate meaningfully in policy processes in which scientific and technical dimensions have become increasingly prominent? Is the modern democratic state now so large and fragmented that no person or group can effectively control it? These are some of the questions implicit in the issue of state complexity.

State complexity has three key dimensions. First, *structural complexity* can be seen most clearly in the sheer number and range of organizations that make up the executive in modern democracies. The state in the United States and in the major European democracies, for example, consists of hundreds if not thousands of separate organizations—a bewildering variety of executive departments, bureaus, and agencies that perform an array of regulatory, judicial, implementational, and advisory roles.

Complexity of structure is closely related to *functional complexity.* The functions of government in the nineteenth, and into the twentieth, century were in essence the classic liberal functions of defense, diplomacy, and the provision of a basic framework of laws. With the development and expansion of the welfare state after World War II, and with efforts by governments to harness the potential of rapid advances in scientific and technological knowledge, the roles assumed by the state have changed greatly in both number and type. Further, the mass publics in Western democracies by and large expect states to take prime responsibility for all issues that impinge upon the quality of life.

The third key dimension of state complexity is the *boundary problem*: where does the state end and the private sphere begin? It is commonly argued that the boundaries between the public and the private have become blurred. Private bodies, such as business groups, labor unions, and professional associations, often perform public functions; at the same time, many public bodies operate in part as private organizations.

The problem of complexity for democracy arises from the ways in which bodies on the fringes of the state interact, their distance from formal lines of accountability to elected politicians, and the often abstruse technical content of their policy functions.

Confronted with this reality, North American and European political scientists have attempted to devise new models of policy processes in Western democracies. In the United States, political scientists working within the established pluralist tradition have developed the concept of *subgovernments*. Pioneered by J. Leiper Freeman (in *The Political Process*, 1955), this body of work stressed the need to study U.S. policy making in terms of subsystems. Interactions among congressional committees, executive agencies, and powerful pressure groups in certain policy sectors came to be called *iron triangles*. The totality of public policy outcomes, in Freeman's view at least, reflected in large measure decisions taken by constitutionally minor, and seemingly politically insignificant, actors who dealt with the details of policy within certain areas such as education, health, and agriculture. Later U.S. writers have picked up these themes, often stressing the possibility of private interests becoming dominant within subgovernments.

Similarly, British political scientists from the end of the 1970s have developed models of *policy networks* and *policy communities* in an attempt to capture the nature of fragmented policy making. Policy networks and communities, in essence, are groupings of state and private individuals and organizations that are dependent on each other's resources to achieve their policy goals. There may be a number of different types of networks—for example, professionalized networks dominated by qualified experts, or producer networks dominated by one or more private corporations.

In Britain especially, such networks are based around government departments; the British legislature is weak, and policy networks further isolate Parliament from policy making. Indeed, the first major British text on policy communities, *Governing under Pressure* by Jeremy Richardson and Grant Jordan (1979), was subtitled "Politics in a Post-parliamentary Democracy." In an influential later account of policy networks in Britain, R. A. W. Rhodes (*Beyond Westminster and Whitehall*, 1988) argued that policy networks had become "as central a feature of the national government environment as some of the hoary old chestnuts of the constitution, less prominent and debated but a more determinant influence."

The implications of complexity and fragmentation for the strength and effectiveness of democracy are far from clear, but they are considerable. The effective sidelining of elected legislatures is merely the first of them. Second, cabinet ministers and department heads often have little possibility of understanding and controlling the enormous and fragmented executive structures of which they are the nominal heads. Third, as the technical content of policy has grown, the chances for effective lay participation in policy making have diminished. Fourth, there is the ever present danger of ungovernability: the complexity of the tasks that governments face, matched by the complexity of the institutions established for the management and resolution of policy problems, may stand as an obstacle to effective decision making. Finally, many observers have feared that as complexity breeds ineffectiveness, it erodes the legitimacy of democratic government in the eyes of the citizenry.

Perhaps, as Danilo Zolo has argued (in *Democracy and Complexity*, 1992), state complexity should lead us to abandon any grand hopes for strengthening popular participation and accountability in contemporary democracies. As the famous, and much criticized, analysis of democracy offered by Joseph Schumpeter (in *Capitalism, Socialism, and Democracy*, 1942) suggested, perhaps democracy can be no more than a method for deciding by election which group of elite leaders will occupy the top government positions for a limited period.

See also *Bureaucracy; Civil service; Corporatism; Decision making; Legitimacy; Schumpeter, Joseph; Science; Technology.*

Michael Saward

BIBLIOGRAPHY

European Journal of Political Research 21 (February 1992). Special issue on policy networks.

Lowi, Theodore J. *The End of Liberalism.* New York and London: Norton, 1969.

Marsh, David, and R. A. W. Rhodes, eds. *Policy Networks in British Government.* Oxford and New York: Oxford University Press, 1992.

Rhodes, R. A. W. *Beyond Westminster and Whitehall: Subcentral Governments of Britain.* London: Unwin Hyman, 1988.

Zolo, Danilo. *Democracy and Complexity: A Realist Approach.* Cambridge: Polity Press, 1992.

Confucianism

Chinese school of political thought founded by Confucius (c. 551–c. 479 B.C.). Although the current Chinese term for *democracy,* literally "rule of the people," was not introduced into the Chinese vocabulary until the nineteenth century, democratic principles of governance have been part of Confucianism for millennia.

Confucius spoke of the ideal of a Grand Commonwealth in which the governing elite would be elected and composed of people of talent and virtue. Since then, Chinese scholars have looked to the ideas of Confucius as the starting point for their own political reform proposals—from Mencius, in the third century B.C., who expanded on Confucius's ideas, to Kang Youwei, a nineteenth-century statesman and Confucian scholar, who advocated extreme egalitarianism, worldwide democracy, and abolition of nation-states.

In the twentieth century, discussion in China and elsewhere has centered on the nature of Confucianism and its impact on the future of China and the world. Some Sinologists in the West have dismissed Confucianism as an outmoded and negative force hindering the modernization of Asian nations. A similar stance was taken by Chinese scholars during the May Fourth Movement, an intellectual revolution that swept China in the wake of World War I. However, the current importance of Confucianism in several modern democraticizing Asian societies—particularly Taiwan, Hong Kong, and Singapore—forces the West and China to reconsider the importance of Confucianism and its compatibility with modern democratic ideals.

Confucian democratic ideals—as opposed to European ruling traditions—are embodied by the concept of the

An idealized image of Confucius, drawn generations after his death, shows him standing in the Chinese National Academy of Learning.

Mandate of Heaven, which portrays the emperor not only as the son of Heaven but also as the first servant of the state. Mencius expanded on this idea, stating that an emperor may rule only so long as the people's needs are met. If the emperor fails in this mission, any commoner may try to depose him and assume his role as leader. The Confucian mandate thus stands in stark contrast to the European idea of a monarch who holds divine right to the throne by birth and bloodline.

Confucius and Confucian Ideals

Confucius was born in Lu, the center of Zhou culture, and now the city of Qufu in Shandong Province. He lost his father at the age of three and was largely self-taught under the guidance of his mother. For much of his life he traveled among warring princes, seeking patronage and expounding upon his political philosophy in an effort to promote peace. Not until he was past fifty did Confucius enter government, rising to the position of minister of justice. He had to resign after only three years, however, and was once again obliged to travel from state to state seeking patronage. Throughout his life, Confucius had three goals: to serve government, to teach youth, and to record Chinese culture for posterity.

A great advocate of order and dignity, Confucius preached against the growing chaos in China, stressing the responsibilities inherent in human relationships: between ruler and subject, father and son, husband and wife, elder brother and younger brother, and friend and friend. He believed that the first step toward the transformation of a disordered world was recognition and fulfillment of each individual's proper place in society. To Confucius, the concept of individual human rights (as defined in Western democracies) was subordinate to this sense of contractual social obligation emphasizing the individual's responsibility to a greater group, such as family and nation.

Confucius believed the world would develop in three stages. The first stage would be an age of disorder; the second would be a period in which all states begin to enjoy order and peace; and the Grand Commonwealth would emerge in the third stage. Confucius thus held the Grand Commonwealth, under which a talented and virtuous elite would be elected to govern, to be the highest ideal of society. This elite was to be made up of gentlemen who had received a literary as well as a moral education that stressed truth, honor, and the promotion of just government. Breaking with tradition, Confucius held that a man was a gentleman due to his character, rather than his bloodline.

Members of the ruling elite were expected to act with the highest degree of moral responsibility as an ethical example for all people. In return, this elite would have authoritarian powers. Confucius saw this system as the best alternative to the state of warfare then current between feudal lords and aristocratic families.

Confucius advocated *ren*—humanity or benevolence—as the highest good. He viewed the princely, or superior, man as the ideal being and the cultivation of life as the supreme duty of man. Confucius emphasized moral perfection for the individual and proper conduct based on morality for society.

Ren expresses the Confucian ideal of cultivating benevolence, developing one's faculties, sublimating one's personality, and upholding the right to education, the right to subsistence, and the right to social and political mobility without distinction according to class. *Ren* could be cultivated through filial behavior and fraternal love, which

Confucius saw as the cornerstones of society. If practiced by successive dynasties, filial behavior and fraternal love would serve as the bond of social solidarity and the connection between generations. Grievances were to be resolved through a process of mutual accommodation. Under the influence of Confucianism, the Chinese state thus developed a consensual model of governance, rather than following the more legalistic and adversarial Western model.

Because *ren* applied to rulers and ruled alike, it represented a new and democratic ideal of society. Confucius was not merely idealistic, however. He also outlined three essential elements of good government that would make the practice of *ren* possible: abundance of goods, adequate armaments, and the confidence of the people. Of the three, Confucius held the greatest to be the confidence of the people, without which he said there would be no government. This theory was later expanded by Mencius into the doctrine of people's sovereignty.

Because of his desire for order in Chinese society and his disdain for the prevailing chaos of his times, Confucius also placed much emphasis on the ruler to the disadvantage of the ruled. Although Confucian doctrine was dependent on the egalitarian ideals of *ren*, as well as many other principles, many rulers in China unfortunately chose to ignore the more democratic principles and focus instead on the authoritarian aspects of Confucianism.

Disciples and Interpreters of Confucius

Mencius (c. 372–c. 289 B.C.) elaborated on Confucius's ideas about the role of the people in government in his doctrine of people's sovereignty. Born near Confucius's hometown in Shandong during a period of civil strife and political instability, Mencius studied under disciples of Confucius. Like Confucius, he traveled for most of his life, offering advice on social and political reforms to feudal lords. Also like Confucius, he failed to win royal support for his political doctrines and had to content himself with teaching and writing in his last years. Although he did not win political favor during his lifetime, Mencius later was recognized by the Chinese literati as the Second Sage—the greatest philosopher after Confucius.

According to Mencius, good government should come upward from the people instead of downward from the ruling class. The people are not only the root but also the final judge of government. A major element of this doctrine is the Confucian theory of the Mandate of Heaven, on which Mencius elaborated. Because the opinion of the people is of supreme significance in the affairs of the state, the people have the right to depose a wicked king. Mencius thus spoke favorably of the popular revolutions of the past that had ended with the overthrow of the rulers Jie and Zhou, whose autocracy and thievery from the people had caused them to lose the Mandate of Heaven.

Above all, Mencius emphasized the ruler's duty to enrich the people, arguing that virtue and peace could not come as long as hunger and cold were the order of the day. Rebellion was justified under such conditions, since the sovereign did not hold an innate right to rule. Mencius also viewed government officials as the nation's public servants, bearing the sovereign's charge to nourish the people, rather than as the private retainers of the sovereign.

The third great developer of Confucian thought was the philosopher Hsün-tzu (Xun Zi), whose life as a social and political reformer was much like that of Confucius. While the exact dates of Hsün-tzu's birth and death are not known, he is believed to have lived to witness the end of the Warring States period (402–221 B.C.), when the state of Qin conquered all its rival states and unified China for the first time (in 221 B.C.). Like Mencius, Hsün-tzu held that a contented, economically well-off populace was the basis of good government. He believed that a sovereign could win the allegiance of his people only by his noble character, not by brute force. Hsün-tzu thus conceived of the sovereign's power as derived from the general will of the people, rather than from a special commission from Heaven. Like Mencius, he supported the right of the people to revolt against the ruler who failed in four duties: nourishing, governing, employing, and protecting the people. However, whereas Mencius represents the more idealistic wing of Confucianism, Hsün-tzu was a pragmatist who emphasized social control to offset what he saw as the basic weakness of human nature.

The Chinese Imperial State

Confucianism became the predominant philosophy in China only after the imperial system was consolidated under the Qin (255–206 B.C.) and Han (205 B.C.–A.D. 220) dynasties. The first Qin emperor, a harsh Legalist monarch, took drastic measures to eradicate dangerous doctrines, burning books and burying scholars alive. Although the Han rulers disapproved of the violent methods of the Qin, they also realized the wisdom of maintaining political unity through unity of thought. Upon the recommendations of Han Confucian scholars, the

Han emperor Wudi organized within the Imperial Court a board of scholars with five faculties, each specializing in one of the five Confucian classics. The board expanded from 50 to 3,000 scholars in the second half of the first century B.C. and to 30,000 scholars in the second century A.D. At the same time, many other scholars of Confucianism were named in the outlying districts throughout China. These scholars became the backbone of China's elite.

Han emperors also established an examination system based on the five classics of Confucianism. By the first century A.D., a hundred scholars each year were said to enter government service through a process resembling modern civil service examinations, which continued throughout successive dynasties. The Confucian-based examination system helped to free common people from feudal bondage by opening up channels of economic, social, and political mobility. Through this examination system, for example, several commoners rose to the position of prime minister of China during the Han dynasty.

Although Confucian ideas did not evolve into structured democratic institutions, Confucianism did divide China into separate state and family structures, which together formed the nation-state. At the top of imperial China was the bureaucratic state, in which the Confucian scholar held exclusive political responsibility under the emperor. At the base was a kinship-centered society headed by a magistrate.

Confucianism demanded that the Chinese people demonstrate loyalty both to the state and to the family. For example, district magistrates, who often were clan elders, would not carry out absurd demands of the state that went against the welfare of the districts and their families. Thus the kinship systems existing in China throughout the dynasties provided a shield against strong-arm tactics of the imperial state.

Since the Han dynasty, China's political system has also made some provision for the distribution of powers. Although the emperor, as the source of all powers, held the exclusive right to exercise legislative, executive, and judicial powers, the powers of examination and impeachment were exercised independently by his ministers in order to ensure an efficient and honest government. For example, the imperial censors were expected to oversee and, when necessary, criticize members of the administration, including the emperor. The Chinese emperor, like the British Crown, stood above the law but was subject to the restraints of the institutions and practices of Confucian ethics and customs. Although this separation of the power of the emperor (monarch) from that of the bureaucracy suffered certain setbacks during the Ming dynasty (1368–1644), when the office of the prime minister was abolished, it nevertheless remained a basic feature of traditional Chinese government for centuries.

As time went on, the content of Confucianism went through numerous metamorphoses. Many early Confucian democratic ideas were at times deemphasized or even ignored. At other times, the idea of people's sovereignty was held up by a small group of scholars or even a single scholar, as in the case of Huang Zongxi (1609–1695). Huang criticized China's growing tendency toward despotism during the Ming dynasty and analyzed the political and economic weaknesses of seventeenth-century China in his first important work, *A Plan for the Prince*.

Huang was rare among Confucianists in attaching importance to the form or system of government rather than simply to the moral character of the ruler and his officials. Whereas Confucianists historically had ignored or been hostile to the concept of law, which they associated with the totalitarian concepts of the violent Legalists under the Qin dynasty, Huang emphasized the importance of law in preventing corruption among the ruling elite and in the civil service examination process.

Unfortunately, Huang's pleas fell on deaf ears and attracted no mass following. Under the Manchu-led Qing dynasty (1644–1911), the last dynasty before the republic, China developed along increasingly authoritarian lines into a so-called benevolent despotism. In doing so, it moved away from Confucian democratic ideals, while remaining committed to Confucian concepts of a strong leader who looked after the welfare of his people.

The Challenge of Modernization

It was not until the last years of the nineteenth century that the issue of democracy for China was raised again, this time by the last great Confucian scholar in China, Kang Youwei (1858–1927). In a series of memorials to the emperor, the last of which was written in 1898, Kang set forth a whole program of reform, including the adoption of a constitution, the creation of a parliament, and a total revision of the educational system. He convinced the emperor that these reforms were essential in order for China to survive.

In the summer of 1898 the Qing dynasty's Emperor Guangxu issued a series of reform edicts based on Kang's proposals, instituting what became known as the Hundred Days' Reform (June 11–September 20). Perhaps most significant was Kang's attempt to revitalize Confucius's concept of the Grand Commonwealth into a modern One World theory. Kang maintained that evolution toward the final one world (the third stage of evolution as envisioned by Confucius) would be a long and gradual process involving abolition of the "nine boundaries" of the contemporary world: nation, class, race, sex, family, occupation, disorder (inequality), kind (separation of people and animal), and suffering. Kang worked out a long chart of the Confucian principles of the three ages as part of his vision of uniting various nations under a universal parliament. Although a coup d'état in the royal house brought about an early end to Kang's reforms, his attempt to bring about a world government built on the concept of unity, equality, and peace must remain a great addition to the history of political thought, just as his writing remains one of the most interesting treatises on democracy with Confucian characteristics.

After the fall of the Qing dynasty and the establishment of a republic in 1911, Confucianism began to come under frequent attack. In the May Fourth Movement of 1919, student-led demonstrations led to a wide-ranging iconoclastic attack on the Confucian tradition. Many prominent reformers of the time were partisans of Western science and democracy who viewed Confucianism as a form of reactionary traditionalism. The intellectual debates of the republican era largely centered on two camps: Confucianists versus the advocates of Westernization. The movement to bring wholesale Westernization to China ended abruptly, however, with the establishment of a Communist government under Mao Zedong in 1949.

Although there has been a long tradition of hostility toward established religion and philosophy in contemporary China, Confucian tradition has been incorporated in support of communist ideology. Mao himself was fundamentally influenced by two Confucian scholars, Kang Youwei and Liang Qichao. In his writings, Mao borrowed two elements of Confucianism in particular: first, the idea that knowledge must lead to action and that action must be based on knowledge, and, second, the ideal of the commonwealth, which Mao identified with communism. As Mao strove to disassociate his ideology from China's past, however, he did not give credit to Confucianism for these concepts. Furthermore, during the violent political upheaval of the Cultural Revolution (1966–1976), the government waged a virulent anti-Confucian campaign throughout China.

Since the late 1970s China's top leader, Deng Xiaoping,

and his followers have adhered to a policy of preserving what they believed to be the best of the cultural heritage of Confucianism. They made use of Confucian ethics and literature to elucidate Deng's doctrines, such as a desire for social and political order, and a sense of a new commonwealth guided by the cultivation of one's faculties and extension of one's services to the party and society. The government spent millions of dollars to repair the temples and mansions of Confucius and his descendants that were damaged by the Red Guards during the Maoist era.

China by the mid-1990s showed definite signs of a revival of Confucian studies, under the broad rubric of "socialism with Chinese characteristics." Articles on Confucianism began to reappear in Chinese newspapers during the reform movement of the 1980s and early 1990s. Confucianism is, in fact, making a theoretical comeback to provide communism with a new moral anchor. The government has sponsored many conferences and symposia linking new interpretations of Confucianism to Deng Xiaoping's policies.

Confucian Revival in East Asia

Beyond the borders of mainland China, Confucianism has developed significantly since the 1960s, as the so-called Four Tigers of the Pacific Rim—Hong Kong, Taiwan, Singapore, and South Korea—have incorporated Confucian ideas to varying degrees into the governments and social structures of their rapidly modernizing societies. The governments have combined the traditional benevolent authoritarian ruler with a democratically elected parliament and instituted a virtuous elite through a civil service examination system, creating a strong bureaucracy independent of politicians.

Interregional communication among Confucian scholars from these areas has led to lively intellectual exchanges. The New Asia College of the Chinese University in Hong Kong, founded on the principle of revitalizing the true spirit of Confucianism, has played a key role in coordinating regional efforts to promote Confucian learning and has trained a new generation of scholars in the study of various dimensions of Confucian culture.

In Taiwan, Confucianism was part of the mandatory curriculum under Chiang Kai-shek's government in conjunction with its anticommunist policy. The government in fact designated September 28 as the birthday of Confucius and made it a national holiday. Interest in Confucianism increased in the 1970s as a new generation of young

scholars was encouraged to investigate the spirit of Confucianism in the modern world.

In Singapore concern over the moral and world outlook of younger Singaporeans prompted the government to introduce Confucianism into school curriculums in the 1980s. Scholars and experts on Confucianism were invited from the United States, China, and Taiwan to help the Ministry of Education develop a model curriculum. At the urging of Lee Kuan Yew, a senior leader and former prime minister, Confucian ethics was identified as among the principles forming the "national ideology" of the country in 1991.

Although Confucianism has evolved greatly over the millennia, it remains a vibrant political philosophy in modern Asian democracies. The historic Western view of Confucianism as a quasi-religious system of ethics should broaden as Western understanding and contact with Asia increases. As a political theory, Confucianism insists on the sovereignty of the people and on the government's devotion to the well-being of its people. As such, Confucianism in its ideal form is not merely sovereignty of the people but rather rule of the people, or democracy.

See also *China; May Fourth Movement; Singapore; South Korea; Taiwan.*

Winberg Chai and May-lee Chai

BIBLIOGRAPHY

Chai, Chu, and Winberg Chai. *Confucianism.* Woodbury, N.Y.: Barron's, 1973.

Chai, Winberg, Carolyn Chai, and Cal Clark, eds. *Political Stability of Economic Growth: Case Studies of Taiwan, South Korea, Hong Kong and Singapore.* Dubuque, Iowa: Kendall/Hunt, 1994.

Chan, Wing-tsit. *A Source Book in Chinese Philosophy.* Princeton: Princeton University Press, 1963.

Confucius. *The Sacred Books of Confucius and Other Confucian Classics.* Edited and translated by Chu Chai and Winberg Chai. New Hyde Park, N.Y.: University Books, 1965.

Creel, H. G. *Chinese Thought from Confucius to Mao Tse-tung.* Chicago: University of Chicago Press, 1953.

deBary, W. T. *The Liberal Tradition in China.* New York: Columbia University Press, 1983.

Fung Yu-lan. *A History of Chinese Philosophy.* 2 vols. Translated by Derk Bodde. Princeton: Princeton University Press, 1952.

Hsiung, James C., and Chung-ying Cheng, eds. *Distribution of Power and Rewards: Proceedings of the International Conference on Democracy and Social Justice East and West.* Lanham, Md.: University Press of America, 1991.

Metzger, Thomas. *Escape from Predicament: Neo-Confucianism and China's Evolving Political Culture.* New York: Columbia University Press, 1977.

Tu, Wei-ming. *Way, Learning, and Politics: Essays on the Confucian Intellectual.* Albany: State University of New York Press, 1991.

Congo, Republic of

See *Africa, Subsaharan*

Consent

One of the central justifying concepts in democratic political theory. Defenders of democracy commonly argue that democracy's superior moral legitimacy derives from the fact that democratic governments act with the consent or authorization of their citizens. Sometimes the claim is that popular consent is necessary for just or legitimate government. The American Declaration of Independence, for example, asserts that governments derive "their just powers from the consent of the governed." But even when the claim is that consent is only one possible source of political legitimacy, democratic political society is still thought to be especially suitable for realizing consensual legitimacy.

Justification by appeal to consent is understandably central to the philosophical structure of liberal thought. Liberals generally conceive of individuals as self-conscious choosers, whose plans and choices are morally valuable and hence merit respect. Free consent is regarded as the primary mechanism through which individual liberty may justifiably be limited, for consent is a clear source of created obligations that is nonetheless plainly consistent with respect for individual liberty and choice. Consensual undertaking of obligations is one among many possible uses of individual liberty, a use that can morally justify the increased restrictions necessary for beneficial social interaction. Within liberal societies a showing of free, informed consent by one party is normally taken to justify or remove liability for the actions of another. Thus the maxim *Volenti non fit injuria* (The willing person is not wronged) governs transactions as diverse as business dealings, medical treatment, and sexual relations.

Consent may be defined as a kind of act by which one attempts to alter the existing structure of rights and duties, normally by freely assuming new obligations and authorizing others to act with respect to one in ways that would otherwise be impermissible for them. Consent is often taken (as in John Locke's political philosophy) to include all sources of self-assumed obligations, including not only what we might normally call consenting but also promising, contracting, and entrusting. But whatever the specific definition, we must distinguish consent in this active sense (as a ground of special obligations and rights) from weaker notions of consent as an attitude of approval or of consent as mere passivity or acquiescence.

In democratic theory, discussions of consent usually involve debates over and developments of the consent theory of political obligation and authority. In its simplest form this theory maintains that the consent of each person to political membership is the only possible source of the person's obligations to obey the law and support the state and of the state's authority over or right to command the person. But political obligation and authority have also been alleged to rest not on direct, personal consent but on tacit (or indirect) personal consent, on consent given by others (such as one's ancestors or the majority of one's fellow subjects), or on hypothetical consent (usually understood as the consent that would be given by rational contractors).

Appeals to tacit consent have always been important within consent theory, for little in the behavior of most citizens resembles the giving of express or direct consent to the authority of their governments. Appeals to the consent of others to justify an individual's obligations have been found unpersuasive by most modern theorists. And appeals to hypothetical consent (following the lead of Immanuel Kant) have again become popular in this century, in an effort to focus attention not on what persons actually agree to but on what they ought to agree to. Here, as in the case of appeals to tacit consent, the motive is partly to show that reasonable political institutions can still be justified in terms of consent, despite the seeming absence of actual consent to these institutions by those subject to them.

Proponents of traditional, nonhypothetical consent theory have argued in three ways for a strong connection between legitimizing consent and democratic government. First, some have argued (following John Locke) that the choice to continue residing in a country that one is free to leave counts as giving one's personal (tacit) consent to the authority of that country's government. Because democracies typically grant their citizens the right of free exit, citizens of democracies will, according to this argument, typically be consenters. Second, others have maintained that possessing or exercising the right to vote in democratic elections constitutes consent to the authority of elected governments and free acceptance of the obligation to obey. Finally, some have claimed that full and direct participation in the processes that determine the requirements of political life is the only way to give meaningful political consent and that only in a democracy is such participation possible.

Against the last of these claims, it can be argued that democratic societies today permit few citizens, if any, to pursue full, direct participation. Against the second claim, skeptics maintain that mere possession of a right to vote is not an act that one performs and so can hardly count as an act of consent. Moreover, far too few citizens in democracies either vote regularly or fully understand the political processes for many of them to be characterized fairly as giving free, informed consent to their governments with their votes. Against the first claim, critics argue (following David Hume) that the choice to continue residing in one's country of birth cannot for many be understood as a free choice, given the high cost of emigration. Furthermore, few people understand their continued residence to involve any morally significant choice at all.

In an effort to answer these objections, proponents of consent theory continue to refine their positions. Those who are persuaded by the objections, however, tend to fall into one of three camps. Some—for example, the contemporary philosopher John Rawls—turn from actual consent to hypothetical consent as their primary justifying concept. Others abandon altogether the ideal of government by consent and attempt to justify democratic government in other terms (such as procedural fairness). And the most radical skeptics embrace philosophical anarchism, which contends that no political societies, democracies included, are morally legitimate.

See also *Contractarianism; Hobbes, Thomas; Justifications for democracy; Liberalism; Locke, John; Obligation.*

A. John Simmons

BIBLIOGRAPHY

Beran, Harry. *The Consent Theory of Political Obligation.* London: Croom Helm, 1987.
Hume, David. "Of the Original Contract." In *Hume's Moral and Political Philosophy,* edited by Henry D. Aiken. New York: Hafner, 1975.
Kleinig, John. "The Ethics of Consent." *Canadian Journal of Philosophy.* Supp. vol. 8 (1982): 91–118.
Locke, John. *Two Treatises of Government.* Edited by Peter Laslett. Cambridge: Cambridge University Press, 1960.
Rawls, John. *A Theory of Justice.* Cambridge: Harvard University Press, Belknap Press, 1971; Oxford: Oxford University Press, 1973.
Simmons, A. John. *Moral Principles and Political Obligations.* Princeton: Princeton University Press, 1979.
———. *On the Edge of Anarchy: Locke, Consent, and the Limits of Society.* Princeton: Princeton University Press, 1993.
Singer, Peter. *Democracy and Disobedience.* New York: Oxford University Press, 1974.

Conservatism

A democratic political philosophy that favors limited government, advocates moderate change, and has doubts about the value and extent of the modern administrative and welfare state. It is common for writers on conservatism to begin by protesting that the term and the phenomenon it describes are hard to pin down or else by noting that it is contrary to the spirit of conservatism to attempt a rigorous account of its principles. Both reservations are in part correct.

First, it is difficult to define conservatism by referring to a fixed set of positions. On an array of issues—from economic policy to questions of social organization, from foreign policy to basic moral principles—conservatives will be found to differ among themselves, sometimes quite dramatically.

Second, it is true that much conservative thought rejects the idea that politics can be understood and managed by applying systems of abstract ideas to practical circumstances. This antipathy to excessive rationalism—to what is now often called social engineering—began with Edmund Burke's objections to the French Revolution. Burke, an English political philosopher and politician of the eighteenth century, believed that the French Revolution was doomed because it rested on the utopianism of the Enlightenment—on the hope that long-established orders based on religion, tradition, and aristocratic privilege could be replaced overnight by a society deduced from the abstract principles of equality and individual natural rights. Burke taught conservatives to mistrust what they take to be the lure of idealism and the utopian hopes of intellectuals. Hence to this day many conservatives resist the temptation to spin out a conservative system and object when others attribute one to them.

But it is possible to heed this objection and at the same time to identify the fundamental issues that matter to conservatives and ultimately determine their several points of view on more concrete and changeable matters. These fundamental issues are the balance between liberty and equality, the question of progress and history, and the character of democracy. Already from this brief list we can see that conservatism as we know it today is quite new. In earlier times people did not presume that there was any equality to be balanced with liberty, did not believe in progress and history, and did not think democracy was a serious possibility to be debated.

These ideas were first broached in the seventeenth century and did not burst forth until the American and French Revolutions at the end of the eighteenth century. It is telling that Burke's political positions were developed in response to these two great events, and one could say without exaggeration that his conservatism is thus paradigmatic: conservatism today almost always takes for granted that change is inevitable, that democracy is good, and that all human beings are born as moral equals. In other words, conservatism stands within, and is in large part defined by, the Enlightenment principles with which it was at first at odds.

Evolution of Conservative Thought

The term *conservatism* did not even become current until the 1830s, when it was imported from France to England and was used to designate the Tory Party as it had been defined by Burke and his followers. In France the term referred to those who, under Burke's influence, had serious doubts about the effects of the French Revolution. So one could say with some justification that the term really originated in England. But having suffered the revolution and its aftermath, European conservatives were more inclined than were the English to reject the principles of the Enlightenment altogether. Thinkers such as Joseph de Maistre and the Vicomte de Bonald in France, and Adam Müller and Klemens von Metternich in Austria, rejected wholly the ideas of republican government and the separation of church and state—and especially rejected the ideas of progress and equality. To them, such ideas ignored disastrously the divine right of kings and the natural depravity of the human race.

In England, however, the revolutionary settlement of 1688 (which resulted in the overthrow of the king, James II) involved an agreement between the Whigs, who wished to limit the king's prerogative, and moderate Tories on the basically Whiggish principle of parliamentary supremacy.

English conservatism thus very early gave up the doctrine of divine right and monarchical absolutism and was therefore able to make its peace with the idea of progress and with an expanding franchise, even if it did not accept fully the Whiggish idea (derived from John Locke, the seventeenth-century English philosopher) that all legitimate government originates in a contract of free and equal individuals or the more radical utilitarianism of thinkers like Jeremy Bentham (1748–1832) and John Stuart Mill (1806–1873). Unlike most European conservatives, English politicians like Burke and Benjamin Disraeli—who as Tory prime minister (1868 and 1874–1880) began the tradition of conservative social reform—saw conservatism as the complex of ideas, traditions, and moral dispositions that moderates inevitably change. Thus they accepted, albeit reluctantly, the most important aspect of modern times.

The same and more could be said for conservatism in America. Because the United States has no monarchical or aristocratic roots, it has never doubted fundamentally the principles of democracy, equality, and progress. As the French historian and political observer Alexis de Tocqueville pointed out in the mid-nineteenth century, the framing of the American Constitution was a conservative event that consolidated a political order embodying these revolutionary forces of the modern spirit. And so he claimed that in America there would be no really deep partisan differences. In Tocqueville's view the Americans agreed about everything fundamental, with the important disagreements appearing only in diluted quarrels about nuance and degree.

Certainly by the end of World War II, in 1945, this description could be said to apply to the whole of the Western world. The monstrous course of fascism put an end to all forms of conservatism that were opposed in principle to the modern age—that is, to secularism, equality, representative democracy, and the culture of science and technology. No conservative can be found today—at least not in a genuine democracy—who favors monarchy, aristocracy, or theocracy or who thinks that mystical nationalism is a serious or desirable alternative to the modern democratic state.

Modern Interpretations

Even in the United States, where ideological consensus runs so deep, it is possible to speak of liberals and conservatives who disagree on important matters. Surely there is a difference between twentieth-century presidents Woodrow Wilson and Franklin Delano Roosevelt, on the one hand, and Calvin Coolidge and William Graham Sumner (the famous theorist of laissez-faire, or minimal, government), on the other. So what are the principles of modern conservatism? To see them, we return to the fundamental issues mentioned earlier. To speak very broadly, the project of modernity aims to establish political and social life on three principles: (1) individuals are born free and equal, with no one warranted by nature or God to rule others without their consent; (2) the progressive conquest of nature means that poverty can be reduced to a level that makes genuine cooperation possible; (3) democracy of a limited kind—"liberal democracy"—is the particular form of government to which free and equal individuals will consent.

No one in our time denies that individuals are born free and equal and that they should be governed only by those to whom they have given their consent. But there is disagreement about the meaning of liberty and equality and the relation between them. In modern democracies the hope is that individuals will be equally free to become whatever their natural endowments and efforts will allow. No artificial barriers—including the power of government—should stand in their way. This interpretation means that individuals should be equally free to become unequal in their accomplishments. Often, however, bad luck or the stifling effects of social class get in the way of equal opportunity, and even legitimate inequalities tend to ossify into illegitimate ones, as might be said to happen when wealth and privilege are inherited rather than earned. And so in the name of equality of opportunity, it can be argued that political power should be used to restrict the liberty of some individuals for the sake of others, usually by way of redistributing income and other opportunities.

Thus, while there may be no disagreement about liberty and equality at the level of general principle, there are serious differences of opinion about which inequalities are legitimate and about how far individual liberty should be restrained in order to remedy illegitimate inequalities. On this issue, conservatives tend to judge inequalities in mature democratic societies to be legitimate and not the result of rigid, and thus unfair, advantages. They likewise think that it can do more harm than good to give government the power to remedy unfair advantages when unfair advantages do occur. In general, it could be said that con-

servatives favor liberty over equality—or, more precisely, that they understand equality as formal equality of opportunity and freedom as independence from political coercion.

Again, no one in our time doubts that democratic government requires what might be called the project of rationalism—the complex of ideas and practices that includes the separation of church and state, individualism and free markets, constitutionalism, and, perhaps most important, the science and technology that are essential for a rising standard of living. But there are disagreements about how completely this project can produce a fully rational society and about whether history is a force that leads inevitably to progress.

Conservatives believe in the separation of church and state. But, not expecting the complete victory of reason over the whole of life, they tend to think that no society can function well without the influence of religion and morality and that public policy must take this fact into account. They also think that the justice and efficiency of markets are diminished, not improved, by centralized and politicized planning. And they have doubts about the extent to which problems such as crime and poverty can be solved by social engineering, which uses the methods and approaches of science and technology. Conservatives tend to doubt that history is a force that makes all innovation turn out for the better. Consequently, they usually worry more than do liberals about the consequences of what is done in the name of progress. And while in general they favor capitalism and free enterprise, a long tradition of conservative thought bemoans the way modern life corrodes old ways, coarsens manners, and levels the depths and contours of cultural life. We see this point of view in such writers and cultural critics as Jonathan Swift, Samuel Taylor Coleridge, James Fenimore Cooper, Henry Adams, T. S. Eliot, José Ortega y Gasset, and Malcolm Muggeridge, to name but a few.

Finally, in our time there is almost unanimous agreement among conservatives that democracy is a form of limited government—that it should be liberal democracy. When used in this way, the term *liberal* is not taken in its usual American sense to mean an ideological preference for big government or progressive social policy. Rather, it refers to the idea that government should derive from popular consent and have as its ultimate goal the securing of private liberty. No one today seriously thinks that modern democracies could or should be like the democracies of the ancient Greeks, which were small, homogeneous, and dedicated to the formation of the citizens' moral character and conception of the good. Preliberal forms of democracy lacked the institution of civil society, the realm of social and economic relations that exists apart from government but under its protection. In a liberal democracy, government is popular, but its purpose is to safeguard and maximize the private liberty that is exercised in civil society. In civil society, individuals are free to buy and sell, to worship as they please, to think and speak as they wish, and to pursue their own conceptions of happiness and the good life. In a liberal democracy, democratic politics is not considered a good in itself, as it was in ancient times; rather, democracy is good because it is the only real guarantee of equal and individual liberty.

But within this broad modern agreement about democracy, there is room for disagreement about how democratic a government must be in order to accomplish its liberal purpose. Conservatives tend to mistrust attempts to bring democracy closer to the people and do not think that more democracy is always better than less. They agree with the spirit of James Madison's view, expressed in the *Federalist* No. 63. There Madison (later president of the United States, 1809–1817) said that the key to successful popular sovereignty was "the total exclusion of the people in their collective capacity" from the government. In a well-ordered democracy, only representatives of the people wield the levers of government; there is no assembly in which all the people exercise the specific functions of government.

Thus conservatives generally have doubts about populist devices—such as the initiative and referendum, the party primary, and proportional representation—intended to get around the distance imposed by the U.S. Constitution between the people and their representatives in government. They are more comfortable than are liberals and progressives with the need for secrecy in government, with the independence and vigor of executive power, and with the influence of and need for elites in politics and society. But at the same time, conservatives have doubts about the expanding power of bureaucracy and the administrative state, which liberals and progressives see as necessary engines of equality and efficiency. Conservatives are thus open to democratic "revolts" against the tendency for government to intrude into private and social life.

Partisan Identifications and Divisions

In terms of the main political parties in the older democracies, conservatism has its home in the Republican Party in the United States, the Conservative Party in the United Kingdom, the Gaullist Party (currently the Rally for the Republic) and the Union for French Democracy in France, the Christian Democratic Union in Germany (and the Christian Democratic Parties in the rest of continental Europe), the Likud bloc in Israel, the Progressive Conservatives in Canada, the National and Liberal Parties in Australia, and the National Party in New Zealand. In recent years the electorates in most democratic countries have become less well defined ideologically—in large part because they are less clearly divided by class, education, and religion—and the end of the cold war has accelerated this development.

The traditional parties of both left and right have thus lost much of their cohesion, and it is likely that new ones will appear and old ones will be defined by new concerns. Furthermore, the almost global fiscal crisis facing the modern welfare state has forced the parties of the left in a rightward direction. But whatever their new form and particular policies, conservative parties will continue to side with the interests of business. They will appeal more to rural and suburban voters than to city dwellers, and more to the better off than to the less well off, and they will resonate more comfortably with middle-class sensibilities and interests than with those of the so-called chattering classes (intellectuals, journalists, educators, and publicly employed professionals). Most important, they will confront any new problems and concerns—whether problems of the environment, ethnic and linguistic identities, regional interests, or social issues associated with mature capitalism—from the general standpoint of the conservative principles outlined previously.

It cannot be concluded, however, that all conservatives are the same, for there are important differences that have divided them and will continue to divide them. Perhaps most significant is the difference between conservatives in the tradition of Burke and those who are the heirs of what was once called radicalism—what today we would call laissez-faire libertarianism. This difference emerged as early as the mid-nineteenth century, when the Conservative Party in England was split on the issue of free trade versus tariffs that protected domestic agricultural interests. The followers of Disraeli favored protection, rural interests and traditions, and, somewhat later, paternalistic social reform from above. On the other side were those who favored free trade and took a more individualistic, business-oriented, even utilitarian view of human nature and society.

This division, which is still visible in England in the split between the more traditional, or Disraelian, conservatives and the followers of Margaret Thatcher (prime minister, 1979–1990), and in Australia in the difference between the National and Liberal Parties, can be seen in conservative parties around the globe. It is impossible to imagine Burke uttering Thatcher's now famous remark: "There is no such thing as society. There are individual men and women, and there are families."

Burke objected to revolutionary rationalism because it did not grasp the true nature of human society. According to the partisans of the French Revolution and radicals like Thomas Paine (a pamphleteer of both the American and French Revolutions and Burke's adversary), society is simply an aggregation of free and equal individuals endowed with the natural right to consent to any government that they deem necessary for their happiness and liberty. For Burke, however, the individual's right to self-government must be mediated through historically determined communities characterized by class hierarchy, established orders of hereditary property, and ancient systems of customs, moral habits, and prejudices. The people could be represented in a constitutional order but certainly not directly: the representatives of the people would act for the society as a whole and would be under no binding instructions from their constituents, who need not all have the right to vote. For Burke, an abstract or theoretical doctrine of individual liberty was merely utopian—and dangerously so—if it ignored the complex moral and material articulation of society.

Traditional Conservatives and Libertarians

Although no conservative today would propose Burkeianism in all its details, the spirit of Burke is evident in contemporary conservatives who approve of privileged elites, who see religion and morality as important for society, and who doubt progressive optimism. It is on these matters that the libertarians part company with their conservative colleagues. Libertarians like Margaret Thatcher and the Austrian economist Friedrich von Hayek reject elitism and traditions of noblesse oblige. They deny that government should have any interest in morality or religion and tend to think that anything standing in the way

of economic enterprise—such as tradition, nostalgia for rural life, or worry about the erosion of moral habits—is an illegitimate constraint on individual liberty. Although they think that government planning, social engineering, and income redistribution do nothing but harm, they have faith that individual free enterprise and the mechanism of the market will do nothing but good. The libertarian conservative is inclined to think that the problems of society and human life in general—war, poverty, disputes about justice, and economic instability—are caused by the dysfunctional effects of illegitimate government power. When the reach of the state is constrained to its proper limits, these problems will disappear.

Modern conservatives are divided by their degree of adherence to what we have referred to as Enlightenment rationalism. Libertarians owe more to Thomas Paine and to utilitarians such as Bentham and Mill than they do to Burke, and they believe more in progress than do their more traditional colleagues. They see the individual as a rational, free, autonomous economic actor, and they are inclined to think that there are no defects and contradictions in the human condition that right reason cannot in principle overcome. The more traditional conservative, on the other hand, thinks that human nature is crooked wood. Reason, democracy, and capitalism can bend it—but never perfectly and not without appeals to passion, belief, morality, and tradition.

The libertarian will oppose the welfare state on both moral and practical grounds. On the one hand, there is no moral obligation for resources to be transferred from the rich to the poor; on the other hand, the state's redistributive interference in the economy is the ultimate cause of the poverty that it is our supposed obligation to relieve. The more traditional conservative likewise will not see the welfare state (or the idea that the rich should be taxed at a higher proportional rate than the less well off) as a redistributive duty but may well see it as necessary for the political integration of any modern, industrialized democracy. The libertarian conservative is in principle opposed to any attempt by the state to influence the character of the citizen—whether by encouraging religion, limiting free speech, outlawing narcotics and pornography, and so on. The traditional conservative will often support such policies, believing that good character is essential for democratic liberty and that both capitalism and technological change, however necessary, can erode the social supports that such character requires.

It is important to remember that the traditional-libertarian divide is not fixed hard and fast. As one would expect in political life, the unalloyed libertarian or traditional conservative is hard to find, even though most conservatives lean more or less strongly in one or the other direction. And so it is difficult to predict specific policy preferences with precision. Thus in the United States the more libertarian conservatives may or may not be internationalists in foreign policy, and the same ambivalence is true for more traditional conservatives. In England, libertarians may be less inclined toward European integration, because they fear its domination by European socialists, and yet more inclined toward global involvement; more traditional conservatives may be more European and less global. It can also be the other way around.

Although libertarians are almost always in favor of free trade, it is less easy to predict how more traditional conservatives in Europe, the United Kingdom, and the United States will come down on this often contentious issue. In America it is hard to predict what libertarians and traditional conservatives will think about abortion rights. Some libertarians may think that such a matter is an individual decision, while others may see the fetus as an individual bearing rights to be protected by the state. Some traditionalists may see abortion as a practice that degrades good character, while others may see it as essential for limiting the spread of dependency among the poor. And in all democracies, a small minority of "far right" conservatives of both kinds will tend toward extremist politics. Thus libertarians can be inclined toward antielitist but aggressive populism, and traditionalists can be inclined toward vaguely anticapitalist populism or toward nationalism, religious fundamentalism, and xenophobia.

All conservatives were anticommunist during the cold war. But while the collapse of communism has had its unsettling effects on their self-understanding, it has not settled the fundamental issues that concern conservatives in the old democracies and even in the new ones arising around the world. Conservatives believe that as long as a government is democratic, the temptation will always exist for it to bid for votes from the various clients of the welfare state and from those producer groups—whether business or labor—who might gain from government economic policy or suffer from the dislocations and changes associated with capitalism.

And so despite their differences, and the difficulty of predicting them, today all conservatives agree in general that the modern welfare state has a dangerous tendency to grow beyond due measure and to threaten the economic well-being and expansion that is essential to democratic liberty. All likewise agree that government management of the economy must be kept to a practicable minimum, because governments are always moved more by political than by economic considerations. And all—even most libertarians—likewise oppose what they see as the relentless egalitarianism of modern life: the ever increasing tendency to leveling, mass culture, and individual dependency that often seems to threaten liberty and equality, properly understood.

Guardians Against the State

Tocqueville has given us the best account of the modern situation as seen from the conservative point of view. In *Democracy in America* (1835–1840), he explained that in the modern age no one can legitimately question the view that all human beings are endowed with equal rights to liberty and the pursuit of happiness. But equality of opportunity comes to be judged by equality of results. As equality progresses, individuals become stronger and more independent than they were in more aristocratic times. But they also become more isolated from each other and at the same time weaker in comparison to the gargantuan power of public opinion and mass taste. Similarly, individuals who love equality become increasingly indignant at the inevitable inequalities that will always exist, even though, considered objectively, all are better off and inequalities tend to shrink.

For all these reasons there is an inevitable tendency for democratic individuals—progressively weakened and increasingly indignant—to see the centralized, administrative state as the solution to their dissatisfaction. It is no moral offense to be dependent on the state, for it is at once like no particular person and also the result of the individual's consent. The paradoxical result is an individual who will assert a right to vote but who is otherwise incapable of independent life. The danger that stalks modern democracy is not harsh tyranny imposed from without but a soft and enervating despotism that grows slowly from within.

Despite their many differences on matters both large and small, there are today no conservatives who would dissent wholly from Tocqueville's view. Virtually all are democrats. But all agree, more or less explicitly, that the task for conservatives is to prevent the dangers to democracy that spring from democracy. They may disagree about some of the means but not about the end.

See also *Burke, Edmund; Laissez-faire economic theory; Liberalism; Paine, Thomas; Tocqueville, Alexis de; Welfare, Promotion of.*

Jerry Weinberger

BIBLIOGRAPHY

Burke, Edmund. *Reflections on the Revolution in France,* with Thomas Paine's *The Rights of Man.* Garden City, N.Y.: Anchor Books, 1973.

Hayek, Friedrich A. von. *The Constitution of Liberty.* Chicago: University of Chicago Press, 1960.

Hearnshaw, F. J. C. *Conservatism in England.* London: Macmillan, 1933; New York: Fertig, 1968.

Kirk, Russell. *The Conservative Mind: From Burke to Eliot.* 6th ed. Chicago: Regnery/Gateway, 1978.

———. *The Conservative Reader.* New York: Viking Penguin, 1982.

Novak, Michael. *The Spirit of Democratic Capitalism.* New York: Simon and Schuster, 1982.

Ortega y Gasset, José. *The Revolt of the Masses.* New ed. New York and London: Norton, 1964.

Rossiter, Clinton. *Conservatism in America, 1770–1945.* New York: Knopf, 1966.

Tocqueville, Alexis de. *Democracy in America.* Translated by George Lawrence. Garden City, N.Y.: Anchor Books, 1969.

Weiss, John. *Conservatism in Europe.* London: Thames and Hudson, 1977.

Consolidation

A process of transforming the accidental arrangements, prudential norms, and contingent solutions that have emerged during the uncertain struggles of a political transition into institutions that are reliably known, regularly practiced, and normatively accepted by the participants, citizens, and subjects of such institutions. Democracies are not supposed to be fully consolidated. Unique among political types, they possess the potential for continuous change and even self-transformation. By a process of deliberation and collective choice among the citizenry, democracies can not only peacefully remove governments from power but also alter their basic structures and practices.

This abstract reflection clashes, however, with the everyday experience of well-established democracies. Not only do their patterns and norms become structured in highly predictable and persistent ways, but considerable effort is expended to make it quite difficult to change these structures. So-called founding generations write constitutions that attempt to bind subsequent ones to a specific institutional format and set of rights. They also draft statutes and codes that render certain kinds of political behavior punishable, create specific constituencies and reward particular clienteles, make difficult (or even exclude) the entry of new parties into the electoral arena, confer monopolistic recognition on certain associations, and even try to make these constitutions and laws almost impossible to amend. Although constitutions can be ignored, policies can be reversed, and laws can be changed in response to public pressures, it can be difficult and costly to do so even in the most loosely structured and recently consolidated of democracies.

It has been said that uncertainty of persons and policies is the central characteristic of a democracy. If so in theory, this uncertainty is heavily conditioned in democratic practice by relative certainties. For citizens to tolerate the possibility that opponents might occupy or influence positions of government and even pursue different and possibly damaging courses of action requires a great deal of mutual trust—backed by a great deal of structural reassurance. The consolidation of democracy can be seen as the process that makes such trust and reassurance possible and that therefore also makes possible regular, uncertain, and yet circumscribed competition for office and influence.

Embodying Consent and Invoking Assent

How does democracy accomplish and legitimate such a delicate task? What is the underlying operative principle that provides the necessary elements of trust and reassurance? The simple answer is the consent of the people; the more complex answer is that it all depends on the contingent consent of politicians and the eventual assent of citizens—all acting under conditions of bounded uncertainty.

The challenge for democratic consolidators is to find a set of institutions that embody contingent consent among politicians, that are capable of invoking the eventual assent of citizens, and that can therefore limit the abnormally high degree of uncertainty that is characteristic of most transitions from autocracy. They do not necessarily have to agree on a set of goals or substantive policies that generate widespread consensus. Disagreements on goals and policies will furnish much of the content for subsequent democratic competition. This "democratic bargain" can vary a good deal from one society to another, depending on inequalities and cleavage patterns within the citizenry, as well as such subjective factors as the degree of mutual trust, the standard of fairness, the willingness to compromise, and the legitimacy of different decision rules.

When a society changes from one political regime to another, it initially passes through a period of considerable uncertainty in which it is unclear where its efforts are leading. During this period, regression to the previous status quo is possible. The transition period can vary in length, depending in large measure on the mode of regime change that has been adopted, but it must end eventually. The psychic and material costs are simply too great for those active in politics to endure indefinitely. Although there will always be some for whom the exhilaration of participating in a continuous "war of movement" remains an end in itself, most of these actors look forward to settling into a "war of positions" with known allies, established lines of cleavage, and predictable opponents, or to resuming their other careers or pursuits.

Specifying the Type of Democracy

When some form of autocracy is changed to a democracy, rather than the reverse, the problem of consolidation takes on special characteristics. For one thing the number and variety of people who are potentially capable of proposing new rules and practices increases greatly. Moreover, these empowered citizens (and the groups they form) have much more autonomy in deciding whether they will accept the rules and practices being offered to them. This is not to suggest that modern political democracies are anarchies in which individuals are free to choose their own norms and to act without regard for the norms of others. But the problem of reducing uncertainty and ensuring the orderly governance of the political unit as a whole is likely to be more acute in a new democracy than, say, in the aftermath of implanting an autocracy.

Democracy does not, however, seek to remove all sources of uncertainty. A polity in which there was no uncertainty about which candidates would win elections, what policies the winners would adopt, or which groups would be likely to influence their choice of those policies could hardly be termed democratic. But the uncertainty that is embedded in all democracies is bounded. Not just any actor can enter the competitive struggle, practice any tactic, raise any issue, cooperate with others in any way, and expect to hold office or exercise influence. Not just any policy can be decided by any procedure—even by the

overwhelming majority—and then be imposed on any segment of the population—even if that minority was represented in the decision-making process. What the exercise of democracy begins to do during the transitional period is to reduce "abnormal" uncertainty to "normal" uncertainty, and it does this through the generation of formal rules and informal practices. Sets of these rules and practices that manage to acquire some autonomy and to reproduce themselves successfully over time become institutions.

All successful democratizations have involved four processes of institutional choice: the formation of a party system, the formation of an interest associational system, the drafting and approval of a constitution, and the submission of the military to civilian control. Unless all four of these processes take place, there is very little likelihood of an eventual consolidation. Their timing, however, is variable, and these differences in sequence contribute much to differences in outcome. *When* something is accomplished may be as important as *what* has been accomplished. For example, in some fortunate cases, civilian control over the military may have been accomplished largely by the previous authoritarian regime. In others, the newly incumbent rulers may be able to agree quickly on reinstituting some ancient or recent constitution and thereby save themselves possible conflicts over the definition of key rules and institutions.

As a process, democratic consolidation involves choosing these institutions. Much of this process takes place in an open, deliberative fashion and manifests itself in formal public acts: the drafting and ratifying of a constitution, the passing of laws by the parliament, the issuance of executive decrees and administrative regulations. Some elements of consolidation, however, emerge more incidentally and unself-consciously from the ongoing "private" arrangements within and between the organizations of civil society and from the often informal interactions between these organizations and various agencies of the state.

One major implication of the preceding discussion is that no single institution or rule defines consolidated democracy. Not even such prominent candidates as majority rule, territorial representation, competitive elections, parliamentary sovereignty, a popularly elected executive, or a "responsible" party system can be taken as its distinctive hallmark. It may be easier to agree on what has been called the procedural minimum without which no type of democracy could exist: secret balloting, universal adult suffrage, regular elections, partisan competition, associational freedom, and executive accountability. But underlying these accomplishments and flowing from them are much more subtle and complex relations that define both the substance and the form of nascent democratic regimes.

Forming a Professional Stratum and Coping with a Dilemma

The consolidation of modern democracy involves both the choice of institutions and the formation of a political stratum. Although this group may vary a great deal in its origins, openness, diversity, interests, coherence, and longevity, most of its members will be representatives of organizations (with differing degrees of authenticity). They are also increasingly likely to be professionals (of differing degrees of dedication to the job). Most members of this small group live not "for politics" but "from politics." Depending on the mode of transition, they may include various proportions of actors from the former autocracy and those recruited from the ranks of the previously excluded. Most important for the long-run future of democracy, they have every reason to develop a loyalty to the existing rules of the game—since these are the rules by which they entered the profession and that may eventually enable them to enter government.

This emphasis on the likely emergence of a distinctive political stratum during the transition and its professionalization during consolidation has important implications for the choice of institutions. It establishes a major dilemma within its core: representatives will have to design a set of rules and practices that they, as politicians, can agree on and live with and that their members and followers, as citizens, can assent to and are willing to support.

A stable solution to these demands may be difficult to find, especially in the climate of exaggerated expectations that tends to characterize the transition to democracy. The choices are intrinsically conflictual: politicians, grouped into different parties, prefer rules that will best ensure their own reelection or eventual access to office; citizens, assembled into different social groups, want rules that will best ensure the accountability of their representatives. The choices are also extrinsically consequential. Once they are translated, through the uncertainties of elections and influence processes, into governments that begin to produce public policies, the rules and practices applied will affect rates of economic growth, willingness to invest, variation in the value of currency, competitiveness in foreign mar-

kets, access to education, perceptions of cultural deprivation, racial balance, and even national identity. To a certain extent, these substantive matters are anticipated by the actors involved and incorporated in the compromises they make with regard to procedures. But there is nonetheless considerable room for error and unintended consequence.

Exploring the Conditions of Consolidation

To paraphrase Karl Marx, those who would consolidate democracy may be making their own history but not under conditions or at moments of their own choosing. The list of factors that could possibly influence—even determine, some would say—the choices they make is virtually endless. The literature on existing, stable democracies tends to stress "prerequisites," such as the level of development, the rate of economic growth, the distribution of wealth, the size of the middle class, the dynamism of the bourgeoisie, the existence of private property rights, the level of literacy and mass education, the existence of stable borders and national identities, the supportiveness of the international system, the extent of linguistic or ethnic homogeneity, and the presence of proper civic attitudes or of a "Western" (in particular, Protestant) culture. Even such relatively idiosyncratic features as having been colonized by the British or having been defeated and occupied by the armed forces of a foreign democracy have been associated with successful democratization.

No one is likely to contest that these conditions have contributed to consolidation in the past and probably can facilitate it in the present. What is less clear is whether those countries that do not score so well on them are irrevocably condemned to failure. Unfortunately, all the changes in regime since 1974 have occurred in socioeconomic settings that lack several of these properties; some have virtually none of them.

Consolidators must also confront one of the major paradoxes of modern democracy. Most citizens support this form of political domination and accord it legitimacy because they expect it to change their living conditions for the better. More concretely, as the French political observer Alexis de Tocqueville recognized in the 1830s, many will expect to use public power to redistribute material goods and symbolic satisfactions more equally throughout the population. No democracy that wishes to reproduce itself over the long run can afford to ignore this passion for equality.

To consolidate themselves in the short to medium run,

however, the institutions of democracy must reflect existing conditions—conditions that are often highly unequally distributed. If this were not already enough of a challenge, these institutions cannot be based exclusively on the principle of one citizen, one vote. They must somehow recognize that social groups, even minorities that stand no chance of winning an election or referendum, have varying intensities of interest and passion concerning different issues. It is prudent, as well as ethical, to ensure that such voices be somehow "weighed" and not just "counted" in the policy process. It may even be desirable to protect these economic, social, ethnic, or cultural minorities by enshrining their rights in formal institutions, not just by making informal arrangements.

Coping with Cleavages and Capacities

Democracy requires cleavages in the society and the dispersion of political capacity among the citizenry. A polity without predictable and significant sources of differentiation would find it very difficult to organize stable patterns of electoral competition or associational bargaining.

Political sociology offers two major orienting hypotheses concerning these patterns. First, whatever cleavages exist in a society should be distributed in such a way that their impact is not cumulative. Ideally, each source of differentiation—class, sector, age, gender, race, language, and religion, for example—should cut across all the others so that no group is permanently and simultaneously disadvantaged on more than one ground. Because this is virtually impossible to accomplish, even in the most "pluralist" of societies, the effect of cumulative discrimination can be mitigated if individuals have a substantial possibility of mobility across categories during their lifetime.

Second, whatever the level of resources in a given society, no group—private or public—should have a monopoly or even concentrated control over any of them. If this condition proves impossible for reasons of economic efficiency, social prejudice, or historical accident, it is better that there be as many levels of political aggregation as possible, that there be as many resource bases as possible, and that the process of converting them into political power at any given level should be as variable and difficult to calculate as possible.

These are general and abstract conditions, not specific prerequisites. Three views are currently held regarding the conditions that must be satisfied before democracy has any chance of consolidating. First, Dankwart Rustow argues that there must be a prior consensus, rooted in obscure historical events and memories, on national boundaries and identity. Second, according to Barrington Moore, Jr., there should be no dominant class of large, precapitalist landowners who do not produce primarily for the market and who require the use of coercion to sustain their labor forces. Finally, Guillermo O'Donnell maintains that there should not be such substantial urban inequalities in income, wealth, and decent living standards that privileged groups cannot conceive of the underprivileged as "fellow citizens."

Presumably, if any of these conditions were not satisfied, it would be impossible to consolidate any type of democracy. All the prerequisites for consolidation can be met through the choice of appropriate rules and practices.

Finding and Valuing Rules

Regime consolidation, then, involves converting patterns into institutions and endowing what are initially fortuitous interactions, episodic arrangements, and ad hoc solutions with sufficient autonomy and value that they stand some chance of persisting. Citizens and politicians respond by adjusting their expectations to the likelihood of persistence and come to regard these emergent rules as given and even desirable.

When democracy is being consolidated, the predominant rules will address competition for office or influence, cooperation in the formation of governments or oppositions, and contingency in the mobilization of consent and assent. The predominant resource should be citizenship, although under the conditions of modern, indirect, and liberal democracy, citizens usually act through representatives and are free to mobilize other, much less equally distributed, resources such as money, property, status, expertise, and "connections" in their efforts to capture office or influence policy.

The mere existence of these rules is, however, insufficient to ensure consolidation. To become institutions, these rules must be successfully legitimated. They must come to be valued in and by themselves, not just for the instrumental and momentary benefits they bring. The normative expectations must not be set too high, however. In most established democracies, high levels of positive identification, ethical approval, and participatory enthusiasm are rarely the norm. Indeed, their authorities and representatives are typically regarded with some skepticism, if not scorn. Although intensely democratic values may be very much present and very important during the transition, what seem to suffice in the longer run are diffuse feelings among the citizens of the "naturalness" or "adequateness" of their regime. As long as there is a consensus that the new rules and emerging institutions conform better to prevailing standards than conceivable alternatives, or that normatively "superior" forms of governance are too difficult or costly to attain, regime legitimation is likely to settle in—along with a certain amount of disenchantment among the citizenry with what has been accomplished.

But politicians will not always agree on the rules of competition and cooperation, and, even if they do, citizens will not always give their assent. Few countries have been successful in their first effort at consolidating democracy. The reason is that it is difficult to find a set of institutions that are both appropriate for existing socioeconomic conditions and capable of satisfying future expectations.

This difficulty does not mean that most of the countries in which new democracies have emerged since 1974 will regress to their previous autocratic forms of government. Many of these fifty or so countries seem destined to remain unconsolidatedly democratic for the foreseeable future, if only because no feasible alternative mode of domination is available. Democracy in its most generic sense will likely persist, but it will less frequently be consolidated into a specific and reliable set of rules or practices.

See also *African transitions to democracy; Democratization, Waves of; Military rule and transition to democracy.*

Philippe C. Schmitter

BIBLIOGRAPHY

Dahl, Robert. *After the Revolution: Authority in a Good Society.* New Haven and London: Yale University Press, 1970.

———. *Dilemmas of Pluralist Democracy.* New Haven and London: Yale University Press, 1982.

Moore, Barrington, Jr. *Social Origins of Dictatorship and Democracy.* Boston: Beacon Press, 1966; Harmondsworth: Penguin Books, 1991.

O'Donnell, Guillermo. "On the State: Democratization and Some Conceptual Problems: A Latin American View with Glances at Some Postcommunist Countries." *World Development* 21 (August 1993): 1355–1370.

Przeworski, Adam. "Some Problems in the Study of the Transition to Democracy." In *Transitions from Authoritarian Rule: Prospects for Democracy.* Vol. 3. Edited by Guillermo O'Donnell and Philippe C. Schmitter. Baltimore: Johns Hopkins University Press, 1986.

Rustow, Dankwart. "Transitions to Democracy: Toward a Dynamic Model." *Comparative Politics* 2 (April 1970): 337–363.

Schmitter, Philippe C., and Terry Lynn Karl. "What Democracy Is . . . and Is Not." *Journal of Democracy* 3 (summer 1991): 75–88.

Constitutionalism

A method of organizing government that depends on and adheres to a set of fundamental guiding principles and laws. The relation between constitutionalism and democracy, that is, between limited government and self-government, remains one of the most important but least understood subjects in political theory. Surprisingly enough, even commentators with diametrically opposite political views often agree that there is an inherent tension between these two paramount liberal values or political practices.

Progressives ask, How can political officials be responsive to the will of today's electorate if they must follow rules laid down by long-dead ancestors—rules that a majority today cannot easily change and that are interpreted by unelected judges who are institutionally insulated from public opinion? Does not constitutional democracy ask government to obey two masters: the framers and the voters? And why should the people accept restrictions that, by a strange coincidence, turn out to serve the interests of social elites?

Conservatives reason otherwise, and come to different conclusions, but nevertheless concur that constitutional restrictions are fundamentally antidemocratic. They believe, however, that this is a good reason to celebrate constitutionalism; they cite the danger of majority tyranny and stress the need to protect individual rights against democratic excesses. Constitutionalism, as they see it, is a curb on the follies and cruelties of popular rule.

This surprising meeting of the minds between conservatives and progressives is reinforced by the dichotomy of positive and negative liberty. Having a voice in the election of those who make the laws under which we live (democracy) is not the same as being protected in our private lives from governmental bullying and interference (constitutionalism). The two aims are not merely different; it is said that they point in opposite directions.

A constitution is an antimajoritarian device, conservatives contend, because its admirable goal is the legal entrenchment of imprescriptible rights against the frivolous voting-day behavior of fleeting electoral majorities. A constitution is an antimajoritarian device, progressives reply, because its disreputable goal is the legal entrenchment of social privileges, guaranteed by property rights and freedom of contract, against the will of democratic majorities. By giving exceptional legal status to fundamental rights, both sides agree, a constitution insulates certain values against potentially dissatisfied majorities.

Any antithesis that appeals strongly, as this one does, to both sides of the political spectrum will prove enormously resilient and difficult to overturn. Nevertheless, the idea of an inherent tension between constitutionalism and democracy is empirically unconfirmed and theoretically inadequate. First, among functioning democracies in the world today, all but Great Britain, Israel, and New Zealand operate within frameworks established by written constitutions. (And there are some solemnly documented and difficult-to-change features in these systems as well.) Second, the purported contradiction between limited government and self-government depends on untenable conceptions of the two terms. Stated briefly, the contradiction assumes that the principal function of a constitution is negative (to prevent tyranny) and that the principal aim of democracy is positive (to implement the will of the majority).

If these definitions were sound, constitutionalism and democracy *would* be intrinsically at odds. But they are not sound. The primary function of a liberal constitution—as this novel political form emerged in the United States at the end of the eighteenth century—is to constitute democracy, that is, to put democracy into effect. A constitution is an instrument of government. It is a way of organizing the people for self-rule. To understand the mutually supportive relation between limited government and self-government, we need to examine, among other topics, the democracy-reinforcing role of individual rights in constitutional systems.

How to Rule the Rulers

It is crucial to distinguish between *voluntaristic democracy* and *deliberative democracy*. In the former a preexistent will is simply expressed by the people, and the people's representatives must implement it. In the latter the people's will is shaped and reshaped through an ongoing process of public disagreement and discussion. The latter conception is superior, both normatively and empirically. But for expository purposes, we begin with voluntaristic

democracy and make a simplifying assumption that we will later call into question. Let us assume that all members of the democratic electorate have at the outset a perfectly clear understanding of their own opinions on policy questions and that a coherent electoral majority has already been formed. Under such idealized conditions, democracy is indistinguishable from majoritarianism and simply demands that the electoral majority's viewpoint be put into effect. Even such a crudely voluntaristic or non-deliberative form of self-rule, it turns out, presupposes constitutionalism of a rather sophisticated kind.

If the majority of the electorate knows perfectly well what it wants, its relation to its elected representatives can be thought of as a principal-agent relation. Decision-making power is lodged in the people, while public officials serve as the people's proxies. An elected deputy, from this perspective, can be compared with a lawyer who represents a client or an ambassador who represents a state. All principal-agent relations raise the sticky issue of how to monitor the activity of the agent, how to make sure that the agent implements the instructions of the principal and does not act secretly and deviously for private advantage, partisan ideology, or whim.

Principals have a hard time monitoring agents for the same reason that they need an agent in the first place: the time, skills, and organizational resources at their disposal do not allow them to do the job themselves. In the case of democracy, periodic elections are by far the most important technique for subordinating the actions of the agents to the wishes of their principal.

But electoral accountability alone, however indispensable, is not sufficient for this purpose. Indeed, elected officials will often succeed in cloaking their actions, whatever purposes these actions serve, with fine-sounding rhetoric about the public good. (This is the residual core of truth in the otherwise misleading commonplace that constitutionalism is essentially antidemocratic: liberal constitutions are designed to prevent public officials from illegitimately invoking the name of the people to support policies that conflict with the wishes of the public.)

In any case, even majoritarianism requires that periodic elections be supplemented by a cluster of auxiliary precautions. What all these auxiliary precautions have in common is *plural agency*. That is, constitutionalism attempts to solve the principal-agent problem not only by institutionalizing periodic elections but also by appointing multiple agents who can monitor each other. Seen in this light, the separation of powers is an innovative use of the old precept, divide and rule. By dividing the "ruling class" of agents against itself, the popular majority can enforce its wishes (at least some of the time) even against those who directly control the levers of power.

Crucial separations and mutual checks that can serve this monitoring function include divisions between executive and legislative branches in presidential systems, divisions between chambers in bicameral systems, and divisions between levels of government in federal systems. Somewhat overlapping jurisdictions laid down in the constitutional text ensure that turf-conscious elected officials will inspect with jealousy the behavior of rival officials in different branches of government. Institutional self-interest alone, without any particular commitment to the public good, will encourage mutual surveillance and whistleblowing in case of misbehavior.

As noted, the people at large is too busy and too poorly organized to engage in full-time monitoring of its political agents. But if officials in one branch of government discern a palpable electoral advantage in disclosing the questionable actions of officials in another branch, they will alert the people to activities that ostensibly contradict the public interest and public opinion. Understood in this way, the separation of powers is a perfectly democratic arrangement.

In short, a constitution is an indispensable instrument of government, even in a purely majoritarian system. A constitution is the way the people rules itself, and it therefore includes a variety of indirect methods for monitoring and controlling the people's political agents. It is vital for constitutionalism, as a result, that the fundamental ground rules, which are meant to serve this function, cannot be changed by ordinary lawmaking procedures in an elected assembly. The British do not have such a system, for Parliament's transcendent and uncontrollable authority extends beyond ordinary legislation to the fundamental structure of government. At one point, for instance, the British Parliament unilaterally replaced triennial elections with septennial elections, continuing itself in office four years beyond the term for which its members were elected by the people. A relatively rigid constitution with fixed-calendar elections, such as the American Constitution, was designed explicitly to prevent such antidemocratic usurpations of power.

The U.S. Framers sought to establish a clear legal basis for the limited government that existed in Britain only by tradition and usage. Although it may exist in practice, limited government remains legally baseless as long as the sovereign power to change the constitution is lodged in the government itself. To provide a legal basis for limited government, the American Framers followed the ideas of the English philosopher John Locke, lodging sovereign power *outside* the government, in the people itself. Constitutionalism, in the minds of U.S. Framers James Madison and Alexander Hamilton, did not depend on rules laid down by God or fixed by custom.

Constitutionalism is self-conscious and voluntaristic, a product of enlightened popular sovereignty. Because democratic citizens have common sense, they clearly recognize the need for a variety of indirect techniques for enforcing their will on public officials.

But what about judicial review? How can we justify democratically a system in which judges insulated from public opinion can unilaterally capsize the decisions of electorally accountable politicians? If democratically elected officials always implemented the wishes of the people faithfully, there would be no democratic justification for judicial review. But because elected officials are constantly tempted to invoke the name of the people to legitimize self-interested or partisan actions, the judiciary has an important role to play in the democratic system of plural agency.

This role of the judiciary is especially important because constitutional provisions are not self-clarifying and constitutional rights are not self-specifying. Constitutions need to be interpreted on an ongoing basis, and the judiciary, which specializes in this function, makes a vital contribution to the political process by which a democratic public decides what its constitution means today. This is not necessarily an undemocratic arrangement—although it sometimes can be—because the judiciary does not have the final and unreviewable say but merely exerts influence in a system where it too can be checked by other branches. Constitutions can be amended, and, in the American case at least, the Supreme Court's appellate jurisdiction can be restricted by Congress.

To summarize: if the principal objectives of constitutionalism are, first, to prevent elected officials from escaping periodic submission to electoral competition and, second, to create a divided government in which rival officials will call public attention to actions against the public interest, then constitutionalism is obviously not undemocratic. Although undemocratic practices persist in every constitutional system, they owe more to human nature than to constitutionalism itself. The democratic public needs a constitution to enforce its will, at least occasionally, on its officials. Constitutionalism is the method by which potentially abusive, corrupt, and negligent rulers are, to some extent, ruled by those they try to rule.

Enabling Versus Obstructionist Constitutionalism

The foregoing argument assumes the validity of the voluntaristic or majoritarian conception of democracy—that democracy is a system designed to implement the preexistent will of the majority. This is an inadequate view of democracy, but it has an important point to teach. It helps us formulate a very simple and clear refutation of the unspoken assumption, common in political theory, that a liberal constitution has essentially one function, to prevent tyranny, including majority tyranny—that is, the majoritarian violation of individual rights.

This assumption is not wrong, but it is one-sided and incomplete. The theoretical challenge is to understand all the important functions in a broader context. All existing constitutions are multifunctional. If we want to speak exclusively about the preventive functions of constitutions, we could say that liberal constitutions are designed, at a minimum, to prevent not only tyranny but also anarchy, corruption, instability, paralysis, unaccountability, unjustified secrecy, and uninformed decision making. This list brings us closer to a realistic appreciation of the many-sided contribution of constitutionalism to democracy. But why focus on preventive functions?

A distinction should be drawn between the enabling and the disabling purposes of constitutions. A one-sided emphasis on inhibiting or constraining functions is a notable defect of much constitutional theory. That constitutions are not merely prohibitory is spectacularly demonstrated by the American example. The U.S. Constitution framed at Philadelphia in 1787 was meant not simply to prevent the tyranny of the majority; it was meant also to bring a new country into being and to enable its citizens to rule themselves.

If we reconsider our expanded list of the preventive functions of democratic constitutions, we can easily tease out the positive or enabling ends. A constitution crafted to avoid paralysis and instability is meant to create stable and effective government. One noteworthy example is the constructive vote of no confidence, introduced into the 1949 constitution of the Federal Republic of Germany. Under the no-confidence procedure, the parliament can-

not topple the cabinet unless it can simultaneously agree on a new candidate to replace the outgoing chancellor. Another provision meant to strengthen the executive vis-à-vis the assembly was included in the 1958 French constitution and is called the pledge of responsibility: a government bill becomes law automatically, without a parliamentary vote, unless a motion of censure is lodged and won. The French constitution also strengthens the executive by giving it considerable control over the parliamentary agenda.

These provisions are obviously sculpted not to prevent tyranny but rather to enhance cabinet stability in the face of a fragmented and rambunctious assembly and, in general, to improve the government's capacity to govern. Many constitutional provisions, including all grants of emergency power, are of this sort. They are not simply obstructionist. They also help organize the political process, distributing powers and giving them a direction, establishing a division of labor meant to foster specialization and enhance the contributions of the major political actors.

Constitutional Rights as Preconditions of Democracy

Positive constitutionalism seems an appropriate title to apply to the structure of democratic constitutions. The rules of the game—establishing, say, a presidential or a parliamentary system—do not simply throw roadblocks in front of public officials. They make political life possible in the first place. But what about the rights provisions? We do not want the right, say, to a fair trial to depend simply upon the say-so of a temporary electoral majority. Hence constitutionalism entrenches rights beyond the reach of ordinary democratic processes. But this does not necessarily mean that rights are somehow antidemocratic or should be conceived as stone-hard limits to the otherwise untrammeled will of the people. To see rights in a more positive light, we need to reevaluate the concept of democracy with which we began. Rights are an essential feature of any democratic constitution because democracy is not voluntaristic but deliberative.

Some rights arise from the needs of representative government. Voting rights, which define one of the main avenues for citizen participation in the democratic system, immediately come to mind. Legislation that unfairly restricts voting rights erodes the most essential precondition of a well-functioning democracy. Such procedural rights, therefore, should be constitutionally entrenched on strictly democratic grounds. While an electoral system is the most important guarantee of accountable government, some nonelected officials (for instance, judges) can reasonably be given custodial responsibility for the fair allocation of voting rights. Elementary knowledge of human nature suggests that no assembly benefiting from malapportionment can be expected to redesign the districting system in anything like a fair manner. Paradoxically, therefore, democracy demands that elected officials sometimes obey unelected ones. But what about other basic rights?

The key to positive constitutionalism lies in communication rights—freedom of speech, freedom of the press, and freedom of assembly. Indeed, a persuasive argument can be made that freedom of discussion is the primary right in any democratic constitution. (This is not to denigrate freedom of religion, freedom of contract, or the right to a fair trial.) Freedom of speech and freedom of the press illustrate the truth that rights can be productive, not merely protective—in this case useful for generating intelligent and publicly acceptable solutions to collective problems—and that they are designed to protect not the lone individual but fragile channels of social communication. Such freedoms also help us rethink our two basic concepts, constitutionalism and democracy. Attention to communication rights makes it clear, for example, why we need to distinguish sharply between democracy and majoritarianism or between deliberative and voluntaristic democracy.

Majoritarianism is a purely neutral decision-making procedure, noncommittal about outcomes, compatible with any sort of decision, brilliant or barbarous, that the majority wants to make. Under majoritarianism, decisions are legitimized by their source alone, not by their content. Democracy is a slightly different system, not wholly voluntaristic but deliberative as well, and painstakingly designed to improve the chances that relatively intelligent collective decisions will be made. Put simply, democracy does not entail blind deference to what the majority happens to think today. This is the main reason why democracy cannot easily survive or flourish outside a constitutional framework.

Why should an electoral majority be constitutionally prohibited from outlawing or silencing its critics? To answer this question is to understand the difference between majoritarianism and democracy. Voting rights might be used to implement the preexistent will of the majority. Freedom of discussion, by contrast, is meant to help the people improve its thinking about public issues and to learn what it wants to do through public debate. A democratic constitution strives to organize a people in such a way as to improve the thoughtfulness and fact-mindedness of public deliberation. Moreover, if a majority makes a decision after having engaged in an uncensored public debate, the outvoted minority will be more likely to view it as a legitimate decision, to be accepted and obeyed. For this reason, government by discussion enhances the effectiveness, not merely the intelligence, of public policy.

A Tool for the Community

Early critics of constitutionalism argued that a democratic public, rather than deferring to a "higher law" that it had created by its own discretion, would impatiently throw off that law at the first crisis. But secular democracies have produced relatively stable constitutions because constitutions are enabling, not merely disabling. They can be accepted voluntarily by a democratic people, for practical reasons, as an indispensable means for achieving widely desired aims. In the cases of freedom of speech and freedom of the press, a democratic people will accept rigid restrictions on majority discretion (for instance, the majority can never prevent its decisions from being publicly criticized) because this is the best means yet discovered for improving the quality of collective decisions, for bringing out the excellence of democracy. Freedom of speech is not based on radical skepticism but, to the contrary, on the firm belief that some policy outcomes are objectively superior to others.

There is nothing particularly strange about this arrangement, as a homely example reveals. Individuals will often want to talk things over with a friend before making a momentous decision in life, because they realize that such a back-and-forth will change the way they think about a problem and its possible solutions. They voluntarily throw themselves into a situation that will clarify their thinking and even transform their preferences. They do this because they want to discover what they really think, or what they would want if they were smart. Freedom of discussion, in political life, is publicly embraced because it promises to do something similar—to bring out and lend authority to the considered will of the people.

Representation also plays a vital role in this process. The relation between the people and its representatives cannot, ultimately, be compared with the relation between principals and agents because democratic representatives, unlike mere emissaries, help the represented discover what they really want. Voting rights are not simply a vehicle for registering a preexistent popular will; they are a method for involving citizens in a process through which the popular will is hammered out and improved by discussion.

Earlier, to explain the uses of constitutionalism under voluntaristic democracy, we described the people's attitude toward its elected officials as primarily one of distrust. There is a lot to this characterization, but it is also incomplete. We choose representatives to specialize in tasks that we need to have done but that we do not have time to do ourselves. What representatives do for us is not simply to make deals but, just as important, to concentrate on major public issues, exchange viewpoints with other deputies representing far-flung constituencies, and engage in mind-clarifying debate. Ordinary citizens need representatives to specialize in issues in order to help them find out what, as citizens, they believe and desire.

Democratic legislatures, as is well known, are also forums for striking bargains among interest groups. There is nothing particularly unsavory or sinful about such deals. The point of the deliberative theory of constitutional democracy is not to denigrate groups for acting on their interests but rather to put interest group bargaining into perspective. In fact, most groups do not have clear interests on many vital public issues, and there remains a good deal of room for the deliberative processes, for the attempt to discover the public interest on some important questions through wide-open discussion in the assembly and in the media.

Democratic citizens want to make good decisions today because, among other reasons, they realize that they will pay the costs of bad decisions tomorrow. An understandable concern for their own future leads democratic citizens to favor a system in which mistakes can be corrected. They embrace constitutionalism for this reason too: not only because it increases the probability of intelligent decision making, but also because it maximizes the opportunity for intelligent self-correction later. The present electoral majority will willingly submit to irritating criticism of its decisions by the opposition because it knows that it may want to change its mind in the future and that it needs to hear and consider, on an ongoing basis, possible reasons for doing so. Constitutional democracy, we might say, is self-correcting democracy. A liberal constitution is the way a democratic nation strives to make itself into a community that can adapt intelligently to new circumstances and continue to learn.

Democracy and Nonpolitical Rights

Not all constitutional rights arise from the needs of representative government. Freedom of religion and the right to a fair trial come to mind. But the relations between such rights and democratic politics are important and need to be explored. First of all, such rights cannot easily be defended in a nondemocratic regime, where power wielders are electorally unaccountable and media coverage is likely to be censored. Second, such rights seem to be indispensable preconditions for democratic politics. Respect for private rights creates a favorable atmosphere for peaceful electoral competition, democratic discussion, and partisan compromise. Any regime, including a majoritarian one, that respects rights will thereby enhance its legitimacy and hence its effectiveness—that is, the general public willingness to cooperate with its decisions.

The dependence of vocal and effective political opposition on the private wealth generated by a system of property rights is often mentioned in this context. To acknowledge the democratic function of property rights, it should be said, is neither to deny that such rights promote other valuable goals, such as material well-being and personal independence, nor to ignore the likelihood that accumulated riches will be used to buy political favors undemocratically.

Freedom of religion can be analyzed in the same light. Democratic citizens need to agree on freedom of religion because this right, by narrowing the range of issues over which governmental authorities can claim jurisdiction, provides an essential precondition for fruitful and cool-headed public cooperation, including democratic debate, in a multidenominational society.

But these are not the only reasons to doubt the traditional opposition between political democracy and the constitutional entrenchment of nonpolitical rights. The meaning of such rights, it should be noticed, is neither fixed unambiguously in the U.S. Constitution nor elaborated by the judiciary alone. What freedom of speech, free exercise of religion, or equal protection mean in practice is decided by intense and drawn-out political struggles, in which public debate plays an important role. Because rights, in their concrete significance and implementation, are elaborated democratically, it is not quite accurate to view them as unmovable barriers erected against the popular will.

The question of the original or ultimate source of these rights will probably never be answered unequivocally. But there is no overwhelming reason to locate this origin in divine command or immemorial custom. All we need to claim, or can justify claiming, is that a democratic public, to operate within the constraints of a liberal constitution, must have already arrived at a fairly stable consensus on basic rights, however vague and susceptible to political interpretation such a consensus remains. Such a claim sidesteps the unanswerable question of the metaphysical origin of rights and stops at the common-sensical recognition that a political culture where such rights are not widely accepted will probably be inhospitable to democracy.

The Amending Power

The essence of the so-called countermajoritarian dilemma lies in the fact that constitutional provisions are more difficult to revise than ordinary statutes. If democratic constitutions were wholly unchangeable, the countermajoritarian dilemma would be an irresoluble contradiction, an unjustifiable subordination of the present to the past and of the democratic public to unelected judges. But the rigidity of constitutions is relative, not absolute, so long as the road to constitutional amendment lies open. Judges, for instance, can be democratically overruled simply by changing the constitution they are entrusted to enforce.

Through the amending formula, the framers of a constitution share their authority over the constitutional framework with their descendants. They do this because they know that their foresight is limited. By building flexibility and adaptability into the constitution, they hope to increase the chances that it will survive and retain public support in unforeseen circumstances. Democratic citizens accept the authority of elected officials because the latter can be ousted from office in the next election. Similarly, they obey laws because they know that these laws can be changed. The legitimacy of authority in a democratic system, in other words, depends on the institutionally maintained opportunity for revision—an opportunity that can play an important role even when it is not used. The same rule applies to democratic constitutionalism.

But why will a secular and future-oriented democratic public, saddled with an imperfect constitution, accept a relatively stringent amending formula? Democratic citizens will accept a relatively rigid and imperfect constitution, first of all, because they understand that it would be a terrible waste of time and effort to be constantly haggling over the rules of the game. Procedural difficulties, by preventing hasty decisions, are meant to improve the quality of successful constitutional revisions, as well as to increase the likelihood that such fundamental changes will garner broad public support.

(Amendments are not the only way to introduce flexibility into a constitution, it should be mentioned parenthetically. One reason successor generations continue to accept a charter framed by distant ancestors is that constitutional provisions are gradually adapted to current circumstances by judicial interpretation. The judicial reinterpretation of the commerce clause is a notable example in American constitutional history. The commerce clause of Article I of the U.S. Constitution gives Congress the power to regulate interstate commerce. The provisions of the Civil Rights Act of 1964 apply to all activities in interstate commerce. The Supreme Court increased the law's effectiveness by broadly defining what is considered to be within interstate commerce. By helping adjust the meaning of the Constitution to a new society unknown to the Framers, judges sometimes serve a democratic function that supplements, rather than contradicts, the role of elected representatives. The possibility of explicit amendment, not to mention the mortality of legally irremovable judges and the subsequent appointment of their successors by democratically elected officials, lessens the chances that the judiciary will exercise this function with no regard to public opinion.)

Democratic acquiescence in an inherited constitution does not mean that citizens believe the document to be above reproach. Even if all citizens concede that the constitution needs improvement, they might not concur on the one right way to amend it. In such circumstances, they will often agree to stick with the inherited framework, not as the best possible constitution, but as the best constitution they are likely to get given the current state of political disagreement in the community. They accept the constitution not as a work of perfection but as better than, or at least as good as, any new constitution they could presumably fashion through democratic discussion and compromise.

The ordinary democratic electorate does not ratify the constitution only in exceptional or rare moments, therefore, but also by tacit consent, by continuing to act, on a daily basis, under the rules it lays down. Constitutional democracy is not the rule of the dead over the living but rather the self-rule of the living with help consciously accepted from the dead.

See also *Checks and balances; Hamilton, Alexander; Judicial systems; Justifications for democracy; Locke, John;*

Madison, James; Majority rule, minority rights; Separation of powers, United States Constitution. See constitutions in Documents section.

Stephen Holmes

BIBLIOGRAPHY

Ackerman, Bruce A. *We the People.* Cambridge, Mass., and London: Harvard University Press, 1991.

Beer, Samuel. *To Make a Nation: Rediscovery of American Federalism.* Cambridge: Belknap Press, Harvard University Press, 1993.

Friedrich, Carl. *Constitutional Government and Democracy.* Waltham, Mass.: Blaisdell, 1968.

Hamilton, Alexander, James Madison, and John Jay. *The Federalist Papers.* New York: Mentor, 1961.

Hayek, Friedrich A. von. *The Constitution of Liberty.* Chicago: University of Chicago Press, 1960.

Holmes, Stephen. *Benjamin Constant and the Making of Modern Liberalism.* New Haven: Yale University Press, 1984.

———. *Passions and Constraint: On the Theory of Liberal Democracy.* Chicago: University of Chicago Press, 1995.

Levinson, Sanford, ed. *Responding to Imperfection: The Theory and Practice of Constitutional Amendment.* Princeton: Princeton University Press, 1995.

Lijphart, Arend, ed. *Parliamentary versus Presidential Government.* Oxford: Oxford University Press, 1992.

Meiklejohn, Alexander. *Political Freedom: The Constitutional Powers of the People.* New York: Harper, 1960.

Mill, John Stuart. *Considerations on Representative Government.* Buffalo: Prometheus Books, 1991.

Sunstein, Cass. *Free Speech and the Problem of Democracy.* New York: Free Press, 1993.

———. *The Partial Constitution.* Cambridge, Mass., and London: Harvard University Press, 1993.

Contractarianism

A long and important tradition in political thought that evolved from the idea of an original contract on which political order is based. Among its exponents were Thomas Hobbes, Benedict de Spinoza, and John Locke in the seventeenth century and Jean-Jacques Rousseau and Immanuel Kant in the eighteenth. John Rawls and others continue the tradition, in modified form, today.

Contract theorists have put the tradition to varied political uses, but they share a common strategy. Each version of the theory describes a situation without government—a "state of nature," to use Rousseau's term—and then describes the conditions in which government would be introduced by general agreement. Contractarianism has been used to provide a basis for political obligation, for we are obliged to do what we have contracted to do. It has also been used as a basis for resistance or revolution, for obligation is canceled when the terms of a contract are broken. In short, the notion of a social contract has been used to define and justify the ground rules upon which politics is carried on.

Hobbes, Locke, and Rousseau

The ground rules are just, contractarians maintain, if they were agreed to or would have been agreed to (we shall return to this distinction). Contractarianism is, then, a theory of consent, and so we may expect it to have an important connection with democracy. But we must distinguish between the ongoing need for popular consent, which is part of a democratic system, and initial consent to a constitution, which contractarian theories require. It is quite possible that people might give initial consent to undemocratic systems.

Hobbes is instructive here. Because people are approximately similar in their capacities, he argued, there is no natural basis for order: all may reasonably hope to get what they want by relying on their strength and wit. So order must be artificial, the product of agreement. But how can the agreement be enforced? Hobbes imagines a special kind of agreement that immediately creates its own enforcement mechanism. All agree to lay down their right to live by their own strength and wit, on condition that one person, "the sovereign," retains this right. The sovereign, or ruler, is thus empowered to do whatever is necessary to preserve his own office; and because the value of his office will increase with the tranquillity and prosperity of his society, he will have a direct personal interest in exercising this absolute power prudently. Hobbes does not rule out democracy: the sovereign could in principle be one person (as he preferred) or a group or an assembly. But the legitimacy of Hobbes's system does not depend on the renewal of popular consent; the initial act of consent is binding and forbids resistance to government.

Locke, however, developed a theory in which ongoing consent was given considerable importance. Like Hobbes, he maintained that the natural state would be one of equality, a state in which no one would owe obedience to any other person. Unlike Hobbes, he maintained that even in such a state, people would seek to follow and to enforce a set of rules because they would grasp that the equality of human beings entails principles of mutual respect ("natural law"). They would actively try to ensure that they and their neighbors were treated respectfully by others and would protect their own and their neighbors' lives and property. But they would see that the private enforcement of natural law is inefficient and uneven and that a public agency would do it better. So they would unanimously agree to form a "civil society," a social group that has undertaken to obey a single political authority.

By majority decision the society would entrust the power of enforcing natural law to some person or group. In any case, Locke believed, there would have to be a means to raise revenue, and so there would have to be an elected assembly at which property owners, through their representatives, would give their consent to taxation. Moreover, whoever has been entrusted with the power to govern must maintain the support of a majority of the people, who retain the right to revoke the trust for sufficiently serious cause. Both of these provisions (no taxation without representation and the right of revolution) have been important in the American democratic tradition. It must be noted, however, that the extent of Locke's notion of "the people" has long been a matter of debate.

With Jean-Jacques Rousseau we arrive at a contractarian theory imbued with a democratic spirit. In Rousseau's hands the tradition becomes an instrument of radical social and political critique. In *Discourse on the Origins of Inequality* (1775) Rousseau maintains that existing society could owe its origins only to a duplicitous social contract in which the rich tricked the poor into perpetuating inequality. In the state of nature we all have something to lose, said the rich, so let us create law and government to confirm us in our possessions. And the poor agreed, forgetting that some had much more to lose than others.

But in *The Social Contract* (1762), Rousseau describes a quite different contract, one that would produce a legitimate political order. It resembles Hobbes's contract in creating an absolute power: here, however, the absolute power is to be held by the people themselves. All surrender their rights to the society as a whole, on two conditions. First, the society will establish equality of right—that is, no one will enjoy any right that is not universally enjoyed. Second, the criterion of all subsequent legislation will be the "general will"—that is, public decisions will be made in the light of the general interest, not on the basis of what some coalition of special interests happens to want. This looks very much like a theory of democracy, in which "the people" is sovereign, and the shared interests of the people take precedence over any partial interests. As it happens, however, Rousseau did not describe his theory as demo-

cratic. He reserved the term *democracy* to describe a system in which the people not only make but also execute the laws—a system that he considered utopian.

Criticisms

Over the years contractarian theories have attracted many criticisms. One of these is the obvious objection that with a few exceptions there *was* no social contract. Coercion and custom, or some blend of the two, explain how societies have come to be. Another objection is that even if there had been a social contract, it is not clear why it should be binding. Those who made it would be bound by it, but why should we? Hobbes and Locke respond in roughly similar ways to these objections. Hobbes maintains that submission to those in power is equivalent to adopting a social contract, for in both cases people are preferring obedience to insecurity. Locke has a notoriously difficult doctrine of "tacit consent," according to which any enjoyment of the amenities of a society amounts to agreeing to obey its laws. As for Rousseau, the critique does not apply, for neither of his two discussions involves the claim that some past event has led to a present obligation.

But contractarianism can take another escape route here. Instead of claiming that a social contract or some substitute for it has actually taken place, the contract can become a purely hypothetical device, a thought experiment. If there were no government, why and on what terms would we agree to create one? In thinking about this, we may settle upon a general reason for government's existence, and a list of things that governments must and must not do, if they are to be worth having. We can then measure the system of government that we do have against the one that we would have chosen.

This method is a powerful way of criticizing political institutions. But it poses two problems. First, although people are certainly bound by agreements that they did make, they are not bound by ones that they would have made, however rational and sensible. If you had asked me yesterday for five dollars, I would have agreed. But that does not mean that you can come to me today and say that I owe you five dollars because I would have agreed if you had asked me yesterday. Your demand stands on its own merits, and the fact that I would have agreed yesterday means nothing. This difficulty leads directly to the second problem. When we make use of a hypothetical agreement, we are appealing to a set of background principles that we think people would have used in making an agreement—principles such as fairness or human equality or the importance of freedom. But why should we not just appeal directly to those principles and say that a political system is legitimate if it is fair or equal or free?

John Rawls

This question certainly applies to the most important current contractarian theory, that of John Rawls, as elucidated in *A Theory of Justice* (1971). Among Rawls's most striking ideas is a thought experiment that he terms "the original position." Suppose that we face the task of agreeing on a set of basic political principles for a society, but that none of us knows what position we would occupy in it: we are under "a veil of ignorance." Rawls suggests that we would arrive at three ideas. First, we would want to ensure that, wherever we ended up in the society, we would enjoy some basic liberties. Second, we would want to ensure that, whatever talents we ended up having, opportunities to exercise them would be open to us. Third, we would be particularly anxious about the condition of those who would have the least advantaged position, where, after all, we might end up ourselves. It would not make sense for us to prohibit any inequality at all, because some inequalities may indirectly benefit everyone, by providing incentives. But we would want to say that there should be only as much inequality as was necessary to improve the well-being of the least advantaged.

Rawls's device is a way of drawing out the implications of a basic sense of moral equality. It prevents us from making any privileged claim on the basis of some attribute or talent that we happen to have, by denying us knowledge of our attributes and talents and requiring us to adopt principles that we would agree to live by whatever our attributes and talents happened to be. But why not just appeal to the idea of moral equality? What does the device of a hypothetical agreement add? This is a much-discussed issue. In Rawls's defense, we may say that an important part of the idea of moral equality is that each person should believe that the principles that he or she favors should be open to every other person: that what is to be politically enforced must be given a fully public justification. Rawls's contractarianism attempts to meet this condition, by seeking a justification that anyone, in given circumstances, would agree to.

Rawls's theory has also been criticized. To a theorist of radical individualism such as Robert Nozick, Rawls implausibly detaches individuals from their talents: if talents do not belong to those who possess them, who do they belong to? To deny people the rewards that their talents earn is a form of exploitation. To a communitarian theorist such as Michael Sandel, Rawls implausibly detaches individuals from their socially produced beliefs: given that I believe something profoundly, what does it matter what I would hold if I did not know what I believed?

In these disputes the democrat will side with Rawls. If we believe that a society's political arrangements must be acceptable to all its members, and if we believe that acceptance must be a matter of critical acceptance, or public justifiability, we will see Rawls's contractarianism as a major asset to democratic theory.

See also *Consent; Hobbes, Thomas; Kant, Immanuel; Locke, John; Natural law; Rousseau, Jean-Jacques; Spinoza, Benedict de; Utilitarianism.*

Richard Vernon

BIBLIOGRAPHY

Dworkin, Ronald. "The Original Position." In *Reading Rawls,* edited by Norman Daniels. Oxford: Blackwell, 1975.
Hobbes, Thomas. *Leviathan.* New York: Collier, 1962.
Lessnoff, Michael. *Social Contract.* London: Macmillan, 1982.
Locke, John. *Second Treatise of Government.* Cambridge: Cambridge University Press, 1960.
Nozick, Robert. *Anarchy, State and Utopia.* New York: Oxford University Press, 1974.
Rawls, John. *A Theory of Justice.* Cambridge: Harvard University Press, Belknap Press, 1971; Oxford: Oxford University Press, 1973.
Riley, Patrick. *Will and Political Legitimacy.* Cambridge and London: Harvard University Press, 1982.
Rousseau, Jean-Jacques. *The Social Contract.* Harmondsworth, England: Penguin Books, 1968.
Sandel, Michael. *Liberalism and the Limits of Justice.* Cambridge and New York: Cambridge University Press, 1982.

Corporatism

One of several possible arrangements through which organized interests can mediate between their members—individuals, families, firms, communities, and groups—and various entities, especially agencies of the state or government. Central to this process is the role of associations, permanently established and staffed, which specialize in and seek to identify, advance, and defend interests by influencing and contesting public policies. Unlike political parties—the other principal intermediaries in modern polities—these organizations neither present candidates for electoral approval nor accept direct responsibility for forming governments.

Corporatism, either as a practice in political life or as a concept in political theory, has always been politically controversial. It has been heralded as a novel and promising way of ensuring harmony between conflicting social classes. It also has been condemned as a reactionary and antidemocratic formula for suppressing the demands of autonomous associations and movements.

After the collapse of fascism in Italy, National Socialism in Germany, and various other authoritarian regimes that flourished in Europe between the end of the First World War and the end of the Second World War (1919–1945)—all of which claimed to be practicing some form of corporatism—the concept more or less disappeared from the lexicon of respectable political discourse. The exceptions were in Francisco Franco's Spain and António de Oliveira Salazar's Portugal, where the practice was left anachronistically on display until both countries "transited" to democracy in the mid-1970s.

At almost the same time, scholars from several countries and academic disciplines revived the concept to describe certain features of the politics of advanced democratic polities that did not seem adequately accounted for by pluralism, the dominant model that had been applied to state-society relations. Austria, Finland, Norway, and Sweden were especially singled out as "neocorporatist" countries in which this type of interest politics was prevalent. Important traces of neocorporatist practice in the making of macroeconomic policy have been observed in Australia, Belgium, Denmark, the Federal Republic of Germany, the Netherlands, and even in postauthoritarian Portugal and Spain. Great Britain and Italy attempted similar arrangements in the 1960s and 1970s without success. Elsewhere, for example, in France, Canada, and the United States, neocorporatism seems confined to specific sectors or regions.

Once the authoritarian-fascist-statist variety of corporatism had been virtually extinguished—first by the wave of democratizations that came after World War II and later by the wave that began in 1974—it became increasingly clear that small European countries with well-organized interest associations and highly vulnerable, internationalized economies were most successful in practicing the more bottom-up or societal version of neocorporatism. The tendency was all the more marked if these countries also had strong social democratic parties, stable electoral preferences, relative cultural or linguistic unity, and neutral foreign policies. Indeed, those that had the most difficulty sustaining such social pacts had weaker social democracies, more volatile electorates, and deep divisions over military and security issues—for example, Denmark and the Netherlands. Belgium's relative lack of success can be traced to its split into rival linguistic groups.

Protracted neocorporatism at the national or macroeconomic level has been convincingly linked to certain desirable outcomes: less unruliness of the citizenry, lower strike rates, more balanced budgets, greater fiscal effectiveness, lower rates of inflation, less unemployment, less instability at the level of political elites, and less tendency to exploit the "political business cycle"—all of which suggests that countries scoring high on neocorporatism have been more governable. This does not, however, make them more democratic.

Since its rediscovery in the mid-1970s, corporatism has borne the burden of its past association with fascism and other forms of authoritarian rule. To describe a polity or practice as corporatist was practically synonymous with accusing it of being undemocratic. Moreover, certain of corporatism's enduring features seemed to confirm this suspicion: organizations replaced people as the principal participants in political life; specialized professional representatives gained at the expense of generally interested citizens; privileged (if not exclusive) access was accorded to particular associations; monopolies were recognized and even extolled at the expense of overlapping and competing intermediaries; organizational hierarchies reaching up to very comprehensive national associations diminished the autonomy of more local and specialized organizations.

As inquiry into corporatism expanded, however, judgment about its effect on democracy shifted. For one thing, many of the countries that are manifestly corporatist are also obviously democratic in the sense that they protect the full range of civic freedoms, define citizenship in the broadest fashion, hold regular competitive elections of uncertain outcome, hold political authorities accountable for their actions, and pursue public policies that seem responsive to popular demands. Some corporatist countries, especially those in Scandinavia, have been in the vanguard of experimentation with such advanced democratic measures as worker participation in management, open disclosure of policy processes, ombudsman arrangements for hearing citizen complaints, public financing of political parties, and even profit-sharing arrangements with workers to extend popular ownership of the economy.

In addition, it soon became apparent that corporatist arrangements have a substantial effect on the conditions under which competing interests can participate in the influence process. Although the spontaneous, voluntaristic, and episodic relations of pluralism seem freer in principle, in practice they produce greater inequality of access to those in power. Privileged groups with smaller numbers, concentrated resources, and more compact location have a natural advantage over larger, dispersed groups such as workers and consumers. Corporatism tends to even out the distribution of resources across more comprehensively organized categories and to guarantee at least a formal parity of access to the making of decisions. Moreover, the direct incorporation of associations into subsequent implementation processes may ensure greater responsiveness to group needs than is possible through the arm's-length relationship that separates the public and the private realms under pluralism.

Evaluations of the impact of corporatism on democracy depend very much on which qualities of democracy one chooses to stress. Seen from the perspective of encouraging the participation of individuals in the decisions that collectively affect them and of ensuring that all public authorities accord equal access to all citizens' demands, corporatist arrangements have a negative effect. If one asks whether those in power can be held effectively accountable for their actions and whether those actions are likely to be responsive to citizen needs, corporatism is bound to be judged more positively. The effect of corporatism on the central mechanism of democracy—competitiveness—is more ambiguous. On the one hand, corporatism diminishes competitiveness by eliminating the struggle between rival associations for membership and access. On the other hand, it enhances competitiveness by encouraging rival conceptions of common interest to express themselves within the same association.

Most of today's democracies are being transformed by the practice of modern corporatism. Organizations are becoming citizens alongside, if not in the place of, individuals. Accountability and responsiveness are increasing, but at the expense of participation and access. Competitiveness is less interorganizational and more intraorganizational. Although the pace is uneven, the acceptance is unequal, and the outcome by no means unequivocal, democracy is becoming more "interested," more "organized," and more "indirect."

See also *Associations; Authoritarianism; Fascism; Multiethnic democracy.*

Philippe C. Schmitter

BIBLIOGRAPHY

Berger, Suzanne, ed. *Organizing Interests in Western Europe: Pluralism, Corporatism, and the Transformation of Politics.* Cambridge and New York: Cambridge University Press, 1981.

Cawson, Alan. *Corporatism and Political Theory.* Oxford and New York: Blackwell, 1986.

Lehmbruch, Gerhard, and Philippe C. Schmitter, eds. *Patterns of Corporatist Policy-Making.* Beverly Hills, Calif., and London: Sage Publications, 1982.

Schmitter, Philippe C. "Democratic Theory and Neo-Corporatist Practice." *Social Research* 50 (winter 1983): 885–928.

———. "Interest Intermediation and Regime Governability in Contemporary Western Europe and North America." In *Organizing Interests in Western Europe,* edited by Suzanne Berger. Cambridge and New York: Cambridge University Press, 1981.

Schmitter, Philippe C., and Gerhard Lehmbruch, eds. *Trends toward Corporatist Intermediation.* Beverly Hills, Calif., and London: Sage Publications, 1979.

Williamson, Peter J. *Varieties of Corporatism: A Conceptual Discussion.* New York: Macmillan, 1985.

Corruption

The abuse of public resources for private gain. The term *corruption* has had different connotations in different historical periods. In its classical conception, political corruption was seen as the degeneration of the political system. For Niccolò Machiavelli, this involved the decline of citizen virtue and civic-mindedness. For Montesquieu, it meant the perversion of a good political order into an evil one. For Jean-Jacques Rousseau, it resulted inevitably from the struggle for power.

Later the definition of political corruption became more specific, differentiating corruption from other societal problems. First, corruption involves a deviation from the laws and regulations, as when public administrators abuse their office to obtain private advantages. Second, the resources exchanged in corruption result in material advantages, as when a favorable public decision is paid for with money. Corruption thus is one form of influence of money on politics. Third, corruption almost always involves clandestine transactions.

Even in this stricter definition, corruption refers to a wide variety of phenomena; it is therefore necessary to distinguish different types. One way to do so is by the actors involved: corruption can implicate politicians or bureaucrats, at the local or national level. Moreover, the abuses of power can benefit an individual, a family, a group of friends, an ethnic group, an institution, or a political party. The resources exchanged also vary: the gain may be direct or indirect, the exchange may involve money or services, and the resources exchanged may be more or less valuable. The structure of corruption varies as well, according to the degree of continuity and stability of the exchanges, the number of actors involved, and the presence or absence of extortion. The basis of loyalty that allows for the development of a corrupt exchange can vary from personal friendship to party membership. Finally, the degree of deviation from societal norms can be more or less serious, according to standards set by the law or public opinion.

Causes

What causes, or allows for, this deviation? Explanations address the phenomenon at different analytic levels. As with other deviant behaviors, the individual's decision to participate in corrupt exchanges depends on the probability of being discovered and punished, the severity of the potential punishment, and the expected rewards, as compared with the available alternatives. Assuming that human behavior is dominated by the pursuit of material interests, political economists have singled out factors that influence the rational choice of an individual to participate in corruption. These factors range from the types of markets where corrupt exchanges develop to the degree of competition in elections.

One variable that is strongly related to corruption is the intervention of the state in the organization of economic life. The proliferation of laws and regulations, the growth of the public sector, and the expansion of the welfare system all increase the opportunities for engaging in corruption. The opportunities also increase with the extent of discretion exercised by civil servants. Corruption implies deviation from the main principles that are supposed to govern public bureaucracies: rationality, anonymity, and universalism.

The occasions for political corruption increase when controls on the activity of public administrators are frag-

ile. When the division of power between political actors and the public bureaucracy, as well as between the government and the judiciary, is unclear, it is difficult to discover and punish cases of corruption. And research has shown that political corruption tends to be more widespread in authoritarian or totalitarian regimes, where public opinion and the press are unable to denounce corruption.

In democracies, corruption tends to grow along with the costs of political representation. This is especially true when politicians acquire votes through personal exchanges with voters. Thus there is likely to be an inverse correlation between the level of generalized support for the regime—or the legitimacy of the institutions—and the cost of political representation. The higher the level of support, the lower the cost of representation, and vice versa.

Furthermore, normative conflicts are likely to lead to corruption. These result from the presence within a society of different value systems and moral codes. Such conflicts occur when loyalty to primary or secondary groups interferes with loyalty to the state and other political groups and widens the gap between codified laws and accepted practices. In particular, corruption spreads when social relationships based on traditional exchanges penetrate into domains that should be based on different, modern interactions.

If corruption develops because of confusion about the borders between state and society, and between traditional and modern values, it can be expected to grow during phases of transition. This will be the case particularly during the processes of development, as well as when established elites are suddenly penetrated by newcomers who are greedy for money and power and who have a weak sense of allegiance to the state.

One thus could conclude that corruption should disappear in modern, stable democratic societies. Instead, growing state intervention in economic and social life has increased the occasions for political corruption. At the same time, new technologies have increased the cost of electoral campaigns, and the professionalization of political careers has increased the number of those who have to make a living from politics rather than living for politics, to use the famous distinction proposed by Max Weber. Corruption has not disappeared, and according to some studies it has tended to spread along different lines: from above, because corruption among leaders reduces the moral integrity of their followers, and from below, because petty corruption requires the complicity of elites. It also moves from one institution to another, because the spread of corruption reduces its unit costs and increases the general connivance of the population as well as the opportunity to find a partner for illegal exchanges.

Consequences

The dynamics of corruption should be kept in mind in discussing its consequences. Social scientists are divided on this point. The so-called functionalist school has emphasized the positive functions of corruption, calling it a functional dysfunction, through which new norms replace old ones and allow for adaptation between different subsystems (such as the cultural and the economic).

Similarly, it has been said that in some processes of modernization political corruption permits the integration of ethnic groups while facilitating the relations of citizens with an impersonal and remote government bureaucracy. According to this view, corruption would help to overcome the difficulties associated with the expansion of participation within weak political institutions. Moreover, it would be preferable to violence: violence delegitimizes the political system, while corruption strengthens the relations between the citizens and the party.

From a similar perspective, some studies on developing countries have claimed that corruption has positive economic functions. It allows entrepreneurs to overcome bureaucratic obstacles, thereby stimulating investment, innovation, and managerial skills. These views are controversial, especially with regard to situations in which corrupt exchanges are generalized, as opposed to sporadic instances of corruption. Economists have observed that the income from political corruption is more likely to be used for consumption than for investment and that corruption favors not the most courageous entrepreneurs but those who have the best political connections. In this way, corruption wastes public resources and also destroys the market, because it rewards political ties more than economic competitiveness and privileges unearned income over entrepreneurial activity.

Corruption has dangerous consequences for politics. Although political corruption is more widespread in nondemocratic regimes, it is particularly dangerous for democracy because it undermines two of the major principles on which democracies are based: the equality of citizens' rights and the transparency of the political decision-making process. Bribes open the way for privileged access to the state for those who are willing to pay and can afford the price. This situation may leave noncorrupt citizens with the belief that one "counts" only if one has the right personal contacts with those who hold power. Because of its illegal nature, corruption increases the range of public decisions that are made in secrecy.

The spread of corruption also influences the most important intermediaries between the state and the citizens: political parties. Parties lose their capacity to make collective demands and are transformed into machines for the organization of profitable economic business. The political personnel changes accordingly, as a class of "business" politicians is created. These politicians regard politics as a source of rapid personal enrichment. They use the money obtained through corruption to buy votes and thus to extend their power into other political arenas.

The effect of these changes is a declining capacity of the administrative system to satisfy general demands and produce public goods. All these processes tend to delegitimize democratic institutions. At the same time the weakening of democratic institutions leads to further corruption. As corruption spreads, citizens' rights are transformed into favors. The more generalized corruption is, the more the citizens need to find a political protector—and the more they are ready to pay for this protection.

Remedies

Several remedies have been suggested to stop the spread of corruption before it leads to economic and political crisis. These policy measures aim at changing the utility function of corruption, by increasing its costs and reducing the expected rewards. For example, legislation in various countries has addressed the cost of politics and, in particular, the amount and sources of party financing, as well as the types of expenses allowed for electoral campaigns. Legislation also has addressed the power of political parties with regard to the public administration and the system of internal controls on public bureaucracies (through administrative controls and accounting procedures as well as ombudsman systems for public complaints).

Other measures have attempted to increase the "moral costs" of corruption by introducing codes of conduct for public servants and private entrepreneurs, emphasizing the merit system of appointment in state bureaucracies, and stimulating pride in public service. Even if these remedies fail to eliminate corruption, they may be sufficient to prevent it from spreading so much that it could become a threat to the stability of democracy.

Donatella della Porta

BIBLIOGRAPHY

Ackerman, Susan Rose. *Corruption: A Study in Political Economy.* New York and London: Academic Press, 1978.

Friedrich, Carl J. *The Pathology of Politics: Violence, Betrayal, Corruption, Secrecy, and Propaganda.* New York: Harper and Row, 1972.

Huntington, Samuel P. *Political Order in Changing Societies.* New Haven and London: Yale University Press, 1968.

Key, V. O. *The Techniques of Political Graft in the United States.* Chicago: University of Chicago Press, 1936.

Merton, Robert. *Social Theory and Social Structure.* New York: Free Press, 1957.

Pizzorno, Alessandro, and Donatella della Porta. "Geschäftspolitiker in Italien: Überlegungen im Anschluss an eine Studie über politische Korruption." *Kölner Zeitschrift für Soziologie und Soziopsychologie* 14 (1993): 439–464.

Costa Rica

The wealthiest and most developed country of Central America, located between Panama and Nicaragua, and the only stable democracy in the region. With a gross domestic product of $1,900 per person for a population of 2.8 million, a life expectancy at birth of seventy-five years, and a literacy rate of 93 percent, Costa Rica is rivaled in wealth and development only by Cuba in Central America and the Spanish Caribbean. Costa Rica is also the most democratic country in the region, the only stable democracy in Central America, and one of the few in Latin America.

Historical Background

Sparsely settled by agricultural and hunter-gatherer peoples before 1500, Costa Rica was discovered by Columbus and settled by Spaniards in the sixteenth century. Throughout the colonial era, it remained the poorest and least developed of the provinces of Guatemala. Costa Rica gained independence from Spain in 1821. Its history over the next six decades (1821–1882) was marked by a series of personal hegemonies or outright dictatorships. The periods between dictatorships were generally unstable, with occasional armed conflict. Constitutions were regularly adopted by new governments to legitimate their authority, but they were rarely effective in controlling political behavior. Suffrage was very tightly restricted by property, literacy, and gender requirements.

Costa Rica first became integrated into the world economy as an agricultural producer. It became heavily dependent on coffee exports by the mid-nineteenth century. The coffee-growing elite directly dominated politics from 1849 to 1882; even after this period, most presidents and other members of the political elite have come from this class.

After 1882 the constitution had increasing importance as a framework for political action. The Constitution of 1871 survived many instances in which the opposition came to power against the will of the incumbents. Literacy rates and numbers of voters increased as a result of public education, which began in the 1880s. Political parties began to be organized in the 1890s, reflecting rising levels of political participation. Nevertheless, politics remained under the control of a narrow elite. It was still possible for leaders to establish personal hegemony; after 1910 they did so primarily through the Republican Party machine. During the first third of the twentieth century, Costa Rican politics was dominated by two genteel politicians, Ricardo Jiménez and Cleto González Víquez. Jiménez served as president three times, and González twice. A short-lived military regime, from 1917 to 1919, was forced out by elite and mass resistance within the country and by U.S. opposition. During the 1920s and 1930s political parties became better organized, and political participation gradually increased.

The large-scale export of bananas under foreign control began in the 1890s. The political elite of Costa Rica was better able to cope with this development than its weaker counterparts in other Central American countries. While the United Fruit Company virtually controlled the state in Honduras, it had to bargain with the government in Costa Rica. In the 1930s a militant banana workers' union was organized by the Popular Vanguard (Communist Party).

Move Toward Democracy

The crucible of contemporary Costa Rican democracy was the turbulent decade of the 1940s. Rafael Angel Calderón Guardia was the Republican machine candidate for president in 1940, and he quickly took control of the party from his predecessor, León Cortés Castro. But Calderón proved to be far more than a traditional political boss. He sought to consolidate his own hegemony through several moves whose significance long outlasted his own hold on power. For the first time, a Costa Rican president used a populist strategy of appealing to and providing benefits for the working class and the poor. The keystone of his approach was the new social security system, supplemented by laws and administrative action to encourage and support the organization of labor unions. These measures caused a deep split with the major coffee growers and other business interests, who had been long accustomed to having a government at their disposal. Calderón also tended to use corrupt means to stay in power. This tendency provoked increasingly militant opposition from an emerging social democratic sector led by José Figueres Ferrer, among others. Calderón's principal allies were the Catholic Church (he was strongly inspired by social Christian thinking) and, after 1942, the Communist Party.

Like most countries of Latin America, Costa Rica does not permit the immediate reelection of a president. In 1944 Calderón left the presidency in the hands of his close ally, Teodoro Picado. Conflict erupted when he sought a second term in 1948. Calderón lost the presidential vote to conservative publisher Otilio Ulate, but he won a majority in Congress. Alleging fraud on the part of the opposition, Calderón asked Congress to annul the presidential election. Congress agreed. Figueres, who had been prepared for insurrection for months, rose in revolt. After six bloody weeks, his Army of National Liberation was victorious.

Shortly after the war, Figueres and Ulate signed a pact recognizing Ulate's victory, while allowing Figueres to head a provisional junta to draft a new constitution and call a constituent assembly. Acting by decree, the junta continued the major social and labor legislation of the Calderón period. It nationalized banking and electric power, set up the structure for overall state guidance of the economy, and abolished the army. The constitution drafted by the junta sought to make a decisive break with individualism, replacing it with a strong, democratic state empowered to act in defense of the common interest in social and economic matters. However, Ulate's Unión Nacional decisively defeated the Social Democrats in elections for the Constituent Assembly. As a result, the Constitution of 1949 was merely a moderate amendment of the 1871 document.

Since 1949 Costa Rica has had a mature democracy. The Constitution of 1949 provides for the president and the fifty-seven members of the unicameral National Assembly to be elected simultaneously every four years. Elections come under the jurisdiction of the Supreme Electoral Tribunal, which is completely independent of the other branches of the government. The tribunal has an exemplary record of supervising honest elections. There is universal adult suffrage, and voting is legally compulsory. Neither the president nor members of the National Assembly may be immediately reelected; since 1969 presidents may not hold the office a second time. Because the constitution confirmed the abolition of the army, internal security has been provided by the civil guard and the rural guard, forces that are traditionally small, lightly armed, and poorly trained. Until 1990 the two forces were commanded by separate ministers.

Political Structure, Parties, and Interest Groups

Compared with most Latin American presidential systems, the Costa Rican presidency is relatively weak. In most administrative matters, the president must act jointly with a minister or with the whole Council of Government, or cabinet. Scores of autonomous institutes and enterprises are insulated both from politics and from presidential control. The president's exercise of extraordinary powers is subject to close legislative restriction.

Although the executive power is comparatively weak, the state in Costa Rica is strong. It has employed a high proportion of the work force and has dominated the economy. Thus the state embodies much of the social democratic vision of Figueres and his allies of the 1940s.

The National Liberation Party has been the anchor of the party system since its founding under Figueres's leadership in 1951. It has manifested an unrivaled combination of organizational permanence and capacity for mass mobilization. Other political sectors, both right and left, have resorted to a succession of ad hoc coalitions to confront the National Liberation Party. The result has been a bipolar party system in which the National Liberation Party has tended to alternate in the presidency with the succession of antiparty coalitions. The party of the incumbent president lost the presidential election in 1953, 1958, 1962, 1966, 1970, 1978, 1982, 1990, and 1994. The National Liberation Party was the beneficiary in both the exceptions to this pattern, in 1974 and 1986. During the 1980s the center-right opposition to the National Liberation Party forged a durable party, the Social Christian Unity Party. The Social Christian Unity Party won the presidency and control of the National Assembly in 1990, with the candidacy of Rafael Angel Calderón Fournier (son of the former president). The National Liberation Party was victorious in 1994, with José María Figueres, also the son of a former president.

The socialist left has been an organized presence in Costa Rica since the formation of the Popular Vanguard Party in 1931. Outlawed from 1949 to 1975, the party was able to function under other names. Other parties on the left were formed in the 1970s and 1980s. Leftist presidential candidates typically receive less than 5 percent of the vote, while leftist electoral coalitions usually elect one or two members of the National Assembly (which is elected on the basis of proportional representation).

The far right is represented most notably by the Free Costa Rica Movement. It has not been a significant electoral force, but it has had significant elite support for decades. The far right assumed new importance during the early 1980s, when the U.S. Central Intelligence Agency (CIA) made extensive use of right-wing elements in Costa Rica, both U.S. expatriates and Costa Ricans. The CIA used these elements to support the U.S.-sponsored counterrevolutionary force, the contras, against the Sandinista regime in Nicaragua.

Political life in Costa Rica is marked by diverse interest groups, which attempt to influence policy by means of administrative or legislative contacts, litigation, or mass action, such as strikes and demonstrations. The business community is well organized. Probably the largest labor union is the one that represents most government workers. Overall, the labor force is not highly unionized, compared with the situation in other Latin American countries. Of growing importance is the Solidarist movement, an employer-sponsored effort to promote workplace organization on the premise of solidarity rather than conflict between employers and employees. Agricultural interests are also extensively organized, though divided by crop, export orientation, and size of holdings. Environmentalists, a newly organized interest, have helped push Costa Rica toward one of the most advanced environmental policies of developing nations.

Costa Rica's commitment to a strong welfare state was challenged by a persistent crisis of international debt and government finance during the 1980s. Under pressure from the International Monetary Fund, successive governments struggled to shrink the state and balance its budget, and to liberalize and privatize its economy, while retaining as much as possible of the old commitments. This effort placed a great strain on the majority of the population, as living standards worsened, public services deteriorated, and unemployment rose. Costa Rica in the early 1990s, however, was in better economic condition than most other countries of Central America and the Spanish Caribbean.

An additional source of strain for Costa Rica was the involvement of all of Central America in a series of civil wars between revolutionary insurgents and status quo forces, the latter supported by the government of the United States. Under President Oscar Arias (1986–1990), Costa Rica played an important role in promoting the peaceful settlement of several simultaneous armed conflicts in the region.

Successful Democracy

Explanations of Costa Rican democracy vary. Explanations based on political economy often cite the country's colonial poverty and lack of a wealthy ruling class of landowners. Some scholars also cite the chronic labor shortage during the coffee boom of the nineteenth century, which kept wages up and permitted the survival of many family farms. Others argue that the emergence of democracy after 1940 required the end of the old coffee oligarchy as a dominant political force, an outcome brought about in two stages, first by Calderón (1940–1948), then by Figueres (1949–1958).

Another line of argument focuses on political culture. Costa Ricans are proud of their political system; they think it represents people like them and believe they can act effectively within it (even though most do not do so).

These patterns are similar to those found in North America and Western Europe. And in spite of economic inequality, Costa Rican elites largely hold egalitarian beliefs, based on the assumption that a poor person has dignity and ought to be treated with respect. This pattern contrasts markedly with countries such as Guatemala and El Salvador.

Finally, an essential factor in Costa Rican democracy is the mutual confidence among elites, built by explicit agreements and implicit accommodations. Without this, political conflict among elites could never have emerged from the polarization of the 1940s or have survived the many political and economic crises since 1949, especially those of the 1980s. The pact between Figueres and Ulate in 1948 and the constitution of 1949 defined a regime in which those two victorious forces would compete. By 1958 Calderón had accepted the terms of that settlement and joined the loose anti–National Liberation Party coalition. Finally, in the 1970s, the left was permitted to join the system as well. Costa Rica thus illustrates the importance of elite consensus and bargaining for managing democracy.

The prolonged, relatively successful practice of democracy in Costa Rica has naturally contributed to consolidation of both a democratic political culture and a pattern of elite compromise. Success breeds success.

See also *Arias Sánchez, Oscar; Caribbean, Spanish; Central America; Figueres Ferrer, José; Political culture.*

John A. Peeler

BIBLIOGRAPHY

Ameringer, Charles D. *Democracy in Costa Rica.* New York: Praeger, 1982.

Cerdas Cruz, Rodolfo. "Colonial Heritage, External Domination, and Political Systems in Central America." In *Political Parties and Democracy in Central America,* edited by Louis W. Goodman et al. Boulder, Colo.: Westview Press, 1992.

Denton, Charles F. *Patterns of Costa Rican Politics.* Boston: Allyn and Bacon, 1971.

Peeler, John A. "Elite Settlements and Democratic Consolidation: Colombia, Costa Rica, and Venezuela." In *Elites and Democratic Consolidation in Latin America and Southern Europe,* edited by John Higley and Richard Gunther. Cambridge and New York: Cambridge University Press, 1992.

Seligson, Mitchell A. "Costa Rica." In *Latin American Politics and Development,* edited by Howard J. Wiarda and Harvey F. Kline. 3d rev. ed. Boulder, Colo.: Westview Press, 1990.

Seligson, Mitchell A., and Miguel Gómez B. "Ordinary Elections in Extraordinary Times: The Political Economy of Voting in Costa Rica." In *Elections and Democracy in Central America,* edited by John A. Booth and Mitchell A. Seligson. Chapel Hill: University of North Carolina Press, 1989.

Vega Carballo, José Luis. "Political Parties, Party Systems, and Democracy in Costa Rica." In *Political Parties and Democracy in Central America,* edited by Louis W. Goodman et al. Boulder, Colo.: Westview Press, 1992.

Côte d'Ivoire

See *Africa, Subsaharan*

Critical theory

A mode of neo-Marxist radical social analysis that emerged during the crisis-ridden final years of the German Weimar Republic, which lasted from 1919 to 1939. The ideas of critical theory came out of the Institute for Social Research, which was founded in Frankfurt, Germany, in 1924.

The institute was an interdisciplinary research organization that brought together philosophers, sociologists, economists, political scientists, and psychologists. After Adolf Hitler's rise to power, members of the "Frankfurt school" went first to Geneva, Switzerland (in February 1933), and then to New York City (in 1935).

The Authoritarian State

Totalitarian movements scored several political victories in Europe in the 1930s, with Italy and Germany coming under fascist governments and the Soviet Union falling under Joseph Stalin's unchallenged control. Max Horkheimer (1895–1973), who was director of the institute, and the neo-Marxist intellectuals grouped around him tried to explain the apparent capitulation of previously radical social movements in the face of European fascism and particularly Nazism. The political traumas of this period, and particularly the collapse of liberal democracy in Germany, encouraged the institute's members to break with pivotal components of orthodox Marxist theory.

Most important, Horkheimer encouraged his colleagues to question the economistic character of traditional Marxism's explanations of collective actions and thus to emphasize the influence of what earlier Marxists had relegated to the so-called superstructure (politics, law, culture, and ideology). This new radical social analysis, which would be called "critical theory," continued to criticize capitalist-bourgeois society in the name of a better, as yet unrealized social order.

The institute's members developed a groundbreaking analysis of how ongoing changes in political and legal institutions, family life, and culture contributed to the growth of authoritarianism. Franz L. Neumann (1900–1953) and Otto Kirchheimer (1905–1965) chronicled the breakdown of traditional liberal legal protections in the Weimar Republic and analyzed the fragility of liberal democratic representative institutions in the face of advancing fascism. In their view, Nazism was the most extreme case of a global trend toward dictatorship, which was facilitated by the demise of crucial political and legal mechanisms that had mediated, though with limited success, between the rights of individuals and the interests of large capitalist cartels and corporations.

Horkheimer and Erich Fromm (1900–1980) led the way in synthesizing Sigmund Freud's theory of psychoanalysis and Marxism. Scholars at the institute argued that the disintegration of the traditional patriarchal family tended to produce personality types vulnerable to mass-based political and social coercion. Dominant, economically independent patriarchal fathers—and the resultant psychological struggles that Freud had associated with the concept of the Oedipus complex—helped to produce (male) offspring capable of some degree of personal autonomy. The fascist experience had shown that the decline of the patriarchal family seemed to make children more open to potentially harmful mechanisms for socialization outside the family.

Horkheimer, Leo Löwenthal (1900–1993), and Theodor Adorno (1903–1969) continued this line of research into the causes of prejudice and the development of authoritarian personality traits after fleeing Germany. The results of this research were published in 1950, in collaboration with other social scientists, as *The Authoritarian Personality*.

Adorno, Löwenthal, Walter Benjamin (1895–1940), and Herbert Marcuse (1898–1979) argued that new forms of mass culture (radio, film, even sports) represented a more thorough subordination of cultural activities to the pressures of capitalism than had occurred in previous periods in the development of bourgeois culture. Benjamin countered the most pessimistic features of his colleagues' argument by focusing on what he considered to be some of the potentially positive aspects of "art in the age of mechanical reproduction." In particular, he suggested that popular media such as film could produce a shock effect that might be mobilized for politically progressive purposes. Nonetheless, the dominant position within the institute was that the capitalist "culture industry" tended to trivialize and even dismantle the most valuable accomplishments of modern culture. Even more disturbingly, the culture industry's ascent contributed to cultural illiteracy and hence conveniently buttressed authoritarian trends. In a 1938 essay on popular music, Adorno went so far as to claim that contemporary society was undergoing a "regression in listening" and increasingly was unable to communicate.

Many of the writings of members of the institute from this period (1937–1945) take on melancholic overtones. Typically, they draw a contrast between the achievements of an earlier phase of bourgeois civilization and contemporary trends, which allegedly suggest the decay of the most progressive bourgeois ideals and institutions. Neumann and Kirchheimer repeatedly compared the progressive features of the traditional liberal rule of law—such as respect for individual rights and fair and equal treatment before the law—with the obvious horrors of fascist law. In addition, they were concerned about the far less terrifying but worrisome dangers posed by the proliferation of discretionary legal standards in welfare-state democracies, which were developed through the power of administrative bodies and often without legislative debate and decision.

Despite Horkheimer's critique of traditional Marxism as giving undue significance to economic factors, the institute's overall theory during this period is dominated by a set of underlying economic assumptions—formulated most clearly by Friedrich Pollock (1894–1970). According to Pollock, modern societies undergo a transition from competitive capitalism (characterized by a large number of relatively independent entrepreneurs and minimal state intervention) to a system of monopoly capitalism (characterized by growing state activity in the economy, the disappearance of the independent entrepreneur, and the rise of cartels and monopolies). The institute's creative inroads into areas traditionally passed over by Marxism ultimately can be interpreted as attempts to explain how these larger economic trends are accompanied by political, legal, cultural, intellectual, and psychological developments.

Divergent Paths

By 1941 the institute's members were engaged in a fierce debate concerning precisely those economic trends that had played such an important background role in their thinking during the 1930s. Neumann and Kirchheimer continued to insist on the analytical superiority of the concept of monopoly capitalism for explaining these trends, whereas Horkheimer and Pollock were more interested in shifts in contemporary capitalism (in particular, the growth of state planning). Horkheimer and Pollock argued that monopoly capitalism was being supplanted by a system of state capitalism in which traditional economic mechanisms were replaced by political mechanisms capable of warding off many of capitalism's economic shortcomings. Capitalism had liberated itself from the endemic economic crises described by earlier Marxists. Social actors formerly considered subversive, such as the industrial working class, were being integrated into the political and economic status quo to a greater extent than had been anticipated even by the institute's own somber analysis just a few years earlier.

The state capitalist model inspired an increasingly pessimistic mode of theorizing. Adorno and Horkheimer outlined a philosophical position that, at least implicitly, conceived fascism to be the pivotal experience of Western modernity and a logical consequence of subterranean trends within it. As the fascist experience allegedly demonstrates, Western rationality was destined to destroy itself. A far-reaching critique of the fundamentals of Western reason, with some similarities to contemporary postmodernist theory, took center stage for Adorno and Horkheimer.

Marcuse, who remained more loyal to traditional Marxism than did his colleagues, struggled to avoid the political paralysis often evident in the later work of Horkheimer and Adorno. He continued to hope that oppositional and subversive social movements would emerge. His writings after World War II, however, were similarly influenced by the concept of "total administration," a term first used by Adorno. The ideas of "one dimensionality" and "total administration" meant that the capitalist-bureaucratic welfare state overruns all aspects of social existence, eliminating all efforts at, and hopes of, radical social transformation.

Neumann and Kirchheimer, by contrast, pursued an innovative alternative version of postwar critical theory. Both argued that the state capitalist model exaggerated the capacities of contemporary political and economic institutions to control social life and to solve economic crises. Their postwar writings (in political sociology as well as in political and legal theory) exhibit a far more subtle understanding of the contradictory and conflict-ridden nature of contemporary welfare state democracies than was formulated by Horkheimer, Adorno, or Marcuse. Neumann's and Kirchheimer's refusal to succumb to the theory of "total integration" clearly heightened their sense of the importance of precisely those institutional mechanisms, such as the rule of law, that play a pivotal role in counteracting inequalities in power in contemporary society—by regulating and curbing the power of corporations through antitrust legislation and by defending individuals' civil and economic rights.

Habermas and the Reconstruction of Critical Theory

Jürgen Habermas (1929–   ) is the most prolific and the most complex of any theorist in the Frankfurt school tradition. A professor of philosophy at the J. W. Goethe University in Frankfurt until his retirement in 1994, he has made significant contributions to moral, social, political, and legal theory as well as actively participating in postwar public debates in Germany. Despite clear differences separating Habermas's version of critical theory from that of first-generation critical theorists, the underlying thrust of his work builds upon that of his predecessors.

In the spirit of continuing the institute's work of the 1930s, Habermas vigorously advocates an interdisciplinary approach that combines philosophical theory with empirical social research. In the process, he has engaged in critical debate with a wide variety of divergent theoretical traditions, ranging from hermeneutics, represented by Hans-Georg Gadamer, to the systems-theory approach, as represented by Niklas Luhmann, and the "power knowledge" approach of Michel Foucault.

Furthermore, Habermas has more rigorously acknowledged the achievements of liberal democracy than did his predecessors at the Institute for Social Research. As early as 1962, his *Structural Transformation of the Public Sphere* aspired to revive the "utopian core" of the bourgeois political traditions—in the simplest terms, an ideal of opinion and consensus formation on public issues through processes of genuinely free and uncoerced communication among participants. While critical theory in the 1930s similarly appealed to the more radical aspirations of the European Enlightenment of the eighteenth century, Habermas has gone further, insisting that these ideals, like freedom, equality, and civic engagement, must be defined through a rigorous moral and political theory.

In synthesizing the views of the German philosophers G. W. F. Hegel and Immanuel Kant, Habermas has developed a moral and political theory called "discourse ethics." Discourse ethics attempts to lay bare the normative presuppositions of democratic legitimacy—namely, the participation of all affected by a norm in a process of free and equal public deliberation regarding the validity of that norm. In a 1993 work, *Faktizität und Geltung* (English translation, *Facticity and Validity,* forthcoming, 1995), Habermas theorizes that the institutional correlate of a discursive concept of political legitimacy would be a multiple, decentered, and free public sphere, situated in civil society.

In the process of retrieving and restating the legacy of Western modernity in science and politics, Habermas has not only distanced himself from the radical critique of Western rationality once advanced by his own teachers (Horkheimer and Adorno), but he has also responded to what he considers the one-sided dismissal of Western modernity and rationalism advanced by theorists such as Jacques Derrida and Jean-François Lyotard.

Since 1989, and with the collapse of authoritarian communism, Habermas's ideas of the public sphere, discourse ethics, and civil society have become influential for those reconstructing democracy in Eastern Europe and the former Soviet Union. As these societies struggle to establish democracy, it becomes increasingly clear that democracy not only refers to a representative system of free elections and a multiparty system but also that it requires a free public sphere of debate and contention as well as the formation among citizens of free associations and organizations that can influence public life. Habermas's theories of discourse ethics, free public sphere, and democratic legitimacy provide inspirations for such efforts.

See also *Fascism; Kirchheimer, Otto; Marxism; Postmodernism; Psychoanalysis.*

Seyla Benhabib and William E. Scheuerman

BIBLIOGRAPHY

Arato, Andrew, and Eike Gebhardt, eds. *The Frankfurt School Reader.* New York: Continuum, 1982.
Habermas, Jürgen. *The Philosophical Discourse of Modernity.* Cambridge: MIT Press, 1987.
———. *The Structural Transformation of the Public Sphere.* Cambridge: MIT Press, 1989.
———. *The Theory of Communicative Action.* Vols. 1 and 2. Boston: Beacon Press, 1987.
Horkheimer, Max. *Between Philosophy and Social Sciences: Selected Early Writings.* Cambridge: MIT Press, 1993.
———, and Theodor Adorno. *Dialectic of Enlightenment.* New York: Continuum, 1972.
Marcuse, Herbert. *One-Dimensional Man.* Boston: Beacon Press, 1964.
Neumann, Franz L., and Otto Kirchheimer. *The Rule of Law under Siege: Selected Essays of Franz L. Neumann and Otto Kirchheimer.* Los Angeles: University of California Press, 1995 (forthcoming).

Critiques of democracy

Critiques of democracy, questioning the basis and goals of democratic political thought, are as old as democracy itself. Inevitably they are influenced by the changes in the concept and practice of democracy over time. In the history of Western political theory, the critics of democracy have usually far outnumbered its advocates. Only relatively recently, beginning with the French Revolution in 1789 and gathering momentum after the revolutions of 1848, has democracy come to be regarded as the goal of every society solicitous of human dignity.

The most dramatic change in the theory and practice of democracy occurred during the transition from direct democracy, as embodied in the institutions of Periclean Athens, to what is described today as liberal or representative or constitutional democracy. Modern scholars vigorously debate how much Athenian direct democracy, instituted by Cleisthenes in the reforms of 508–507 B.C., and modern representative democracy have in common. There is a profound difference between a regime based on the direct participation of all citizens in the popular assembly, like in Athens, or one based on the indirect participation of the people through representation in a legislature, in which political parties play a role. The two concepts overlap somewhat, however, and elements of direct democracy (town meetings, referendums, recall elections, and so forth) are present in most modern liberal democratic regimes. Furthermore, the ancient Athenian democratic ideals of freedom of expression, rotation of office, and equality before the law are also goals of modern representative democracies.

The earliest preserved criticism of democracy is found in the Greek historian Herodotus (485–425 B.C.). Although not an Athenian, Herodotus had spent time in Athens, where presumably he learned much of what he knew both about democracy and its critics. In his *Histories,* he includes a debate over the best form of government. Democracy loses the debate to monarchy; the *demos,* or the common people, are judged to be arrogant and selfish. In addition, they are said to need the protection of the monarch against the few who are rich.

One of the earliest surviving critiques of Athenian democracy by an Athenian is the composition by an unknown author referred to as the "Old Oligarch," probably written between 431 and 424 B.C. Its form is that of a fictitious speech by a cynical and worldly-wise member of the Athenian upper class who detests democracy in principle but who concedes that, because in Athens it has proved to be militarily successful, democracy must be accommodated. The Old Oligarch shudders at what he perceives to be the moral emptiness of democracy, even as he marvels at its economic and military vitality. Democratic Athens, he complains, favors the vulgar and unscrupulous mob at the expense of those who are best in character.

Thucydides (c. 471–400 B.C.), in his *History of the Peloponnesian War,* includes many examples of how Athenian democracy could degenerate into mob rule. In one case he recounts how the greed of the common people led them to demand the invasion of Sicily. During the debate in the assembly, the wiser heads remained silent out of fear of the aroused populace. The invasion, in clear defiance of Pericles' policy of caution, resulted in one of Athens's worst defeats. Thucydides implies that a democracy such as that established in Athens is not stable enough to conduct a prudent long-term foreign policy.

Democracy in the "Canon" of Political Theory

Most authors in the traditional canon of Western political theory have either ignored democracy or criticized it. Plato, who held the democratic regime in Athens responsible for the trial and death of Socrates in 399 B.C., condemned democracy in the *Republic* as the rule of the many trapped in the cave who mistake the shadows for reality. For Plato, democracy meant the rule of license in which all the passions of the soul indiscriminately have their way. Democratic chaos was the prelude to tyranny.

In Plato's *Gorgias,* Socrates criticizes not only the Athenian people but their most famous democratic leaders as well. Pericles and Themistocles are said to have neglected the education of the people in the virtues of justice and moderation. Instead, they built docks and harbors and expanded commerce with outsiders. Plato's dialogues contain many speeches by Socrates denouncing the practice of choosing members of the Council of 500 (or senate) by lot. In these speeches, also summarized by Aristotle in his *Rhetoric,* Socrates asks whether anyone would chose a surgeon or a ship navigator by lot. When the negative reply inevitably follows, Socrates scornfully concludes that it makes as little sense to select political leaders by lot. To Plato's Socrates (and apparently to the historical Socrates as well), political knowledge is a craft analogous to medicine or navigation. The statesman is the physician of the soul.

Particularly in the *Gorgias,* Plato has Socrates criticize democracy on yet another ground: it corrupts public speech or rhetoric. Democratic rhetoric, as perfected by the Sophists, tells the people what they want to hear rather than what they need to hear. Socrates is said to have paid with his life because he refused to go along with this corruption.

Plato may have softened his view later. In the *Statesman,* democracy is described as the worst of the lawful regimes and the best of the lawless ones; in the *Laws,* it is considered one of two "mother constitutions" for the "mixed regime" (the other one being monarchy). Both Plato and Aristotle enumerated six "simple" regimes: the rule of one (monarchy) and its corruption (tyranny); the rule of the few (aristocracy) and its corruption (oligarchy); and the rule of the many (moderate democracy) and its corruption (extreme democracy). The mixed regime resulted from a blending of elements from two or more of the simple regimes, with the requirement that the mixture must contain elements of different numerical categories. That is, it would not do to mix monarchy and tyranny, aristocracy and oligarchy, or the two versions of democracy because they would not adequately restrain their excessive tendencies to favor the one, the few, or the many. Thus Plato's "second best" regime in the *Laws* has some democratic features, including the limited use of the lottery to choose some public officials. Finally, however, it is Plato who is the source of law, although he provides lengthy preambles to the laws designed to win the people's consent. The preambles, which elucidate the theoretical rationale for the laws, were designed to elicit consent rather than blind obedience.

Aristotle's view of democracy seems somewhat more affirmative than Plato's. Still, in both the *Ethics* and the *Politics* he favors polity—a mixture of democracy and oligarchy—as the best practicable regime because polity checks the tendency of the few rich to exploit the many poor as well as the tendency of the many poor to exploit the few who are rich. Aristotle expresses an aversion to rule by many people concentrated in small urban areas, preferring landowners in rural areas as more moderate and less likely to be swayed by demagogues. Both Plato and Aristotle held philosophy to be the highest kind of life, a life that could be led only by those few possessing leisure and virtue. Philosophers are by right the judges of the priorities to be pursued in the city-state because they excel in prudence or practical reason. In the *Politics*, Aristotle proclaims the best regime to be a society in which citizenship is limited to the best persons—in other words, an aristocracy based on character rather than on heredity or wealth.

The Roman statesman Cicero (106–43 B.C.) thought undiluted democracy a disaster and put forward a theory of the mixed constitution (with monarchical, aristocratic, and democratic elements) as the absolutely best regime. In *De republica*, Cicero insists that the Senate, which represents the nobility, is essential to the proper operation of the government, although he grants that the popular assembly, organized into tribes and represented by the ten tribunes of the people, rightly holds veto power in certain areas. Cicero, who had served a term as one of the two consuls, or chief executives, of the Roman Republic, thought the wealthy should control the consulate as well. He also thought it necessary that in emergencies a constitutional dictatorship of six months' duration could be invoked.

Medieval Christian political thought was greatly influenced by the passage in Paul's letter to the Romans enjoining Christians to be subject to the higher powers as ordained by God. Authority descended from God to the rulers and nobility; the common people were conceived of as passive—to be acted upon. Democracy in the early Christian Middle Ages was not explicitly criticized, in part because of the loss of the Greek classical sources. This situation changed in the thirteenth century with the recovery of Aristotle's *Politics*. Thomas Aquinas, Aristotle's major medieval Christian interpreter, rejected democracy in favor of limited monarchy. In *On Kingship*, he extols rule by one: just as God rules the universe and the queen bee rules the hive, so the monarch must rule the multitude. Democracy is against the natural order. Dante Alighieri drew on this analogy even more emphatically in his *On World Monarchy* (1321).

Marsilius of Padua is often mistakenly credited with being a medieval precursor of modern democracy. In his *Defender of Peace* (1324), Marsilius declares that the "weightier part" of the people is the source of law; however, he significantly adds the phrase "in quantity and quality." Marsilius actually deserves to be ranked among the critics of democracy. Withering criticisms of the people's poor judgment and susceptibility to demagogic appeals are scattered throughout his work. It seems more probable, as Leo Strauss has suggested, that his occasional "populism" was camouflage for his support of a new antipapal elite.

Beginnings of Modern Political Theory

Despite his reputation for being an apologist for tyranny, the early sixteenth-century political philosopher Niccolò Machiavelli expressed considerable sympathy for the common people. He even wrote in the *Prince* that there is some truth in the proverb "the voice of the people is the voice of God." The people, however, he wrote in the *Discourses*, constitute only one of the two "humors" in the body politic; the powerful few are the other indispensable force. Machiavelli was also emphatic about the necessity for a single leader to found "new modes and orders." In the *Discourses*, he treated democracy as an unstable form of government and espoused a doctrine often described as civic republicanism rather than democracy. In the *Prince*, he appears to express contempt for the vulgar majority who are easily taken in by appearances. He may, however, have been uncovering the manipulation of public opinion for the many to see.

Thomas Hobbes, in the *Leviathan* (1651), held democracy to be one of the three forms of government, monarchy and aristocracy being the other two. Democracy is a regime in which the sovereign power is lodged in an assembly of all the citizens. Despite his formal neutrality on the question of whether one, few, or many should exercise the sovereign power, Hobbes clearly favored monarchy as the form most likely to produce peace and security. Democracy (direct rule by all the people) is so patently impracticable as to be out of the question. In his *Behemoth*, a history of the English Civil War of the 1640s, Hobbes denounces those democrats who wanted to govern themselves. In Hobbes's view, the common people think only of their selfish interests. They are inclined to be swayed by religious demagogues. Their only proper role is to consent to the rule of the sovereign. Hobbes detested what are today known as interest groups, declaring them to be so many worms in the body politic.

One is tempted to say that John Locke reversed

Hobbes, but this assertion is only partially true. Locke did reject absolute monarchy. Because he grounded government on the original and continuous consent of the property-owning males in the population, Locke is today often hailed as the foremost democratic thinker. To the extent that safeguarding minority rights is thought crucial to democracy, however, Locke is vulnerable to the charge of promoting the "tyranny of the majority." Significantly, in the *Second Treatise,* Locke referred to democracy only twice; he described the political system he advocated as civil government rather than democracy. It seems clear from his emphasis on property and its inevitably unequal possession because of the lack of reason and industry in the mass of men that Locke would have been averse to egalitarian, participatory, and populist versions of democracy. He thought that only those with a stake in the system should decide whether a revolution is justified.

Although widely hailed as the father of modern democracy, Jean-Jacques Rousseau rejected democracy, in the literal sense of government by all or even a majority of the people, as impracticable. In the *Social Contract* (1762), he wrote that a true democracy has never existed and never will exist because it is unthinkable that the people will remain perpetually assembled to discuss and administer public affairs. Indeed, it is a violation of the natural order for the many to govern the few. Only a "people of gods" could govern themselves democratically. It is important, however, to bear in mind Rousseau's sharp distinction between government and legislating. Although the people cannot govern, they should declare the basic legislative principles or constitutional framework within which the magistrates do their daily work.

Even if one were to excise Rousseau's commentary on government from the *Social Contract,* he can be shown to have been more preoccupied with the problem of leadership than with day-to-day rule by the people, collectively considered. He emphasizes the role of the (unelected) founder-legislator in creating the conditions from which a community bound together by a "general will" could emerge. Rousseau's distinction between the general will and the "will of all" has given rise to endless debate as to his meaning. It would appear that to Rousseau we vote properly only when we follow the inner voice of our own idealized selves and vote for the public interest regardless of how it affects us individually. If we selfishly decide issues of public policy on the basis of what we think will be to the advantage of our particular interest group, we will produce a corrupt result. The will of all stands for the mere sum of particular (selfish) wills. Thus a majority—or even a unanimous—vote is only procedurally democratic. A decision that is substantively democratic results only when all or most of the people declare the general will. Rousseau rejected the idea of representative government. The only true legislators are the people; a parliament of representatives (as in England) deprives the people of their right to declare the general will and returns them to slavery after each election.

John Stuart Mill, whose *On Liberty* (1859) is hailed as a classic of liberal democratic thought, was highly suspicious of unqualified majority rule. He feared that newly emerging electoral majorities might themselves become tyrannical and ride roughshod over the privacy of individuals and the legitimate claims of minorities. He also feared the extension of the lowest common denominator of taste to all areas of life in a democracy.

In *Reflections on the Revolution in France* (1790), Edmund Burke, the father of conservatism, refers to undiluted democracy as the most "shameless" thing in the world. A mass democracy is shameless because it acknowledges no standard higher than itself. Such a democracy destroys morality as traditionally understood—that is, as an objective standard discoverable by reason and beyond the reach of majorities. Earlier, in his famous *Speech to the Electors of Bristol,* he declares it to be the duty of the parliamentary representative to be guided by conscience and explicitly rejects any idea that constituents could command him to follow any course of action. Burke's preference for a "natural aristocracy" is reminiscent of Aristotle. Horrified by the violence of the French Revolution, he roundly condemns the notion that will is the source of law, no matter whether it be the will of the many or of the few. Reason and tradition should hold in check the will of both majorities and minorities, of both peoples and kings. Burke's notion of the independent representative is directly opposed to Rousseau's rejection of representative government.

G. W. F. Hegel also opposed the ideas of the French Revolution, such as popular sovereignty and the mandate theory of representation. In his *Philosophy of Right* (1821), Hegel rejects any notion of the people conceived of as a collection of atomistic individuals whose opinion should be binding on those who govern. "The people" is an abstraction and as such has no will to be followed.

In his *Critique of Hegel's Philosophy of the State* (1843), Karl Marx contrasts what he calls true democracy with the false democracy of bourgeois liberal representative government. For Marx, true democracy is not a political system but a condition he later calls "final communism"; it represents the transcending of all political constitutions and the negation of the multiple tyrannies—economic, social, religious, cultural, political—that hitherto have ruled over humans. In *The Communist Manifesto* (1848), Marx and Friedrich Engels state that the first step in the coming working-class revolution is to bring the working class up to the level of the ruling class and achieve democracy. By democracy, Marx does not mean the practices or aspirations of liberalism then current, such as universal suffrage, regular elections, competition of two or more political parties, freedom of the press, and the rule of law. These practices are merely façades for the oppression of the proletariat by the bourgeois ruling class. At best they may be used by the proletariat as part of its strategy to overthrow the liberal order. The *Manifesto* discusses liberal or representative democracy as a "democracy of unfreedom." True freedom involves the end of alienation in all its forms, and the precondition for abolishing alienation is the overthrow of capitalism. (Engels later contended on the basis of the electoral success of the German Social Democratic Party that universal suffrage might hasten the revolution.)

Although critiques of democracy are generally perceived to come from the right, Marx and Engels show that there also exists a left-wing critique. Left-wing critics attack liberal democracy for not being democratic enough. Left-wing critics tend to make a distinction between the people's declared will as distorted and manipulated by its current oppressors and the people's authentic will. The people's true will can express itself only after the class society is transformed into a condition of equality. As the Italian Marxist Antonio Gramsci put it, until now societies have been divided into "those who know" and "those who do not know." The elite, those who know, condition the great majority of people to accept inequality as natural and inevitable. Only through a thoroughgoing revolution in popular culture can those in the majority become aware that they need not remain inert. As democratic citizens they can transform the sociopolitical world and abolish the division between those who know and those who do not.

A controversy exists in contemporary political science over whether the very notion of the people's true will inevitably leads to totalitarianism. J. L. Talmon, who coined the term "totalitarian democracy," argues that this current of thought, originating with Rousseau's concept of the general will and running through Marx to Vladimir Ilich Lenin and Joseph Stalin, uses democratic rhetoric to subvert democracy. According to Talmon, totalitarian democrats have an arbitrary, restricted notion of who qualifies as the people.

Few scholars today go as far as Talmon, and some thinkers who attempt to combine the insights of Marx and Sigmund Freud reject his thesis. In fact, they argue that an authentically radical critique of democracy such as that offered by Marx and Gramsci leads to the opposite of totalitarianism—that is, to a true democracy. Herbert Marcuse is one example of such a radical democratic thinker. Robert Paul Wolff is another.

One could cite many more criticisms of democracy from the classics of political theory. James Madison in *Federalist* No. 10 (1787) wrote that a pure democracy cannot cure discord caused by factions. In his epoch-making work *The Spirit of the Laws* (1748), Montesquieu harbored grave suspicions about democratic republics and clearly preferred aristocratic republics. Montesquieu rejects the idea of popular sovereignty in his famous doctrine of the separation of powers. For Immanuel Kant the only choice is between a republican and a despotic form of government. In a republic the executive and legislative powers are separate; in a despotism they are united. Democracy, which Kant understands as resting on the union of the legislative and executive powers, is inherently despotic, even though the will of the majority rules rather than the will of a single person.

The Elite School

Having set forth the major critiques of democracy in Western political theory, we are now in a position to examine the arguments of the so-called elite school of political theorists in the twentieth century. In common parlance the term "elitist" today has a uniformly derogatory connotation. The assumption is that theorists who emphasize the inevitable rule of elites in any society are antidemocratic and perhaps even profascist. Closer inspection, however, will reveal that increasingly theorists of democracy have come to adopt some version of elite theory, although this tendency is not universally shared. Joseph Schumpeter, Carl J. Friedrich, Robert Dahl, and Seymour Martin Lipset are representative of "realistic" democratic thinking in postwar social science in the United States.

The elite school of thought began about the turn of the twentieth century with Gaetano Mosca, Vilfredo Pareto, and Robert Michels. Mosca is the author of such terms as "the ruling class" and "the political class." Pareto wrote about the "circulation of elites." Michels, in his study of the German Democratic Socialist Party, coined the term "the iron law of oligarchy."

Mosca, who began as early as 1883 to write about the role of elites, or organized minorities, in every society, proclaimed that whether a society labels itself a democracy, an aristocracy, or a monarchy, it will be governed by a minority. Every society is divided into a ruling class (the minority) and a ruled class (the majority). The ruled class does not share in government but only submits to it. Mosca insisted that it is a lie to assert that the masses of the people choose their representatives in representative democracies. On the contrary, their representatives are nominated and elected by organized minorities that force their will on the disorganized majority.

Given Mosca's conclusion that elections are nothing but unequal contests between organized minorities and the disorganized majority, it is somewhat surprising to find him expressing strong opposition to expanding the suffrage. Nonetheless, he declared in 1933 in the final version of his ruling-class theory that universal suffrage is the chief threat to liberal democracy because the masses are more volatile and subject to manipulation by demagogues than are the elites. The experience of the Italian fascist dictatorship appears to have caused Mosca to revise his ideas of the passivity of the masses, who, he thought, had been mobilized by Benito Mussolini in a way that would have been unlikely before universal suffrage and the encouragement of democratic participation.

Writing at the height of the fascist dictatorship, Mosca observed that autocratic regimes have greater staying power than liberal regimes. He thought liberal regimes could flourish only under conditions of economic prosperity and intellectual flowering. Ironically, Mosca alone in the Senate defended liberal parliamentary government when, in 1925, Mussolini pushed through a law declaring the head of the government (himself) no longer responsible to parliament.

Mosca's true successor in the elite school was Guido Dorso, who today is virtually unknown outside Italy. Like Mosca, Dorso, who died in 1947, was from the south of Italy. Dorso divested Mosca's theory of its aversion to the masses by insisting that the strength of liberal democracy rests in the rapid and continuous movement of the most able elements from the rank and file into the ruling class. Dorso also diluted Mosca's notion of the organized mi- nority to the point that any hint of conspiracy disappeared. By stressing continuous competition between sections of the ruling class and the political class through political parties, Dorso gave strong support to liberal democratic institutions. He played a leading role in the resistance movement against the fascist dictatorship, and after the war he supported the left-of-center Action Party.

The French sociologist Maurice Duverger, in *Political Parties* (1951), provided the foundation for a "realistic" theory of democracy in the spirit of Mosca, as revised by Dorso, when he wrote that Abraham Lincoln's famous formula "government of the people, by the people, and for the people" needed to be rewritten as government for the people by an elite derived from the people. Then this maxim could serve as the only definition of democracy compatible with reality.

Ortega on the Triumph of Hyperdemocracy

If the elitist school inaugurated by Mosca, Pareto, and Michels declared the inevitability of minority rule, the Spanish man of letters José Ortega y Gasset argued in *The Revolt of the Masses* (1930) that just the opposite had happened in the West. Writing in a vein somewhat reminiscent of Friedrich Nietzsche (although much more sympathetic to liberalism and socialism than Nietzsche was), Ortega lamented that, while liberal democracy had formerly been animated by devotion to the rule of law, now a kind of hyperdemocracy prevailed, corrupting common people and elites alike. In all areas of life, including art and literature, the "revolt of the masses" had ruined the quality of human existence.

For Ortega, as for Nietzsche, mass democracy is less a governmental form than a cultural disaster. The term "mass man" is not synonymous with the poor or the working classes but is the representative psychological type of current society regardless of income level and education. Education has been destroyed; humanistic learning has been replaced by technical training.

Ortega claimed that democracy, conceived of as the rule of the common people from below, is contrary to the proper ordering of public affairs. It is the destiny of persons of ordinary talents and taste to take direction from cultural elites. By definition, he wrote, the mass of humanity exists only to be raised up by selected minorities who impose standards of morality and taste on them.

Like Mosca, however, Ortega refrained from attacking liberal parliamentary government and specifically endorsed parliamentary institutions. Like Mosca, he rejected

Mussolini's fascism. In effect, he declared the fascist police state to be nothing but hyperdemocracy with a brutal face.

Gentile and Fascism

Italian fascism's aversion to representative democracy was best expressed by the philosopher Giovanni Gentile (1875–1944). Gentile, who held various offices under the Italian fascist dictatorship, wrote much of the article on fascist doctrine published in the *Italian Encyclopedia* in 1932, even though Mussolini had signed his name to it. The article declares fascism's opposition to democratic ideologies. Fascism rejects the possibility of rule by the majority and extols the inequality of human beings as beneficial. Democratic regimes give the illusion that the people are sovereign; in truth, sovereignty is exercised by special interests behind the scenes. In contrast to a regime openly ruled by a king, democracy is a regime with a number of hidden kings who exercise a collective tyranny far worse than that of any avowed tyrant.

The prestige of the word *democracy* was so great in the twentieth century that even fascism found it necessary to claim to be the true democracy. Thus the fascist doctrine declared that, although fascism is opposed to a democracy that reduces the nation to the lowest common denominator of the majority, it is nonetheless the purest form of democracy if the nation is properly organized into a structure of corporate groups, thereby allegedly allowing the best talents in the mass of people to rise to the top. The implication is that the nation's true will is expressed by the one leader, *Il Duce,* Mussolini himself.

In his last work, *Genesis and Structure of Society,* published posthumously in 1946, Gentile expanded on his paradoxical claim that fascism is the true democracy by arguing that authentic democracy rejects privacy and individualism in the name of a complete merger of the individual with the state. Far from the state swallowing up the individual, the reverse occurs in fascist democracy, for the fascist state is the will of the individual in its universality. To justify this centralized and authoritarian view of democracy, Gentile claimed the ancient Greek city-state as his source.

Fascist Intellectual Opponents of Democracy

It is important to recall that critiques of democracy vary widely in substance and intent, and that it is quite possible to have theoretical reservations about democracy while in practice preferring it to alternatives. Conversely, as the discussion of Gentile shows, some prominent intellectuals critical of democracy in varying degrees actively supported the Nazi and fascist dictatorships. Among the most prominent were the philosopher Martin Heidegger, the jurist Carl Schmitt, and the playwright Luigi Pirandello.

Heidegger (1889–1976), author of *Being and Time* (1927) and the leading existentialist philosopher of the twentieth century, joined the Nazi Party shortly after Hitler's accession to power in 1933 and served as rector of the University of Freiburg for ten months. Even after leaving this position, during which he made a number of speeches supportive of Hitler's "national revolution," he clearly remained convinced that National Socialism (Nazism), in principle or at least initially, had the potential of saving Europe from bourgeois democratic nihilism.

In his inaugural address as university rector, Heidegger attacked democracy on numerous grounds. He seemed to endorse an idealized version of Hitler's leadership principle. Modern society, he proclaimed, must be reorganized to combat the corrupting influences of urbanization and runaway technology. A hierarchy of estates must replace mass society. Society must be organized around discipline, work, and "manly service." Multiparty systems have no right to exist; in their place is one party serving a united people with one will and one führer.

In a posthumously published interview with the editors of *Der Spiegel,* conducted in 1966, Heidegger, though repudiating what he euphemistically called the rougher manifestations of National Socialism, remained skeptical of democracy, declaring that he was not convinced that democracy could react creatively to the technological ethos permeating the modern world. Democracy, Heidegger continued, is at best only half true, in part because it operates under the illusion that global technology is something that can easily be controlled or mastered.

Carl Schmitt, a famous legal scholar during the period before Hitler seized power, shared with Heidegger an initial enthusiasm for the Nazi dictatorship, but later his attitude was more reserved. Both Schmitt and Heidegger extolled the sacrifice of the individual to the state in war, which for Schmitt was the essence of politics. In *The Concept of the Political* (1927), Schmitt defined politics in terms of the relationship between friendly states and enemy states. He repudiated cooperative and humanitarian ideas designed to support democracy. During the Nazi regime he authored justifications of Hitler's lawlessness in the name of a decisionist theory of law.

Luigi Pirandello (1867–1936), winner of the Nobel Prize for literature in 1934 and best known for his plays *Six Characters in Search of an Author* and *Henry IV*, became an active supporter of Italian fascism in 1924 when, in a much publicized event, he joined the Fascist Party at the regime's greatest moment of crisis following the murder of the Socialist deputy Giacomo Matteoti. Long before the advent of fascism in the March on Rome of October 28, 1922, Pirandello had become disillusioned with Italian parliamentary democracy. Italian democracy, he made clear in his novel *The Old and the Young* (1909), had betrayed the spirit of the nineteenth-century liberation movement embodied in Giuseppe Garibaldi's military expedition to unify Italy. Pirandello was outraged over what he perceived to be the corruption prevalent in the new national government in Rome after unification in 1870. In the novel he described Italian liberal democracy as a regime covered in mud. He bitterly resented the exploitation of southern Italy by successive liberal governments in Rome. During and after World War I he turned furiously against the Italian Socialist and Communist Parties and called for a rebirth of nationalism. Like Heidegger in Germany with reference to the cruder currents of Nazism, Pirandello gradually distanced himself from the Fascist Party as it set about promoting a rigid social conformity. He never wavered in his public support of Mussolini, however, whom he hailed as the consummate actor imposing his sense of perpetually changing life on the contemporary political scene.

Voegelin and Strauss: Emigré Critics

Eric Voegelin (1901–1985) and Leo Strauss (1899–1973) were the two leading political theorists who emigrated to the United States as refugees from Nazi Germany and Nazi-occupied Austria, respectively. Both thinkers were highly critical of the modern liberal democratic tradition, which neither thought possessed the intellectual and spiritual resources to defend the dignity of the individual against the unprecedented assaults of totalitarian mass movements in the twentieth century. Each sought in different ways to recover the classical (Platonic and Aristotelian) foundations of political science. Unlike Heidegger and Schmitt, Voegelin and Strauss were fiercely antitotalitarian; they resisted Nazism rather than collaborating with it.

Voegelin was especially critical of the Lockean elements in Anglo-American social science. Locke, to Voegelin, was a destroyer of traditions who put nothing in their place.

Strauss inveighed against American political science, with its mélange of positivism, behaviorism, and historicism (a euphemism for Heidegger's philosophy). Both Voegelin and Strauss thought it was vital for the liberal democracies to reconstitute elites capable of shaping the issues to be discussed in elections. They agreed that knowledge of the premodern classics of political theory is essential to understanding the modern crisis of constitutional democracy, which has been called upon to weather the storms of apocalyptic mass movements desirous of transforming politics into a process of inner-worldly salvation through utopian magic.

Conclusion

As the examples of Gentile, Heidegger, Schmitt, and Pirandello show, some twentieth-century critics of democracy promoted fascism and Nazism in varying degrees. Most of the other critics discussed here, however, can scarcely be labeled enemies of the open society or fascist precursors. Indeed, it may well be the case that, to be true to itself, democracy needs thoughtful critics.

See also *Authoritarianism; Classical Greece and Rome; Conservatism; Constitutionalism; Elite theory; Elites, Political; Fascism; Justifications for democracy; Liberalism; Majority rule, minority rights; Marxism; Mass society; Theory, Twentieth-century European.*

Dante Germino

BIBLIOGRAPHY

Dahl, Robert A. *Democracy and Its Critics.* New Haven and London: Yale University Press, 1989.

Gentile, Giovanni. *Genesis and Structure of Society.* Translated by H. S. Harris. Urbana: University of Illinois Press, 1960.

Germino, Dante. *Beyond Ideology: The Revival of Political Theory.* New York: Harper and Row, 1968.

Klosko, George. *The Development of Plato's Political Theory.* New York and London: Methuen, 1986.

Machiavelli, Niccolò. *The Prince* and *The Discourses on Livy.* Vol. 1 of *Machiavelli: The Chief Works.* Edited and translated by A. Gilbert. Durham, N.C.: Duke University Press, 1965.

Marcuse, Herbert. "Repressive Tolerance." In *A Critique of Pure Tolerance.* Boston: Beacon Press, 1969.

Meisel, James H. *The Myth of the Ruling Class.* Ann Arbor: University of Michigan Press, 1958.

Sartori, Giovanni. *The Theory of Democracy Revisited.* 2 vols. Chatham, N.J.: Chatham House, 1987.

Schmitt, Carl. *The Concept of the Political.* Translated by G. Schwab. Rutgers, N.J.: Rutgers University Press, 1976.

Strauss, Leo. *On Tyranny.* Edited and translated by V. Gourevitch and M. Roth. New York: Free Press, 1991.

Talmon, J. L. *The Origins of Totalitarian Democracy.* New York: Praeger, 1961.

Voegelin, Eric. *The New Science of Politics.* 2d ed. Chicago: University of Chicago Press, 1987.

———. *The World of the Polis.* Baton Rouge: Louisiana State University Press, 1957.

Wolin, Richard, ed. *The Heidegger Controversy.* New York: Columbia University Press, 1991.

Croatia

See *Europe, East Central*

Cube law

A mathematical formula (also known as the cube rule of elections) that estimates the relationship between the seats in a legislature and the votes received by major parties, specifically when seats are allocated by plurality in single-member (one-seat) districts. First proposed in 1910 for British elections, the cube law may be the earliest example of an empirical rule in political science that is presented as an equation in measurable variables, reminiscent of the form used in physics. The equation follows:

$$s_A/s_B = (v_A/v_B)^3$$

where s_A and s_B are the seats won by parties A and B respectively, and v_A and v_B are the votes for parties A and B, respectively.

For instance, if the vote ratio is 60:40, the cube law predicts a seat ratio of 77:23; so the smaller of the two parties is heavily underrepresented. Although the cube law is often thought to apply mainly to two-party systems, it can in principle apply to multiparty systems as well. For instance, if the winning party in the example just cited splits into two, the resulting vote distribution of 30:30:40 leads to a seat distribution of 23:23:54, according to the cube law, so that the loser in the two-party example now wins handsomely. The largest party is always overrepresented because it tends to win, however narrowly, in many districts.

The implications for the party system are momentous.

There is strong incentive for political forces to conglomerate into two major parties because any additional parties may obtain votes but hardly any seats. Qualitatively, the result is Duverger's law: seat allocation by plurality in single-member districts leads to a two-party system. Quantitatively, actual data often deviate appreciably from the cube law. Thus the major party overrepresentation can be either milder (as in many U.S. states) or stronger (as in many formerly British island nations) than predicted.

At first the cube law lacked an underlying theoretical model and hence was an empirical rule rather than a law in a scientific sense. The law can now be derived from two more basic ingredients, however. One of them consists of the seat-vote equations

$$s_A/s_B = (v_A/v_B)^n$$

where the exponent 3 of the cube law is replaced by n, given by the ratio of logarithms of total votes (V) and the number of electoral districts (E):

$$n = \log V/\log E$$

The other component is the cube law of assembly sizes, which explains why almost all representative assembly sizes are close (within a factor of two) to the cube root of the population. If this is so, $\log V/\log E$ is close to 3, and the cube law results.

The strong attrition in second-party seats in a number of island nations results from their unusually small assemblies, which lead to $\log V/\log E$ being much greater than 3. However, the low attrition of second-party seats (n is much less than 3, empirically) in many U.S. states cannot be explained by the seat-vote equations. One must resort to qualitative explanations such as the bipartisan gerrymander, the effect of which has not yet been expressed in a quantitative theoretical model.

Thus the laws that underpin the cube law do not fully explain the relation between seats and votes in single-member districts, but they do elucidate the basic mechanisms. The seat-vote equations also apply to plurality elections in multimember districts, to presidential electoral colleges, and, in a modified form, to multimember proportional representation elections.

The generalized form of the cube law (with n instead of 3) may be useful for fine-tuning electoral systems. If a government that uses plurality in single-member districts decides that its seat distribution is overly disproportional to votes, it can reduce this disparity moderately either by increasing the number of districts (and hence the size of the assembly) or by resorting to two- or three-member districts with a proportional representation allocation rule. On the other hand, if this same country has too many parties, their number can be trimmed by reducing the number of districts (either by reducing assembly size or by resorting to seat allocation by plurality in two-member districts), provided that the smaller parties do not have regional strongholds.

In a still broader sense that transcends electoral systems, the cube law generalized as seat-vote equations expresses a law of minority attrition in a variety of selection procedures. For example, if women are underrepresented among assistant professors, they are likely to be even more severely underrepresented among full professors and still more among deans. In sum, the original cube law often fails to fit actual data, but it is a fruitful first stage toward building better quantitative theoretical models of an important aspect of representational democracy.

See also *Districting; Duverger, Maurice; Electoral systems; Party systems; Proportional representation; Small island states; Types of democracy; United Kingdom.*

Rein Taagepera

BIBLIOGRAPHY

Kendall, M. G., and A. Stuart. "The Law of Cubic Proportion in Election Results." *British Journal of Sociology* 1 (1950): 183–197.

Schrodt, Philip A. "A Statistical Study of the Cube Law in Five Electoral Systems." *Political Methodology* 7 (1981): 31–54.

Taagepera, Rein, and Matthew S. Shugart. *Seats and Votes: The Effects and Determinants of Electoral Systems.* New Haven and London: Yale University Press, 1989.

Theil, Henri. "The Desired Political Entropy." *American Political Science Review* 63 (1969): 521–525.

Tufte, Edward R. "The Relationship between Seats and Votes in Two-Party Systems." *American Political Science Review* 67 (1973): 540–547.

Czechoslovakia

Central European nation, bounded by Poland, Germany, Austria, Hungary, and Ukraine, that split into the Czech and Slovak Republics in 1993. Czechoslovakia comprised the Czech Republic (consisting of Bohemia and Moravia) and the Slovak Republic.

Before they were joined at the end of World War I, the Czech Lands and Slovakia had very different histories. The medieval lands of Bohemia and Moravia were closely linked to German culture. Prague was the capital of the Holy Roman Emperor Charles IV in the fourteenth century. As a result of the Thirty Years' War (1618–1648), the Czech Lands came to be controlled by the Hapsburg monarchy, which was centered in Vienna. Slovakia, which came under Hungarian rule in the tenth century, continued to be ruled by Hungary until the end of World War I. Both regions thus were part of the Austro-Hungarian Empire.

Conditions for the development of a national movement were far more favorable and opportunities for citizens to be active in politics were far greater for the Czechs, who were ruled by the Austrian part of the empire, than for the Slovaks. In contrast, the Slovak population faced great pressure to give up its identity and become Hungarian. Educational levels and levels of urbanization were also much lower in Slovakia than in the Czech lands. Bohemia and Moravia were among the most developed regions of the Hapsburg empire; Slovakia was one of the least developed.

Nationhood and Occupation, 1918–1945

Czechoslovakia was created as an independent state in 1918 by the peace settlement that ended World War I. The nation's founding resulted from the efforts of Tomáš Masaryk and other Czech and Slovak leaders as well as the actions of the great powers. The new state brought together Czechs, Slovaks, and smaller numbers of Germans, Hungarians, Ukrainians, Jews, and gypsies, or Romanies, in a common state for the first time.

In contrast to the situation in the other new states of the region, Czechoslovakia's democratic government lasted until it was ended by outside forces. The country's high level of economic development, near-universal literacy, and sizable middle class, particularly in Bohemia and Moravia, made Czechoslovakia favorable ground for democracy. Under the enlightened leadership of Masaryk, Czechoslovakia's leaders weathered economic crisis and social unrest by enacting progressive social policies and incorporating most social groups into the polity.

The country's leaders were not as successful, however, in dealing with ethnic issues. The dissatisfaction of the Sudeten Germans, who resented the loss of their status as members of the ruling group in Austria-Hungary and who suffered economic losses under the new government, provided the pretext for Adolf Hitler's dismemberment of the state. Faced with desertion by his Western allies when they agreed to the Munich Pact of 1938, President Edvard Beneš yielded to Hitler's ultimatum that he cede the Sudetenland to Germany. Germany's occupation of Bohemia and Moravia and the establishment of a Slovak Republic under Hitler's tutelage in March 1939 completed the destruction of interwar Czechoslovakia.

Communism

Liberated primarily by Soviet troops, Czechoslovakia was re-created after World War II. From 1945 to February 1948 the country enjoyed a period of limited pluralism. Yet the leaders of the Communist Party of Czechoslovakia enjoyed a number of advantages. The party system was simplified, and all parties were required to be part of the government. Communist Party members held the key government ministries, including Interior, Agriculture, and Information. The proximity of Soviet troops also benefited the party's leaders. Nonetheless, Beneš, who had headed the government in exile in London during the war, returned as president, and other political forces were also active.

This period of coalition government came to an end in February 1948, when Communist leaders provoked a government crisis over control of the police. Democratic members of the government tried to force new elections by resigning, but Beneš accepted their resignations and allowed the Communists to form a new government. After Beneš resigned in June 1948, the country's new government, led by Communist Party leader Klement Gottwald, began to emulate the Soviet model in earnest. Czechoslovakia's institutional structure was changed to parallel that of the Soviet Union; its new leaders also adopted Soviet-style policies. Censorship was introduced, and contacts with noncommunist states were restricted. The leadership also set up the machinery of central economic planning, with binding five-year plans and ambitious industrialization targets.

The country's new government nationalized industry and collectivized agriculture. Ignoring Czechoslovakia's tradition of light industry, the leaders emphasized the rapid development of heavy industry. They also reoriented the country's trading patterns away from its traditional ties with the West and toward the Soviet Union and other communist countries. Communist leaders attempted to

politicize all areas of life, including education at all levels. They also took steps to improve the status of previously disadvantaged groups, such as agricultural workers and women. The economic base and privileges of those who owned property or had wealth in the past were removed, and egalitarian wage policies were adopted.

The death of Joseph Stalin, head of the Soviet Union, in March 1953 had few repercussions in Czechoslovakia. Antonín Novotný, who replaced Gottwald as head of the party, gave lip service to the need to de-Stalinize, but little changed. Only in the early 1960s, when economic performance seriously deteriorated, did Czechoslovakia's leaders begin to reform the system.

The Prague Spring of the 1960s, also known as the effort to create "socialism with a human face," was characterized by a number of reforms. Censorship was loosened, and debate became more open. Alexander Dubček replaced Novotný as head of the party in January 1968, after severe divisions had split the party's leadership. The people demanded even more radical changes, until the Soviet Union began to feel threatened. Forces of the Warsaw Pact nations (the Soviet bloc) invaded on August 21, 1968. Passive resistance and sporadic open protest by the population continued throughout the last months of 1968 and early 1969. The most dramatic protest was the self-immolation of Czech student Jan Palach in January 1968. Dubček's replacement as the head of the Communist Party by Gustáv Husák in April 1969 clearly signaled the end of reform.

Under Husák's leadership, conservative party leaders attempted to reverse all elements of the reform. This "normalization" strategy succeeded in maintaining political stability for most of the next two decades. Independent activists were concentrated in Charter 77, a human rights group founded in 1977. Charter supporters called attention to the abuses of human rights in Czechoslovakia. Because their numbers were small and most of them were in Prague, however, their effect on the larger society was negligible until the very end of communist rule.

Transition

Czechoslovakia's communist regime continued to be very repressive until its end. Mikhail Gorbachev's policies in the Soviet Union, continued poor economic performance, and a chronic, if low-level, political crisis produced important changes in the last two years of communist rule. Miloš Jakeš, who replaced Husák as head of the party in December 1987, was not a reformer. Most of the others who were added to the top party leadership had backgrounds similar to those of the hard-liners whom they replaced, although they were somewhat younger and less committed to maintaining their predecessors' policies. Increasing numbers of citizens became willing to oppose the regime openly, and the number of independent groups grew.

These factors proved to be important when brutal police beatings of peaceful student demonstrators on November 17, 1989, provoked mass demonstrations that quickly led to the end of communist rule. Encouraged by developments in Poland, Hungary, and East Germany, Czechoslovak citizens took to the streets by the hundreds of thousands to protest police actions and call for the end of communism. Dissidents, including Václav Havel, who quickly came to serve as the symbol of the "Velvet Revolution," founded the Civic Forum in the Czech Lands and Public Against Violence in Slovakia to negotiate. Within three weeks the communist government had resigned. The election of Havel as president of Czechoslovakia in December 1989 capped the victory of the democratic forces.

Czechoslovakia's new noncommunist leaders moved quickly to re-create democratic political life and reorient the country's foreign policy. In the political arena they enacted legal and constitutional reforms to correct the distortions of the communist period. They also recruited many new political leaders and officials to reform the bureaucracy. The widespread desire for change had to be channeled into coherent political directions. A new party system and civic organizations had to be developed, and political values and attitudes that were supportive of democracy had to be fostered. The question of what to do

with the economic assets of the Communist Party and how to come to terms with the communist period also became important issues. One of the most troubling occurrences was the revelation of individuals' collaborations with the secret police.

After a period of indecision, Czechoslovakia's leaders began to re-create a market economy. The first step was to create the legal basis for the return to private ownership of property that had been owned by the state or by cooperatives. The new laws were followed by policies that promoted the establishment of new private businesses and the privatization of existing enterprises. Foreign investors and auctions played an important role in these processes. The keystone of the leadership's approach to privatization, however, was the voucher privatization plan advocated by Václav Klaus, then finance minister, later prime minister. Approximately 80 percent of all eligible citizens participated in this process, which allowed citizens to purchase at minimal cost coupons that could later be exchanged for stock in privatized companies. The country's new leaders also reoriented Czechoslovakia's external economic relations, a step that was given added impetus by the collapse of its trade with the Soviet Union and other formerly communist states in 1991.

President Havel and Foreign Minister Jiří Dienstbier also moved quickly to reassert Czechoslovakia's independence in foreign policy and to regain a place on the European stage. They redefined the country's relationship with the Soviet Union and negotiated the withdrawal of Soviet troops by June 1991. They also reestablished friendly relations with the United States and noncommunist European countries, normalized relationships with Czechoslovakia's neighbors, and actively sought membership in European organizations.

Democratic Czechoslovakia

Conditions for a successful transition from communist to democratic rule were better in Czechoslovakia than in many other postcommunist states. The country's new leaders could draw on Czechoslovakia's previous experience with democratic government and the dominant democratic political culture of the interwar years. The country's high level of development, and, in world terms, educated and skilled labor force also provided a good base for efforts to re-create the market. Czechoslovakia had not benefited from Western technology or trade links during the communist era. As a result the new leaders were faced with very little foreign debt.

The country's new leaders made much progress in re-creating democracy and the market in the first few years after the end of communist rule. As developments in Czechoslovakia illustrate, however, coming to terms with the legacy of four decades of communist rule and re-creating democratic institutions and the market have been extremely complicated processes, even though conditions were favorable to the change.

The end of the Communist Party's monopoly of power was quickly followed by the repluralization of political life. A multitude of new political parties emerged, and voluntary associations and organizations proliferated. Free elections held in June 1990 legitimated the country's new government. Threshold requirements kept the number of parties in the legislature reasonable. In the Czech Lands, Civic Forum emerged as the clear victor in the Federal Assembly and the Czech National Council. In Slovakia, Public Against Violence won the most seats in both houses of the Federal Assembly. The Christian Democratic Movement of former dissident and later Prime Minister of Slovakia Ján Čarnogurský came in a distant second. With 13 percent of the total vote, the Communist Party was the second strongest party in the Czech Lands and the third strongest in Slovakia.

Political preferences in both the Czech Lands and Slovakia remained very fluid, and the umbrella organization that won the 1990 elections soon broke up. After an initial period of great interest and involvement, levels of participation in politics beyond the act of voting decreased, and dissatisfaction with political leaders and political institutions increased. The political values of citizens also continued to reflect the legacy of the communist era.

The transition from communist rule exacerbated many existing social problems and brought new ones. Prostitution, crime, child abuse, and violence against women increased. Drug abuse and trafficking also grew with the end of tight political control and the opening of borders. The transition carried emotional and psychological costs. Although many people welcomed the post-1989 changes, the uncertainty created by the need to adjust to change in almost every sphere of life took its toll on individuals and families and contributed to growing popular dissatisfaction.

Breakup of the Federation

In the first two years after the fall of communism, conflict between Czech and Slovak leaders dominated the political agenda, complicating constitutional and economic reform. The federal system created in 1969 was one of the few elements of the 1968 reforms that survived. Control over decision making remained in Prague, however, and many Slovaks continued to be dissatisfied with Slovakia's position in the federation. With the end of censorship and the repluralization of politics, Slovak leaders called openly for a more equitable position for Slovakia. Despite repeated negotiations, Czech and Slovak leaders were incapable of agreeing on a division of powers between the federal government and the two republics.

Economic issues also contributed to tensions between the two groups. Dissatisfaction with economic and political developments grew quickly in Slovakia. Much of Slovakia's industrialization occurred during the communist period. Many of Czechoslovakia's most inefficient industries, as well as much of its substantial arms industry, were located in Slovakia. As a result, the end of state subsidies and other aspects of the move to the market were much more painful in Slovakia than in the Czech Lands. Unemployment rates in Slovakia were approximately three times those in the Czech Lands for much of 1991 and 1992, and far more Slovak than Czech families lived in poverty.

These factors contributed to the breakup of the Czechoslovak federation at the end of 1992. Historical and emotional factors also played a role. Most Slovaks, like most Czechs, continued to oppose the breakup of the common state even as their leaders negotiated its end. Yet views of the two groups on many of the most important issues differed greatly. Czechs were much more supportive of a rapid move to the market and privatization. Many held views on individual responsibility that led them to oppose systems of state support and control of social life. Slovak citizens had greater reservations about continuing to move rapidly to the market, particularly if the cost was greater unemployment, and they held less favorable attitudes toward privatization. They also were more likely than Czechs to want the state to continue to provide a high level of material security.

The effect of national differences was evident in the results of the June 1992 elections. The Civic Democratic Party, led by free market advocate Klaus, emerged as the strongest political party in the Czech Lands. In Slovakia, on the other hand, the Movement for a Democratic Slovakia of Vladimír Mečiar won the largest share of the vote. Not willing to preside over the dissolution of the state, President Havel resigned after Slovakia's declaration of sovereignty in July 1992.

The peaceful dissolution of the Czechoslovak federation on December 31, 1992, was followed by the creation of the Czech and Slovak Republics on January 1, 1993. Political leaders in both new states declared their intention to continue to consolidate democratic systems and market economies. Political and economic developments have diverged considerably in the two states since independence, however. The Czech economy became the strongest in the region. Unemployment remained at very low levels, and foreign investment increased. Klaus's government enjoyed widespread public support. In Slovakia, the breakup exacerbated existing economic problems. Mečiar was forced out as prime minister in March 1994. The coalition of five parties, ranging from left to right, that replaced him moved quickly to restart the privatization process, encourage foreign investment, and reduce tensions between Slovaks and the country's 600,000-strong Hungarian minority. The Slovak economy began to recover in 1994, and Mečiar's party won the largest share of the vote in the fall parliamentary elections.

See also *Europe, East Central; Havel, Václav; Masaryk, Tomáš Garrigue; World War II.* In Documents section, see *Constitution of The Czech Republic (1993).*

Sharon L. Wolchik

BIBLIOGRAPHY

Ash, Timothy Garton. *The Magic Lantern: The Revolution of 1989 Witnessed in Warsaw, Budapest, Berlin, and Prague.* New York: Random House, 1990.

Havel, Václav. *Disturbing the Peace.* New York: Vintage Books, 1990.

Myant, Martin. *The Czechoslovak Economy, 1948–1988.* Cambridge: Cambridge University Press, 1989.

Skilling, H. Gordon. *Czechoslovakia's Interrupted Revolution.* Princeton: Princeton University Press, 1976.

———. *Samizdat and an Independent Society in Central and Eastern Europe.* Columbus: Ohio State University Press, 1989.

Wolchik, Sharon L. *Czechoslovakia in Transition: Politics, Economics, and Society.* London: Pinter, 1991; New York: St. Martin's, 1992.

INDEX

INDEX

African Party for the Independence of Cape Verde, 24
African Party for the Independence of Guinea and Cape Verde, 24
African People's League for Independence, 20
African Political Systems (Fortes and Evans-Pritchard), 1232
Afrikaner Brotherhood, 1163
Afrikaners, 1161–1162
After the Revolution? (Dahl), 334
Agbakoba, Olisa, 366
Age discrimination, 397
Age of Diminished Expectations, The (Krugman), 804
Age of Reason, The (Paine), 903
Age of Reform, The (Hofstadter), 804
Age requirements for voting, 1328
Agency for International Development, 48
Agnew, Spiro, 596
Agrarian capitalism, 244, 245
Agrarian class relations, 168, 244–247
Agrarian Justice (Paine), 903
Agrarian parties, 925
    Hungary, 580
    portfolio allocation, 544
    Scandinavia, 458, 459, 1104, 1105, 1108
    Switzerland, 458
    Ukraine, 1291
Agrarian Socialism: The Cooperative Commonwealth Federation in Saskatchewan (Lipset), 765, 767
Agu, Amma, 366
Aguiyi-Ironsi, Johnson, 887
Ahmed, Khurshid, 645
Aid policy, 48–50, 627, 998
Aid to Families with Dependent Children, 1192
Akayev, Askar, 84, 85, 716, 717
Akintola, S. L., 887
Akiyode, Toye, 366
Akuffo, Frederick, 530
Alabama paradox, 1014
Alaska, 1137
Albania, 749, 1527
    democratization, 348, 426
    political history, 443, 447–448, 1398
    women's suffrage, 1383
Alberta, 157, 986
Albertus Magnus, 222
Albizu Campos, Pedro, 180
Alcibiades, 1242–1243
Aldrich, John, 1031
Alexander the Great, 76, 478, 1056, 1185
Alexander II (czar of Russia), 900
Alexander, Humberto Noble, 366
Alfarabi, Abu Nasr, 642–643
Alfonsín, Raúl, 73, 354, 839
Alford, Robert, 937
Alford index, 937
Algeria, 38, 796, 1271, 1272, 1277, 1365
    corporatism, 105
    independence movement, 37, 229, 344, 461, 499, 1076, 1077
    Islam, and political practice, 347, 508, 639, 640, 645, 840
    political history, 50–53
    women's rights, 1382, 1383
ʿAli (son-in-law of Muhammad the Prophet), 639
Alien and Sedition Acts of 1789, 786
Alienation. *See* Political alienation
Aliens. *See* Immigration

Aliyev, Heydar, 187
All-India Muslim League, 601
Allegiance, oaths of, 774
Allende Gossens, Salvador, 108, 201, 506, 507, 837
Alliance for Progress, 214, 492, 506, 625
Alliance of Free Democrats, 583
Alliance Party, 3
Almond, Gabriel A., 53–55, 915, 965–967, 969
Alsace-Lorraine, 520, 525, 1262, 1378
Althing (Icelandic parliament), 1104, 1106, 1361
Althusius, Johannes, 55–57, 479
Althusser, Louis, 550, 810, 1256
Altruism, 1086
Amal Party, 735
Amalrik, Andrei, 362
American Antislavery Society, 68
American Association of University Women, 1386
American Civil Liberties Union, 356
American Commonwealth, The (Bryce), 139–141
American Declaration of Human Rights, 625
American Democracy, The (Laski), 723
American Equal Rights Association, 68
American People and Foreign Policy, The (Almond), 54
American Politics (Huntington), 967
American Popular Revolutionary Alliance, 63–64
American Presidency, The (Laski), 722–723
American Revolution. *See* Revolution, American
American Woman Suffrage Association, 68, 1185, 1388, 1389
Americans, ethnic, 57–60
Amin, Idi, 106, 271, 357, 1286
Amir Kabir, 629
Amish community, 759, 1045
Amnesty International, 97, 196, 534, 577, 1404
Anabaptists, 1022, 1045
Anand Panyarachun, 1228–1229
Anarchism, 82, 92, 977
    conditions leading to, 49
    environmentalism and, 440
    ideology, 60–62
    industrial democracy and, 609
    negative liberty and, 125
    populism and, 985
    Protestantism and, 1023
    socialism and, 61, 1148–1150, 1152
    Spain, 1172
Anarcho-syndicalism, 1149
Anarchy, State and Utopia (Nozick), 687
Ancient theory. *See* Classical Greece and Rome
And We Are Not Saved: The Elusive Quest for Racial Justice (Bell), 1253
Andean countries, 62–67
    See also specific countries
Anderson, John, 964
Andorra, 475, 476
Andrew II (king of Hungary), 444
Andropov, Yury Vladimirovich, 1297–1298
Anglican Church, 366, 673, 755, 1022, 1304
Anglo-Irish Agreement of 1985, 637
Angola, 1115, 1405
    natural resources, 24, 35
    political history, 21–25, 28, 29, 31, 33, 37, 38, 47, 267, 622, 868, 990, 1076, 1077, 1136, 1235, 1514
    women's suffrage, 1384
Anguilla, 171, 476, 1137
Ankrah, Joseph, 530
Annapolis Convention, 785
Anne (queen of England), 1304

Antall, József, 583
Anthony, Susan B., 68, 1184, 1185, 1381, 1387–1389, 1455
Anticolonialism, 1233–1235
Anticonstitutional parties, 925
Anti-Fascist People's Freedom League, 151
Antifederalists, 69–70, 479, 786, 1067, 1189–1190, 1316, 1344
Antifoundationalism, 468
Antigua, 171, 172, 476, 1135, 1137, 1355
Anti-Semitism, 1143
    fascism and, 472
    Hitler and Nazism, 358, 359, 473, 474, 526, 1037, 1039, 1394, 1397
    populism and, 985
Antislavery International, 1133
Antisystem parties, 925
Antony, Mark, 217, 254
Anyaoku, E. Chukwuemeka, 270
Apartheid. *See* South Africa
Apology of Socrates (Plato), 1111
Appeals of Communism, The (Almond), 54
Appointment and removal power, 998, 1177
Apportionment, 367
Approval voting, 414
Aprista Party, 64, 838, 987
Aquinas. *See* Thomas Aquinas
Aquino, Benigno, 365
Aquino, Corazon, 943–946, 1385
Arab countries. *See* Islam; Middle East; specific countries
Arab League, 349, 713
Arab Socialist Party, 400
Arab Socialist Union, 400
Arafat, Yasir, 1413
Arawak Indians, 172
Arcos Bergnes, Gustavo, 366
Arendt, Hannah, 253, 359, 692, 815, 1061, 1256, 1259, 1345
Areopagitica (Milton), 190, 505
Areopagus, 252
Arezzo, Italy, 222
Argentina, 129, 138, 196, 748, 829, 1307–1308
    assembly, freedom of, 503
    constitution, text, 1458–1467
    democratization, 66, 350, 352, 354, 424, 837, 838, 1363
    dissident movement, 366
    federalism, 475, 480
    immigration policy, 593
    indirect election of president and senators, 406, 407, 409–410
    measures of democracy, 818
    political history, 70–74, 103, 105, 168, 263
    populism, 72, 838, 987, 988
    privatization, 1048
    terms of office, 1225, 1226
    United Nations membership, 1310
    voter turnout, 66
    voting rights, 1355, 1356
    women's suffrage and other rights, 1384, 1385
Arias Navarro, Carlos, 1193, 1194
Arias Sánchez, Oscar, 74–75, 315
Aris, Michael Vaillancourt, 96
Aristide, Jean-Bertrand, 347, 626, 1534
Aristocracy, 12, 290, 436, 438, 1088, 1222, 1232, 1244, 1245
Aristophanes, 1110, 1279
Aristotle, 776, 1049, 1176
    Arab thinkers influenced by, 642, 643

Chissano, Joaquim, 22, 23
Chou En-lai, 208
Christian democracy
  European parties, 213–214, 458
  Latin America and developing nations, 183,
    184, 214–215
  Maritain influence, 182–183, 213, 799–800
  philosophical origins and tenets, 212–213, 215,
    611, 1187
Christian Democratic Appeal, 778
Christian Democratic International, 408, 931–932
Christian Democratic Movement, 331
Christian Democratic Organization of America,
  932
Christian Democratic parties, 925, 937
  conservatism, 292
  portfolio allocation, 544
  social integration programs, 927
Christian Democratic Party
  Belgium, 779
  Chile, 108, 200–202, 214, 506, 507
  El Salvador, 193
  Germany, 213–214, 422
  Guatemala, 194
  Italy, 183, 212, 213, 342–343, 459, 652–657, 926,
    937
  Lithuania, 119
  Mexico, 828
Christian Democratic People's Party, 583
Christian Democratic Union, 12–14, 183, 292, 422,
  526, 527
Christian Democratic World Union, 931–932
Christian ethics, 670, 673, 690
Christian Frederik (prince of Denmark), 1447
Christian Historical Union, 778
Christian Orthodox Church, 898–900
Christian People's Party, 779
Christian Social Union, 526, 527
Christianity
  Burma, 150
  civic virtue, 1343
  civil religion, 1052–1054
  Declaration of Independence and, 342
  Eastern Europe institutions, 443–448
  egalitarianism and, 397, 398
  Enlightenment theories contrasted. See En-
    lightenment, Scottish
  French Revolution and, 1072
  fundamentalism, 507–509
  Iran, 630, 631
  Judaism compared, 677
  natural law, 878–879
  Ottoman Empire, 1272
  Rousseau criticism, 1088
  science and, 1111
  slavery and, 1128
  See also specific confessions
Christianity and Democracy (Maritain), 213
Chrysanthemum and the Sword (Benedict), 966
Chuan Leekpai, 1229, 1230
Chun Doo Hwan, 1080, 1168–1170
Churches in the Modern State (Figgis), 93
Churchill, Winston, 12, 109, 215–216, 344, 392, 526,
  691, 1352, 1392, 1395
Chuuk, 1137
Chyngyshev, Tursunbek, 717
Cicero, Marcus Tullius, 217, 254, 321, 878, 921, 981,
  1059, 1079, 1240, 1244
Çiller, Tansu, 1273, 1275, 1385
Cincinnatus, 1342
Citizen Politics (Dalton), 918

Citizens' Rights Movement, 1413
Citizenship
  African Americans, 231–233
  alien discrimination, 397
  ancient theory, 217–218, 252, 253, 1009, 1246
  Baltic states, 119–120
  civic education. See Civic education; Educa-
    tion
  contemporary problems, 220–221
  feminist critique, 220
  immigration, 592–593
  liberal and communitarian concepts, 218, 219,
    280, 503
  Middle East, 833–834
  Native Americans, 234
  rights and responsibilities, 219, 397, 1212
  social democracy concept, 1140–1141
  Switzerland, 1203–1204
  voting right, 1353–1357
Citizenship Act of 1924, 234
City Money (Clark and Ferguson), 1214
City-states, communes, and republics, 221–224,
  241, 478, 768, 981, 1361, 1370
Civic culture. See Political culture
Civic Culture, The: Political Attitudes and Democ-
  racy in Five Nations (Almond and Verba),
  54, 915, 965
Civic Democratic Party, 331
Civic education, 111, 392–395, 408, 587–589, 672,
  777, 850, 923, 1260, 1280, 1345
Civic Forum, 330, 331, 558
Civic humanism, 218
Civic nationalism, 221
Civic republicanism, 218–220
Civic virtue, 777
  Antifederalist view, 69–70
  civic education, 111, 392–395, 587–591, 672,
    777, 1345
  classical republican concept, 342, 783–784,
    1058–1061, 1068, 1175, 1204, 1341–1342
  in commercial republics, 12, 1062–1065
  communitarianism and, 277–281
  corruption, 310
  dominant party democracies and, 374
  existentialism and, 466–470
  freedom of assembly and, 503
  Machiavelli view, 1343, 1345
  modern issues, 483, 646, 1345
  Montesquieu view, 189, 849, 850
  political obligation, 895–896
  religious basis, 1052–1054, 1176, 1343
  Rousseau view, 189, 879, 1087–1088, 1343–1344
  Scottish Enlightenment view, 432–435, 1343
  technological innovation and, 1221–1225
  Tocqueville perspective, 1344–1345
  warfare as stimulus, 590–591
Civil conflict. See War and civil conflict
Civil disobedience, 224–226, 503–504, 520–522,
  601, 710, 881, 1163, 1234, 1239, 1254, 1511
Civil law tradition, 161, 679–681
  natural law distinguished, 878
Civil-military relations, 226–230
Civil Movement, 84
Civil Rights Act of 1866, 231
Civil Rights Act of 1964, 15, 233, 305, 490
Civil rights and liberties
  Canada, restrictions, 158–159
  dominant party democracies and, 372–376
  historical development, 1373–1374
  Israel, 1413
  liberalism safeguarding of, 756, 760, 761, 982

  as measures of democracy, 817–821
  national security versus, 725
  Singapore, 1126
  socialism and, 1151
  suspension during U.S. Civil War, 727–728,
    762–763
  United States, 57–60, 189, 225, 231–234, 503,
    661, 700, 708–710, 807, 961, 1017, 1074,
    1143, 1254, 1317–1318, 1325–1328
  what constitute, 231
  women. See Women's rights; Women's suf-
    frage
  See also specific civil liberties
Civil Rights Commission, 233
Civil Rights Commission Authorization Act of
  1976, 233
Civil service
  Baltic states, 117
  bureaucracy distinguished, 145–147, 235
  Canada, 237
  change and reform, 238
  China, 285
  corruption and, 310–313
  Dominican Republic, 378
  France, 236
  Germany, 236–237
  Hegel, German idealist view, 236, 590, 591
  institutional role, 234, 235, 238–239
  machine politics decline, 972
  patterns of organization, 235–238
  power-sharing arrangements and, 857, 860,
    1283
  Soviet Union, 237–238
  Spain, 236
  spoils system, 1177–1180
  state complexity, 281–283
  Sweden, 1104
  United Kingdom, 236, 769
  United States, 236, 237, 768
  Uruguay, 1332
Civil society, 292
  Africa, 32–33, 1231–1238
  aid policies and, 49
  Argentina, 70
  Caribbean countries, 172
  components, 240
  contractarian basis, 307, 879
  definition, 240, 1098
  Eastern Europe movements, 1259–1260
  egalitarianism and, 397
  Hegel theory, 590, 1259
  Middle East, 835–436
  non-Western developments, 241–242
  Poland, 951
  Russia, 1097–1098
  Thatcher changes, 1230–1231
  Ukraine, 1289–1290, 1292
  Western model development, 240–241, 1370
Civil wars
  Angola, 21, 24, 25, 47
  Austria, 858
  Burma, 88
  Cambodia, 89
  Central America, 315
  China, 1363
  Colombia, 260, 858
  conditions leading to, 49, 567–568, 573, 727,
    1029–1030
  Cyprus, 859
  democratization affected by, 1363–1364
  elite consolidation and, 425

Human Rights and Democratic Initiative Program, 48
Humanist socialists, 1151
Humboldt, Wilhelm von, 761
Hume, David, 289, 432–438, 687, 759–760, 813, 978, 982, 1050, 1063
Humphrey, Hubert H., 700
Hundred Days' Reform, 286
Hundred Flowers Movement, 208
Hungarian Democratic Forum, 582, 583
Hungarian Socialist Party, 583–584
Hungary, 795, 933, 1272, 1297
    Catholicism and Christian democracy, 184, 185, 214
    democratization, 348, 354–355, 426, 1393
    dissident movement, 363, 365, 1260
    electoral system, 381
    European Union assistance, 583, 624
    fascist movement, 473
    local government, 769
    market socialism, 386
    political history, 104, 443, 444, 446–450, 578–584, 1398
    Slovakia ruled by, 328
    Soviet Union invasion, 1365
    women's suffrage, 1383
Hunt, E. Howard, 1367
Hunter, Floyd, 336
Huntington, Samuel P., 44, 346, 350, 922, 967, 1237
Hurd, Douglas, 1309
Hurtado Larrea, Osvaldo, 66
Hus, Jan, 1021
Husák, Gustáv, 329
Husayn (son of ʿAli), 639
Hussein, Saddam, 633–634, 641, 870
Hussein, Uday, 634
Hussein bin Talal, 674–676
Hutcheson, Francis, 432, 434
Hutchinson, Anne, 1023
Hyman, Herbert H., 389
Hyperdemocracy, 324

I
Ibn Khaldun, 643
Ibrahim, Abdurreshid, 645
Ibrahim, Saad al-Din, 645
Iceland, 352, 412, 417, 452, 456, 460, 870, 913, 1103–1104, 1105–1108, 1134–1136, 1216, 1361, 1383, 1385
Idaho, 1389
Idealism, German, 559, 585–592
    bureaucracy and civil service, 145, 236, 590
    Kant influence, 695–696
    Rousseau inspiration, 566, 585, 587–589, 1089
    Spinoza influence, 1176–1177
Ideological politics, 434
Ideology and Utopia (Mannheim), 798
Idiagbon, Tunde, 889
Illia, Arturo, 72
Illinois, 59, 189, 971, 973, 1015, 1389
Imanyara, Gitobu, 366, 703
Immigration
    Australia and New Zealand, 98–100
    British Commonwealth politics, 271
    consent and, 288, 593
    ethnic Americans and, 57–60
    France, 501, 502
    immigrants, discrimination against, 232, 397, 593, 1028, 1324–1326
    nationalism and, 876–877
    patterns and policies, 592–593

progressivism and, 1003, 1005, 1326
Switzerland, 1204
terms defined, 592
voting behavior, 1348
Western Europe, 455
Immortale Dei (Leo XIII), 212
Immunity, 596
Immunization, political and voting behavior, 1346–1353
Impeachment, 199, 285, 594–596, 888, 910–911, 1368
Imperiali quota, 1012–1014
Imperialism, 757, 780
Impiety, 189
In a Different Voice (Gilligan), 688
In Defense of Anarchism (Wolff), 107
In Defense of Decadent Europe (Aron), 82
"In Search of Progressivism" (Rodgers), 1004
Inaugural addresses
    Clinton, 1141
    Lincoln, 762
Inca Indians, 263
Income equality, inequality, 460, 514, 596–599, 1264
Income tax. See Taxation
Indentured servitude, 1319
Independence Party
    Iceland, 1106
    Morocco, 852
Independent Labour Party, 909, 1381
Independent Smallholders' Party, 581, 582–583
Independent voters, 937, 1031
India, 147, 226, 510, 627, 673, 731, 1043, 1233
    affirmative action, 14, 15
    British Commonwealth politics, 270
    British rule and decolonization, 263–265, 268, 845, 1234
    Buddhism, 142, 144
    capitalism, 167
    civic consequences of military training, 393
    democratization, 241, 346, 351, 354, 425, 599–602, 905–906, 1076
    districting, 368, 418
    dominant party democracy, 373, 601–602
    election campaigns, 403–404
    electoral system, 412, 416–418, 420
    emigration, 593
    ethnic conflict, 602–604, 674
    federalism, 475, 476, 479, 480, 482
    freedom ranking, 87
    Gandhi and, 520–522
    Hinduism, 521, 561–565
    impeachment, 594
    indirect election, 407
    judicial system, 681, 683, 685
    League of Nations, 1310
    local government, 769
    military rule, 840
    minority rights protection, 792, 858, 861, 862
    Nehru leadership, 880–882
    Nepal relations, 712
    polyarchy, 977
    populism, 986
    racism, 1039
    regional politics, 908, 1116
    slavery and abolitionism, 8
    socioeconomic development, 388
    terms of office, 1225
    voter turnout, 403, 602
    women's suffrage and other rights, 1383–1385
Indiana, 973

Indians. See Native Americans
Indirect rule, 1278
    African colonies, 1233
    See also Representation
Individualism, 982
    citizenship and, 218, 219
    communitarianism opposed, 277–281, 1126
    contractarian theory and, 308
    income inequality, 597
    Macpherson view, 784
    negative liberty and, 125
    political culture, 967
    Puritanism link, 1370
    Rousseau influence, 1089
    speech right and, 190
    Tocqueville view, 815, 1266, 1344–1345
Indochina, 1396, 1397
    See also Cambodia; Laos; Vietnam
Indonesia, 86, 627, 640, 855
    colonial experience, 263, 604–605
    democratization, 346
    dominant party democracy, 373, 374, 1311
    political history, 86, 88, 604–608, 1055
    Sukarno leadership, 1198–1199
    women's suffrage, 1383
Indonesian Communist Party, 606, 607
Indonesian Democracy Party, 607
Indonesian National Party, 606, 607
Induction, 978
Industrial class relations
    capitalism and, 166–171, 722
    compromise, 780, 781
    postindustrial society, 249–250
    post–World War II prosperity and, 248–249
    theory, 247–248
Industrial democracy, 334, 608–610, 941–942, 1141, 1251, 1280
Industrial policy, 804
Industrial relations, 610–613
Industrial Revolution, 263, 277, 897, 936, 1063, 1326
Industrialization, and suffrage expansion, 1356
Inequality, 766, 774
Inflation, 804, 805
Informal norms, 745
Informateurs, 542
Information theory, 804
Inglehart, Ronald, 914, 967, 969, 1018
Ingushetia, 185, 188
Inheritance laws, 438
Initiative and referendum, 514, 1351
    abuse of, 984
    Canada, 160, 162
    conservatism view, 292
    as direct democracy, 319, 367, 772, 1280
    institutional role, 11, 922, 1027–1028, 1034, 1042–1044
    Ireland, 636, 637
    Italy, 657, 1028
    plebiscites, 1284
    populism and, 985
    Switzerland, 456, 743, 770, 916, 1028, 1202–1203, 1205, 1281
    tax revolts, 1212, 1213, 1218
    teledemocracy and, 1281
    Turkey, 1272–1273
    United States, 336, 1027, 1326
    women's suffrage, 1389
Inkatha Freedom Party, 44, 797, 1166
Inkeles, Alex, 353, 354, 390, 966
Innate ideas, doctrine of, 777

L